THE KEY TO YOUR
ROYAL ANCESTORS
THE DESCENDANTS OF EDWARD III FOR 12 GENERATIONS

VOLUME 1

Daniel A. Willis

TABLE OF CONTENTS

INTRODUCTION

At some point everyone has wondered about their ancestors, even if they have done nothing to learn about them. This is part of a more basic question in the collective human consciousness: where do we come from? For those of us who actively seek out our ancestors' stories, this question often becomes refined to more specific questions such as *Am I descended from any of the "Founding Fathers"* or *Am I related to that actor who has the same last name I do?* Along these same lines, many of us want to know if we descend from royalty.

The answer to that last question is, "Yes, you probably do." The remaining unknowns are how far back you have to go to find your royal ancestors and can you prove the path that gets you there. This book is designed to help you accomplish these goals.

One of the reasons we can be so sure that any given person is of royal descent is purely mathematical. For each generation a person goes back, the number of their ancestors doubles. Every person has two parents, four grandparents, eight great-grandparents, and so on. So when you pick a point far enough back in history, say 1066, the year which is reckoned as the beginning of the current British royal family, it becomes numerically difficult to not be descended from a royal.

Assuming a generation is twenty years, the year 1066—955 years ago—is about 46 or 47 generations ago. When you double your ancestors each generation for 46 generations, the number you get is 703 trillion and change. Of course, that is not the actual number of ancestors you had at that time, because there were surely cases of ancestors from multiple lines marrying each other along the way. The point though is to compare that huge number of ancestors to the population of England, which at the time is estimated to only be between 1.5 and 2 million people. Even with cousinly marriages, the numbers suggest any given person living in 1066 is an ancestor of any given person living today who has at least some English ancestry. Therefore, it is reasonably safe to say, if you have any English ancestry, you are descended from William the Conqueror of 1066 fame, who is now numbered as King William I of England. Using the same method, but without bogging you down with all of those numbers, it can also be reasonably assumed that anyone of European descent is a descendant of Charlemagne, who was crowned as the first Holy Roman Emperor in 800 AD. He is now reckoned as King Charles I of France, as well as Holy Roman Emperor Carolus I, and is the ancestor of every French king—and Emperor—since, as well as of William the Conqueror.

This book is going to stick to people of British descent. For our purposes, Britain is defined as the territories of England, Scotland, and Wales. We are also going to focus on the descendants of a later king, Edward III. Using the number of ancestors to population ratio described above, the population of Britain in 1350, the middle of Edward's life, was roughly equivalent to the number of ancestors a baby-boomer—someone born between 1946 and 1964—would have living at that same time. Therefore, it is safe to say anyone living today who is of British descent is a descendant of Edward III.

The primary goal of this book is to provide the researcher with a tool that will help them establish their personal link to Edward III. However, I am not doing all of your work for you. Each line of descent represented in these pages stops at the 12th generation of descent from Edward. So it will be your responsibility to trace back each of your ancestral lines to this time.

Why the 12th generation? For most lines of descent, this generation is living in the late 1600s to late 1700s. By 1770, most of the colonial immigrants to the United States who have proven lines of descent from Edward III were already here. For a person researching their ancestry, getting their line back to the immigrant ancestor is typically the easy part; and yes, I typed that with a straight face. The bigger challenge is tracing those lines across the Atlantic and connecting it to the ancestors on the British side.

Large-scale immigration to Australia and New Zealand did not begin until the 1790s. While the ancestors in this book are equally their ancestors as well as the present–day Americans and Canadians, they will need to work a little further past their immigrant ancestor to get to the generations covered herein.

Not every line of your ancestors is going to lead to a royal line of descent. Just because the mathematical likelihood that you are a descendant of Edward III does not hold true for each one of the roughly one thousand or so ancestors you had living in 1700. So you need to work out all of your ancestral lines to gain the maximum value of this book.

The layout of this book attempts to make it easy to follow. The genealogies are formatted in an outline, which each successive generation being indented one tab space more than their parents. Every effort has been made to include as much genealogical information as possible for each person, but record keeping had definite limitations in the 15th and 16th centuries. For those who carried titles, I have also attempted to state when their title was created or when they succeeded to it, whichever is applicable.

There are many cases where two descendants of Edward III marry each other. When this happens, the children of that marriage will be listed with the father. Before anyone starts yelling about sexism, the reason to do this is simple practicality. It helps keep a surname together in one place. At the bride's location in these instances, a note will be made that the children are with with the other parent. I would recommend using the index to find the other family. keeping in mind this is a two-volume work A diamond symbol is also used to denote spouses who are also a descendant of Edward III. The one exception to this rule is actually made to maintain the spirit of it. The only surviving son of Mary, Queen of Scots is listed with her even though his father is also a descendant. This is to present the royal line of succession in a logical location in the book. For the same reason the descendants of Princess Elizabeth Stuart, daughter of James I and her husband, Frederick V, King of Bohemia, are listed with Elizabeth because it through them that succession to the British Throne passed from the House of Stuart to that of Hanover.

There are a lot of abbreviations used throughout the genealogy, but most are self-explanatory. The few you might not be familiar with deal with the passing of noble titles, such as *cr.* for created, or *suc.* for succeeded. I use standard abbreviations for the counties of Great Britain. If these are not familiar to you, a list can easily be obtained online.

The same is true for the orders of Knighthood, however only a few were founded yet during the period covered by this book. These were the Knights of the Garter (*KG*), of the Bath (*KB*), of the Thistle (*KT*), and of St. Patrick (*KP*). If a person is a "Sir" without having a particular order of knighthood associated with their name, they are a "Knight Bachelor," which means they were simply knighted but not admitted to a chivalric order. There is a third category of knights, which became very numerous after James I came to the Throne in 1603. These are the Baronets, which are essentially hereditary knighthoods.

Place names will be included where known. Anything taking place in Greater London is listed simply as London since the overlap of the counties and neighborhoods there change so often. Counties in the U.S. are written in the standard form of "Fairfax Co, VA" which denotes Fairfax County, Virginia. Irish counties are written as "co Kildare." If a specific town is known for the U.S. events, the county is omitted: "Boston, Mass."

While a lot of genealogies love to give full honor and glory to the fighting men of the past, I choose not to. This is not any political statement about military might but done for purely practical reasons. First, it saves a lot of space to leave military ranks out. A work of this size needs to have space-saving measures wherever it is most expedient. And second, a person's military rank changes throughout their life. Just because someone is remembered by history as General So-and-So, he was not always a general. At the time of his marriage he might have been a Lieutenant, or a Captain when child number three was born, and so forth. To avoid the endless notes about their rise through the ranks, military rank has just been omitted.

Another space-saver is to leave out the children who died young. In the time period this work covers, it was common practice for a woman to give birth to a dozen or so kids so she could end up with three or four survivors. Since this work is designed to help people find their lines of descent, there is not much use for including people who died young enough that they can't possibly have any descendants. My guideline in this regard was to include anyone who lived to be thirteen or more, even if they are recorded as having no children. The reason for including the nuns and priests, for example, is just because they were not supposed to have children, didn't always mean they didn't. If a person researching their ancestry comes across evidence that Father John at the local parish was the biological father of Mary Smith's little bastard, the researcher's many times great-grandparent, then they will also need the information about who Father John was as well as his ancestors. If there are named children in a family, but their fate is not known, I include them. I only exclude those who are actually recorded as dying under age thirteen. If I have documented evidence that a person either died unmarried or without children, it will be noted in the genealogy. A single person who lived well into adulthood who has no such notation can be assumed to have possibly married and/or had children. The lack of evidence of something does not definitively mean it did not occur.

There are a few chapters where most of the descendants are nobles of a European country outside of Britain. To the extent it was practical, the English versions of their titles are used. However, there are places where it just made more sense to use the foreign version because the English translation seemed too awkward. This is often the case with a French Marquis (Italian: Marchese, Spanish: Marqués) and the French title Vicomte, which are not exactly equivalents of an English Marquess or Viscount. When the title Lord is used for a foreign title, it marks the class of nobility that is lower than a Baron such as a French Seigneur, a Dutch Heer, etc. Royal titles are always anglicized, solely to help the researcher. While the Duke of Cleves is a generally recognizable title, the Herzog von Kleve, might not be.

Each chapter will be joined by a narrative text. There are too many people in this book for each one to have a personal bio, but these narratives will be a historical overview of the family and their role in the events of their times. Occasionally, a particularly important person in history may be noted individually, with some emphasis being given to those people who came to the American colonies and became the ancestor of large numbers of people on this continent.

This is a two-volume set. The page numbering continues from Volume 1 to Volume 2, so Volume 2 begins somewhere in six hundreds in pages numbers. The indexes, however, are for their respective volumes only. So, when checking the index to find a family, be sure to check the index of both volumes.

And finally a note about accuracy. Every genealogy builds upon information recorded by previous generations. This information can only be as reliable as the information gathered originally. This book has attempted to verify much of the information in it either directly from original documents, when available, or at least by using sources that documented their own sources for their information. Nonetheless, there is no doubt there will be errors in this work. These are completely unintentional, and prudent steps have been taken to eliminate as many of them as possible. This work will not, nor could it ever, be 100% complete. Usxe it as a toll, along with others in your

5

genealogical pursuits. And keep in mind, there are going to be people simply lost to the past due poor record-keep, or later destruction, etc.

CHAPTER 1
THE ROYAL LINEAGE

Any researcher into this area needs to get a firm grasp on some basic concepts. The first of these is knowing the difference between royal and noble. While all royals are considered noble, only the smallest sliver of nobles are actually royal.

Royalty refers to a reigning sovereign of a country. Technically, it should be limited to a king or queen and their immediate family, but for larger discussions such as this book presents, the term can be expanded to include reigning dukes and princes as well. For example Monaco is a Principality and has a reigning prince, not a king. Technically, everything in Monaco, the reigning family, the palace, etc. should all be called the princely family, or the princely palace, but more informally they are often referred to as "royal" in the same sense that the Windsors and Buckingham Palace are in London.

The word "noble" describes the group of people who make up the nobility. These are people who have titles like Earl, Count, Baron, and a few others, but do not reign over a territory. They are as much a subject of the country's Sovereign as the town beggar is. They receive their title from the Sovereign, usually a King in the time period we are discussing and offer their loyalty to that King.

One area where Britain is different from Europe is how they reckon their nobles. In Europe, if a person is made a Count, all of his children, and all of the descendants in the male line are also titled Count or Countess. In Britain, only the head of the family has the noble title, while all of his descendants are plain commoners. Britain also has an elaborate system of courtesy styles which are used by the children of a noble. This allows them to predicate their first name with Lord, Lady, or Honourable depending on their parents' rank. This system was not codified until the end of the 17th century. Before that, younger sons of nobles rarely carried any style to denote their position. On the other hand, women of a noble family were often called Lady Firstname, out of a sense of chivalry, whether they actually ranked that style or not.

There are five ranks of nobility in Britain, from the lowest: Baron, Viscount, Earl, Marquess, and Duke. If a title equivalent to a Baron was created in Scotland prior to the 1707 formal union with England, they were titled Lord. The style Lord is used very generically to refer to anyone with a title less than Duke. In Queen Elizabeth I's court, one might have been introduced to "My Lords Exeter and Chesterfield," even though the former was a Marquess, and the latter an Earl. Meanwhile, Lord Scott of Buccleuch, —his formal title—might also be visiting from Scotland. This generic use of Lord and Lady has led many to give up trying to learn the intricacies of the British titling system.

The title Duke is also a little tricky. In Britain, dukes are at the highest level of the nobility, but are not royal. However, the British royal family typically gives a ducal title to its male members (like, Prince William, Duke of Cambridge). The person holding the title may be a royal, but the title itself is still only noble. For many territories in continental Europe, a Duke was a reigning sovereign over a Duchy, such as Bavaria or Aquitaine. To add to the confusion, the present-day territories of France, Spain, Portugal, and Italy all had both reigning and non-reigning dukes at the same time.

So, now that you know enough about nobility and royalty to be dangerous, or at least dangerously baffled, let's look at the possibility of your descent from a King/Queen of England (or, after 1707, Great Britain).

In the introduction, we discussed how and why King Edward III is used as the progenitor of the lines of descent covered by this book. But, what about being descended from any more recent British monarchs? The answer to that requires a little bit of a history lesson, but we have to view it in reverse to make the most genealogical sense. Starting with the current sovereign, Queen Elizabeth II, we have to go back several generations before we get to a royal ancestor with any significant number of descendants. Even her great-grandfather, Edward VII's living descendants only number in the one hundred or so range. His mother, Queen Victoria's (1817–1901) descendants, while numbering well over a thousand now, are still pretty well known. At least, *they* all know who they are and from whence they came. Her father, Edward, Duke of Kent, had no additional children, and his father, King George III, only adds a hundred or so additional descendants to our count, despite having fifteen children to start with. George III was the son of Frederick, Prince of Wales. However, all of the descendants of Frederick's other children have either gone extinct or married back to the descendants of George III, so our living descendant count remains unchanged.

Then we hit King George II (1683–1760), Frederick's father. Through his three daughters, the number of royal descendants suddenly jumps to the low tens of thousands. While this might sound like a lot of people, the reality is they are almost all members of European royal and noble families, or at least, very closely related to them. So if you are not noble, and neither is your mother nor your maternal grandmother, I can say with some authority you are not descended from King George II.

The further descendants of his father, however, gives a little more wiggle room. King George I (1660–1727) had only one other legitimate child, a daughter who became Queen of Prussia. She adds a significant number to the living royal descendants today. However, they, like those of George II, still remain in the royal and noble classes.

However, George I also recognized three illegitimate children by his mistress, the Duchess of Kendal. Prior to becoming King, George had been the ruler—called an Elector for reasons not germane to our story—of Hanover in Germany. He only visited his newer realm of Great Britain a couple of times. The Duchess mostly remained in Hanover and their children were raised there. Their descendants have mostly remained on the continent of Europe, often marrying into noble families, so they do not really add any likelihood for royal descent to present day British descendants. The number of living descendants of George I was counted in 2011 by this author assisting a reporter who was covering the wedding of Prince William and Kate Middleton. That number was a bit over 38,000.

There is one persistent, yet pertinent, genealogical myth that needs to be dispelled here since it applies to thousands of Americans living today. One of George's illegitimate children was a daughter, Petronilla, whom he created the Countess of Walsingham. She died childless, despite the attempts by several American genealogists to name her as the mother of the illegitimate children of Swingate Calvert of Maryland, himself a bastard son of one the Barons Baltimore who was a governor of that colony. It is true that Swingate left illegitimate issue, and it is true that Petronilla visited Maryland at a time where she could have encountered Swingate. However, the mother of his children, though not known, was definitely not Petronilla. The most damning evidence is that the children were recorded as being born in Maryland at a time when Petronilla was known to be back in Europe. However, Swingate's descendants should not despair. While they are not descendants of George I, they are descendants of his cousin, King Charles II. We will revisit Charles shortly.

King George I came to the throne through an indirect path, and entirely thanks to the newly passed Act of Settlement of 1705. During the 17th century, Britain had suffered through a civil war, then an eleven year period of not having a king, only to be followed up by a renewal of the Protestant versus Catholic unrest that plagued the Tudor monarchs in the 1500s.

Things came to a head in 1688 when staunchly Protestant William of Orange, son-in-law of the then reigning, and very Catholic, King James II, invaded England is what became known as the Glorious Revolution. William was declared King jointly with his wife, James' daughter Mary, reigning until his death in 1708. Mary had died previously. In 1705, parliament passed the Act of Settlement which established the rules used to this day for the succession to the Throne, with only a minor adjustment being made in the past few years. The Act's purpose was to ensure Protestant inheritance of the Crown and named Anne, Mary's sister as William's heir and her heir—since all of her children had died young—would be the next Protestant cousin, who was also the genealogically most junior one, Electress Sophia of Hanover, mother of the man who became George I. As it turned out Queen Anne outlived Sophia—by only two months—so the Throne went to George.

In doing so, several other branches of the family, all Catholics, were skipped, leading to a fifty-year period of armed invasions by them to reclaim the Throne. The descendants of these lines are called Jacobites, derived from Jacobus, the Latin form of James. The Jacobite male line of descent died out in the mid-1700s, causing their claim to the Throne to pass through several females lines. It currently resides with the elderly and childless Duke of Bavaria. His eventual heir is the current Crown Princess of Liechtenstein.

The king all of these lines have in common is King George's great-grandfather, King James I of England (1566–1625), who was also King James VI of Scotland. His descendants add tens of thousands more names to our list of royal descendants. Most of the legitimate lines

10

lived and continue to live in continental Europe. However, both King James II, and his brother and immediate predecessor, Charles II, left a large number of illegitimate children. James acknowledged four children by his mistress, Arabella Churchill, and Charles acknowledged a whopping thirteen children spread over seven mistresses. The brothers, Charles and James, were grandsons of James I, their father being King Charles I, famous for losing his head at the hands of Parliament in 1649.

Both brothers, via their illegitimate children, have a relatively small number of descendants—a few thousand—living in the former colonies of the United States, Canada, Australia, and New Zealand. This makes them the most recent monarchs that the average person on the street in these countries, as well as in the UK, could reasonably hope to be descended from. However, the reality is that most people are not, as they are only a few thousand in a population of roughly half a billion.

As mentioned before, King James I was King of Scotland (as James VI) before becoming King of England also. His Scots ancestry will be discussed in a later chapter, but for our continued look at the royal descent of English kings, the thing to know is that his great-grandmother, Queen Margaret, wife of James IV of Scotland, was a daughter of King Henry VII of England, and therefore a sister of the famous Henry VIII.

In our quest to find royal descendants, Henry VII (1457–1509), is our next major stop. The monarchs who ruled between him and James I were Henry VIII, Edward VI, Mary I, and Elizabeth I. The first of these was the father of the other three, all of whom died childless. Henry VIII's only other acknowledged child was the illegitimate Henry, Duke of Richmond, who died as a childless teenager.

The remainder of Henry VII's descendants are through his daughters, with the Scots line via Margaret being the senior most. A few of these lines survived the Tudor period and now have several descendants. They mostly continued marrying back into the noble houses right up to the 20th century.

Prior to Henry VII, the royal lineage gets more confusing. The 85 year period between the death of the childless Richard II and the claiming of the Throne by Henry VII was almost entirely consumed with a combination of the Hundred Years War with France and the far more internal Wars of the Roses, which will be reviewed in more detail in the next chapter. For this brief genealogical history, what we need to know is that the wars were over rival claims to the Throne by the Lancaster and the York lines of the Plantagenet family, each descending from a different child of King Edward III, one being through a female line and the other through an unbroken male line.

The York Kings, who had the genealogically superior claim through a female line of descent, were Edward IV, his son Edward V who was murdered as a child, and Richard III, who was Edward IV's brother. The Lancaster Kings, whose claim followed a male only—called Salic—succession were Henry IV, his son, Henry V, and his son, Henry VI. Each of these kings who lived to adulthood left descendants, both legitimate and illegitimate. Some of those lines remain in existence today, but most do not, especially the legitimate ones. During the reigns of Henry VII and Henry VIII, many of their Plantagenet cousins found their death either on the battlefield or on the scaffolds due to persisting rival claims over the Throne. The last of the legitimate male lines of Plantagenet became extinct 1541 with the death of Margaret, Countess of Salisbury, a niece of Kings Edward IV and Richard III. One notable line still in existence is an unbroken line of female descent from Edward and Richard's sister, Anne, which provided the DNA necessary to positively identify Richard's recently found remains.

The Wars of the Roses ended with the decisive Battle of Bosworth Field in 1485, where Richard III, the last male York, was killed, and the victorious Lancaster claimant, Henry Tudor, Earl of Richmond, claimed the Throne as Henry VII. In a twist of irony, Henry's claim was through his mother, despite the Lancastrian stance of sticking to the male lines.

In addition to the aforementioned Lancaster and York kings, there were many daughters in each of these families who married outside of the royal set. Their husbands and children who sided with one or the other of the warring factions usually came to a bad end. Those who remained neutral, or later supported the Tudors, thrived for the most part. This book is largely made up of the descendants from these Plantagenet ladies.

12

CHAPTER 2
THE WARS OF THE ROSES

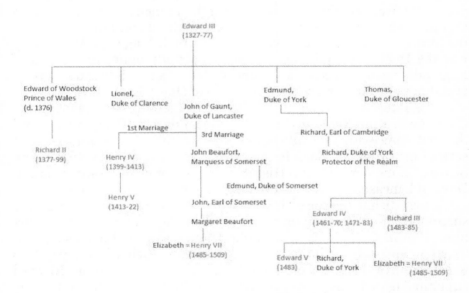

There are far more exhaustive volumes than this book on the subject of the battles between the Lancasters and the Yorks. Here, we have just a brief overview to provide historical context and a timeline of events as they affected the lives of Edward III's descendants enumerated throughout the remainder of this book.

One quick note on the name of this series of battles. Each of the branches of the royal family had adopted a personal badge which was used on their shields and banners to differentiate them from their cousins on a battlefield. The Lancaster line's badge was a red rose. The York's was a white rose. Hence, the name the Wars of the Roses. Furthermore, the hostilities happened in fits and starts with intermittent periods of peace so this period is properly called the Wars (plural) of the Roses.

These wars played out in England at the same time the Hundred Years War was being waged between England and France. This larger conflict was begun by Edward III who attempted to claim the Throne of France upon the death of Charles IV, his maternal uncle. France has always strictly practiced a Salic Law of succession, where the Throne passes to the next male-line heir of the family, even if that means going to a distant cousin. When Charles IV died, the next male-line heir was a cousin, who succeeded as Philippe IV. Edward claimed he deserved the Throne because he was more closely related to Charles, albeit through his mother, Charles' sister. The real stake of this protracted war was the territories along the French side of the English Channel, which switched hands between England and France so often, the locals who lived there rarely knew who their king was. Also in play was the Duchy of Aquitaine, which was already under the Crown of England having been an inheritance from Edward's great-grandmother, Eleanor of Aquitaine, wife of Henry II.

The internal troubles in the House of Plantagenet began during the reign of King Richard II (1367–1400), Edward III's grandson and the last King with an undisputed right to the Throne for the next several centuries. Richard became King as a child, the actual rulers being a Council of Regency. His surviving eldest uncle, John of Gaunt, Duke of Lancaster, held considerable influence over this Council.

Once Richard reached his majority, he proved not to be a very successful king. He relied on a very small circle of advisors, distancing himself from the nobility as a whole. These disaffected nobles banded together and seized the government. It took Richard two years to wrest control back away from them. During this time Richard circumnavigated his government by ruling as a dictator. One unilateral decision he made would come back to haunt him.

John of Gaunt's eldest son, Henry of Bolingbroke, had gotten into a dispute with the Duke of Norfolk. Tensions between these two powerful nobles rose to the point they were going to settle the matter in combat. Richard stepped in, banishing both parties from England, stripping them of their titles and confiscating their lands, a tried and true means of filling the royal coffers.

After John of Gaunt's death, Henry returned to England to reclaim his inheritance. He found a populace who was fed up with their King's tyranny. By the time he reached the capital, several nobles and knights had signed on with him to help fight for his rights. But they chose not to stop there. Instead, they deposed the King, threw him in the Tower of London, and declared Bolingbroke to be King as Henry IV.

Now, since Richard had disinherited Henry, he named a different successor, Edmund Mortimer, Earl of March, who was the representative of the senior most Plantagenet line, albeit through a female. His maternal great-grandfather had been Lionel, Duke of Cambridge, the second son of Edward III. Henry's claim to the Throne came through John of Gaunt, Edward III's third son. The main reason no one seriously disputed Henry in the beginning was because March was still a toddler at the time Richard was overthrown.

Henry's reign started off well enough, but a serious of events in Wales led March's uncle, also named Edmund Mortimer, to join with the Welsh leader, Owain Glyndwr and his brother-in-law Lord Percy—nicknamed Hotspur and heir to the powerful Earl of Northumberland—to launch a rebellion against Henry IV in 1405. The rebellion was quashed after four years of fighting, with Hotspur and Mortimer dying on the battlefield, and Glyndwr going into hiding.

After battling the Welsh, Henry handed a somewhat settled country over to his son when he died in 1413. The new king, Henry V, bolstered his popularity with decisive victories over the French, claiming much of the territory in the northern third of France and northwest Belgium. The treaty negotiated with France even recognized Henry as heir-apparent to his father-in-law, Charles VI of France. At home, Henry made peace with his father's former adversaries, and brought the Mortimer family back into favor as advisors.

By the time Henry V had come to the Throne, Anne Mortimer, March's sister and heiress had married Richard, Earl of Cambridge, son of the 1st Duke of York, who was Edward III's fourth son. Richard and Anne's eldest surviving son would succeed to the Dukedom of York in 1425. He also became the genealogically senior-most heir of Edward III when his mother died.

Henry V died suddenly in 1422 and was succeeded by his infant son as Henry VI. Henry inherited a reasonably peaceful England but a disputed claim to France. Under the treaty signed by his father, baby Henry became King of France upon the death of Charles VI, which was only four months after that of his father. At this point the English, with extensive help from Burgundy, occupied all of northern France including Paris and Rheims, the two cities most closely identified with the French monarchy. The remainder of France was held by Charles' 5th but eldest surviving son, who also claimed the succession as Charles VII. It was this Charles that encountered Joan of Arc, who inspired French forces to rout the English and Burgundian forces from most of the French Territory.

Henry VI's minority was spent under the protection of his uncles, the Dukes of Gloucester and Bedford. When he came of age in 1437, he found a government divided on the question of France. His uncles had pursued a policy of continued warfare, despite suffering several defeats at the hands of Charles VII and Joan of Arc. Henry opted to pursue peace, siding with some junior Lancaster cousins who were also on his council.

This peace was achieved with the Treaty of Tours (1444), but the terms of the treaty were kept secret. It was public knowledge that Henry agreed to marry Margaret of Anjou, Charles VII's niece, but the secret part was that England would turn over Maine and Anjou in northwest France over to Charles. The terms did become public two years later, causing public outcry against the King and his new Queen.

Henry was always a bit of a pliable character, but Margaret had enough backbone for the both of them. She insisted Henry address any disloyalty to them swiftly and severely. First on their hit list were the uncles who criticized Henry's peace initiative with France. Meanwhile, the Duke of York, now viewed as Henry's heir until he had children, was sent to govern over Ireland.

While being the Lord Lieutenant of Ireland might sound like an important, and very difficult, job, it was really just a convenient way to remove York from court when he might benefit from the building anti-Henry sentiments.

The early 1450s were particularly tough for Henry, as England lost even more French possessions until, by 1453, they only held Calais. Losing the Duchy of Guyenne was particularly painful, as it was the last of Eleanor of Aquitaine's inheritance from the 1200s. This series of losses, and a general discontent with the running of the government, prompted York to return from Ireland and claim his proper place on the Council and restore stability to the government. Henry sought to block York's return, largely at the behest of his wife.

York raised an army and began marching on London. Henry raised a similar sized army to meet him. Bloodshed was diverted when the two forces met in a stand-off south of London.

York presented a list of grievances, and demanded the arrest of the King's chief councilor, the Duke of Somerset. Henry agreed, but Margaret intervened to protect the duke, who had become her personal voice in government. Henry's court managed to outmaneuver York, isolating him from any real power once again. Henry's position was further strengthened by the announcement that Margaret was pregnant.

Later that year, with the loss of Bordeaux, the King suffered a mental breakdown. He lived in a state of non-responsiveness for over a year. Even the birth of his son and heir could not bring him out of it. Modern authorities believe he suffered from a form of schizophrenia. York, with the aid of new powerful ally, Richard Neville, Earl of Warwick, was named Regent, Somerset was arrested, and the Queen was isolated from government altogether. York spent the remainder of his regency setting the kingdom's finances and fiscal policy to rights, which were a bit of a mess after the continual battles with France.

On Christmas Day, Henry VI came to his senses and was declared fit to rule again. However, those nobles who has been disenfranchised by him and Queen Margaret were not prepared to allow him to return. They began a whispering campaign against the Queen, suggesting that she was Somerset's lover and that the newly born prince was not really Henry's. Next, they had Parliament name York as Henry's successor, over the child. Margaret and her allies, primarily the Beauforts, a junior branch of the Lancastrian line pushed back, physically removing York from Court. He escaped to the western counties.

York built up a force to respond to this attack and dusted off his claim to the Throne via the senior branch, that of Great-Great-Granddad Lionel, Duke of Cambridge. Margaret, who had taken the de facto position of leader of the Lancastrian forces, sent Henry and an army to meet York.

The first official battle of the Wars of the Roses took place in May 1455 in St. Albans, north of London. The battle ended with several Lancastrian leaders dead, including Somerset. Henry's mind had snapped once again, and he was found hiding, abandoned by all of his advisors. York was once again made Regent but was not yet prepared to declare himself King with Henry still living. Queen Margaret was sequestered with the King, nominally to care for him, but mostly to restrain her from causing more problems.

17

Both sides were actually shocked this dispute rose to a full-fledged battle being fought and strived to reconcile their differences. However, the question of who would succeed Henry, York or the baby Prince Edward, was still a point of contention.

Henry recovered again and relieved York as Protector in early 1456, and Margaret quickly set about undoing everything that York had done. The new Duke of Somerset, son of the previous one, quickly rose to replace his father's position as a favorite of the queen. Margaret also persuaded Henry to travel to the Midlands where they were the most popular and settle their Court at Coventry. This kept him from London where the merchants were now the ones howling at the gates for the loss of trade which had come about from the loss of the French territories.

At the same time, a brutal feud between the Percy and Neville families erupted in northern England. Meanwhile, the southern coast was under constant attack by French pirates, now that France controlled almost all of the ports on the south side of the channel, except Calais. York's great ally, the Earl of Warwick, who was a Neville, distanced himself from his family's fighting in the north, became a popular advocate for the merchants in London, and himself being a capable naval officer, established a base in Calais from which to fight the pirates.

In the spring of 1458, the Archbishop of Canterbury sought to find an end to all of these hostilities and pulled in all sides for a peace conference. The factions in each dispute made concessions in what was thought to be a very balanced agreement that favored neither Lancastrian nor Yorkist. The King even led a triumphant "love procession" into St. Paul's Cathedral where Lancasters and Yorks followed him arm in arm. But it all went to Hell that summer.

The Earl of Warwick began attacking ships from neutral countries such as Spain and their Dutch provinces. Henry demanded he come to court to answer an inquiry. He refused. Soon it was York who was wanted for questioning about Warwick's actions, under suspicion Warwick had turned to piracy himself to raise the funds needed to overthrow the King. York, fearing arrest if he was cut off from his supporters, ignored the summons. Furthermore, he called on Neville's fighting men to join him in the west.

Henry's troops failed to stop Neville's forces from Northumberland, and they were soon merged with York's. At the next battle, one of the Warwick contingents from Calais defected to the

Lancasters, forcing York to withdraw back to Ireland, while his son, now the new Earl of March, went with Warwick back to Calais.

After a bit of regrouping, March and Warwick landed again in England in June 1460, swiftly taking Kent and London, where the King was extremely unpopular. Building a devoted army as they went, Warwick and March headed northward. Henry and his troops met them at Northampton but were soundly defeated.

As per the norm for him, Henry VI again relapsed into a catatonic state and was taken prisoner by the Yorkist armies, returning with him to London. York himself joined them there. While Parliament and the victors were preparing to establish another Protectorate, York walked in and declared he was the rightful King of England by birth and presented the genealogical evidence proving his descent from Lionel, second son of Edward III.

Parliament, not quite prepared to unseat an anointed king, reached an agreement with York called the Act of Accord. With the legitimacy of young Prince Edward still in doubt, they decreed that York would be the successor to Henry VI, stripping the latter's children of all succession rights. In the meantime, he would serve as Protector of the kingdom while Henry was incapacitated. York accepted this offer, as it was the best he was going to get and he knew it.

Queen Margaret and her son fled to Scotland where they obtained the support of Queen Mary, wife of James II. The two queens turned this new alliance into a formidable army using both Scots and Northumberland forces still loyal to the Lancasters, led by the Percy family.

The next military victory went to the Lancasters. In the dead of the 1460-61 winter, Margaret's forces met with York and his army at the Battle of Wakefield, right outside of the town of York. Warwick and the Duke of York both lost their lives in the fighting, with Queen Margaret setting up her Court in her enemies main base, the heart of Yorkshire.

The 18-year-old Edward, Earl of March, was now the 4th Duke of York, and heir to the Throne under the Act of Accord. He promptly proved himself an able commander by soundly defeating the Lancastrian forces in Herefordshire with the forces he was now commanding from the Marshes, the area along the border between England and Wales. Warwick's surviving forces went west to join up with Edward's. Together, they advanced on London, who welcomed them with open arms. People in the streets started chanting "King

Edward, King Edward." Parliament quickly voted to declare the Throne forfeited by Henry, and pronounced Edward IV to be King on March 4th, 1460[1]. However, Edward vowed not to be crowned until Henry VI and Margaret were out of the way.

To this end, Edward and Warwick set out in force, heading north to confront the Lancastrians in what was to be the largest and bloodiest battle of the Wars of the Roses, the Battle of Townton—a small town near York. The combined number of participants is estimated between 60,000 and 70,000, with the casualties being over 20,000. That remains as the record for the largest number of lives lost in a single battle on English soil. The Yorkists scored a rousing victory, killing many of the Lancastrian leaders. Those who survived switched sides, pledging allegiance to Edward. Henry VI and Queen Margaret had remained in York during the fighting and managed to flee to the northern borderlands before Edward reached them. They eventually took refuge in Scotland.

With Henry and Margaret effectively exiled, Edward was crowned King in the summer of 1461 with all the pomp and ceremony that only a Coronation can muster. That ceremony has remained largely unchanged to the present day.

The years that followed were filled with mopping-up exercises. Warwick's brother, John Neville, led Edward's troops in securing the remaining Lancastrian strongholds in the northern counties. Somerset was finally captured and executed after the Battle of Hexham in May 1464. King Henry himself was captured the following year and held in the Tower of London. Edward and James III of Scotland came to an understanding, assuring peace on the Isle of Britain for the time being. Under these terms, Scotland expelled Queen Margaret and her son, who settled in France under impoverished means.

Warwick, now nicknamed the Kingmaker, had done very well for himself at the expense of the Lancastrians. Not only did he have the combined inherited land and wealth of both his father and father-in-law, he also acquired many prized holdings confiscated from the Lancastrian leaders. His political power rose at the same pace, and by 1465 he held several positions of power in Edward's court.

Warwick was of the opinion that an alliance was needed between England and France, now under the rule of Louis XI. Ultimately, he

---

[1] The Julian calendar was still in force at this time. By the Gregorian calendar we use now, this would be 1461.

hoped to regain some of the English holdings on the mainland that France had taken in recent decades. However, while he negotiated a marriage between Edward and one of Louis' daughters, who were all still pre-teens, Edward secretly married Elizabeth Woodville, the widow of a Lancastrian knight. To add to Warwick's misery, Elizabeth's family quickly moved in and started taking positions that had been held by Warwick's family, the Nevilles. Edward also dampened the efforts to negotiate with France, showing a stronger preference towards Louis' biggest enemy, Charles the Bold, Duke of Burgundy.

The final straw came when Edward refused to allow his brothers, George and Richard, the Dukes of Clarence and Gloucester respectively, to marry either of Warwick's daughters. Edward was angling to marry one of them off to Charles of Burgundy's daughter and heiress. Edward was shrewd enough to know that the young Mary of Burgundy was going to make her future husband very wealthy and powerful as she stood to inherit several crowns of small by lucrative duchies and counties in northern Europe in addition to Burgundy. Ultimately his plans came to naught and Mary ended up married to Maximilian Habsburg in the first of a handful of marriages that raised that family from obscurity to being the most powerful family in Europe for centuries.

Warwick, whose vision only included that which involved his own purse, forged an alliance with Prince George, Duke of Clarence, and gave his daughter Isabelle to the prince in marriage against the King's wishes. Warwick and Clarence raised an army against the King and defeated his forces in the Battle of Edgcote Moor in 1469. Shortly after, Edward himself was captured and held prisoner in Middleham Castle, in Yorkshire. Warwick was now the jailor holding two Kings of England. Warwick moved quickly to have the men of the Woodville family captured, tried, and executed for trumped up treason charges.

Revolts from both sides, York and Lancaster alike, began to spring up across the country. The nobles were not prepared to accept the seizure of power by Warwick. With little support on his side, Warwick reluctantly released King Edward, and made a public display of peace with him. However, rebellion broke out in Lincolnshire and, after being quickly put down by Edward's forces, the leaders declared they acted on the instigations of Warwick and Clarence. The conspirators were declared traitors and forced to flee to France.

In a strange case of "the enemy of my enemy is my friend," Warwick, after much enticement by King Louis, entered into an alliance with his former bitter opponent, Queen Margaret. The alliance was a hostile one, but both sides hoped to gain from it, with France's support. Warwick was seeking to control the English Throne through a puppet-king such as Edward IV or his young son, Prince Edward, who was now 17. Margaret was hoping to regain her father's Duchy of Anjou, now under the control of King Louis.

Backed with French forces to compliment the Lancastrian ones already in England, Warwick and Prince Edward invaded in the fall of 1470, quickly taking London and freeing King Henry. At this time, King Edward was in the north putting down more Lancastrian revolts with John Neville fighting at his side. When news reached them that Warwick had invaded, Neville, Warwick's brother, abandoned the King and switched sides. Edward was unprepared for such treachery and ordered his troops to scatter. Edward and his brother, Richard, were forced to flee to the coast at Doncaster in southern Yorkshire.

Meanwhile back in London, Warwick paraded Henry VI through the streets as the restored King. Henry quickly declared King Edward and the Yorkists to be traitors, forcing them to flee to Holland, which was under the control of Edward's pal, the Duke of Burgundy. Warwick and King Edward now made plans to invade each other's land with the backing of their European supporters, the King of France and Duke of Burgundy. Getting involved with a European scheme proved to be Warwick's undoing. Using troops provided by Duke Charles, Edward successfully invaded England and reclaimed his Throne. After a series of small battles, during which the Duke of Clarence switched sides again, now joining his brother, King Edward, Warwick was killed and his troops were forced to withdraw towards Wales.

Queen Margaret landed in Cornwall and sought to take her troops there to combine with the Lancastrian forces in the north. The city of Gloucester withstood her progress until King Edward's forces could arrive to repel Margaret's. The Battle of Tewkesbury in spring 1471 brought Edward the decisive victory he needed. Prince Edward, Henry's only son, was killed during the battle. Shortly afterward Henry was also murdered, leaving Edward of York as the last King standing, for a while.

Some historians consider the 1471 restoration the final act of the Wars of the Roses proper. The Lancasters, as such, were defeated, and all of the legitimate male members of the family were dead. Peace reigned supreme through the rest of Edward's life. However there was an illegitimate line of Lancasters still out there, the Beauforts, now headed up by Margaret Beaufort, daughter of the 1st Duke of Somerset. The Beauforts were descended in the male line from John of Gaunt, the first Duke of Lancaster, but from a son born prior to his parents' marriage, making them illegitimate and therefore not eligible to claim the Throne.

During Edward's reign of peace, he did have to face the problem of his brother, George, Duke of Clarence. Never one to be satisfied with his present condition, George changed his loyalties again, reaching out to Lancastrian factions both abroad and suppressed at home. He was found out and executed in 1478, leaving only the King's two small sons and surviving brother, Richard as male heirs.

King Edward died suddenly in 1483 of natural causes, one of the few men in his family to do so. While his fatal illness was brief, he did have time to add codicils to his will. He named his brother, Richard, as Protector of England during the minority of Edward's sons. Concern swept through the Court, who generally did not like the amount of influence the Queen's family, the Woodvilles, had gained. The new king, 12-year-old Edward V, had even been raised and educated under the care of his uncle, Anthony Woodville, Earl Rivers at Ludlow Castle. While taking Edward from Ludlow to London, Rivers' entourage was stopped by Richard, coming from the north where he was been working on behalf of the Crown when his brother died, and the Duke of Buckingham, a longtime supporter of the Yorks, coming from London. Rivers was arrested and executed after the young king was escorted by his Uncle Richard onward to England.

Young Edward was housed in the Tower of London. While it was used as a prison, there were also apartments there for the royal Family to use when they needed more protection. Richard insisted the Woodvilles were plotting to steal Edward away until he was old enough to rule without a protector, and therefore needed the security the Tower afforded. The Archbishop of Canterbury, an ally of Richard's, convinced Queen Elizabeth to allow her younger son, Richard, Duke of York, to join his brother in the Tower so he would not be lonely.

Once this was done, a clergyman, later identified as Robert Stillington, the Bishop of Bath, came to Richard and told him he had officiated a marriage between Edward IV to one Lady Eleanor Talbot prior to Edward's marriage to Elizabeth Woodville. Lady Eleanor was already conveniently dead and not able to confirm or deny the story. If true, this would mean the Queen's children would be illegitimate. Richard presented this information to Parliament, which voted to declare the young princes in the tower illegitimate and name the Duke of Gloucester as King Richard III.

Shortly thereafter the boys in the tower disappeared and are presumed to have been killed. Historians argue to this day how much involvement Richard had with all of these events. Most agree he conspired to have the boys declared illegitimate so he could take the Throne, but they disagree if he ordered them killed.

After the deaths of King Henry VI and his son, the Lancastrian flame was kept alive by Margaret Beaufort, the senior representative of the illegitimate Lancaster line discussed previously. She argued that her line was legitimated by the subsequent marriage between John of Gaunt and his Beaufort children's mother. Married three times to powerful members of Edward's court, she used every opportunity to push for the rights of her son, Henry Tudor, the Earl of Richmond, to be recognized.

After Richard III was crowned and his nephews disappeared under mysterious circumstances, the Duke of Buckingham led a revolt against Richard in the name of Richmond. Henry did not personally participate in Buckingham's revolt. Even though it failed and Buckingham was executed, the Lancastrian spark was relit, with the scattered Lancaster sympathizers now rallying around his cause. Richard's woes continued that year when his wife and only son both died suddenly.

Henry Tudor had lived most of his life in exile, and was at this point residing in Brittany, an independent Duchy in present-day northwest France. Here he began building an invasion force. He sailed from France on August 1st, 1485, landing in Wales, where his male-line ancestors had been powerful nobles dating back to before Wales was annexed to England.

With forces strengthened by Welsh and mid-landers, Henry marched towards London, meeting up with Richard's troops at Bosworth Field in Leicestershire. Richard was killed, his coronet being placed on Henry Tudor's head that very day as King Henry VII, the first of the House of Tudor.

August 22nd is the date most call the true end of the Wars of the Roses. There were minor skirmishes for the next few years, and Henry spent most of his reign putting down plots to overthrow him, but none came close to succeeding. To shore up his claim to the Throne, Henry married Edward IV's daughter, Elizabeth of York, denying any Yorkish cousins a stronger claim than his. Even in heraldry, Henry made his claim. He melded the badges of the Lancasters, the red rose, and the

Yorks, the white rose, into one emblem of alternating red and white pedals, the Tudor Rose.

CHAPTER 3
EDWARD III AND HIS FAMILY

The story of Edward III actually begins before his birth. His father, Edward II, was a very unpopular king. During his reign England was engaged in a war with Scotland that was not going well. This war was a problem inherited from his father, Edward I, who had invaded Scotland in 1296 and attempted to rule it ever since. This was the time of the great Scottish heroes Robert the Bruce and William Wallace.

The English people's frustration with Edward II was not that the War continued, but that he paid little mind to it and let the generals do as they wanted without showing any leadership from the Throne.

He also held his barons, the people relied on to carry out law and order throughout the kingdom, at arm's length, in favor a small clutch of royal favorites. These favorites were not necessarily selected for their ability in governance, but more for their youthfulness and beauty. One favorite, and likely lover to the King, Piers Gaveston, was a specific point of contention between the King and his nobles. Gaveston had been forced into exile twice by the nobles, only to be recalled by Edward each time. Ultimately, Piers was murdered, leading to open hostility between the King and his barons. When Edward found a new favorite in Hugh de Spencer, the scenario played out much the same way.

Despite Edward's obvious love of men, he dutifully married Isabelle of France, daughter of Philippe IV. Isabelle had four children. By all accounts they were likely Edward's, but as he had his young men, so did she. The two sons are almost surely Edward's as they boasted a physical resemblance to him, but there were questions about the paternity of the two youngest, both daughters. Edward was also not opposed to the time-honored royal tradition of wenching and fathered at least one illegitimate child by an unknown woman. The boy, named Adam, died as a teen in battle, fighting for his father in Scotland.

It was into this mess that the future Edward III was born in 1312, while his father was still grieving from the recent murder of Gaveston. In his youth, Edward was called Edward of Windsor following the tradition of the day that royal children were named for the place they were born. The titles Prince or Princess were not generally used as part of their names, but rather a descriptive term denoting they were of royal blood. The only usage of Prince as a title during this time period was the Prince of Wales, a title Edward of Windsor did not possess himself. He was however made Earl of Chester when he was only twelve days old.

Edward's childhood found him torn between his emotionally distant father, the increasingly unpopular King, and his mother, who maintained a separate household and had taken up with a lover, Roger Mortimer. Mortimer would play the most important role in young Edward's life, though not a positive one. Edward's resistance to Mortimer would shape him into the beloved king he eventually became.

In 1325, the year Edward turned 13, his father was under pressure from the French king to pay homage for the Duchy of Aquitaine, an English possession on the French mainland. The King passed the ducal title to the younger Edward, sending him and his mother—with Mortimer in tow—to pay homage to King Charles IV, Isabelle's brother.

However, while in France, Isabelle and Mortimer raised an army and led an invasion force back to England. There was virtually no resistance to the overthrow of Edward II, who was promptly imprisoned. It took a couple of years of legal wrangling to get Edward to abdicate, during which time Isabelle and Mortimer ruled in his stead. There was no precedent in England for removing a King from power who was still alive. Finally, in early 1327, Edward signed the resignation and the young Earl of Chester was declared King Edward III with Mortimer as his Regent.

While Edward II had been a despised ruler, there was no great love for Mortimer either. A faction, mostly relatives of the former king's lovers and other favorites, plotted to free the elder Edward from captivity. He was eventually moved to Berkeley Castle, where he was reported to have conveniently died in September 1327. The circumstances, or even the reality, of his death continue to be debated to the present day. Most historians accept that he was likely murdered on the orders of the Queen and/or the Regent. However, there is some evidence that he may have escaped—or was released—and lived secretly in Europe for several more years. Since he was a man who often yearned to be free of royal responsibilities, it is quite believable that he could have been happy in exile and would not have tried to reclaim his former position.

But whatever happened on that fateful day in September, Edward III was now a teenaged King reigning under a regency. A part of the support Isabelle had built up while in France just prior to overthrowing her husband included the betrothal of young Edward to Philippa of Hainault, the French king's niece. Their marriage was celebrated in York in January 1328, when the newly crowned King was 15 and Philippa was 13. Despite their youth, they had their first child, a healthy son, two and a half years later.

It was during this period of early marital bliss that Mortimer finally managed to lose the war with Scotland. The treaty of Edinburgh-Northampton gave Scotland her independence back and recognized Robert the Bruce as her King. This loss and the birth of a son seems to be the instigation Edward needed to take direct control of his country away from Mortimer. With the help of his most trusted friends, Edward took Mortimer by surprise, having him quickly tried and executed for treason. The charge stemmed from Mortimer using his regency to line his own pockets and give himself extensive land holdings around the country. Edward declared his Regency to be ended in October 1330.

Edward III reigned for the next 47 years as King. His reign was one of several advancements internally and protracted military engagements abroad. The first few years were spent being involved with an internal conflict in Scotland. After England's defeat in 1328, Edward was only too happy to support those opposing the Bruce family. The alternate candidate for the Throne was Edward Balliol, a member of the family that ruled prior to the English occupation. The Bruce king, Robert II, eventually won out though.

After this Edward was forced to spend the rest of his reign focused on France. Philippe VI, King of France since 1328, confiscated the Duchy of Aquitaine and County of Ponthieu in 1337. Aquitaine is located in southwestern France along the coast just north of Spain, and therefore a particularly vital territory to maintain as it provided England's only access via the sea to southern France.

Rather than pay France homage as his father had done, Edward took the novel approach of declaring himself King of France, claiming the throne as a closer relative to the previous king, Charles IV, who was his maternal uncle. France had always been ruled by Salic law which dictates that the Throne should pass only through the male lines. Under this guideline, the Throne went to Charles' cousin, Philippe. This succession question sparked the Hundred Years War which saw England and France swap territories back and forth continually for more than a century.

Domestically, Edward faced many issues as well. One of the biggest was paying for the ongoing warfare in France. The raising of taxes progressed hand in hand with the more defined role of the House of Commons. Basic principles were established requiring the Crown to prove its need for more tax money and the Commons being the entity to actually approve it and raise the money. In return, the Commons also functioned as the means which the common folk could petition the Crown for redress of grievances, the most common being mistreatment at the hands of a crown official.

Edward's reign also saw the Black Death, a bubonic plague pandemic, reach England in the 1340s. Over seven years it killed an estimated 40% of England's population, although this number is highly speculative due to uncertainty about the size of the population before the plague hit. Edward lost one of his own daughters to the outbreak.

Edward's reign saw an expansion, as well as a more defined role, for the nobility. While his immediate predecessors had been mostly at odds with the peerage, Edward developed a rapport, even comradery with them. He expanded their ranks by creating new nobles at a rate unheard of before. He introduced the concept of using the title Duke as a non-reigning noble title and meant for it to be an honor that could be carried by the king's relatives. He also established the Order of the Garter, an order of chivalry which remains the highest in the United Kingdom to this day. The order was meant to mirror the Round Table of Camelot, with its limited number of members and the equality of all members when they met as an order.

Meanwhile on the more personal home front, Edward and Philippa continued having children, lots of children. Of the thirteen Philippa bore, nine survived to adulthood. Of these, six provided them with grandchildren. In time, Edward would use these children to cement marital alliances with several European powers in his ongoing fight with France. Despite the continued state of war, Edward passed a stable Throne to his grandson—his son had predeceased him—in 1377. Both Edward and Philippa are buried in Westminster Abbey, holding one of the more prominent positions there.

Their first child, Edward, is known to history as the Black Prince, although the origin of the name is still unclear. In 1348, he would become the first Knight of his father's new Order of the Garter. He was also the first English Duke when his father created the title Duke of Cornwall for him in 1337. Furthermore, the Duchy of Cornwall is special in that it is automatically bestowed upon the eldest son of the Monarch. In 1952, when Elizabeth II became queen, Prince Charles, then three years old, automatically became the Duke of Cornwall. He was created Prince of Wales a little later, just as Edward was in 1343.

Prince Edward was a military man. He participated in several campaigns during his 46 years. He was allowed to marry his cousin, Joan of Kent, whom he had been raised with. Joan was twice a widow and brought children from her previous marriages to the match. Likewise, Edward had a handful of illegitimate children he took responsibility for. Together the royal couple had only two children, yet another Edward, who died young, and Richard who would eventually succeed his grandfather as King.

Edward also served as his father's representative in Aquitaine. He and Joan maintained what was called one of the most fashionable European courts in Auvergne, the capital. Unfortunately, a combination of a long-living father and a life of a warrior lead to his demise during Edward III's lifetime, so the Black Prince never became King. Instead, Edward III was succeeded in 1377 by his grandson, Richard.

King Richard II was originally called Richard of Bordeaux. For the first twelve years of his reign, power was exercised by a Council of Regents until he reached his majority in 1389. The beginning of his reign was harmonious enough, but as he aged, he displayed a varying temperament and is now believed to have suffered from a personality disorder. In 1397, he either executed or exiled any voice of dissention from his circle of advisors and launched into a period referred to as "The Tyranny."

After the death of his uncle, John of Gaunt, Richard disinherited John's heirs, prompting them to raise an army and fight back. John's son, Henry of Bolingbroke, effectively reclaimed his rightful place and ultimately deposed Richard, laying the groundwork for the Wars of the Roses. Richard died in captivity in mid-February 1400, likely starved to death.

31

Richard had married twice to foreign princesses, but neither left heirs. After his deposition, his throne was claimed by Henry of Bolingbroke as Henry IV.

Edward III's second child was his eldest daughter, Isabella of Woodstock. Like most first born daughters, she was believed to be her father's favorite. Being considered as unduly willful, and a bit spoiled, Isabella did not marry until she was 33, then considered well into middle age. When she did marry, it was for love with a man seven years her junior. She chose Enguerrand VII, Lord of Coucy, a minor but wealthy nobleman from present-day north central France. They met when Enguerrand was exchanged as a hostage for the captive Jean II of France. In time he became an integral part of the English royal family. Their descendants make up a large portion of what today is the Belgian nobility. Additionally, one line leads to the House of Bourbon which succeeded to the throne of France in 1589, Spain in 1700, Parma in 1748, Sicily in 1759, and Luxembourg in 1964. Their reign in Spain and Luxembourg continues today.

Edward and Philippa's second daughter, Joan, was engaged to marry Pedro, future King of Castile. However, she succumbed to bubonic plague on the trip to Spain to meet her intended husband.

Their second son, and fourth child, was Lionel of Antwerp. His role in Edward's reign was as the king's representative in Ireland. In preparation for the task he was married to an Irish heiress, Elisabeth de Burgh, Countess of Ulster. Ireland had been under the forced rule of the English since the 12th century. It was a land of constant rebellion and upheaval. Lionel made a real effort at taming this wild island to the west, but after some mild initial successes, finally threw up his hands in disgust and returned to England. As his father started handing out the new title of Duke to his family members, Lionel got the third one to be created, Duke of Clarence.

Lionel and Elizabeth had only one child, a daughter, Philippa. She inherited her mother's Irish estates and title, Countess of Ulster. Through marriage she also became the Countess of March when she married Edmund Mortimer, the 3rd Earl. Edmund was the great-grandson of Roger Mortimer, lover of Queen Isabelle, Edward III's mother.

Philippa was the heiress-presumptive to her cousin, Richard II, a position that passed to her son, Roger, 4th Earl of March, upon her death in 1382, and then to his infant son, Edmund the 5th Earl, in 1398. However, when Richard II was deposed the following year, the Throne was usurped by Henry of Bolingbroke, Duke of Lancaster.

Weak attempts to press for Edmund's rights we quickly put down by the Lancastrian king's forces. When he came of age, Edmund chose instead to play nice with his cousin the King and was given a position on his Council.

Edmund died childless in 1425, his estates and the claim to the Throne passing to his sister, Anne's, family. Anne had married the Earl of Cambridge, heir to the Duke of York. Their son would take up the claim and actively fight against the Lancasters for the Throne. The Yorks will be discussed further in their own chapter.

Philippa, Countess of Ulster's other descendants are through her daughters, Elizabeth and Philippa. They too have their own chapters, "The Percys" and "The Hastings," later in this book. The Percy descendants are so numerous they are further divided into three chapters covering the Percy, the Clifford, and the Wentworth lines.

Edward III's third surviving son—there was an additional boy, William of Hatfield, who died in infancy—was John of Gaunt, later created Duke of Lancaster. Gaunt was the medieval English rendering of Ghent, now in Belgium, John's birthplace.

The Dukedom of Lancaster was the second Dukedom, behind only Cornwall, created, but not for John. It was created for Henry of Grosmont, a great-grandson in the direct male line of King Henry III (reigned 1216-1272). John of Gaunt married Henry's only daughter and heiress, eventually inheriting all of Henry's extensive holdings in the northern portion of England. When John received the re-created title Duke of Lancaster in 1362, he was already the largest landowner in England, aside from the King.

Blanche of Lancaster, Henry of Grosmont's daughter and John's first wife, died a few years later, leaving John with a son and two daughters. John, being a third son and not seeing any real possibility of becoming King of England, set his sight on foreign thrones. To this end, he married Constanza—called Constance in England—of Castile, a rival heiress of King Pedro. The marriage of Constance's parents was of questionable validity, so her claim to her father's throne was disputed by her uncle, Enrique II, who successfully wrested control away from her. Despite this loss, Constance was still called Queen of Castile and her husband, was King *jure uxoris* (by right of marriage).

Constance never managed to reclaim possession of Castile, but her daughter, Catherine, married Enrique's son, joining the rival claims.

While married to Constance, John began a longstanding relationship with Katherine Swynford, the governess to his elder daughters. He and Mrs. Swynford, a widow, had four children, who were surnamed Beaufort: John, Henry, Thomas, and Joan. Two years after the death of Queen Constance, John married Katherine in 1396. Their children, now adults, were legitimated with the permission of both King Richard II and the Pope. The descendants of John of Gaunt are numerous and covered by no less than twelve of the chapters in this book.

Edward's fourth surviving son, Edmund of Langley, is the founder of the other branch of the Wars of the Roses, the Yorks. He was created Duke of York in 1385 having served several years with the lower title Earl of Cambridge. A capable, but not exceptional, military commander, Edmund has been largely relegated in history to the position expected for a fourth son.

When his older brother John set his sights on Constance of Castile, Edmund was betrothed to her younger sister, Isabella. The couple had two sons and a daughter, whose descendants will be examined in a later chapter.

The next three children of Edward III and Philippa of Hainault were all daughters, Blanche, Mary, and Margaret. Blanche died in infancy, and the other two, while they did marry, left no children. Mary of Waltham was married to Jean IV, Duke of Brittany. This was a politically motivated arrangement to give Edward troops and support for his claim on the French throne. Margaret of Windsor eventually married her childhood pal, John Hastings, a grandson of the infamous Roger Mortimer. John's father had been created Earl of Pembroke, a title to which he succeeded. Margaret was John's third wife, and although she had no children with him, his descendants from previous marriages are represented among the descendants of Lionel of Antwerp, Duke of Clarence.

Thomas of Woodstock, the youngest of Edward III's brood, was eventually titled Duke of Gloucester, having first been the Earl of Buckingham. Thomas' principle military record was involvement in a dispute over the succession of the Duchy of Brittany. The Duchy was claimed by both Thomas' brother-in-law, John of Monfort and by Charles of Blois, a many times great-nephew of England's King Stephen. Thomas fought on behalf of his brother-in-law, who eventually won the day.

During the reign of Richard II, Thomas became the leader of the nobles who were opposed to the tyranny of the King, called the Lords Appellant. While these lords had some initial successes, Richard eventually gained the upper hand and had them all executed or exiled.

34

Thomas was arrested and imprisoned in Calais, awaiting trial. Before the case could be heard though, he was murdered in his cell, likely on the orders of the King, his nephew.

Thomas married Eleanor de Bohun, a daughter of the Earl of Hereford. They had five children, but only his daughter, Anne, had children of her own. Her descendants will be explored in the Stafford chapter.

Edward III also had three illegitimate children by a later-in-life mistress, Alice Perrers. She later married William de Windsor. These children, John. Joan, and Jane Plantagenet, all married but none of them had further issue.

Edward III, King of England and France (13 Nov 1312 Windsor Castle–
21 Jun 1377 Sheen [present-day Richmond]) son of Edward II, King of
England & Isabella of France; suc. father as King 1 Feb 1327; claimed to have
succeeded maternal uncle, Charles IV, as King of France 1 Feb 1328[2]
= 24 Jan 1328 York; **Philippa of Hainault** (24 Jun 1314 Valenciennes – 15
Aug 1369 Windsor Castle) daughter of William I, Count of Hainault & Jeanne
of Valois

I. **Prince Edward, Prince of Wales**, KG, Duke of Cornwall, Earl of
   Chester, Prince of Aquitaine (a.k.a. the Black Prince) (15 Jun 1330
   Woodstock Palace – 8 Jun 1376) cr. Earl 18 May 1333, Duke 17 Mar 1337,
   and Prince of Wales 12 May 1343[3]; KG (the first one) 1348
   = 10 Oct 1361; **Princess Joan, Countess of Kent** (29 Sep 1328 – 7 Aug
   1385 Wallingford Castle,Berkshire) daughter of Prince Edmund, Earl of
   Kent (a son of Edward I) & Margaret Wake, 3rd Baroness Wake of Liddell;
   she =1st Thomas Holland; =2nd (bigamously) William Montacute, 1st Earl of
   Salisbury
   A. **Richard II, King of England and France** (6 Jan 1367 Bordeaux –
      ca.14 Feb 1400 Pontefract Castle) suc. grandfather 21 Jun 1377; abdicated
      (by force) 29 Sep 1399
      =1 22 Jan 1382 Westminster Abbey; **Anne of Bohemia** (11 May 1366 – 7
      Jun 1394 Sheen Manor) daughter of Charles IV, Roman Emperor &
      Elisabeth of Pommerania
      =2 31 Oct 1396; **Isabelle of Valois** (9 Nov 1389 Paris – 13 Sep 1409
      Blois) daughter of Charles VI, King of France & Isabelle of Bavaria; =2nd
      Charles, Duke of Orleans
      no issue
   issue by **Edith de Willesford** (... – after 1385):
   B. **Sir Roger de Clarendon** (ca.1350 Clarendon, Wilts. – 1402) executed
      = ...; **Margaret Fleming** (...) daughter of John Fleming, Baron de la
      Roche
      no issue
   issue by ...:
   C. **Sir John Sounder** (... – bef.1376)

II. **PRINCESS ISABELLA, COUNTESS OF BEDFORD** (1332–1379)

---

[2] The English claim to the Throne of France would continue until the reign of George III and
each King and Queen of England during this period was also styled King or Queen of France.
However, the male lines of Hugh Capet were the *de facto* Kings of France during the entire
period.
[3] Edward was the first heir-apparent to be titled Prince of Wales, etc. Since then, every heir-
apparent has become Duke of Cornwall automatically and was cr. Prince of Wales sometime
later if they lived so long.

see: Chapter 26

III. **Princess Joan of England** (19 Dec 1333 – 1 Jul 1348 Loremo, France) unm.

IV. **Prince Lionel** (of Antwerp[4]) **of England KG, Duke of Clarence** (29 Nov 1338 Antwerp – 7 Oct 1368 Alba, Piedmont, Italy) cr. Duke Nov 1362; KG 1361
=1 15 Aug 1352 Tower of London; **Elizabeth de Burgh, 4th Countess of Ulster, 5th Baroness of Connaught** (6 Jul 1332 Carrickfergus Castle, near Belfast – 10 Dec 1363 Dublin) daughter of William de Burgh, 3rd Earl of Ulster & Maud of Lancaster[5]; suc. father 6 Jun 1333
=2 28 May 1368 Milan; **Violante Visconti** (1354 Pavia – Nov 1386 Pavia) daughter of Galeazzo II, Lord di Pavia & Bianca of Savoy; =2nd Secondotto, Marchese di Montferrat; =3rd (her first cousin) Ludovico Visconti, Lord di Lodi
issue of 1st (none by 2nd):
A. **Philippa, 5th Countess of Ulster** (16 Aug 1355 Eltham Palace, Kent – 5 Jan 1382 Cork) suc. mother 10 Dec 1363
= ca.1368 Reading; **Edmund Mortimer, 3rd Earl of March** (1 Feb 1352 – 27 Dec 1381) son of Roger Mortimer, 2nd Earl of March & Philippa Montacute; suc. father 26 Feb 1360
1. **LADY ELIZABETH (MORTIMER) PERCY CAMOYS** (1371 – 1417)
see: Chapter 8
2. **Roger Mortimer, 4th Earl of March, 6th Earl of Ulster** (11 Apr 1374 – 20 Jul 1398) suc. father 27 Dec 1381 and mother 5 Jan 1382
= 7 Oct 1388; **Lady Alinore Holland** (1373 Upholland, Lancs. – Oct 1405) daughter of Thomas Holland, 2nd Earl of Kent & Lady Alice Fitzalan; =2nd Edward Charleton, 5th Baron Cherleton
a. **Lady Anne Mortimer** (27 Dec 1390 co. Westmeath, Ireland – 21 Sep 1411 King's Langley, Herts.)
= ca.1406; ♦**Richard, 3rd Earl of Cambridge** (ca.1375–1415)
Children are listed with other parent
b. **Edmund Mortimer, 5th Earl of March, 7th Earl of Ulster** (6 Nov 1391 – 18 Jan 1425 in Ireland) suc. father 20 Jul 1398
= ...; ♦**Lady Anne Stafford** (... – 20 Sep 1432) daughter of Edmund Stafford, 5th Earl of Stafford & Anne of Gloucester; =2nd John Holland, 2nd Duke of Exeter
no issue
c. **Lady Eleanor Mortimer** (... – 1418)

---

[4] It was the custom of the day to style princes by their birthplace.
[5] Maud was a male-line great-granddaughter of King Henry III.

= ca.1408; **Sir Edward de Courtenay** (1388 – Aug 1418) son of
Edward de Courtenay, 11th Earl of Devon & Maud Camoys
no issue

    3. **Lady Philippa Mortimer** (21 Nov 1375 – 26 Sep 1400)
=1 1389; **John Hastings, 3rd Earl of Pembroke** (Oct 1372 – 30 Dec
1389) killed in a jousting tournament; son of John Hastings, 2nd Earl of
Pembroke[6] & Anne Manny, 2nd Baroness Manny; =1st ♦Elizabeth of
Lancaster
=2 15 Aug 1390; **Richard Fitzalan KG, 11th Earl of Arundel, 9th
Earl of Surrey** (1346 – 21 Sep 1397) son of Richard Fitzalan, 10th Earl
of Arundel & Eleanor of Lancaster[7]; =1st Elizabeth de Bohun
=3 aft.Apr 1398; **Sir Thomas Poynings, 5th Baron St,John of
Basing** (... – 7 Mar 1429) son of Luke de Poynings, 4th Baron St. John of
Basing & Isabella St.John
no surviving issue

    4. **Sir Edmund Mortimer** (9 Nov 1376 – 1409)
= 1402; **Catrin Glyndwr** (... – 1413) daughter of Owain Glyndwr &
Margaret Hamner
no surviving issue

V. JOHN OF GAUNT, DUKE OF LANCASTER (1340–1399)
see: Chapter 5

VI. EDMUND OF LANGLEY, DUKE OF YORK (1341–1402)
see: Chapter 4

VII. Princess Mary of England (10 Oct 1344 Waltham – Dec 1362
Abingdon)
= 3 Jul 1361 Woodstock Palace; **Jean V, Duke of Brittany** (1339 – 1 Nov
1399) son of Jean IV, *de jure* Duke of Brittany & Jeanne of Flanders; =2nd
Joan Holland; =3rd Juana of Navarre
no issue

VIII. Princess Margaret of England (20 Jul 1346 Windsor Castle – after
1 Oct 1361)
= 13 May 1359 Reading; **John Hastings KG, 2nd Earl of Pembroke**
(ph.29 Aug 1347 Sutton Valence - 16 Apr 1375) son of Laurence Hastings, 1st
Earl of Pembroke & Agnes Mortimer, KG 1369; =2nd Anne Manny
no issue

---

[6] The 2nd Earl's first wife had been ♦Princess Margaret, daughter of King Edward III.
[7] Eleanor was a male-line great-granddaughter of King Henry III, and sister to Maud, Countess
of Ulster.

IX. **Prince Thomas** (of Woodstock) **of England, Duke of Gloucester**, Earl of Essex, Earl of Buckingham **KG** (7 Jan 1355 Woodstock, Oxon – 9 Sep 1397 Calais) murdered in prison; cr. Earl of Buckingham 16 Jul 1377, Earl of Essex 22 Jun 1380, and Duke 6 Aug 1385; KG1380; attainted 1397 = ca.1375; **Lady Eleanor de Bohun** (ca.1366 – 3 Oct 1399 London) daughter of Humphrey de Bohun, 7th Earl of Hereford & Joan FitzAlan

  A. **Humphrey of Gloucester, 2nd Earl of Buckingham** (ca.1381 – 2 Sep 1399) suc. father 9 Sep 1397; unm.

  B. **ANNE, COUNTESS OF STAFFORD** (1383 – 1438) see: Chapter 18

  C. **Joan of Gloucester** (1384 – 16 Aug 1400) = aft.1392; **Gilbert Talbot, 5th Baron Talbot** (1383 – 19 Oct 1419) son of Richard Talbot, 4th Baron Talbot & Ankaret Lestrange; suc. father 7 Sep 1396 no issue

  D. **Isabella of Gloucester** (12 Mar 1385/6 – ca.Apr 1402) unm.

issue by **Alice Perrers** (ca.1348 – 1383) = William de Windsor:
X. **Sir John de Southeray, Kt** (ca.1364 – aft.1383) Kt. 1377 =1377 (dv.1380); **Mary Percy** (1367 – 25 Aug 1394) daughter of Henry Percy, 3rd Baron Percy & Joan, Baroness Orreby; =2nd John de Ros, 5th Baron de Ros no issue

XI. **Jane Plantagenet** (ca.1365 – ...) = ...; **Robert Northland** (...) no known issue

XII. **Joan Plantagenet** (ca.1366 – bef.Jan 1431/2) = ...; **Robert Skerne** (... – 9 Apr 1437 Kingston upon Thames) no issue

CHAPTER 4
YORK

Although Edmund of Langley, Duke of York was the fourth surviving son of Edward III, his descendants would become the genealogically senior English line when his son, the Earl of Cambridge, married the heiress of the Duke of Clarence, Edward III's second son. This leap-frogging of the York line in front of the Lancaster line set up the rival claims for the Wars of the Roses as we have already seen.

Edmund was part of the double marriage package of two English princes—John of Gaunt being the other—with two daughters of King Pedro of Castile. Edmund got the younger one, Isabella. Neither sister was a princess since they were both daughters of the King's mistress rather than his wife. Isabella lived a life as scandalous as her mother, and died mostly unmourned at age of 37, leaving Edmund with three children, Edward, Constance and Richard.

Edward succeeded his father as Duke in 1402. He was close to his cousin, Richard II, and served with him in several of his military campaigns. He married twice but left no children before being slain at the Battle of Agincourt (1415), one of the major battles of the Hundred Years War.

His sister Constance married two men from the Beauchamp family and their descendants will be discussed in a later chapter.

The youngest child of Edmund of Langley was Richard, Earl of Cambridge. The remainder of this chapter are descended from him, as are all Kings and Queens of England, Great Britain, and the United Kingdom from Edward IV onwards, with the lone exception of Henry VII, who was only married to a descendant.

Richard, himself being the younger son of a fourth son, had no great grants of land or other wealth, so lived largely off of the estate of his wife, Anne Mortimer, who was quite the heiress acquiring the money of both the Clarence branch of the royal family through her mother, and that of her paternal lineage, the Mortimers. This marriage also brought Richard closer in succession to the Throne, a point that was set aside when Henry of Bolingbroke usurped the Throne from Richard II.

Much of the lives of Richard's senior male line has been discussed along with the Wars of the Roses. The abbreviated version here is that his son became the 3rd Duke of York, and his grandsons were Kings Edward IV and Richard III. His daughter, Anne, married Sir Thomas Grey and their ancestors will be discussed in their own chapter.

Richard, 3rd Duke of York, in addition to his life-long battles against the Lancasters, was known for the large number of progeny he fathered. He and his wife, Cecily Neville, had thirteen children, although nearly half of them died young. His surviving children included the previously mentioned Kings, a third son, George, and three daughters, Anne, Elizabeth, and Margaret, who all made notable impacts on history.

Anne, the eldest surviving daughter, married twice, but her progeny by the first husband died out within a generation. By the second husband, Thomas St. Leger, their sole child, Anne would become the common ancestress of many lines that would later emigrate to the New World and form many of the founding families of the United States, as well as produce several U.S. Presidents who served in the 19th and 20th centuries.

Elizabeth, the middle surviving York sister, was the olive branch that ended the War of the Roses when she was married to King Henry VII. In addition to their famous son, Henry VIII, Elizabeth gave her husband several daughters who were used to cement alliances abroad and quell rebellious nobles at home. They will be discussed in more detail in the Beaufort/Tudor chapter.

Margaret, the youngest York girl, was married to Charles the Bold, Duke of Burgundy. While this marriage did much to strengthen the bonds between the two countries, it did not produce any children.

However, Margaret was the step-mother of Maria of Burgundy, one of the wealthiest, and therefore most sought after, heiresses of all of Europe. Margaret helped negotiate the marriage of Maria to Maximilian Habsburg, laying the cornerstone of the soon-to-be vast Habsburg Empire.

George, Duke of Clarence, a brother to Kings Edward IV and Richard III, would likely have been lost to history if it were not for Shakespeare dispatching him by drowning in a vat of wine, an event that probably did not actually happen. However, George's children do share a special place in the Royal Family. His son, the Earl of Warwick, was the last legitimate male Plantagenet, dying in 1499. Warwick's sister, Margaret, Countess of Salisbury was the absolute last Plantagenet, regardless of gender, living on to 1541. Both came to bad ends.

This position as the remaining Plantagenets, made them rivals to the Tudors claim on the Throne. After all, Henry VII took the Crown by force, with very week genealogical claims to it. It was for this reason that the descendants of the Duke of Clarence spent most of their lives either in the Tower or in exile abroad. Warwick was locked up at age ten when Henry took the Throne and was kept there until his eventual execution fourteen years later.

Margaret had married Sir Richard Pole and had four sons. They were a devoutly Catholic family and ran afoul of Henry VIII when he established the Church of England as a Protestant church. One of the sons, Reginald, was a Catholic Cardinal and served as the last Roman Catholic Archbishop of Canterbury. The eldest and third sons, Henry and Geoffrey, were both accused of conspiring against Henry and were convicted of treason. Henry was beheaded, but Geoffrey had managed to escape to the continent and lived the rest of his life abroad. Both Henry and Geoffrey have left numerous descendants, although the male line became extinct within a few generations. The youngest son escaped such problems by dying of natural causes shortly after Henry converted the Church.

Margaret herself did not fare so well. Since Henry could not get his hands on neither the Cardinal nor his brother Geoffrey, he took out their punishment on their elderly mother. She was locked up in the Tower for two and half years. Though never convicted of a crime, Henry ordered her execution. Despite her age, she put up a fight on the way to the ax, having to be physically forced onto the chopping block. Between her struggling and the bungling of the inexperienced executioner it took eleven swings of the axe to carry out the sentence.

It was considered one of the most gruesome executions in British history.

To this day, there is a school of thought that Henry VII was a usurper and all the Sovereigns to come after him were equally unentitled to the throne. The proponents of this theory support a line of succession that would have continued through Richard III's family. Since his only child was already dead, the next heirs would be the children of his brother George, Duke of Clarence. His sons both died childless, leaving Margaret, Countess of Salisbury as the "Yorkist claimant." This claim continues through her granddaughter, Catherine, Countess of Huntingdon and currently resides in the person of the 15th Earl of Loudoun, a rice farmer in Australia.

The remainder of the descendants of the House of York are through Edward IV's illegitimate children by his mistress, Elizabeth Wayte. Some of these lines of descent still remain untraced, however, many of the ones we do know about became families of baronets once that title was created in the early 17th century.

|

Prince Edmund (of Langley), **Duke of York, Earl of Cambridge KG** (5 Jun 1341 Kings Langley, Hertfordshire – 1 Aug 1402 Kings Langley) KG 1361; cr. Earl 1362; cr. Duke 3 Aug 1385

=1 Mar/Apr 1372; **Infanta Isabel of Castile LG** (ca.1355 – 23 Dec 1392 Kings Langley) LG 1378; daughter of Pedro, King of Castile & Maria de Padilla

=2 ca.4 Nov 1393; **Lady Joan Holland LG** (ca.1380 – 12 Apr 1434) LG 1399; daughter of Thomas Holland, 2nd Earl of Kent & Alice FitzAlan; she =2nd William de Willoughby, 5th Baron Willoughby de Eresby; =3rd Henry le Scrope, 3rd Baron Scrope of Masham; =4th Sir Henry Blomflete

issue of 1st (none by 2nd):

A. **Edward** of Norwich, **2nd Duke of York** etc. 1st Earl of Rutland, Earl of Cork, Duke of Aumale (1373 Norwich – 25 Oct 1415 Agincourt) killed in battle; cr. Rutland 1390 (for father's lifetime); cr. Cork 1394 and Aumale in 1397; suc. father 1402; resigned Cambridge 1414
   = ...; **Philippa de Mohun** (bef.1376 – 17 Jul 1431 Carisbrooke Castle, Isle of Wight) daughter of John de Mohun, 2nd Baron de Mohun & Joan Berghersh; =1st Walter FitzWalter; =2nd Sir John Golafre
   no issue

B. **Constance of York** (ca.1374 – 29 Nov 1416 Reading)
   = 7 Nov 1379; **Thomas le Despencer, 1st Earl of Gloucester** 2ndBaron le Despencer **KG** (22 Sep 1373 – 13 Jan 1400 Bristol) executed; son of Edward le Despencer, 1st Baron le Despencer; suc. father 1375; cr. Earl 1397; KG 1399; titles forfeitd Jan 1400/1

   1. **Richard le Despencer, 4th Baron Burghersh KB** (30 Nov 1396 – Oct 1414 Merton, Surrey) KB 8 Apr 1413; suc. granduncle Aug 1409
      = aft.23 May 1412; ◆**Lady Eleanor Neville** (ca.1397 Reby Castle, Durham – 1472) daughter of Ralph Neville, 1st Earl of Westmorland & Lady Joan Beaufort; =2nd ◆Henry Percy, 1st Earl of Northumberland
      no issue

   2. **Isabel le Despencer** (26 Jul 1400 Cardiff – 27 Dec 1439 Tewkesbury, Glos.)
      =1 27 Jul 1411 Tewkesbury; **Richard Beauchamp, 1st Earl of Worcester**, 2nd Baron Bergavenny (bef.1397 – 18 Mar 1421/2 Meaux, France) Killed in battle; son of William Beauchamp, 1st Baron Bergavenny & Joan FitzAlan; suc. father 18 May 1411, cr. Earl Feb. 1420/1
      =2 26 Nov 1423 Hanley Castle, Worcs.; **Richard Beauchamp, 13th Earl of Warwick**, 5th Baron Burghesh, Count d'Aumâle (25 Jan 1381/2 Salwarpe, Worcs. – 30 Apr 1439 Rouen) son of Thomas Beauchamp, 12th Earl of Warwick & Margaret Ferrers; he =1st Elizabeth Berkeley; suc. father 8 Apr 1401; cr. Count 1419
      issue of 1st:
      a. **Elizabeth Beauchamp, 3rd Baroness Bergavenny** (16 Sep 1415

Hanley Castle, Worcs. – 18 Jun 1448) suc. father 1421/2
= 1424; ♦**Edward Neville, 1ˢᵗ Baron Abergavenny** (... – 1476)
Children are listed with other parent
issue of 2ⁿᵈ:
  b. **Henry Beauchamp, 1ˢᵗ Duke of Warwick**, 14ᵗʰ Earl of Warwick,
     etc. (22 Mar 1424/5 – 11 Jun 1445) suc. father 1439, cr. Duke 5 Apr 1445
     which became extinct up on his death
     = 1434; ♦**Lady Cecily Neville** (... – 28 Jul 1450) daughter of Richard
     Neville & Alice Montagu, 5ᵗʰ Countess of Salisbury; =2ⁿᵈ John Tiptoft, 1ˢᵗ
     Earl of Worcester
     no surviving issue
  c. **Lady Anne Beauchamp** (13 Jul 1429 – 20 Sep 1492)
     = 1434; ♦**Richard Neville, 16ᵗʰ Earl of Warwick** (1428 – 1471)
     Children are listed with other parent
C. **Richard** of Conisburgh, **3ʳᵈ Earl of Cambridge** (ca.1375 Conisburgh
   Castle, Yorks. – 5 Aug 1415 Southampton, Hants.) executed; suc. brother
   1414
   =1 Jun 1406; (his first cousin) ♦**Lady Anne Mortimer**[8] (27 Dec 1390
   Westmeath, Ireland – 21 Sep 1411 Kings Langley) daughter of Roger
   Mortimer, 4ᵗʰ Earl of March & Lady Alinore Holland
   =2 ca.1414; **Matilda Clifford** (... – 26 Aug 1446) daughter of Thomas
   Clifford, 6ᵗʰ Baron de Clifford & Elizabeth de Ros; =1ˢᵗ John Neville, 6ᵗʰ
   Baron Latimer
   issue of 1ˢᵗ (none by 2ⁿᵈ):
   1. **Lady Isabella Plantagenet** (1409 – 2 Oct 1484)
      = 1426; ♦**Henry Bourchier, 1ˢᵗ Earl of Essex** (1409–1483)
      Children are listed with other parent
   2. **Richard Plantagenet, 3ʳᵈ Duke of York**, etc. 4ᵗʰ Earl of Cambridge,
      6ᵗʰ Earl of March, 8ᵗʰ Earl of Ulster (21 Sep 1411 Kings Langley – 30 Dec
      1460 Wakefield, Yorkshire) killed in battle; suc. mother as senior claimant
      to Throne and in March and Ulster at birth; suc. father as Earl Aug 1415;
      suc. uncle as Duke Oct 1415
      = bef. Oct 1429; ♦**Lady Cecily Neville** (3 May 1415 Raby Castle,
      Durham – 31 May 1495) daughter of Ralph Neville, 1ˢᵗ Earl of
      Westmorland & Lady Joan Beaufort
      a. **Lady Anne Plantagenet** (10 Aug 1439 – 14 Jan 1476)
         =1 1447; ♦**Henry Holland, 3ʳᵈ Duke of Exeter** (1430 – 1475)
         =2 1473; **Sir Thomas St.Leger** (... – 8 Nov 1483)
         issue of 1ˢᵗ:
         Children are listed with other parent
         issue of 2ⁿᵈ:

---

[8] On 14 Feb 1400, Lady Anne, later Countess of Cambridge, should have succeeded Richard II
as Queen, but the Throne was taken in conquest by the Duke of Lancaster instead.

(I) **Anne St.Leger** (1466 Ulcombe, Kent – 21 Apr 1526)
= 1490; **George Manners, 11ᵗʰ Baron de Ros** (bef.1470 – 23 Oct 1513 Toutney, France) son of Sir Robert Manners & Eleanor de Ros; suc. maternal uncle 15 Oct 1508

A) **Thomas Manners, 1ˢᵗ Earl of Rutland** 12ᵗʰ Baron de Ros **KG** (bef.1492 – 20 Sep 1543) suc. father 1513; cr. Earl 18 Jun 1525; KG 1525
=1 21 Feb 1512/3; **Elizabeth Lovell** (... – aft.26 Oct 1513) daughter of Sir Robert Lovell
=2 ...; **Eleanor Paston** (... – 1551) daughter of Sir William paston & Bridget Heydon
issue of 2ⁿᵈ (none by 1ˢᵗ):

1) **Henry Manners, 2ⁿᵈ Earl of Rutland** etc. (... – 17 Sep 1563) suc. father 1543
=1 3 Jul 1536; ◆**Lady Margaret Neville** (... – 13 Oct 1559) daughter of Ralph Neville, 4ᵗʰ Earl of Westmorland & Lady Catherine Stafford
=2 1560; ◆**Hon. Bridget Hussey** (ca.1526 – 12 Jan 1600/1) daughter of John Hussey, 1ˢᵗ Lord Hussey & Lady Anne Grey; =1ˢᵗ Sir Richard Morrison; =3ʳᵈ Francis Russell, 2ⁿᵈ Earl of Bedford
issue of 1ˢᵗ (none by 2ⁿᵈ):

a) **Lady Elizabeth Manners** (...)
= 1573; ◆**Sir William Courtenay** (1553–1630)
Children are listed with other parent

b) **Edward Manners, 3ʳᵈ Earl of Rutland** etc. (12 Jul 1549 – 14 Apr 1587) suc. father 1563
= 6 Jun 1573; **Isabel Holcroft** (ca.1552 – 14 Jan 1605/6) daughter of Sir Thomas Holcroft

(I) **Elizabeth Manners, 15ᵗʰ Baroness de Ros** (Jan 1575/6 – 19 May 1591) suc. father 1587
= 1589; ◆**William Cecil, 2ⁿᵈ Earl of Exeter** (1566–1640)
Children are listed with other parent

c) **John Manners, 4ᵗʰ Earl of Rutland** (bef.1552 – 24 Feb 1587/8) suc. brother Apr 1587
= bef.1575; **Elizabeth Charlton** (... – 21 Mar 1594/5) daughter of Francis Charlton & Cicilia Fitton

(I) **Roger Manners, 5ᵗʰ Earl of Rutland** (6 Oct 1576 – 26 Jun 1612) suc. father 1588
= 5 Mar 1598/9; **Elizabeth Sydney** (20 Nov 1585 – 8 Aug 1612) daughter of Sir Philip Sydney & Frances Walsingham
no issue

(II) **Francis Manners, 6ᵗʰ Earl of Rutland** 17ᵗʰ Baron de Ros, 1ˢᵗ Baron Roos **KG** (1578 – 17 Dec 1632) suc. brother 1612; suc. cousin as Baron de Ros 27 Jun 1618; cr. Baron Roos 22 Jul 1616; KG 1616
=1 6 May 1602; **Frances Knyvett** (... – bef.26 Nov 1605)

daughter of Sir Henry Knyvett & Elizabeth Stumpe; =1st Sir
William Bevill

=2 aft.26 Oct 1608; ♦**Cecily Tufton** (1587 – 9 Sep 1653)
daughter of Sir John Tufton, 1st Baronet & Christian Browne;
she =1st Sir Edward Hungerford

issue of 1st (none surviving of 2nd):

(A) **Catherine Manners, 18th Baroness de Ros** (1603 – Oct
1649 Waterford, Ireland) suc. father 1632

=1 1620; ♦**George Villiers, 1st Duke of Buckingham**
(1592–1628)

=2 bef.12 Apr 1635; **Sir Randal MacDonnell, 1st
Marquess of Antrim** 2nd Earl of Antrim, Viscount Dunluce
(1609 – 3 Feb 1682) son of Randal MacDonnell, 1st Earl of
Antrim & Alice O'Neill; =2nd Rose O'Neill; suc. father 10 Dec
1636; cr. Marquess 26 Jan 1644/5, but that title became
extinct upon his death

issue of 1st (none by 2nd):

Children are listed with other parent

(III) **George Manners, 7th Earl of Rutland** (ca.1580 – 29 Mar
1641) suc. brother 1632

= 3 Mar 1605; **Frances Carey** (... – bef.1656) daughter of Sir
Edward Carey & Katherine Knyvett; =1st Ralph Baesh

no issue

(IV) **Hon. Sir Oliver Manners** (ca.1582 – ...)

(V) **Lady Bridget Manners** (...)

= ...; **Robert Tyrwhitt** (...) son of William Tyrwhitt

(A) **William Tyrwhitt** (...)

= ...; ♦**Hon. Catherine Browne** (...) daughter of Anthony
Browne, 2nd Viscount Montagu & Lady Jane Sackville

(1) **Francis Tyrwhitt** (...)

= ...

(a) **Catherine Tyrwhitt** (...)

= ...; **Sir Henry Hunloke, 2nd Baronet** (1645 – 1715)
son of Sir Henry Hunloke, 1st Baronet & Mariana Hickman
1648

Has further generations of issue

(VI) **Lady Elizabeth Manners** (... – Mar 1653/4)

= 1609; ♦**Emmanuel Scrope, 1st Earl of Sunderland**
(1584–1630)

Children are listed with other parent

(VII) **Lady Mary Manners** (...) unm.

(VIII) **Lady Frances Manners** (22 Oct 1588 Winkbourne,
Notts. – ca.1643)

= 1603; ♦**William Willoughby, 3rd Baron Willoughby**
(1584–1617)

Children are listed with other parent

2) **Lady Gertrude Manners** (... – 13 Jan 1566/7)
= 1539; ♦**George Talbot, 6ᵗʰ Earl of Shrewsbury** (1522–1590)
Children are listed with other parent
3) **Lady Anne Manners** (... – aft.27 Jun 1549)
= 1536; ♦**Henry Neville, 5ᵗʰ Earl of Westmorland** (ca.1524–1564)
Children are listed with other parent
4) **Lady Frances Manners** (... – Sep 1576)
= 1556; ♦**Henry Neville, 4ᵗʰ Baron Abergavenny** (aft.1527–1587)
Children are listed with other parent
5) **Hon. Roger Manners** (... – 1607)
6) **Hon. Sir Thomas Manners** (...)
= ...; **Theodosia Newton** (...) daughter of Sir Thomas Newton
a) **Sir Charles Manners** (...)
= ...
(I) **Anne Manners** (...)
= ...; **Sir George Carey** (... – 27 May 1678) son of Sir Edward Carey
(A) **Edward Carey** (... – 15 Jul 1718)
= ...; ♦**Mary Pelson** (...) daughter of Richard Pelson & Lady Anne Villiers
(1) **William Carey** (... – 1 Dec 1750)
= ...
(a) **Edward Carey** (...)
= ...; **Camilla** Annabella **Fleming** (...) daughter of Gilbert Fleming & Lady Camilla Bennet
Has further generations of issue
(b) **George Carey** (1731 – 1 Dec 1805)
=1 ...; **Cecilia Fagnani** (...)
=2 ...; **Frances Stonor** (...) daughter of Thomas Stonor & Mary Biddulph; =1ˢᵗ Thomas Giffard, 22ⁿᵈ of Chillington
Has further generations of issue by both
(2) **George Carey** (1685 – 1 Oct 1758)
= Jul 1723; ♦**Hon. Anne Clifford** (...) daughter of Hiugh Clifford, 2ⁿᵈ Baron Clifford of Chudleigh & Anne Preston
no issue
(B) **Constantia Carey** (...)
= ...; ♦**George Blount** (...–1702)
Children are listed with other parent
b) **Anne Manners** (...)
= ...; **William Vavasour** (1569 – bef.1626) son of Ralph Vavasour & Ursula Fairfax
(I) **Sir Thomas Vavasour, 1ˢᵗ Baronet** (... – bef. Mar 1635/6)
cr. Baronet 24 Oct 1628
= ...; **Ursula Giffard** (...) daughter of Walter Giffard

(A) **Sir Walter Vavasour, 2nd Baronet** (ca.1612 – aft.13 Aug 1666) suc. father 1636
= 8 Mar 1636; ♦**Hon. Ursula Belasyse** (ca.1617 – ...) daughter of Thomas Belasyse, 1st Viscount Fauconberg & Barbara Cholmley
  (1) **Sir Walter Vavasour, 3rd Baronet** (ca.1644 – 16 Feb 1712/3) suc. father 1666
  = ...; **Jane Crossland** (...) daughter of Sir John Crossland & Bridget Fleming
  no issue4
(B) **William Vavasour** (...) unm.
(C) **Thomas Vavasour** (... – 1644 Marston Moor) killed in battle
(D) **John Vavasour** (...) unm.
(E) **Peter Vavasour** (... – 23 Nov 1659)
= ...; **Elizabeth Langdale** (...) daughter of Philip Langdale
  (1) **Sir Walter Vavasour, 4th Baronet** (ca.1659 – 1740) suc. cousin 1713; unm.
  (2) **Peter Vavasour** (ca.1667 – 6 Jun 1735)
  = ...
    (a) **Sir Walter Vavasour, 5th Baronet** (... – 13 Apr 1766) suc. uncle 1740
    =1 ...; **Elizabeth Vavasour** (...) daughter of Peter Vavasour
    =2 Apr 1741; **Hon. Dorothy Langdale** (... – 25 Apr 1751) daughter of Marmaduke Langdale, 4th Baron Landgale & Hon. Elizabeth Widdrington
    Has further generations of issue by 2nd
(F) **Mary Vavasour** (... – 24 Dec 1631) a nun
(G) **Frances Vavasour** (...)
= ...; **Alphonso Thwen** (...)
issue ?
7) **Hon. Oliver Manners** (... – 1563)
8) **Lady Catherine Manners** (...)
= ...; **Sir Henry Capell** (...) son of Sir Edward Capell & Anne Pelham
a) **Sir Arthur Capell** (... – Apr 1632)
= ...; ♦**Margaret Grey** (...) daughter of Lord John Grey
(I) **Sir Henry Capell** (... – 29 Apr 1622)
= ...; **Theodosia Montagu** (...) daughter of Sir Edward Montagu & Elizabeth Harington
(A) **Arthur Capell, 1st Baron Capell** (20 Feb 1603/4 – 9 Mar 1648/9 London) executed; cr. Baron 5 Aug 1641
= 28 Nov 1627 Watford, Herts.; **Elizabeth Morrison** (bef.23 Mar 1610/1 Watford – 26 Jan 1660/1) daughter of Sir Charles Morrison, Baronet & Hon. Mary Hicks

(1) **Hon. Anne Capell** (...)
= ...; **John Strangways** (...)
issue ?

(2) **Hon. Mary Capell** (bef.16 Dec 1630 Herts. – 7 Jan 1714/5 London)
=1 1648; ◆**Henry, Lord Beauchamp** (1626–1654)
=2 1657; ◆**Henry Somerset, 1st Duke of Beaufort** (1629–1700)
issue of 1st:
Children are listed with other parent
issue of 2nd:
Children are listed with other parent

(3) **Arthur Capell, 1st Earl of Essex** Viscount Malden, 2nd Baron Capell (bef.28 Jan 1631/2 Hadham, Herts. – 13 Jul 1683 London) suicide while prison; suc. father 1649; cr. Earl etc. 20 Apr 1661
= 19 May 1653; ◆**Lady Elizabeth Percy** (1 Dec 1636 – 5 Feb 1717/8) daughter of Algernon Percy, 4th Earl of Northumberland & Lady Anne Cecil

　　(a) **Algernon Capell, 2nd Earl of Essex** etc. (28 Dec 1670 – 10 Jan 1710) suc. father 1683
　　= 28 Feb 1691/2; ◆**Lady Mary Bentinck** (1679 – 20Aug 1726) daughter of Hans William Bentinck, 1st Earl of Portland & Anne Villiers; =2nd Rt.Hon. Sir Conyers Darcy
　　has further generations of issue

　　(b) **Lady Anne** de Vere **Capell** (ca.1675 – 14 Oct 1752)
　　= 1688; ◆**Charles Howard, 3rd Earl of Carlisle** (1669–1738)
　　Has issue beyond the 12 generation limit in the male line

(4) **Hon. Elizabeth Capell** (bef.4 Jun 1633 Hadham – 30 Jul 1678)
= bef.1653; ◆**Charles Dormer, 2nd Earl of Carnarvon** (1632–1709)
Children are listed with other parent

(5) **Henry Capell, Baron Capell of Tewkesbury KB** (bef.6 Mar 1637/8 – 30 May 1696 Chapelizod, co Dublin) cr. Baron 11 Apr 1692 but it became wexinct upon his death; KB 1661
= 16 Feb 1658/9; **Dorothy Bennet** (... – 7 Jun 1721 Kew, Surrey) daughter of Richard Bennet & Mary Leman
no issue

(6) **Hon. Theodosia Capell** (bef.3 Jan 1639/40 Hadham – Mar 1661/2)
= 25 Jan 1660/1; **Henry Hyde, 2nd Earl of Clarendon** Viscount Cornbury Baron Hyde (2 Jun 1638 – 31 Oct 1709) son of Edward Hyde, 1st Earl of Claredon & Frances

Aylesbury; =2nd Flower Backhouse; suc. father 19 Dec 1674
   (a) **Edward Hyde, 3rd Earl of Clarendon** etc. (28 Nov
      1661 – 31 Mar 1723 London) suc. father 1709
      = 10 Jul 1688 Totteridge, Herts.; ♦**Katherine O'Brien,
      8th Baroness Clifton** (29 Jan 1673 – 11 Aug 1706 NY)
      daughter of Henry, Lord O'Brien & Katherine Stuart, 7th
      Baroness Clifton
      Has further generations of issue
(B) **Elizabeth Capell** (... – 6 Apr 1660)
   = 6 Nov 1628; **Sir William Wiseman, 1st Baronet** (... – 1
   Jul 1643) son of Thomas Wiseman & Alice Myles; cr. Baronet
   29 Aug 1628
   (1) **Sir William Wiseman, 2nd Baronet** (1630 – 14 Jan
      1684/5) suc. father 1643
      =1 26 Oct 1659; **Anne Prescot** (... – 11 May 1662) daughter
      of Sir John Prescot
      =2 16 May 1664; **Arabella Hewett** (... – 1705) daughter of
      Sir Thomas Hewett, 1st Baronet & Margaret Lytton
      issue of 2nd (none by 1st):
      (a) **Sir Thomas Wiseman, 3rd Baronet** (bef.16676 – 1
         May 1733) suc. father 1685; unm.
      (b) **Sir Charles Wiseman, 4th Baronet** (bef.27 Aug
         1676 – 3 Jun 1751) suc. brother 1733; unm.
      (c) **John Wiseman** (bef.14 Dec 1679 – ...)
         = ...; **Penelope ...** (...)
         Issue extinct 1774
   (2) **Very Rev. Capel Wiseman** (aft.1630 – Sep 1683) Dean
      of Raphoe, Bishop of Dromore
   (3) **Sir Edmund Wiseman** (1633 – 8 May 1704)
      = 18 Apr 1670; **Elizabeth Waldo** (... – 8 Dec 1694)
      daughter of Daniel Waldo
      (a) **Edmund Wiseman** (1671 – Oct 1741)
         = 3 Nov 1697; **Maria Harnage** (...) daughter of Edmund
         Harnage
         Has further generations of issue
   (4) **Theodosia Wiseman** (...)
      = 7 Apr 1662; **Sir Anthony Craven, Baronet** (...) son of
      Thomas Craven & Margaret Craven
      no issue
   (5) **Elizabeth Wiseman** (...)
      = ...; **Robert Tyderleigh** (...)
      issue ?
(C) **Anne Capell** (...)
   = ...; **Thomas Westrow** (...)
   (1) **Dorothy Westrow** (...)
      = ...; **Edward Hulse** (bef.18 Mar 1631/2 – 3 Dec 1711) son

of William Hulse & Anne ...
    (a) **Sir Edward Hulse, 1ˢᵗ Baronet** (1682 – 10 Apr 1759)
    cr. Baronet 7 Feb 1738/9
    = 15 Jan 1712/3; **Elizabeth Levett** (... – 15 Jan 1741/2)
    daughter of Sir Richard Levett
    Has further generations of issue
    (b) **William Hulse** (... – Aug 1761)
    (c) **Anne Hulse** (... – 30 Jan 1745) unm.
    (d) **Mary Hulse** (... – Oct 1721) unm.
b) **Mary Capell** (... – 12 Oct 1633)
= 10 Jul 1586; **Humphrey Mildmay** (... – 9 Aug 1613) son of Sir
Walter Mildmay & Mary Walsingham
(I) **Sir Humphrey Mildmay** (...)
= Jul 1616; **June Croftes** (...) daughter of Sir John Croftes
issue ?
(II) **Anthony Mildmay** (...)
Had issue, but is now extinct
(III) **Sir Henry Mildmay** (... – ca.1664/5)
= 6 Apr 1619; **Anne Halliday** (... – 12 Mar 1656/7) daughter of
William Halliday & Susane Rowe
    (A) **Henry Mildmay** (... – bef.14 Mar 1704)
    = 30 Aug 1674; **Alice Bramston** (... – 20 Jan 1691/2)
    daughter of Sir Moundiford Bramston
        (1) **Halliday Mildmay** (1675 – 18 Nov 1696)
        = ...; **Ann Bawden** (... – ca.1698) daughter of Sir John
        Bawden
            (a) **Letitia Mildmay** (bef.17 Aug 1694 – 2 Oct 1749)
            = 1706; ♦**Humphrey Mildmay** (1692–1761)
            Has issue beyond the 12 generation limit in the male line
    (B) **William Mildmay** (1623 – ...)
    (C) **Susan Mildmay** (...)
    (D) **Anne Mildmay** (...)
    (E) **Mary Mildmay** (...)
9) **Lady Elizabeth Manners** (... – 8 Aug 1570 Frodsham, Ches.)
= ...; **Sir John Savage** (ca.1525 – 5 Dec 1597) =2ⁿᵈ Elinor
Cotgrave
a) **Margaret Savage** (1549 – 7 Apr 1597)
= ...; **William Brereton, 1ˢᵗ Baron Brereton** (bef.6 Feb 1550
Brereton Hall, Ches. – 1 Oct 1631) son of Sir William Brereton &
Jane Warburton; cr. baron 11 May 1624
(I) **Hon. Mary Brereton** (28 Dec 1580 – Apr 1640)
= 1608; **Henry O'Brien, 4ᵗʰ Earl of Thomond** (1588–1639)
Children are listed with other parent
(II) **Hon. Sir John Brereton** (ca.1591 – 23 Dec 1629)
= ...; **Anne Fitton** (...) daughter of Sir Edward Fitton, 1ˢᵗ
Baronet & Anne Barrett

(A) **William Brereton, 2ⁿᵈ Baron Brereton** (28 Feb 1611 – Apr 1664) suc. grandfather 1631
= ...; ♦**Lady Elizabeth Goring** (... – Nov 1687) daughter of George Goring, 1ˢᵗ Earl of Norwich & Hon. Mary Neville
  (1) **William Brereton, 3ʳᵈ Baron Brereton** (bef.4 May 1631 – 7 Mar 1679/80 London) suc. father 1664
  = bef.1659; ♦**Hon. Frances Willoughby** (... – Sep 1680) daughter of Francis Willoughby, 5ᵗʰ Baron Willoughby & Hon. Elizabeth Cecil
    (a) **John Brereton, 4ᵗʰ Baron Brereton** (2 Dec 1659 – 1718 Brereton) suc. father 1680
    = 26 Jun 1686; **Mary Tipping** (ca.1655 – Feb 1714/5) daughter of Sir Thomas Tipping Elizabeth Beconshaw
    no issue
    (b) **Francis Brereton, 5ᵗʰ Baron Breton** (1 May 1662 – Apr 1722 London) suc. brother 1718, but title became extinct upon his death; unm.
  (2) **Hon. Elizabeth Brereton** (... – ca.1723) unm.
(B) **Jane Brereton** (...)
= ...; **Sir Robert Holte, 2ⁿᵈ Baronet** (... – 1679) son of Edward Holte; suc. grandfather 14 Dec 1654
  (1) **Sir Charles Holte, 3ʳᵈ Baronet** (ca.1649 – 20 Jun 1722) suc. father 1679
  = ...
    (a) **Sir Clobert Holte, 4ᵗʰ Baronet** (1682 – 1729) suc. father 1722
    = ...
    Has further generations of issue
(C) **Mary Brereton** (...)
b) **Sir John Savage, 1ˢᵗ Baronet** (1550 – 1615) cr. Baronet 1611
= ...; **Mary Alington** (ca.1548 – ...) daughter of Sir Richard Alington & Jane Cordell
(I) **Grace Savage** (...)
= ...; **Sir Richard Wilbraham, 1ˢᵗ Baronet** (... – 1643) son of Thomas Wilbraham & Frances Cholmondeley; cr. Baronet 1621
(A) **Elizabeth Wilbraham** (...)
= 1648; ♦**Sir Humphrey Brigges, 2ⁿᵈ Baronet** (1615– 1691)
Children are listed with other parent
(B) **Sir Thomas Wilbraham, 2ⁿᵈ Baronet** (... – ca.1660) suc. father 1643
= ...; **Elizabeth Wilbraham** (...) daughter of Roger Wilbraham & Mary Baber de Tew
  (1) **Ralph Wilbraham** (... – bef.1660)
  = ...; **Christiana Leigh** (...) daughter of Edward Leigh
    (a) **Elizabeth Wilbraham** (...)

= ...; ◆**Sackville Tufton** (1647–1721)
Children are listed with other parent
(b) **Sir Thomas Wilbraham, 3ʳᵈ Baronet** (ca.1630 –
1692) suc. grandfather ca.1660, but title became extinct
upon his death
= ...; **Elizabeth Mytton** (1631 – 1703) daughter of Edward
Mytton
Has further generations of issue
(2) (a daughter) **Wilbraham** (...)
= 27 May 1657; **Mytton Davies** (...)
(a) **Catherine Davies** (...)
= ...; **Sir William Williams, 2ⁿᵈ Baronet** (ca.1665 – Oct
1740) son of Sir William Williams, 1ˢᵗ Baronet & Margaret
Cyffin; =1ˢᵗ Jane Thelwall; suc. father 11 Jul 1700
no issue
(II) **Thomas Savage, 1ˢᵗ Viscount Savage** 2ⁿᵈ Baronet
(ca.1586 – 20 Nov 1635) suc. father 1615; cr. Viscount 1626
= 14 May 1602; ◆**Elizabeth Darcy, Countess Rivers**
(1584 – 9 Mar 1650/1) daughter of Thomas Darcy, 1ˢᵗ Earl
Rivers & Mary Kitson; cr. Countess ad personam 1641
(A) **Lady Anne Savage** (... – 16 Jun 1696)
= ...; ◆**Robert Brudenell, 2ⁿᵈ Earl of Cardigan** (1607–
1703)
Children are listed with other parent
(B) **John Savage, 2ⁿᵈ Earl Rivers** Viscount Colchester, Baron
Darcy, 2ⁿᵈ Viscount Savage, 3ʳᵈ Baronet (... – 10 Oct 1654) suc.
father 1635; suc. maternal grandfather by special remainder
25 Feb 1639/40
=1 ...; ◆**Hon. Catherine Parker** (...) daughter of William
Parker, 13ᵗʰ Baron Morley & Elizabeth Tresham
=2 ...; **Mary Ogle** (...)
issue of 1ˢᵗ:
(1) **Thomas Savage, 3ʳᵈ Earl Rivers** etc. (ca.1628 – 14 Sep
1694 London) suc. father 1654
=1 ...; ◆**Elizabeth Scrope** (...) natural daughter of
Emmanuel Scrope, 1ˢᵗ Earl of Sunderland & Martha Jeanes
=2 8 Aug 1684 London; **Lady Arabella Bertie** (ca.1656 –
28 Feb 1716/7) daughter of Robert Bertie, 3ʳᵈ Earl of Lindsey
& Mary Massingberd
issue of 1ˢᵗ (none by 2ⁿᵈ):
(a) **Richard Savage, 4ᵗʰ Earl Rivers** etc. (... – 1712) suc.
father 1694
= ...
Has further generations of issue
(b) **Lady Arabella Savage** (...)
= ...; **Sir Erasmus Norwich, 3ʳᵈ Baronet** (...) son of Sir

Roger Norwich, 2nd Baronet & Catherine Fermor; suc.
father 23 Sep 1691
no issue
(2) **Lady Jane Savage** (... – 6 Jun 1676)
=1 1653; ♦**George Brydges, 6th Baron Chandos** (1620–
1655)
=2 21 Oct 1655 London; **Sir William Sedley, 4th Baronet**
(... – 1656) son of Sir John Sedley, 2nd Baronet & Elizabeth
Savile; suc. brother 1641
=3 1657; **George Pitt** (... – 27 Jul 1694) son of Edward Pitt
& Rachel Morton
issue of 1st:
Children are listed with other parent
issue of 3rd (none by 2nd):
(a) **Elizabeth Pitt** (...)
=1699; ♦**Thomas FitzWilliam, 4th Viscount
FitzWilliam** (ca.1640 – 1704) daughter of William
FitzWilliam, 3rd Viscount FitzWilliam & Mary Luttrell; =1st
♦Mary Stapleton
Has further generations of issue
(b) **George Pitt** (...)
= ...
Has further generations of issue
(c) **Mary Pitt** (... – Aug 1739)
= bef.1694; ♦**Sir Charles Browne, 2nd Baronet**
(aft.1663–1751)
Children are listed with other parent
(3) **Lady Elizabeth Savage** (... – 16 Jul 1665)
= ...; ♦**William Petre, 4th Baron Petre** (1626–1683)
Children are listed with other parent
issue of 2nd:
(4) **Hon. Peter Savage** (...)
(C) **Hon. Thomas Savage** (1606 – Feb 1655)
= ...; **Elizabeth Whitmore** (1605 – ...) daughter of Sir
William Whitmore & Margaret Beeston; =2nd ♦Hon. Sir
Edward Somerset
(1) **Elizabeth Savage** (1634 – 1685)
= ...; **Marmaduke Langdale, 2nd Baron Langdale**
(1628 – 1703) son of Marmaduke Langdale, 1st Baron
Langdale & Lenox Rodes; suc. father 5 Aug 1661
(a) **Hon. Jane Langdale** (...)
= ...; **Sir Hugh Smithson, 3rd Baronet** (... – 2 Mar
1733) son of Sir Jerome Smithson, 2nd Baronet
Has further generations of issue
(b) **Marmaduke Langdale, 3rd Baron Langdale** (1656 –
12 Dec 1718 York) suc. father 1703

= 1679; **Frances Draycott** (1659 – ...) daughter of Sir Richard Draycott & Mary Blomer
Has further generations of issue
(D) **Lady Jane Savage** (...)
= 1622; ♦**John Paulet, 5th Marquess of Winchester** (1598–1675)
Children are listed with other parent
(E) **Lady Elizabeth Savage** (...)
= Sep 1634; **John Thimbleby** (...)
issue ?
(F) **Lady Dorothy Savage** (ca.1611 – 6 Dec 1691)
= 1637; ♦**Charles Howard, 2nd Earl of Berkshire** (1615–1679)
Children are listed with other parent
(G) **Lady Henrietta Maria Savage** (...)
= ...; **Ralph Sheldon** (1623 – 24 Jun 1684) son of William Sheldon & Hon. Elizabeth Petre
issue ?
c) **Eleanora Savage** (1557 – ...)
=1 1577; **Sir Henry Bagenal** (1556 – 14 Aug 1598) killed in battle; son of Sir Nicholas Bagenal & Eleanora Griffith
=2 ...; **Sir Sackville Trevor** (...) son of John Trevor & Mary Bruges
issue of 1st (none by 2nd):
(I) **Anne Bagenal** (...)
= ...; **Rt.Rev. Lewis Bayly** (... – 26 Oct 1631) Bishop of Bangor
(A) **Nicholas Bayly** (...)
= ...; **Dorothy Hall** (... – Feb 1714)
(1) **Sir Edward Bayly, 1st Baronet** (... – 28 Sep 1741) cr. Baronet 4 Jul 1730
= 28 Aug 1708; **Dorothy Lambart** (... – 16 Aug 1745) daughter of Hon. Oliver Lambart & Eleanor Crane
(a) **Sir Nicholas Bayly, 2nd Baronet** (1709 Anglesey, Wales – 9 Dec 1782 London) suc. father 1741
=1 19 Apr 1737 London; **Caroline Paget** (1707 – 7 Feb 1766 Anglesey) daughter of Thomas Paget & Mary Whitcombe
=2 aft.1766; **Anne Hunter** (... – 18 May 1818)
Has further generations of issue by 1st
(b) **Very Rev. Edward Bayly** (aft.1710 – ...) Archdeacon of Dublin
= 13 Jan 1738; **Catherine Price** (...) daughter of James Price; =1st John Savage
Has further generations of issue
(c) **Lambart Bayly** (aft.1711 – ca.1747)
= Jan 1743; **Elizabeth Rotton** (...) daughter of John
57

Rotton
Has further generations of issue
    (d) **Charles Bayly** (aft.1712)
    = ...; **Anne Graves** (...)
    issue ?
  (II) **Arthur Bagenal** (...)
  = ...; **Magdalen Trevor** (...) daughter of Sir Richard Trevor;
  she =2nd ... Tyringham
    (A) **Nicholas Bagenal** (... – 1712)
    =1 ...; **Lady Anne** Charlotte **Bruce** (...) daughter of Robert
    Bruce, 2nd Earl of Elgin & Lady Diana Grey
    =2 ...; **Sydney Grosvenor** (...) daughter of Roger Grosvenor
    & Christian Myddleton
    issue of 1st (none by 2nd):
      (1) **Elizabeth Bagenal** (...)
      = ...; **Rev. Henry Rowlands** (...)
      issue ?
  (III) **Gryffyth Bagenal** (...) unm
  (IV) **John Bagenal** (...) unm
  (V) **Roger Bagenal** (...) unm
  (VI) **Eleanor Bagenal** (...)
  =1 ...; **Sir Robert Salusbury** (...)
  =2 ...; **Thomas Needham** (...) son of Robert Needham &
  Frances Aston
  issue ?
  (VII) **Mary Bagenal** (...)
  = ...; **Thomas Bodville** (...)
  issue ?
  (VIII) **Elizabeth Bagenal** (...) unm.
  (IX) **Jane Bagenal** (...)
  = ...; **Robert Griffith** (...)
  issue ?
10) **Hon. Sir John Manners** (1527 – 4 Jun 1611)
  = ...; ♦**Dorothy Vernon** (1531 – 24 Jun 1584) daughter of Sir
George Vernon & Margaret Tailboys
a) **Sir George Manners** (... – 23 Apr 1623)
  = 1 Aug 1593; **Grace Pierrepont** (...) daughter of Sir Henry
Pierrepont & Frances Cavendish
  (I) **John Manners, 8th Earl of Rutland** (10 Jun 1604 – 29 Sep
  1679) suc cousin 29 Mar 1641
  = 1628 Barnwell Castle, Northants; ♦**Hon. Frances Montagu**
  (8 Aug 1613 – 19 May 1671) daughter of Edward Montagu, 1st
  Baron Montagu & Frances Cotton
    (A) **Lady Frances Manners** (2 Dec 1630 – 2 Dec 1660)
    = 1646; ♦**John Cecil, 4th Earl of Exeter** (1628–1678)
    Children are listed with other parent

(B) **Lady Grace Manners** (1632 Haddon, Derbys. – 15 Feb 1699/1700)

=1 bef.1666; **Patrick Chaworth, 3rd Viscount Chaworth** (bef.20 Jun 1635 – Jun 1693) son of John Chaworth, 2nd Viscount Chaworth & Hon. Elizabeth Noel; suc. father Jun 1644

=2 aft.1693; ♦**Sir William Langhorne, Baronet** (... – 26 Feb 1714/5) son of William Langhorne & Mary Oxenbridge; cr. Baronet 1668, but it became extinct upon his death

issue of 1st (none by 2nd):

(1) **Hon. Juliana Chaworth** (ca.1655 – 9 Nov 1692)
   = bef.1682; **Chambre Brabazon, 5th Earl of Meath** 6th Baron Brabazon, Baron of Ardee (ca.1645 – 1 Apr 1715) son of Edward Brabazon, 2nd Earl of Meath & Mary Chambré; suc. brother 22 Feb 1707/8

   (a) **Lady Frances Brabazon** (... – 4 Nov 1751)
      = ...; **Hon. Henry Ponsonby** (aft.1680 – 11 May 1745 Fontenay, France) killed in battle; son of William Ponsonby, 1st Viscount Duncannon & Mary Moore
      Has further generations of issue

   (b) **Lady Juliana Brabazon** (...)

   (c) **Chaworth Brabazon, 6th Earl of Meath** etc (1686 – 14 May 1763) suc. father 1715
      = 13 Dec 1731; **Juliana Prendergast** (... – 12 Dec 1758) daughter of Sir Thomas Prendergast, 1st Baronet & Penelope Cadogan
      no issue

   (d) **Lady Mary Brabazon** (...)
      = ...; **Rev. William Tisdall** (...)
      issue ?

   (e) **Lady Catherine Brabazon** (...)
      = ...; **Thomas Hallowes** (...)
      Has further generations of issue

   (f) **Edward Brabazon, 7th Earl of Meath** etc. (bef.24 Nov 1691 – 24 Nov 1772) suc. brother 1763
      = ca.1720; **Martha Collins** (... – 24 Apr 1762) daughter of Rev. William Collins
      Has further generations of issue

(C) **Lady Margaret Manners** (... – bef.30 Aug 1682)
   = ca.1665; ♦**James Cecil, 3rd Earl of Salisbury** (1646–1683)
   These descendants are beyond the 12 generation limit in the male line.

(D) **Lady Dorothy Manners** (... – Jun 1698)
   = 1669; ♦**Anthony Ashley-Cooper, 2nd Earl of Shaftesbury** (1652–1699)

Children are listed with other parent

(E) **Lady Elizabeth Manners** (... – 7 Dec 1700)
= 17 Sep 1669; **James Annesley, 2ⁿᵈ Earl of Anglesey**
Baron Annesley, 3ʳᵈ Viscount of Valentia, Baron Mountnorris
(ca.1645 – 1 Apr 1690) son of Arthur Annesley, 1ˢᵗ Earl of
Anglesey & Elizabeth Altham; suc. father 6 Apr 1686
(1) **Lady Elizabeth Annesley** (... – dec 1725)
= ...; **Robert Gayer** (...) son of Sir Robert Gayer
(a) **Anne Gayer** (...)
= ...; **Rev. Francis Annesley** (bef.1701 – 1 May 1740) son
of Francis Annesley & Elizabeth Martin
Has further generations of issue
(2) **James Annesley, 3ʳᵈ Earl of Angelesey** etc (bef.13 Jul
1674 – 21 Jan 1701/2) suc. father 1690
= 28 Oct 1699 London (dv.1701); ♦**Lady Catherine
Darnley** (ca.1681 – 13 Mar 1743) natural daughter of James
II, King of England & Catherine Sedley, Countess of
Dorchester; =2ⁿᵈ John Sheffield, Duke of Buckingham
(a) **Lady Catherine Annesley** (1700 – 18 Jan 1735/6)
=1 25 Sep 1718; **William Philips** (bef.11 Oct 1698 – 1 Feb
1729/30) son of Sir Constantine Phipps & Catherine
Sawyer
=2 ...; **John Sheldon** (...)
Has further generations of issue by 1ˢᵗ
(3) **John Annesley, 4ᵗʰ Earl of Anglesey** etc. (bef.18 Jan
1676 – 18 Sep 1710) suc. brother 1686
=21 May 1706; ♦**Henrietta Maria Stanley, 4ᵗʰ Baroness
Strange** (ca.1687 – 26 Jun 1718) daughter of William
Stanley, 9ᵗʰ Earl of Derby & Lady Elizabeth Butler; =2ⁿᵈ John
Ashburham, 1ˢᵗ Earl of Ashburnham
(a) **Lady Elizabeth Annesley** (... – 23 Apr 1718) unm.
(4) **Arthur Annesley, 5ᵗʰ Earl of Anglesey** etc. (aft.1677 –
1 Apr 1737) suc. brother 1710
= ca.1701; **Hon. Mary Thompson** (... – 22 Jan 1718/9
Woodstock, Oxon) daughter of John Thompson, 1ˢᵗ baron
Haversham & Lady Farnces Annesley
no issue

(F) **John Manners, 1ˢᵗ Duke of Rutland** Marquess of
Granby, Baron Manners, 9ᵗʰ Earl of Rutland (29 May 1638 –
10 Jan 1711) suc. father 1679; cr. Baron 30 Apr 1679, and Duke
etc. 29 Mar 1703
=1 15 Jul 1658; ♦**Lady Anne Pierrepont** (9 Mar 1630/1 –
bef.Jan 1696/7) daughter of Henry Pierrepont, Marquess of
Dorchester & Hon. Cicelia Bayning
=2 20 Nov 1671; **Lady Diana Bruce** (... – 15 Jul 1672)
daughter of Robert Bruce, 2ⁿᵈ Earl of Elgin & Lady Diana Grey;

she =1st Sir Seymour Shirley, 5th Baronet
=3 8 Jan 1673/4; ♦**Hon. Catherine Noel** (10 Aug 1657 – 24 Jan 1732/3) daughter of Baptist Noel, 3rd Viscount Campden & Lady Elizbaeth Bertie
issue of 3rd (non surviving by others):
(1) **Lady Catherine Manners** (1675 – 7 Mar 1722)
 = Sep 1692; **John Levenson-Gower, 1st Baron Gower** 5th Baronet (7 Jan 1674/5 – 31 Aug 1709) son of Sir William Levenson-Gower, 4th Baronet & Lady Jane Granville
 (a) **John Levenson-Gower, 1st Earl Gower** Viscopunt Trentham, 2nd Baron Gower etc. (10 Aug 1694 – 25 Dec 1754) suc. father 1709; cr. Earl etc. 8 Jul 1746
 =1 136 Mar 1711/2; ♦**Lady Evelyn Pierrepont** (bef.19 Sep 1691 – 26 Jun 1727) daughter of Evelyn Pierrpont, 1st Duke of Kingston-upon-Hull & Lady Mary Feilding
 =2 31 Oct 1733 London; **Penelope Stonhouse** (... – 19 Aug 1734 Trentham, Staffs.) daughter of Sir John Stonhouase, 3rd Baronet & Penelope Dashwood; =1st Sir Henry Atkins, 4th Baronet
 =3 16 May 1736; ♦**Lady Mary Tufton** (6 Jul 1701 – 19 Feb 1785) daughter of Thomas Tufton, 6th Earl of Thanet & Lady Catherine Cavendish; =1st Anthony Grey, 3rd Baron Lucas
 Has further generations of issue by 1st and 3rd
 (b) **Hon. William Levenson-Gower** (... – 13 Dec 1756) = 26 May 1730; **Anne Grosvenor** (...) daughter of Sir Thomas Grosvenor, 3rd Baronet & Mary Davis
 Issue is extinct
 (c) **Hon. Thomas Levenson-Gower** (... – 12 Aug 1727) unm.
 (d) **Hon. Baptist Levenson-Gower** (... – 4 Aug 1782) unm.
 (e) **Hon. Jane Levenson-Gower** (... – 10 Jun 1726) = 5 Jan 1719; **John Proby** (... – 16 Mar 1762) son of William Proby & Henrietta Cornwall
 Has further generations of issue
 (f) **Hon. Katherine Levenson-Gower** (bef.12 Nov 1701 – ...)
(2) **John Manners, 2nd Duke of Rutland** etc. **KG** (18 Sep 1676 – 22 Feb 1721) suc. father 1711
 =1 23 Aug 1693; ♦**Catherine Russell** (23 Aug 1676 – 30 Oct 1711) daughter of Rt.Hon. William, Lord Russell & Lady Rachel Wriothesley
 =2 1 Jan 1713; **Hon. Lucy Sherard** (1685 – 27 Oct 1751) daughter of Bennet Sherard, 2nd Baron Sherard & Elizabeth Christopher

issue of 1st:

(a) **John Manners, 3rd Duke of Rutland** etc (21 Oct 1696 – 29 May 1779) suc. father 1721
= 27 Aug 1717; **Hon. Bridget Sutton** (30 Nov 1699 – 16 Jun 1734) daughter of Robert Sutton, 2nd Baron Lexinton & Margaret Hungerford
Has further generations of issue

(b) **Lady Catherine Manners** (... – 18 Feb 1780)
= 29 Oct 1726; **Rt.Hon. Henry Pelham** (1696 – 6 Mar 1754) son of Thomas Pelham, 1st Baron Pelham & Lady Grace Holles
Has further generations of issue

(c) **Lady Frances Manners** (...)
= 2 Sep 1732; **Hon. Richard Arundell** (bef.1698 – 1759) son of John Arundell, 2nd Baron Arundell & Barbara Slingsby
no issue

(d) **Lord William Manners** (aft.1696 – 1772)
Has further generations of issue with his mistress

(e) **Lady Elizabeth Manners** (ca.1709 – 22 Mar 1730)
= ...; **John Monckton, 1st Viscount Galway** Baron Killard (1695 – 15 Jul 1751) son of Robert Monckton & Theodosia Fountaine
Has further generations of issue

issue of 2nd:

(f) **Lord Sherard Manners** (1713 – 13 Jan 1742) unm.

(g) **Lady Caroline Manners** (... – 10 Nov 1769)
=1 2 Oct 1734; **Sir Henry Harpur, 5th Baronet** (1708 – 7 Jun 1748) son of Sir John Harpur, 4th Baronet & Catherine Crew; suc. father 24 Jun 1741
=2 17 Jul 1753; **Sir Robert Burdett, 4th Baronet** (28 May 1716 – 13 Feb 1797) son of Robert Burdett & Hon. Elizabeth Tracy; =1st Elizabeth Sedley; suc. grandfather 28 May 1716
Has further generations of issue by 1st

(h) **Lady Lucy Manners** (ca.1717 – 18 Jun 1788)
= 28 Oct 1742; **William Graham, 2nd Duke of Montrose** Marquess of Graham, Earl of Kincardine, Earl Graham, Viscount of Dundaff, Lord Aberuthven, Mugdock, and Fintry, Baron Graham 5th Marquess of Montrose, Earl of Kincardine Lord Graham and Mugdock, 11th Lord Graham, 9th Earl of Montrose (27 Aug 1712 – 23 Sep 1790 London) son of James Graham, 1st Duke of Montrose & Lady Christian Carnegie; suc. father 7 Jan 1742
Has further generations of issue

(i) **Lord Robert Manners** (ca.1721 – 31 May 1782)

= 1 Jan 1756; **Mary Diggs** (ca.1737 – 22 Feb 1829)
Has further generations of issue
(3) **Lady Dorothy Manners** (1681 – 27 Apr 1734)
= 1707; ♦**Baptist Noel, 3rd Earl of Gainsborough**
(1684–1714)
These descendants are beyond the 12 generation limit in the male line
(G) **Lady Anne Manners** (ca.1655 –...)
= Apr 1672; ♦**Scrope Howe, 1st Viscount Howe** (Nov 1648 – 26 Jan 1712) son of John Howe & Lady Arabella Scrope; =2nd Hon. Juliana Alington; cr. Viscount 16 May 1701
no issue
(II) **Elizabeth Manners** (...)
= 1616; **Robert Sutton, 1st Baron Lexinton** (... – 13 Oct 1668) son of Sir William Sutton & Susan Cony; =2nd Anne Palmes; =3rd Mary St.Leger; cr. Baron 21 Nov 1645
no issue
(III) **Eleanor Manners** (...)
= 1622; **Lewis Watson, 1st Baron Rockingham** (14 Jul 1584 – 12 Jan 1652/3) son of Sir Edward Watson; =1st ♦Catherine Bertie; cr. Baron 1645
(A) **Hon. Grace Watson** (... – Mar 1658)
= ...; **Sir Edward Barkham, 2nd Baronet** (1628 – 1688) son of Sir Edward Barkham, 1st Baronet & Frances Berney; he =2nd ♦Frances Napier; suc. father 2 Aug 1667
no issue
(B) **Edward Watson, 2nd Baron Rockingham** (30 Jun 1630 – 22 Jun 1689)
= 1654; ♦**Lady Anne Wentworth** (...) daughter of Thomas Wentworth, 1st Earl of Stafford & Lady Arabella Holles
(1) **Lewis Watson, 1st Earl of Rockingham** 3rd Baron Rockingham (29 Dec 1655 – 19 Mar 1723/4) suc. father 1689; cr. Earl 9 Oct 1714
= 17 Jul 1677; **Lady Catherine Sondes** (1657 – 1695) daughter of George Soundes, 1st Earl of Feversham & Mary Villiers
(a) **Edward, Viscount Sondes** (... – 21 Mar 1722)
= 21 Mar 1708/9; ♦**Lady Katherine Tufton** (24 Apr 1693 – 13 Feb 1733/4) daughter of Thomas Tufton, 6th Earl of Thanet & Lady Catherine Cavendish
Has further generations of issue
(b) **Lady Margaret Watson** (...)
= 8 Apr 1725; **John Monson, 1st Baron Monson** KB (ca.1693 – 1748) son of George Monson & Anne Wren; cr. Baron 28 May 1728; KB 1725
Has further generations of issue

(c) **Lady Mary Watson** (...)
= ...; **Wray Saunderson** (...) son of Nicholas Saunderson
& Elizabeth Wray
issue ?
(d) **Lady Arabella Watson** (...)
= ...; **Sir Robert Furnese, 2ⁿᵈ Baronet** (1687 – 1733)
son of Sir Henry Furnese & Anne Brough
Issue extinct 1776
(2) **Hon. Thomas Watson-Wentworth** (... – 1723)
= 1689; **Alice Proby** (...) daughter of Sir Thomas Proby, 1ˢᵗ
Baronet & Frances Cotton
(a) **Thomas Watson-Wentworth, 1ˢᵗ Marquess of
Rockingham** Earl of Malton, Viscount Higham, Baron
Malton, **KB** (... – 14 Dec 1750) cr. Baron 1728, Earl 1734,
and Marquess 1746
= 22 Sep 1716; ◆**Lady Mary Finch** (1701 – 30 May 1761)
daughter of Daniel Finch, 7ᵗʰ Earl of Winchilsea & Hon.
Anne Hatton
Has further generations of issue
(3) **Hon. Eleanor Watson** (... – 1705)
= 25 Oct 1679; **Thomas Leigh, 2ⁿᵈ Baron Leigh** 3ʳᵈ
Baronet (bef.17 Jun 1652 – 12 Nov 1710) son of Hon. Sir
Thomas Leigh & Jane FitzMaurice; =1ˢᵗ Elizabeth Brown
(a) **Lady Eleanor Leigh** (... – 1756)
= 1709; ◆**Thomas Verney** (1691–1710)
*These descendants are beyond the 12ᵗʰ generation in the
father's line*
(b) **Edward Leigh, 3ʳᵈ Baron Leigh** (13 Jan 1683/4 – 9
Mar 1737/8) suc. father 1710
= 11 Sep 1705; **Mary Holbech** (...) daughter of Thomas
Holbech & Elizabeth Paulet
Has further generations of issue
(c) **Hon. Charles Leigh** (1686 – 28 Jul 1749)
= 1716; **Lady Barbara Lumley** (... – 4 Jan 1755) daughter
of Richard Lumley, 1ˢᵗ Earl of Scarborough & Frances Jones
issue ?
(d) **Hon. Lewis Leigh** (1690 – 1706) unm.
(4) **Hon. Arabella Watson** (... – 1735)
= ...; **Sir James Oxenden, 2ⁿᵈ Baronet** (1641 – 1708) son
of Sir Henry Oxenden, 1ˢᵗ Baronet & Elizabeth Meredith; =1ˢᵗ
Elizabeth Chute; suc. father 1686
issue ?
(IV) **Frances Manners** (... – 1652)
= ...; **Nicholas Saunderson, 2ⁿᵈ Viscount Castleton** Baron
Saunderson, 2ⁿᵈ Baronet (ca.1595 – 13 Nov 1640) son of
Nicholas Saunderson, 1ˢᵗ Viscount Castleton & Mildred Elltoft;

suc. father 17 May 1631

(A) **Hon. Mildred Saunderson** (... – 8 May 1656)
= 3 Jul 1651; ♦**Thomas Belasyse, 1ˢᵗ Earl of Fauconberg**
(bef.16 Mar 1627/8 – 31 Dec 1700) son of Hon. Henry Belasyse
& Grace Barton; =2ⁿᵈ ♦Mary Cromwell
no issue

(B) **Nicholas Saunderson, 3ʳᵈ Viscount Castleton** (ca.1627
– 1641) suc. father 1640; unm.

(C) **Peregrine Saunderson, 4ᵗʰ Viscount Castleton**
(ca.1628 – 1650) suc. brother 1641; unm.

(D) **George Saunderson, 5ᵗʰ Viscount Castleton** (12 Oct
1631 – 27 May 1714 Sandbeck, Yorks.) suc. brother 1650
=1 bef.Mar 1656; ♦**Grace Belasyse** (... – 16 Nov 1667)
daughter of Hon. Henry Belasyse & Grace Barton
=2 14 Feb 1674/5 London; **Sarah Evelyn** (... – Oct 1717)
daughter of Sir John Evelyn & Elizabeth Cooke; =1ˢᵗ Sir John
Wray, 1ˢᵗ Baronet; =2ⁿᵈ Thomas Fanshawe, 2ⁿᵈ Viscount
Fanshawe
issue of 1ˢᵗ (none by 2ⁿᵈ):

(1) **James Saunderson, Earl Castleton** Baron Saunderson
6ᵗʰ Viscount Castleton etc. (... – 23 May 1723 Richmond,
Surrey) unm. suc. father 1714; cr. Earl 18 Jun 1720, but all
titles became extinct upon his death

(2) **Hon. Nicholas Saunderson** (...)
= ...; **Elizabeth Wray** (...) daughter of Sir John Wray, 3ʳᵈ
Baronet & Sarah Evelyn
Issue is extinct

(V) **Dorothy Manners** (...)
= ...; **Sir Thomas Lake** (... – 1653) son of Sir Thomas Lake &
Mary Ryder
issue ?

B) **Hon. Eleanor Manners** (... – 13 Sep 1547)
= 1524; ♦**John Bourchier, 2ⁿᵈ Earl of Bath** (1499–1561)
Children are listed with other parent

C) **Hon Sir Richard Manners** (...)
= ..; **Margaret Dymoke** (... – 1550) daughter of Sir Robert Dymoke
& Anne Cresmore; =1ˢᵗ Sir Richard Vernon

1) **John Manners** (...)

D) **Hon. Sir Oliver Manners** (...)

E) **Hon. Anne Manners** (...)
= ...; **Sir Henry Capel** (...)
issue ?

F) **Hon. Elizabeth Manners** (...)
= bef.1513; **Thomas Sandys, 2ⁿᵈ Baron Sandys** (...) son of
William Sandys, 1ˢᵗ Baron Sandys & Margaret Bray
issue ?

G) **Hon. Margaret Manners** (...)
 =1 ...; **Sir Henry Strangways** (...)
 =2 ...; **Robert Heneage** (...)
 issue ?
H) **Hon. Catherine Manners** (1511 – aft.1547)
 = ca.1526; **Sir Robert Constable** (bef.1495 – 12 Oct 1558) son of
 Sir Marmaduke Constable & Barbara Soothill
 1) **Sir Marmaduke Constable** (... – 1 Feb 1575)
  = 1547; ♦**Hon. Jane Conyers** (1522 – 1558) daughter of
  Christopher Conyers, 2nd Baron Conyers & Anne Dacre
  a) **Sir Philip Constable** (1547 – 14 Jul 1619)
   = 1567; ♦**Margaret Tyrwhitt** (1552 – ...) daughter of Sir Robert
   Tyrwhitt & Elizabweth Oxenbrige
   (I) **Robert Constable** (1568 – 1599)
    = 1590; **Jane Dolman** (1580 – ...) daughter of Thomas Dolman
    & Elizabeth Vavasour
    issue ?
   (II) **Roger Constable** (1569 – 3 Apr 1625)
    = 1599; **Mary Cotton** (...)
    issue ?
   (III) **Francis Constable** (1573 – aft.20 Jul 1617)
    = 1603; **... Lengar** (...) daughter of John Lengar
    issue ?
   (IV) **Sir Marmaduke Constable** (ca.1574 – 3 Apr 1632)
    = 25 Nov 1593; **Frances Metham** (...) daughter of Thomas
    Metham & Catherine Bellasis
    (A) **Sir Philip Constable, 1st Baronet** (ca.1595 – 1664) cr.
     Baronet 1642
     = ...; **Anne Roper** (...) daughter of Sir William Roper
     (1) **Sir Marmaduke Constable, 2nd Baronet** (Apr 1619 –
      1680) suc. father 1664
      = 17 Mar 1648/9; **Anne Sherburne** (...) daughter of
      Richard Sherburne & Elizabeth Walmesley
      (a) **Sir Philip** Mark **Constable, 3rd Baronet** (25 Apr
       1651 – 1710)
       = ...; **Anne Radclyffe** (...) daughter of Francis Radclyffe,
       1st Earl of Derwentwater & Catherine Fenwick
       Has further generations of issue
     (2) **Catherine Constable** (1630 – 30 Apr 1681)
      = ...; ♦**Edward Sheldon** (1624–1676)
      Children are listed with other parent
   (V) **Michael Constable** (1578 – 1615)
    = 1602; **Frances Tyndall** (...)
    issue ?
   (VI) **Barbara Constable** (1581 – ca.1610)
    = ...; **Sir Thomas Metham** (1575 – 2 Jul 1644)

(A) **Barbara Metham** (1602 – 20 May 1626)
   = 1625; **Thomas Dolman** (1582 – 13 Jul 1639) son of Sir
   Robert Dolman & Eleanor Mallory; =1st Temperance Watson
   no issue
(VII) **Frances Constable** (4 Jul 1584 – 18 Nov 1613)
   = 1597; **Walter Rudston** (...)
   issue ?
(VIII) **Jane Constable** (29 Apr 1589 – 15 Jul 1630)
   = 1613; **Robert Sothby** (bef.30 Mar 1583 – 26 Nov 1652) son
   of Roger Sothby & Elizabeth Hungate
   (A) **Marmaduke Sothby** (... – 26 Sep 1681)
     = ...
     (1) **Robert Sothby** (bef.30 Aug 1657 – ...)
   (B) **William Sothby** (20 Nov 1621 Burnby, Yorks. – ...)
     = ...; **Dorothy Gray** (...)
     (1) **John Sothby** (1677 – ...)
       = ...; **Elizabeth Camplishon** (...)
       (a) **Thomas Sothby** (...)
         = ...
         Has further generations of issue
       (b) **Robert Sothby** (ca.1706 – ...)
         = ...
         Has further generations of issue
2) **Barbara Constable** (...)
   = ...; ♦**Sir William Babthorpe** (1524–1581)
   Children are listed with other parent
3) **Everilda Constable** (...)
   = ...; **Thomas Crathorne** (...)
 a) **Katherine Crathorne** (...)
   = ...; **Ralph Creyke** (...) son of William Creyke
   (I) **Robert Creyke** (...)
     = ...; **Margaret Thornborough** (...) daughter of George
     Thornborough
     (A) **Catherine Creyke** (3 Jan 1618/9 – ...)
       = bef.1640; ♦**James Boyd, 9th Lord Boyd** (1597–1654)
       Children are listed with other parent
   (II) **Gregory Creyke** (...)
     = ...
     (A) **Gregory Creyke** (...)
       = ...
       (1) **Ralph Creyke** (...)
         = ...
         (a) **Rev. John Creyke** (...)
           = ...
           Has furhter generations of issue
   (III) **Everilda Creyke** (...)

= ...; **Christopher Maltby** (...)
(A) **Everilda Maltby** (...)
  = ...; **Sir George Wentworth** (...) son of Michael
  Wentworth; =1st ♦Hon. Anne Fairfax
  (1) **Frances Wentworth** (...)
    = ...; **Thomas Grantham** (...)
    (a) **Elizabeth Grantham** (...)
      = ...; **Sir Geoffrey Palmer, 3rd Baronet** (12 Jun 1655 –
      29 Dec 1732) son of Sir Lewis Palmer, 2nd Baronet & Jane
      Palmer; suc. father 1714
      no issue
    (b) **Dorothy Grantham** (...)
      = ...; **James Holt** (...)
      Has further generations of issue

b. **Edward IV, King of England, France and Ireland** (28 Apr 1442
Rouen – 9 Apr 1483 Windsor Castle) suc. father as 4th Duke of York, etc.
1460; overthrew Henry VI 1461; was exiled 1470–71 by Henry VI;
decisevely won the Throne back 1471
= ca.1 May 1464 Grafton Regis; **Lady Elizabeth Woodville** (ca.1437
Grafton Regis, Northants. – 8 Jun 1492 London) daughter of Richard
Woodville, 1st Earl Rivers & Jacquetta of Luxembourg; =1st Sir John Grey
I) **Princess Elizabeth of York** (11 Feb 1466/7 Westminster Palace –
  11 Feb 1503/4 Richmond Palace)
  = 1486; ♦**Henry VII, King of England** (1457 – 1509)
  Children are listed with other parent
II) **Princess Mary of York** (11 Aug 1467 Windsor – 23 May 1482
  Greenwich)
III) **Princess Cecily of York** (20 Mar 1469/70 Westminster Palace –
  24 Aug 1507 Sandown, Isle of Wight)
  =1 ... (ann.); **Ralph Scrope** (later 9th Baron Scrope of Marsham) (... –
  17 Sep 1515) son of Thomas Scrope, 5th Baron Scrope of Marsham; suc.
  niece 1502; =2nd Eleanor Windsor
  =2 1487; **John Welles, 1st Viscount Welles KG** (1450 – 9 Feb
  1498/9 London) son of Lionel Welles, 6th Baron Welles & Margaret
  Beauchamp; cr. Viscount bef.1 Sep 1487; KG 1485
  no surviving issue
IV) **Edward V, King of England, France, and Ireland** (2 Nov 1470
  Westminster Abbey – 29 Dec 1483 Tower of London) murdered; suc.
  father 9 Apr 1483; deposed 25 Jun 1483[9]
V) **Prince Richard** of Shrewsbury, **1st Duke of York** (17 Aug 1473

---

[9] The marriage of Edward IV was declared invalid making his children illegitimate and therefore ineligible to succed.

Shrewsbury – 29 Dec 1483 Tower of London) murdered

VI) **Princess Anne of York** (2 Nov 1475 Westminster Palace – 23 Nov 1511)

= 4 Feb 1495/6 Greenwich; **Thomas Howard, 3rd Duke of Norfolk**, 2nd Earl of Surrey (1473 – 25 Aug 1554 Kenninghall, Norfolk) son of Thomas Howard, 2nd Duke of Norfolk & Elizabeth Tylney no surviving issue

VII) **Princess Catherine of York** (14 Aug 1479 Eltham, Kent – 15 Nov 1527 Tiverton, Devon)

= Oct 1495; **William Courtenay, 1st Earl of Devon, KB** (ca.1475 – 6 Jun 1511) son of Edward Cortenay, Earl of Devon (1485 creation) & Elizabeth Courtenay; KB 1487; cr. Earl 9 May 1511

A) **Henry Courtenay, Marquess of Exeter**, 2nd Earl of Devon **KG** (ca.14969 – Jan 1538/9 London) executed; suc. father 1511; cr. Marquess 18 Jun 1525; KG 1521; all title forfeited when convicted of treason 1538/9

=1 aft.Jun 1515; ◆**Elizabeth Grey, 3rd Baroness Lisle** (25 Mar 1504/5 – Apr 1519) daughter of John Grey, 2nd Viscount Lisle & Lady Marcella Howard; suc. father at birth

=2 25 Oct 1519; **Hon. Gertrude Blount** (ca.1504 – 25 Sep 1558) daughter of William Blount, 4th Baron Mountjoy & Elizabeth Say issue of 2nd (none by 1st):

1) **Edward Courtenay, Earl of Devon** (1526 – 18 Sep 1556 Padua, Italy) cr. Earl 3 Sep 1553, but it became extinct upon his death

B) **Lady Margaret Courtenay** (ca.1499 – bef.15 Apr 1526)

= ca.15 Jun 1514; ◆**Henry Somerset, 2nd Earl of Worcester**, etc. (ca.1496 – 26 Nov 1549) son of Charles Somerset, 1st Earl of Worcester & Elizabeth Herbert, (3rd) Baroness Herbert; =2nd Elizabeth Browne; suc. mother 1513 and father 1526 no issue

VIII) **Princess Bridget of York** (10 Nov 1480 Eltham – 1517 Dartford, Kent) a nun

issue by **Elizabeth Wayte**[10] (...) daughter of Thomas Wayte; =1st ... Lucy:

IX) **Arthur Plantagenet, 1st Viscount Lisle** (ca.1462 Calais – 3 Mar 1542 Tower of London) cr. Viscount 25 Aug 1523, but title went extinct upon his death

=1 12 Nov 1511; **Elizabeth Grey, 6th Baroness Lisle** (ca.1470 –

---

[10] Elizabeth's background is pretty much unknown. There is a school of thought that Elizabeth Wayte and Elizabeth Lucy were different people, but there is no real evidence one way or the other.

1525/6) daghter of Edward Grey, 1st Viscount Lisle & Elizabeth Talbot, 5th Baroness Lisle; =1st Edmund Dudley
=2 ...; **Honora Grenville** (1493 – 1566) daughter of Sir Thomas Grenville & Isabella Gilbert; =1st Sir John Bassett
issue of 1st (none by 2nd):
A) **Frances Plantagenet** (...)
=1 ...; (her step-brother) **John Bassett** (1520 – 1541) son of Sir John Bassett & Honora Grenville
=2 ...; **Thomas Monke** (ca.1515 – ca.1583)
issue of 2nd (none by 1st):
1) **Margaret Monke** (... – Oct/Nov 1619)
= ca.1575; **Hugh Acland** (... – 22 May 1622) son of John Acland & Margaret Radcliffe
  a) **Sir Arthur Acland** (1570 Broad Clyst, Devon – 26 Dec 1610) Kt 1606
  = ...; **Eleanor Mallet** (1573 Wooleigh, Devon – 10 Aug 1608) daughter of Robert Mallet & Elizabeth Rolle
    (I) **Sir John Acland, 1st Baronet** (ca.1591 – 24 Aug 1647) cr. Baronet 24 Jun 1644
    = bef.1635; **Elizabeth Vincent** (... – bef.25 Jan 1650/1) daughter of Sir Francis Vincent, 1st Baronet & Sarah Paulet
      (A) **Sir Francis Acland, 2nd Baronet** (... – 1649) unm.; suc. father 1647
      (B) **Eleanor Acland** (... – Jun 1717)
      = ...; **Sir John Davie, 2nd Baronet** (bap.6 Dec 1612 – Jul 1678) son of Sir John Davie, 1st Baronet & Juliana Strode; =2nd Triphonea Reynell; =3rd Mary Glanville; =4th Amy Parker; suc. father Oct 1656
      no issue
      (C) **Susanna Acland** (... – 5 Feb 1696 Stoke Dabernon, Surrey)
      =1 ...; **Edward Halsall** (ca.1632 – bef.1660)
      =2 ca.1660; **John Carleton** (... – 20 Jul 1703 London)
      no issue
      (D) **Sir John Acland, 3rd Baronet** (ca.1636 – 1655) suc. brother 1649
      = bef.1654; ♦**Margaret Rolle** (... – ca.1673) daughter of Dennis Rolle & Hon. Margaret Poulett; =2nd Henry Ayshford
        (1) **Margaret Acland** (... – 26 Mar 1691)
        = Mar 1675; **John Arundell, 2nd Baron Arundell of Trerice** (1 Sep 1649 Richmond, Surrey – bef.21 Jun 1698) son of Richard Arundell, 1st Baron Arundell of Trerice & Gertrude Bagge; =2nd Barbara Slingsby
          (a) **John Aundell, 3rd Baron Arundell of Trerice** (25 Feb 1677/8 – 24 Sep 1706 London) suc. father 1698
          = ...; **Jane Beaw** (ca.1674 – 20 Jun 1744) daughter of William Beaw & Frances Bowsie

Has further generations of issue
  (b) **Hon. Gertrude Arundell** (... – 23 Sep 1709)
=1 1 Dec 1702; **Peter Whitcombe** (... – Sep 1704) =1st
Elizabeth Sherard
=2 2 Oct 1707; **Sir Bennet Hoskins, 3rd Baronet** (28
Jan 1674/5 – 17 Dec 1711) son of Sir John Hoskins, 2nd
Baronet & Jane Lowe
Has further generations of issue
  (2) **Sir Arthur Acland, 4th Baronet** (ca.1655 – 1672) unm.
suc. father 1655
(E) **Sir Hugh Acland, 5th Baronet** (ca.1639 – Mar 1713/4)
suc. nephew 1672
= 1674; **Anne Daniel** (ca.1654 – Mar 1727/8) daughter of Sir
Thomas Daniel
  (1) **John Acland** (ca.1675 – May 1703
= 24 Mar 1695/6; **Elizabeth Acland** (...) daughter of
Richard Acland
  (a) **Sir Hugh Acland, 6th Baronet** (bap.26 Jan 1696/7 –
29 Jul 1728) suc. grandfather 1714
= May 1721; **Cicely Wrothe** (...) daughter of Sir Thomas
Wrothe, 3rd Baronet & Mary Osbaldeston; =2nd Rev.
Thomas Troyte
Has further generations of issue
  (b) **Richard Acland** (... – 1735 London)
= ...; **Anne Burrell** (... – 1771)
Has further generations of issue
  (c) **Elizabeth Acland** (... – ca.Mar 1738)
= 1 Mar 1724/5; **Sir John Davie, 6th Baronet** (27 Jul
1700 – Aug 1737) son of Sir John Davie, 5th Baronet &
Elizabeth Richards) suc. father Dec 1727
Has further generations of issue
(II) **Elizabeth Acland** (1596 Killerton, Devon – ...)
= ...; **Sir Anthony Vincent, 2nd Baronet** (1594 Stoke
d'Abernon, Surrey – 1642) son of Sir Francis Vincent, 1st
Baronet & Sarah Paulet; suc. father 1640
(A) **Sir Francis Vincent, 3rd Baronet** (1621 – 1670) suc.
father 1642
=1 1645; **Catherine Pitt** (1622 London – 16 Feb 1653/4)
daughter of George Pitt
=2 ...; **Elizabeth Vane** (...) daughter of Rt.Hon. Sir Henry
Vane & Frances D'Arcy
issue of 1st (none by 2nd):
  (1) **Sir Anthony Vincent, 4th Baronet** (bef.1646 – 1674)
suc. father 1670
= ...; **Anne Austin** (...) daughter of Sir James Austin; =2nd
Thomas Fowke

no issue
- (2) **Sir Francis Vincent, 5th Baronet** (1646 Stoke d'Abernon – 10 Feb 1735/6) suc. brother 1674
  = ...; **Rebecca Ashe** (1645 London – 19 Aug 1725 Stoke d'Abernon) daughter of Jonathan Ashe & Rebecca Leaver
  - (a) **Sir Henry Vincent, 6th Baronet** (10 Jul 1685 Stoke d'Abernon – 10 Jan 1757 Stoke d'Abernon) suc. father 1736
    = ...; **Elizabeth Sherman** (1685 London – 25 May 1759 Stoke d'Abernon) daughter of Bezaliel Sherman & Annie Norton
    Has further generations of issue
  - (b) **Frances Vincent** (...)
    = ...; **William Ward** (...) son of William Ward
    Has further generations of issue
- b) **Elizabeth Acland** (...)
  = ...; **Thomas Coplestone** (ca.1598 – 1648) son of Anthony Coplestone & Margaret Larder
  no issue
- c) **William Acland** (1578 Acland Barton, Devon – 16 Dec 1644 Landkey, Devon)
  = 6 Feb 1622 Swimbridge, Devon; **Johanna Shore** (1588 – 1663 Exeter)
  - (I) **William Acland** (11 Jan 1623/4 – ...)
    = 24 Apr 1651 London; **Ann Shrowsbridge** (ca.1625 – ...)
    - (A) **William Acland** (21 Mar 1650/1 – ...)
    - (B) **Elizabeth Acland** (22 Sep 1653 – ...)
    - (C) **Christopher Acland** (26 Aug 1655 – ...)
    - (D) **Annis Acland** (25 Aug 1657 – ...)
    - (E) **John Acland** (15 Nov 1659 – Mar 1702)
      = 7 Oct 1687 London; **Ellinor Cope** (ca.1658 – ca.1699 Surrey) daughter of William Cope & Elinor ...
      - (1) **Mary Acland** (27 Mar 1681/2 – ...)
      - (2) **Anne Acland** (13 Mar 1688/9 – ...)
      - (3) **John Acland** (25 Mar 1689/90 – ...)
      - (4) **William Acland** (2 Nov 1690 – ...)
        = ...; **Mary ...** (...)
        - (a) **Ellinor Acland** (23 Oct 1726 – ...)
        - (b) **Ann Acland** (13 May 1736 – ...)
        - (c) **John Acland** (26 Aug 1739 – 1819) (twin)
          = 4 Mar 1764 London; **Mary Newbolt** (...)
          Has further generations of issue
        - (d) **Elizabeth Acland** (26 Aug 1739 – ... (twin)
        - (e) **Thomas Acland** (4 Sep 1743 – ...)
      - (5) **Thomas Acland** (28 Apr 1691 Rotherhithe, Surrey – ca.1747 London)
      - (6) **Ellinor Acland** (23 Aug 1892 – ...)

(7) **Headley Acland** (12 Jun 1694 Rotherhithe – 1739
  London)
(8) **Elizabeth Acland** (17 Apr 1698 Rotherhithe – Sep 1700)
(F) **Thomas Acland** (26 Nov 1660 – ...)
(G) **James Acland** (3 Feb 1664/5 – ...)
B) **Elizabeth Plantagenet** (1516 London – 1569 Essex)
  = bef.1544; **Sir Francis Jobson**[11] (1514 – 11 Jun 1573
Monkwike, Essex) son of William Jobson; Kt.1549/50
1) **John Jobson** (...)
  = ...; **Elizabeth Pexall** (...) daughter of Sir Richard Pexall
  a) **Pexall Jobson** (ca.1574 Essex – ...)
    = ...; **Clement Medley** (...)
    (I) **Katherine Jobson** (... – 1625 Rosedumon, Ireland)
      = 7 Feb 1613 Whatfield, Suffolk; **Robert Harland** (...)
      issue ?
2) **Edward Jobson** (1536 London – 12 Jan 1609)
  =1 ...; **Mary Markaunt** (ca.1543 Dunham Hall, Essex – ...)
  daughter of Edmund Markaunt
  =2 ...; **Mary Bode** (ca.1543 – ca.1572) daughter of John Bode
  issue of 2nd (none by 1st):
  a) **Mary Jobson** (...)
    = ...; **George Brooke** (...)
    issue ?
  b) **Elizabeth Jobson** (...)
3) **Henry Jobson** (...)
4) **Thomas Jopson** (...)
  = ...; **Dame Mary Wytham, 1st Baronetess** (bap.30 Jun 1579
  Ledsham, Yorks. – 5 May 1662 Ledsham) daughter of William
  Wytham & Eleanor Neale; =2nd Thomas Bolles; cr. Baronetess 19
  Dec 1635[12]
  a) **Thomas Jobson** (... – 26 Aug 1653)
    =1 31 Jul 1626 Worksop, Notts.; **Anne Stringer** (...) daughter
    of Nicholas Stringer
    =2 ...; **Sarah Baker** (...) daughter of Gregory Baker
    issue of 1st (none by 2nd):
    (I) **Sir William Jopson, 2nd Baronet** (ca.1635 – bef.1673) suc.
      grandmother 1662, but baronetcy became extinct upon his
      death
      = ...; **Lucy Tindall** (...) daughter of Henry Tindall; =2nd Sir
      John Jackson, 1st Baronet

---

[11] The name is spelled Jobson and Jopson interchangably throughout the records.

[12] The only instance of a woman being cr. Baronetess in her own right.

(A) **Lucy Jopson** (... – 4 Sep 1724)
  = 1686; **Robert Ridgeway, 4th Earl of Londonderry**,
Viscount Gallen-Ridgeway, Baron Ridgeway, 4th Baronet (... –
7 Mar 1713/4) son of Weston Ridgeway, 3rd Earl of
Londonderry & Mary Temple; suc. father 1672, but all titles
became extinct upon his death
  (1) **Lady Frances Ridgeway** (...)
    =1 10 Mar 1717; **Thomas Pitt, 1st Earl of Londonderry**,
    Baron Londonderry (ca.1688 – 12 Sep 1729) son of Thomas
    Pitt & Jane Innes; cr. Baron 1719 and Earl 1726
    =2 Dec 1732; **Robert Graham** (
    (a) **Thomas Pitt, 2nd Earl of Londonderry**, etc. (ca.
      1717 – 24 Aug 1734) killed in a fall from a horse; suc. father
      1729; unm.
    (b) **Ridgeway Pitt, 3rd Earl of Londonderry**, etc. (ca.
      1721 – 8 Jan 1765) unm.; suc. brother 1734, but his titles
      became extinct upon his death
    (c) **Lady Lucy Pitt** (...)
      = ...; **Pierce Meyrick** (Jul 1752 Llanfierian, Anglesey – ...)
      son of Owen Meyrick & Ann Lloyd
      Has further generations of issue
  (2) **Lady Lucy Ridgeway** (... – 16 Jul 1732)
    = 3 Oct 1716; **Arthur Chichester, 4th Earl of Donegall**,
    5th Viscount Chichester, Baron Chichester (28 Mar 1695 – 30
    Sep 1757) son of Arthur Chichester, 3rd Earl of Donegall &
    Lady Catherine Forbes; suc. father 10 Apr 1706
    no issue
5) **Mary Jobson** (...)
C) **Bridgit Plantagenet** (1513 London – 1 Jan 1558 London)
  = ...; **William Cawarden** (ca.1510 London – 1559 East Horsley,
Surrey) son of William Cawarden
1) **Sir Thomas Cawarden** (ca.1529 London – Feb 1587/8 Essex)
  = ...; **Elizabeth Robinson** (ca.1535 Harlow, Essex – ca.1574)
  a) **John Carden** (1555 – ca.1620)
    =1 1572 Caldecote, Warks.; **Mary** Anne **Byrd** (1551 Broxton,
    Ches. – 1620) daughter of Henry Byrd & Anne Phelkin
    =2 9 Nov 1608 London; **Judith Empson** (...)
    issue of 1st:
    (I) **John** Samuel **Carden** (1575 Carden, Ches – ca.1620 Isle of
      Wight Co, VA)
      = ...; **Elizabeth Hedger** (1578 England – ... in England)
      (A) **John Carden** (1602 London – 1685 Isle of Wight Co, VA)
        = 10 May 1625 Wootten, Kent; **Joan** Elizabeth **Grant** (Jun
        1604 Trowbridge, Wilts. – 1688 Isle of Wight Co, VA)
        daughter of Robert Grant
        (1) **Robert Carden** (1630 London – 18 Feb 1684

Rappahannock Co, VA) arrived in VA 1674

= ca.1652 London; **Elizabeth Moss** (1634 England – 1688 Rappahannock Co) daughter of Edward Moss

    (a) **John Carden** (1655 Rappahannock Co – 16 May 1739 Rappahannock Co.)

        = 20 Jan 1693 Essex Co, VA; **Mary** Anne **Parker** (1670 Rappahannock Co. – 1703 Rappahannock Co.) daughter of Thomas Parker & Elinor ...

        Has further generations of issue

X) **Elizabeth Plantagenet** (ca.1464 – ...)

= ...; ♦**Thomas Lumley** (... – 1487)

Children are listed with other parent

XI) **Grace Plantagenet** (... – aft.1492) unm.

c. **Edmund, Earl of Rutland** (17 May 1443 Rouen – 30 Dec 1460 Wakefield) killed in battle

d. **Princess Elizabeth of York** (22 Apr 1444 – btw. Jan 1503/May 1504)

= bef. Feb 1458; **John de la Pole, 2nd Duke of Suffolk KG** (27 Sep 1442 – btw.Oct 1491/ Oct 1492) son of John de la Pole, 1st Duke of Suffolk & Alice Chaucer; =1st ♦Lady Margaret Beaufort

I) **John de la Pole, Earl of Lincoln** (ca.1463 – 16 Jun 1487 East Stoke, Notts.) killed in battle; cr. Earl 1467, but it became extrinct upon his death; designated heir-pesumptive by Richard III ca.1485 and continued as Yorkist Claimant during the reign of Henry VII

= ...; **Lady Margaret FitzAlan** (... – aft.1493) daughter of Thomas FitzAlan, 17th Earl of Arundell & Lady Margaret Woodville

no issue

II) **Edward de la Pole** (1466 – 1485) a priest

III) **Elizabeth de la Pole** (ca.1468 – aft.1489)

= ...; **Henry Lovell, 8th Baron Morley** (bef.1474 – 1489) son of Sir William Lovel & Eleanor Morley, 7th Baroness Morley; suc. mother 1476

no issue

IV) **Edmund de la Pole, 3rd Duke of Suffolk**, 1st Earl of Suffolk **KG** (1471/2 – 4 May1513) executed; suc. brother as York pretender 1487 and father as Duke 1492; The title was demoted to an Earldom 1492

= bef.10 Oct 1496; **Margaret Scrope** (... – bef.Feb 1515) daughter of Sir Richard Scrope & Eleanor Washburne

no issue

V) **Humphrey de la Pole** (1454 – 1513) a priest

VI) **Anne de la Pole** (1476 – 1495) a nun

VII) **Catherine de la Pole** (ca.1477 – 1513)

= ...; **William Stourton, 5th Baron Stourton** (1457 – 17 Feb 1523/4) son of William Stourton, 2nd Baron Stourton & Margaret Chideoke; =2nd Thomasine Wrottesley; suc. nephew Feb 1486/7

no issue

VIII) **Sir William de la Pole** (ca.1478 – Oct/Nov 1539 London) died
while imprisoned for 37 years
= ca.1497; **Hon. Catherine Stourton** (... – 25 Nov 1521) daughter of
William Stourton, 2nd Baron Stourton & Margaret Chideoke; =2nd
♦Henry de Grey, 4th Earl Grey (of Codnor)
no issue
IX) **Richard de la Pole** *de jure 4th Duke of Suffolk* (1480 – 24 Feb
1525 Pavia, Italy) styled himself Duke after brother's death in 1513
even though his elder brother, William, was alive, albeit imprisoned
issue by ...[13]:
A) **Marguerite de la Pole** (1520 – ca.1599)
= 21 May 1539 Fontainbleau; **Sibeud de Trivoley, Lord de
Brenieu** (... – bef.1568) son of Guillaume de Trivoley, Lord de
Brénieu & Louise du Rochain
1) **Louise de Trivoley** (...)
= 1568; **Jean de Montchenu** (...)
a) **Lucrèce de Montchenu** (...)
=1 1590; **Hughes de Calignon** (...)
=2 ...; **Alexandre de Bardonnenche** (...)
issue of 1st:
(I) **Magdelene de Calignon** (... – 1629)
issue of 2nd:
(II) **César de Bardonnenche** (...)
2) **Eleonore de Trivoley** (ca.1543 – 1606)
= 28 Jul 1564 Cosne Cours-sur-Loire; **Jean II de Secondat,
Lord de Roques** (1515 – 1599)
a) **Jeanne de Secondat, Lady de Romefort** (1563 – 1618)
= 1583; **Antoine, Marquis de Frontenac**, Lord de Buade
(ca.1570 – 1625)
(I) **Henri de Buade, Count de Palluau**, Lord de Culêtre
(1585 – aft.1623)
= ...; **Anne Phélypeaux** (9 Nov 1595 – 1632) daughter of
Raymond Phélypeaux & Claude Gobelin
(A) **Louis de Buade, Count de Frontenac** (22 May 1622
Saint-Germain-en-Laye – 28 Nov 1698 Québec, Canada)
= 27 Jun 1648 Paris; **Anne de La Grange-Trianon** (...)
daughter of Charles de La Grange-Trianon, Lord de Neuville &
Marquerite Blanquet
no issue
(B) **Marie Henriette de Baude** (1623 – 1676)
= 1637; **Henri Louis Habert de Montmor** (1600–1679)

---

[13] The mother of Richard's child is not known for sure, but has been said to possibly be Marie
of Sicily

(1) **Claude Madeleine Habert de Montmor** (... – 1713)
= 1 Jul 1677; **Bernard du Rieu, Lord de Blanville** (... – 1702)

   (a) **Anne Louise de Rieu** (4 Jun 1678 Paris – ...)
   = ...; **Jean Étienne de Thomassin, Marquis de Saint Paul**, Vicomte de Reillane, Baron de Rognac, Lord di Fuveau (21 Oct 1661 Aix-en-Provence – 22 Jul 1739 Aix-en-Provence) son of Jean-Baptiste de Thomassin, Marquis de Saint Paul & Gabrielle d'Arbaud
   Has further generations of issue

   (b) **Madeline** Elisabeth **de Rieu** (...)
   = 24 Jul 1700; **Pierre Eléonor de la Ville de Férolles, Marquis de Férolles** (... – 4 Aug 1705 Caybee, Guyana) son of Pierre de La Ville de Férolles, Lord de Férolles & Marie de Meulles; Gov. of Guyana 1691–1705
   no issue

   (c) **Jean Louis de Rieu, Lord de Fagis** (30 Aug 1682 – aft.1728) unm.

(2) **Louis Habert de Montmor** (... – 1686)
= 1661; **Marie Claude Phélypeaux** (1644 – 1661) daughter of Louis Phélypeaux, Lord de Pontchartain & Marie Suzanne Talon
no issue

(3) **Father Habert de Montmor** Bishop of Perpignan (1644 – 1695) a priest

(4) **Jean-Louis de Montmor, Lord de Monmor** (... – 1720) unm.

(5) **Anne-Louise Habert de Montmor** (... – 1680)
= ...; **Nicolas Jehannot de Bartillat** (... – 28 Sep 1718) son of Étienne Jehannot de Bartillat, Baron d'Huriel & Catherine Lucas

   (a) **Étienne Michel Jehannot de Bartillat** (... – 1 Jul 1690)
   = ...; **Eléonore Suzanne Passart** (...) daughter of François Passart, Lord de Saclay & Andrée Lucas
   no issue

   (b) **Joachim Jehannot de Bartillat** (1680 – ...)
   = 10 Mar 1706; **Marie Françoise Le Bel** (1690 – 30 Aug 1748) daughter of Michel Le Bel & Marie Françoise Ferrand
   Has further generations of issue

(6) **Henri-Louis Habert de Montmor** (... – 1680)
= ...; **Anne Morin** (... – 1715)
no issue

(C) **Anne de Buade** (... – 6 Jan 1685)
= 1643; **François d'Espinay-Saint-Luc, Marquis de Saint Luc**, Count d'Estelan (... – Apr 1670) son of Thimoléon

d'Espinay-Saint-Luc, Count d'Estelan & Henriette de
Bassompierre
(1) **François d'Espinay-Saint-Luc, Marquis de Saint-
Luc**, etc. (... – 9 Jul 1694) suc. father 1670
= 8 Jan 1674; **Marie de Pompadour** (... – Oct 1723)
daughter of Jean de Pompadour, Marquis de Pompadour &
Marie de Rochechouart-Pontville, Vicomtesse de
Rochechouart
(a) Marie Anne **Henriette d'Espinay-Saint-Luc, Lady
de Saint-Luc**, et de Pompadour, Vicometesse de
Rochechouart (21 Nov 1674 Paris – 1731)
= ...; **François de Rochechouart-Pontville** (...) son of
Louis Joseph de Rochechouart-Pontville, Baron du
Bâtiment & Jeanne Marie de Pérusse des Cars; =2nd Marie
de Saint-Gestin de Themergat
no issue
(D) **Geneviève de Buade** (...)
= ...; **Claude de Bourdeilles, Count de Montrésor**
(1606 – 1663) son of Henri de Bourdeilles, Baron de
Bourdeilles & Madeleine de La Châtre
no issue
(II) **Gabrielle de Buade** (...)
= 1625; **Louis, Baron de l'Isle de Noé** (...) son of Urbain de
Noé, Baron de l'Isle-Noé & Marie de Mauléon
(A) **Marguerite de Noé** (...)
(B) **Anne de Noé** (... – 8 Oct 1734)
= 18 Apr 1697 L'Isle de Noé; **Pierre de Luppé, Count du
Garrané** (Aug 1657 Lacassagne – 27 Feb 1729) son of
François de Luppé, Lord du Garrané & Marie de Castaing
(1) **Louis de Luppé, Count du Garrané** (1699 Auch – 15
Sep 1774 château de La Cassagne)
= 31 Oct 1725 Pavie; **Sidonie Colbert, Lady de la
Grimenaudière** (17 Jul 1704 Sainte Soulle – 9 Dec 1778
Auch) daughter of François Colbert, Lord de Saint-Mars &
Charlotte Lee
(a) **Pierre** Charles Joseph **de Luppé, Marquis de Luppé**
(13 Jul 1729 – 5 Feb 1806)
= 22 Dec 1762; **Marie-Madeleine d'Angosse** (...)
daughter of Etienne d'Angosse, Baron d'Angosse & Marie
d'Incamps
Has further generations of issue
(b) **Thérèse de Luppé** (1741 – 1809)
= ...; **Bernard de Fiancette** (...)
Has further generations of issue
(c) **Anne** Marie Thérèse Elisabeth **de Luppé** (...)
= ...; **Guy de Léaumont** (...) son of Jean-François de

Léaumont & Jeanne de Patras
Has further generations of issue
(C) **Marie de Noé** (...)
= 1649; **Étienne de Montaut** (...) son of François de
Montaut & Paule de Faudoas
  (1) **Roger de Montaut, Marquis de Montaut** (...)
  = ...; **Catherine de Martres** (...)
    (a) **Philiberte de Montaut** (...)
    = 3 Sep 1716; **Nicolas de Comminges, Lord de
    Sieuras et de Lastronques** (...) son of Jeande
    Commingues, Lord de Sieuras & Marie de Canals
    Has further generations of issue
    (b) **Françoise de Montaut** (... – 1746)
    =1 ...; **Louis de Vignes** (1648 – 1714) son of Jean Vignes
    & Jacquette Barbedor
    =2 3 Feb 1717 Montpelier; **Henri, Marquis de
    Roquefeuil** Vicomte de Gabriac, Lord de Tournemire, de
      Laroque, de Blacardy, and du Pin (... – 18 Jan 1744
      Montpelier) son of François-Fulcrand de Roquefeuil, Lord
      de Gabriac & Marie de Tour du Pin, Lady de La Roque et
      d'Arènes
    Has further generations of issue
  (2) **Françoise de Montaut, Lady de Saint-Sivié** (... – Sep
  1734)
  = 1699; **Louis de Salgues de Lescure** (...) son of François
  de Lascure, Lord de Lescure & Anne de Tubières de Caylus
    (a) **Alphonse de Salgues de Lescure** (...)
    = Feb 1714; **Henriette Elisabeth de Granges de
    Surgères** (bef.1691 – 9 Feb 1778) daughter of François de
    Granges de Surgères, Marquis de Fiocellière & Françoise de
    La Chassaigne
    Has further generations of issue
(D) **Jean de Noé** (...)
(E) **Pierre de Noé** (...)
(F) **Philibert de Noé** (...)
(G) **Clément de Noé** (...)
(H) **Roger de Noé, Marquis de Noé** (1626 – 1700)
= 1666; **Marguerite de Pouy** (1646 – 1705) daughter of Jean
de Pouy, Lord de Marignac & Anne de Narbonne
  (1) **Gabrielle de Noé** (...)
  = 23 Feb 1693; **François de Péguilhan, Lord de
  Larboust** (...) son of César de Péguilhan, Lord de Belbèze &
  Isabeau d'Astorg, Vicomtesse de Larboust
    (a) **Urbain de Péguilhan, Lord de Larboust** (...)
    = 25 Nov 1724 Toulouse; **Anne de Pillotte** (...) daughter
    of Jean-Baptiste de Pillotte, Lord de Saint-Clément &

Jeanne de Pourtalès
Has further generations of issue
(b) **Anne de Péguilhan** (...)
= ...; **Joseph de Casteras, Lord de Casteras** (28 Oct 1670 Mourède – ...) son of Lisier de Casteras & Angélique de Jaulin
no issue
(c) **Elizabeth de Péguilhan** (...)
= 28 Dec 1715; **François Cao de Benos, Baron de Les** (1692 – 1724)
Has further generations of issue
(2) **Anne Françoise de Noé** (...)
(3) **Marc Roger de Noé, Marquis de Noé** (1673 – 1733)
= 2 May 1714 Paris; **Charlotte Colbert** (... – aft.1735) daughter of François Colbert, Lord de Saint-Mars & Charlotte Lee
(a) **Jacques Roger, Marquis de Noé** (...)
= 1746; **Jacquette de Taffanel de La Jonquière** (1722 – ...) daughter of Pierre Jacques de Taffanel, Marquis de La Jonquière & Marie Angélique de La Valette
Has further generations of issue
(b) **Vicomte Louis de Noé** (... – aft.1790) Mayor of Bordeaux
= 1752; **Madeleine** Elisabeth Flavie **de Cohorn de la Palun** (...) daughter of Louis Alexandre de Cohorn de la Palun & Jeanne Lucrèce de Silvecane de Camaret
Issue extinct by 1800
(c) **Marc Antoine de Noé** Bishop of Lescar (1724 – ...) a priest
(d) **Dominique de Noé** (...) unm.
(e) **Thérèse Charlotte de Noé** (...)
= 9 Jan 1744; **Jaime Joaquin de Labay, Marquês de Viela** (...)
Issue extinct by 1800
(4) **Louis** Jérôme **de Loé, Count de Noé** (3 Jun 1691 L'Isle de Noé – 21 Dec 1730) killed in a duel
= 1725; **Marie Anne de Bréda** (1708 – 1761) daughter of Pantaléon de Bréda & Elisabeth Bodin
(a) **Louis Panaléon de Noé, Marquis de Noé** (8 Nov 1728 Haiti – 25 Feb 1816)
= 1776; ♦**Charlotte de Noé** (... – 10 Sep 1833 L'Isle de Noé) daughter of Jacques Roger de Noé, Marquis de Noé & Jaquette de Taffanel de La Jonquière
Has further generations of issue
(b) **Anne Charlotte de Noé** (1729 – 1788)
= 14 Apr 1754; **Juan Francisco** Gabriel **de Polastron,**

3rd Count de Polastron (1722 Montpellier – 13 Jul 1794 Paris) son of Juan Bautista de Polstron, 2nd Count de Polastron & Françoise de Mirman; =1st Jeanne Charlotte Hérault
Has further generations of issue
(5) **Urbain de Noé** (...)
(I) **Andrée de Noé** (...)
= ...; **Jean Pierre de Siregand** (...) son of Hercule de Siregand & Georgette de Sers
  (1) **Jean Pierre** Gaston **de Siregand** (4 Mar 1640 – 12 Sep 1709)
  =1 ...
  =2 14 Jan 1700; **Marie Anne de Rochechouart** (...) daughter of Jean-François de Rochechouart, Baron de Clermont & Jeanne de Foix-Rabat
  issue of 1st (none by 2nd):
    (a) **Jean François** Gaston **de Siregand** (1673 – 1717)
    = ...; **Catherine de La Roche de Gensac** (...)
    Has further generations of issue
    (b) **Roger de Siregand** (1675 – 1743)
    (c) **Jeanne Rose de Siregand** (... – 1712)
    (d) **Urbaine-Andrée de Siregand** (... – aft.1729)
    = ...; **Pierre-Gaston d'Orbessan, Lord de Labalut** (...) son of Jean-François d'Orbessan, Lord de Lissac & Anne de Vendômois
    Has further generations of issue
  (2) **Louis de Siregand** (1647 – ...)
  (3) **Roger de Siregand** (21 Jun 1649 – ...)
(III) **Anne de Buade** (...)
= 19 Jun 1620; **Clément de La Roque-Bouillac, Lord de Loupiac et de Saint-Géry** (27 Jun 1595 – 18 Mar 1647 Rabastens) son of Georges de La Roque-Bouillac, Lord de Bouillac & Antoinette de Baulac
  (A) **Louis de La Roque-Bouillac, Baron de Miers** (1621 Rabastens – ...)
  = 14 Dec 1653; **Françoise de Rollet** (1638 – aft.1710)
    (1) **Gilles de La Roque-Bouillac** (1655 Rabastens – 1737 Rabastens)
    = 1700; **Marthe d'Yzarn** (1659 Castres – ...) daughter of Benoît d'Yzarn, Lord de Varagnes & Jeanne de Saillard
    no issue
  (B) **Isabeau de La Roque-Bouillac** (11 Aug 1622 – 30 Dec 1681)
  = 18 Nov 1643; **François de Bonnet de Maureilhan** (30 May 1611 Maureilhan – ...) son of Pierre de Bonnet, Lord de Maureilhan & Françoise de La Jugie

(1) **Joseph de Bonnet, Baron de Maureilhan** (... – 1 Dec
1710 Béziers)
= 8 Oct 1680; **Jeanne de Raymond-Lasbordes** (...)
daughter of Jacques de Raimond, Lord de Laurac & Louise
de Saint-Jean
   (a) **Joseph** Guillaume **de Bonnet de Maureilhan** (Jan
   1687 Béziers – ...)
   = ...; **Elisabeth de Boyer** (...) daughter of Henri-Joseph
   de Boyer, Baron de Sorgues & Jacquette de Murviel
   Has further generations of issue
   (b) **Barthélémy de Bonnet de Maureilhan** (24 Aug 1693
   Maureilhan – 19 Oct 1762 Béziers)
   = 13 Jan 1722 Béziers; **Marguerite Dumas de Manse** (8
   Feb 1702 Béziers – 19 Feb 1738 Béziers) daughter of Henri
   Dumas de Manse, Lord de La Vidalle & Catherine
   Dautrivay
   Has further generations of issue
(C) **Gabrielle de La Roque-Bouillac** (6 Oct 1626
Rabastens – 1655)
= 16 Jun 1647; **Jean François de Raynaldy, Lord de
Marmont, de Rulhe, et de Calzins** (... – 1684) son of Jean
de Raynaldy, lord de Colobiés & Anne de Durrieu
   (1) **Jean-François de Raynaldy** (...)
   = 1695; **Marie-Adélaïde del Puech** (...) daughter of Jean
   del Peuch & Marie de Borel
      (a) **Louis de Raynaldy** (...)
      (b) **Marie de Raynaldy** (...)
      (c) **Henriette de Raynaldy** (...)
   (2) **Jean de Raynaldy** (12 Jun 1648 Villefranche-de-
   Rouergue – 28 Sep 1713 Saint-Michel-Campes)
   = 15 Feb 1682 Toulouse; **Catherine de Sapte** (...)
      (a) **Jean-Bernard Raynaldy** (...)
      (b) **Marie de Raynaldy** (...)
      = 1714; **Jean-François de Cahuzac, Lord de Verdier**
      (...) son of François de Cahuzac & Anne de Clergue
      Has further generations of issue
      (c) **Elisabeth de Raynaldy** (...)
      (d) **Françoise de Raynaldy** (...)
      (e) **Pierre de Raynaldy** (...)
   (3) **Isabeau de Raynaldy** (18 Jan 1654 Villefranche – 3 Apr
   1707 Villefranche)
   = 30 Nov 1667 Villefranche; **Guillaume de Campmas,
   Lord d'Elves** (1643 Villefranche – 1710) Mayor of
   Villefranche 1670; son of Nicolas de Campomas & Antoinette
   de Garibal
      (a) **Nicolas de Campmas, Vicomte d'Elves** (1668 – 24

Jun 1748 Saint-Rémy)

(b) **Jean de Campmas** (27 Nov 1670 Villefranche – ...) a priest

(c) **Marie de Campmas** (1670 Villefranche – 27 Aug 1743 Villefranche)

= 16 Feb 1693 Villefranche; **Jean de Raynal, Lord de Ginais** (24 Oct 1652 Villefranche – 7 Mar 1710 Villefranche) son of Étienne de Raynal, Lord de Farrou & Antoinette de Pomayarols

Has further generations of issue

(d) **François de Campmas** (8 Jan 1677 Villefranche – 15 May 1739)

= 16 Sep 1710 Villefranche; **Agnès de Roucoules** (...) daughter of Honoré Roucoules & Agnès de Raynaldy

Has further generations of issue

(e) **Catherine de Campmas** (2 Sep 1683 Villefranche – ...)

= 27 Jan 1711 Villefranche; **Jean Dintilhac, Lord de Cabanes** (6 Jan 1671 Villefranche – ...) son of Jean-Jacques Dintilhac & Marguerite de Loupiac

Has further generations of issue

(4) **Marie de Raynaldy** (..

(D) **Father François de La Roque-Bouillac** (1641 – ...) a priest

b) **Marie Anne de Secondat** (1566 – ...)

= 1595; **Jean d'Harambure, Baron de Picarassy** (1553 – ...) son of Bertrand d'Harambure & Florence de Belsunce

(I) **Henri d'Harambure** (...)

= 1648; **Marguerite Hatte** (...)

(A) **Jean d'Harambure, Lord de Romefort et des Augères** (...)

= 26 Apr 1681; **Elisabeth de Piozet** (...) daughter of Paul de Piozet, Lord de Vignaux & Jeanne de Piozet

(1) **Paul d'Harambure, Lord de Romfort et de la Chèvrerie** (14 May 1683 Preuilly-sur-Claise - ...)

= 9 Nov 1715 Yzeures-sur-Creuse; **Marie Anne de Moussy** (...) daughter of Claude de Moussy, Lord de La Grange & Madeleine de Montbel

(a) **Anne** Marguerite **d'Harambure** (13 Jan 1719 – ...)

= 20 Feb 1748; **René Antoine Pierres, Lord d'Epigny et de Fontenailles** (...) son of René Pierres, Lord de Fontenailles & Marguerite de Cothereau de Grandchamp

Has further generations of issue

(b) **Madeleine** Sylvie **d'Harambure** (...)

= 17 Nov 1774 Yzeures; **Gabriel Louis de Ferrou, Lord de Mondion** (26 Apr 1714 – 19 Mar 1784) son of François de Ferrou, Lord de Mondion & Marguerite Amaury

83

no issue
- (c) **Louis François** Alexandre **d'Harambure, Baron d'Harambure** (13 Feb 1742 – 27 Mar 1828 Yzeures)
  =1 28 Nov 1771; **Anne** Rosalie Nicole **Bazin** (...)
  =2 18 Dec 1797; **Françoise** Madeline **Mégissier de La Martinère** (31 Jan 1768 Tours – 2 Feb 1832 Tours) daughter of François Mégissier de la Martinère & Martine Pinceloup de La Grange
  Has further generations of issue by both
- (II) **Jean d'Harambure** (...)
  = ...; **Marie Tallemant** (...) daughter of Gédéon Tallemant & Anne de Rambouillet
  issue ?
- c) **Jason de Secondat** (1567 – ...)
- d) **Pierre IV de Secondat, Lord de Roques** (3 May 1571 Agen – 16385 Agen)
  = 21 Aug 1600 Bordeaux; **Anne de Pontac** (1580 – 18 Aug 1673) daughter of Jean de Pontac, Lord du Chalard & Marie de Lahet
  - (I) **Gaston de Secondat, Baron de Roquefort** (12 Apr 1625 Bordeaux – 1693)
    = 1647; **Gabrielle, Lady des Gardès** (...) daughter of Jean des Gardès, Lord de Calayrac & Marthe de Pau
    - (A) **Geoffroy de Secondat, Baron de Roquefort** Lord des Gardès (31 Jul 1665 – 1724)
      = 26 Aug 1706; **Louise de Raymond** (bef.1680 – ...) daughter of Gratien de Raymond, Lord du Suquet & Marguerite Anceau
      - (1) **Jean** Tiburce Godefroy **de Secondat** (...)
        = ...; **Marie Louise** Hélène **de Cunolio d'Espalais** (...)
        - (a) **Jean** Godefroy **de Secondat, Baron de Roquefort** (8 Nov 1741 Agen – 9 Jan 1825 Boé)
          = 1778; **Marie Bernardine de La Myre, Lady de Douazac** (bef.1758 Cahors – 22 Sep 1833 Boé) daughter of Jean François de La Myre & Marie Anne de Lautron
          Has further generations of issue
      - (2) **Gratién de Secondat** (1709 – 1786)
        = 30 Jan 1753 Agen; **Marie Françoise de Jayan** (... – bef.8 Oct 1796) daughter of François de Jayan & Marie Boissié
        - (a) **Marie Louise de Secondat** (bef.1760 – 1823 Agen)
          = 26 Jan 1779; **Jean Joseph de Raymond, Lord de La Garde**, etc. (24 Jul 1747 Agen – 30 Nov 1802 Agen) son of Gilbert de Raymond & Marie Anne de Guiidon de Gardes
          Has further generations of issue
        - (b) **Sophie de Secondat** (1769 – 1850) unm.
        - (c) **Anne de Secondat** (2 Aug 1770 Agen – 21 Apr 1847)

= 17 Sep 1796 Agen; **Nicolas** Philippe Célerin **West** (3 Feb 1774 – 15 Sep 1838) son of Nicolas West & Elisabeth Laubry
Has further generations of issue
    (d) **Marie Félicité de Secondat** (1781 – 1861) unm.
    (3) **Marc Antoine** Martial **de Secondat** (...)
    (4) **Louise** Marie Anne **de Secondat** (...)
    = ...; **Jean de Bazon, Baron de Baulens** (...)
    (a) **Jacquette de Bazon** (...)
    = ...; **Jean de Bazon** (...)
    Has further generations of issue
  (B) **Jean de Secondat** (1669 – 1730)
  = 1699; **Marie de Touton** (...) daughter of François de Touton & Marie de Crozat
    (1) **Godefroy de Secondat** (12 Jul 1702 Agen – 6 Mar 1774 Agen)
    =25 Mar 1745 Clairac; ♦**Denise de Secondat de Montesquieu** (23 Feb 1727 Bordeaux – 23 Feb 1800 Agen) daughter of Charles Louise de Secondat de Montesquieu, Baron de Labrède & Jeanne de Lartigue
    (a) **Joseph** Cyrille **de Secondant de Montesquieu, Baron de Roquefort** (1748 – 1829)
    = 1789; **Jacqueline** Henriette **de Menou** (1762 – 24 Jan 1837) daughter of Louis Joseph, Count de Menou & Bonne Cochon de Maurepas
    Has further generations of issue
 (II) **Marie de Secondat** (...)
 (III) **Marguerite de Secondat** (ca.1630 – ...)
 (IV) **Jean de Secondat** (...)
e) **Marguerite de Secondat** (1575 – ...)
= ...; **Clément de La Roque-Boulliac, Lord de La Fage** (...) son of Joseph de La Roque-Bouillac & Anne de Lyon
 (I) **Joseph de la Roque-Bouillac** (...)
  = bef.1620; **Marguerite de Alaire** (...)
  (A) **Clément de La Roque-Bouillac** (... – aft.1654)
  = ...; **Isabeau de Montagu** (...) daughter of Jean-Charles de Montagu, Baron de La Lande & Quitterie de Belcastel
    (1) **Charles de La Roque-Bouillac** (...)
    = 1695; **Jeanne del Puech de Cagnac** (...)
    (a) **Guillaume de Roque-Bouillac, Lord de Fraisse** (...)
    = 1736; **Jeanne Charlotte de La Tour** (...)
    Has further generations of issue
f) **Jacob de Secondat, Baron de Montesquieu** (12 Dec 1576 Agen – 1619 Agen) cr. Baron 12 Aug 1606
= 9 Mar 1610 Agen; **Marguerite de Sevin** (1587 – 1683) daughter of Guillaume de Sevin, Lord de Beauregard & Antoinette

de Ranse

(I) **Anne Antoinette de Secondat** (bef.1611 – ...)
= 1627; **Jehan Poute, Lord de Château de Dompierre**
(1606 – 1669) son of Claude Poute, Lord des Forges & Marie
Marguerite de Durfort
(A) **Louise Poute** (...)
= 21 Mar 1659; **Honoré de La Chassaigne, Lord de
Montjouan** (... – 1666)
(1) **Jacques Honoré de La Chassaigne, Lord de
Mountjouan** (... – bef.1720)
= ...; **Jeanne de Jovion de Drouilles** (...)
(a) **Jacques de La Chassaigne, Lord de Drouilles** (...)
=1 21 Jan 1727 Oradour-sur-Glane; **Jeanne Louise de
Lescours** (... – 26 Dec 1733) daughter of François-Louis
de Lescour, Marquis de Lescours & Elisabeth Green
=2 ...; **Charlotte de Roffignac** (...) daughter of Claude
François, Marquis de Roffignac & Catherine de La Borie
no issue
(2) **Marie Thérèse de la Chassaigne** (...)
= ...; **François Père, Lord de Confolens** (...)
issue ?
(3) **Antoinette de La Chassaigne** (...)
= 19 Feb 1675; **René de La Rye, Lord de Fresne-
St.Coutant** (...) son of Jean de La Rye, Lord de l'Aubuge &
Marie de La Tousche
(a) **Jean de La Rye, Lord de La Coste** (...)
= ...; **Antoinette Pigné de Nouic** (...)
Has further generations of issue
(b) **Renée de La Rye** (...)
= 16 Dec 1726 Saint-Bonnet-de Beliac; **Jean Martin,
Lord de La Goutte-Bernard** (1707 – 1759)
Has further generations of issue
(B) **François Poute, Lord de Dompierre** (1637 – 1700)
= 28 Mar 1671 Nieul-le-Virouil; **Marie Arnoul** (...) daughter
of Léon Arnoul, Baron de Nieuil le Viroul & Marguerite de
Rabaines
(1) **Marie Poute** (26 Feb 1672 – ...)
= 16 Aug 1688 Prissac; **Jacques-César Couraud, Lord de
La Roche-Chevreux** (... – 20 Feb 1710) son of Honoat
Couraud, Lord de La Roche-Chevreux & Anne de Brilhac
(a) **François César Couraud, Lord de La Roche-
Chevreux** (...)
= 6 Jan 1737; **Marie Catherine de Pierre-Buffière**
(1713 – ...)
Has further generations of issue
(b) **François-Gabriel** César **Couraud, Lord de Salvert**

(...)
= ...; **Françoise** Marquerite **Douat** (...)
Has further generations of issue
(c) **Marie Geneviève Couraud** (1690 – ...)
(d) **Jacques César Couraud** (...)
(e) **Gabriel César Couraud** (...)
(2) **Anna Poute** (1689 – 1725 Saint-Pardoux)
= 16 Feb 1705; **Antoine du Pouget de Nadaillac** (4 Feb 1673 Aubusson – 19 Jan 1741 Saint-Pardoux) son of François du Pouget, Marquis de Nadaillac & Françoise de Douhet
   (a) **François du Pouget de Nadaillac, Baron de Saint-Pardoux** (15 Dec 1705 Saint-Pardoux – 1748)
   = ...; **Marie Anne** Françoise Félicité **Le Mastin de Buaillé** (... – 1782) daughter of Charles Le Mastin de Buaillé & Anne Louise de La Rochefoucauld
   Has further generations of issue
   (b) **Anne du Pouget de Nadaillac** (20 Mar 1709 Saint-Pardoux – ...)
   = 26 Dec 1748; **Jacques du Ligondès, Marquis de Ligondès** (... – 15 Dec 1749) son of Gaspard du Ligondès, Lord de Châteaubodeau & Antoinette de Saint-Julien
   Has further generations of issue
(3) **Jean-Baptiste Poute, Count de Nieul** (bef.1690 – ...)
=1 ...; **Marie Anne** Marguerite **Arnoul** (...)
=2 ...; **Anne Louise de La Rochefoucauld** (1706 – ...) daughter of François de La Rochefoucauld, Marquis de Surgères & Angélique Lee
issue of 1st:
   (a) **Marie Thérèse Poute de Nieuil** (...)
   = 16 Sep 1748; **Ranaud de Courbon, Marquis de Blénac** (... – 1787)
   issue ?
issue of 2nd:
   (b) **Arnoul-Claude Poute, Marquis de Nieuil** (22 Jul 1730 – 19 Apr 1806 Poitiers)
   = 1 Apr 1762 Cramard; **Jeanne des Francs** (5 Feb 1744 – 2 Mar 1809 Poitiers) daughter of Etienne, Marquis des Francs & Jeanne Milon
   Has further generations of issue
   (c) **Alexis** Benjamin François **Poute, Count de Nieuil** (29 Jun 1731 Nieuil-le-Virouil – 31 Aug 1787 Poitiers) unm.
   (d) **Jeanne Poute de Nieuil** (...)
(4) **Agnès Poute** (...)
= 20 Sep 1729; **Jacques du Rousseau de Ferrières** (...)
   (a) **Marie du Rousseau de Ferrières** (...)
   = 18 Apr 1740; **Léonard** Louis **Guingand, Lord de**

Saint-Mathieu (8 Jun 1715 Limoges – 5 Oct 1748) son of
Martial Guingand, Lord de Saint-Mathieu & Catherine
Limousin
Has further generations of issue
(C) **Jehan Poute** (26 Feb 1639 Dompierere-les-Eglises – 14
Sep 1719 Dompierre)
= 27 Nov 1680 Benest; **Marie Caillou de Sainte-Terre**
(bef.1660 – 21 Jul 1716 Benest)
(1) **Louis Poute** (30 Aug 1688 Benest – 1734)
= 7 Jan 1710 Benest; **Marguerite Pinot de Puybaudet** (17
Dec 1685 Confolens – 1762 Benest) daughter of Isaac Pinot &
Marie Ribiere
(a) **François Poute de Puybaudet** (1720 – 1795)
= ...; **Marie d'Hugonneau** (...) daughter of Jean
Hugonneau & Marie Michell
Has further generations of issue
(D) **Marguerite Poute** (... – 30 Jul 1678 Paris)
= 11 Aug 1644 Dompierre; **François de Raymond, Lord du
Cluzeau** (... – 12 Dec 1672) son of François de Raymond, Lord
du Cluzeau & Isabeau Marrand
(1) **Gabriel-François de Raymond, Lord du Haut et Bas
Monteil** (...)
= 3 Feb 1676 Paris; **Catherine Sanguiniere** (bef.1653 – ...)
daughter of Pierre Sanguiniere & Margueritye Dupuy de
Marques
(a) **Louise de Raymond** (...)
= 18 Mar 1704 Montbas; **Pierre Barton, Count de
Montbas** (25 Mar 1681 – 12 Jan 1756 Montbas) son of
François Barton, Count de Montbas & Anne Aubert
Has further generations of issue
(II) **Gaston de Secondat, Baron de Montesquieu** (1612
Agen – 2 Aug 1678 Bordeaux)
= 16 Feb 1634; **Anne Jeanne Dubernet** (1610 – 27 Dec 1675)
daughter of Joseph Dubernet & Catherine de Benoist
(A) **Jean Baptiste de Secondat de Montesquieu** (... –
1716)
= ...; **Marguerite de Caupos** (...) daughter of Jean de
Caupos & Marie de Baleste
(1) **Jean de Secondat de Montesquieu** (1671 – ...)
(B) **Jacques de Secondat, Baron de Montesquieu** (29 Dec
1654 Bordeaux – 15 Nov 1713)
= 25 Sep 1686 La Brède; **Marie-Françoise de Pesnel de La
Brède** (28 Oct 1665 La Brède – 13 Oct 1696 Bordeaux)
daughter of Pierre de Pesnel, Baron de La Brède & Marie de La
Serre
(1) **Marie de Secondat de Montesquieu** (1685 – ...)

= ...; **Bénigne** Jérôme **du Trousset d'Hériqourt** (...) issue ?

(2) **Charles-Louis de Secondat, Baron de Montesquieu et de Labrède**[14] (18 Jan 1689 La Brède – 10 Feb 1755)
= 30 Apr 1715 Bordeaux; **Jeanne Catherine de Lartigue** (1689 – 13 Jul 1770 Bordeaux) daughter of Pierre, Lord de Lartigue & Elisabeth de Pauzie

  (a) **Jean Baptiste de Secondat, Baron de Roduefort**, etc. (12 Feb 1716 Martillac – 17 Jun 1795 Bordeaux)
= 30 Aug 1740; **Marie** Catherine Thérèse **de Mons** (...) daughter of François Joseph de Mons & Marie Thérèse Ménoire
Issue became extinct in 1835

  (b) **Marie-Catherine de Secondat de Montesquieu** (1717 La Brède – 1784 Landiras)
= 19 Nov 1738 La Brède; **Joseph** Vincent **de Guichaner d'Armajan** (1707 – 1766) son of François de Giuchaner d'Armajan & Marthe de Chambert
Has further generations of issue

  (c) **Denise de Secondat de Montesquieu** (23 Feb 1727 Bordeaux – 23 Feb 1800 Agen)
= 1745; ♦**Godefroy de Secondat** (1702–1774)
Children are listed with other parent

(3) **Thérèse de Secondat de Montesquieu** (1681 – 1772) unm.

(4) **Joseph de Secondat de Montesuieu** (1694 – 1754)

(C) **Marguerite de Secondat de Montesquieu** (...)
= ...; **Jacques Dunoyer** (...)

(1) **Marie Dunoyer** (...)
= ...; **Charles de Guérin** (...) son of Etyienne de Guérin & Marie Lescuyer
issue ?

(III) **Henri de Secondat** (...)
= ...; **Marie de Rance, Baroness de La Perche** (...) daughter of André de rance, Baron de La Perche & Marie de Maillet

(A) **Étienne de Secondat, Baron de La Perche** (...)
= 26 Oct 1677 Agen; **Sereine de Raymond** (1655 – ...)

(1) **Marguerite de Secondat** (...)
= 9 Sep 1700; **François de Cours, Lord de Thoumazeau** (1658 Castillonès – ...) son of Jean Cours, Lord de Puiguiraud & Marie de Guyon de Favas

---

[14] A noted political philosopher.

(a) **Étienne de Cours, Lord de Thomazeau** (27 May 1701 Castillonès – 7 Jun 1772 Castillonès) = 14 Nov 1721 Castillonès; **Catherine Monnel** (1705 – ...) daughter of Pierre Monnel & Catherine Roy
Has further generations of issue

(b) **Joseph** François Bernard **de Cours** (4 Feb 1703 Castillonès – 3 Jul 1738 Penne-d'Agenais) = ...; **Antoinette de Lard** (19 May 1715 Penne-d' Agenais – ...) daughter of Paul de Lard & Jeanne de Marboutin
no issue

(c) **Jacques de Cours** (...) = 1760; **Marie Anne Littée** (1740 – ...) daughter of François Littée & Catherine Carreau
Has further generations of issue

(d) **François** Étienne **de Cours** (17 Apr 1719 Castillonès – ...)

(2) **Jean Baptiste de Secondat, Baron de La Perche** (...) = ...; **Luce Monnel** (...) daughter of Pierre Monnel & Catherine Roy

(a) **Serène de Secondat** (... – 26 Dec 1788) = 15 Jul 1736; **Gérard Dupleix, Lord de Cadigan** (1716 – ...) son of Charles Dupleix, Lord de Cadignan & Jeanne de Gerboux
Has further generations of issue

g) **Léonor de Secondat** (1578 – ...)

h) **Suzanne de Secondat** (bef.1581 – ...) = ...; **François d'Estrades** (...) son of Jean d'Estrades, Lord de Bonel & Antoinette Arnoul

(I) **Godefroy d'Estrades** (...) = ...; **Marie de Lallier** (...) daughter of Jacques de Lallier, Lord du Pin & Marguerite de Burtio de La Tour

(A) **Gabriel** Joseph **d'Estrades** (... 12 Aug 1699) killed in battle

(B) **Louis, Marquis d'Estrades** (... – 1711) Mayor of Bordeaux 1674, Gov. of Dunkerque 1686
=1 ...; **Charlotte Thérèse de Runes** (... – 25 Nov 1682) daughter of Charles de Runes, Marquis de Fouquesolles & Jeanne Lambert d'Herbigny
=2 ...; **Marie Anne Blouin** (...) daughter of Jérôme Blouin & Marie Armande Sénéchal
issue of 1st:

(1) **Godefroy** Louis, **Count d'Estrades** (... 1717) = 1691; **Charlotte La Normant** (... – 1730) daughter of Charles Le Normant & Marie Parthon

(a) **Louis** Godefroy, **Marquis d'Estrades** (1717 – 1769)

Mayor of Bordeaux
= ...; **Marie Jeanne** Charlotte **de Saintonge** (...)
daughter of Jean de Saintonge, Lord de Richemont &
Catherione Blanchet
no issue
  (b) **Jeanne** Renée **d'Estrades** (16 Apr 1700 – 4 Nov 1725
  Montpellier)
  = 11 Aug 1720; **Henry de Baschi, Marquis de Pignan**,
  Baron de Las Rabes (13 May 1867 Pontpellier – 1725) cr.
  Marquis 1721
  Has further generations of issue
  (c) **Marie Charlotte d'Estrades** (...)
  = ...; **Pierre** Jean **Romanet** (14 Jun 1685 Paris – ...) son
  of Jean Romanet & Marie Dorson
  Issue extinct by 1755
issue of 2nd:
  (2) **Louise** Françoise Armande **d'Estrades** (...)
  = ...; **Pierre** Charles **Lambert d'Herbigny, Marquis de
  Thibouville** (...) son of Henry Lambert d'Herbigny &
  Elisabeth Rouillé
  (a) **Perre-Armand Lambert d'Herbigny** (... – 23 Jun
  1737)
  (b) **Elisabeth Lambert d'Herbigny** (...)
  = 13 Sep 1728; **François** Guillaume **Briçonet, Count
  d'Auteuil** (...) son of Guillaume Briçonnet, Marquis de
  Rozay & Charlotte Croiset
  issue ?
  (c) **Marie Armande Lambert d'Herbigny** (...)
  = 7 Aug 1725 Rouen; **Jean Baptiste Le Sens, Lord de
  Folleville** (1702 Rouen – 30 Mar 1732) son of Jean Le
  Sens, Lord de Folleville & Renée Boullais de Catteville
  Has further generations of issue
3) **Sebastienne de Brénieu** (...)
= 1584; **Andre Bérenger, Lord de Pipet** (...) son of Claude
Bérenger, Lord de Pipet & Margueirte de Dorgeoise
a) **Alexandre Bérenger, Lord de Pipet** (...)
= 10 May 1617; **Isabeau de Perrinet** (...)
 (I) **Pierre de Bérenger, Baron de Violes** (...)
 = 16 Aug 1646; **Louise de Langes** (...)
 (A) **Rose de Bérenger** (...)
 = 11 Feb 1688; **Alexandre de Gallifeet** (... – 1719) son of
 Pierre de Gallifeet & Marquerite de Bonfils
 (1) **Louis François, Marquis de Gallifeet** (1 Feb 1695 –
 1778)
 = 1 Mar 1730; **Denise Pucelle** (...) daughter of Omer
 Pucelle & Marie Dominique Talon

issue ?
   (B) **Frédéric de Bérenger** (1655 – ...)
   = 11 Oct 1707; **Marguerite de Mirman** (1679 – 1720)
   daughter of Henri Huguenot de Mirman, Lord de Robiac &
   Marthe d'Audiffret
   issue ?
 b) **Madelaine de Bérenger** (1590 – 16 Aug 1624)
  = 1607; **Jean de Lamorte** (7 Jun 1576 – ...) son of Jean François
  de Lamorte & Marguerite d'Armand
  (I) **Pierre de Lamorte, Lord de Laval** (...)
  = ...; **Anne d'Armand** (...)
  (A) **Pierre Charles de Lamorte-Laval** (1657 – 1743)
  = 25 Sep 1685; **Almade Alexandrine de La Tour du Pin-
  Montauban** (bef.1666 – 5 Sep 1724 LaMotte-Chalancon)
  daughter of Alexandre de La Tour du Pin-Montauban, Lord de
  la Chaux & Lucrèce du Puy-Montbrun de Villefranche
   (1) **Jean René de Lamorte-Laval** (Jan 1701 – 1744)
   = 7 Jul 1736; **Louise Marie Manent** (... – 2 Sep 1738)
   daughter of Aymard de Manent & Laure de l'Homme
   (a) **Thérèse de Lamorte-Laval** (...)
   = 6 Dec 1755 **François de Chastelard** (Jun 1717 – 1755)
   son of Christophe de Chastelard & Marguerite de Roux-
   Déagent
   Has further generations of issue
  (II) **Madeleine de Lamorte** (... – 1693)
  = 1630; **Charles Tonnard** (...)
  (A) **Olympe de Tonnard** (...)
  = 12 Nov 1651 Grenoble; **Jean de Vaulserre, Baron des
  Adrets** (...)
   (1) **César de Vaulserre, Baron des Adrets** (...)
   = 11 May 1700 Paris; **Marguerite Landais** (7 Nov 1663
   Paris – ...) daughter of Étienne Landais & Elisabeth du Val
   (a) **Apollinaire** Etienne **de Vaulserre des Adrets** (...)
   = 9 Dec 1755 Grenoble; **Marie** Anne Marc Joséphine **de
   Bally** (...) daughter of François Joseph de Bally &
   Françoise Pourroy
   Has further generations of issue
4) **Catherine de Brénieu** (1540 – ...)
= ...; **Jean de Colombe** (...)
 a) **Françoise Colombe** (...)
 = ...; **Christophe Copier** (...)
 (I) **Catherine Copier** (...)
 = 6 Jun 1588; **Jean de La Rochette** (... – 1656) son of Jacques
 de La Rochette & Claire de Cosu
 (A) **Catherine de La Rochette** (...)
 = 1624; **Pierre de Giry** (...) son of Antoine de Giry & ... du

Bosquet
(1) **Pierre de Giry** (... – 1682)
= ...; ♦**Marie de la Rochette** (1625 – ...) daughter of Jean
Jacques de Rochette & Catherine de Soleysel
(a) **Jean François de Giry** (3 Aug 1652 Lyon – 1719 Lyon)
= 1690; **Marie-Antoinette Jacquier** (...) daughter of
Jacques Jacquier, Baron de Cornillion & Antoinette-
Catherine de La Farge
Has further generations of issue
(B) **Marcelin de La Rochette** (15 Nov 1602 – 1678)
= ...; **Marguerite Pichon** (...)
(1) **Jean Baptiste de La Rochette** (24 Jun 1632 – 12 Dec
1689)
= 26 Nov 1666; **Marguerite de Chaves de La Chavas**
(... – 19 Dec 1689) daughter of Jean de Chaves de La Chavas,
Lord du Col & Jeanne de Sauzéa
(a) **Jean Marcelin de la Rochette** (19 Jan 1670 – ...)
= 22 Dec 1711; **Marguerite de Chomel** (...) daughter of
Christophe de Chpomel, Lord du Mont & Catherine Faure
Has further generations of issue
(2) **Jacques de La Rochette** (13 Aug 1634 – ...)
= ...; **Catherine Sabot** (...)
(a) **Marcellin de La Rochette, Lord de Villdemont** (...)
= 24 Feb 1686; **Marie Vincent** (...) daughter of Jean
Baptiste Vincent & Anne Barallon
Issue became extinct in 1783
(C) **Jean Jacques de Rochette** (...)
= 29 Apr 1621; **Catherine de Soleysel** (...) daughter of Vital
de Soleysel
(1) **Catherine de La Rochette** (... – 1674)
= ...; **Jacques de Fouris** (...)
issue ?
(2) **Marguerite de la Rochette** (...)
= ...; **Michel du Bois de Gallerande** (...)
(a) **Marie du Bois de Gallerande** (... – 7 Aug 1699 Lens-
Lestang)
= 7 Dec 1672 Hauterives; **Claude Chuin** (9 Jun 1646
Lens-Lestang – 20 Apr 1694 Lens-Lestang)
Has further generations of issue
(3) **Marie de La Rochette** (1625 – ...)
= ...; ♦**Pierre de Giry** (...–1682)
Children are listed with other parent
(D) **François de La Rochette** (...)
= 20 Aug 1620; **Marguerite Thomas** (...)
(1) **Paul de La Rochette, Lord de la Beyssonière** (...)
= 5 Jul 1677; **Ursule du Fornel** (...)

issue ?

(E) **Paul de La Rochette, Lord de Bobnigneux** (30 Jul 1610 – ...)
= 1645; **Jeanne de Parchas** (...) daughter of Marcellin de Parchas & Clémence de La Roue
(1) **Gabriel Joseph de La Rochette, Lord de Bobnigneux** (... – 1706)
= ...; **Madeleine Laurenson de Saint-Didier La Seauve** (...)
(a) **Henri de La Rochette, Lord de Bobnigneux** (23 Nov 1681 – 16 Oct 1764)
= 22 Sep 1721; **Anne Marie d'Inguimbert de Pramiral** (...) daughter of Jean Bapiste d'Ingiumbert de Pramiral & Marie Pernette du Fournel
no issue

(F) **Fleurie de La Rochette** (...)
= 20 Feb 1618 Saint-Saveur-en-Rue; **Gabriel Mottot** (...)
(1) **Jean Mottot** (1 Feb 1619 Saint-Saveur-en-Rue – 14 May 1688 Sainbt-Saveur-en-Rue)
= 14 Feb 1645 Saint-Saveur-en-Rue; **Catherine Dumas** (28 May 1623 Saint-Saveur-en-Rue – 25 Dec 1698 Saint-Saveur-en-Rue) daughter of François Dumas & Marquerite Despinasse
(a) **Catherine Mottot** (1661 Saint-Saveur-en-Rue – 11 Apr 1692 Saint-Saveur-en-Rue)
= 26 Nov 1686 Saint-Saveur-en-Rue; **Barthélémy Oriol** (19 Jul 1660 Saint-Saveur-en-Rue – 19 Sep 1711 Saint-Saveur-en-Rue) son of Jacques Oriol & Anne Celle
Has further generations of issue

5) **Jacques de Trivoley, Lord de Brenieu** (... – 1622)
= 30 Nov 1584; **Anne de Taillefer** (...) daughter of Antoine de Taillefer, Lord de Mauriac & Jeanne de Ségur
a) **Marie de Brénieu** (...)
= ...; **Guy de Lestonnac, Lord du Parc** (4 Mar 1563 – 15 Nov 1612) son of Richard de Lestonnac & Jeanne Eyquem de Montaigne
issue ?
b) **Jeanne de Brénieu** (...)
= 24 Jun 1602; **Joseph Eyquem de Montaigne, Lord de Bussaguet** (... – 12 Oct 1627 Bordeaux) son of Geoffrey Eyquem de Montaigne, Lord de Bussaguet & Pirrine Guillet
(I) **Henry Eyquem de Montaigne** (...)
= 26 May 1624 Saintes; **Marguerite Blanchard** (...) daughter of Pierre Blanchard & Esther Goy
issue ?
(II) **Antoine Eyquem de Montaigne** (... – 27 Aug 1649 Saint-

Savinien) priest
(III) **Marie Eyquem de Montaigne** (...)
= bef.1627; **Jean de Massiot** (...)
(A) **Jeanne de Massiot** (28 Feb 1629 – ...)
= 22 Jun 1649; **Nicolas Maron** (...) son of Micolas Maron &
Jeanne Blanc
issue ?
(IV) **Guillaume Eyquem de Montaigne** (...)
(V) **François Eyquem de Montaigne** (8 Apr 1625 Bordeaux –
...)
= ...; **Thérèse du Solier** (...)
(A) **Jeanne Eyquem de Montaigne** (1660 – 13 May 1737
Belluire)
= 9 Jun 1686 Bordeaux; **Paul Clément de Laage de
Volude** (... – 16 Aug 1712) son of Paul de Laage de Volude &
Marie de Mauvise
(1) **Paul François, Marquis de Laage de Volude** (1688 –
1754)
= 18 Jun 1730; **Marie Louise de La Rochefoucauld** (...)
(a) **Jeanne Françoise de Laage de Volude** (3 Jul 1732
Belluire – ...)
(b) **François Paul de Laage de Volude** (10 Sep 1734
Belluire – ...)
= ...; **Marie Jeanne** Claudine **de Kergariou** (1745 – ...)
daughter of Joseph de Kergariou & Marguerite des Fages
Has further generations of issue
(B) **Michel Eyquem de Montaigne, Lord de Beausoleil**
(1665 – ...)
= ...; **Catherine de Viaut** (...)
(1) **Jean Baptiste Eyquem de Montaigne, Lord de
Beausèjour** (...)
= 21 Sep 1739 Bordeaux; **Marguerite de Combabessouze**
(18 Nov 1715 Bordeaux – ...) daughter of Nicolas de
Combabessouze & Thérèse de Gascq
(a) **Joseph Eyquem de Montaigne, Lord de
Beauséjour** (... – 1815)
= ...; **Thérèse de Galatheau** (...)
Has further generations of issue
(VI) **Raymond Eyquem de Montaigne** (... – bef.1639)
(VII) **Charlotte Eyquem de Montaigne** (...) a nun
(VIII) **Madeleine Eyquem de Montaigne** (...) a nun
6) **Pierre de Brénieu** (...) a priest
7) **Claude de Brénieu** (...) a priest
8) **Justine de Brénieu** (...)
= ...; **Jean de Rivière** (...)
issue ?

9) **Marquerite de Brénieu** (...)
= ...; **Claude Dorgeoise, Lord de Montferrier** (...) son nof
Antoine Dorgeoise
a) **Pierre Dorgeoise, Lord de Montferrier** (...)
= ...; **Madeleine de Bonne** (...)
(I) **Lucrèce Dorgeoise** (...)
= 13 Jan 1669; **Charles de Baudan, Lord de Villeneuve** (29
Apr 1604 Nîmes – 1 Mar 1671 Lyon) son of Guillaume de
Baudan, Lord de Villeneuve & Jacqueline de Solier; =1st
Gabrielle de Barnier
(A) **Théodore de Baudan** (...)
(B) **Pierre de Baudan** (...)
(II) **Charles Dorgeoise** (...)
e. **Princess Margaret of York** (3 May 1446 Fotheringhay Castle,
Northants. – Mechelen [now Belgium])
= 3 Jul 1468 Damme; **Charles** (the Bold), **Duke of Burgundy** (10 Nov
1433 Dijon – 5 Jan 1477 Nancy) son of Philippe (the Good), Duke of
Burgundy & Infanta Isabella of Portugal; =1st Catherine of France; =2nd
Isabelle de Bourbon
no issue
f. **Prince George, 1st Duke of Clarence** Earl of Salisbury, Earl of
Warwick **KG** (21 Oct 1449 Dublin – 18 Feb 1478 Tower of London)
executed; cr. Duke and KG 1461
= 11 Jul 1469; ♦**Lady Isabel Neville** (5 Sep 1451 Warwick Castle – 22
Dec 1476 Tewkesbuey Abbey) daughter of Richard Neville (the
Kingmaker), 16th Earl of Warwick & Lady Anne de Beauchamp
I) **Margaret Plantagenet, 8th Countess of Salisbury** (14 Aug 1473
Farleigh Hungerford Castle, Som. – 27 May 1541 London) executed;
restored to earldom of Salisbury 1512
= Nov 1487; **Sir Richard Pole KG** (1462 – bef.18 Dec 1505) son of
Sir Geoffrey Pole & Edith St.John; KG 1499
A) **Henry Pole, 1st Baron Montagu** (ca.1492 Ellesborough,
Bucks. – 9 Jan 1538/9 London) executed; cr. Baron 12 Oct 1514; Kt.
1513; titled were forfeited upon conviction
= bef. May 1520; ♦**Hon. Jane Neville** (ca.1484 – bef.26 Oct 1538)
daughter of George Neville, 2nd Baron Abergavenny & Margaret
Fenne
1) **Hon. Catherine Pole**[15] (1511 – 23 Sep 1576)
= 1532; ♦**Francis Hastings, 2nd Earl of Huntingdon** (1514 –
1561)

---

[15] Catherine's descendants continue the "Yorkist Claim" to the Throne to this day, based on
the school of thought that Henry VII was an usurper and all the monarchs since then are
illegitimately on the Throne.

Children are listed with other parent

2) Hon. Lucy Pole (...)[16]

3) Hon. Thomas Pole (... – 1526)
= ...; **Elizabeth Wingfield** (...)
no issue

4) Hon. Henry Pole (ca.1521 – aft.Sep 1542 London) died while imprisoned; unm.

5) Hon. Winifred Pole (ca.1525 Ellesborough – 1580)
=1 ...; ♦**Sir Thomas Hastings** (1515 – 1558)
=2 ...; **Sir Thomas Barrington** (1530 Barrington Hall, Essex – 1586) son of John Barrington & Elizabeth Bonham
issue of 2nd (none by 1st):

a) **Sir Francis Barrington, 1st Baronet** (1560 Barrington Hall – 3 Jul 1628) Kt. 1603; cr. Baronet 29 Jun 1611
= 1579; **Joan Cromwell** (Hinchingbrooke, Hunts.– ca.1641) daughter of Sir Henry Cromwell & Joan Warren

(I) **Sir Thomas Barrington, 2nd Baronet** (ca.1585 – Sep 1644) suc. father 1628
=1 bef.1605; **Frances Gobert** (...) daughter of John Gobert
=2 ...; **Judith Lytton** (... – bef.1657) daughter of Sir Rowland Lytton & Anne St.John; =1st Sir George Smith
issue of 1st (none by 2nd):

(A) **Sir John Barrington, 3rd Baronet** (1605 – 24 Mar 1682/3) Kt.1638; suc. father 1644
= bef.1643; **Dorothy Lytton** (... – 27 Oct 1703 London) daughter of Sir William Lytton & Ann Slaney

(1) **Thomas Barrington** (... – 1681)
= 8 Nov 1664; **Lady Anne Rich** (...) daughter of Robert Rich, 3rd Earl of Warwick & Lady Anne Cavendish; =2nd Sir Richard Franklin, 2nd Baronet

(a) **Sir John Barrington, 4th Baronet** (16 Oct 1670 – 26 Nov 1691 London) unm.; suc. grandfather 1683

(b) **Sir Charles Barrington, 5th Baronet** (aft.1670 – 29 Jan 1714/5) suc. brother 1691
=1 20 Apr 1693 London; **Bridget Monson** (ca.1674 – Dec 1699) daughter of Sir John Monson & Judith Pelham
=2 1700; **Lady Anna** Marie **FitzWilliam** (ca.1677 – Jul 1717 Bath) daughter of William FitzWilliam, 1st Earl FitzWilliam & Anne Cremor
no issue

(c) **Anne Barrington** (1675 – 17 Nov 1729)
= 17 Nov 1698 London; **Charles Shales** (1670 – 1734)

---

[16] If Lucy lived to adulthood, she did not leave children.

Has further generations of issue
  (2) **John Barrington** (...)
    = ...; **Elizabeth Hawkins** (...) daughter of Edward Hawkins
    (a) **Sir John Barrington, 6th Baronet** (ca.1673 – Aug
      1717) suc. cousin 1715
      = ...; **Susan Draper** (... – ca.1750) daughter of George
      Draper
      Has further generations of issue
  (B) **Sir Gobert Barrington** (... – 1695)
    =1 ...; **Lucy Wiseman** (...) daughter of Sir William Wiseman
    =2 ...; **Elizabeth ...** (...) =1st Hugh Lawton
    issue of 1st (none by 2nd):
    (1) **Sir Francis Barrington** (...)
      = ...; **Elizabeth Shute** (...) daughter of Samuel Shute
      no issue
  (C) **Oliver Barrington** (...)
  (D) **Lucy Barrington** (...)
    =1 ...; **William Cheney** (...)
    =2 ...; **Sir Toby Tyrrell, 2nd Baronet** (... – 1671) son of Sir
    Edward Tyrrell, 1st Baronet & Elizabeth Kingsmill; =1st
    Elizabeth Windebank; suc. father 1656
    (1) **Sir Thomas Tyrrell, 3rd Baronet** (... – 14 Oct 1705) suc.
      father 1671
      = ...; **Frances Blount** (25 Oct 1648 – 7 Jun 1699) daughter
      of Sir Henry Blount & Hester Wase
      (a) **Sir Henry Tyrrell, 4th Baronet** (ca.1670 – 6 Nov
        1708) suc. father 1705
        = ...; **Hester Blount** (26 Dec 1673 – ...) daughter of
        Charles Blount & Eleanor Tyrrell
        Has further generations of issue
      (b) **Hester Tyrrell** (...)
        = ...; **John Sheppard** (30 Jan 1663 – ...) son of John
        Sheppard & Ellen Herne
        Has further generations of issue
(II) **Ruth Barrington** (...)
  = ...; **Sir William Lytton** (ca.1590 – Aug 1660) son of Sir
  Rowland Lytton & Anne St.John; =1st Anne Slaney
  no issue
(III) **Mary Barrington** (... – 1666)
  = ...; **Sir Gilbert Gerard, 1st Baronet** (23 Oct 1587 – 6 Jan
  1670) son of William Gerard & Dorothy Ratcliff; cr. Baronet
  1620; =1st Charlotte Miriam
  (A) **Sir Francis Gerard, 2nd Baronet** (12 Oct 1617 – Dec
    1680) suc. father 1670
    = ca.1648; **Isabel Cheeke** (... – 1670) daughter of Sir Thomas
    Cheeke & Lady Essex Rich

(1) **Charles Gerard, 3rd Baronet** (1653 – 1701) suc. father 1680

= 9 Feb 1675/6; ♦**Hon. Honora Seymour** (... – 1731) daughter of Charles Seymour, 2nd Baron Seymour & Hon. Elizabeth Alington

(a) **Elizabeth Gerard** (...)
=1 ...; **Warwick Lake** (...)
=2 ...; **Miles Stapleton** (...)
Has further generations of issue

(2) **Francis Gerard, 4th Baronet** (aft.1653 – 1704) suc. brother 1701

= ...

(a) **Isabella Gerard** (ca.1688 – 10 Aug 1762)
=1 bef.1726; **Sir John Fryer, Baronet** (14 Sep 1671 Bucks. – 11 Sep 1726) son of Francis Fryer & Susannah Boulter; =1st Katherine Weedon; =2nd Dorcas Roberts; cr. Baronet 13 Dec 1714
=2 11 May 1738; **Henry Temple, 1st Viscount Palmerston** (ca.1673 – 10 Jun 1757) son of Sir John Temple & Jane Yarner; =1st Anne Houblon; cr. Viscount 12 Mar 1722/3
no issue

(3) **Cheeke Gerard, 5th Baronet** (1662 – 1716) suc. brother 1704, but Baronetcy became extinct upon his death

(B) **Winifred Gerard** (1625 – 5 Apr 1694)

= ...; **Tristram Conyers** (5 Sep 1619 – 6 Aug 1684) son of William Conyers & Mary Harvey

(1) **John Conyers** (6 Mar 1650 – 10 Mar 1725)
= ...; **Mary Lee** (... – 1702) daughter of George Lee & Cecily Goodwin

(a) **Edward Conyers** (1683 – 23 Apr 1742 Epping, Essex)
= ...; **Matilda Fermor** (... – 1741)
Has further generations of issue

(b) **Elizabeth Conyers** (... – 1758)
= ...; **Sir Herbert** Perrott **Pakington, 5th Baronet** (... – 27 Sep 1748) son of Sir John Pakington, 4th Baronet & Hester Perrott; suc. father 13 Aug 1727
Has further generations of issue

(c) **Dorothy Conyers** (... – Mar 1726)
= ...; **Sir Charles Mordaunt, 6th Baronet** (1697 – 7 Mar 1778) son of Sir John Mordaunt, 5th Baronet & Penelope Warburton; suc. father 6 Sep 1721
no issue

(2) **Gerard Conyers** (1649 – 20 Jul 1737) Lord Mayor of London 1722–1723
= ...; **Anne Lethieullier** (... – 16 Dec 1728) daughter of

Christophe Lethieullier & Jeanne du Quesne
no issue
(C) **Joan Gerrard** (...)
(D) **Henry Gerrard** (...)
(E) **Sir Gilbert Gerrard** (ca.1618 – 1683)
(IV) **Robert Barrington** (ca.1595 Barrington Hall – 26 Feb 1640)
= ...; **Dorothy Eden** (ca.1600 – ...) daughter of Sir Thomas Eden & Mary Darcy; =2nd Walter Barrett
(A) **Thomas Barrington** (1625 – ...)
(V) **Joan Barrington** (ca.1599 – ca.1653)
= ...; **Sir Richard Everard, 1st Baronet** (ca.1595 – 1680) son of Hugh Everard & Mary Bond; cr. Baronet 29 Jan 1629; =2nd Frances Elwes
(A) **Sir Richard Everard, 2nd Baronet** (1625 – 1694) suc. father 1680
=1 ...; **Elizabeth Gibb** (1625 – ...) daughter of Sir Henry Gibb, 1st Baronet & Ann Gibbs
=2 ...; **Jane Finet** (...) daughter of Sir John Finet
issue of 1st (none by 2nd):
(1) **Sir Hugh Everard, 3rd Baronet** (1655 Langley, Essex – 1706) suc. father 1694
= ...; **Mary Brown** (1655 – 1707) daughter of John Brown
(a) **Sir Richard Everard, 4th Baronet** (1683 Langley – 17 Feb 1733 Langley) Gov. of North Carolina 1725–1731
= ...; **Susanna Kidder** (1683 – 1739) daughter of Rt.Rev. Richard Kidder, Bishop of Bath & Elizabeth ...
Has further generations of issue
(B) **Winifred Everard** (...)
= ...; **Sir William Lucklyn, 1st Baronet** (of Waltham) (ca. 1633 – 1678) son of Sir William Lucklyn, 1st Baronet (of Little Waltham) & Mildred Capell; cr. Baronet 15 Nov 1661
(1) **Ann Lucklyn** (...)
= ...; **Sir Henry Palmer, 3rd Baronet** (... – 19 Sep 1706) son of Sir Thomas Palmer, 2nd Baronet & Elizabeth Shurley; suc. father 20 Apr 1656
no issue
(2) **Sir William Lucklyn, 2nd Baronet** (... – 1700) unm.; suc. father 1678, but the Baronetcy became extinct upon his death
(C) **Joan Everard** (...)
= ...; **Richard Cutts** (... – 1669)
(1) **John Cutts, Baron Cutts** (ca.1661 – 1707 Dublin) cr. Baron 12 Dec 1690, but title went extinct upon his death
=1 1690; **Elizabeth Clarke** (... – 1693) daughter of George Clarke

100

=2 31 Jan 1697; **Elizabeth Pickering** (... – 1697) daughter
of Sir Henry Pickering, 2nd Baronet & Philadelphia Downing
=3 12 Mar 1700; **Dorothy Weld** (...) daughter of Sir John
Weld; =2nd Edward Pickering
no issue

(2) **Anne Cutts** (...)
= ...; **John Thurbarne** (5 May 1636 – Jan 1713) son
of James Thurbarne & Ellen ...; =2nd Mary Croke
no issue

(VI) **Elizabeth Barrington** (ca.1593 Barrington Hall – ...)
=1 ...; **Sir James Altham** (ca.1593 – ...)
=2 ...; **Sir William Masham, 1st Baronet** (1592 – 1656) son
of William Masham & Alice ...; cr. Baronet 20 Dec 1621
issue of 1st:

(A) **Joan Altham** (ca.1606 Latton, Essex – ...)
= ...; **Sir Oliver St.John** (25 Jun 1598 Wooten,
Wilts. – 31 Dec 1673) son of Oliver St.John & Sarah
Bulkeley; =2nd Elizabridge Oxenbridge

(1) **Joanna St.John** (1631 Longthorp, Northants. – 1705)
= ...; ♦**Sir Walter St.John, 3rd Baronet** (1622–1708)
Children are listed with other parent

(2) **Sir Francis St.John** (ca.1632 High Lover, Essex – ...)
=1 ...; **Mary Wakering** (...) daughter of Dionsis Wakering
=2 14 May 1674; **Mary Foorthe** (ca.1649 – ...)
issue of 2nd (none surviving by 1st):

(a) **William St.John** (ca.1675 Longthorpe – ...)
(b) **Joan St.John** (ca.1676 Longthorpe – ...)
(c) **Mary St.John** (ca.1678 Longthorpe – ...)
(d) **Walter St.John** (ca.1680 Longthorpe – ...)
(e) **Oliver St.John** (ca.1682 Longthorpe – ...)
(f) **Elizabeth St.John** (ca.1684 Longthorpe – ...)
(g) **Sir Francis St.John** (ca.1687 Longthorpe – Sep 1756)

(3) **Catherine St.John** (ca.1634 High Lover – ...)
= ...; **Henry St.John** (Jul 1628 – Sep 1679) son of Sir John
St.John, 1st Baronet & Anne Leighton
no issue

(4) **William St.John** (ca.1637 High Lover – ...)
issue of 2nd:

(B) **Sir William Masham, 2nd Baronet** (... – 1663) suc.
father 1656
= ...; **Elizabeth Trevor** (...)

(1) **Sir Francis Masham, 3rd Baronet** (ca.1646 – 7 Feb
1723) suc. father 1663
=1 ...; **Mary Scott** (1649 – 1685) daughter of Sir William
Scott, 1st Baronet & Catherine Fortrey
=2 ...; **Damaris Cudworth** (18 Jan 1659 – 20 Apr

1708) daughter of Ralph Curworth & Damaris Cradock
issue of 1st:
   (a) **Samuel Masham, 1st Baron Masham**, 4th Baronet
     (1678 – 16 Oct 1758) suc. father 1723; cr.Baron 1712
     = 1707; **Abigail Hill**[17] (1670 – 6 Dec 1734) daughter of
     Francis Hill & Elizabeth Jennings
     Has further generations of issue
   issue of 2nd:
   (b) **Francis** Cudworth **Masham** (Jun 1686 – 25 May 1731)
(C) **Francis Masham** (...)
(VII) **Winifred Barrington** (...)
= ...; **Sir William Meux** (ca.1579 – 27 Aug 1638) son of Sir
John Meux & Cecily Button; =2nd Elizabeth Gerard
(A) **Sir John Meux, 1st Baronet** (... – Feb 1657) cr. Baronet
1641
   = ...; ♦**Elizabeth Worsley** (...) daughter of Sir Richard
   Worsley, 1st Baronet & Frances Neville
   (1) **Sir William Meux, 2nd Baronet** (... – 1697) suc. father
     1657
     =1 ...; **Mabel Dillington** (...) daughter of Robert
     Dillington & Hannah Webb
     =2 ...; **Elizabeth Browne** (...) daughter of George Browne
     issue of 2nd (none by 1st):
     (a) **Elizabeth Meux** (... – 22 Apr 1756)
        = 2 May 1710; **Sir John Miller, 2nd Baronet** (... –
        29 Nov 1721) son of Sir William Miller, 1st
        Baronet & Hannah ...; suc. father 2 Dec 1705
        Has further generations of issue
     (b) **Sir William Meux, 3rd Baronet** (ca.1685 – 6
        Mar 1706) suc. father 1697, but baronetcy became
        extinct upon his death; unm.
     (c) **Jane Meux** (... – 1750) unm.
     (d) **Anne Meux** (... – 1742) unm.
   (2) **Henry Meux** (... – Dec 1701) unm.
   (3) **John Meux** (... – 1649) unm.
   (4) **Anne Meux** (... – 1728) unm.
   (5) **Elizabeth Meux** (... – bef.1728) unm.
(B) **Jane Meux** (...)
   = ...; **... Meade** (...)
   issue ?
(C) **Cecily Meux** (... – 1697) unm.
(VIII) **Francis Barrington** (...)

---

[17] Abigail was a favorote of Queen Anne and was her hair dresser.

= ...; **... Doucet** (...) daughter of Richard Doucet
(A) **Francis Barrington** (...)
(IX) **John Barrington** (... – 1631 the Netherlands)
= ...; **Marie Pinaule** (...)
issue ?
c) **John Barrington** (...)
B) **Cardinal Reginald Pole, Archbishop of Canterbury**[18]
(Mar 1500 – 17 Nov 1558) cr. Cardinal 1536
C) **Sir Geoffrey Pole** (ca.1502 – Nov 1558) Kt. 1529
= bef.9 Jul 1528; **Constance Pakenham** (1498 – aft.12 Aug
1570) daughter of Sir Edmund Pakenham
1) **Margaret Pole** (ca.1528 Lordington House, Sussex –...)
= ...; **Walter Windsor** (... – 20 Aug 1558) son of William
Windsor, 2nd Baron Windsor & Elizabeth Cowdrey[19]
a) **Winifried Windsor** (6 Oct 1576 Minchinhanpton, Glos. – 10
Jun 1929 Otley, Suffolk)
= ...; **John Gosnold** (1568–1628)
issue ?
2) **Arthur Pole** (1531 Lordington, Sussex – 1570 London)
died in prison
= 1562; **Mary Holland** (... – bef.16 Nov 1570) daughter of Sir
Richard Holland & Eleanor Harbottle; =1st ♦Sir Thomas Percy
no issue
3) **Thomas Pole** (ca.1532 – 2 Nov 1570 Tower of London)
= ...; **Mary ...** (... – ca.Mar 1576) =1st John Lewes; =3rd Francis
Cotton
no issue
4) **Catherine Pole** (ca.1535 – Sep 1598)
= ...; **Sir Anthony Fortescue** (...)
a) **John Fortescue** (...)
= ...
(I) **Elizabeth Fortescue** (... – aft.16 Apr 1652)
= ...; ♦**Sir John Beaumont, 1st Baronet** (1582 – 1627)
Children are listed with other parent
5) **Mary Pole** (1538 Lordington, Sussex – ...)
= ...; **William Cuffaud** (...)

---

[18] He was the last Catholic Archbishop of Canterbury serving from 1555-1558 during the reign of Mary I. He died within 12 hours of Mary, freeing Elizabeth I to appoint a Protestant Archbishop.
[19] It is unclear which of his father's two wives that Walter is the son of. He is listed as the 6th son of Lord Windsor, so it is likely he is the sone fo the 2nd wife, Elizabeth. However the first wife was Margaret Sambourne, just in case that turns out to be wrong.

a) **Alexander Cuffaud** (...)
b) **Mary Cuffaud** (ca.1564 – ...)
= ...; **Richard Lambe** (...)
(I) **Mary Lambe** (... – 1675 Leuven, Flanders)
6) **Edmund Pole** (1541 Lordington – aft.12 Aug 1570 London) died in prison
7) **Geoffrey Pole** (1546 Lordington – bef.9 Mar 1590/1)
= bef. 1573; **Catherine Dutton** (... – aft.1608)
a) **Arthur Pole** (ca.1575 – 23 Jun 1605 Rome) murdered; unm.
b) **Geoffrey Pole** (ca.1577 – bef.7 Jan 1619) murdered; unm.
8) **Henry Pole** (...)
9) **Elizabeth Pole** (...)
= ca.1546; **William Neville** (...) of Torksey, Lincs.
issue ?
10) **Ann Pole** (...)
=1 ...; **Thomas Hildersham** (...)
=2 ...; **... Ward** (...)
issue of 1st:
a) **Arthur Hildersham** (6 Oct 1563 Stetchworth, Cambs. – 1632)
= 5 Jan 1590/1; **Anne Barfoot** (... – 1639)
(I) **Samuel Hildersham** (1594 Ashby de la Zouch, Leics. – Apr 1674 Ashby de la Zouche)
= ...; **Mary Goodyear** (...) daughter of Sir Henry Goodyear
issue ?
(II) **Sarah Hildersham** (...)
(III) **Timothy Hildersham** (1600 Ashby – 1633 Ashby)
(IV) **Nathaniel Hildersham** (1602 Ashby – 1647 Ashby)
D) **Sir Arthur Pole** (ca.1502 – aft.10 May 1527) Kt. 1523
= bef. 24 Oct 1522; **Jane Lewkenor** (ca.1503 – 1562) daughter of Sir Roger Lewkenor & Eleonor Tuchet; =1st Sir Christopher Pickering; =3rd Sir William Barentyne
1) **Margaret Pole** (1527 Racton, Sussex – ...)
= ...; **Sir John FitzHerbert** (...)
issue ?
2) **Mary Pole** (1529 Racton – ...)
= ...; **Sir John Stanley** (...)
issue ?
3) **Jane Pole** (...)
4) **Henry Pole** (...)
E) **Lady Ursula Pole** (ca.1504 – 12 Aug 1570)
= 1519; ♦**Henry Stafford, 1st Baron Stafford** (1501 – 1563)
Children are listed with other parent
II) **Edward Plantagenet, 17th Earl of Warwick** (25 Feb 1475 Warwick – 28 Nov 1499 Tower of London) executed; unm.
g. **Richard III, King of England, Ireland and France** (2 Oct 1452

Fotheringhay Castle – 22 Aug 1485 Bosworth Field, Leics.) killed in battle; cr. Duke of Gloucester KG, KB 1461; suc. nephew 26 Jun 1483 = 12 Jul 1472 Westminster Abbey; **Lady Anne Neville** (11 Jun 1456 Warwick Castle – 16 Mar 1485 London) daughter of Richard Neville, 16th Earl of Warwick & Lady Anne de Beauchamp; =1st

♦Prince Edward (of Westminster), Prince of Wales

a. **Prince Edward** (of Middleham), **Prince of Wales** etc. (Dec 1473 Middleham Castle, York – 31 Mar 1484 Middleham Castle)

CHAPTER 5
LANCASTER

As we have seen previously, the Lancasters are descended from John of Gaunt, 1st Duke of Lancaster and third surviving son of Edward III. This family is actually broken into two parts, those of unquestioned legitimacy, descended from John's first two marriages, and the Beauforts, who were born prior to John marrying thirdly to their mother. The latter will be discussed in their own chapter, which is next.

The legitimate male line has been thoroughly discussed in the chapter on the Wars of the Roses. There were a few other sons along the way, but the only two who lived to adulthood did not leave legitimate children. Of John's legitimate daughters, three produced further descendants and two have their own chapters: Portugal and Holland. The third daughter was Catherine, who married her cousin, King Enrique III of Castile.

For those who are a little geographically challenged in a historical sense, Castile, which by this time was combined with Léon, covered roughly the northwest quarter of present day Spain and included the cities of Madrid on its eastern border and Toledo on its southern one. The borders within the Iberian Peninsula were rather fluid during this time period as there were constant battles between the rival factions of Castle, Aragon (northeast Spain – today called the Basque region), Muslim-held Andalusia (southern Spain), and Portugal.

The two primary lines ruling in Spain were the Houses of Castile and Aragon which were actually the same family descended from two brothers in the 11th century. They maintained a long tradition of marrying their first cousins, and sometimes even closer. As the gene pool got weaker and weaker, both of these families came very close to extinction. They finally came down to one heiress in Castile—the granddaughter of Enrique III and Catherine of Lancaster—and one heir in Aragon. Of course they married. Not only did their union bring about the unification of Spain, but also the potential end to their royal family. This couple is Ferdinand and Isabel, best known to Americans as the sponsors of Christopher Columbus'[20] voyages to the New World.

Fortunately for Spain, Ferdinand and Isabel had the good sense to seek out fresh blood, at least for two of their children. Their only son died young, so they were left with four daughters. Juana, the eldest, was married to a German princeling of the up and coming Habsburg family, Archduke Philipp. He was a product of the marriage of the century: Maximilian von Habsburg and Duchess Maria of Burgundy. The marriages of Philipp and his siblings placed a huge swath of land reaching from the Atlantic Ocean to the steppes of Russia under direct Habsburg control.

The youngest Spanish princess, Catalina (called Catherine in England) was married off to Prince Arthur, the eldest son of English King Henry VII. Arthur died shortly thereafter, and Catherine then married his brother, Henry, gaining historical fame as Catherine of Aragon, Henry VIII's first wife. The rest of the story of Spain will be covered in the chapter on the Habsburgs.

Like the Yorks, the bulk of the descendants of the Lancasters is through illegitimate lines. In this case, it is via Antigone Plantagenet, the illegitimate daughter of Humphrey, Duke of Gloucester, himself a younger son of King Henry IV. While a large number of her descendants have served in the English Parliament, an even larger number can be found in the United States. Several lines settled in the area from Philadelphia to the Chesapeake Bay and now number in the tens, if not hundreds, of thousands of Americans.

These gateway families for American descendants include the Lloyd and Norris families of Philadelphia, the Prestons and Moores of Maryland, the Owens of Delaware, and the Littleton and Lewis families of Virginia, among others.

---

[20] Christopher Columbus is an anglicized version of his name. He was actually called Cristobal Colón in Spain and Cristobal Colombo in his native Italy.

Edward III

|

Prince John (of Gaunt), **1ˢᵗ Duke of Lancaster KG** (6 Mar 1340 Ghent –
3 Feb 1399 Leicester Castle) KG 1361; cr. Duke 13 Nov 1362
=1 19 May 1359 Reading Castle; **Blanche of Lancaster** (25 Mar 1345
Bolingbroke Castle, Lindsey – 12 Sep 1368 Tutbury Castle, Staffordshire)
daughter of Henry (of Grosmont), Duke of Lancaster[21] & Isabelle de
Beaumont
=2 12 Sep 1371 Rochefort; **Infanta Constanza of Castile** (1354 Castile –
24 Mar 1394 Leicester Castle) daughter of Pedro, King of Castile & Maria de
Padilla
=3 **KATHERINE, DUCHESS OF LANCASTER** (1350 – 1403)

issue of 1ˢᵗ:
A. **QUEEN PHILIPPA OF PORTUGAL**(1359 – 1415)
   see: Chapter 28
B. **ELIZABETH, DUCHESS OF EXETER** (1363 – 1426)
   see: Chapter 12
C. **Henry IV, King of England and France** (3 Apr 1367
   Bolingbroke Castle – 20 Mar 1413 London) overthrew Richard II
   and declared King 30 Sep 1399
   =1 5 Feb 1381 Rochford Hall, Essex; **Lady Mary de Bohun** (ca.1368 – 4
   Jun 1394 Petersborough Castle, Northants.) daughter of Humphrey de
   Bohun, 7ᵗʰ Earl of Hereford & Joan FitzAlan
   =2 7 Feb 1403; **Joanna of Navarre** (ca.1370 Pamplona – 10 Jun
   1437 London) daughter of Charles II, King of Navarre & Jeanne de
   Valois; =1ˢᵗ Jean V, Duke of Brittany
   issue of 1ˢᵗ (none by 2ⁿᵈ):
   1. **Henry V, King of England and France** (16 Sep 1386
      Monmouth, Wales – 31 Aug 1422 château de Vincennes, near
      Paris) suc. father 20 Mar 1413
      = 2 Jun 1420 Troyes Cathedral; **Catherine of France** (27 Oct
      1401 Paris – 3 Jan 1437 London) daughter of Charles VI, King of
      France & Isabeau of Bavaria; =2ⁿᵈ Owen Tudor[22]
      a. **Henry VI, King of England and France** (6 Dec 1421
         Windsor Castle – 21 May 1471 Tower of London) likely murdered; suc.
         father 31 Aug 1422; overthrown by Edward IV 4 Mar 1461; restored 3
         Oct 1470 but was generally held captive until his death.
         = 23 Apr 1445 Titchfield, Hants.; **Marguerite d'Anjou** (23 Mar 1430
         Pont-a-Mousson, Lorraine – 25 Aug 1482 Anjou) daughter of René, King

---

[21] Henry was a male-line great-grandson of King Henry III.
[22] By her second husband, Catherine was the paternal grandmother of King Henry VII.

109

of Naples & Isabelle, Duchess of Lorraine

I) **Edward** (of Westminster), **Prince of Wales** etc. (13 Oct 1453 Palace of Westminster – 4 May 1471 Tewkesbury) killed in battle
= Dec 1470; **Lady Anne Neville** (11 Jun 1456 Warwick Castle – 16 Mar 1485 Palace of Westminster) daughter of Richard Neville, 16th Earl of Warwick & Anne de Beauchamp; =2nd ♦Richard III, King of England
no issue

2. **Thomas of Lancaster, 1st Duke of Clarence KG** (1387 London – 22 Mar 1421 Baugé, France) killed in battle; KG 1402; cr. Duke 1414
= 1411; **Lady Margaret Holland** (1385 – 31 Dec 1439 London) daughter of Thomas Holland, 5th Earl of Kent & Lady Alice FitzAlan; =1st ♦John Beaufort, 1st Earl of Somerset
no issue by marriage
issue by ...:

a. **Sir John Clarence** (1387 – 1421) unm.

3. **John of Lancaster, 1st Duke of Bedford** Earl of Kendal, Earl of Richmond, **KG** (20 Jun 1389 – 14 Sep 1435 Rouen) KG 1402; cr. Duke 1414
=1 14 Jun 1423 Troyes; **Anne of Burgundy** (1404 – 14 Nov 1432 Paris) daughter of Jean II, Duke of Burgundy & Margarete of Bavaria
=2 22 Apr 1433 Therouenne; **Jacquetta of Luxembourg** (ca.1416 – 30 May 1472) daughter of Pierre de Luxembourg, Count de St.Pol & Marguerite de Baux
no surviving issue by marriages
issue by ...:

b. **Mary Plantagenet** (ca.1420 – ...)
= ca.1439; **Pierre de Montferrand** (ca.1411 – Jul 1454 Poitiers) executed; son of Bertrand de Montferrand & Isabeau de Preissac

I) **François de Montferrand** (1440 – 1501)
= ca.1485; **Bernardine de Lavedan** (ca.1460 – ...)

A) **Thomas de Montferrand, Baron de Landiras** (ca.1490 – ...)
= 1520; **Yolande Carriou** (...) daughter of François de Carriou & Isabeau de Lenencourt

1) **Pierre de Montferrand, Lord de la Trave** (... – 1540)

2) **Gaston de Montferrand, Baron de Montferrand** (...)
= ...; ...

a) **Pierre de Montferrand** (...)

b) **Gaston de Montferrand, Marquis de Montferrand** (ca.1540 – 1597)
= ...; **Jeanne de Lestonac** (1556 – 1640)

(I) **François de Montferrand** (...)

3) **Jean de Montferrand, Baron de Portets** (1520 – 1574)
=1 ca.1550; **Jacquette Rayet** (ca.1520 – ...) daughter of Pierre Rayet & Bonaventure de Belhade
=2 ...; **Marguerite Grignols** (ca.1520 – 1561)
issue of 1st (none by 2nd):

a) **Marguerite de Montferrand** (1550 – 1595)
= 13 Sep 1573; **François de Sentout** (ca.1540 – 1595) son of
Jean de Sentout & Geyonne de Ségur
(I) **Jean de Sentout** (ca.1574 – ...)
= ...; **Anne de Brethon** (...)
(A) **Jean Jacques de Sentout** (...)
= ...; **Isabeau de Gères** (...)
(1) **Anne de Sentout** (ca.1645 – 1687)
= ...; **François de Pontac, Lord d'Anglades** (1627 –
1692)
(a) **Joseph de Pontac** (1669 – 1729)
(b) **Françoise de Pontac** (1674 – 1743)
(c) **Léon de Pontac** (...)
(d) **Dénis de Pontac** (...)
(e) **Jean Jacques de Pontac** (...)
(f) **Delphine de Pontac, Lady de Landiras** (...)
(2) **Jean François de Sentout, Lord de Loubens** (1647 –
...)
= ...; **Marie de Loyac** (...)
(a) **Jean Jacques de Sentout** (...)
(II) **François de Sentout** (1575 – 1641)
= ...; **Anne d'Eclezia** (...)
issue ?
b) **Gaston de Montferrand, Baron de Landiras** (1551 –
ca.1597 Bordeaux)
= 12 Sep 1573 Bordeaux; **St. Jeanne de Lestonnac**[23] (27 Dec
1556 Bordeaux – 2 Feb 1640 Bordeaux) daughter of Richard de
Lestonnac & Jeanne Eyquem de Montaigne; canonized 15 May
1949
(I) **Gaston de Montferrand** (1574 – 1597) unm.
(II) **François de Montferrand, Baron de Landiras** (1578 –
1619)
= 13 Jul 1600 Bordeaux; **Marguerite de Cazalis** (1580 – ...)
daughter of Bernard, Lord de Cazalis & Marguerite Blanc
(A) **Jeanne de Montferrand** (1608 – 1685) a nun
(B) **Françoise de Montferrand** (1610 – 1655 Villeneuve-sur-
Lot) a nun
(C) **Bernard de Montferrand, Marquis de Landiras** (...)
cr. Marquis 1651
= 21 Oct 1646; **Delphinette de Pontac** (1627 – ...) daughter
of Geoffroy de Pontac & Anne du Duc
(1) **Marie-Catherine de Montferrand** (10 Nov 1654

---

[23] Patron saint of abuse victims, widows and pewople rejected by religious orders.

Bordeaux – 9 Sep 1731 Villeveuve-sur-Lot) a nun
(2) **François-Joseph de Montferrand** (...)
(3) **Léon de Montferrand, Marquis de Landiras** (1659 –
6 May 1717) suc. father
=1 ...; **Elisabeth de Rizancourt** (...)
=2 13 Sep 1700; **Catherine de Meslon** (10 Jan 1683 – 19
Apr 1724 Bordeaux) daughter of Jean André de Meslon, Lord
des Combes & Marie-Esther de Saint-Cric
issue of 2nd (none by 1st):
(a) **Delphine de Montferrand** (1702 – ...)
= 1720; **François de Brassier, Baron de Senignan** (...)
son of Etienne de Brassier & Suzanne Dabadie
Has further generations of issue
(b) **François-Armand de Monrferrand, Marquis de
Landiras** (1704 – 18 Aug 1761 Bordeaux) suc. father 1717
= 1 Sep 1721; **Thérèse Jeanne du Hamel** (... – 29 Aug
1761)
Issue extinct by 1751
(c) **Henriette** Catherine Olive **de Montferrand** (...) a nun
(d) **Marie** Catherine Lucie **de Montferrand** (1707 – ...) a
nun
(4) **Louise de Montferrand** (...) a nun
(5) **François de Montferrand, Lord d'Escouasse** (... – 24
Feb 1674)
= 29 Nov 1665; **Marthe Blanc** (...) daughter of Guillaume
Blanc, Lord de Coucoury & Marie de Pontcastel
no issue
(D) **Guy de Montferrand** (...)
(III) **Marthe de Montferrand** (1580 - ...) a nun
(IV) **Jeanne de Montferrand** (1587 – 5 Nov 1635)
= 22 Dec 1608; **François de Chartres, Baron d'Arpaillan**
(... – aft.1644) son of Jean de Chartres, Lord d'Arpaillan &
Françoise de Puch
(A) **Marie de Chartres** (...) a nun
(B) **Jean de Chartres** (...)
= 16 Sep 1642; **Eléonore de La Chassaigne** (...) daughter of
Geoffroy de La Chassaigne, Lord de Pressac & Isabeau de
Camain
issue ?
(C) **Françoise de Chartres** (...)
= bef.1657; **Louis de Rebleys, Lord de Labarthe** (...)
issue ?
(V) **Madeleine de Montferrand** (1588 – ...) a nun
c) **Catherine de Montferrand** (...)
= 1580; **Antoine de Chanteloube** (...)
(I) **Bonaventure de Chanteloube** (...)

= 4 Aug 1608; **Richard d'Aulède** (...)
(A) **Antoine d'Aulède** (...)
  = ...; **Marie de Cabjus** (...)
  (1) **Pierre d'Aulède** (...)
    = ...; **Jeanne de Rosier** (...)
    (a) **Louis Bertran d'Aulède, Lord de Pardaillan** (...)
      = 15 Jul 1706; **Jeanne Blondel de Joigny** (...) daughter
      of Claude Charles Blondel de Joigny, Marquis de
      Bellebrune & Marie Ferrand
      Has further generations of issue
d) **Barbe de Montferrand** (...)
e) **Marie de Montferrand** (... – 1581)
  = ...; **Bernard de Faverolles** (...)
  issue ?
f) **Galienne de Montferrand** (...)
issue of 2nd:
g) **Jacquette de Montferrand** (...)
  = ...; **François de La Cropte de Saint-Abre** (...)
  (I) **Jeanne de La Cropte** (...)
  = 1599; **Guillaume de Leymarie** (... – bef.1651) son of
  Giullaume de Leymarie & Barbe de Saint-Astier
  (A) **Fronton de Leymarie** (bef.1641 – ...)
    = ...; **Isabeau de Chilhaud** (...)
    (1) **Jean de Leymarie** (...)
      = 1686; **Marie d'Andrieu** (...)
      (a) **Jean de Leymarie, Lord de La Roche** (...)
        = 28 Dec 1708 Mensignac; **Marguerite de Sanzillon** (...)
        daughter of Armand de Sanzillion, Lord de Mensignac &
        Judith de Bayly
        Has further generations of issue
  (II) **François de La Cropte de Saint-Abre** (...)
  = 13 Feb 1614; **Antoinette de Jousserand** (...) daughter of
  Pierre de Joussaerand, Lord de Moys & Gabrielle de r
  (A) **Jean de La Cropte, Marquis de Saint-Arbe** (... – 16
    Jun 1674)
    = 22 Dec 1650; **Catherine de Salignac** (...) daughter of
    Achille de Salignac & Catherine de
    (1) **Jean** Isaac François **de La Cropte, Marquis de Saint-
      Abre** (... – 1727)
      = Mar 1677; **Marie-Anne de La Rochefoucauld** (... –
      1711) daughter of Louis Antoine de La Rochfoucauld & Anne
      Garnier
      (a) **François de La Cropte de Saint-Abre** (... – 1716)
        unm.
      (b) **Marie-Louise de La Cropte de Saint-Abre** (...)
    (2) **Léonard de La Cropte de Saint-Abre, Lord de**

Serillac (18 Nov 1666 – Jan 1719 Surin)
=1 16 Nov 1695; **Jeanne du Reclus** (... – 26 Nov 1704
Surin) daughter of François du Reclus & Jacqueline de
Salignac
=2 1708; **Renée Desmier** (...) daughter of Louis Desmier &
Gabrielle Berland
issue of 1st:
(a) **Henri-Joseph de La Cropte, Marquis de Saint-
Abre** (12 Mar 1702 – ...)
= 1730; **Marguerite-Claude Garnier** (...)
Has further generations of issue
issue of 2nd:
(b) **Louise** Françoise **de la Cropte de Saint-Abre** (18 Nov
1709 Surin – ...)
(c) **Marie Anne** Andrée **de La Cropte de Saint-Abre** (23
Nov 1710 Surin – ...)
(d) **Henri** Anne **de La Cropte de Saint-Abre** (17 May
1712 Surin – ...)
= 1747 Crazannes; **Marie Gabrielle de Durport de
Civrac** (...) daughter of Aimery de Durport de Civrac &
Gabrielle de Sainte-Maure
Has further generations of issue
(e) **Marie-Françoise de La Cropte de Saint-Abre**
(1714 – ...)
= 1744; **François Joumard Tison d'Argence** (1719 –
...) son of Annet Joumard Tison d'Argence & Jeanne Guy
de Puyrobert
Has further generations of issue
(B) **François de La Cropte de Saint-Abre** (...)
(C) **Louise de La Cropte de Saint-Abre** (... – bef.1677)
= 1 Oct 1647; **Pons de Salignac de La Mothe-Fénelon**
(1601 – Mar 1663 Sarlat-la-Canéda) son of François de
Salignac, Baron de Mothe-Fénelon & Marie de Bonneval
(1) **François Fénelon, Archbishop of Cambrai** (1695 – 7
Jan 1715) a priest
h) **Isabeau de Montferrand** (...)
= ...; **Raymond de Fontbride** (...)
(I) **Raymond de Fontbride** (...)
= 26 Sep 1608; **Bertrade de Born** (...) daughter of Jean de
Born & Marquerite Martineau
issue ?
(II) **Gratianne de Fontbride** (...)
=1 1593; **Pierre de Laborde** (...) son of Jeannot de Laborde &
Marguerite de Lerm
=2 30 Apr 1607; **Geoffroy de Vimeney** (...)
issue ?

(III) **Marguerite de Fontbride** (...)
    = ...; **... Guilhemin** (...)
    issue ?
4) **Jeanne de Montferrand** (...)
    = ...; **Jean de Portepain, Lord de la Salle de Pujols** (...)
    a) **Jean de Portepain** (...)
    b) **Marthe de Portepain** (...)
5) **Françoise de Montferrand** (...)
    issue by ...:
6) **Étienne de Montferrand** (... – 20 May 1540)
B) **Pierre de Montferrand** (...)
C) **Catherine de Montferrand** (...)
D) **Jeanne de Montferrand** (...
II) **Thomas de Montferrand** (...)
III) **Bertrand de Montferrand** (...)
IV) **Matilde de Montferrand** (...)

4. **Humphrey of Lancaster, 1st Duke of Gloucester,** Earl of Pembroke
KG (3 Oct 1390 – 23 Feb 1447) KG 1400; cr. Duke 1414
=1 bef.Mar 1423 Hadleigh, Essex (ann.1428); **Jacqueline of Bavaria,
Countess of Hainault** (16 Aug 1401 Hainault – 8 Oct 1436 Treylingen
Castle, near Leiden) daughter of Wilhelm II, Duke of Bavaria &
Marguerite of Burgundy; suc. father in Hainault 31 May 1417; =1st Jean,
Dauphin of France; =2nd Jean IV, Duke of Brabant; =4th François,
Siegneur de Borselen
=2 Jan 1428; **Eleanor Cobham** (ca.1400 Sterborough Castle, Kent – 7
Jul 1452 Beaumaris Castle, Anglesey) imprisoned from 1442; daughter of
Sir Reynald Cobham, 3rd Lord Cobham & Eleanor Culpeper
no surviving issue by marriages
issue by ...:
a. **Arthur of Gloucester** (... – 1447)
b. **Antigone Plantagenet** (btw.1425/28 – aft.1450)
    =1 ...; **Henry Grey, 2nd Earl of Tankerville** (ca.1419 – 13 Jan
    1449/50) son of John Grey, 1st Earl ofTankerville & Joan
    Charleston, 6th Baroness of Powis; suc. father 22 Mar 1421 and
    mother 17 Sep 1425[24]
    =2 ...; **Jean d'Amancy** (...)
    issue of 1st (none by 2nd):
    I) **Richard Grey, 3rd Earl of Tankerville** (5 Nov 1436 Pontesbury,
       Salop. – 17 Dec 1466) suc. father 1450; Tankerville (being in France)
       was lost 1453; titles were attainted 1459

---

[24] The Earls of Tankerville were never technically titled Baron, so when the son of the 3rd
Earl was called to Parliament as Baron Grey of Powis, it was considered a new cration.

= bef. 12 Jan 1458/9; **Hon. Margaret Tuchet** (... – 2 Fen
1480/1) daughter of James Tuchet, 5th Baron Audley & Eleanor
Holland; =2nd Sir Robert Vaughan
A) **John Grey, 1st Baron Grey of Powis** (1460 – 1497) cr.
  Baron 15 Nov 1482
  = ...; **Lady Anne Herbert** (...) daughter of William Herbert, 1st
  Earl of Pembroke
  1) **John Grey, 2nd Baron Grey of Powis** (1485 – 1504) suc.
    father 1497
    = ...; ♦**Hon. Margaret Sutton** (...) daughter of Edward Sutton,
    2nd Baron Dudley & Cecily Willoughby
    a) **Edward Grey, 3rd Baron Grey of Powis** (Jan 1503 Powys
      Castle – 2 Jul 1551 Powys)
      = 1525; ♦**Lady Anne Brandon** (2 Jun 1510 Bishops Lynn,
      Norfolk – 1542 Bishops Lynn) daughter of Charles Brandon, 1st
      Duke of Suffolk; =2nd Randall Haworth
      no issue by marriage
      issue by **Jane Orwell** (1510 – 1598) daughter of Sir Lewis
      Orwell:
      (I) **Anne Grey** (ca.1541 – ...)
        = ...; **Christopher Haywood** (...)
        issue ?
      (II) **Jane Grey** (ca.1543 – ...)
        = ...; **William Booth** (...)
        issue ?
      (III) **Cecily Grey** (1545 – ...)
        = ...; **Humphrey Freeman** (...)
        isue ?
      (IV) **Edward Grey** (1547 Powys, Montgomerys. – aft.1601
        Buildwas, Salop.)
        = ca.1563; **Chrysogena Giffard** (...) daughter of Sir John
        Giffard & Elizabeth Throckmorton
        (A) **Edward Grey** (ca.1578 – ...)
        (B) **Walter Grey** (ca.1580 – ...)
        (C) **Andrew Grey** (ca.1582 – ...)
        (D) **Thomas Grey** (ca.1584 – ...)
          = ..; **Anna Dudley** (ca.1588 Cleobury, Salop. – ...)
          issue ?
        (E) **Devereux Grey** (ca.1586 – ...)
        (F) **Jane Grey** (1588 – ...)
          =1 ...; **William Sheldon** (
          =2 ...; **William Leighton** (1565 Alberbury, Salop. – 1637
          Alberbury) son of Sir Edward Leighton & Anne Darrell
          issue ?
        (G) **Lettice Grey** (ca.1589 – ...)
        (H) **Cecilia Grey** (ca.1591 – 1653)

= ...; **George French** (1565 – 1647) =1st Anne Lytton
issue ?
(I) **Chysogena Grey** (1592 – ...)
= ca.1610; **Sir Morton Brigges, 1st Baronet** (ca.
1587 – ca.1650) son of Humphrey Brigges & Ann
Moreton; cr. Baronet 12 Aug 1641
(1) **Sir Humphrey Brigges, 2nd Baronet** (ca.1615 –
ca.May 1691) suc. father ca.1650
=1 ca.1630; **Elizabeth Cary** (1 Sep 1611 – ...) daughter
of Sir Philip Cary & Elizabeth Bland)
=2 ca.1648; ◆**Elizabeh Wilbraham** (...) daughter of Sir
Richard Wilbraham, 1st Baronet & Grace Savage
=3 16 Jun 1691; **Ann ...** (...)
=4 ...; **Magdalen Corbet** (... – bef. Nov 1693) daughter
of Sir John Corbet, 1st Baronet & Ann Mainwaring
issue of 2nd (none by others):
(a) **Sir Humphrey Brigges, 3rd Baronet** (ca.1650 –
1699) suc. father 1691
= ...; **Barbara Wyndham** (7 Nov 1649 – bef.1699)
daughter of Sir Wadham Wyndham & Barbara Clarke
Has further generations of issue (but extinct by 1767)
(2) **Robert Brigges** (...)
= ...
(a) **Martha Brigges** (...)
=1 ...; **Richard Spencer** (...)
=2 10 Oct 1668; **Sir John Stonhouse** (ca.1639 – 1700)
son of Sir John Stonhouse, 1st Baronet & Margaret Lovelace
Has further generations of issue
(V) **Walter Grey** (...)
(VI) **Andrew Grey** (...)
(VII) **Thomas Grey** (...)
b) **Hon. Anthony Grey** (...)
B) **Hon. Elizabeth Grey** (ca.1462 Weshpool – ...)
= ...; **Sir John Ludlow KB** (ca.1459 Hodnet, Salop. – 23
Dec 1495) son of Sir Rchard Ludlow & Isabel Pembrugge
1) **Alice Ludlow** (ca.1482 Stokesay, Salop. – 28 Aug 1531)
= ..; **Humphrey Vernon** (1476 Haddon, Derbys. – Aug
1542 Hodnet) son of Sir Henry Vernon & Anne Shirley
a) **Benedicta Vernon** (1504 – ...)
b) **Henry Vernon** (...)
c) **Catherine Vernon** (...)
d) **George Vernon** (1520 Hodnet – 1553 Hodnet)
= ...; **Elizabeth Pigot** (ca.1522 Chetwynd, Salop – ...)
daughter of Thomas Pigot & Elizabeth Onley
(I) **John Vernon** (1546 Hodnet – 1592 Hodnet)
= ...; ◆**Elizabeth Devereux** (ca.1541 Devereux Castle,

Carmarthens. – 1583) daughter of Sir Richard Devereux & Dorothy Hastings

(A) **Elizabeth Vernon** (ca.Jan 1572 Hodnet – 23 Nov 1655 Hodnet)

= 1598; ♦**Henry Wriothesley, 3ʳᵈ Earl of Southampton** (1573 – 1624)

Children are listed with other parent

(B) **Sir Robert Vernon** (1577 – 1625)

= ...; **Mary Needham** (...) daughter of Sir Robert Needham & Frances Aston

(1) **Sir Henry Vernon, 1ˢᵗ Baronet** (16 Dec 1606 – Apr 1676) cr. Baronet 23 Jul 1660

= 1636; **Elizabeth White** (...) daughter of Sir Richard White

(a) **Elizabeth Vernon** (... – 1685)

= 1675; **Robert Cholmondeley** (.... – 1679) son of Thomas Cholmondeley & Jane Tollemache

Has further generations of issue

(b) **Sir Thomas Vernon, 2ⁿᵈ Baronet** (... – 5 Feb 1682) suc. father 1676

= 9 Sep 1675; ♦**Elizabeth Cholmondeley** (...) daughter of Thomas Cholomondeley & Jane Tollemache

Issue extinct by 1725)

(C) **Susan Vernon** (...)

= ...; **Sir Walter Levenson** (1551 – 20 Oct 1602) son of Sir Richard Levenson & Mary Fitton; =1ˢᵗ Anne Corbet

no issue

e) **Thomas Vernon** (... – 17 Jan 1556/7)

= ...; **Eleanor Shirley** (ca.1528 Staunton Harold, Leics. – 28 Apr 1565 Staunton Harold) daughter of Ralph Shirley & Amee Lolle; =2ⁿᵈ Nicholas Browne

(I) **Walter Vernon** (1551 – 11 Jan 1592/3)

= ca.1582; **Mary Littleton** (1560 – 17 Dec 1622) daughter of Sir Edward Littleton & Alice Cockayne; =2ⁿᵈ ♦John Vernon

(A) **Sir Edward Vernon** (1584 Houndhill, Staffs. – 1657)

= 23 Jul 1605 Cound, Salop.; ♦**Margaret Vernon** (Sep 1592 – Jan 1656) daughter of Henry Vernon & Dorothy Heveningham

(1) **Dorothy Vernon** (ca.1615 – ...)

(2) **Henry Vernon** (1616 Houndhill – 9 Mar 1658/9)

= ...; **Muriel Vernon** (...) daughter of Sir George Vernon & Jane Corbet

(a) **George Vernon** (1636 Sudbury – 13 Jul 1702) (twin)

=1 ...; **Dorothy Shirley** (... – 1680) daughter of Sir Robert Shirley, 4ᵗʰ Baronet & Catherine Okeover

=2 ...; **Margaret Onely** (...) daughter of Edward Onely
=3 ...; **Catherine Vernon** (...) daughter of Sir Thomas
Vernon & Ann Weston
Has further generations of issue
(b) **Henry Vernon** (1636 – ...) (twin)
= ...; **Margaret ...** (...)
Has further generations of issue
(3) **Anne Vernon** (1620 – 15 Jan 1688)
(4) **Margaret Vernon** (... – 26 Oct 1658)
= ...; **Robert Dobyns** (...)
no issue
(5) **Walter Vernon** (... – 1650) unm.
(6) **Edward Vernon** (... – 1687)
(7) **John Vernon** (1632 – 1693)
= ...; **George Harpur** (... – 1658) son of Sir Richard
Harpur
issue ?
(B) **Elizabeth Vernon** (...)
= ...; **Sir Henry Merry** (...)
issue ?
(II) **Barbara Vernon** (...)
(III) **Dorothy Vernon** (...)
= bef.1580; ♦**Job Throckmorton** (ca.1545 – 1601)
Children are listed with other parent
II) **Hon. Humphrey Grey** (ca.1438 Pontesbury – ...)
= ...; **Eleanor Tuchet** (ca.1450 Heileigh, Staffs. – ...) daughter of
James Tuchet,5th Baron of Audley & Eleanor Holland
A) **John Grey** (1469 Montgomerys. – ...)
= ...; **Ellen verch Owen** (1460 Montgomerys. – ...)
1) **Elizabeth Grey** (1480 Llwydiarth, Montgomerys. – ...)
= ...; **John Vaughan** (1470 Llwydiarth – ...) son of Howell
Vaughan & Elen ferch John
a) **Howell Vaughan** (ca.1500 Glyncorrwg, Glamorgan –
...)
b) **Owen Vaughan** (aft.1500 Llwydiarth – ...)
= ...; **Margaret verch Owen** (ca.1510 Hergfest,
Montgomerys. – ...)
issue ?
c) **Margaret Vaughan** (...)
d) **Ann Vaughan** (1510 Talgarth, Brecons. – ...)
= ...; **John Gaines** (ca.1510 – 1606 Aberbran,
Brecons.) son of John Games & Jennet Harvard
(I) **Thomas Gaines** (ca.1535 Aberbran – 1579 New, Brecons.)
= ...; **Elinor Morgan** (1552 Llanhennock,
Monmouths. – 1634) daughter of John Morgan & Elizabeth
Lewis

(A) **John Gaines** (1520 Newton, Brecons. – ...)
= ...; **Jane Havard** (ca.1537 Aberbran – ...) daughter of
Richard Havard
(1) **Sir John Gaines** (1559 Newton – 1606 Newton)
(II) **Joan Gaines** (aft.1535 – ...)
= ...; **David Gwyn** (1532 Carmarthen – ...)
issue ?
III) **Lady Elizabeth Grey** (1440 Pontesbury – 1501 Salop.)
= 1465; **Sir Roger Kynaston** (ca.1430 Ellesmere, Salop. – 28
Oct 1495 Shrewsbury) son of Griffith Kynaston & Margaret
Hord; =1st Elizabeth Cobham
A) **Humphrey Kynaston** (22 Apr 1468 Marton in Middle –
May 1534)
=1 ...; **Margred ferch William** (1498 – ...) daughter of
Williamus ap Griffith
=2 ...; **Isabella ferch Maredudd** (ca.1495 – ...) daughter of
Maredudd ap Howell & Thomasina Ireland
issue of 1st:
1) **Isabella Kynaston** (...)
= ...; **John Trevor** (...)
issue ?
issue of 2nd:
2) **Ellen Kynaston** (...)
= ...; **John Tanat** (...)
issue ?
3) **Jane Kynaston** (...)
= ..; **Owain ap Maredudd** (...)
issue ?
4) **Thomas Kynaston** (ca.1510 Hordley, Salop. – 1549)
=1 ...; **Gwen ferch Maredudd** (1515 – ...) daughter of Marudd
ap Rhys
=2 ...; **Susanna Onslow** (1514 Walford, Salop. – ...)
issue of 1st (none by 2nd):
a) **Jane Kynaston** (1540 Stanwardine, Salop. – 23 Dec 1588)
= ...; **Robert Corbet** (1523 Wem, Salop. – 30 Jan 1594
Baschurch, Salop.) son of Sir Robert Corbet & Hon. Anne
Windsor
(I) **Richard Corbet** (ca.1553 Salop. – 10 Mar 1625 in Spain)
= ...; **Joan Burton** (ca.1568 Condover, Salop. – ...)
issue ?
(II) **Roger Corbet** (ca.1559 Salop. – ... in Spain)
(III) **Thomas Corbet** (1562 Stanwardine – 18 Mar 1614
Moreton Corbet, Salop.)
(IV) **Arthur Corbet** (ca.1566 Salop. – ...)
= ...; **Margaret Corbet** (1579 Moreton Corbet – 11
Apr 1659 Frodeley, Salop.) daughter of Sir Vincent Corbet

& Frances Humfreston; =2nd Sir Thomas Scriven
no issue
(V) **Reginald Corbet** (ca.1568 Salop. – …)
(VI) **Gertrude Corbet** (ca.1572 Salop. – 4 Apr 1643)
= …; **Thomas Baldwin** (1546 Salop. – 1614)
issue ?
(VII) **Jane Corbet** (ca.1573 Salop. – …)
= …; **Edward Hanmer** (1570 Salop. – …)
issue ?
(VIII) **Susanna Corbet** (…)
=1 …; **William Young** (1566 Salop. – 11 Feb 1597
Wolstanton) son of William Young & Anne Sneyd
=2 …; (her brother-in-law) **Edward Young** (1570
Thannington – 16 May 1617 Tenterden, Kent) son of
William Young & Anne Sneyd
issue of 2nd (none by 1st):
(A) **Elizabeth Young** (1601 Starnbrook, Beds. – …)
= …; **John Cobb** (Feb 1586 Starnbrook – …)
issue ?
(B) **Jeanne Young** (18 May 1606 Chislet, Kent – …)
(C) **Catherine Young** (…)
(IX) **Margaret Corbet** (1576 Salp. – …)
= …; ♦**Francis Kynaston** (1572 Little Ness, Salop. – …)
issue ?
5) **Robert Kynaston** (…)
6) **Margaret Kynaston** (ca.1515 Knoking, Salop. – …)
= …; **John ap Ieuan Lloyd** (…) son of Ievan Lloyd & Gwenhfar …
a) **Humphrey Lloyd** (ca.1550 Duffnyn, Montgomerys. –
1571 Somme, Picardie, France)
= …; **Maud Wynne** (1554 Duffnyn – …)
(I) **Katrin Lloyd-Wynne** (ca.1575 Duffnyn – 1636
Montgomerys.)
= … **John Lloyd** (né ap David) (1575 Dolobran,
Montgomerys. – 25 May 1636 Duffnyn) son of David
ap Dafydd & Ales ferch Llwyd
(A) **Charles Lloyd** (1613 Dolobran – 17 Aug 1757 in Wales)
= …; ♦**Elizabeth Stanley** (1616 Knockyn, Salop. – 1641 in
Wales) daughter of Sir Thomas Stanley & Sarah Burton
(1) **Charles Lloyd** (9 Dec 1637 Dolobran – 26 Nov
1698 Birmingham)
=1 …; **Sarah Elizabeth Lort** (2 Nov 1633 Stackpole,
Pembs. – 2 Nov 1685 Pembs.) daughter of Sampson Lort &
Olive Phillips
=2 …; **Ann Lawrence** (… – 2 Mar 1708)
issue of 1st (none by 2nd):
(a) **Charles Lloyd** (1662 – 21 Jan 1747)

= ..,; **Sarah Crowley** (7 Nov 1675 Rowley Regis, Staffs. –
1743) daughter of Ambrose Crowley & Sarah Morris
Has further generations of issue

(b) **Sampson Lloyd** (26 Feb 1664 Dolobran – 3 Jan
1724 Birmingham)
=1 ...; **Elizabeth Goode** (...)
=2 ...; **Mary Crowley** (15 Sep 1677 Kingswinford, Staffs. –
1771) daughter of Ambrose Crowley & Sarah Morris
Has further generations of issue

(c) **George Lloyd** (1665 – 17 Nov 1683)

(d) **Elizabeth Lloyd** (1673 – 18 Oct 1711)
= ...; **John Pemberton** (...)
issue ?

(2) **John Lloyd** (1638 Dolobran – 1695)
= ...; **Jane Gresham** (...) daughter of Sir Thomas Gresham
(a) **John Lloyd** (...)
(b) **Samuel Lloyd** (...)
(c) **Jane Lloyd** (...)

(3) **Elizabeth Lloyd** (1639 – ...)
= ...; **Henry Parry** (...)
issue ?

(4) **Thomas Lloyd** (17 Feb 1640 Dolobran – 10 Sep 1694
Philadelphia, PA) immirated to PA in 1683; Lt. Gov. of PA
1690–93
=1 ...; ◆**Mary Jones** (... in Wales – 11 Nov 1683
Philiaelphia) daughter of Gilbert Jones & Mary Littleton
=2 ...; **Patience Wilson** (1656 Gardiner, NY – 30
June 1724 Philadelphia) =1st Robert Story
issue of 1st (none by 2nd):

(a) **Hannah Lloyd** (21 Sep 1661 Dolobran – 25 Feb
1727 Philadelphia)
=1 ...; **John Delaval** (... – 10 Jun 1693
Philadelphia) son of Thomas Delaval
=2 ca.1700; **Richard Hill** (5 Oct 1659 Anne
Arundel Co. MD – 5 Jul 1729 Sussex Co. DE)
issue of 2nd (none surviving by 1st):
Has further generations of issue

(b) **Rachel Lloyd** (20 Jan 1667 Dolobran – 15 Aug
1716 Philadelphia)
= 16 Jul 1688 Philaelphia; **Samuel Preston** (1665
Patuxent, MD – 10 Sep 1743 Philadelphia) son of
Richard Preston & ... Marsh; =2nd Margaret
Langdale; Mayor of Philadelphia 1711–1714
Has further generations of issue

(c) **Robert Lloyd** (14 Jan 1669 Llanfor, Wales – 29
May 1714 Bryn Mawr, PA)

= ...; **Lowry Jones** (ca.Jan 1680 Llangelynnin,
Wales – 25 Nov 1762 Philadelphia) daughter of Rees
Jones & Hannah Price
Has further generations of issue
(d) **Mordecai Lloyd** (7 Dec 1669 Doloran – 1694
Hardy Co. VA[now WV])
(e) **John Lloyd** (3 Feb 1671 Dolobran – 5 Oct 1692
Jamaica)
(f) **Mary Lloyd** (27 Mar 1674 Dolobran – 15 Oct
1744 Philadelphia)
= ca.1700; **Isaac Norris** (21 Jul 1671 London – 4 Jun 1735
Philadelphia) son of Thomas Norris & Mary Moore
Has further generations of issue
(g) **Thomas Lloyd** (15 Sep 1675 Landerval, Wales –
17 Sep 1748 Philadelphia)
=1 ...; **Jane MacMahon** (...)
=2 ...; **Sarah Young** (1676 Bristol, England – 1740)
daughter of William Young & Ann Elizabeth Rousby
Has further generations of issue
(h) **Elizabeth Lloyd** (1 Mar 1677 London – 22 Jul
1704 Somerset Co. PA)
= ...; **Daniel Zachary** (19 May 1671 Beaconsfield, Bucks. –
...[25]) son of Thomas Zachary & Rebecca Murford
issue ?
(i) **Deborah Lloyd** (1 Mar 1682 Dolobran – 1721)
= ...; **Mordecai Moore** (ca.1660 Ireland – 1721
Anne Arundel Co.) son of Richard Moore
Has further generations of issue
7) **Thomasina Kynaston** (...)
B) **Lancelot Kynaston** (1469 – ...)
C) **Mary Kynaston** (1470 Hordley – ...)
=1 ...; **Sir Rhys ap Thomas KG**[26] (1449 Dynevor,
Carmarthens. – 1525) KG 1505
=2 ...; **Howell ap Jenkin** (1467 Tywyn, Merioneths. – 1494Nannau,
Merioneths.) so of Jenin ap Iorwerth & Ellyw ferch Grufudd
issue of 1st:
1) **Margred verch Rhys**[27] (...)

---

[25] He retuned to England after death of Elizabeth.
[26] A supporter of Henry Tudor, he is believed to have delivered the death blow to Richard III at Boswoth in 1485.
[27] The Welsh were very late to adopt the use of surnames. Instead they used a system of Patrinominals "ap David" would mean son of David and "verch David" would mean daughter of David. in the 16th century these morphed into surnames, but not on a consistent basis.

= ...; **Henry Wyriott** (...)
a) **Elspeth Wyriott** (...)
  = ...; **Rhys Bowen** (...)
  (I) **Henry Bowen** (1556 Upton Castle, Pembs. – 20 May 1621)
  = ...; **Elin ferch Owen** (ca.1560 Anglesey – ...) daughter of
  Owen ap Hugh & Sibyl Griffith
  issue ?
b) **Thomas Wyriott** (...)
  = ...; **Isabel verch Thomas** (...) daughter of Thomas ap Lewis
  (I) **Anne Wyriott** (... – 1525)
  = ...; **William Perrot** (...) son of John Perrot & Elizabeth
  Elliott
  (A) **John Perrot** (ca.1510 – 1575)
    = ...; **Jane Lloyd Vaughan** (1512 – ...) daughter of John
    Lloyd Vaughan & Alice Perrot
    (1) **Katherine Perrot** (1530 – 1614)
    = ...; **John ap Rhys** (ca.1528 – 1598) son of William
    ap Rhys & Elizabeth Bateman
    (a) **Thomas Rice** (ca.1570 – 1650)
      =1 ...; **Margaret Mercer** (ca.1580 Lancs. – 1 May 1610
      Tenby, Pembs.) daughter of William Mercer & Johanna
      Lovelace
      =2 ...; **Alice ...** (... – 1665)
      Has further generations of issue
    (b) **Elspeth Rice** (...)
    = ...; **... Barlow** (...)
    issue ?
    (c) **William Rice** (...)
    (d) **Janet Rice** (...)
  (B) **Thomas Perrot** (...)
    = ...
    (1) **Jane Perrot** (...)
    = ...; **Walter Philpin** (...)
    issue ?
  (C) **Rose Perrot** (...)
    = ...; **John Griffith** (...)
    issue ?
c) **George Wyriott** (...)
  = ...; **Jane Phillips** (ca.1534 Picton Castle, Pembs. – ...)
  daughter of Sir John Phillips & Elizabeth Griffith
  (I) **Elizabeth Wyriott** (...)
issue of 2nd:
2) **Humphrey ap Hwyel** (ca.1494 Tywyn, Merioneths. – 1545)
  = ...; **Anne Herbert** (ca.1496 – ...) daughter of Sir Richard
  Herbert & Margaret Craddock
  a) **Jane verch Humphrey** (1516 Tywyn – ...)

= ...; **Gruffydd ap Hywell of Nannau** (1520 Nannau –
1550) son of Hywell ap David & Elin Salusbury
(I) **Hugh Nannau** (1542 Nannau – 4 May 1603 Nannau)
  = ...; **Annest Vaughan** (ca.1546 Llanddwywe,
  Merioneths. – 1627 Nannau) daughter of Rhys Vaughan &
  Gwen verch Gruffydd
  (A) **Gruffydd Nannau** (11 Jun 1568 Nannau – 1609 Nannau)
    = ...; **Elin Wynn** (ca.1570 Dolgelley, Merioneths. –
    1600 Nannau) daughter of John Wynn & Mary Owen
    (1) **Elizabeth Nannau** (ca.1580 – bef.1630)
      = ...; **Humphrey Owen** (1580 – 1646) son of Robert Owen
      & Elizabeth verch Robert; =2nd ♦Catherine Nannau
      (a) **Owen Owen** (1625 – ...)
      (b) **Hugh Owen** (1626 – ...)
      (c) **John Owen** (1627 – ...)
      (d) **Robert Owen** (20 Oct 1628 Dolgelly – May 1686 New
        Castle Co, DE)
        = ...; **♦Jane Vaughan** (ca.1627 Dolocraw, Merioneths. –
        May 1685 New Castle Co.) daughter of Robert Vaughan &
        Catherine Nannau
        Has further generations of issue
      (e) **Henry Owen** (...)
      (f) **Samuel Owen** (1629 – ...)
      (g) **Ann Owen** (1631 – ...)
      (h) **Elizabeth Owen** (1632 – ...)
      (i) **William Owen** (1636 – ...)
      (j) **Elin Owen** (1637 – ...)
      (k) **Humphrey Owen** (...)
    (2) **Hugh Nannau** (ca.1586 Nannau – ...)
      = ...; **Anne ...** (...)
      issue ?
    (3) **John Nannau** (ca.1588 Nannau – ...)
    (4) **William Nannau** (ca.1590 Nannau – ...)
      = ...; **Elin Edwards** (...)
      (a) **John Nannau** (...)
        = ...
        Has further generations of issue
    (5) **Anne Nannau** (ca.1592 Nannau – ...)
    (6) **Catherine Nannau** (12 Dec 1594 Nannau – 25
      Jan 1662 Wales)
      = ...; **Robert Vaughan** (1592 Hengwrt,
      Merioneths. – 16 May 1667 Dolgelly) son of Hywel
      Vaughan & Margaret Owen
      (a) **Howell Vaughan** (ca.1620 Hengwrt – ...)
      (b) **Ynyr Vaughan** (ca.1622 Hengwrt – 1668)
      (c) **Hugh Vaughan** (ca.1625 Hengwrt – ...)

= ...; **Elizabeth Meyrick** (...)
issue ?
(d) **Jane Vaughan** (ca.1627 Dolocraw,
Merioneths. – May 1685 New Castle Co.)
= ...; ♦**Robert Owen** (1628 – 1686)
Children are listed with other parent
(e) **Gruffydd Vaughan** (20 Oct 1628 Hengwrt – 29
Aug 1700)
= ...; **Catherine Jones** (...)
issue ?
(f) **Margaret Vaughan** (ca.1630 Hengwrt – ...)
(g) **Ellin Vaughan** (ca.1634 Hengwrt – ...)
(B) **Robert Nannau** (1570 Nannau – ...)
(C) **Rhys Nannau** (1572 Nannau – ...)
(D) **Richard Nannau** (1574 Nannau – ...)
= ...; **Ellin Lloyd** (...)
issue ?
(E) **Edward Nannau** (1576 Nannau – ...)
= ...; **Elizabeth Gwyn** (...)
issue ?
(F) **Jane Nannau** (1580 Nannau – ...)
(G) **Ellen Nannau** (1581 Nannau – ...)
(H) **Margaret Nannau** (1578 Nannau – ...)
= ...; **Robert Lloyd** (...)
issue ?
(I) **Gwen Nannau** (1582 Nannau – ...)
= ...; **John Hughes** (...)
(1) **Jane Hughes** (...)
(J) **Mary Nannau** (1586 – ...)
(II) **Sion ap Gruffydd** (ca.1542 – ...)
= ...; **Elspeth verch Lloyd** (ca.1539 – ...)
(A) **Lewis ap Sion** (ca.1561 Llangdadock,
Carmarthens. – 1654)
= ...; **Ellin Rees** (1559 – ...) daughter of Howell Rees
(1) **Rees ag Lewis** (ca.1600 Llanfihangel, Pembs. – 1649)
= ...; **Catherine Ellis** (1595 – ...)
(a) **Ellis ap Rhys** (ca.1624 Dyffryn Ardudey,
Merioneths. – 1685)
= ...; **Anne Humphrey** (1634 Llangelynin,
Merioneths. – 1650 Dolgelly) dau of Humphrey ap
Hugh & Elizabeth Powell
Has further generations of issue
(III) **John ap Gruffydd** (1542 Nannau – ...)
=1 ...; **Elspeth Lloyd** (...)
=2 ...; **Elizabeth Lewis** (...)
issue of 2nd (none by 1st):

(A) **Lewis ap John** (...)
= ...; **Ellen Lewis** (...)
(1) **Rhys ap Lewis** (...)
= ...; **Catherine Lewis** (...)
(a) **Ellis ap Rhys** (...)
= ...; **Ann Rhys** (...)
Has further generations of issue
(IV) **Margaret Nannau** (1544 Nannau – ...)
= ...; **William ap Tudor** (...) son of Tudor ap Gruffydd
issue ?
(V) **Elizabeth Nannau** (1546 Nannau – ...)
= ...; **Robert Lloyd** (...)
issue ?
(VI) **Anne Nannau** (1548 Nannau – ...)
D) **Jane Kynaston** (1470 Salop. – ...)
= ca.1484; **Roger Thornes** (1468 Shelvock, Salop. – Apr 1531
Shelvock) son of Thomas Thornes and Mary Isabel Corbet
1) **John Thornes** (1482 Shelvock – 1535)
= ...; **Elizabeth Astley** (1486 Patshull, Staffs. – ...) daughter of
Richard Astley & Jane Otley
a) **Richard Thornes** (1499 Andover, Hants. – 1585 Condover,
Salop.)
=1 ...; **Margaret Vychan** (ca.1505 – ...) daughter or Ieuan
Vychan
=2 ...; Georgina (**Polly**) **Buckley** (1513 – 1581) daughter of
Curtis Buckley & Daisy Richards
issue of 1st (none by 2nd):
(I) **Alice Thornes** (1530 Condover – 21 Mar 1596
Munslow, Salop.)
= ...; **Rev. John Littleton** (ca.1510 Frankley, Salop. – 30 Nov
1560 Munslow) son of Thomas Littleton & Anne Botreaux
(A) **Thomas Littleton** (ca.1548 Munslow – Jan 1622
Munslow)
= ...; **Frances Lutley** (1562 Munslow – ...) daughter of
Adam Lutley & Elizabeth Cresset
(1) **Sir Adam Littleton, 1st Baronet** (1590 Salop. – 6
Sep 1647 North Ockendon, Essex) cr. Baronet 1642
= ...; **Audrey Poyntz** (1597 North Ockendon – 1648 North
Ockendon) daughter of Thomas Poyntz & Jane Peryam
(a) **Anne Littleton** (1622 – 1655)
= ...; **Thomas Powys** (1617 – 21 Apr 1671) son of Thomas
Powys & Elizabeth Smith; =2nd Mary Cotes
Has further generations of issue
(b) **Sir Thomas Littleton, 2nd Baronet** (ca.1621 – 14 Apr
1681) suc. father 1647
= Oct 1637; ♦**Hon. Anne Lyttleton** (21 Aug 1623 – ...)

daughter of Edward Lyttleton, Baron Lyttleton & Anne or
Jane Lyttleton

Has further generations of issue (but extinct by 1709)

(c) **Edward Littleton** (...)

= ...

Has further generations of issue

(2) **Rev. Thomas Littleton** (1590 Oxford – ...)

(3) **Rev. George Littleton** (1599 Stoke Milburgh,
Salop. – Nov 1675 Munslow)

(4) **Joan Littleton** (...)

(5) **John Littleton** (...)

(6) **Cecilia Littleton** (...)

(B) **Sir Edward Lyttleton** (23 Mar 1549 Hanly,
Salop. – 1622 Penkridge, Staffs.)

= ...; **Mary Walter** (1 Nov 1565 Salop. – 23 Oct 1633 Ludlow,
Salop.) daughter of Edmund Walter & Mary Hakluyt

(1) **Anne Lyttleton** (1583 – ...)

= ...; **Humphrey Salwey** (1575 – 1652)

(a) **Richard Salwey** (1615 – 1685)

= ...; **Anne Waring** (...) daughter of Richard Waring &
Hannah Colman

issue ?

(b) **Edward Salwey** (1603 – ...)

= ...; **Dorothy Dryden** (...) daughter of Sir Erasmus
Dryden & Frances Wilkes

Has further generations of issue

(2) **Jane Lyttleton** (1587 – 31 Aug 1657)

= ...; **Richard Knightley** (1580 Stafford, Staffs. – 1
Sep 1650 Fawsley, Northants.) son of Thomas
Knightley & Elizabeth Shuckburgh

(a) **Jane Knightley** (1606 Fawsley – 1661)

=1 ...; **John Thomson** (...)

=2 ...; **Peregrine Gastrell** (...)

Has further generations of issue

(b) **William Knightley** (...)

(c) **Devereux Knightley** (...)

(d) **Edward Knightley** (1611 Fawsley – 1659)

(e) **Elizabeth Knightley** (12 Mar 1612 Gnosall,
Staffs. – 12 Dec 1637 Preston Bagot, Warks.)

= ...; **William Randall** (...)

no issue

(f) **Walter Knightley** (...)

(g) **Bridget Knightley** (1616 Fawsley – 27 Feb
1638 Fawsley) unm.

(h) **Sir Richard Knightley, KB** (1617 Fawsley – 29
Jun 1661 Northants.) KB 30 Jan 1648/9

=1 ca.1637; **Elizabeth Hampden** (... – 1643) daughter
of John Hampden & Elizabeth Simeon
=2 aft.1643; **Ann Courteen** (1614 London – 1 Feb
1703 Fawsley) daughter of Sir William Courteen &
Hester Tyron; =1st Essex Devereux
Has further generations of issue
  (i) **Valentine Knightley** (1620 Fawsley – 1671)
  (j) **Lucy Knightley** (a son) (23 Apr 1623 London – 22 Oct
    1691 Daventry, Northants.)
    = ...; **Elizabeth Dent** (1653 Essex – 21 Jan 1711 Daventry)
    Has further generations of issue
  (k) **Mary Knightley** (1628 Stafford – 19 Jun 1949)
    = ...; **John Shelton** (ca.1613 – 30 Mar 1663 Wrest
    Bromwich, Staffs.) =2nd Elizabeth Holland
    no issue
(3) **Edward Lyttleton, Baron Lyttleton** (1589 – 27 Aug
  1645) cr. Baron 1641, but it became extinct upon his death
  =1 ...; **Anne/Jane Lyttleton** (1600 – 1623) daughter of
  John Lyttleton & Muriel Bromley
  =2 aft.1623; **Elizabeth Jones** (1595 – aft.1645) daughter
  of Sir William Jones & Margaret Griffith; =1st Richard Wynn,
  she =3rd Sir George Calverley
  issue of 1st:
  (a) **Hon. Anne Lyttleton** (21 Aug 1623 Mounslow – ...)
    = 1637; ♦**Sir Thomas Littleton, 2nd Baronet**
    (1624 – 1681)
    Children are listed with other parent
(4) **James Lyttleton** (1592 – 1645)
(5) **Thomas Lyttleton** (ca.1593 – 1645)
(6) **John Lyttleton** (ca.1596 – 1657)
  = ...; **Jane Newport** (...)
  issue ?
(7) **Sir Timothy Lyttleton** (ca.1598 – 1649)
(8) **Priscilla Lyttleton** (1600 – 1662)
  = ...; **Perrot Rice** (1595 – 1650)
  issue ?
(9) **Mary Lyttleton** (ca.1602 – 1649 Wales)
  = ...; **Gilbert Jones** (ca.1590 Montgomery, Wales –
  1650) son of Gilbert Jones & Joan Moore
  (a) **Edward Jones** (1621 – ...)
  (b) **Anne Jones** (1623 – 1664)
    = ...; **John Butler** (1610 Pembs. – 1655 Pembs.)
    son of Hugh Butler & Elizabeth Perrot
    Has further generations of issue
  (c) **Gilbert Jones** (...)
  (d) **Littleton Jones** (ca.1626 Welshpool, Monts. – ...)

(e) **James Jones** (1634 Welshpool – ...)
(f) **Bridget Jones** (1641 Welshpool – ...)
(g) **Mary Jones** (... – Nov 1683 Philadelphia, PA)
= ...; ♦**Thomas Lloyd** (1640 – 1694)
Children are listed with other parent
(h) **Roger Jones** (1645 Welshpool – ...)
(lo) **Nathaniel Lyttleton** (22 Dec 1605 Henley,
Salop. – 1654 VA) immigrated to VA 1635
= bef.Jun 1640; **Ann Southey** (1620 England – 028
Oct 1656 Northampton Co. VA) daughter of Henry
Southey & Elizabeth ...; =1st Charles Harmar
(a) **Edward Littleton** (1642 – 25 Jun 1663)
=1 ...; **Sarah Douglas** (1646 – 1659) daughter of
Edward Douglas & Isabella Dale
=2 ...; **Frances Robins** (1641 Cherrystone, VA –
1680 Accomack Co. VA) daughter of Obedience
Robins & Grace Neale; =2nd Francis Pigott
Has further generations of issue
(b) **Southey Littleton** (1643 Accomac, VA – 1680
Accomoc)
= ...; **Sarah Bowman** (1647 Accomack Co. – 1677
Northampton Co.) daughter of Edmund Bowman &
Margaret ...
Has further generations of issue
(c) **Esther Littleton** (1648 Accomack Co. – 1724
Accomack Co.)
=1 ...; **John Robins** (7 May 1636 Cherrystone – 28
May 1709 Cherrystone) son of Obedience Robins
& Grace Neale
=2 ...; **William Whittington** (1649 Accomack
Co. – 1720 Somerset Co. MD)
issue of 1st (none by 2nd):
Has further generations of issue
(II) **Thomas Thornes** (1520 – 1587)
= ...; **Mary Wigmore** (1520 – ...)
(A) **Francis Thornes** (Oct 1550 Candleshoe, Lincs. – 7 Oct
1601 Candleshoe)
= ...; **Jane Cavendish** (1558 – 3 Sep 1608 Candleshoe)
(1) **John Thorne** (ca.1580 Candleshoe – Jun 1621)
= ...; **Constance ...** (ca.1584 Essex – 2 Sep 1617
Somersby, Lincs.)
(a) **Susannah Thorne** (4 Oct 1608 Candleshoe – ...)
(b) **Cavendish Thorne** (Jul 1610 Candleshoe – ...)
(c) **John Thorne** (3 Jul 1614 Candleshoe – ...)
(d) **William Thorne** (31 Jul 1617 Candleshoe – ...
Queens Co. NY)

      (e) **Peter Thorne** (...)
    (B) **Richard Thornes** (...)
    (C) **Nicholas Thornes** (...)
  b) **Galfrid Thornes** (...)
  =1 ...; **Anne Fowler** (...) daughter of Roger Fowler
  =2 ...; **Jane Kynaston** (...) daughter of Thomas Kynaston &
  Alice Harnage
  issue of 1st (none by 2nd):
  (I) **Nicholas Thornes** (...)
    = ...; **Margaret Wrottesley** (...) daughter of Walter
    Wrottesley & Isabel Harcourt
    (A) **Francis Thornes** (ca.1606 – ...)
      = ...; **Beatrice Corbet** (...) daughter of Sir Andrew Corbet
      & Elizabeth Boothby
      (1) **Thomas Thornes** (1630 – ...)
        =1 ...; **Elizabeth Langley** (...) daughter of John Langley
        =2 ...; **Hester Courteen** (...) daughter of Sir William
        Courteen & Hester Tryon; =2nd ◆Sir Thomas Littleton, 1st
        Baronet
        no issue
      (2) **Elizabeth Thornes** (...)
        = ...; **Sir Vincent Corbet, 2nd Baronet** (ca.1642 – 4
        Feb 1681 London) son of Sir Vincent Corbet, 1st
        Baronet & Sarah Monson; suc. father Jan 1657
        (a) **Sir Vincent Corbet, 3rd Baronet** (1670 – 1688) suc.
        father 1681; baronetcy became extinct upon his death
E) **Margaret Kynaston** (...)
  = ...; **Richard Hanmer** (...) son of Griffith Hanmer & Eleanor
Dutton
  1) **Ermine Hanmer** (ca.1506 – ...)
    = ...; **Sir Edward Puleston** (ca.1500 Wrexham, Flints. –
    1567) son of Sir Roger Puleston & Joan Hanmer
    a) **Roger Puleston** (ca.1524 Wrexham – 29 Aug 1571)
      = ...; **Anne Grosvenor** (ca.1526 Chester, Ches. – ...) daughter
      of Richard Grosvenor & Catherine Cotton
      (I) **Richard Puleston** (1525 Wrexham – ...)
        = ...; **Anne Lewis** (1520 Bulcot, Oxon. – ...) daughter of
        David Lewis
        (A) **Sir John Puleston** (ca.1540 Anglesey, Wales –
        Aug 1599 Worthenbury, Flints.)
        = ...; **Elizabeth Woolrich** (ca.1540 Salop. – ...) daughter
        of John Woolrich
        (1) **Margaret Puleston** (ca.1565 Newport,
        Monmouths. – 1658 Anglesey)
        = ...; ...; **Robert** William **Lewis** (1560 Newport – 21 Aug
        1657 New Kent Co., VA) son of Hugh Lewis & Agnes Griffith

(a) **Richard Lewis** (1590 Anglesey – 4 May 1616
Brecknocks.)
(b) **Hugh Lewis** (ca.1575 Anglesey – ...)
= ...; **Margaret Wynne** (...) daughter of William Wynne
issue ?
(c) **John Lewis** (22 Feb 1592 Llantilio, Monmouths. – 21
Aug 1657 New Kent Co. VA) immigrated to VA ca.1653
= 21 Nov 1630 Monmouths.; **Lydia Warner**
(ca.1610 Monmouths. – Jan 1680 Gloucester Co.)
daughter of Thomas Warner & Elizabeth Sotherton
Has further generations of issue
(d) **Anne Lewis** (...)
= ...; **David Owen** (...)
Has further generations of issue
(2) **Roger Puleston** (ca.1636 – 13 Jul 1667)
= ...; **Jane Mostyn** (1646 – 1704) daughter of Sir Roger
Mostyn; =1ˢᵗ Sir John Trevor
(a) **Sir Roger Puleston** (1663 – 28 Feb 1697
London)
=1 ...; **Martha Rider** (...) daughter of William Rider
=2 ...; **Catherine Edwards** (... – 24 Jun 1685) daughter
of William Edwards
Has further generations of issue
(b) **Susan Puleston** (...)
= ..; **Eubule Thelwell** (...) son of Eubule Thelwell
& Mary Parry
Has further generations of issue
(II) **Roger Puleston** (28 Apr 1587 – ...)
= ...; ◆**Magdalen Hanmer** (...) daughter of Sir Thomas
Hanmer & Catherine Salter
(A) **Sir Roger Puleston** (ca.1566 – 1618)
= ...; **Susanna Bromley** (...) daughter of Sir George
Bromley & Joan Waverton
issue ?
(B) **George Puleston** (... – 1634)
= ...; **Jane Price** (...) daughter of ◆Cadwaladr Price &
Catherine Lloyd
issue ?
(III) **Catherine Puleston** (...)
= ...; **Sir Richard Trevor** (1558 – 1638) son of John
Trevor & Mary Brydges
(A) **Magdalen Trevor** (...)
= ...; **... Bagnall** (...)
issue ?
(B) **Dorothy Trevor** (...)
= ...; ◆**Sir John Hanmer, 1ˢᵗ Baronet** (1590 – 1624)

Children are listed with other parent
(C) **Mary Trevor** (...)
= ...; **Evan Lloyd** (... – 17 Apr 1637)
(1) **William Lloyd** (...)
= ...; **Anne Vaughan** (...) daughter of Richard Vaughan
& Catherine Wynne
issue ?
(2) **John Lloyd** (...)
= ...; **Margaret Thelwall** (...) daughter of Sir Bevis
Thelwall & Elizabeth Allen
(a) **Sir Evan Lloyd, 1st Baronet** (1622 – 1663) cr.
Baronet 21 Jun 1647
= ...; **Anne Williams** (...) daughter of Sir Charles
Williams
Has further generations of issue
2) **Sir Thomas Hanmer** (... – 20 Feb 1545)
= ...; **Jane Brereton** (ca.1486 – ...)
a) **Sir Thomas Hanmer** (1 Feb 1526 Wrexham – 1583)
= ...; **Catherine Salter** (...) daughter of Thomas Salter
(I) **John Hanmer** (... – 1604)
= ...; **Jane Salesbury** (...) daughter of Sir John Salesbury &
Jane Middleton
(A) **Sir Thomas Hanmer** (... – 18 Apr 1619)
=1 18 Nov 1585; ♦**Anne Talbot** (...) daughter of Sir John
Talbot & Catherine Petre
=2 1597 or 98; **Katherine Mostyn** (...) daughter of Sir
Thomas Mostyn & Ursula Goodman
issue of 1st:
(1) **Catherine Hanmer** (ca.1586 – ca.1608) unm.
(2) **Sir John Hanmer, 1st Baronet** (ca.1590 – aft.19
Jun 1624) cr. Baronet 8 Jul 1620
= ...; ♦**Dorothy Trevor** (...) daughter of Sir Richard
Trevor & Catherine Puleston
(a) **Sir Thomas Hanmer 2nd Baronet** (ca.1612 – 6
Oct 1678) suc. father 1624
=1 21 Dec 1631; **Elizabeth Baker** (...) daughter of Sit
Thomas Baker
=2 bef.1648; **Susan Hervey** (...) daughter of Sir
William Hervey & Susan Jermyn
Has further generations of issue
(b) **Katherine Hanmer** (...)
= ...; **Edward Kynaston** (1613 – 1656)
issue ?
(c) **John Hanmer** (... – 1643 Little Dean, Glos.) murdered
(d) **David Hanmer** (...) unm.
(e) **Mary Hanmer** (...)
133

issue of 2nd:

    (3) **Thomas Hanmer** (...)
      = ...; **Mary Hill** (...) daughter of Osmeri Hill
      no issue
    (4) **Roger Hanmer** (... – 1673)
  b) **Elizabeth Hamner** (... – 1560)
    = ...; **John Conwy** (ca.1518 – ca.1559) son of Thomas
  Conwy & Alice Chantrel
  (I) **John Conwy** (ca.1538 – 1579)
    =1 ...; **Anne Salesbury** (...) daughter of Robert Salesbury
    =2 ...; **Anne Gruffudd** (...) daughter of Gruffudd ab Ieuan
  ap Llywelyn Fynchan; =1st John Mutton
  issue of 1st (none by 2nd):
  (A) **John Conwy** (bef.1558 – ca.1605)
    = ...; **Margaret Mostyn** (...) daughter of Piers Mostyn
    (1) **Sir John Conwy** (21 Jun 1575 – 1641)
      = 23 Jul 1589; **Mary Morgan** (... – 19 Jan 1642)
      daughter of Edward Morgan
    (2) **William Conwy** (... – aft.1654)
      = aft.2 Jun 1623; **Luce Mostyn** (...) daughter of Thomas
      Mostyn & Anne Hughes
      (a) **Sir Henry Conway, 1st Baronet** (1630 – 1669)
        cr. Baronet 25 Jul 1660
        = bef.20 Nov 1662; **Mary Lloyd** (... – bef.1687)
        daughter of Sir Richard Lloyd & Margaret Sneyd
        Has further generations of issue
      (b) **Robert Conwy** (aft.1631 – ...)
 3) **Dorothy Hanmer** (...)
  = ...; **Edward Brereton** (...)
  issue ?
F) **Joan Kynaston** (...)
 = ...; **Thomas Stury** (...) son of John Stury & Anne Corbet
1) **Thomas Stury** (... – 1585)
 = ...; **Katherine Carew** (...) daughter of Thomas Carew &
 Elizabeth Courtney
 a) **Thomas Stury** (... – 2 Jul 1597)
  = ...; **Eleanor Mackworth** (...) daughter of John Mackworth
  Elizabeth Hosier
  issue ?
G) **Elizabeth Kynaston** (...)
 = ...; **John Eyton** (...)
1) **Elizabeth Eyton** (...)
 = ...; **John Trevor** (...) son of Sir Edward Trevor & Anne Kyffin
 issue ?
H) **Jana Kynaston** (1466 – ...)
5. **Princess Blanche of England** (1392 Petersborough Castle – 22

May 1409 Haguenau, Alsace)
= 6 Jul 1402 Cologne; **Ludwig III, Elector of the Palatine** (23
Jan 1378 – 30 Dec 1436 Heidelberg) son of Rupert, Roman
Emperor & Elisabeth of Nuremberg; suc. father as Elector 1410;
he =2nd Mathilde de Savoy

   a. **Hereditary Prince Rupert of the Palatine** (22 Jun 1406
   Heidelberg – 1426) unm.

  6. **Princess Philippa of England** (4 Jun 1394 Petersborough
  Castle – 7 Jan 1430 Linköping, Sweden)
  = 26 Oct 1406 Lund; **Erik of Pomerania, King of Sweden, Norway,
  and Denmark** (ca.1382 Rügenwalde, Pomerania – 3 May 1459
  Rügenwalde) son of Wartislaw VII, Duke of Pomerania & Marie of
  Mecklenburg-Schwerin; declared King of Norway (as Eirik III) 1389; King
  of Denmark (as Eric VII) 1396, and Sweden (as Erik I) 1396
  no issue

issue of 2nd:

D. **Catherine of Lancaster** (31 Mar 1373 Hertford Castle, Herts. – 2
Jun 1418 Valladolid)
= bef.17 Sep 1388; **Enrique III, King of Castile and Léon** (4 Oct
1379 Burgos – 25 Dec 1406 Toledo) son of Juan I, King of Castile and Léon
& Infanta Leonor of Aragon; suc. father 9 Oct 1390

  1. **Infanta Maria of Castile** (14 Sep 1401 Segovia – 7 Sep 1458 Valencia)
  = 12 Jun 1415 Valencia; **Alfonso V, King of Aragon and Naples** (1396
  Medina del Campo – 27 Jun 1458 Castell dell'Ovo, Naples) son of
  Fernando I, King of Aragon & Leonor de Albuquerque, 3rd Countess de
  Albuquerque; suc. father in Aragon 2 Apr 1416; conquered Naples 2 Jun
  1442
  no issue

  2. **Infanta Catalina of Castile, Duchess of Villena** (1403 –
  1439) recevied the Dukedom 1427
  = 1448; **Infante Enrique of Aragon, 4th Count de Albuquerque**,
  Count de Ampurias (1400 – 15 Jun 1445) son of Fernando I, King of
  Aragon & Leonor de Albuquerque, 3rd Countess de Alburquerque; =2nd
  Peatriz de Pimentel; suc. mother 1435
  no issue

  3. **Juan II, King of Castile and Léon** (6 Mar 1405 Toro – 20 Jul
  1454 Valladolid) suc. father 2 Jun 1418
  =1 1418; **Infanta Maria of Aragon** (ca.1396 – 18 Feb 1445
  Villacastin) daughter of Fernando I, King of Aragon & Leonor de
  Albuquerque, 3rd Countess de Albuquerque
  =2 22 Jul 1447; ◆**Dona Isabel de Portugal** (1428 – 15 Aug 1496
  Arévalo) daughter of Infante João, Constable of Portugal & Isabel de
  Barcelos
  issue of 1st:

   a. **Enrique IV, King of Castile and Léon** (5 Jan 1424
   Valladolid – 11 Dec 1474 Madrid) suc. father 20 Jul 1454

=1 1440 (ann.1453); **Blanca of Navarre** (later **Queen Blanca II**) (9 Jun 1424 Olite – 2 Dec 1464 Orthez) daughter of Juan II, King of Aragon & Blanca I, Queen of Navarre; suc. as nominal queen 1461 (was incarcerated, never ruled)
=2 May 1455 (without papal dispensation); ♦**Infanta Joana of Portugal** (20 Mar 1439 Almada – 12 Dec 1475 Madrid) daughter of Duarte I, King of Portugal & Infanta Leonor of Aragon
issue of 2ⁿᵈ (none by 1ˢᵗ):[28]

I) **Infanta Juana of Castile** (21 Feb 1462 – 12 Apr 1530)
  = 30 May 1475 (without papal dispensation); (her uncle) ♦**Afonso V, King of Portugal** (15 Jan 1432 Sintra – 28 Aug 1481 Lisbon) son of Duarte I, King of Portugal & Infanta Leonor of Aragon; =1ˢᵗ ♦Dona Isabel de Coimbra; suc. father 13 Sep 1438
  no issue
issue of 2ⁿᵈ:
b. **Isabel I, Queen of Castile and Léon** (22 Apr 1451 Madrigal de las Altas Torres – 26 Nov 1504 Medina del Campo) suc. half-brother 11 Dec 1474
= 19 Oct 1469 Valladolid; **Fernando II, King of Aragon** (10 Mar 1452 Sos del Rey Católico – 23 Jan 1516 Madrigalejo) son of Juan II, King of Aragon & Juana Enriquez; =2ⁿᵈ Germaine de Foix; suc. father 20 Jan 1479; Regent of Castile 1504 and again 1506–1516
  I) **Isabel, Princess of Asturias** (2 Oct 1470 Dueñas – 23 Aug 1498 Zaragoza) suc. as Princess 4 Oct 1497
    =1 1490; ♦**Infante Afonso of Portugal** (18 May 1475 – 13 Jul 1491) son of João II, King of Portugal & Dona Leonor de Viseu
    =2 1497; ♦**Manuel I, King of Portugal** (1469 – 1521)
    issue of 2ⁿᵈ (none by 1ˢᵗ):
    see:
  II) **Juan, Prince of Asturias** (30 Jun 1478 Seville – 4 Oct 1497 Salamanca) became Prince at birth
    = 3 Apr 1497 Burgos; ♦**Archduchess Margarete of Austria** (10 Jan 1480 – 1 Dec 1530 Mechelen, Flanders) daughter of Maximilian, Roman Emperor & Maria, Duchess of Burgundy; =2ⁿᵈ Philibert II, Duke of Savoy
    no issue
  III) **Juana, Queen of Castile and Aragon** (6 Nov 1479 Toledo – 12 Apr 1555 Tordesillas) suc. mother 26 Nov 1504 and father 23 Jan 1516, reigning under the Regency of her

---

[28] Most historicans agree that Infanta Juana was not the daughter of Enrique IV, but that of her mother's lover, Béltran de la Cueva. In fact, she is generally known as Juana la Beltraneja as a reflection of her paternity.

husband, then her father, then her son due to mental instability

= 1496; ◆**Archduke Philipp of Austria** (1478 – 1506)
Children are listed with other parent

IV) **Infanta Maria of Aragon and Castile** (29 Jun 1482
Córdoba –7 Mar 1517 Lisbon)

= 1500; ◆**Manuel I, King of Portugal** (1469 – 1521)
see: 1050

V) **Infanta Catalina of Aragon and Castile** (16 Dec 1485
Madrid – 7 Jan 1536 Kimbolton Castle, Cambridgeshire)

=1 14 Nov 1501 London; ◆**Prince Arthur, Prince of Wales**
etc. (20 Sep 1486 Winchester – 2 Apr 1502 Worcester) son of
Henry VII, King of England & Elizabeth of York

=2 1509; ◆**Henry VIII, King of England** (1491 – 1547)
issue of 2nd (none by 1st):
see:

c. **Alfonso, Prince of Asturias** (17 Nov 1453 Tordesillas – 5 Jul
1468 Cardeñosa) became Prince 20 Jul 1454

issue of 3rd (born prior to marriage legitimated Feb 1396/7):
see: Chapter 6

CHAPTER 6
BEAUFORT AND TUDOR

The Lancasters had another branch on their family tree, the Beauforts. These are the initially illegitimate descendants of John of Gaunt by his mistress, later his third wife, Katherine Swynford. Katherine's only place in history, before finding John's bed, was being a sister-in-law to the poet Chaucer.

All four of the Beaufort children were born prior to John and Katherine's marriage. After the event, all four were legitimated by both the Vatican and by Parliament, with the proviso that they had no succession rights to the Crown, a point forgotten towards the end of the York reigns.

The eldest son, named for his father, was given the title Earl of Somerset, which would be elevated to Duke in the next generation. The Somerset Dukes played the role of advisors to the Lancaster kings and generally did the day-to-day job of defending their crown. This usually proved to be a fatal position, and the male line died out with the 3rd Duke, who was executed shortly after the 1471 Battle of Tewkesbury. His only son and heir also fell in that battle. This Duke was actually from the second creation of the Dukedom. The first Duke was attainted and executed for treason, his titles being forfeited. His brother was later given a new creation of the title, also being reckoned as the 1st Duke. The remaining two Dukes were his heirs.

There is a more successful illegitimate line, descended from the 2nd Duke and his mistress, a largely forgotten soul named Joan Hill. Their only surviving son, Charles, was given the surname Somerset for his father's title and was eventually entitled himself as the Earl of Worcester. Today his descendants, who eventually rose to yet another creation of the Dukedom of Beaufort, represent the only living male-line Plantagenets, and have remained closely connected to the royal court. For example, the most recently deceased Duke was married to a first cousin of King George VI, the current Queen's father. The current Duke is his childless predecessor's distant cousin.

The descendants of the Beaufort daughters are a very interesting lot, and many of them lead to prominent families in present-day Britain and the United States. Three such ladies will have their own stories told in their own chapters, but two of note remain here. Lady Eleanor, daughter of the 1st Duke of Somerset (second creation), and Lady Spencer by marriage, is the ancestress to roughly half of this chapter. Her male line of Spencer descendants quickly died out and are not the same branch as the late Diana, Princess of Wales. However, the female lines of descent lead to the Pagets, the Careys, the Knowles, the Wests, the Pelhams, and several others who became prominent families throughout the original American colonies.

The other Beaufort woman of note was Lady Margaret, the much married daughter of the original Duke of Beaufort and the senior-most great-granddaughter in the male line of John of Gaunt. Her early years were spent racking up an impressive number of widowhoods— four in all—being successively the Duchess of Suffolk, Countess of Richmond, Lady Stafford, and the Countess of Derby. However, for all of this martial success, she only had one child to show for it: Henry Tudor, Earl of Richmond and later King Henry VII.

After the extinction of the male line of her house, Margaret wasted no time staking the Lancaster claim to the Throne for her son, then a lad of only fourteen. She sent him off to Brittany, where he lived with and learned the art of war under the tutelage of Duke François II, one of Margaret's many in-laws.

Meanwhile she remained in the court of Edward IV, paying the expected amount of homage to the York King, and his hated Queen, Elizabeth Woodville. As Elizabeth kept spitting out one daughter after another, Margaret regularly reminded the King that there was still a Plantagenet heir out there in the person of her son. Edward named Henry his heir-presumptive, a position which he soon lost again when the blessed Prince of Wales was finally born, followed less than three years later by a Duke of York. In due course, Edward's two younger brothers also married and each had a son. Henry's chances at the Throne became more and more remote.

Then the series of events that ended the House of York began. As they have been well described in previous chapters, we will fast forward to 1485 when Henry VII was crowned the first Tudor king. Henry's claim on the Throne was sketchy from the get-go. He was a descendant of the junior branch of the junior branch of the royal family, through a female, who was herself descended from the line that was originally illegitimate and only legitimated without succession rights. He had to shore up his position—fast.

So he first had Parliament declare the setting aside of Edward IV's children was in error, being based on hearsay, with no evidence that there had been an earlier marriage on the King's part. This made those numerous surviving daughters all legitimate again. Then he married Elizabeth, the eldest surviving of them.

The marriage of King Henry VII and Elizabeth of York was no love match. In time, they found a place of mutual respect and friendship which was needed to produce four surviving children. The eldest son's name was a good indication of how Henry felt about his reign. He had effectively ended 85 years of fighting over the Throne. He continued to put down remaining rebellious cousins rather easily. And he joined the houses of Lancaster and York into one House of Tudor. To mark his great success, he named his first son Arthur, marking what he was sure was to be an era as glorious as Camelot.

Fate disagreed. Arthur died at the age of fifteen, leaving the Throne, and his new wife, to be taken over by his younger brother, Henry. There has been so much written about Henry VIII that there is nothing to be added here save to note the important detail for our purposes. Henry had no grandchildren. Though it took six wives and a mistress, Henry fathered four children. But none of them produced further heirs. He was duly succeeded by his only legitimate son, Edward VI, followed by his two daughters, Mary and Elizabeth.

With the reign of Queen Elizabeth I, Henry VII got his glimpse of Camelot again as England experienced its Golden Age. But her reign also brought an end to the nearly 450-year rule of the Plantagenets, whether they be called Anjou, Lancaster, York, or Tudor. But as the saying goes: the Queen is dead, Long Live the King! The family may end, but the Throne does not.

Henry VII also left two daughters, Margaret and Mary. Both became Queens, Margaret of Scotland and Mary of France. Margaret's family will be viewed in further detail in the next chapter about the Stewarts.

Although Mary married King Louis XII, 30-plus years her senior, she was widowed within fifteen months, and still childless. Her second marriage was a romantic tale of secret love with her brother's best friend—Charles Brandon, who had been created Duke of Suffolk— ending in elopement and banishment from court. She and her husband could not have been happier. It also led to three children, an unmarried son who died before he was twenty, and two daughters who married noblemen found in other chapters.

One quick note about Mary's elder daughter, Frances, as it pertains to the succession. Frances was a mother of only daughters, the eldest of whom was Jane Grey. Jane's mother and father-in-law schemed and had Jane declared Queen upon the death of Edward VI in an effort to prevent the staunchly Catholic Mary Tudor from becoming Queen. This failed effort only lasted the six days that it took Mary to reach London. Jane, and all of those who plotted on her behalf, found their way to the gallows quick enough.

As previously noted though, the succession does continue. After the demise of the Tudors, the Throne passed, with surprisingly little bloodshed, to the closest heir descended from Margaret Tudor, Queen of Scotland. Her great-grandson, King James VI, took the Throne of England as James I.

Edward III

|

John (of Gaunt), Duke of Lancaster

|

issue of 3rd (born prior to marriage, legitimated Feb 1396/7):

E. **John Beaufort, Marquess of Somerset and Dorset 1st Earl of Somerset, KG** (bet.1371/73 château de Beaufort, Anjou – 16 Mar 1409/10 London) cr. Earl 10 Feb 1396/7 and Marquess (ad personam) 29 Sep 1397 = bef.28 Sep 1397; **Lady Margaret Holland** (1385 – 31 Dec 1439 London) daughter of Thomas Holland, 5th Earl of Kent & Lady Alice FitzAlan; =2nd ♦Thomas, 1st Duke of Clarence

  1. **Lady Margaret Beaufort** (ca.1400 – Nov 1449)
    = aft.1421; **Thomas Courtenay, 5th Earl of Devon** 6th BaronCourtenay (1414 – 3 Feb 1457/8 Abingdon, Oxon.) son of Hugh Courtenay, 4th Earl of Devon & Anne Talbot; suc. father 16 Jun 1422

    a. **Lady Joan Courtenay** (...)
      =1 ...; ♦**Sir Roger Clifford** (1437 – 1485) executed; son of Thomas Clifford, 8th Baron de Clifford & Joan Dacre
      =2 aft.1485; **Sir William Knyvet** (...)
      no issue

    b. **Lady Elizabeth Courtenay** (...)
      = ...; **Sir Hugh Conway** (ca.1453 – btw.12 Mar 1517 & 23 May 1518) son of John Conway & Alice Minshall; =2nd Joice ...; knighted Jan 1485/6
      no issue

    c. **Thomas Courtenay, 6th Earl of Devon**, etc. (1432 – 3 Apr 1461 York) executed; suc. father 3 Feb 1457/8; titles forfeited
      = Sep 1456; **Marie d'Anjou** (...) illegitimate daughter of Charles, Count de Maine
      no issue

    d. **Henry Courtenay** (... – 4 May 1466 Salisbury) executed

    e. **John Courtenay, 7th Earl of Devon**, etc. (ca.1435 – 4 May 1471 Tewkesbury, Glos.) killed in battle. Knighted 1460; restored to titles 9 Oct 1470; titled forfeited again 14 Apr 1471; upon his death his titles became extinct; unm.

  2. **Henry Beaufort, 2nd Earl of Somerset** (bap.26 Nov 1401 – 25 Nov 1418) unm.; suc. father 16 Mar 1409/10

  3. **John Beaufort, 1st Duke of Somerset** Earl of Kendal, 3rd Earl of Somerset, etc. **KG** (bef. 24 Mar 1403/4 – 27 May 1444 Wimborne, Dorset) possibly suicide; suc. as Earl of Somerset, etc. 25 Nov 1418; cr. Duke etc. 28 Aug 1443; KG ca.1440
    = bet.1439/42; **Margaret Beauchamp** (... – 8 Aug 1482 Wimborne) daughter of John Beauchamp & Edith Stourton; =1st Sir Oliver St.John; =3rd Sir Lionel de Welles

    a. **Lady Margaret Beaufort** (31 May 1443 Bletsoe Castle, Beds. – 29 Jun 1509 London)

143

=1 bef.7 Feb 1450 (ann.1453); ◆**John de la Pole, 2nd Duke of Suffolk** (27 Sep 1442 – ca.1492) son of William de la Pole, 1st Duke of Suffolk & Alice Chaucer; suc. father 1450
=2 1 Nov 1455 Bletsoe Castle; **Edmund Tudor, 1st Earl of Richmond** (ca.1430 Much Hadham Castle, Herts. – 3 Nov 1456 Carmarthen Castle, Wales) son of Sir Owen Tudor & Catherine of France; cr. Earl 23 Nov 1452
=3 ca.1462; ◆**Sir Henry Stafford** (... – 4 Oct 1471) son of Humphrey Stafford, 1st Duke of Buckingham & Lady Anne Neville
=4 bef.Oct 1473; ◆**Thomas Stanley, 1st Earl of Derby**, 2nd Baron Stanley, **KG** (ca.1435 – 29 Jul 1504 Latham, Kent) son of Thomas Stanley, 1st Baron Stanley & Joan Goushill; =1st ◆Lady Eleanor Neville; KG 1483; suc. father 1459; cr. Earl 27 Oct 1485
issue of 2nd (none by others):

I) **Henry VII, King of England** and France (28 Jan 1457/8 Pembroke Castle, Wales – 21 Apr 1509 Richmond Palace) suc. father as Earl of Richmond 3 Nov 1456; proclaimed King 22 Aug 1485
= 18 Jan 1486 London; ◆**Princess Elizabeth of York** (11 Feb 1466 Palace of Westminster – 11 Feb 1503 London) daughter of Edward IV, King of England & Elizabeth Woodville

A) **Arthur, Prince of Wales**, etc. **KG, KB** (20 Sep 1486 London – 2 Apr 1502 Ludlow Castle, Salop.) cr. Duke of Cornwall 20 Sep 1486; KB 1489; cr. Prince of Wales 29 Nov 1489; KG 1491
= 14 Nov 1501 London; ◆**Infanta Doña Catalina of Aragon** (16 Dec 1485 Madrid – 7 Jan 1536 Kimbolton Castle, Herts.) daughter of Fernando II, Kingof Aragon & Isabel I, Queen of Castile; =2nd ◆Henry VIII, King of England
no issue

B) **Princess Margaret of England** (28 Nov 1489 Palace of Westminster – 18 Oct 1541 Methven, Perths.)
=1 1503; ◆**James IV, King of Scotland** (1473 – 1513)
=2 4 Aug 1514 Kinnoul (dv.1528); **Archibald Douglas, 6th Earl ofAngus**, 2nd Lord Douglas (ca.1490 – Jan 1457/8 Tantallon Castle) son of George, Master of Angus & Elizabeth Drummond; suc. grandfather 9 Sep 1513; =1st Lady Margaret Hepburn; =3rd Margaret Maxwell
issue of 1st:
Children are listed with other parent
issue of 2nd:
1) **Lady Margaret Douglas** (18 Oct 1515 Harbottle Castle, Northumb. – 9 Mar 1578)
= 1544; ◆**Matthew Stuart, 4th Earl of Lennox** (1516 – 1571)
Children are listed with other parent

C) **Henry VIII, King of England**, Ireland, and France (28 Jun 1491 Greenwich Palace – 28 Jan 1547 Whitehall) suc. father 21 Apr 1509; proclaimed King of Ireland 1542

=1 11 Jun 1509 Greenwich (ann.1536); ◆**Infanta Doña
Catalina of Aragon** (16 Dec 1485 Madrid – 7 Jan 1536
Kimbolton Castle, Herts.) daughter of Fernando II, King of Aragon
& Isabel I, Queen of Castile; =1ˢᵗ ◆Arthur, Prince of Wales
=2 25 Jan 1533 Palace of Westminster; ◆**Anne Boleyn,
Marchioness of Pembroke** (ca.1501 Blickling, Norfolk – 19 May
1536 Tower of London) executed; daughter of Thomas Boleyn, 1ˢᵗ Earl
of Wiltshire & Lady Elizabeth Howard; cr. Marchioness 1 Sep 1532
=3 30 May 1536 Whitehall; ◆**Jane Seymour** (1509/10 Wolf
Hall, Wilts. – 24 Oct 1537 Hampton Court) daughter of Sir John
Seymour & Margaret Wentworth
=4 6 Jan 1540 Greenwich (ann.1540); **Duchess Anne of Cleves,**
Duchess of Jülich and Berg, Countess von der Mark (22 Sep 1515
Düsseldrof – 17 Jul 1557 Chelsea Old Palace, London) daughter of
Johann III, Duke of Cleves & Duchess Marie of Jülich and Berg
=5 28 Jul 1540 Hampton Court; ◆**Catherine Howard**
(ca.1525 London – 13 Feb 1542 Tower of London) executed;
daughter of Lord Edmund Howard & Joyce Culpeper
=6 12 Jul 1543 Hampton Court; **Catherine Parr** (1512
London – 5 Sep 1548 Sudeley Castle, Glos.) daughter of Sir
Thomas Parr & Maud Green; =1ˢᵗ ◆Sir Edward Burgh; =2ⁿᵈ
◆John Neville, 3ʳᵈ Baron Latymer; =4ᵗʰ ◆Thomas Seymour,
1ˢᵗ Baron Seymour of Sudeley[29]
issue of 1ˢᵗ:
1) **Mary, Queen of England** etc. (18 Feb 1516 Greenwich –
    17 Nov 1558 St. James' Palace) suc. half-brother 6 Jul 1553
    = 25 Jul 1554 Winchester, Hants.; ◆**Felipe II, King of Spain** (21
    May 1527 Valladolid, Castile – 13 Sep 1598 El Escorial, Madrid) son
    of Charles V, Roman Emperor & Izabel de Aziz, Infanta of Portugal;
    he =1ˢᵗ ◆Maria de Aziz, Infanta of Portugal; =3ʳᵈ Elisabeth of France;
    and =4ᵗʰ ◆Archduchess Anna of Austria
    no issue
issue of 2ⁿᵈ:
2) **Elizabeth I, Queen of England**, etc. (7 Sep 1533
    Greenwich – 24 Mar 1603 Richmond Palace) suc. half-sister
    17 Nov 1558
issue of 3ʳᵈ (none by other marriages):
3) **Edward VI, King of England**, etc. (12 Oct 1537 Hampton
    Court – 6 Jul 1553 Greenwich) suc. father 28 Jan 1547/8
issue by **Elizabeth Blount** (ca.1502 – ca.1540) daughter of Sir
John Blount; =1ˢᵗ Gilbert Tailboys, Baron Tailboys; =2ⁿᵈ

---

[29] Thomas was a brother of Jane Seymour, Henry VIII's 3ʳᵈ wife.

Edward Clinton, 1st Earl of Lincoln:

4) **Henry Fitzroy, Duke of Richmond** (1519 – 22 Jul 1536)
cr. Duke 18 Jun 1525
= aft. 26 Nov 1533; ♦**Lady Mary Howard** (... – ca.1555)
daughter of Thomas Howard, 3rd Duke of Norfolk & Lady
Elizabeth Stafford
no issue

D) **Princess Mary** Rose **of England** (18 Mar 1496 Richmond
Palace – 25 Jun 1533 Westhorpe, Suffolk)
=1 9 Oct 1514 Abbéville, France; **Louis XII, King of France**
(27 Jun 1462 Blois – 1 Jan 1515/6 Paris) son of Charles, Duke
of Orleans & Duchess Maria of Cleves; =1st Jeanne of France;
he =2nd Anne, Duchess of Bretagne; suc. as King 1498
=2 31 Mar 1515 Paris; **Charles Brandon, 1st Duke of Suffolk**
(1484 – 22 Aug 1545) son of Sir William Brandon &
Elizabeth Bruyn; =1st Anne Browne; =2nd ♦Lady Margaret
Neville; =4th Katherine Willoughby, Baroness Willoughby de
Eresby; cr. Duke 1504
issue of 2nd (none by 1st):

1) **Henry Brandon, 1st Earl of Lincoln** (11 Mar 1515/6
London – 1 Mar 1533/4) unm.; cr. Earl 1525

2) **Lady Frances Brandon** (16 Jul 1517 – 20 Nov 1559
Godalming, Surrey)
=1 1533; ♦**Henry Grey, 1st Duke of Suffolk** (1517–1554)
Children are listed with other parent

3) **Lady Eleanor Brandon** (1519/20 – 27 Sep 1547
Brougham Castle, Cumbria)
= 1537; ♦**Henry Clifford, 2nd Earl of Cumberland** (1517 – 1570)
Children are listed with other parent

issue by ...:
b. **Thomasine Beaufort**[30] (ca.1434 – aft.1469)
= bef.6 Oct 1447; **Reynold Grey, 7th Baron Grey** (ca.1421 – 22 Feb
1493/4) son of Richard Grey, 6th Baron Grey & Margaret Ferrers; suc.
father Aug 1442

I) **John Grey, 8th Baron Grey** (... – 3 Apr 1499) suc. father 22 Feb
1493/4
=1 ...; ♦**Anne Grey**[31] (...) daughter of Edmund Grey, 1st Earl of Kent &
Lady Catherine Percy
=2 ...; **Elizabeth Vaughan** (... – 15 Jan 1514/5) daughter of Thomas
Vaughan; =1st Sir Thomas Cokesey; =3rd 1st Baron Mounteagle

---

[30] Thomasine was also known as Taclyn and Jacinta.
[31] John and Anne were distant cousins, both being great-great-great-grandchildren of the 2nd
Baron Grey in the male line.

issue of 1st (none by 2nd):

A) **Edmund Grey, 9th Baron Grey** (ca.1469 – 5 May 1511) suc. father 3 Apr 1499
= bef.May 1505; **Florence Hastings** (...) daughter of Sir Ralph Hastings & Anne ...

1) **Hon. Elizabeth Grey** (9 Mar 1491 Wilton on Wye, Herefords. – 29 Dec 1559 Winchombe, Glos.)
= 1512 Wilton on Wye; **John Brydges, 1st Baron Chandos** (9 Mar 1491/2 Cubberley, Glos. – 12 Apr 1557 Winchcombe) son of Sir Giles Brugge & Isabel Baynham

a) **Hon. Elizabeth Brydges** (1515 – 1557)
= ...; **John Tracy** (...) daughter of William Tracy & Agnes Digby

(I) **Sir John Tracy** (ca.1544 Toddington, Glos. – 25 Sep 1591)
= ca.1569 Glos.; **Anne Throckmorton** (ca.1548 Torthworth, Glos. – ...) daughter of Sir Thomas Throckmorton & Margaret Whittington

(A) **John Tracy, 1st Viscount Tracy** Baron Tracy (ca.1750 Toddington – 1647) cr Viscount 12 Jan 1642/3
= ca.1590; **Anne Shirley** (...) daughter of Sir Thomas Shirley

(1) **Robert Tracy, 2nd Vicount Tracy** (1593 Toddington – 8 May 1662) suc. father 1647
=1 bef.1617; ♦**Bridget Lyttleton** (...) daughter of John Lyttleton & Meriel Bromley
=2 ...; **Dorothy Cocks** (... – 1685) daughter of Thomas Cocks
issue of 1st:

(a) **John Tracy, 3rd Viscount Tracy** etc. (1617 – 8 Mar 1686/7) suc. father 1662
= ca.1655; **Hon. Elizabeth Leigh** (... – 1688) daughter of Thomas Leigh, 1st Baron Leigh & Mary Egerton
Has further generations of issue

(b) **Hon. Horace Tracy** (bef.28 Jun 1618 – ...)
issue of 2nd:

(c) **Hon. Robert Tracy** (ca.1655 – 11 Sep 1735)

(2) **Hon. Horace Tracy** (bef.28 Jun 1618 – ...)
= ...

(a) **Robert Tracy** (ca.1655 – 11 Sep 1735)
= ...
Has further generations of issue

(B) **Dorothy Tracy** (... – Mar 1612)
=1 bef.1593; **Edward Bray** (... – bef.1593)
=2 ca.1593; **Edward Conway, 1st Viscount Conway** (... – 3 Jan 1630/1) son of Sir John Conway & Helen Greville

(1) **Edward Conway, 2nd Viscount Conway** (bef.10 Aug 1594 – 26 Jun 1655) suc. father 1631
= Oct 1621; ♦**Frances Popham** (ca.1597 – 7 May 1671)

daughter of Sir Francis Popham & Ann Dudley
- (a) **Edward Conway, Earl of Conway**, 3rd Viscount
  Conway (ca. 1623 – 11 Aug 1683) suc. father 1655; cr. Earl
  (which became extinct upon his death)
  = ...; ♦**Hon. Elizabeth Booth** (... – 4 Jul 1681) daughter
  of George Booth, 1st Baron Delamer & Lady Elizabeth Grey
  no issue
- (b) **Hon. Dorothy Conway** (... – 1665)
  = Sep 1654; **Sir George Rawdon, 1st Baronet** (1604
  Rawdon, Yorks. – 18 Aug 1684) son of Francis Rawdon &
  Dorothy Aldborough
  Has further generations of issue
- (2) **Hon. Helen Conway** (... – Aug 1629)
  = 9 Apr 1627; **Sir William Smith** (... – 5 Mar 1631) son of
  Sir William Smith & Bridget Fleetwood; =1st Anne Croft
  - (a) **Edward Smith** (ca,1630 – Jan 1652) unm.
- (3) **Hon. Sir Thomas Conway** (...)
- (4) **Hon. Ralph Conway** (...)
- (5) **Hon. Frances Conway** (...)
  = ...; ♦**Sir William Pelham** (...)
  Children are listed with other parent
- (6) **Hon. Brilliana Conway** (...)
  = ...; **Sir Robert Harley** (...)
  - (a) **Sir Edward Harley** (bef.1645 – 8 Dec 1700)
    = ...; **Abigail Stephens** (...) daughter of Nathaniel
    Stephens & Catherine Beale
    Has further generations of issue
- (7) **Hon. Mary Conway** (...)
- (C) **Mary Tracy** (18 May 1581 Toddington – 25 Dec 1671 Little
  Ouseburn, Yorks.)
  =1 bef. 1607; **William Hoby** (... – bef.1607)
  =2 Nov 1607 Toddington; **Horatio de Vere, Baron Vere**
  (1565 Walkes Colne, Essex – London) son of Geoffrey de Vere
  & Elizabeth Hardkyn; cr. Baron 24 Jul 1625, but title became
  extinct upon his death
- (1) **Hon. Elizabeth de Vere** (ca.1608 London – Dec 1683)
  = 1626; ♦**John Holles, 2nd Earl of Clare** (1595–1666)
  Children are listed with other parent
- (2) **Hon. Mary de Vere** (1608 in the Netherlands – 15 Nov
  1669 Mereworth Kent)
  =1 1628; **Sir Roger Townshend, 1st Baronet** (ca.1596 – 1
  Jan 1636/7) son of Sir John Townshend & Anne Bacon; cr.
  Baronet 16 Apr 1617
  =2 21 Jun 1638 London; ♦**Mildmay Fane, 2nd Earl of
  Westmorland** (1602–1666)
  issue of 1st:

(a) **Sir Roger Townshend, 2ⁿᵈ Baronet** (21 Dec 1628 – 1678 Geneva) unm. suc. father 1637

(b) **Horatio Townshend, 1ˢᵗ Viscount Townshend**
Baron Townshend, 3ʳᵈ Baronet (bef.16 Dec 1630 – 7 Dec 1687) suc. brother 1678, cr. Viscount 11 Dec 1682
=1 bef.13 Apr 1659; ◆**Mary Lewknor** (... – 1673) daughter of Sir Edward Lewnor & Elizabeth Russell
=2 27 Nov 1673; **Mary Ashe** (... – Dec 1685) daughter of Sir Joseph Ashe, 1ˢᵗ Baronet & Mary Wilson
Has further generations of issue by 2ⁿᵈ

(c) **Mary Townshend** (...)
= 1650; **Thomas Crew, 2ⁿᵈ Baron Crew** (ca.1624 – 30 Sep 1697) son of John Crerw, 1ˢᵗ Baron Crew & Jemima Waldegrave; =2ⁿᵈ Anne Armyne; suc. father 12 Dec 1679
Has further generations os issue

(d) **Vere Townshend** (...)
= 30 Aug 1660; ◆**Sir Ralph Hare, 1ˢᵗ Baronet** (... – 12 Jul 1671) son of John Hare & Hon. Elizabeth Coventry; =1ˢᵗ Susan Alington; =3ʳᵈ Elizabeth Chapman
no issue

(e) **Jane Townshend** (...)
= ...; **John Windham** (...)
issue ?

(f) **Anna Townshend** (... – 1 Feb 1667)
= ...; **William Cartwright** (...)
issue ?

(g) **Edith Townshend** (...) unm.
issue of 2ⁿᵈ:
Children are listed with other parent

(3) **Hon. Catherine de Vere** (ca.1613 Brielle, the Netherlands – aft.27 Mar 1648)
=1 ...; ◆**Oliver St.John** (1613–1641)
=2 1640; ◆**John Poulett, 2ⁿᵈ Baron Poulett** (1615–1665)
issue of 1ˢᵗ:
More than 12 generations down in father's line
issue of 2ⁿᵈ:
Children are listed with other parent

(4) **Hon. Anne de Vere** (1618 the Netherlands – 16 Oct 1665 Bolton Percy, Yorks.)
= 1637; ◆**Thomas Fairfax, 3ʳᵈ Baron Fairfax** (1612–1671)
Children are listed with other parent

(5) **Hon. Dorothy de Vere** (ca.1620 the Ntherlands – ...)
= ...; **John Wolstenholme** (...) son of Sir John Wolstenholme, 1ˢᵗ Baronet
issue ?

b) **Hon. Mary Brydges** (1519 – 1606)
= ...; ♦**George Throckmorton** (1533–1612)
Children are listed with other parent
c) **Edmund Brydges, 2nd Baron Chandos** (bef.1522 – 11 Mar 1572/3) suc. father 1557
= ca.1548; **Hon. Dorothy Bray** (ca.1530 – 31 Oct 1605) daughter of Edmund Bray, 1st Baron Braye & Jane Halliwell; =2nd William Knollys, 1st Earl of Banbury
(I) **Giles Brydges, 3rd Baron Chandos** (ca.1548 – 21 Feb 1593/4) suc. father 1573
=bef.Sep 1573; ♦**Lady Frances Clinton** (... – 12 Sep 1623) daughter of Edward Clinton, 1st Earl of Lincoln & Hon. Ursula Stourton
(A) **Hon. Elizabeth Brydges** (ca.1578 – Oct 1617)
= 1603; **Sir John Kennedy** (...)
no issue
(B) **Hon. Catharine Brydges** (ca.1580 – 29 Jan 1656/7 London)
= 26 Feb 1608/9 London; **Francis Russell, 4th Earl of Bedford** 5th Baron Russell, 2nd Baron Russell (bef.19 Oct 1587 Watford, Herts. – 9 May 1641) son of William Russell, 1st Baron Russel & Elizabeth Long; suc. father 9 Aug 1613 and cousin 3 May 1627
(1) **Lady Margaret Russell** (... – Nov 1676)
=1 21 Mar 1631/2 London; ♦**James Hay, 2nd Earl of Carlisle** (ca.1612 – 30 Oct 1660) son of James JHay, 1st Earl of Carlisle & Lady Honora Denny; suc. father 1636
=2 1 Aug 1667; ♦**Edward Montagu, 2nd Earl of Manchester** (1602 – 5 May 1671) son of Henry Montagu, 1st Earl of Manchester & Catherine Spencer; =1st Susannah Hill; =2nd ♦Lady Anne Rich; =3rd Eswsex Cheeke; =4th Eleanor Wortley; suc. father 1642
no issue
(2) **William Russell, 1st Duke of Bedford** Marquess of Tavistock, Baron Howland, 5th Earl of Bedford etc. **KG** (Aug 1616 – 7 Sep 1700 London) suc. father 1641; cr. Duke etc. 11 May 1694; KG 1672
= 11 Jul 1637 London; ♦**Lady Anne Carr** (9 Dec 1615 London – 10 May 1684 Woburn, Beds.) daughter of Robert Carr, Earl of Somerset & Lady Frances Howard
(a) **Francis, Lord Russell** (1638 – 14 Jan 1677/8) unm.
(b) **Rt.Hon. William, Lord Russell** (29 Sep 1639 – 21 Jul 1683 London)
= 31 Jul 1669 Titchfield, Hants.; ♦**Lady Rachel Wriothesley** (ca.1636 – 29 Sep 1723 London) daughter of Thomas Wriothelesy, 4th Earl of Southampton &

Rachel de Massue; =1ˢᵗ Francis, Lord Vaughn
Has further generations of issue
(c) **Lord James Russell** (aft.1640 – 22 Jun 1712)
=1 ...; **Elizabeth Wright** (...) daughter of Sir Edmund
Wright & Jane Mills; =1ˢᵗ Sir John Trott, Baronet
=2 ...; **Elizabeth Lloyd** (... – 1 Dec 1736) daughter of
Richard Lloyd & Tyrphena Lisle; =2ⁿᵈ Sir Henry
Houghton, 5ᵗʰ Baron Houghton
Has further generations of issue by 2ⁿᵈ
(d) **Lord Edward Russell** (ca.1642 – 1714)
= 6 Oct 1689; **Frances Williams** (ca.1654 Penrhyn,
Caernarvons. – 30 Jun 1714) daughter of Sir Robert
Williams, 2ⁿᵈ Baronet & Jane Glynne; =1ˢᵗ Robert Lloyd
no issue
(e) **Lady Diana Russell** (... – 13 Dec 1701)
=1 1667; ♦**Greville Verney, 9ᵗʰ Baron Willoughby
de Broke** (1649–1668)
=2 1675; ♦**William Alington, 3ʳᵈ Baron Alington**
(1641–1685)
issue of 1ˢᵗ:
Children are listed with other parent
issue of 2ⁿᵈ:
Children are listed with other parent
(f) **Lady Margaret Russell** (...)
= 18 Nov 1691; ♦**Edward Russell, 1ˢᵗ Earl of Orford**
(1653 – 26 Nov 1727) son of Hon. Edward Russell &
Penelope Hill
no issue
(3) **Lady Catherine Russell** (1618 – 1 Dec 1676)
= 1630; ♦**Robert Greville, 2ⁿᵈ Baron Brooke** (1607–
1643)
Children are listed with other parent
(4) **Lady Anne Russell** (ca.1620 – 26 Jan 1696/7)
= ...; ♦**George Digby, 2ⁿᵈ Earl of Bristol** (1612–1677)
Children are listed with other parent
(5) **Hon. Edward Russell** (... – 21 Sep 1665)
=aft.1643; **Penelope Hill** (... – ca.1694) daughter of Sir
Moyses Hill & Alice MacDonnel; =1ˢᵗ Arthur Wilmot; =2ⁿᵈ
Sir William Brooke
(a) **William Russell** (...) unm.
(b) **Francis Russell** (... – 1 Oct 1696) Gov. of Barbados
1694-96
= 30 Apr 1691; ♦**Hon. Catherine Grey** (... – 11 Oct
1694 Barbados) daughter of William Grey, 1ˢᵗ Baron
Grey; =1ˢᵗ Sir Edward Mosely, 2ⁿᵈ Baronet; =2ⁿᵈ Charles
North, 5ᵗʰ Baron North

no issue

(c) **Laetitia Russell** (... – 9 Jan 1721/2)
= ...; **Thomas Cheeke** (...)
Has further generations of issue

(d) **Edward Russell, Earl of Orford** Viscount Barfleur, Baron of Shingay (1653 – 26 Nov 1727) cr. Earl etc 7 May 1697, but titles became extinct upon his death
= 12 Nov 1691; ◆**Lady Margaret Russell** (...) daughter of William Russell, 1st Duke of Bedford & Lady Anne Carr
no issue

(6) **Lady Diana Russell** (ca.1624 – 30 Jan 1694/5)
= 28 Apr 1642 London; **Francis Newport, 1st Earl of Bradford** Viscount Newport, 2nd Baron Newport (23 Feb 1619/20 – 19 Sep 1708 London) son of Richard Newport, 1st Baron Newport & Rachel Leveson; suc. father 8 Feb 1650/1; cr. Viscount 11 Mar 1674/5 and Earl 11 May 1694

(a) **Richard Newport, 2nd Earl of Bradford** etc. (3 Sep 1644 – 14 Jun 1723 London) suc. father 1708
= 20 Apr 1681; ◆**Mary Wilbraham** (... – 3 Dec 1737 High Ercall, Salop.) daughter of Sir Thomas Wilbraham, 3rd Baronet & Elizabeth Mytton
Has further generations of issue

(b) **Lady Diana Newport** (...)
= ...; ◆**Thomas Howard** (...)
Beyond the 12th generation on the father's line

(c) **Lady Katherine Newport** (...)
= Dec 1681; ◆**Henry Herbert, 4th Baron Herbert** (ca.1640 – 21 Apr 1691) son of Richard Herbert, 2nd Baron Herbert & Lady Mary Egerton; suc. brother 9 Dec 1678
no issue

(d) **Lady Elizabeth Newport** (...)
=1 aft.1663; ◆**Sir Henry Lyttleton, 2nd Baronet** (... – 24 Jun 1693) son of Sir Thomas Lyttleton, 1st Baronet & Catherine Crompton; =1st ◆Philadelphia Carey; suc. father 22 Feb 1649/50
=2 1702; **Edward Harvey** (1658 – 1736) son of Daniel Harvey & Elizabeth Montagu; =1st Elizabeth Harvey
no issue

(e) **Thomas Newport, Baron Torrington** (1654/5 High Ercall – 27 May 1719) cr. Baron 20 Jun 1716 but it became extinct upon his death
=1 ...; **Lucy Atkyns** (... – ca.1696) daughter of Sir Edward Atkyns & Elizabeth Lucy
=2 22 Jul 1700 London; **Penelope** Mary **Bridgeman** (... – 1705) daughter of Sir Orlando Bridgeman, 1st

Baronet & Mary Cave
=3 aft.1705; **Anne Pierrepont** (... – 17 Feb 1734/5)
daughter of Robert Pierrepont & Anne Murray
no issue

  (7) **Hon. Francis Russell** (...) unm.
  (8) **Hon. John Russell** (...)
(II) **William Brydges, 4ᵗʰ Baron Chandos** (ca.1552 – 18 Nov
  1602) suc. brother 1594
= ...; **Mary Hopton** (... – Oct 1624) daughter of Sir Owen
Hopton & Anne Itchingham
  (A) **Grey Brydges, 5ᵗʰ Baron Chandos** (bef.6 Mar 1578
    Purton, Wilts. – 10 Aug 1621 Spa, Germany) suc. father 1602
    = 28 Feb 1607/8; ♦**Lady Anne Stanley** (May 1580 – 8 Oct
    1647 London) daughter of Ferdinando Stanley, 5ᵗʰ Earl of
    Derby & Alice Spencer; =2ⁿᵈ ♦Mervyn Tuchet, 2ⁿᵈ Earl of
    Castlehaven
    (1) **Hon. Elizabeth Brydges** (... – Mar 1678/9)
      = bef.1631; ♦**James Tuchet, 3ʳᵈ Earl of Castlehaven**
      (ca.1617 – 11 Oct 1684 KIleash, co Tipperary) son of Mervyn
      Tuchet, 2ⁿᵈ Earl of Castlehaven & Elizabeth Barnham; =2ⁿᵈ
      Elizabeth Graves; suc. father 1631
      no issue
    (2) **Hon. Anne Brydges** (...)
    (3) **George Brydges, 6ᵗʰ Baron Brydges** (9 Aug 1620 –
      Feb 1654/5) suc. father 1621
      =1 14 Dec 1637 Totteridge; ♦**Lady Susan Montagu** (... –
      Apr 1652) daughter of Henry Montagu, 1ˢᵗ Earl of
      Manchester & Margaret Crouch
      =2 17 Jan 1652/3 Hedgerley, Bucks.; ♦**Jane Savage** (... – 6
      Jun 1676) daughter of John Savage, 2ⁿᵈ Earl Rivers &
      Catherine Parker; =2ⁿᵈ Sir William Sedley, 4ᵗʰ Baronet; =3ʳᵈ
      George Pitt
      issue of 1ˢᵗ:
      (a) **Hon. Catherine Brydges** (... – 21 Aug 1682)
        = 14 Oct 1681; **Richard Parsons, 1ˢᵗ Viscount Rosse**
        Baron Oxmantown, 3ʳᵈ Baronet (ca.1656 – 30 Jan 1702/3)
        son of Sir William Parsons, 2ⁿᵈ Baronet & Hon. Catherine
        Jones; =1ˢᵗ Anne Walsingham; =3ʳᵈ ♦Elizabeth Hamilton;
        suc. father 31 Dec 1658; cr. Viscount 2 Jul 1681
        no issue
      (b) **Hon. Margaret Brydges** (...)
        = ...; **Sir Thomas Skipwith, 2ⁿᵈ Baronet** (...) son of Sir
        Thomas Skipwith, 1ˢᵗ Baronet
        issue ?
      (c) **Hon. Elizabeth Brydges** (bef.25 Mar 1651 – 3 Feb
        1718)

=1 20 Aug 1673; ◆**Edward Herbert, 3ʳᵈ Baron Herbert** (ca.1633 – 9 Dec 1678) son of Richard Herbert, 2ⁿᵈ Baron Herbert & Lady Mary Egerton; =1ˢᵗ Anne Myddleton; suc. father 1655

=2 aft.1684; ◆**William O'Brien, 2ⁿᵈ Earl of Inchiquin** (ca.1640 – Jan 1691/2) son of Morrogh O'Brien, 1ˢᵗ Earl of Inchiquin & Elizabeth St.Leger; =1ˢᵗ ◆Lady Margaret Boyle; suc. father 1674

=3 bef.Aug 1694 (ann.aft.1697); ◆**Charles Howard, 4ᵗʰ Baron Howard** (... – 29 Apr 1715) son of William Howard, 4ᵗʰ Baron Howard & Frances Bridgman; suc. father 1694

no issue

issue of 2ⁿᵈ:

(d) **Hon. Lucy Brydges** (... – 12 Jul 1689)
= ...; ◆**Adam Loftus, Viscount Lisburne** (...–1691)
Children are listed with other parent

(4) **William Brydges, 7ᵗʰ Baron Brydges** (aft.1620 – Aug 1676) suc. brother 1655
= ...; **Susan Kerr** (... – Oct 1672)
no issue

(B) **Hon. Beatrice Brydges** (...)
= ...; **Sir Henry Poole** (1588 Sapperton, Glos. – 1645) son of Sir Henry Poole & Anne Wroughton

(1) **Sir William Poole** (1619 Sapperton – 1651)
= ...; **Meriell Tracy** (...)

(a) **Sir Henry Poole** (... – aft.1661)

(C) **Hon. Giles Brydges** (... – 28 Aug 1628)

(D) **Hon. William Brydges** (...)

(E) **Hon. Frances Brydges** (1580 – 1663)
=1 1603; **Sir Thomas Smith** (... – bef.1610)
=2 1610; ◆**Thomas Cecil, 1ˢᵗ Earl of Exeter** etc. (5 Mar 1542 – 8 Feb 1622/3) son of William Cecil, 1ˢᵗ Baron of Burghley & Mary Cheke; =1ˢᵗ ◆Hon. Dorothy Neville; suc. father 1598; cr. Earl 1605
no issue

d) **Hon. Katherine Brydges** (1524 – Apr 1566)
= 1556; ◆**Edward Dudley, 4ᵗʰ Baron Dudley** (...–1586)
Children are listed with other parent

e) **Hon. Charles Brydges** (1528 – 9 Apr 1619)
= ...

(I) **Sir Giles Brydges, 1ˢᵗ Baronet** (ca.1573 – 12 Sep 1637) cr. Baronet 17 May 1627
= ...; **Mary Scudamore** (... – bef.Sep 1634) daughter of Sir James Scudamore & Mary Throckmorton

(A) **Sir John Brydges, 2ⁿᵈ Baronet** (1623 – 21 Feb 1651/2

London) suc. father 1637

= ...; **Mary Peale** (...) daughter of James Pearle; =2nd Sir
William Powell, 1st

(1) **James Brydges, 8th Baron Chandos** 3rd Baronet (Sep
1642 – 16 Oct 1714) suc. father 1652; suc. distant cousin as
Baron 1676

= 4 May 1665; **Elizabeth Bernard** (5 Feb 1642/3 – 26 May
1719) daughter of Sir Henry bernard & Emma Charlton

(a) **Hon. Mary Brydges** (19 Feb 1665/6 – 13 Jun 1703)
= 28 Nov 1689; **Theophilius Leigh** (ca.1643 – 10 Feb
1724/5) son of William Leigh & Joanna Perry
Has further generations of issue

(b) **Hon. Elizabeth Brydges** (21 Jun 1668 – 23 Dec 1739)
= 24 Dec 1691 London; **Alexander Jacob** (1651 – 31 Mar
1725) son of Robert Jacob & Margaret Packer
Has further generations of issue

(c) **Hon. Jon. Emma Brydges** (11 Jun 1669 – Jun 1738)
= ...; **Edmund Chamberlayne** (1670 – 1755) son of John
Chamberlayne & Mary Savage
Has further generations of issue

(d) **James Brydges, 1st Duke of Chandos** Marquess of
Carnarvon, Earl of Carnarvon, Viscount Wilton, 9th Baron
Chandos, 4th Baronet (9 Jan 1673/4 – 9 Aug 1744 London)
suc. father 1714; cr. Earl and Viscount 9 Oct 1714; cr. Duke
etc. 29 Apr 1719

=1 27 Feb 1695/6 London; **Mary Lake** (18 Jul 1668
London – 15 Dec 1712 London) daughter of Sir Thomas
Lake & Rebecca Langham

=2 4 Aug 1713 London; ♦**Cassandra Willoughby** (... –
18 Jul 1735) daughter of Francis Willoughby & Emma
Barnard

=3 18 Apr 1736; **Lydia** Catherine **van Hatten** (3 Nov
1693 – 19 Nov 1750 Shaw Hall, Berks.) daughter of John
van Hatten & Lydia Davall
Has further generations of issue by 1st

(e) **Hon. Rev. Henry Brydges** (...)
= ...
Has further generations of issue

f) **Hon. Stephen Brydges** (1530 – ...)

g) **Hon. Richard Brydges** (1532 Cerney North, Glos. – 8 Jan
1592 Cerney North) (twin)

h) **Hon. Anthony Brydges** (1532 Cernet North – 1584) (twin)

i) **Hon. Frances** Mary **Brydges** (1533 – 1559)

j) **Hon. Henry Brydges** (1534 – 1615)
= ...; **Alice ...** (...)

(I) **Anne Brydges** (...)

= ...; **William Wright** (...)
  (A) **Stanguide Wright** (...)
  (B) **Giles Wright** (...)
  (C) **Anne Wright** (...)
(II) **Dorothy Brydges** (... – 1655)
= ...; **Thomas Dennis** (...)
  (A) **Margaret Dennis** (...)
  (B) **Alice Dennis** (...)
  (C) **Catherine Dennis** (...)
  (D) **Morris Dennis** (...)
  (E) **Elizabeth Dennis** (...)
  (F) **Thomas Dennis** (1610 – ...)

2) **George Grey, 10th Baron Grey** (ca.1493 – bef.15 Jan 1514/5) suc. father 5 May 1511
3) **Thomas Grey, 11th Baron Grey** (ca.1496 – 30 Oct 1517) suc. brother bef.15 Jan 1514/5
4) **Richard Grey, 12th Baron Grey** (ca.1505 – 15 Oct 1521) suc. brother 30 Oct 1517
5) **William Grey, 13th Baron Grey KG** (ca.1509 – 15 Dec 1562 Cheshunt, Herts.) suc. brother 15 Oct 1521; KG 1557
= ...; ♦**Lady Mary Somerset** (...) daughter of Charles Somerset, 1st Earl of Worcester & Elizabeth West; =2nd Robert Carre
  a) **Arthur Grey, 14th Baron Grey KG** (1536 Hammes, France – 14 Oct 1593 Whaddon, Bucks.) suc. father 15 Dec 1562; knighted 1560; KG 1572
  =1 ca.1553; **Dorothy la Zouche** (...) illegitimate daughter of Richard la Zouche, 9th Baron Zouche
  =2 ...; **Jane** Sibell **Morrison** (... – Jul 1615) daughter of Sir Richard Morrison & Bridget Hussey; =1st Edward, Lord Russell
  issue of 1st:
  (I) **Hon. Elizabeth Grey**(...)
  = ...; **Sir Francis Goodwin** (...)
    (A) **Arthur Goodwin** (...)
    = ...
      (1) **Jane Goodwin** (... – 21 Apr 1658)
      = 1637; ♦**Philip Wharton, 4th Baron Wharton** (1613 – 1695/6)
      Children are listed with other parent
  issue of 2nd:
  (II) **Thomas Grey, 15th Baron Grey** (ca.1575 Whaddon – 9 Jul 1614 Tower of London) knighted 1599; suc. father 14 Oct 1593; titles attainted and forfeited 1603; condemned to death but reprieved, died in prison; upon his death the Barons Grey (of

Wilton) became extinct[32]

(III) **Hon. Bridget Grey** (... – 28 Jul 1648)
= ...; **Sir Rowland Egerton, 1ˢᵗ Baronet** (... – Oct 1646) son
of Sir John Egerton & Margaret Stanley; cr. Baronet 5 Apr 1617

(A) **Sir John Egerton, 2ⁿᵈ Baronet** (... – 1674) suc. father 1646
= ...; **Anne Wintour** (... – 1681) daughter of George Wintour

(1) **Sir John Egerton, 3ʳᵈ Baronet** (... – 4 Nov 1729) suc.
father 1674
=1 ...; **Elizabeth Holland** (... – 31 May 1701)
=2 ...; **Anne Wolferstan** (... – 12 Apr 1726) daughter of
Francis Wolferstan
issue of 1ˢᵗ (none by 2ⁿᵈ):

(a) **Sir Holland Egerton, 4ᵗʰ Baronet** (ca.1689 – 25 Apr
1730) suc. father 1729
= 27 Mar 1712; **Eleanor Cave** (... – 26 Sep 1734) daughter
of Sir Roger Cave & Mary Bromley; =2ⁿᵈ John Brooke
Has further generations of issue

(b) **John Egerton** (... – 19 Dec 1704) unm.

(c) **Rev. William Egerton** (...)
= ...
issue ?

(2) **Bridget Egerton** (...)
=1 1663; **Ralph Thickness** (1640 – ...) son of Ralph
Thickness & Margaret Middlemore
=2 ...; **Timothy Hildyard** (...)
issue of 1ˢᵗ (none by 2ⁿᵈ):

(a) **Ralph Thickness** (1663 – ...)
= ...; **Elizabeth Stockton** (...)
Has further generations of issue

(b) **John Thickness** (...)
= 1692; **Joyce Blencowe** (...) daughter of Thomas
Blencowe
Has further generations of issue

(c) **Frances Thickness** (...)
= ...; **Charles Fletcher** (...)
issue ?

(d) **Elizabeth Thickness** (...)
= ...; **John Hough** (...)
issue ?

(3) **Margaret Egerton** (...)

---

[32] The Barony Grey of Wilton would be recreated for a descendant of Thomas' sister, Bridget
in 1784 who would later be further created Earl Grey.

= ...; **Winsdor Finch** (...)
issue ?
(4) **Anne Egerton** (...)
= ...; **John Gardner** (...)
issue ?
(B) **Sir Philip Egerton** (... – Aug 1698)
= ...; **Catherine Conway** (... – Aug 1698) daughter of Piers Conway
(1) **John Egerton** (...) unm.
(2) **Rev. Philip Egerton** (... – 6 Mar 1726)
= ...; **Frances Offley** (...) daughter of William Offley
(a) **Philip Egerton** (...)
= ...; **Frances Jeffreys** (...) daughter of Sir Griffith Jeffreys
no issue
(b) **Rowland Egerton** (...)
(c) **John Egerton** (... – 1770)
= ...; **Elizabeth Brock** (...) daughter of William Brock
Has further generations of issue
(d) 5 daughters – no further details known
(3) **Mary Egerton** (...)
= bef.1682; **Richard Bulkeley, 3rd Viscount Bulkeley** (1658 – 9 Aug 1704) son of Robert Bulkeley, 2nd Viscount Bulkeley & Sarah Harvey; suc father 18 Oct 1688
(a) **Richard Bulkeley, 4th Viscount Bulkeley** (19 Sep 1682 – 4 Jun 1724 Bath) suc. fazther 1704
=12 Feb 1702/3; **Ladfy Bridget Bertie** (ca.1682 – 13 Jun 1753 Thame, Oxon.) daughter of James Bertie, 1st Earl of Abingdon & Eleanora Lee
Has further generartions of issue
(C) **Sybilla Egerton** (ca.1605 – 1661)
=1 bef.1649; **Edward Bellot** (... – bef.1649)
=2 11 Sep 1649; **Sir Edmund Anderson, 1st Baronet** (10 Aug 1605 Redborune, Herts. – Jan 1660/1 Broughton, Lincs.) son of William Anderson & Joan Essex; =1st Mary Wood; cr. Baronet 11 Dec 1660
no issue
4. **QUEEN JOAN OF SCOTLAND** (ca.1404 –1445)
see: Chapter 19
5. **Thomas Beaufort, Count of Perche** (1405 – 1432) unm.; claimed the county of Perche from Dec. 1427[33]

---

[33] The land was actually held by Jean II, Duke of Alençon.

6. **Edmund Beaufort, 1st Duke of Somerset,** Marquess of Dorset, Earl of Dorset, 1st Count of Mortain, 4th Earl of Somerset, **KG** (ca.1406 – 22 May 1455 St.Albans) killed in battle; cr. Count 22 Apr 1427; KG bef.5 May 1436; Earl of Dorset 28 Aug 1442; Marquess 24 Jun 1443; and Duke 31 Mar 1448; suc. as Earl of Somerset 27 May 1444

= bet.1431/5; **Lady Eleanor Beauchamp** (ca.1408 – ca.1467 Baynard's Castle, London) daughter of Richard Beauchamp, 13th Earl of Warwick & Elizabeth Berkeley; =1st Thomas de Ros, 8th Baron de Ros; =3rd Walter Rokesley

a. **Lady Eleanor Beaufort** (... – 16 Aug 1501)

=1 ca.Apr 1458; **James Butler, 5th Earl of Ormonde** (24 Nov 1420 – 1 May 1461) beheaded by Yorkists; son of James Butler, 4th Earl of Ormonde & Elizabeth Beauchamp; =1st Avice Stafford; suc. father 22 Aug 1452

=2 ca.1470; **Sir Robert Spencer** (1446 – aft.13 Mar 1491/2) son of Robert Spencer & Anna Smyth; =1st Anne Pecke

issue of 2nd (none by 1st):

I) **Catherine Spencer** (bef.1480 – Oct/Nov 1542)
   = bef.1502; ◆**Henry** Algernon **Percy, 4th Earl of Northumberland** (1478 – 1527)
   Children are listed with other parent

II) **Margaret Spencer** (bef.1480 – 16 Aug 1501 Engle, Devon)
   = 1490; **Thomas Carey** (... – ca.21 Jun 1536) son of Sir William Cary & Anne Fulford

   A) **Sir John Carey** (ca.1495 – 9 Sep 1552 Herts.)
      = ...; **Joyce Denny** (24 Jul 1506 – 1560/1) daughter of Sir Edmund Denny & Mary Troutbeck

      1) **William Carey** (bef.1538 – 1612)
      2) **Sir Wymond Carey** (6 Mar 1538 – 13 Apr 1612)
         = ...; **Catherine Jemingham** (ca.1549 – 14 Feb 1614) daughter of John Jemingham & Hon. Catherine Brooke
         no issue
      3) **Sir Edward Carey** (ca.1540 – 18 Jul 1618)
         = aft.1568; **Katherine Knyvett** (1547 – 20 Dec 1622 Aldenham, Herts.) daughter of Sir Henry Knyvett & Anne Pickering; =1st Henry Paget, 2nd Lord Paget
         a) **Elizabeth Carey** (1570 Cockington – ...)
            = 20 Nov 1586; **John Savile, 1st Baron Savile** (1556 – 31 Aug 1630) son of Sir Robert Savile & Anne Hussey; =1st Katherine Willoughby; cr. Baron 1627
            (I) **Thomas Savile, 1st Earl of Sussex**, Viscount Savile, Baron of Castlebar, 2nd Baron Savile (14 Sep 1590 Doddington Pigot, Lincs. – ca.1659) cr. Viscount and Baron of Castlebar 1628; suc. father 1630; cr. Earl 1644
               =1 ca.1620 **Frances Sondes** (1592 – 1640) daughter of Sir Thomas Sondes & Margaret Brooke; =1st Sir John Levenson

=2 aft. Nov 1640; **Lady Anne Villiers** (...) daughter of
Christopher Villers, 1st Earl of Anglesey & Elizabeth Sheldon
issue of 2nd (none by 1st):
(A) **Lady Frances Savile** (... – 6 Jun 1695)
  = 1668; ♦**Francis, Lord Brudenell** (... – 1698)
  Children are listed with other parent
(B) **Lady Elizabeth Savile** (...)
  = ...; ♦**Hon. John Touchet** (...)
  Children are listed with other parent
(C) **James Savile, 2nd Earl of Sussex**, etc. (1647 – 1671) suc.
  father 1659, but titles became extinct upon his death
  = 1671; **Anne Wake** (...) daughter of Robert Wake
  no surviving issue
(II) **Frances Savile** (1604 Pomfert, Yorks. – 30 Jan 1663
Pomfert)
= ...; **Thomas Bradley** (1594 Pomfert – 1636) son of
Francis Bradley & Francisca Watkins
(A) **Savile Bradley** (1622 Pomfert – ...)
(B) **John Bradley** (1623 Pomfret – ...)
(C) **Francis Bradley** (1625 – 1689 Fairfield, CT)
  = ... in CT; **Ruth Barlow** (1638 Fairfield – 22 Oct
  1689 Fairfield) daughter of John Barlow & Ann Ward
  (1) **John Bradley** (ca.1664 – 1703 Fairfield)
    = ...; **Hannah Sherwood** (1672 – 1730)
    (a) **Abigail Bradley** (1695 Bridgeport, CT – 22 Apr
      1772 Kent, CT)
      = ...; **Ephram Hubbell** (11 Oct 1694 Stratford,
      CT – 4 Nov 1780 Kent, CT) son of Samuel
      Hubbell & Temperence Nichols
      Has further generations of issue
  (2) **Ruth Bradley** (1664 Fairfield Co. CT – 1700 Fairfield Co.)
    = ...; **Thomas Williams** (1659 CT – 17 Apr 1727
    Fairfield Co.) son of Richard Williams
    (a) **Thomas Williams** (1683 New London, CT – 29
      Sep 1769 Fairfield)
      = ...; **Esther Smith** (ca.1685 Fairfield – ...) daughter of
      Samuel Smith & Sarah Frost
      Has further generations of issue
  (3) **Abigail Bradley** (1667 – ...)
  (4) **Francis Bradley** (1670 Fairfield – 4 Dec 1716 Fairfield)
    = ...; **Sarah Jackson** (Mar 1680 Fairfield – 16 Apr
    1753) daughter of Joseph Jackson & Mary Godwin
    (a) **Francis Bradley** (29 May 1699 Greenfield, CT –
      3 Apr 1786 Fairfield)
      = ...; **Mary Sturges** (8 Aug 1699 Greenfield – 8
      Apr 1794) daughter of John Sturges & Abigail Wheeler

Has further generations of issue
(b) **Gershom Bradley** (7 Dec 1712 Greenfield – 7
Jan 1795 Greenfield)
=1 ...; **Sarah Sherwood** (...)
=2 ...; **Elizabeth Osborn** (...)
=3 ...; **Jane Dimon** (...)
=4 ...; **Deborah Dimon** (...)
Has further generations of issue by 3rd and 4th
(5) **Daniel Bradley** (1670 Fairfield – 1 Jul 1713
Fairfield)
= ...; **Abigail Jackson** (1672 Fairfield – 1714
Fairfield) daughter of Joseph Jackson & Mary Godwin
(a) **Daniel Bradley** (11 Jun 1704 Fairfield – 3 Apr
1765 Ridgefield, Fairfield, Co.)
=1 ...; **Esther Burr** (31 Jan 1702 Fairfield – 29
Dec 1741 Fairfield) daughter of Daniel Burr &
Elizabeth Pinckney
=2 ...; **Sarah Scribner** (... – 1783) daughter of Thomas
Scribner & Mary Abbott
Has further generations of issue
(b) **James Bradley** (1712 – 1786)
= ...; **Abigail Sanford** (1713 – ...) daughter of Ezekiel
Sanford & Rebecca Gregory
Has further generations of issue
(c) **Abigail Bradley** (1706 Fairfield – 1803)
= ...; **Solomon Sturges** (1698 – 7 Jul 1779) son of
Joseph Sturges & Sarah Judson
Has further generations of issue
(d) **Martha Bradley** (1702 – ...)
= ...; **Ebenezer Hull** (1697 – 1745 Reading,
Fairfield Co.) son of Cornelius Hull & Sarah Hull
Has further generations of issue
(6) **Joseph Bradley** (ca.1676 – ...)
(7) **Mary Bradley** (ca.1679 – ...)
(D) **Barbara Bradley** (1631 Pomfret – ...)
(E) **Thomas Bradley** (1633 Pomfret – 1665 Virginia)
= ...; **Alice Damton** (1636 Broseley, Salop. – 30 Jan
1665) daughter of John Damton
(1) **John Bradley** (21 Feb 1656 Bethall, Salop – in
Virginia)
(2) **Thomas Bradley** (1658 – ...)
(3) **Mary Bradley** (1659 – ...)
(4) **Lawrence Bradley** (16 Apr 1661 Broseley – 30
Nov 1712 Broseley)
= ...; **Eleanor ...** (1665 – ...)
(a) **Lawrence** Augustine **Bradley** (26 Dec 1689 Broseley –

1 Jun 1784 Orange Co. NC) immigrated to colonies bef.
1732

= **Elizabeth Lillard** (1710 Culpeper Co. VA – Jun 1788
Culpeper Co.) daughter of Jean Lillard & Sarah Glassel
Has further generations of issue

(b) **John Bradley** (1693 Broseley – ...)

(c) **William Bradley** (1699 Broseley – ...)

(d) **Thomas Bradley** (1702 – ...)

(e) **Richard Bradley** (1707 – ...)

(f) **Andrew Bradley** (...)

b) **Frances Carey** (1571 Cockington, Devon – 1644)

=1 ...; **Ralph Baesh** (... – 1598)

=2 3 Mar 1605; ◆**George Manners, 7ᵗʰ Earl of Rutland**
(1580 – 29 Mar 1641) son of John Manners, 4ᵗʰ Earl of
Rutland & Elizabeth Charlton; suc. brother 17 Dec 1632
issue of 1ˢᵗ (none by 2ⁿᵈ):

(I) **Sir Edward Baesh** (1 Jan 1594 – Dec 1653)

= ...; **Mary Montagu** (1615 – ...) daughter of Sir Charles
Montagu & Mary Whitmore
no issue

c) **Katherine Carey** (1573 Cockington – 24 Sep 1635)

= 15 Jan 1597; **Sir Henry Longueville** (1575 Blunham, Beds. –
17 May 1621) son of Arthur Longueville & Anne Middleton

(I) **Sir Edward Longueville, 1ˢᵗ Baronet** (bap.23 Apr 1604
Aldenham, Herts. – Aug 1661) cr. Baronet 17 Dec 1738

= ca.1631; **Margaret Temple** (... – Aug 1665 Buckingham)
daughter of Sir Thomas Temple, 1ˢᵗ Baronet & Hester Sandys

(A) **Margaret Longueville** (1628 – 1688)

= ...; ◆**John Digby** (1627 – 1723)
Children are listed with other parent

(B) **Sir Thomas Longueville, 2ⁿᵈ Baronet** (ca.1631 –
25 Jun 1685 Wolverton, Bucks.) suc. father 1661

=1 bef.1662; **Mary Fenwick** (... – 1683) daughter of Sir
William Fenwick & Elizabeth Radclyffe

=2 7 May 1685 London; **Catherine Peyton** (1641 –
30 Dec 1715 London) daughter of Sir Thomas Peyton, 2ⁿᵈ
Baronet & Cecilie Clerke
issue of 1ˢᵗ (none by 2ⁿᵈ):

(1) **Sir Edward Longueville, 3ʳᵈ Baronet** (1662 – Aug 1718
Bichester, Oxon.) killed in a horse race; suc. father 1685

= ...; ◆**Mary Longueville** (... – 1766) daughter of Edward
Longueville & Mary Sylvester; =1ˢᵗ John Lawton
no issue

(2) **Margaret Longueville** (... – Nov 1677)

= ...; **Sir William Stych, Baronet** (... – 1697) son of
William Stych & Magdalen Betham; =2ⁿᵈ Elizabeth ...; cr.

Baronet 8 Oct 1697
no surviving issue
   (3) **Elizabeth Longueville** (...)
   = ...; **Sir Miles Stapleton** (...)
   issue ?
  (C) **Edward Longueville** (...)
  = ...; **Mary Sylvester** (...)
   (1) **Sir Thomas Longueville, 4ᵗʰ Baronet** (... – 1759
   Wrexham, Denbighs.) suc. cousin (and brother-in-law) 1718,
   but the baronetcy became extinct upon his death
   = ...; ♦**Maria Margaretta Conway** (... – Aug 1730)
   daughter of Sir John Conway, 2ⁿᵈ Baronet & Margaretta
   Digby
    (a) **Maria Margaretta Longueville** (1722 – ...)
    =1 ...; **John** Thomas **Jones** (... – 29 Oct 1749 Wrexham)
    =2 ...; **Joseph Taylor** (...)
    Has further generations of issue
   (2) **Mary Longueville** (... – 1766)
   = ...; **Sir Edward Longueville, 3ʳᵈ Baronet** (1662 – Aug
   1718 Bichester, Oxon.) killed in a horse race; suc. father 1685
   no issue
(II) **Catherine Longueville** (... – 1627)
= aft.1620; **Roger Jones, 1ˢᵗ Viscount Ranelagh**, Baron
Jones (1612 – 1643) Killed in battle; son of Most Rev. Thomas
Jones, Archbishop of Dublin & Margaret Purdon; =1ˢᵗ Hon.
Frances Moore; Kt. 1607; cr. Viscount etc. 25 Aug 1628
  (A) **Hon. Elizabeth Jones** (ca.1629 co Meath – Apr 1704)
  = ...; **Robert Sandys** (1620 Northbourne, Kent – 1684
  in Ireland) son of Sir Edwin Sandys & Catherine Bulkeley
   (1) **Robert Sandys** (1645 – 1703)
   = ...; **Mary Reynolds** (1650 – ...) daughter of John
   Reynolds
    (a) **Edwin Sandys** (...)
    = ...; **Jane Donnelan** (...)
    Has further generations of issue
    (b) **William Sandys** (...)
    (c) **Robert Sandys** (...)
    (d) **James Sandys** (...)
    (e) **John Sandys** (...)
    (f) **Elizabeth Sandys** (... – 1683)
    = ... **Henry Piers** (1667 – 1705)
    Has further generations of issue
    (g) **Richard Sandys** (...)
    (h) **Catherine Sandys** (...)
   (2) **Margaret Sandys** (...)
   (3) **Elizabeth Sandys** (...)

(4) **Edwin Sandys** (...)
(5) **Joan Sandys** (...)
(6) **Francis Sandys** (...)
(7) **Catherine Sandys** (... – 1681)
= ...; **Chidley Coote** (1644 Kilmallock, co. Limerick – 1702) son of Chidley Coote & Alice Philips
(a) **Ann Coote** (ca.1678 – ...)
= 1699; **Bartholomew Purdon** (...) son of Bartholomew Purdon & Alicia Jephson
Has further generations of issue
(b) **Rev. Chidley Coote** (1678 co. Limerick – 2 Aug 1720 Limerick)
= ...; **Janet Evans** (1682 – Feb 1763) dau, of Rt.Hon. George Evans & Mary Eyre
Has further generations of issue
(c) **Elizabeth Coote** (...)
(d) **Catherine Coote** (ca.1680 – ...)
= 1715; **Henry Boyle, 1st Earl of Shannon**, Viscount Boyle, Baron Castlemartyr (1682 – 1764) son of Henry Boyle & Lady Mary O'Brien; =2nd Lady Henrietta Boyle; cr. Earl etc. 1756
no issue
(e) **Robert Coote** (...)
(III) **Elizabeth Longueville** (...)
d) **Henry Carey, 1st Viscount Falkland**, Lord Carye (ca.1576 – ca.Sep 1633) cr, Viscount etc. 10 Nov 1620
= 27 Jun 1602; **Elizabeth Tanfield** (... – Oct 1639) daughter Sir Lawrence Tanfield & Elizabeth Symonds
(I) **Hon. Catherine Carey** (...)
= 2 Aug 1622; ♦**James Home, 2nd Earl of Home**, Lord Dunglas, 7th Lord Home (ca.1607 – ca.Feb 1633) son of Alexander Home, 1st Earl of Home & Mary Dudley; suc. father 5 Apr 1619; =2nd Lady Grace Fane
no issue
(II) **Lucius Carey, 2nd Viscount Falkland**, etc. (1610 – 20 Sep 1643 Newbury, Berks.) killed in battle; suc. father 1633
= ...; **Letitia Morison** (1610 – ca.Feb 1646/7) daughter of Sir Richard Morison & Elizabeth Harington
(A) **Lucius Carey, 3rd Viscount Falkland**, etc. (bap.5 Jul 1632 – 27 Sep 1649 Montpelier, France) unm.; suc. father 1643
(B) **Henry Carey, 4th Viscount Falkland**, etc. (21 Nov 1634 – 2 Apr 1663) suc. brother 1649
= 14 Apr 1653; **Rachel Hungerford** (... – 24 Feb 1717/8) daughter of Sir Anthony Hungerford & Rachel Jones
(1) **Anthony Carey, 5th Viscount Falkland**, etc. (15

Feb 1656 – 24 May 1694) suc. father 1663
= ...; **Rebecca Lytton** (... – 1709) daughter of Sir
Rowland Lytton & Rebcca Chapman
no surviving issue

(III) **Hon. Lawrence Carey** (5 Oct 1613 – 1642 Swords,
co. Dublin) killed in action; unm.

(IV) **Hon. Victoria Carey** (1620 Wickham, Hants. – 1694)
=1 ...; **Sir William Uvedale** (1587 Wickham – ca.Nov 1682
Wickham) son of Sir William & Mary Norton; =1st ♦Anne Carey
=2 14 Aug 1653; **Bartholomew Price** (...)
issue of 1st (none by 2nd):

(A) **Victoria Uvedale** (1642 – 18 Nov 1679 Wickham)

(B) **Elizabeth Uvedale** (bap.8 Jun 1646Wickham –
15 Dec 1696 Wickham)
=1 bef.1668; **Sir William Berkeley** (... – bef.1668)
killed at sea
=2 1668; ♦**Edward Howard, 2nd Earl of Carlisle**
(1646 – 1692)
issue of 2nd (none by 1st):
Beyond the 12th generation on the father's line

(V) **Hon. Patrick Carey** (ca.1623 Ireland – 15 Mar 1657/8)
= 1653; **Susan Uvedale** (... – 25 Jul 1658) daughter of
Francis Uvedale

(A) **Edward Carey** (bap.25 Apr 1656 – bef.24 Nov 1692)
= ...; ♦**Hon. Anne Lucas** (... – 1709) daughter of Charles
Lucas, 2nd Baron Lucas & Lady Penelope Leke; =2nd
Hon. Archibald Hamilton

(1) **Lucius Carey, 6th Viscount of Falkland**, etc. (27
Aug 1887 – 31 Dec 1730) suc. cousin 24 May 1694;
styled by the Jacobites as 1st Earl of Falkland
=1 5 Oct 1704; **Dorothy Molyneux** (... – 26 Jun
1722) daughter of Francis Molyneux
=2 ...; **Laura Dillon** (... – 12 Jul 1741) daughter of
Arthur Dillon, Count Dillon & Christina Sheldon
Has issue by both born after 1700

(2) **Frances Carey** (... – 17 Feb 1768)
= Sep 1705/6; **John FitzGerald, Earl Grandison**,
5th Viscount Grandison (ca.1684 – 14 May 1766)
son of Hon. Edward FitzGerald & Katherine
FitzGerald; suc. as Viscount 16 Dec 1699; cr. Earl
11 Sep 1721, which became extinct up on his death

(a) **Elizabeth FitzGerald, 1st Countess Grandison**,
Viscountess Villiers, Viscountess Grandison (... –
29 May 1782) cr. Viscountess Grandison 10 Apr
1746 and Countess 19 Feb 1767
=1 12 Jun 1739; **John Mason** (... – 26 Mar 1759)

=2 15 Feb 1763; **Charles** Montigue **Halifax** (...)
Has further generations of issue
  (b) **James, Lord Villiers** (bef.1715 – 12 Dec 1732)
  = 10 Jul 1728; **Jane Butler** (– 20 Dec 1751) daughter of
  Richard Butler; =2ⁿᵈ ♦Lucius Cary, 7ᵗʰ Viscount Falkland
  no surviving issue
e) **Adolphus Carey** (ca.1578 Berkhamstead, Herts. – 10
Apr 1609 London)
  = 9 Aug 1596; ♦**Ann Corbet** (... – 1601) daughter of Sir
  Robert Corbet & Anne St.John
  no issue
f) **Sir Philip Carey** (... – ca.Jun 1631)
  = ...; **Eilzabeth Bland** (... – 1623) daughter of Richard Bland
  (I) **Elizabeth Carey** (1 Sep 1611 Great Berkhamsted,
    Herts. – ...)
    = ca.1630; **Sir Humphrey Brigges, 2ⁿᵈ Baronet** (ca.1615 –
    ca.May 1691) son of Sir Morton Brigges, 1ˢᵗ Baronet &
    Chrisogena Grey; =2ⁿᵈ Elizabeth Wilbraham; =3ʳᵈ Anne ...; =4ᵗʰ
    Magdalen Corbet; suc. father ca.1650
    no issue
  (II) **Ann Carey** (10 Jun 1615 London – Jan 1671/2)
    = bef.1638; ♦**William Willoughby, 6ᵗʰ Baron Willoughby**
    (1616 – 1673)
    Children are listed with other parent
g) **Muriel Carey** (ca.1579 Cockington – 15 May 1600)
  = 23 Oct 1597; **Sir Thomas Crompton** (... – 16 May 1659
  Abbeville, France) murdered; son of Thomas Crompton & Mary
  Hudson
  (I) **Catherine Crompton** (1599 Driffield, Yorks. – 1666
    Arely Hall, Worcs.)
    = ...; ♦**Sir Thomas Lyttleton, 1ˢᵗ Baronet** (1593 – 1650)
    Children are listed with other parent
  (II) **Thomas Crompton** (...)
  (III) **Richard Crompton** (...)
  (IV) **John Crompton** (...)
  (V) **Anne Crompton** (...)
  (VI) **Margaret Crompton** (...)
  (VII) **Barbara Crompton** (...)
h) **Anne Carey** (10 Aug 1585 – bef.1660)
  = 16 Sep 1607; **Francis Leke, 1ˢᵗ Earl of Scarsdale**,
  Baron Deincourt, Baronet (1581 – 9 Apr 1665) son of Sir
  Francis Leke & Frances Swifte; cr. Baronet 22 May
  1611, Baron 26 Oct 1624, and Earl 11 Nov 1645
  (I) **Hon. Francis Leke** (...) killed in battle in France
  (II) **Nicholas Leke, 2ⁿᵈ Earl of Scarsdale**, etc. (1 Oct
    1612 – 27 Jan 1681) suc. father 1665

= ...; **Lady Frances Rich** (...) daughter of Robert Rich, 2ⁿᵈ
Earl of Warwick

(A) **Robert Leke, 3ʳᵈ Earl of Scarsdale**, etc. (9 Mar
  1654 – 27 Dec 1707) suc. father 1681
  = 11 Feb 1672; **Mary Lewis** (ca.1658 – ...) daughter of Sir
  John Lewis, Baronet & Sarah Foote
  no issue

(B) **Hon. Richard Leke** (...)
  = ...; **Mary Molyneux** (...) daughter of Sir John Molyneux,
  3ʳᵈ Baronet & Lucy Rigby

  (1) **Nicholas Leke, 4ᵗʰ Earl of Scarsdale**, etc. (... –
    1736) unm.; suc. uncle 1707, but his titles became
    extinct upon his death
  (2) **Frances Leke** (...)
  (3) **Lucy Leke** (...)

(III) **Hon. Edward Leke** (...) killed in battle
(IV) **Hon. Charles Leke** (...) killed in battle
(V) **Lady Anne Leke** (1614 – ...)
  = ...; **Henry Hildyard** (1608 Winestead, Yorks. – ...)

(A) **Henry Hildyard** (1637 Winestread – ...)
  = ...; **Dorothy Grantham** (...) daughter of Sir Thomas
  Grantham & Dorothy Alford

  (1) **Christopher Hildyard** (1664 – 1719)
    = ...; ♦**Jane Pitt** (1665 – ...) daughter of George Pitt &
    Lady Jane Savage

    (a) **Dorothy Hildyard** (...)
      = ...; **George Clayton** (...)
      Has further generations of issue

(VI) **Lady Catherine Leke** (...)
  = ...; **Cuthbert Morley** (...)
  issue ?

(VII) **Lady Frances Leke** (... – 29 Jul 1682)
  = ...; ♦**Jenico Preston, 7ᵗʰ Viscount Gormanston** 10ᵗʰ
  Baron Preston (... – 17 Mar 1690/1) son of Nicholas Preston, 6ᵗʰ
  Viscount Gormanston & Mary Barnewall; =2ⁿᵈ Hon. Margaret
  Molyneux; suc. father 28 Jun 1643
  no issue

(VIII) **Lady Penelope Leke** (... – 1705)
  = ...; **Charles Lucas, 2ⁿᵈ Baron Lucas** (1631 – 1688)
  son of Sir Thomas Lucas & Mary Byron; suc. uncle by
  special remainder 2 Jul 1671

(A) **Hon. Anne Lucas** (... – 1709)
  = ...; ♦**Edward Carey** (1656 – 1692)
  Children are listed with other parent

(B) **Hon. Penelope Lucas** (...)
  = ...; **Isaac Selfe** (...)

  (1) **Anne Selfe** (1696 – 15 May 1733)
   = ca.20 May 1720; **Thomas Methuen** (... – 2 Jan
   1737/8) son of Anthony Methuen & Gertrude Moore
   (a) **Paul Methuen** (16 May 1723 – 22 Jan 1795)
    = 25 Jun 1749; **Catherine Cobb** (... – 21 May
    1779) daughter of Sir George Cobb, 3rd Baronet
    Has further generations of issue
  i) **Jane Carey** (ca.1595 – ca.1632)
   = Apr 1608; **Sir Edward Barrett, Lord Barrett of
   Newburgh,** Baronet (21 Jun 1581 Aveley, Essex – ca.Dec 1644)
   son of Charles Barrett & Christian Mildmay; =2nd Catherine Fenn;
   Kt.1608; cr. Lord and Baronet 17 Oct 1627, but all titles became
   extinct upon his death
   no issue
 B) **William Carey** (1500 – 22 Jun 1529)
  = 4 Feb 1520/1; ♦**Lady Mary Boleyn**[34] (ca.1502 – 19 Jul
  1543) daughter of Thomas Boleyn, Earl of Wiltshire & Lady
  Elizabeth Howard; =2nd ♦Sir William Stafford
 1) **Katherine Carey** (ca.1524 – 1569)
  = 1540; **Sir Francis Knollys KG** (1511 – 19 Jul 1596) son
  of Robert Knollys & Lettice Peniston
  a) **Lettice Knollys** (1540/1 – 25 Dec1634)
   =1 ca.1563; ♦**Walter Devreaux, 1st Earl of Essex**
   (1539 – 1576)
   =2 1578; ♦**Robert Dudley, 1st Earl of Leicester** (1532 – 1588)
   =3 1589; **Sir Christopher Blount** (1565 Kidderminster,
   Worcs. – 18 Mar 1601 London) executed
   issue of 1st (none by others):
   Children are listed with other parent
  b) **Henry Knollys** (ca.1542 – 1582)
   = 1565; **Magaret Cave** (...) daughter of Rt.Hon. Sir Ambrose
   Cave & Margery Willington
   (I) **Lettice Knollys** (... – 1655)
   = bef.19 Jun 1602; **William Paget, 4th Baron Paget** (1572 –
   29 Aug 1628 London) son of Thomas Paget, 3rd Baron Paget &
   Nazarth Newton; suc. father 19 Mar 1603/4
   (A) **Hon. Katherine Paget** (...)
    = 19 Aug 1641; **Sir Anthony Irby** (1605 – 1681) son
    of Sir Anthony Irby & Elizabeth Peyton; =1st Farnces
    Wray; =2nd Margaret Smyth; =3rd Margaret Barkham

---

[34] Sister of Queen Anne Boleyn, she was a mistress of King Henry VIII prior to Henry meeting
her sister.

(1) **Anthony Irby** (... – 1684)
  = ...; **Mary Stringer** (...) daughter of John Stringer
  (a) **Sir Edward Irby, 1st Baronet** (... – 11 Nov
    1718 Kingscliffe, Northants.) cr. Baronet 13 Apr 1704
    = 1706; ♦**Dorothy Paget** (... – Oct 1734) daughter of
    Hon. Henry Paget & Mary O'Rorke
    Has further generations of issue
(2) **Isabella Irby** (bef.1669 – ca.Dec 1685)
  = ...; ♦**William Paget, 6th Baron Paget** (1637 – 1712)
  Children are listed with other parent
(B) **Hon. Margaret Paget** (...)
= ...; **Sir William Hicks, 1st Baronet** (1596 – 9 Oct
1680) son of Sir Michael Hicks & Elizabeth Coulson;
cr. Baronet 21 Jul 1619
  (1) **Sir William Hicks, 2nd Baronet** (1629 Rook
    Holes, Essex – 1703) suc. father 1680
    = 13 Feb 1660/1 Shenley, Herefords.; **Martha**
    Agnes **Coningsby** (...) daughter of Sir Henry Coningsby
    & Hester Campbell
    (a) **Sir Henry Hicks, 3rd Baronet** (1666 – 1755)
      suc. father 1703
    (b) **Mary Hicks** (1670 – 1710)
      = 19 Oct 1693; ♦**James Darcy, 1st Baron Darcy of
      Navan** (ca.1650 – 19 Jul 1731) son of James Darcy & Isabel
      Wyvill; =1st Bethia Payler; =2nd Anne Stawel; =4th Margaret
      Garth; cr. Baron 13 Sep 1721
      no issue
    (c) **Margaret Hicks** (1672 – ...)
      = ...; **Anthony Wharton** (...)
      Has further generations of issue
    (d) **William Hicks** (1674 – ...)
    (e) **John Hicks** (1676 – ...)
    (f) **Charles Hicks** (1677 Aldenham, Northants. – ...)
      = ...; **Mary Coningsby** (bef.18 Dec 1684 – 10 Oxt
      1739) daughter of John Coningsby & Mary Aram
      Has further generations of issue
    (g) **Hester Hicks** (1680 – ...)
    (h) **Elizabeth Hicks** (1684 – ...)
    (i) **Anne Hicks** (1686 – ...)
  (2) **Lettice Hicks** (...)
    = 1651; ♦**Arthur Chichester, 1st Earl of Donegall**
    (1606 – 1675)
    Children are listed with other parent
  (3) **Sir Michael Hicks** (...)
    = ...
    (a) **Howe Hicks** (...)

= ...

Has further generations of issue[35]

(C) **William Paget, 5ᵗʰ Baron Paget** (13 Spr 1609 – 19
Oct 1678 London) suc. father 29 Aug 1628
= 28 Jun 1632 London; **Lady Frances Rich** (... –
ca.1672 London) daughter of Henry Rich, 1ˢᵗ Earl of
Holland & Isabel Cope

(1) **William Paget, 6ᵗʰ Baron Paget** (10 Feb 1637 –
26 Feb 1712/3 London) suc. father 1678
=1 20 Jul 1661; **Frances Pierrepont** (bef.1644 –
Oct/Nov 1681 London) daughter of Hon. Francis
Pierrepont & Elizabeth Bray
=2 ...; ♦**Isabella Irby** (bef.1669 – ca.Dec 1685) daughter
of Sir Anthony Irby & Hon. Katherine Paget
issue of 1ˢᵗ (none surviving by 2ⁿᵈ):

(a) **Henry Paget, 1ˢᵗ Earl of Uxbridge**, Baron
Burton, 7ᵗʰ Baron Paget (ca.1663 – 30 Aug 1743
London) suc. father 1713; cr. Baron Burton 1 Jan
1711/12 and Earl 19 Oct 1714
=1 2 Jan 1685/6; **Mary Catesby** (... – 3 Nov 1734)
daughter of Thomas Catesby & Margaret Samwell
=2 7 Jun 1739; **Elizabeth Bagot** (3 Mar 1674
Blithfield, Staffs. – 2 Sep 1749) daughter of Sir Walter
3ʳᵈ Bagot, 3ʳᵈ Baronet & Jane Salesbury
Has further generations of issue

(b) **Hon. William Paget** (aft.1663 – ca.Aug 1684) unm.

(2) **Hon. Henry Paget** (ca.1643 – ...)
=1 bef.1683; **Anne Sandford** (... – 15 Dec 1683)
daughter of Robert Sandford
=2 29 Mar 1684; **Mary O'Rorke** (...) daughter of HUgh
O'Rorke & Joan Reynolds
issue of 2ⁿᵈ (none surviving of 1ˢᵗ):

(a) **Thomas Paget** (... – 1741)
= ...; **Mary Whitcombe** (... – 15 Feb 1740/1) daughter
of Peter Whitcombe & Elizabeth Sherard
Has further generations of issue

(b) **Dorothy Paget** (... – ca. Oct 1834)
= 1706; ♦**Sir Edward Irby, 1ˢᵗ Baronet** (... – 1718)
Children are listed with other parent

(3) **Hon. Diana Paget** (ca.1648 – Aug 1707)
= 26 Mar 1670; **Sir Henry Ashurst, 1ˢᵗ Baronet** (8

---

[35] His male line of descendants continue the Baronets who were elevated to Earls St. Aldwyn.

Sep 1645 – 13 Apr 1711) son of Henry Ashurst &
Judith Reresby; cr. Baronet 21 Jul 1688
 (a) **Frances Ashurst** (... – 23 Jun 1643)
  = ca.1710; **Sir William Allen, 1st Baronet** (... – 19
  Oct 1725) né Anguish; son of Edmund Anguish &
  Alice Allen; cr. Baronet 14 Dec 1699
  Has further generations of issue
 (b) **Sir Henry Ashurst, 2nd Baronet** (... – 17 May
  1732) suc. father 1711, but the baronetcy became
  extinct upon his death
  = bef. Jan 1711; **Elizabeth Draper** (... – bef.1738)
  daughter of Sir Thomas Draper, 1st Baronet & Mary Cary
  no issue
 (4) **Hon. Lettice Paget** (ca.1649 – ...)
  = ...; **Richard Hampden** (...)
  issue ?
 (5) **Hon. Frances Paget** (ca.1653 – ...)
  = ...; **Rowland Hunt** (...)
  issue ?
 (6) **Hon. Penelope Paget** (ca.1655 – ...)
  = ...; **Philip Foley** (12 May 1648 – Dec 1716) son of
  Thomas Foley & Anne Browne
  (a) **Robert Foley** (...)
   = ...; **Mary Markland** (...) daughter of Rev. Ralph Foley
   Has further generations of issue
  (b) **Paul Foley** (7 Jun 1684 – 27 Nov 1739)
   = ...; **Elizabeth Turton** (...) daughter of William Turton
   Has further generations of issue
 (6) **Hon. Anne Paget** (ca.1659 – ...)
(II) **Elizabeth Knollys** (1579 – 1621)
 = ...; **Sir Henry Willoughby, Baronet** (14 Sep 1579 –
20 Nov 1649 Lavenham, Suffolk) son of Sir John
Willoughby & Frances Hun; cr. Baronet 29 Jun 1611
but title became extinct upon his death
 (A) **Mary Willoughby** (14 May 1605 Derby – 1633
  Wilne, Derbys.)
  = ...; **Sir Henry Griffith, 2nd Baronet** (1603 Burton Agnes,
  Yorks. – 1666 Burton Agnes) son of Sir Henry Griffith, 1st
  Baronet & Elizabeth Throckmorton; suc. father 1620; =2nd
  Dorothy Bellingham; =3rd Margaret Wortly
  no issue
 (B) **Catherine Willoughby** (1610 – 30 Jun 1673) unm.
 (C) **Anne Willoughby** (ca.1614 – 2 Jun 1688 Wilne)
  =1 ...; **Sir Thomas Aston, 1st Baronet** (29 Sep 1600 –
  24 Mar 1645) son of John Aston & Maud Needham;
  cr. Baronet 25 Jul 1628

=2 ...; ♦**Hon. Anchitell Grey** (ca.1624 – 8 Jul 1702)
son of Henry Grey, 1st Earl of Stamford & Lady Anne Cecil
issue of 1st (none by 2nd):
  (1) **Sir Willoughby Aston, 2nd Baronet** (5 Jul 1640 –
    14 Dec 1702) suc. father 1645
    = ...; **Mary Offley** (3 Feb 1649 – 22 Jan 1711) daughter
    of John Offley & Mary Broughton
      (a) **Sir Thomas Aston, 3rd Baronet** (17 Jan 1665 –
        16 Jan 1724) suc. father 1702
        = ...; **Catherine Widdrington** (Nov 1676 – 10 Apr 1752)
        Has issue biorn after 1700
      (b) **Magdalene Aston** (7 Apr 1672 – 30 Aug 1709)
        = ...; **Thomas Norris** (30 May 1653 – Jun 1700)
        son of Thomas Norris & Catherine Garway
        Has further generations of issue
      (c) **Richard Aston** (... – 24 Nov 1741)
        = ...; **Elizabeth Warren** (...)
        Has further generations of issue
      (d) **Mary Aston** (...)
        = ...; **Hugh Chamberlain** (1664 – 1728) son of
        Hugh Chamberlain & Dorothy Brett
        Has further generations of issue
  (2) **Magdalen Aston** (ca.1642 – 1694)
    = ...; **Sir Robert Burdett, 3rd Baronet** (11 Jan 1640
    Bamcott, Warks.– 18 Jan 1716) son of Sir Francis
    Burdett, 2nd Baronet & Elizabeth Walter; =2nd Mary
    Brome; suc. father 30 Dec 1696
    no issue
  (D) **Frances Willoughby** (14 Oc 1607 – ...) unm.
c) **Mary Knollys** (1542 – 1593)
  = ...; **Edward Stalker** (...)
  issue ?
d) **Edward Knollys** (1546 – 1580)
e) **William Knollys, 1st Earl of Banbury**, Viscount
  Wallingford, Baron Knollys **KG** (ca.1547 – 25 May 1632
  London) Kt. 1586; KG 1615; cr. Baron 13 May 1603,
  Viscount 7 Nov 1616, and Earl 18 Aug 1626
  =1 bef.1573; **Dorothy Bray** (ca.1530 – 31 Oct 1605) daughter
  of Edmund Braye, 1st Baron Bray & Jane Halliwell;
  Edmund Brydges, 2nd Baron Chandos
  =2 23 Dec 1605; ♦**Lady Elizabeth Howard** (11 Aug 1586
  Saffron Walden, Essex – 7 Apr 1658) daughter of Thomas
  Howard, 1st Earl of Suffolk & Katherine Knyvett; =2 Edward Vaux,

4th Baron Vaux

issue of 2nd (none by 1st):

(I) **Edward Knollys,** *de jure 2nd Earl of Banbury, etc.*[36]
(10 Apr 1627 Rotherfield Greys, Oxon. – bef.Jun 1645
Pas-de-Calais, France) murdered; unm.; suc. father 1632

(II) **Nicholas Knollys,** *de jure 3rd Earl of Banbury, etc.* (3
Jan 1630/1 Harrowden, Northants. – 14 Mar 1673/4
Boughton, Northants.) suc. brother 1645
=1 ...; ♦**Lady Isabella Blount** (... – ca.Feb 1654/5) daughter
of Mountjoy Blount, 1st Earl of Newport & Hon. Anne Boteler
=2 4 Oct 1655 Stapleford, Leics.; **Anne Sherard** (... – 6
Mar 1679/80) daughter of William Sherard, 1st Baron
Sherard & Abigail Cave

issue of 1st:

(A) **Katherine Knollys** (...)
  = ...; **John Law** (...)
   (1) **Katherine Law** (ca.1711 – 14 Oct 1790 London)
   = ... **William Knollys** (15 Oct 1694 – Jun 1470) son
   of Charles Knollys & Catherine Lister
   no issue

issue of 2nd:

(B) **Charles Knollys** *de jure 4th Earl of Banbury, etc.* (3
Jun 1662 Boughton – 26 Aug 1740 Dunkirk, France)
=1 16 May 1689 London; **Elizabeth Lister** (7 Jun
1663 South Carlton, Lincs. – ca.Dec 1699) daughter of
Michael Lister & Ann Burrell
=2 30 Apr 1702 London; **Mary Woods** (... – 12 May
1762 Bath) daughter of Thomas Woods & Mary Harwood

issue of 1st:

  (1) **Sir Charles Knowles, 1st Baronet,** *de jure 5th Earl
  of Banbury, etc.* (15 Oct 1694 London – 9 Dec 1777) (twin)
  suc. father 1740; cr. Baronet 31 Oct 1765; Gov. of Jamaica
  1752–56
  =1 23 Dec 1740; **Mary Allenye** (... – 16 Mar 1742)
  daughter of John Allenye & Mary Terrill
  =2 29 Jul 1750; **Maria Magdalena** Theresa **de
  Bouget** (... – 6 Mar 1796) daughter of Henri François,

---

[36] While they were recognized sons of William, Earl of Banbury, there was debate that Elizabeth's children were actually the natural sons of Lord Vaux, who became their step-father. The House of Lords refused to seat them as Peers based on their likely illegitimacy. The descendants of the de jure 3rd Earl continued to appeal this decision, but it has never been reversed.

Count de Bouget
Has issue by both born after 1700

(2) **William Knowles** (15 Oct 1694 London – Jun 1740 London) (twin)
= ...; ♦**Mary Katherine Law** (ca.1711 – 14 Oct 1790 London) daughter of John Law & Katherine Knollys
no issue
issue of 2nd:

(3) **Rev. Charles Knowles** (26 Mar 1703 – 13 Mar 1771 Burford, Oxon.)
= ...; **Martha Hughes** (... – Sep 1771)
Has further generations of issue

(C) **Anne Knollys** (...)
=1 ...; **Charles Fry** (1644 – 1670) son of William Fry & Dorothy Drake
=2 ...; **Sir John Briscal** (...)
issue of 1st (none by 2nd):

(1) **Mountjoy Fry** (19 Oct 1668 – ...)

f) **Sir Robert Knollys KB** (ca.1547 – 1619) KB 1603
= ca.1585; **Catherine Vaughan** (...) daughter of Rowland Vaughan

(I) **Lettice Knollys** (...)
= ...; **Framingham Gawdy** (1589 – 1655 Norfolk)

(A) **Sir William Gawdy, 1st Baronet** (24 Sep 1612 – 18 Aug 1669) cr. Baronet 13 Jul 1663
= ...; **Elizabeth Duffield** (... – 1653) daughter of John Duffield

(1) **Bassingbourne Gawdy** (... – bef.Aug 1669)

(2) **Sir John Gawdy, 2nd Baronet** (1639 – 1709) suc. father 1669
= ...

(a) **Sir Bassingbourne Gawdy, 3rd Baronet** (... – 1724) suc. father 1709, but titel became extinct upon his death

g) **Maud Knollys** (1548 – ...)

h) **Elizabeth Knollys** (15 Jun 1549 – 1605)
= 1578; **Sir Thomas Leighton** (ca.1555 – 1611 Guernsey) son of John Leighton & Joyce Sutton

(I) **Elizabeth Leighton** (ca.1573 – ...)
= ...; **Sherrington Talbot** (1577 – 1642) son of Sir John Talbot & Olive Sherrington; =2nd Mary Washbourne

(A) **Sherrington Talbot** (... – 1677)
= 13 Oct 1627; ♦**Jane Lyttleton** (...) daughter of John Lyttleton & Meriel Bromley

(1) **Elizabeth Talbot** (... – 1709)
= ...; **Henry Davenport** (... – 1698)

(a) **Henry Davenport** (1677 – 1731)
=1 ...; **Mary Chardin** (1670 – ...)
=2 ...; **Barbara Ivory** (... – 1748) daughter of Sir John
Ivory & Anne Talbot
Has further generations of issue by both
(2) **Sir John Talbot** (1630 – 13 Mar 1713/4 Laycock Abbey,
Wilts.)
=1 11 Dec 1653 Ebrington, Glos.; **Elizabeth Keyt** (...)
daughter of Sir John Keyt, 1st Baronet
=2 ...; ♦**Barbara Slingsby** (...) daughter of Sir Henry
Slingsby, 1st Baronet & Barbara Bellasyse
issue of 1st:
(a) **Sherrington Talbot** (bef.30 Mar 1656 – ...) unm.
issue of 2nd:
(b) **Anne Talbot** (1665 – 1720)
= ...; **Sir John Ivory** (1655 – 1695)
Has further generations of issue
(c) **Barbara Talbot** (ca.1671 – 31 Jan 1763)
= 11 Jul 1689; **Henry Yelverton, 1st Viscount de
Longueville** (ca.1664 – 24 Mar 1703/4) son of Sir Henry
Yelverton, 2nd Baronet & Susan Longueville, 13th Baroness
Grey; suc. brother as Baroent and Baron Grey 17 May 1679;
cr. Viscount 21 Apr 1690
Has further generations of issue
(d) **Gilberta Talbot** (15 Feb 1675 – 1746) unm.
(B) **Sir Gilbert Talbot** (...) unm.
(II) **Thomas Leighton** (1584 – ...)
= ...; **Mary Zouche** (...)
issue ?
(III) **Anne Leighton** (ca.1595 – ...)
= ...; ♦**Sir John St.John, 1st Baronet** (1585–1648)
*These descendants are further down than 12 genearations in
the father's line*
i) **Sir Francis Knollys** (ca.1550 – 1648)
= ...; **Lettice Barrett** (1555 Hanham, Glos. – 1620
Reading, Berks) son of John Barrett & Elizabeth Braytoft
(I) **Sir Francis Knollys** (ca.1588 – 1643)
married twice and left issue, no further details known
(II) **Richard Knollys** (1590 – ...)
(III) **Leticia Knollys** (1591 – Mar 1666 Reading)
=1 ...; **Sir Thomas Vachell** (1560 – 1638)
=2 ...; **John Hampden** (1595 Great Hempden, Bucks. –
24 Jun 1643 Thame, Oxon) died of wounds received in
battle; son of William Hampden & Elizabeth Williams;
he =1st Elizabeth Symeon
no issue

j) **Richard Knollys** (1552 – 1596)
= ...; **Jane Heigham** (... – 1631) daughter of Sir John
Heigham & Martha Yelverton
(I) **Sir Robert Knollys** (1589 – 1659)
= ...; **Joan Wolstenholme** (... – 1660) daughter of Sir John
Wolstenholme & Catherine Fanshawe
(A) **William Knollys** (1620 – 1664)
= ...; **Margaret Saunders** (...) daughter of John Saunders
& Margaret Evelyn
issue ?
(B) **Leticia Knollys** (...)
= ...; **Sir John Corbet, 2nd Baronet** (ca.1620 – 24 Feb
1665) son of Sir John Corbet, 1st Baronet & Anne
Mainwaring; suc. father Jun 1662
(1) **Sir John Corbet, 3rd Baronet** (1642 – 1695) suc.
father 1665
= 28 Nov 1658 Woodford, Essex; **Theophilia
Cambell** (... – bef.1672) daughter of James Cambell &
Hon. Theophilia Mohun
(a) **Sir Robert Corbet, 4th Baronet** (1670 – 1740)
suc. father 1695
= ...
Has further generations of issue
(II) **Francis Knollys** (...)
= ...; **Alice Beecher** (1599 – 1670) daughter of William
Beecher & Judith Quarles; =2nd Sir Henry Huncks. Gov.
of Barbados
(A) **Dorothy Knollys** (21 Oct 1633 Stamford, Lincs. – ...)
= ...; **William Byam** (9 Mar 1622 Luccombe, Som – Dec 1670
Antigua) son of Edward Byam & Elizabeth Eaglesfield
(1) **William Byam** (22 Nov 1652 – ...)
(2) **Mary Byam** (1653 – 1690)
= ...; **... Nedham** (...)
issue ?
(3) **Alice Byam** (6 Oct 1656 – ...)
(4) **Willoughby Byam** (23 Dec 1657 Antigua – 1690)
= ... **Rebecca Winthrop** (...)
(a) **William Byam** (...)
= ...; **Mary Yeamans** (...)
Has further generations of issue
(5) **Edward Byam** (9 Jan 1662 Suriname – 4 Dec 1741)
= ...; **Lydia Thomas** (1670 St.John's, Antigua – 22
Dec 1744 Harpenden, Herts.) daughter of William
Thomas & ... Tomlinson; =2nd Samuel Martin
Has further generations of issue
(III) **Henry Knollys** (...)

k) **Anne Knollys** (19 Jul 1555 – 30 Aug 1608 Lansium, Hants.)
= 19 Nov 1571; **Thomas West, 2nd Baron Delaware**
(ca.1556 – 24 Mar 1601/2) son of William West, 1st Baron
Delaware & Elizabeth Strange; suc. father 30 Dec 1595
(I) **Hon. Lucy West** (1572 Wherwell – ...)
(II) **Hon. Elizabeth West** (11 Sep 1573 Wherwell,
Hants. – 16 Jan 1633 Valence, Dorset)
=1 ...; **Sir Herbert Pelham** (ca.1546 Bucksheep, Sussex – 4
Dec 1620 Fordington, Dorset) son of Anthony Pelham &
Margarret Uckthorpe; =1 Catherine Pelham
=2 ...; **Sir Richard Saltonstall** (ca.1586 – Oct 1661
Yorks.) son of Samuel Saltonstall & Anne Ramsden;
he =1st Grace Kaye; =3rd Martha Cammock
issue of 1st:
(A) **Elizabeth Pelham** (27 Apr 1604 Hellingly,
Sussex – 1 Nov 1628)
= ...; **John Humphrey** (ca.1596 Chaldon, Dorset – 23
Mar 1651 Sandwich, Kent) son of John Humphrey ;
he =1st Mary ...; =3rd Hon. Susan Clinton
(1) **Anne Humphrey** (bef.17 Dec 1625 Fordingham,
Dorset – 17 Dec 1693 Swansea, MA)
=1 ...; **William Palmes** (ca.1620 Ireland – 1668
Ardfinnan, co. Tipperary) son of Stephen Palmes
=2 aft.1668; **Rev. John Myles** (ca.1621 Newton-
Clifford, Herefords. – 3 Feb 1684 Swansea) son of
Walter Myles & Susannah Palmes; had 2 previous
unknown wives
issue of 1st:
(a) **Jonathan Palmes** (1650 – ...)
(b) **Ann Palmes** (1659 – ...)
= ...; **Nicholas Lange** (1668 Boston – 1728 Swansea) son
of Richard Lange & Catherine Woods
Has further generations of issue
(c) **Elizabeth Palmes** (1663 Boston – ...)
= ...; **Griffin Edwards** (...)
issue ?
(d) **Susannah Palmes** (1665 Swansea – 9 Oct 1747 Groton,
CT)
= ...; **Samuel Avery** (14 Aug 1664 New London, CT – 1
May 1723 New London) son of James Avery & Joana
Greenslade; =1st Sarah Walker
Has further generations of issue
issue of 2nd:
(e) **Hannah Myles** (5 Jan 1673 Rehoboth, MA – 1741
Swansea)
= ...; **Isaac Mason** (15 Jul 1667 Rehoboth – 25 Jan 1742

Swansea) son of Sampson Mason & Mary Butterworth
Has further generations of issue
(B) **Thomas Pelham** (...)
(D) **Anne Pelham** (...)
= ...; **Edward Clarke** (...)
issue ?
(E) **Jonathan Pelham** (...)
issue of 2nd:
(F) **John Saltonstall** (1632 – ...)
(III) **Hon. Robert West** (3 Jan 1575 Wherwell – 1594
London)
= ...; **Elizabeth Cocke** (1579 Herts. – 1645) daughterof Sir
Henry Cocke & Ursula Bury; =2nd Sir Richard Lucy, 1st
Baronet; =3rd Sir Robert Oxenbridge
no issue
(IV) **Hon. Margaret West** (ca.1576 – ...)
= ...; **Samuel Johnson** (...)
issue ?
(V) **Thomas West, 3rd Baron Delaware** (9 Jul 1577
Wherwell – 6 Jun 1618 at sea enroute to
Virginia) suc. father 1602; Gov. of Virginia 1611–1618
= 25 Nov 1602 London; **Cecily Shirley** (... – ca.Jul
1662) daughter of Sir Thomas Shirley & Anne Kempe
(A) **Hon. Cecily West** (1612 Newstead, Hants. – Feb
1638 Southampton)
=1 bef.1626; **Sir Francis Bindlosse** (ca.1603 – 25 Jul
1629) son of Sir Robert Bindlosse & Mary Eltoft
=2 ...; **John Byron, 1st Baron Byron** (ca.1599 – Aug
1652) son of Sir John Byron & Anne Molyneux; =2nd
Hon. Eleanor Needham; cr. Baron 24 Oct 1643
issue of 1st (none by 2nd):
(1) **Drororthy Bindlosse** (1626 – 16 Aug 1684)
= 7 Aug 1648; **Sir Charles Wheler, 2nd Baronet**
(1620 – 26 Aug 1683) son of William Wheler &
Eleanor Puleston; suc. cousin under special
remainder 6 Aug 1666
(a) **Trevor Wheler** (... – 12 Oct 1678) unm.
(b) **Dorothy** Elizabeth **Wheler** (...)37
(c) **Sir William Wheler, 3rd Baronet** (1654 – 23
Feb 1708/9) suc. father 1683

---

37 ThePeerage.com and Wikipedia say she married a Count of Nassau, but I have not been
able to find her in the Nassau family tree.

= 15 Jan 1695/6; **Teresa Widdrington** (...) daughter of
Hon. Edward Widdrington
Has further generations of issue
  (d) **Sir Fancis Wheler** (ca.1656 – 19 Feb 1694)
= 12 Nov 1685; **Arabella Clifton** (...) daughter of
Clifford Clifton
Has further generations of issue
  (2) **Sir Robert Bindlosse, Baronet** (8 May 1624 –
Nov 1688) cr. Baronet 16 Aug 1641, but it became
extinct upon his death
= ...; **Rebecca Perry** (... – ca.Jun 1708) daughter of
Hugh Perry & Catherine Fenn
    (a) **Cecilia Bindlosse** (1645 – 19 Jan 1729/30)
= ...; **William Standish** (1645 – 8 Jun 1703)
issue ?
  (3) **Francis Bindlosse** (...)
(B) **Henry West, 4th Baron Delaware** (3 Oct 1603 – 1
Jun 1628) suc. father 6 Jun 1618
= Mar 1624/5; **Isabella Edmunds** (Nov 1607
Brussels – ca.1675) daughter of Sir Thomas Edmunds
  (1) **Charles West, 5th Baron Delaware** (Feb 1626 –
22 Dec 1687) suc. father 1628
= 25 Sep 1642 London; **Anne Wilde** (... – ca.May
1703) daughter of John Wilde
    (a) **Hon. Charles West** (1645 – 22 Jun 1684)
=1 ...; **Mary Huddleston** (... – bef.Dec 1678) daughter
of Ferdinando Huddleston & Dorothy Hunle
=2 26 Dec 1678; **Elizabeth Pye** (...) daughter of Sir
Edmund Pye, Baronet & Catherine Lucas
no issue
    (b) **Hon. Cecilia West** (1659 – ...)
= ...; **William Beaw** (11 Dec 1665 Adderbury,
Oxon. – 1738) son of William Beaw & Frances
Bourchier; =1st Margaret Lyster
no issue
    (c) **John West, 6th Baron Delaware** (ca.1663 – 26
May 1723 London) suc. father 1687
= Jun 1691; **Margaret Freeman** (... – 31 Jan
1737/8) daughter of John Freeman
Has issue by 1st born after 1700
(C) **Hon. Lucy West** (ca.1613 Newstead, Notts. – 1660
Southampton, Hants.)
= ...; **Sir Robert Byron** (1611 – aft.1643) son of Sir
John Byron & Anne Molyneux
  (1) **Cecily Byron** (1634 Hants. – ...)
= 1665; **Charles Balfour** (...) son of William Balfour

(a) **Lucy Balfour** (...)
  =1 ...; **Hugh McGill** (...)
  =2 ...; **Blayney Townley** (...)
  issue ?
(2) **Lucy Byron** (1638 Hants. – ...)
(3) **Mary Byron** (1642 – ...)
(D) **Hon. Martha West** (1615 – ...)
  = ca.1645; **William Woodward** (ca.1620 – 1695)
  (1) **Philemon Woodward** (ca.1646 – ...)
  (2) **John Woodward** (ca.1648 – ...)
  (3) **Samuel Woodward** (ca.1651 – ...)
  (4) **Martha Woodward** (ca.1655 – ...)
    =1 ca.1675; **William Bigger** (...)
    =2 ca.1681; **Gideon Macon** (...)
    =3 14 May 1702; **Nathaniel West** (...)
    issue ?
  (5) **Anne Woodward** (aft.1655 – ...)
issue by "**Rachel**" (1600 VA – 1646 VA) =1st Raleigh Croshaw:
(E) **Totopotomoi** (aka **Toby West**) (1616 Sussex – 1 Jan 1656
  Richmond, VA) Chief of the Pamunkey tribe in 1649
  = ...; (his first cousin) **Cockacoseske** (ca.1640 –
  ca1686) daughter of Openchancanough & Cleopatra
  Powhatan[38]
  no issue
(VI) **Hon. Penelope West** (9 Sept 1582 Wherwell – 1619
  Boston, Lincs.)
  = ca.1599; **Herbert Pelham**[39] (ca.1580 Hastings, Sussex – 20
  Jul 1724 Boston, Lincs.) son of Sir Herbert Pelham &
  Catherine Thatcher
  (A) **Herbert Pelham** (1601 Boston – 1 Jan 1673
    Bewer's Hamlet, Essex)
    =1 ...; **Jemima Waldegrave** (Oct 1602 Lawford,
    Essex – 1638) daughter of Thomas Waldegrave &
    Margaret Olmstead
    =2 ...; **Elizabeth Bossville** (1617 Earls Colne, Essex –
    25 Aug 1659 Bures, Essex) daughter of Godfrey Bossville
    & Margaret Greville; =1st Roger Harlakenden
    issue of 1st:
    (1) **Nathaniel Pelham** (1632 – ...)
    (2) **Penelope Pelham** (ca.1632 Bures – 7 Dec 1703

---

[38] Cleopatra (her English name) was a sister of Pocahontas.
[39] Herbert was step-son of Penelope's sister, Elizabeth.

Marshfield, MA)
= ...; **Josiah Winslow** (22 May 1629 Plymouth, MA – 18 Dec 1680 Marshfield) son of Edward Winslow[40] & Susannah White

(a) **Elizabeth Winslow** (8 Apr 1664 Marshfield – 11 Jul 1735 Pembroke, MA)
= ...; **Stephen Burton** (1650 in England – 22 Jul 1693 Grafton, NH) son of Stephen Burton; =1st Elizabeth Brenton
Has further generations of issue

(b) **Isaac Winslow** (17 Jul 1670 Marshfield – 14 Dec 1738 Marshfield)
=1 ...; **... Prence** (...) daughter of Thomas Prence
=2 ...; **Sarah Wensley** (11 Aug 1673 Boston, MA – 16 Dec 1753) daughter of John Wensley & Elizabeth Paddy
Has issue by both born after 1700
issue of 2nd:

(3) **Edward Pelham** (ca.1650 Newport, RI – 1720)
= ...; **Freelove Arnold** (20 Jul 1661 – 20 Sep 1730)

(a) **Edward Pelham** (... – 1740)
= ...; **Arabella Williams** (1683 – ...) daughter of JOhn Williams & Anna Guthrie; =2nd John Holman
issue ?

(B) **Penelope Pelham** (... – 28 May 1702 Boston, MA)
= ca.1642; **Richard Bellingham** (1592 Boston, Lincs. – 7 Dec 1672 Boston, MA) son of William Bellingham & Frances Amcotts; =1st Elizabeth Backhouse; Gov. of MA 1641–42, 1654–55, and 1665–1672
no surviving issue

(VII) **Hon. Catherine West** (27 Dec 1583 Wherwell – 1650)
= ...; **Nicholas Strelby** (...)
issue ?

(VIII) **Hon. Francis West** (28 Oct 1586 Salisbury, Wilts. – 1634 Duxbury, MA) served in first VA House of Burgesses
=1 ca.1625; **Margaret Whitney** (1590 – bef.Mar 1627/8) =1st ...; =2nd William Powell; =3rd Edward Blayney
=2 Mar 1627/8; **Temperence Flowerdew** (ca.1587 – Dec 1628) daughter of Anthony Flowerdew & Martha Garrett; =1st Richard Barrow; =2nd Gov. Sir George Yeardley

---

[40] A Mayflower passenger (along with his wife) and Gov. of Plymouth Colony.

=3 ...; **Jane Davye** (1586 Southampton, Hants. – 1640
Northampton Co. VA) daughter of Sir Henry Davye
issue of 1st:
(A) **Elizabeth West** (1627 – 1670)
issue of 3rd (none by 2nd):
(B) **Francis West** (1632 – ...)
  = ...
   (1) **Francis West** (1653 – bef.1679)
    = ...; **Elizabeth Gilliam** (1654 Surry Co, VA – 15 Feb 1715
    Surry Co) daughter of John Gilliam & Margery Henshaw;
    she =2nd William Bevin; =3rd Francis Maybury
    (a) **John West** (ca.1673 VA – aft.3 Aug 1742 Amelia Co, VA)
    (b) **Francis West** (1674 Albemarle C o, VA – 1738 Amelia
     Co)
     = ...; **Elizabeth ...** (ca.1709 – ...)
     Has further generations of issue
    (c) **Robert West** (...)
    = ...; **Mary ...** (...)
    issue ?
(IX) **Hon. Helena West** (15 Dec 1587 Wherwell – 1602
Wherwell)
= 1608 Ballgalget, co Down; **William** Watkins **Savage** (1569
Winchester, Hants. – 16 Jan 1627 Taunton, Som.)
(A) **John Savage** (ca.1610 Taunton – ...)
(B) **Cecily Savage** (ca.1612 Taunton – ...)
(C) **Anne Savage** (ca.1613 Ches. – 16 Jun 1696 London)
(X) **Hon. Anne West** (13 Feb 1588 Wherwell – 1670
Shelton, Norfolk)
=1 ...; **John Pellet** (... – 22 Oct 1625)
=2 aft.1625; **Christopher Swale** (... – 7 Sep 1645)
=3 aft.1645; **Leonard Lechford** (... – Nov 1673)
issue of 1st:
(A) a daughter (...)
(B) a daughter (...)
(C) a daughter (...)
issue of 2nd (none by 3rd):
(D) **Christopher Swale** (...)
(E) **Elizabeth Swale** (...)
(XI) **Hon. Lettice West** (24 Nov 1589 Wherwell – 28 Jul
1645 Matlock, Derbys.)
= ...; **Sir Henry Ludlow** (ca.1577 Warminster, Wilts. –
13 Oct 1639 Matlock, Derbys.) son of Sir Edmund Ludlow &
Bridget Coker
(A) **William** Joseph **Ludlow** (May 1600 Matlock – 2 Nov 1667
  Southampton, NY)
  = ...

(1) **Edmund Ludlow** (...)
  = ...
  (a) **Edmund Ludlow** (10 Jul 1714 – 28 Feb 1787)
    = ...; **Bodicoate ...** (...
    Has further generations of issue
  (b) **Thomas Ludlow** (21 Nov 1715 – ...)
(B) **Henry Ludlow** (1603 Maiden Bradley, Wilts. – 1698)
(C) **Edmund Ludlow** (ca.1605 Matlock – ...)
  = ...
  (1) **Katherine Ludlow** (...)
  (2) **Elizabeh Ludlow** (...)
  (3) **Edmund Ludlow** (...)
  (4) **John Ludlow** (...)
  (5) **Anne Ludlow** (...)
  (6) **William Ludlow** (...)
(D) **Anthony Ludlow** (ca.1607 Matlock – 17 Mar 1681
  Southampton, NY)
(E) **Obadiah Ludlow** (ca.1609 Matlock – ...)
(F) **Elizabeth Ludlow** (ca.1610 – ...)
  = ...; **Robert Corbet** (1606 Baschurch, Salop. – 1676
  Baschurch) son of Thomas Corbet & Margaret Scriven
  (1) **Robert Corbet** (ca.1635 – ...)
  (2) **Thomas Corbet** (1636 – ...)
  (3) **Lettice Corbet** (1638 – 1714)
    = ...; **Richard Barrett** (1618 – 1669)
    (a) **Richard Barrett** (1664 – 1704)
      = ...; **Susanna Vaughn** (...)
    Has further generations of issue
  (4) **Andrew Corbet** (1640 – ...)
  (5) **Elizabeth Corbet** (ca. 1643 – ...)
    = ...; **George Clive** (1640 Walford, Salop – 1690)
    (a) **Thomas Clive** (12 Aug 1673 Walford – 10 Dec 1711
      Baschurch)
      = ...; **Elizabeth Amplett** (... – 1738 Salop)
    Has further generations of issue
    (b) **George Clive** (...)
    (c) **William Clive** (...)
  (6) **Margaret Corbet** (ca.1646 – ...)
  (7) **Mary Corbet** (ca.1650 – ...)
(G) **Clemence Ludlow** (ca.1617 Huntington, NY – ...)
(H) **John Ludlow** (1626 Matlock – 8 Apr 1650 Matlock)
(XII) **Hon. John West** (14 Dec 1590 Wherwell – Mar
  1659 King William Co. VA)
= ...; ◆**Ann Percy** (ca.1613 – 1661 James City, VA)
daughter of Hon. George Percy & Anne Floyd
(A) **John West** (1632 – 1691)

= 1654; **Unity Croshaw** (... – 30 Oct 1693) daughter
of John Crowhaw
(1) **Anne West** (ca.1655 West Point – 1708 New Kent Co.)
= ...; **Henry Fox** (ca.1650 London – 17 Nov 1714
King William Co.) son of John Fox & Anne ...
 (a) **Richard Fox** (ca. 1673 New Kent Co. – ...)
 (b) **Henry Fox** (ca.1674 New Kent Co. – 1750
 Brunswick, VA)
 =1 ...; **Mary Claiborne** (... – 1714 King William Co.)
 daughter of William Claiborne & Elizabeth Ludman
 =2 ...; **Mary ...** (... – aft.1716)
 Has issue by both born after 1700
 (c) **John Fox** (ca.1676 London, England – ca.1730
 Spottsylvania Co. VA)
 = ...; **Frances Lightfoot** (...) daughter of John
 Lightfoot & Elizabeth Taylor
 Has further generations of issue
 (d) **Anne Fox** (20 May 1684 New Kent Co. – 4 May 1733)
 = ...; **Thomas Claiborne** (16 Dec 1680 Sweet Hall, King
 William Co. – 16 Aug 1732 Sweet Hall)
 Has further generations of issue
 (e) **Thomas Fox** (1686 New Kent Co. – ...)
 = ..; **Mary Tunstall** (...)
 Has further generations of issue
(2) **Ursula** Unity Susanna **West** (24 Dec 1658 Drayton,
 Somerset, England – 12 May 1708 Elsing Green, King
 William Co.)
 = ...; **George** Thomas **Martin** (ca.1656 King William Co. –
 ca.1715 South Carolina) son of George Martin & Winifred
 Lewis
 a) **Amelia** Anne **Martin** (ca.1674 New Kent Co. –
 1714 New Kent Co.)
 = ...; **Thomas Mims** (22 Apr 1681 Middlesex,
 Hanover Co. VA – 28 Apr 1712 New Kent Co.)
 son of Thomas Mims & Anne Stanford
 Has further generations of issue
(3) **Nathaniel West** (ca.1665 West Point – 1723
 New Kent Co., VA)
 = ...; **Martha Woodward** (1660 King William Co. –
 1723 King William Co.) daughter of William
 Woodward & Martha West; =1st Gideon Macon;
 and =2nd William Biggers
 (a) **John** William **West** (1702 King William Co. – ...)
 = ...; ◆**Martha Huntingdon** (1704 Surrey Co.
 VA – ...) daughter of William Huntingdon & Jane ...
 Has further generations of issue

(b) **Unity** Susannah **West** (ca.1702 – 9 Jul 1753King
William Co.)
= ...; **William Dandridge**[41] (29 Dec 1689
London – 25 Aug 1743 King William Co.) son of
John Dandridge & Bridget Dugdale
Has further generations of issue
(4) **John West** (1676 – 1734)
= 15 Oct 1698 Elizabeth City Co. VA; **Judith Armistead**
(...) daughter of Anthony Armistead & Hannah Ellyson
(a) **Charles West** (... – after 1780) unm.
(5) **Thomas** Oliphant **West** (ca.1685 West Point –
King William Co.)
= ...; **Agnes** Frances **Claiborne** (ca.1670 – 1720 King
William Co.) daughter of Thomas Clairborne & Sarah Fenn
Has further generations of issue
issue by **Cockacoeske** (1640 – 1686) recognized as Queen of
the Pamunkey tribe by the Virginia colonial government 1656;
she married ♦Totopotomoi (aka Toby West):
(6) **John West** (ca.1657 – ...)
= ...; **Elizabeth Rose** (...)
(a) **Thomas West** (...)
= ...; **Sarah ...** (...)
Has further generations of issue
(XIII) **Hon. Nathaniel West** (30 Nov 1592 Lansium
Hants. – 1623 Charles City Co., VA)
=1 ...; **Elizabeth Sagar** (... – 1621)
=2 aft.1621; **Frances Greville** (ca.1598 Glos. – May
1633 Warwick Co. VA) daughter of Giles Greville & Sarah
Payne; =2nd Abraham Percy; =3rd Samuel Matthews
issue of 2nd (none by 1st):
(A) **Alice West** (aft.1621 Charles City Co. – 31 Mar
1673 Isle of Wight Co. VA)
=1 ...; **Thomas Harris** (10 Jun 1616 Cheeksea,
Essex – 10 Jun 1672 Isle of Wight Co.) son of John
Harris & Dorothy Calcott
=2 ...; **John Sojourner** (...)
issue of 1st (none by 2nd):
(1) **John Harris** (1636 Isle of Wight Co. – 1713 Isle of Wight
Co.)
=1 ...; **Margaret Hobbs** (1636 – 1688)
=2 aft.1688; **Ann Martin** (1644 – 1733) daughter of

---

[41] Uncle of Martha Dandridge Washington, the first First Lady of the United States.

Joseph Martin & Martha Tomlin
issue of 1st (none by 2nd)
- (a) **Edward Harris** (1663 – 1734)
  = ...; **Mary Turner** (1667 – 1733) daughter of John
  Turner & Mary Tomlin
  Has further generations of issue
- (b) **Margaret Harris** (1670 – ...)
  = ...; **Charles Stuart** (1666 – 1692)
  Has further generations of issue
- (2) **Thomas Harris** (1637 Charles City Co. – 7 Oct
  1688 Isle of Wight Co.)
  = ...; **Ann Martin** (1642 Isle of Wight Co. – 14 Mar
  1688 Isle of Wight Co.) daughter of Thomas Martin &
  Martha Tomlin
  - (a) **Ann Harris** (ca.1655 Isle of Wight Co. – 17 Jul
    1739 New Kent)
    = ...; **Bridgeman Joyner** (2 Jun 1654 Isle of Wight
    Co. – 1 Oct 1719 Isle of Wight Co.) son of Thomas
    Joyner & Sarah Edwards
    Has further generations of issue
  - (b) **Jane Harris** (ca.1658 – 3 Dec 1700 Isle of Wight Co.)
    =1 ...; **Richard** Edwin **Jones** (1666 Isle of Wight
    Co. – 22 May 1721 Isle of Wight Co.) son of
    Arthur Jones & Martha Baratt; =1st Sarah Legare
    =2 ...; **Edward Jones** (ca.1656 Isle of Wight Co. –
    15 Jul 1730 Isle of Wight Co.) son of Edward
    Jones & Mary ferch Hugh
    Has further generations of issue
  - (c) **Edward Harris** (ca.1663 Charles City Co. – 25
    Mar 1734 Isle of Wight Co.)
    = ...; **Mary Turner** (ca.1666 Isle of Wight Co. –
    27 Apr 1733 Isle of Wight Co.) daughter of John
    Turner & Mary Tomlin; =1st John Kendrick
    Has further generations of issue
  - (d) **John Harris** (1665 Isle of Wight Co. – 10 Dec
    1711 Date, MO [then French terriroty])
    =1 ...; **Sarah Tyner** (1668 Isle of Wight Co. –
    1711 Chowan Co. NC) daughter of Nicholas Tyner &
    Margaret Oliver
    =2 ...; **Mary ...** (... – 1713)
    =3 ...; **Mildred ...** (...)
    Has issue by 1st and 2nd born after 1700
  - (e) **Thomas Harris** (1667 Isle of Wight Co. – 1712
    Isle of Wight Co.)
    = ...; **Judith Edwards** (1690 Spotsylvania Co.
    VA – 1727 Isle of Wight Co.) daughter of Robert

Edwards & Mary Hunt
Has further generations of issue
(f) **Robert Harris** (1674 Isle of Wight Co. – 1739
Isle of Wight Co.)
= ...; **Ann Fulgham** (1681 Isle of Wight Co. – 4
Nov 1740 Isle of Wight Co.) daughter of Michael
Fulgham & Ann Izard
Has further generations of issue
(g) **George Harris** (ca.1676 Isle of Wight Co. – 22
Aug 1720 Isle of Wight Co.)
= ...; **Martha ...** (...)
Has further generations of issue
(h) **Martin Harris** (1676 Isle of Wight Co. – 1750
Isle of Wight Co.)
(i) **William Harris** (1677 Isle of Wight Co. – 1740
Isle of Wight Co.)
(j) **Dorothy Harris** (1672 Isle of Wight Co. – ...)
(3) **Ann Harris** (1638 Isle of Wight Co. – 1699 Isle of
Wight Co.)
(4) **Mary Harris** (ca.1639 Isle of Wight Co. – 10 Jun
1672)
(5) **Edward Harris** (1642 Isle of Wight Co. – 1677
Isle of Wight Co.)
= ...; **Martha Hardy** (1644 Isle of Wight Co. – 4
Apr 1676 Isle of Wight Co.)
(a) **Edward Harris** (1672 Isle of Wight Co. – 1739 Isle of
Wight Co.)
= ...; **Mary Thorpe** (1680 – 1781)
Has further generations of issue
(b) **John Harris** (1670 Isle of Wight Co. – 1712)
(6) **Martha Harris** (ca.1644 Isle of Wight Co. – ...)
= ...; **John Jennings** (1650 – ...)
(a) **Sarah Jennings** (1676 New Kent, VA – ...)
= ...; **John Luck** (1675 New Kent – 1712 New
Kent Co. VA) son of Richard Luck
Has further generations of issue
(B) **Nathaniel West** (1622 London – 1670 Princess Anne Co.
VA)
(XIV) **Hon. Eleanor West** (1593 Lansium – 1660)
(XV) **Hon. Matthew West** (...)
= ...
(A) **Robert West** (...)
= ...
(1) **John West** (...)
= ...
(a) **Robert West** (...)

Has further generations of issue
(XVI) **Hon. Walkinge West** (...)
l) **Sir Thomas Knollys** (1558 – ca.Aug 1596)
m) **Catherine Knollys** (1559 – ...)
=1 1578; ♦**Gerald, Lord Garrat** (1559 – 1580)
=2 aft.1580; **Sir Philip Boteler** (1560 – Jan 1592) son of
Sir Philip Boteler & Anne Conningsby
issue of 1st:
Children are listed with other parent
issue of 2nd:
(I) **Sir John Boteler, KB** (bap.10 Dec 1587 – Feb 1653/4) KB
1626
= bef. 1624; **Anne Spencer** (... – Nov 1638) daughter of Sir
Richard Spencer
(A) **Philip Boteler** (1627 – ...)
= ...; **Elizabeth Landham** (ca.1630 – ...)
(1) **Anne Boteler** (1658 – 1692)
= ...; **Lionel Copley** (1648 – 12 Sep 1693 in MD)
Gov. of Maryland 1692–93
(a) **Lionel Copley** (16 Jul 1677 – ...)
= ...; **Mary Wilson** (...)
issue ?
2) **Henry Carey, 1st Baron Hunsdon KG** (4 Mar 1525 – 23
Jul 1596 London) cr. Baron 13 Jan 1558/9; KG 1561
= 21 May 1545; **Ann Morgan** (1529 – 19 Jan 1607/8) daughter
of Sir Thomas Morgan & Anne Whitney
a) **Hon. Katherine Carey** (1547 – 25 Feb 1603)
= Jul 1563; **Charles Howard, 1st Earl of Nottingham** 2nd
Baron Howard **KG** (ca.1536 – 14 Dec 1624) son of William
Howard, 1st Baron Howard & Margaret Gamage; =2nd Lady
Margaret Stuart; suc. father 21 Jan 157283; cr. Earl 22 Oct
1596; KG 1574
(I) **Lady Elizabeth Howard** (... – Jan 1646)
=1 bef.1599; ♦**Sir Robert Southwell** (...–1599)
=2 1604; ♦**John Stewart, Earl of Carrick** (...–ca.1644)
issue of 1st:
Children are listed with other parent
issue of 2nd:
Children are listed with other parent
(II) **Lady Frances Howard** (bef.1572 – 7 Jul 1628)
=1 1590; ♦**Henry Fitzgerald, 12th Earl of Kildare**
(1562–1597)
=2 27 May 1601; **Henry Brooke, 11th Baron Cobham** (22
Nov 1564 – 24 Jan 1618/9 London) son of William Brooke,
10th Baron Cobham & Frances Newton
issue of 1st (none by 2nd):

Children are listed with other parent

(III) **William Howard, 3ʳᵈ Baron Howard** (27 Dec 1577 –
28 Nov 1615) suc. father during his lifetime
= 7 Feb 1596/7; **Hon. Anne St.John** (... – 7 Jun 1638)
daughter of John St.John, 2ⁿᵈ Baron Saint John of Bletso &
Catherine Dormer

(A) **Hon. Elizabeth Howard** (19 Jan 1602/3 – 15 Nov
1671)
= 1621; ◆**John Mordaunt, 1ˢᵗ Earl of Peterboroough**
(1599–1644)
Children are listed with other parent

(IV) **Charles Howard, 2ⁿᵈ Earl of Nottingham** etc. (17
Sep 1579 – 3 Oct 1642) suc. father 1624
=1 19 May 1597; **Charity Whit** (...) daughter of Robert
Whit; =1ˢᵗ William Leche
=2 22 Apr 1620; **Mary Cokayne** (... – 6 Feb 1650/1)
daughter of Sir William Cokayne & Mary Morris
no issue

b) **George Carey, 2ⁿᵈ Baron Hunsdon KG** (bef.1556 – 8
Sep 1603) suc. father 1596; KG 1597
= 29 Dec 1574; **Elizabeth Spencer** (29 Jun 1552
Althorp, Northants. – 25 Feb 1618) daughter of John Spencer
& Katherine Kitson; =2ⁿᵈ Ralph Eure, 3ʳᵈ Baron Eure

(I) **Hon. Elizabeth Carey** (24 May 1576 – 23 Apr 1635)
= 1595; ◆**Sir Thomas Berkeley** (1575 – 1611)
Children are listed with other parent

c) **John Carey, 3ʳᵈ Baron Hunsdon** (ca.1556 – 4 Apr
1617 Hunsdon, Herts.) suc. brother 1603
= 20 Dec 1576 Little Chester, Essex; **Mary Hyde** (... – 4
Apr 1627) daughter of Leonard Hyde; =1ˢᵗ Richard Peyton

(I) **Hon. Anne Carey** (...)
= ...; **Sir Francis Lovell** (...) son of Thomas Lovell &
Alice Huddleston
issue ?

(II) **Hon. Charles Carey** (1578 Hunsdon – bef.Apr 1617)

(III) **Henry Carey, 1ˢᵗ Earl of Dover**, Viscount Rochford, 4ᵗʰ
Baron Hunsdon, **KB** (ca.1580 – Apr 1666 Hunsdon) KB 1610;
suc. father 1617; cr. Viscount 6 Jul 1621 and Earl 8 Mar 1627/8
=1 bef.1608; **Judith Pelham** (21 Jun 1590 Laughton, Sussex –
Oct 1629) daughter of Sir Thomas Pelham, 1ˢᵗ Baronet & Mary
Walsingham
=2 6 Jul 1630 London; **Mary Morris** (10 May 1573 London – 8
Jan 1648/9 Kingston, Surrey) daughter of Richard Morris &
Maude Daborne; =1ˢᵗ Sir William Cokayne
issue of 1ˢᵗ (none by 2ⁿᵈ):

(A) **John Carey, 2ⁿᵈ Earl of Dover**, etc. **KB** (ca.1608 –

26 May 1677) suc. father 1666, but the Earldom and
Viscountcy became extinct upon his death
=1 9 May 1628; ♦**Lady Dorothy St.John** (... – 28 Jun 1628)
daughter of Oliver St.John, 1st Earl of Bolingbroke & Elizabeth
Paulet
=2 2 Dec 1630 London; (his step-sister) **Abigail
Cokayne** (26 Aug 1610 London – 10 Feb 1687/8
London) daughter of Sir William Cokayne & Mary Morris
issue of 2nd (none by 1st):
(1) **Lady Mary Carey** (6 Oct 1631 – 19 Jan 1695/6 London)
  = 25 Apr 1655; **William Heveningham** (... – 20 Feb 1677)
  (a) **Abigail Heveningham** (... – 11 May 1686)
    = 22 Jun 1676 London; **Sir John Newton, 3rd Baronet**
    (ca.1651 – 12 Feb 1733/4) son of Sir John Newton, 2nd
    Baronet & Mary Eyre; =2nd Susanna Wharton; suc. father
    31 May 1699
    Has further generations of issue
(B) **Hon. Sir Pelham Carey** (ca.1612 – ...)
= ...; **Mary Jackson** (1609 – 1680) daughter of Sir John
Jackson; =2nd George Peyler
no issue
(C) **Lady Mary Carey** (1615 – 1672)
= ...; ♦**Thomas Wharton** (1615 – 1684)
Children are listed with other parent
(IV) **Hon. Blanche Carey** (... – 6 Nov 1651)
=1 bef.1605; **Christopher Peyton** (... – bef.1605)
=2 16 Jun 1605; **Sir Thomas Wodehouse, 2nd Baronet**
(... – 18 Mar 1658) son of Sir Philip Wodehouse, 1st
Baronet & Grizell Yelverton; suc. father 30 Oct 1623
issue of 2nd (none by 1st):
(A) **Jane Wodehouse** (...)
  = ...; **Sir Hugh Wyndham** (1602 – 1684)
  (1) **Rachael Wyndham** (ca.1645 – 16 Feb 1708/9)
    = Aug 1663; ♦**John Digby, 3rd Eal of Bristol** , etc.
    (ca.1635 – 18 Sep 1698) son of George Digby, 2nd
    Earl of Bristol & Lady Anne Russell; =1st Alice
    Bourne; suc. father 20 Mat 1676/7
    no isue
(B) **Sir Philip Wodehouse, 3rd Baronet** (24 Jul 1608 –
6 May 1681) suc. father 1658
= 10 Jul 1634 Lambeth, Surrey; ♦**Lucy Cotton** (... – 26 Jun
1684) daughter of Sir Thomas Cotton, 2nd Baronet & Margaret
Howard
  (1) **Blanche Wodehouse** (...)
    = 6 Feb 1661 Kimberley, Norfolk; **Sir Jacob Astley,
    1st Baronet** (ca.1639 – 17 Aug 1729) son of Edward

Astley & Elizabeth Astley; cr. Baronet 26 Jun 1660

(a) **Jacob Astley** (ca.1665 – 9 Jun 1681 Oxford)

(b) **Sir Philip Astley, 2ⁿᵈ Baronet** (20 Jul 1667 – 7 Jul 1739) suc. father 1729
    = 2 Dec 1690 London; **Elizabeth Bransby** (ca.1672 – 30 Mar 1738) daughter of Thomas Bransby & Elizabeth ...
    Has issue by 1ˢᵗ born after 1700

(2) **Sir Thomas Wodehouse** (... – 29Apr 1671) Kt.1663
    = ...; **Anne Armyne** (1652 – 1719) daughter of Sir William Armyne, 1ˢᵗ Baronet & Anne Crane; =2ⁿᵈ Thomas Crew, 2ⁿᵈ Baron Crew; =3ʳᵈ Arthur Herbert, 1ˢᵗ Earl of Torrington

    (a) **Sir John Wodehouse, 4ᵗʰ Baronet** (23 Mar 1669 – 6 Aug 1764) suc. grandfather 1681
        =1 17 Jun 1700; **Elizabeth Benson** (... – 5 Jan 1700/1) daughter of Robert Benson & Doroty Jenkins
        =2 ...; **Hon. Mary Fermor** (... – 24 Oct 1729) daughter of William Fermor, 1ˢᵗ Baron Leominster
        Has further generations of issue

    (b) **Anne Wodehouse** (... – 1727)
        = 2 Dec 1685; **Sir Nicholas le Strange, 4ᵗʰ Baronet** (2 Dec 1661 – 18 Dec 1724) son of Sir Nicholas le Strange, 3ʳᵈ Baronet & Mary Coke; suc. father 13 Dec1669
        Has further generations of issue

(3) **Edmond Wodehouse** (... – 5 Sep 1727)
    =1 ...; **Mercy Parker** (...) daughter of Sir Philip Parker; she =1ˢᵗ William Guybon
    =2 ...; **Anne Anguish** (...) daughter of John Anguish
    issue of 1ˢᵗ (none by 2ⁿᵈ):

    (a) **Lucy Wodehouse** (...)
        = ...; ♦**Lewis Monoux** (...)
        see: below

(4) **John Wodehouse** (...)
    = ...; ♦**Anne Strutt** (...) daughter of Sir Denner Strutt, Baronet & Elizabeth Wodehouse; =1ˢᵗ William Samwell
    issue ?

(5) **Margaret Wodehouse** (1646 Kimberley – ...)
    = ...; **Thomas Savage** (1644 Elmley Castle, Worcs. – 1694 Elmley Castle) son of Thomas Savage & Mary Hare

    (a) **Thomas Savage** (ca.1669 Elmley Castle – 22 Apr 1694 Elmely Castle)

    (b) **Anne Savage** (1671 Elmley Castle – ...)

    (c) **Lucy Savage** (ca.1673 Elmley Castle – ...)

    (d) **Jane Savage** (ca.1675 Elmley Vastle – ...)

(C) **Grizzel Wodehouse** (14 Jan 1609 – ...)
(D) **Mary Wodehouse** (...)
  = ...; **Sir Humphrey Monoux, 1ˢᵗ Baronet** (... –
  1676) cr. Baronet 4 Dec 1660
  (1) **Sir Humphrey Monoux, 2ⁿᵈ Baronet** (1640 –
    1685) suc. father 1676
    = ...
    (a) **Sir Philip Monoux, 3ʳᵈ Baronet** (1679 – 1707)
      suc. father 1685
      = ...; **Dorothy Harvey** (...) daughter of William Harvey
      & Dorothy Dycer
      Has further generations of issue
    (b) **Frances Monoux** (...)
      = ...; **Sir Edward Gould** (... – 1728) son of James
      Gould & Catherine Westcombe
      no issue
    (c) **Alice Monoux** (1670 – 1749)
      = ...; **Sir John Cope, 6ᵗʰ Baronet** (1673 – 1749)
      son of Sir John Cope, 5ᵗʰ Baronet; suc. father 1721
      Has further generations of issue
  (2) **Lewis Monoux** (...)
    = ...; ♦**Lucy Wodehouse** (...) daughter of Edmond
    Wodehouse & Mary Mercy
    (a) **Humphrey Monoux** (...)
      = ...; **Mary Savage** (...) daughter of Thomas Savage &
      Elizabeth Grimes
      Has further generations of issue
    (b) **Lewis Monoux** (...)
      = ...
      Has further generations of issue
(E) **Anne Wodehouse** (ca.1617 – 1 Jun 1653)
  = 16 Jan 1633 Norwich, Norfolk; **Robert Suckling** (25 May
  1602 Woodten Hall, Norfolk – 2 Jul 1689 Wotton, Norfolk)
  son of Charles Suckling & Mary Drury; =2ⁿᵈ ♦Margaret
  D'Oyley
  (1) **Charles Suckling** (... – 28 Apr 1673)
  (2) **Blanche Suckling** (...)
  (3) **Anne Suckling** (ca.1638 – 24 Oct 1662)
    = 23 Apr 1660 Woodton; **Augustine Scottow** (...)
    issue ?
  (4) **Elizabeth Suckling** (ca.1639 – ...)
    = 10 Jul 1667 Woodton; **Abraham Castell** (...)
    issue ?
  (5) **Robert Suckling** (1641 Woodton – 30 Nov 1707
    Woodton)
    = 16 Nov 1669 Barningham, Suffolk; **Sarah**

Shelton (... – 5 Nov 1695 Woodton) daughter of
Maurice Shelton & Elizabeth Kemp

(a) **Elizabeth Suckling** (7 Jan 1670 Woodton – ...)
= 21 Aug 1692 Woodton; **John Mathews** (...)
issue ?

(b) **Mary Suckling** (28 May 1672 Barsham, Suffolk –...)
= 10 Nov 1734 Woodton; **Robert Howman** (...)
no issue

(c) **Robert Suckling** (10 Jun 1673 Woodton – 23 Mar 1732)

(d) **Shelton Suckling** (1675 – ...)

(e) **Rev. Maurice Suckling** (1676 Woodton – 21 Sep 1730)
= 1723; **Marianne Turner** (1691 – 5 Jul 1768) daughter
of Sir Charles Turner, 1st Baronet & Mary Walpole
Has further generations of issue

(f) **Charles Suckling** (28 Apr 1677 Woodton – 8 Oct 1727)

(g) **Sarah Suckling** (1 Apr 1678 Woodton – 13 Sep 1711
Woodton)

(h) **Anne Suckling** (ca.1680 – ...)
= ...; **Thomas Berney** (...) son of John Berney
issue ?

(i) **Jane Suckling** (21 Oct 1681 Norwich – ...)

(j) **Henry Suckling** (11 Dec 1683 Norwich – 25 Mar 1737
Woodton)

(k) **Edmund Suckling** (... – aft.1707)

(l) **John Suckling** (2 Apr 1689 Woodton – 3 Dec 1733)
= ...; **Anne Berney** (...) daughter of John Berney

(m) **Philip Suckling** (25 Jul 1690 Woodton – aft.1707)

(6) **Lucy Suckling** (ca.1650 – ...)

(7) **Philip Suckling** (15 Nov 1652 Woodton – 28 Jun 1679)

(F) **Elizabeth Wodehouse** (15 Apr 1621 – 6 Nov 1651)
= ...; **Sir Denner Strutt, Baronet** (...) cr. Baronet 1641, but
it became extinct upon his death

(1) **Anne Strutt** (...)
=1 ...; **William Samwell** (...)
=2 ...; ♦**John Wodehouse** (...) son of Sir Philip
Wodehouse, 3rd Baronet & Lucy Cotton
issue ?

d) **Henry Carey** (...)

e) **Sir Edmund Carey** (1558 Hunsdon – 12 Sep 1637)
=1 ...; **Mary Crocker** (... – bef.1596) daughter of Christpher
Crocker & Anne le Strange
=2 aft. 1594; ♦**Hon. Elizabeth Neville** (1545 – 21 Jun
1630) daughter of John Neville, 4th Baron Latymer & Lady
Lucy Somerset; =1st Sir John Danvers
=3 aft.Jun 1630; **Judith Humphrey** (...) daughter of Dr.
Lawrence Humphrey

issue of 1st (non by others):

(I) **Sir Robert Carey** (21 Mar 1582/3 – ...)
= ...in the Netherlands; **Aletta van Hogenhove** (...)

  (A) **Sir Horatio Carey** (1619 – aft.1652)
  = ...; **Pernel Harrington** (...) daughter of Robert
  Harrington

    (1) **Robert Carey, 6ᵗʰ Baron Hunsdon** (bef.1652 –
    1692 La Hogue, Normandy, France) suc. 2ⁿᵈ Earl of
    Dover as Baron 1677
    = aft.1659; ♦**Margaret Clifton** (... – Feb 1697/8) daughter
    of Sir Gervase Clifton, 1ˢᵗ Baronet & Lady Frances Clifford;
    she =1ˢᵗ Sir John South; =2ⁿᵈ Sir William Whichcote
    no issue

  (B) **Ernestus Carey** (1621 – 1680)
  = ...; **St.John Salveyn** (... – 1649) daughter Thomas Salveyn

    (1) **Robert Carey, 7ᵗʰ Baron Hunsdon** (bef.1649 –
    11 Sep 1702) unm.; suc. cousin 1692

  (C) **Ferdinando Carey** (1625 – 1662)
  = ...; **Isabella Oem** (ca.1635 – 22 Dec 1701 Venlo,
  Netherlands)

    (1) **William Carey** (... – 7 Nov 1683)
    = ...; **Gertrude de Vlaming van Oudsthoorn** (14 Jun
    1658 The Hague – 26 Jun 1688 Amsterdam) daughter of
    Cornelius de Vlaming van Oudsthoorn & Claesje Hooft

      (a) **William** Ferdinand **Carey, 8ᵗʰ Baron Hunsdon** (14
      Jan 1684 Maastricht, Netherlands – 12 Jun 1765) suc.
      cousin 1702, but barony went extinct upon his death
      = 11 Jan 1717/8 London; **Grace Waldo** (ca.1683 – 9 May
      1729) daughter of Sir Edward Waldo & Elizabeth
      Shuckburgh; =1ˢᵗ Sir Nicholas Wolstonholme
      no issue

(II) **Catherine Carey** (...)
= ...; **Francis Rogers** (...)
issue ?

(III) **Anne Carey** (...)
= ...; **Sir William Uvedale** (ca.1581 – 1652) son of William
Uvedale & Mary Norton; Kt.1613; =2ⁿᵈ ♦Victoria Carey
issue ?

(IV) **Sir Ferdinando Carey** (1 Feb 1590 Hunsdon – 1663
Maastricht)
= ...; **Philippa Throckmorton** (...) daughter of John
Throckmorton & Dorothy Saunders

  (A) **Mary Carey** (... – ca.Dec 1695)
  = aft.1659; **Sir Alexander Fraser, 1ˢᵗ Baronet** (ca.1607 –
  28 Apr 1681 London) son of Adam Fraser; cr. Baronet 2 Aug
  1673

     (1) **Carey Fraser** (1660 – 13 May 1709)

     = 1678; ◆**Charles Mordaunt, 3rd Earl of Peterborough** (1658 – 1735)

     Children are listed with other parent

     (2) **Sir Peter Fraser, 2nd Baronet** (... – 1729) unm.; suc. father 1681, but baronetcy became extinct upon his death

    (B) **Philadelphia Carey** (... – 4 May 1696)

    = 1657/8; ◆**Thomas Wentworth, 5th Baron Wentworth** (1613 – 1665)

    Children are listed with other parent

    (C) **Elizabeth Carey** (...)

    =1 ...; **Francis Staunton** (...)

    =2 ...; **Sir Thomas Fortescue** (ca.1620 – 1710) son of Sir Faithful Fortescue & Hon. Anne Moore; =1st Sydney Kingsmill issue of 1st (none by 2nd):

     (1) **Philippa Staunton** (1640 – 5 Aug 1723 Utrecht, Netherlands)

     = 21 Apr 1660; **Roelof van Arkel, Lord van Broekhuizen** (1632 – 16 May 1709)

      (a) **Carel** Justis **Roelof van Arkel, Lord van Burgst** (23 Jul 1688 Doorn, Netherlands – 28 Dec 1767 Doorn)

      = 20 Dec 1711 Rhenen, Netherlands; **Constantia** Isabell **Smissaert** (5 Dec 1682 The Hague – 1731 Doorn)

      Has further generations of issue

    (D) **Sir Edmund Carey** (...)

    = ...; **Ann Gerard** (...)

     (1) **Charlotte Carey** (...)

     = ...; **Brian Fairfax** (...)

     issue ?

    (E) **Aletta Carey** (...)

    = 29 Nov 1650; **Sir Gelyn Quirijnssen** (...) Kt. 1655

    issue ?

    (F) **Dorothy Carey** (...)

    = ...; **Thomas Throckmorton** (...)

    issue ?

    (G) **Simonia Carey** (...)

    = ...; **Bernard Skelton** (...)

    issue ?

f) **Robert Carey, 1st Earl of Monmouth**, Baron Carey (1560 – 12 Apr 1639) cr. Baron 6 Feb 1621/2 and Earl 5 Feb 1625/6

= 20 Aug 1593; **Elizabeth Trevannion** (...) daughter of Sir Hugh Trevannion & Sybilla Morgan

    (I) **Henry Carey, 2nd Earl of Monmouth**, etc. KB (27 Jan 1595/6 Denham, Bucks. – 1661) KB 1616; suc. father 1639, but titles became extinct upon his death

    = 1620; **Lady Martha Cranfield** (...) daughter of Lionel

Cranfield, 1st Earl of Middlesex & Elizabeth Shepherd
(A) **Lionel, Lord Carey** (ca.1622 – bef. 1649)
(B) **Henry, Lord Carey** (1623 – 5 Nov 1649)
 = ...; **Mary le Scrope** (bef.1630 – 1 Nov 1680
 Moulins, France) illeg. daughter of Emmanuel Scrope, 1st
 Earl of Sunderland & Martha Jeanes; =2nd Charles
 Powlett, 1st Duke of Bolton
 (1) a daughter
(C) **Lady Anne Carey** (ca.1626 – 15 Jan 1688/9)
 =1 23 Sep 1641 **James Hamilton, 1st Earl of Clanbrassill**,
 2nd Viscount Claneboye (... – 20 Jun 1659) son of James
 Hamilton, 1st Viscount of Claneboye & Janes Philipps; suc.
 father 1644; cr. Earl 7 Jun 1647
 =2 1668; **Sir Robert Maxwell of Orchardtoun, 2nd
 Baronet** (... – 1693) son of Sir Robert Maxwell of
 Orchardtoun, 1st Baronet & Anne Maclellan; suc.
 father bef.1673
 issue of 1st (none by 2nd):
 (1) **James Hamilton, 2nd Earl of Clanbrassill**, etc.
  (ca.1647 – 12 Jan 1675) suc. father 1659, but his titls
  became extinct upon his death
  = May 1667; ◆**Lady Alice Moore** (... – 25 Dec 1677 Dublin)
  daughter of Henry Moore, 1st Earl of Drogheda & Hon. Alice
  Spencer; =2nd John Hamilton, 2nd Lord Bargeny
  no surviving issue
(D) **Lady Elizabeth Carey** (ca.1630 – 14 Dec 1676)
(E) **Lady Mary Carey** (ca.1632 – 9 Dec 1719)
 = ...; **Wiliam Fielding, 3rd Earl of Denbigh**, Baron of
 Newnham Paddockes, 2nd Baron St.Liz, 2nd Viscount
 Callan, Baron Fielding (29 Dec 1640 – 23 Aug 1685)
 son of George Fielding, Earl of Desmond & Bridget Stanhope;
 he =1st Mary King; suc. uncle as Earl, etc. 28 Nov 1675 and
 father as Viscount etc. 31 Jan 1665
 no issue
(F) **Lady Martha Carey** (ca.1635 – 23 Jan 1705)
 = ...; **John Middleton, 1st Earl of Middleton**
 (ca.1608 – 3 Jul 1674 Tangiers, Morocco) son of
 Robert Middleton & Helen Strachan; =1st Grizel
 Durham; cr. Earl 1656
 (1) **Lady Elizabeth Middleton** (1672 – 1748)
  = ...; **William Spelman** (...)
  issue ?
(II) **Lady Philiadelphia Carey** (...)
 = 1611; ◆**Hon. Sir Thomas Wharton** (1588 – 1622)
 Children are listed with other parent
(III) **Hon. Thomas Carey** (1616 – 1649)

= ...; **Margaret Smith** (... – aft.1648) daughter of Sir
Thomas Smith; =2nd Edward Herbert
(A) **Philadelphia Carey** (... – 2 Aug 1663)
  = bef.1663; ♦**Sir Henry Lyttleton, 2nd Baronet** (... –
24 Jun 1693) son of Sir Thomas Lyttleton, 1st Baronet
& Catherine Crompton; =2nd Lady Elizabeth Newport;
suc. father 22 Feb 1649/50
no issue
(B) **Elizabeth Carey** (ca.1632 – 5 Apr 1679)
  = 1656; ♦**John Mordaunt, 1st Viscount Mordaunt**
(1626 – 1675)
Children are listed with other parent
g) **Philadelphia Carey** (... – 3 Feb 1626/7)
= 1584; ♦**Thomas Scrope, 10th Baron Scrope** (1567 –
1609)
Children are listed with other parent
h) **Margaret Carey** (... – 1605)
= ...; **Sir Edward Hoby** (...) son of Sir Thomas Hoby &
Elizabeth Cooke
issue ?
issue by **Emilia Lanier** (1569 – 1645):
i) **Henry Lanier** (1592 – ...)
issue by ...
j) **Very Rev. Valentine Carey** (... – 1626) Bishop of Exeter
D) **Margaret Carey** (1496 – 1560)
E) **Edward Carey** (1498 – 1560)
F) **Mary Carey** (1501 – 1560)
= ...; **John Delaval** (1493 – 1562)
issue ?
b. **Lady Elizabeth Beaufort** (... – bef.1472)
= ...; **Sir Henry FitzLewis** (...)
I) **Mary FitzLewis** (ca.1465 – aft.1488)
= aft.1473; **Anthony Woodville, 2nd Earl Rivers** (ca. 1440 –
25 Jun 1483) son of Richard Woodville, 1st Earl Rivers &
Jacquetta of Luxembourg; =1st Elizabeth Scales, 8th Baroness
Scales; suc. father 12 Aug 1469
no issue
c. **Henry Beaufort, 2nd Duke of Somerset** etc. (26 Jan 1435/6 –
15 May 1464 Hexham, Northumberland) executed; suc. father
22 May 1456
issue by **Joan Hill** (...):
I) **Charles Somerset, 1st Earl of Worcester KG** (ca.1460 – 15
Apr 1526 Windsor) KG 1498; cr. Earl 1 Feb 1513/4
=1 2 Jun 1492; **Elizabeth Herbert, (3rd) Baroness Herbert**
(ca.1476 – bef. 21 Mar 1513) daughter of William Herbert, 3rd
Earl of Pembroke & Mary Wydeville; suc. father 16 Jul 1491

=2 aft.1513; **Elizabeth West** (...) daughter of Thomas West,
8th Baron la Warre & Elizabeth Mortimer

=3 aft.1514; **Eleanor Sutton** (... – bef.1549) daughter of
Edward Sutton, 2nd Baron Dudley & Cicely Willoughby; =2nd
Leonard Gray, 1st Viscount Grane

issue of 1st:

A) **Henry Somerset, 2nd Earl of Worcester, 4th Baron
Herbert** (ca.1496 – 26 Nov 1549 Monmouthshire, Wales
suc. mother bef.1513; suc. father 15 Apr 1526

=1 ca.15 Jun 1514; ♦**Lady Margaret Courtenay** (ca.1499 –
bef.15 Apr 1526) daughter of William Courtenay & Princess
Catherine of England

=2 bef.1527; **Elizabeth Browne** (... – 1565) daughter of Air
Anthony Browne & Lady Lucy Neville

issue of 2nd (none by 1st):

1) **Lady Lucy Somerset** (1524 – 23 Feb 1583)
   = ca.1545; ♦**John Neville, 4th Baron Latymer** (1520 – 1577)
   see:

2) **William Somerset, 3rd Earl of Worcester**, etc. KG (ca.
   1527 – 21 Feb 1588/9 London) suc. father 26 Nov 1549; KG 1570
   =1 bef.19 May 1550; **Christian North** (... – aft.20 Mar
   1563/4) daughter of Edward North, 1st Baron North & Alice Squire
   =2 aft. 1564; **Theophilia Newton** (... – aft.1589) daughter
   of Sir John Newton & Margaret Poyntz; =2nd William Paratt

   issue of 1st (none by 2nd):

   a) **Edward Somerset, 4th Earl of Worcester**, etc. KG(ca.
      1550 – 3 Mar 1627/8 London) suc. father 21 Feb 1588/9; KG 1593
      = Dec 1571; **Lady Elizabeth Hastings** (1546 – 24 Aug
      1621 London) daughter of Francis Hastings, 2nd Earl
      Huntingdon & Catherine Pole

      (I) **Lady Katherine Somerset** (ca.1575 – 30 Oct 1624)
          = 8 Nov 1596; **William Petre, 2nd Baron Petre** (24 Jun 1575
          West Horndon, Essex – 1637 West Horndon) son of John Petre,
          1st Baron Petre & Mary Waldegrave; Kt,1603; suc. father 11 Oct
          1613

          (A) **Hon. Elizabeth Petre** (1597– 1657)
              = 1611; **William Sheldon** (ca.1589 Beoley, Worcs. –
              1659) son of Edward Sheldon & Elizabeth Markham

              (1) **Ralph Sheldon** (1 Aug 1623 Beoley – 24 Jun
                  1684 Weston, Warks.)
                  = 1647; ♦**Hon. Henrietta Maria Savage** (... –
                  1663) daughter of Thomas Savage, 1st Viscount Savage
                  & Elizabeth Darcy, Countess Rivers
                  no issue

          (B) **Robert Petre, 3rd Baron Petre** (22 Sep 1599
              Ingatestone, Essex – 23 Oct 1638) suc. father 1637

= 1620; **Hon. Mary Browne** (ca.1603 – 13 Jan 1684/5) daughter of Anthony Browne, 2nd Viscount Montagu & Jane Sackville

(1) **Hon. Mary Petre** (1624 – 1672)
= 1638; ♦**Hon. Edward Stourton** (1617 – 1644)
Children are listed with other parent

(2) **William Petre, 4th Baron Petre** (ca.1626 – 5 Jan 1683/4 Tower of London) died a prisoner; suc. father 1638
=1 ...; ♦**Lady Elizabeth Savage** (... – Jul 1665) daughter of John Savage, 2nd Earl Savage & Catherine Parker
=2 bef.15 Apr 1675; **Bridget Pincheon** (1652 – 1695) daughter of John Pincheon & Anne Kynnion issue of 2nd (none by 1st):

  (a) **Hon. Mary Petre** (25 Mar 1679 – Jun 1704)
  = 1696; **George Heneage** (3 Aug 1674 – 31 Dec 1731) son of George Heneage & Mary Kemp; =2nd Elizabeth Hemloke
  Has further generations of issue

(3) **John Petre, 5th Baron Petre** (24 Jun 1629 – 22 Jan 1684/5) unm.; suc. brother 1683

(4) **Thomas Petre, 6th Baron Petre** (5 Dec 1633 – 4 Jan 1706/7) suc. brother 1685
= ...; **Mary Clifton** (...) daughter of Sir Thomas Clifton, Baronet

  (a) **Robert Petre, 7th Petre** (17 Mar 1689/90 – 22 Mar 1713/4) suc. father 1707
  = 1 Mar 1711/2; **Catherine Walmsley** (... – 31 Jan 1785) daughter of Bartholomew Walmesley;=2nd
  ♦Charles Stourton, 15th Baron Stourton
  Has further generations of issue

(5) **Hon. Dorothy Petre** (...)
= ...; **John Thimbelby** (...)'son of Sir John Thimbelby
no issue

(C) **Hon. Mary Petre** (ca.1600 – 14 Oct 1640)
= 20 Nov 1616; **Sir John Roper, KB** (ca.1591 – 27 Feb 1627) son of Sir Christopher, 2nd Baron Teynham & Catherine Seborne; KB 1616

(1) **Christopher Roper, 4th Baron Teynham** (20 Apr 1621 – 23 Oct 1673) suc. uncle 1628
=1 1640; **Mary Englefield** (... – 1 Dec 1647) daughter of Sir Francis Englefield, 1st Baronet & Jane Browne
=2 ...; **Philadelphia Knollys** (ca.1621 – Nov 1655) daughter of Sir Henry Knollys; =1st Sir John Mill

=3 ...; **Margaret FitzMaurice** (...)
issue of 2nd (none by others):
  (a) **Christopher Roper, 5th Baron Teynham** (... –
  24 July 1689) suc. father 1673
    = 1674; ♦**Hon. Elizabeth Browne** (... – aft.1686)
    daughter of Francis Browne, 3rd Viscount Mantagu &
    Lady Elizabeth Somerset
    Has issue by 1st and 3rd born after 1700
  (2) **Hon. Elizabeth Roper** (...)
  = ...; **Sir John Arundell** (... – 1701) son of Sir John
  Arundell & Elizabeth Brocke; =2nd Anne Aundell
    (a) **Elizabeth Arundell** (1655 – 1690)
    = ...; **Sir Henry Bedingfield, 2nd Baronet** (1636 –
    1704) son of Sir Henry Bedingfield, 1st Baronet &
    Margaret Paston; =2nd ♦Anne Howard
    Has further generations of issue
    (b) **Frances Arundell** (...)
    = ...; **Sir Richard Bellings** (ca.1622 – 30 Oct
    1716) son of Richard Bellings & Margaret Butler
    Has further generations of issue
(D) **Hon. William Petre** (1601 – 1677)
(E) **Hon. Thomas Petre** (1605 – ...)
(F) **Hon. Edward Petre** (1603 – 1664)
(G) **Hon. Catherine Petre** (1607 – 1681)
  = ...; **Sir John Caryll** (1603 – 1679) son of John
  Caryll & Hon. Mary Dormer
  (1) **John Caryll** (2 Nov 1626 Harting, Sussex – 4 Sep
  1711 St.Germain-en-Laye, France) cr. Baron Caryll
  in the Jacobite Peerage, with remainder to brother.
    = ...; **Margaret Drummond** (... – 1656)
    no issue
  (2) **Robert Caryll** (...)
    = ...
    (a) **John Caryll** (...)
  (3) **Philip Caryll** (1642 – 1688)
    = ...; **Mary Erle** (1646 – 1685)
    (a) **John Caryll** (1680 – 1742 Rusper, Surrey)
    = ...; **Jane Stone** (1680 – ...)
    Has further generations of issue
(H) **Hon. John Petre** (1608 – 1696)
=1 ...; **Elizabeth Pordage** (... – 1658)
=2 aft.1658; **Elizabeth Pincheon** (... – aft.1671)
=3 aft.1671; **Frances White** (1632 – 1711) daughter of
Richard White & Lady Catherine Weston
issue of 1st:
(1) **John Petre** (...)

= ...; **Mary Mannock** (...)
   (a) **Joseph Petre** (bef.1746 – 1721)
   = ...; **Catherine Andrews** (...)
   Has further generations of issue
issue of 2nd (none by 3rd):
   (2) **Benjamin Petre** (10 Aug 1672 – 22 Dec 1758)
(I) **Hon. Henry Petre** (27 Mar 1611 – 1648)
(J) **Hon. George Petre** (1613 – 26 Feb 1649)
= ...; **Anne Fox** (...) daughter of Henry Fox & Mary Gage;
she =1st John Mostyn
issue ?
(II) **Henry Somerset, 1st Marquess of Worcester, 5th
Earl of Worcester**, etc. (ca.1576/7 – 18 Dec 1646
London) died under while in custody of
Parliamentarians; suc. father 3 Mar 1627/8; cr.
Marquess 2 Mar 1642/3
= 16 Jun 1600 Ludgate; **Hon. Anne Russell** (... – 8 Apr
1639 London) daughter of John Russell, 3rd Baron
Russell & Elizabeth Cooke
(A) **Edward Somerset, 2nd Marquess of Worcester**,
   etc. (ca.9 Mar 1302/3 Raglan Castle, Monmouth – 3
   Apr 1667 London) suc. father 18 Dec 1646
   =1 ca.1628; **Elizabeth Dormer** (... – 31 May 1635
   London) daughter of Sir William Dormer & Alice ...
   =2 Aug 1639; ♦**Lady Margaret O'Brien** (... – 26 Jul
   1681) daughter of Henry O'Brien, 4th Earl of
   Thomond & Mary Brereton; =2nd Donogh Kearney
   issue of 1st (none surviving by 2nd):
   (1) **Henry Somerset, 1st Duke of Beaufort, 3rd
     Marquess of Worcester**, etc. KG (ca.1629 – 21 Jan
     1699/ 1700 Badminton, Glos.) suc. father 3 Apr
     1667; KG 1672; cr. Duke 2 Dec 1682
     = 17 Aug 1657; ♦**Hon. Mary Capell** (bap.16 Dec
     1630 Hadham Parva, Herts. – 7 Jan 1714/5 London)
     daughter of Arthur Capell, 1st Baron Capell &
     Elizabeth Morrison; =1st ♦Henry, Lord Beauchamp
     (a) **Charles, Marquess of Worcester** (25 Dec 1660
       London – 13 Jul 1698 in Wales) killed ion a
       carriage accident
       = 5 Jun 1682 Wanstead, Essex; **Rebecca Child**
       (ca.1666 – 17 Jul 1712) daughter of Sir Josiah
       Child, 1st Baronet & Mary Atwood; =2nd John
       Granville, Baron Granville of Potheridge

Has further generations of issue[42]
(b) **Lord Arthur Somerset** (aft.1661 – ...)
= ...; **Mary Russell** (...) daughter of Sir William
Russell, Baronet & Hester Rouse; =1st Hugh Cotton
Has further generations of issue
(c) **Lady Mary Somerset** (1664 – 19 Nov 1733)
= 3 Aug 1685 Great Badminton, Glos.; **James Butler, 2nd
Duke of Ormonde**, Marquess of Ormonde, Earl of
Brecknock, Baron Butler, 13th Earl of Ormonde, 5th
Viscount Thurles, 7th Earl of Ossory, 3rd Lord Dingwall, **KG**
(29 Apr 1665 – 16 Nov 1745) son of Thomas Butler, 6th Earl
of Ossory & Lady Amelia de Nassau; =1st Lady Anne Hyde;
KG aft.1688; suc. father 30 Jul 1680; suc. grandmother as
Lord Dingwall 21 Jul 1684, and grandfather to the
remainder of the titles 21 Jul 1688
Has further generations of issue, but extinct in 1750
(d) **Lady Henrietta Somerset** (ca.1669/70 – 10 Aug
1715 Audley End, Essex)
=1 1686; ♦**Henry, Lord O'Brien** (1670 – 1690)
=2 1 May 1705; ♦**Henry Howard, 6th Earl of
Suffolk, 1st Earl of Bindon,** Baron Chesterford
(ca.1670 – 19 Sep 1719) son of Henry Howard, 5th
Earl of Suffolk & Mary Stewart; =1st Lady Auberie
O'Brien; suc. father 10 Dec 1709; cr. Earl of
Bindon 30 Dec 1706
issue by 1st (none by 2nd):
Children are listed with other parent
(e) **Lady Anne Somerset** (22 Jul 1673 – 17 Feb
1763 Snitterfield, Warks.)
= 4 May 1691 Badminton, Glos.; **Thomas Coventry, 2nd
Earl of Coventry**, Viscount Deerhurst, 6th Baron
Coventry (ca.1662 – Aug 1710) son of Thomas Coventry, 1st
Earl of Coventry & Winifred Edgcumbe; suc. father 15 Jul
1699
Has further generations of issue
(2) **Lady Anne Somerset** (1631 – 1662)
= 1652; ♦**Henry Howard, 6th Duke of Norfolk**
(1628 – 1684)
Beyond the 12th generation on the father's line
(3) **Lady Elizabeth Somerset** (ca.1634 – 16 MAR 1690/1)
= 1654; ♦**William Herbert, 1st Marquess of Powis**

---

[42] Charles' descendants are the only surviving male line of Plantagenet, albeit an illegitimate one.

(1626 – 1696)

Beyond the 12th generation on the father's line

(B) **(Lord) Father Thomas Somerset** (... – 30 Aug 1678 Dunkirk) a priest

(C) **Sir John Somerset** (aft.1604 – ...)
= ...; ♦**Hon. Mary Arundell** (ca.1617 – ...) daughter of Thomas Arundell, 1st Baron Arundell of Wardour & Anne Philipson

(1) **Henry Somerset** (...)
= ...; **Hon. Anne Aston** (ca.1643 – ...) daughter of Walter Aston, 2nd Lord Aston of Forhar & Mary Weston

(a) **Edward** Maria **Somerset** (bef.1670 – 1711)
=1 1690 in England; ♦**Clare Calvert** (1670 Anne Arundell Co. MD – 1694 England) daughter of Charles Calvert, 3rd Baron Baltimore & Jane Lowe
=2 1694 in England; (his sister-in-law) ♦**Anne Calvert** (1674 Anne Arundell Co. – ...) daughter of Charles Calvert, 3rd Baron Baltimore & Jane Lowe
no issue

(2) **Thomas Somerset** (... – 1671)

(3) **Charles Somerset** (...)
= ...; **Catherine Baskerville** (...) daughter of Walter Baskerville; =1st George Sawyer

(a) **Charles Somerset** (...)

(b) **Henry Somerset** (

(c) **Elizabeth Somerset** (

(d) **Mary Joanna Somerset** (... – 1697 Calvert Co. MD)
=1 ...; **... Lowther** (... – bef.1695)
=2 ca.1695 MD; **Richard Smith** (... – 1714) son of Richard Smith
issue of 2nd (none by 1st):
Has further generations of issue [43]

(D) **Lady Elizabeth Somerset** (ca.1618 – 1684)
= 1637; ♦**Francis Browne, 3rd Viscount Montagu** (1610 – 1682)
Children are listed with other parent

(III) **Thomas Somerset, 1st Viscount Somerset** (aft. 1578 – 1650) cr. Viscount 8 Dec 1626 (became extinct

---

[43] Including a great-granddaughter, Ann, who was the 2nd wife of Anthony Drane of Prince George's Co. MD. She adopted her step-son, David Drane/Drain, the great x4 grandfather of the author. The Drane family is traced to the 20th century in this author's *Legends, Half-Truths, and Cherished Myths of the Drane Family*.

upon his death)

= 1631; **Hon. Helen Barry** (...) daughter of David
Barry, 5th Viscount Barry & Ellen Roche; =1st John
Power; =2nd Thomas Ormonde, 10th Earl of Ormonde
no surviving issue

(IV) **Hon. Sir Charles Somerset, Kt.** (ca.1580 – ...)
= ...; **Elizabeth Powell** (...) daughter of Sir William Powell

(A) **Elizabeth Somerset** (... – bef.Oct 1706)
= bef.1657; **Sir Francis Anderton, 1st Baronet** (ca.
1628 – 9 Feb 1678 Paris) son of Christopher Anderton
& Aletheia Smith

  (1) **Sir Charles Anderton, 2nd Baronet** (1657 – 30
    Dec 1691) suc. father 9 Feb 1678
    = bef.1676; **Margaret Ireland** (ca.1659 – 26 Aug 1720
    London) daughter of Laurence Ireland & Anne Scarisbrick

    (a) **Sir Charles Anderton, 3rd Baronet** (... – 1705
      St.Omer, France) suc. father 30 Dec 1691; +unm.

    (b) **Sir James Anderton, 4th Baronet** (... – 5 Oct
      1710 St.Omer) suc. brother 1705; +unm.

    (c) **Brother** (Sir) **Laurence Anderton, 5th Baronet**
      (ca.1680 – 4 Oct 1724 London) a monk; suc.
      brother 5 Oct 1710

    (d) **Sir Francis Anderton, 6th Baronet** (aft.1681 –
      12 Feb 1760 Lydiate, Lancs.) suc. brother 4 Oct
      1724; upon his death, Baronetcy became extinct
      = ca.1707; **Frances Bedingfeld** (... – bef.1741)
      daughter of Sir Henry Bedingfeld, 2nd Baronet &
      Elizabeth Arundell
      no issue

(B) **Frances Somerset** (...)
= bef.1662; **Sir Henry Browne, 1st Baronet** (ca.
1639 – 1689)
Children are listed with other parent

(V) **Lady Blanche Somerset** (ca.1584 – 28 Oct 1649
Winchester, Hants.)
= 1607; ◆**Thomas Arundell, 2nd Baron Arundell of
Wardour** (1586 – 1643)
Children are listed with other parent

(VI) **Lady Catherine Somerset** (ca.1585 – ...)
= Jan 1607/8; ◆**Thomas Windsor KB, 6th Baron Windsor**
(29 Sep 1591 – 6 Dec 1642) son of Henry Windsor, 5th Baron
Windsor & Anne Revett; suc. father 6 Apr 1605; KB 1610
no issue

(VII) **Hon. Sir Edward Somerset** (ca.1588 – Mar 1629)
= ...; **Elizabeth Whitmore** (1605 – ...) daughter of Sir William
Whitmore & Margaret Beeston; =1st Hon. Thomas Savage

no issue
(VIII) **Lady Elizabeth Somerset** (ca.1590 – ...)
= ...; **Sir Henry Guildford** (...)
no issue
(IX) **Lady Frances Somerset** (ca.1596 – ...)
= ...; **Sir Edward Morgan, 1st Baronet** (1573
Llantarnam Abbey, Glamorgan, Wales – 24 Jun 1643
Glamorgan) son of William Morgan; cr. Baronet 12
May 1642; =1st Elizabeth Englefield
no issue
b) **Lady Elizabeth Somerset** (...)
= ...; **William Windsor** (...) son of William Windsor, 2nd Baron
Windsor & Margaret Sambourne
no issue
c) **Lady Lucy Somerset** (ca.1554 – Jan 1604)
= ...; **Henry Herbert** (... – Jan 1596) son of Thomas Herbert &
Anne Lucy
(I) **Lewis Herbert** (1577 – ...) (twin)
(II) **William Herbert** (1577 – ...) (twin)
(III) **Eleanor Herbert** (ca.1578 – ...)
= ...; **William Rawlins** (...)
issue ?
(IV) **Christian Herbert** (ca.1582 – 1634)
=1 ...; **William Winter** (...) son of William Winter
=2 ...; **George Milbourne** (... – 1637)
issue of 2nd (none by 1st):
(A) **Henry Milbourne** (...)
(B) **Mary Milbourne** (...)
=1 ...; **John Bonnet** (...)
=2 ...; **Charles Herbert** (... – 1662) son of Edward
Herbert & Susana Old
issue of 2nd (none by 1st):
(1) **Catherine Herbert** (... – 1692)
(2) **Margaret Herbert** (...)
(3) **Mary Herbert** (... – 1728)
(V) **Elizabeth Herbert** (1584 – 1640)
= ...; **Giles Herbert** (...)
issue ?
(VI) **Joan Herbert** (1588 – 1650)
= ...; **Henry Lewis** (... – 1637)
(A) a son (...)
= ...
(1) **Thomas Lewis** (...)
4) **Thomas Somerset** (ca.1530 – 27 May 1587 Tower of
London) unm.
5) **Francis Somerset** (bef.1532 – 22 Jul 1563 Le Havre)

killed in battle
6) **Lady Eleanor Somerset** (...)
=1 ...; **Sir Roger Vaughan** (1516 Porthami, Brecons. – 16 Jun 1571
Porthami) son of Sir William Vaughan & Catherine Havard
=2 ...; **Henry Johns** (ca.1532 Albemarles, Carmarthens. – 24 Sep
1586) son of Sir Thomas Johns & Mary Berkeley; =1st Cathine
Morgan; =3rd Elizabeth Salesbury; =4th Elizabeth Herbert
issue of 1st (none by 2nd):
a) **Joan Vaughan** (...)
7) **Lady Jane Somerset** (... – 16 Oct 1597)
= ...; **Sir Edward Maunsell** (1531 – 5 Aug 1595) son of
Sir Rhys Maunsell & Cecily Danbridgecourt
a) **Elizabeth Maunsell** (...)
= ...; **Sir Walter Rice** (ca.1562 – ca.1636) son of Griffith
Rice & Elinor Jones
(I) **Henry Rice** (ca.1590 – ca.1651)
= ...; **Margaret Lewis** (...) daughter of Sir Edward Lewis
(A) **Walter Rice** (... – bef.1681)
=1 ...; **Elizabeth Deere** (...) daughter of Piers Deere
=2 1673: **Dorothy Vaughan** (... – 6 Nov 1687) daughter
of Sir William Vaughan; =1st Robert Brandling
issue of 1st (none by 2nd):
(1) **Elizabeth Rice** (...)
= ...; **Richard Middleton** (...)
issue ?
(2) **Griffith Rice** (1664 – 27 Sep 1729)
=1 28 Aug 1690; **Catherine Hoby** (... – 4 May
1717) daughter of Philip Hoby
=2 aft.1717; **Eliza Morgan** (...) daughter of John Morgan
issue of 1st (none by 2nd)"
(a) **Philip Rice** (...)
(b) **Elizabeh Rice** (...)
= ...; **Thomas Lloyd** (... – bef.1721)
issue ?
(c) **Catherine Rice** (...)
= ...; **William Brydges** (... – 24 Sep 1764)
issue ?
(d) **Edward Rice** (1694 – 5 Apr 1727)
= ...; **Lucy Trevor** (...) daughter of John Trevor
Has further generations of issue
(B) **Sir Edward Rice** (... – bef.1664) unm.
b) **Sir Thomas Mansel, 1st Baronet** (of Mansel) (... – 20
Dec 1631) Kt.1593; cr. Baronet 22 May 1611
=1 30 May 1582; **Hon. Mary Mordaunt** (...) daughter of
Lewis Mordaunt, 3rd Baron Mordaunt & Elizabeth Darcy
=2 ...; **Jane Powell** (...) daughter of Thomas Powell; =1st John

Fuller; =2nd John Bussey
issue of 1st (none by 2nd):

(I) **Sir Lewis Mansel, 2nd Baronet** (ca.1594 – 4 Apr
1638) suc. father 1631
=1 aft.1603; **Lady Katherine Sydney** (...) daughter of
Robert Sydney, 1st Earl of Leicester & Barbara Gamage
=2 ...; **Katherine Lewis** (...) daughter of Sir Edward Lewis
=3 25 Aug 1627; ♦**Lady Elizabeth Montagu** (... – bef.1657)
daughter of Henry Montagu, 1st Earl of Manchester & Catherine
Spencer; =2nd Sir Edward Sebright, 1st Baronet
issue of 3rd (none by others):

(A) **Sir Henry Mansel, 3rd Baronet** (ca.1630 – ca.
1640) suc. father 1638

(B) **Sir Edward Mansel, 4th Baronet** (ca.1637 – 17
Nov 1706) suc. brother ca.1640
= ca.1665; **Martha Carne** (...) daughter of Edward Carne

(1) **Sir Thomas Mansell, 1st Baron Mansell**, 5th Baronet
(ca.1668 – 10 Dec 1723) suc. father 1706; cr. Baron 1 Jan
1711/2
= 18 May 1686; **Martha Millington** (... – 10 Jun 1718)

(a) **Hon. Martha Mansell** (...)

(b) **Hon. Elizabeth Mansell** (...)

(c) **Hon. Mary Mansell** (...)
= ...; **John** Ivory **Talbot** (1691 – 1772)
Has further generations of issue

(d) **Hon. Robert Mansell** (2 Nov 1695 – 23 Apr 1723)
= ca.Apr 1718; **Anne Shovel** (... – 20 Oct 1741)
daughter of Sir Cloudesley Shovel & Elizabeth Hill;
she =2nd John Blackwood
Has further generations of issue[44]

(e) **Sir Christopher Mansell, 3rd Baron Mansell**,
etc. (aft.1696 – 26 Nov 1744) unm.; suc. nephew 1744

(f) **Bussy Mansell, 4th Baron Mansell**, etc.
(aft.1697 – 29 Nov 1750) suc. brother 1744
=1 17 May 1724; **Lady Elizabeth Hervey** (9 Dec
1697 – Sep 1727) daughter of John Hervey, 1st Earl of
Brstol & Elizabeth Felton
=2 13 Mar 1728/9; **Lady Barbara Villiers** (... – 11 Jun
1761) daughter of William Villiers, 2nd Earl of Jersey &
Judith Herne; =1st Sir William Blackett, 2nd Baronet
Has further generations of issue by the 2nd

---

[44] An only son who became the 2nd Baron but died unm. 29 Jan 1743/4.

(II) **Arthur Mansel** (...)
  = 1621; **Jane Price** (...) daughter of William Price; =2ⁿᵈ
  ♦Sir Anthony Mansel
  no issue
c) **Sir Francis Mansel, 1ˢᵗ Baronet** (of Muddlescombe)
  (... – ca.1628) cr. Baronet 14 Jan 1621/2
  =1 ...; **Catherine Morgan** (...) daughter of Henry Morgan
  =2 ...; **Dorothy Stepney** (...) daughter of Alban Stepney &
  Mary Phillips
  issue of 1ˢᵗ:
  (I) **Sir Walter Mansel, 2ⁿᵈ Baronet** (25 Jul 1586 – Apr
    1640) suc. father 1628
    = 11 Dec 1623; **Elizabeth Fotherby** (... – 11 Sep 1643)
    daughter of Charles Fotherby
    (A) **Elizabeth Mansel** (21 Oct 1631 – ...)
      = ...; **Thomas Broome** (... – 1673)
      issue ?
    (B) **Sir Francis Mansel, 3ʳᵈ Baronet** (9 May 1633 – 27
      Oct 1654) unm.; suc. father 1640
  (II) **Francis Mansel** (... – 1 May 1655)
  (III) **Sir Anthony Mansel** (aft.1587 – 27 Oct 1644
    Newbury, Berks.) killed in battle; Kt.1629
    = ...; **Jane Price** (...) daughter of William Price; =1ˢᵗ
    ♦Arthur Mansel
    (A) **Sir Edward Mansel, 4ᵗʰ Baronet** (... – bef.10 Mar
      1690/1) suc. cousin 1654
      = ...; **Jane Wyndham** (... – bef.1692) daughter of
      Humphrey Wyndham; =1ˢᵗ Sir Roger Lort, 1ˢᵗ Baronet
      (1) **Dorothy Mansel** (...)
        = ...; **Samuel Townsend** (23 Sep 1692 – 1859)
        Has further generations of issue
  (IV) **Richard Mansel** (... – ca.1635)
    = 14 Feb 1612/3; **Catherine Morgan** (... – 27 Feb
    1631/2) daughter of Rees Morgan
    (A) **Anthony Mansel** (6 Mar 1613/4 – Dec 1670)
      = ...; ♦**Mary Carne** (... – Aug 1667) daughter of Sir
      Edward Carne & Ann Williams
      (1) **Anthony Mansel** (... – ca.1679) unm.
      (2) **Sir Richard Mansel, 5ᵗʰ Baronet** (6 Feb 1641 –
        aft.Mar 1691) suc. cousin Mar 1691
        = ...; **Alice Davies** (... – Aug 1691) daughter of Rees Davies
        (a) **Sir Richard Mansel, 6ᵗʰ Baronet** (bef.1670 –
          1696) unm.; suc. father 1691
        (b) **Sir William Mansel, 7ᵗʰ Baronet** (15 Mar
          1670 – ca.1732) suc. brother 1696
          = 18 Oct 1700; **Amy Cox** (29 Jun 1684 – ...) daughter

of Sir Richard Cox, 1ˢᵗ Baronet
Has further generations of issue
issue of 2ⁿᵈ:
(V) **John Mansel** (8 Dec 1611 – ...)
= ...; **Mary Vaughan** (...) daughter of Sir Henry Vaughan
(A) **Henry Mansel** (... – bef.1683)
= ...; ♦**Frances Stepney** (...) daughter of Sir John Stepney,
1ˢᵗ Baronet & Jan Mansel; =2ⁿᵈ ♦Rawleigh Mansel
(1) **Sir Edward Mansel, 1ˢᵗ Baronet** (of Trimsaran)
(... – 19 Feb 1719/20) cr. Baronet 22 Feb 1696/7
= ...; **Dorothy Vaughan** (... – Sep 1721)
Has further generations of issue
(VI) **Edward Mansel** (... – May 1671)
= ...; **Honor Lloyd** (... – Dec 1660) daughter of Thomas Lloyd
(A) **Rawleigh Mansel** (...)
= ...; ♦**Frances Stepney** (...) daughter of Sir John Stepney,
1ˢᵗ Baronet & Jane Mansel; =1ˢᵗ ♦Henry Mansel
no issue
(VII) **Jane Mansel** (... – aft. Jan 1628/9)
= ...; (her uncle) **Sir John Stepney, 1ˢᵗ Baronet**
(ca.1581 – 21 Jul 1626) son of Alban Stepney & Mary
Phillips; cr. Baronet 24 Nov 1621
(A) **Sir Alban Stepney, 2ⁿᵈ Baronet** (ca.1607 – 1628)
unm.; suc. father 1626
(B) **Sir John Stepney, 3ʳᵈ Baronet** (1618 – ca.1676)
suc. brother 1628
= ...; **Magdalen Jones** (...) daughter of Sir Henry Jones
issue ?
(C) **Frances Stepney** (...)
=1 ...; ♦**Henry Mansel** (... – bef.1683)
=2 ...; ♦**Rawleigh Mansel** (...)
issue of 1ˢᵗ (none by 2ⁿᵈ):
Children are listed with other parent
(D) a son (...)
= ...
(1) **Sir John Stepney, 4ᵗʰ Baronet** (1632 – 1681) suc.
uncle 1676
= ...; **Justina van Dyck** (...) daughter of Sir Anthony van
Dyck (the painter)
(a) **Sir Thomas Stepney, 5ᵗʰ Baronet** (ca.1668 –
1745) suc. father 1681
= ...; **Margaret Vaughan** (...) daughter of Walter
Vaughan
Has further generations of issue
(VIII) **Cicely Mansel** (...)
= ...; **George Jones** (...)

issue ?
(IX) **Rawleigh Mansel** (1622 – 1674)
= ...; **Ann Phillips** (...) daughter of Sir Richard Phillips
no issue
d) **Cecily Maunsell** (...)
= ...; **Sir Rowland Williams** (...)
(I) **Ann** Maunsell **Williams** (...)
= ...; **Sir Edward Carne** (...)
(A) **Mary Carne** (... – Aug 1667)
= ...; ◆**Anthony Mansel** (1614 – 1670)
Children are listed with other parent
e) **Rhys Maunsell** (... – 1596 Carrickfergus, co Antrim)
executed following the Battle of Carrickfergus; unm.
f) **Anthony Maunsell** (...)
= ...; **Mary Morgan** (...) daughter of Henry Morgan
no issue
g) **Charles Mansfield** (... – aft.1598) legally changed name
h) **Philip Maunsell** (...)
=1 ...; **Catherine Mathew** (...) daughter of William Mathew;
she =1st Lewis Rowland
=2 ...; **Elizabeth Mansel** (...) daughter of Henry Mansel
issue of 1st:
(I) **Thomas Maunsell** (...)
= ...; **Jane Gwyn** (...) daughter of David Gwyn
(A) **Edward Maunsell** (... – aft.1685)
= ...; **Anne Gorges** (...) daughter of Sir Theobald Gorges
issue ?
(B) **Philip Maunsell** (...)
(C) **Roderic Maunsell** (...)
(D) **Thomas Maunsell** (... – bef.1704)
= ...; **... Tenby** (...) daughter of Ray Tenby
issue ?
(II) **Dorothy Maunsell** (... – 1673)
= ...; **David Vaughan** (... – 1673) son of Thomas Vaughan
issue ?
issue of 2nd:
(III) **Mary Maunsell** (...)
i) **Christopher Maunsell** (...)
= ...; **Ann Worseley** (...) daughter of Sir Robert Worseley
(I) **Jane Maunsell** (...)
(II) **Hope Maunsell** (...)
(III) **Dorothy Maunsell** (...)
(IV) **Catherine Maunsell** (...)
= ...; **Rev. Marmaduke Mathew** (...)
issue ?
(V) **Elizabeth Maunsell** (...)

j) **Edward Maunsell** (...)

k) **Henry Maunsell** (... – aft.1585)

l) **William Maunsell** (...) unm.

m) **Mary Maunsell** (...)
= ...; **Christopher Turberville** (...)
issue ?

n) **Anne Maunsell** (...)
= ...; **Edward Carne** (...)
issue ?

o) **Sir Robert Maunsell** (1573 – bef.20 Jun 1656) Kt.1596
=1 bef.1600; **Elizabeth Bacon** (...) daughter of Sir Nicholas
Bacon, 1st Baronet & Anne Butts
=2 1617; **Anne Roper** (...) daughter of Sir John Roper
no issue

8) **Lady Anne Somerset** (1538 – 17 Oct 1596 Namur)
= 1558; ◆**Thomas Percy, 1st Duke of Northumberland**
(1528 – 1572)
see:

issue of 2nd:

B) **Lady Mary Somerset** (...)
=1 ...; ◆**William Grey, 13th Baron Grey KG** (ca.1509 –
1562)
=2 ...; **Robert Carre** (... – 16 Sep 1590) son of Robert Carre
issue of 1st (none by 2nd):
Children are listed with other parent

d. **Lady Margaret Beaufort** (... – 1474)
=1 1455; ◆**Humphrey, Earl of Stafford** (... – 1457)
=2 aft.1455; **Sir Richard Dayrell** (1429 Ramsbury, Wilts. – 6
Aug 1489)
issue of 1st:
Children are listed with other parent
issue of 2nd:

I) **Margaret Dayrell** (ca.1465 Ramsbury – ...)
= bef.1483; **James Touchet, 7th Baron Audley** (ca.1463
Heleigh Castle, Staffs. – 28 Jun 1497 London) executed; son
of John Touchet, 6th Baron Audley & Anne Echingham; =2nd
Joan Bourchier; suc. father 26 Sep 1490; attainted 1497

A) **John Touchet, 8th Baron Audley** (ca.1483 – bef.20 Jan
1557/8) restored 1512
= ...; **Mary Griffin** (...) daughter of John Griffin & Emmote
Wheathill

1) **George Touchet, 8th Baron Audley** (... – Jun 1560) suc.
father bef.20 Jan 1557/8
=1 30 Aug 1538; **Elizabeth Tuke** (...) daughter of Sir
Brian Tuke & Grizel Boughton
=2 23 Jan 1559/60 Chester; **Joan Platt** (...)

issue of 1ˢᵗ (none by 2ⁿᵈ):
a) **Henry Touchet, 10ᵗʰ Baron Audley** (... – 30 Dec 1563)
suc. father Jun 1560
= ...; **Elizabeth Sneyd** (... – Dec 1609 Thelwall, Ches.) daughter
of Sir William Sneyd & Anne Barrowe; =2ⁿᵈ Stephen Bagot
(I) **George Touchet, 1ˢᵗ Earl of Castlehaven**, Baron
  Audley of Orier, 11ᵗʰ Baron Audley (ca.1551 – 20 Feb
  1616/7) suc. father 30 Dec 1563; cr. Earl 6 Sep 1616
  =1 bef.28 Aug 1584; **Lucy Mervyn** (... – bef.Apr 1610)
  daughter of Sir James Mervyn & Amy Clark
  =2 29 Apr 1611 London; **Elizabeth Noel** (1590 – aft.8
  Dec 1644) daughter of Sir Andrew Noel & Mabel
  Harington; =2ⁿᵈ Sir Pierce Crosbie, Baronet
  issue of 1ˢᵗ (none by 2ⁿᵈ):
  (A) **Lady Eleanor Touchet** (1590 – 1652)
    =1 Mar 1609; **Sir John Davies** (16 Apr 1569
    Chicksgrove Manor, Wilts. – 8 Dec 1626 Englefield
    House, Berks.) son of John Davies & Mary ...
    =2 aft.1626; **Sir Archibald Douglas** (...)
    issue of 1ˢᵗ (none by 2ⁿᵈ):
    (1) **Lucy Davies** (20 Jan 1612/3 Dublin – 14 Nov
      1679)
      = 1623; ♦**Ferdinando Hastings, 6ᵗʰ Earl of
      Huntingdon** (1609 – 13 Feb 1656)
      Children are listed with other parent
  (B) **Mervyn Touchet, 2ⁿᵈ Earl of Castlehaven** etc.
    (ca.1593 – 14 May 1631 London) executed⁴⁵; suc.
    father 20 Feb 1616/7; Barony of Audley was forfeited,
    but the Irish titles passed to his son.
    =1 bef.1619; **Elizabeth Barnham** (... – bef.1624)
    daughter of Benedict Barnham & Dorothy Smith
    =2 22 Jul 1624 London; ♦**Lady Anne Stanley** (May
    1580 – Oct 1647 London) daughter of Ferdinando
    Stanley, 5ᵗʰ Earl of Derby & Alice Spencer; =1ˢᵗ Grey
    Brydges, 5ᵗʰ Baron Chandos
    issue of 1ˢᵗ (none by 2ⁿᵈ):
    (1) **James Touchet, 3ʳᵈ Earl of Casthaven**, etc.
      (ca.1617 – 11 Oct 1684 Kilcash, co. Tipperary) suc.
      father 14 May 1631
      =1 bef.1631; ♦**Hon. Elizabeth Brydges** (... – Mar
      1678/9) daughter of Grey Brydges, 5ᵗʰ Baron

---

⁴⁵ Lord Castlehaven was convicted of sodomy (with several male servants) and rape, by
restraining his wife while one of his male lovers raped her.

Chandos & Lady Anne Stanley
=2 Jun/Jul 1679; **Elizabeth Graves** (... – 1720)
no issue
(2) **Lady Frances Touchet** (1617 – ...)
= ...; **Hon. Richard Butler** (... – 1701) son of
Thomas, Viscount Thurles & Elizabeth Poyntz
(a) **Walter Butler** (... – 1700)
= ...; **Lady Mary Plunkett** (...) daughter of Christopher
Plunkett, 2nd Earl of Fingall & Mabel Barnewall
Has further generations of issue
(b) **Frances Butler** (... – Jan 1709)
= ...; **Sir Patrick Barnewall, 3rd Baronet** (ca.
1630 – bef.1702) son of Sir Richard Barnewall, 2nd
Baronet & Julia Aylmer; suc. father 6 Jul 1679
Issue extinct 1758
(c) **John Butler** (... – 1715)
= ...; **Katherine Aylmer** (...) daughter of James
Aylmer; =1st Nicholas Plunkett
Has further generations of issue
(d) **Elizabeth Butler** (...)
= ...; **Sir Redmond Everard, 2nd Baronet** (... –
1687) son of Sir Richard Everard, 1st Baronet; suc.
father 1650
Has further generations of issue
(e) **Mary Butler** (... – 28 Mar 1737)
= ca.1665; **Christopher, Lord Delvin** (... –
bef.1680) son of Richard Nugent, 2nd Earl of
Westmeath & Mary Nugent
Has further generations of issue
(3) (Hon.) **Brother George Touchet** (... – ca.1689) a monk
(4) **Mervyn Touchet, 4th Earl of Castlehaven**, etc.
(... – 2 Nov 1686) suc. brother 11 Oct 1684
= ...; **Lady Mary Talbot** (... – Mar 1710/1) daughter
of John Talbot, 10th Earl of Shrewsbury & Mary
Fortescue; =1st Charles Arundell
(a) **James Touchet, 5th Earl of Castlehaven**, etc.
(... – 12 Aug 1700) suc. father 2 Nov 1686
= ...; **Anne Pelson** (... – Jun 1733) daughter of
Richard Pelson & Lady Anne Villiers
Has further generations of issue[46]

---

[46] The Earldom became extinct in 1777 and all legitimate lines of descent became extinct in 1973. The descendants of an illegitimate daughter of the 19th Baron Audley remain extant.

(b) **Hon. John Touchet** (...)
= ...; ♦**Lady Mary Savile** (...) daugter of Thomas
Savile, 1st Earl of Sussex & Lady Anne Villiers
Has further generations of issue
(5) **Lady Lucy Touchet** (... – 1662)
=1 ...; **John Anketell** (...)
=2 ...; **Hon. Garrett FitzMaurice** (... – Dec 1632
Louvain [Belgium]) son of Patrick FitzMaurice, 15th
Baron of Kerry and Lixnow & Jane Roche
issue of 1st:
(a) **Frances Anketell** (...)
= ...; **Thomas O'Grady** (...) son of Darby O'Grady
& Faith Standish
Has further generations of issue
issue of 2nd:
(b) (**Father Cyprian**) Richard **MitzMaurice** (...) a
   priest
(c) **Eleanor FitzMaurice** (...)
= ...; **Sir Turlough MacMahon, 2nd Baronet** (... –
aft.1683) son of Sir Teague MacMahon, 1st
Baronet; suc. father ca.1673, but barontcy became
extinct upon his death
no issue
(d) **Catherine FitzMaurice** (...)
=1 ...; **James Berry** (...)
=2 ...; **John Stevenson** (...)
issue ?
(6) **Lady Dorothy Touchet** (... – 10 Feb 1635)
= ...; **Edmund** Roe **Butler** (later **4th Viscount
Mountgarret**) (ca.1595 – 5 Apr 1679) son of
Richard Butler, 3rd Viscount Mountgarret &
Margaret O'Neill; =2nd Anne Tresham, =3rd
Elizabeth Simeon; suc. father 1651
(a) **Richard Butler, 5th Viscount Mountgarret**
   (... – 27 Feb 1707)
=1 Sep 1661; **Emilian Blundell** (... – 1682) daughter of
William Blundell & Anne Haggerston
=2 aft.1682; **Margaret Shee** (...) daughter of Richard
Shee; =1st Gilbert Butler
issue of 1st (none by 2nd):
Has further generations of issue
(b) **Hon.Margaret Butler** (...) unm.
(c) **Hon. Elizabeth Butler** (...)
= ...; **... Sutton** (...)
no issue
(7) **Lady Mary Touchet** (...)

= ...; **Sir Henry Wingfield, 4th Baronet** (ca.1655 – 1677) son of Sir Richard Wingfield, 2nd Baronet & Mary Wintour; suc. brother 1671

(a) **Sir Henry Wingfield, 5th Baronet** (ca.1673 – 1712) suc. father 1677

(b) **Sir Mervyn Wingfield, 6th Baronet** (ca.1675 – aft.1727) suc. brother 1712, but on his death the baronetcy became extinct

= ...; **Mary Dalton** (...) daughter of Theobald Dalton
Has further generations of issue

(C) **Sir Ferdinando Touchet KB** (...)

= ...; ... (...) =1st Sir John Rodney
no issue

(D) **Anne Touchet** (...)

= ...; **Edward Blount** (...)
issue ?

(E) **Elizabeth Touchet** (...)

=1 ...; **Sir John Stawel, KB** (...) son of Sir John Stawel & ... Dyer

=2 ...; **George Legh** (... – 24 Mar 1617) son of Robert Legh & Eleanor Spurstow; =1st Elizabeth Leycester
issue of 1st (none by 2nd):

(1) **John Stawel** (...)

=1 ...; **Catherine Hext** (...) daughter of Sir Edward Hext

=2 ...; **Ursula Austen** (...) daughter of Sir Robert Austen, 1st Baronet & Anne Muns
issue of 1st:

(a) **Ralph Stawel, 1st Baron Stawel** (... – 1689) cr. Baron 15 Jan 1683/4

=1 ...; **Ann Ryves** (...) daughter of John Ryves

=2 ...; **Abigail Pitt** (...) daughter of William Pitt
Has further generations of issue

(b) **John Stawel** (...)
issue of 2nd:

(c) **Ursula Stawel** (... – 13 Aug 1697)

= 18 Mar 1685/6 Ramsbury, Wilts.; ♦**John Sheffield, 1st Duke of Buckingham and Normandy** Marquess of Normanby, **3rd Earl of Mulgrave**, 5th Baron Sheffield **KG** (8 Sep 1647 – 16 Mar 1705/6 Buckingham House [later Palace]) son of Edmund Sheffield, 2nd Earl of Mulgrave & Lady Elizabeth Cranfield; =2nd Hon. Catherine Greville; he =3rd Lady Catherine Darnley; suc. father as Earl and Baron 24 Aug 1658; KG 1674; cr. Marquess 10 May 1694; cr. Duke 23 Mar 1702/3
Issue extinct 1764

(d) **Elizabeth Stawel** (ca.1681 – ca.1725)
= ca.1696; (her first cousin) **Sir Robert Austen, 3ʳᵈ Baronet** (19 Mar 1663 Bexley, Kent – ca.Jun 1706) son of Sir John Austen, 2ⁿᵈ Baronet & Rose Hale; suc. father 1698
Issue extinct by 1758
(F) **Mary Touchet** (...)
= ...; **Sir Thomas Thynne** (...) son of Sir John Thynne & Joan Hayward
(1) **Sir James Thynne** (... – 12 Oct 1670)
= ...; **Lady Isabella Rich** (6 Oct 1623 – ...) daughter of Henry Rich, 1ˢᵗ Earl of Holland & Isabel Cope
no issue
(2) **Sir Thomas Thynne** (...)
= 6 Sep 1642; **Stuarta Balquanquill** (...) daughter of Walter Balquanquill
(a) **Thomas Thynne** (1648 – 12 Feb 1681/2) murdered
= (secretly) 15 Nov 1681; ◆**Lady Elizabeth Percy** (26 Jan 1666/7 – 23 Nov 1722) daughter of Joceline Percy, 5ᵗʰ Earl of Northumberland & Lady Elizabeth Wriothesley; =1ˢᵗ Henry, Earl of Ogle; she =3ʳᵈ ◆Charles Seymour, 6ᵗʰ Duke of Somerset
no issue
(G) **Christian Touchet** (ca.1587 – bef.1646)
= ...; **Sir Henry Mervyn** (1583 – 1646) son of Edmund Mervyn & Anna Jephson
(1) **Sir Audley Mervyn** (... – aft.1666)
(II) **Hon. Anne Touchet** (... – Jul 1579 Runcorn, Ches.)
= ...; **Thomas Brooke** (1549 – 1622) son of Richard Brooke; =2ⁿᵈ Elizabeth Merbury; =3ʳᵈ Eleanor Gerard
(A) **Sir Richard Brooke** (14 Mar 1571 – 10 Apr 1632)
=1 ...; **Jane Chaderton** (...) daughter of Rt.Rev. William Chaderton, Bishop of Chester
=2 ...; ◆**Katherine Neville** (...) daughter of Sir Henry Neville & Anne Killigrew
issue of 2ⁿᵈ (none by 1ˢᵗ):
(1) **Sir Henry Brooke, 1ˢᵗ Baronet** (1611 – 1664) cr. Baronet 12 Dec 1662
= ca.1635; **Mary Pusey** (...) daughter of Timothy Pusey
(a) **Sir Richard Brooke, 2ⁿᵈ Baronet** (ca.1635 – Feb 1709/10) suc. father 1664
= Apr 1656 Frodsham, Ches.; **Francisca** Posthuma **Legh** (...) daughter of Rev.Thomas Legh & Lettice Calveley
Has further generations of issue
(b) **Henry Brooke** (aft.1635 – ...)
(B) **George Brooke** (18 Jun 1574 – ...) drowned; unm.
(C) **Margaret Brooke** (25 Dec 1576 – ...)

= ...; **... Warburton** (...)
issue ?
(D) **Eleanor Brooke** (29 Oct 1578 – ...)
= ...; **John Brooke** (...)
issue ?

e. **Lady Anne Beaufort** (1435 London – bef.28 Nov 1496)
= ...; **Sir William Paston** (28 May 1434 Paston, Norfolk – 1496)
I) **John Paston** (...)
= ...

A) **Bridget Paston** (...)
= ...; **Sir Edward Coke** (1549 – 3 Sep 1633) son of Robert Coke &
Winifred Knightley; =2nd ♦Lady Elizabeth Cecil; Kt.1603
1) **Henry Coke** (...)
= ...; **Margaret Lovelace** (...) daughter of Richard Lovelace
a) **Richard Coke** (...)
= ...; **Mary Rous** (...) daughter of John Rous, 1st Baronet
(I) **Robert Coke** (... – 16 Jan 1678/9)
= ...; **Lady Anne Osborne** (1657 – 1722) daughter of
Thomas Osborne, 1st Duke of Leeds & Lady Bridget
Bertie; =2nd Horatio Walpole
(A) **Edward Coke** (... – 13 Apr 1707)
= ...; ♦**Cary Newton** (... – 4 Aug 1707) daughter of Sir
John Newton, 3rd Baronet & Abigail Heveningham
(1) **Thomas Coke, Earl of Leicester**, Viscount Coke,
Baron Lovel **KB** (17 Jun 1697 – 20 Apr 1759) KB
1725; cr. Baron 28 May 1728, and Earl etc. 9 May
1744, all of which became extinct upon his death
= 3 Jul 1718; ♦**Margaret Tufton, 19th Baroness
Clifford** (16 Jun 1700 – 28 Feb 1775 Holkham,
Norfolk) daughter of Thomas Tufton, 6th Earl of Thanet
& Lady Catherine Cavendish; suc. father 30 Jul 1729
no surviving issue
(2) **Anne Coke** (...)
= ...; **Philip Roberts** (...)
Has further generations of issue
(3) **Edward Coke** (... – Aug 1733) unm.
(4) **Robert Coke** (...)
= 13 Jun 1733; **Jane Wharton, 7th Baroness
Wharton** (1706 – 1761) daughter of Thomas Wharton,
1st Marquess of Wharton & Lucy Loftus; =1st John
Holt; suc. father 12 Apr 1715
no issue
(5) **Carey Coke** (... – 11 Jun 1734)
= 1716; **Sir Marmaduke Wyvill, 6th Baronet**
(ca.1692 – 1754) son of Sir Marmaduke Wyvill, 5th
Baronet & Henrietta Yarburgh; suc. father 1722

no issue

2) **Arthur Coke** (... – 6 Dec 1629)
= ...; **Elizabeth Walgrave** (... – 14 Nov 1627) daughter of Sir
George Walgrave
issue ?

3) **Clement Coke** (... – 23 May 1629)
= ...; **Sarah Reddish** (...) daughter of Alexander Reddish & ...
Langley
   a) **Sir Edward Coke, 1st Baronet** (... – bef.1669) cr.
      Baronet 30 Dec 1611
      = 1644; **Catherine Dyer** (...) daughter of Sir William Dyer
      (I) **Sir Robert Coke, 2nd Baronet** (29 Apr 1645 – 1688)
         suc. father bef.1669
         = ...; **Sara Barker** (... – ca.Feb 1685)
         no issue
      (II) **Sir Edward Coke, 3rd Baronet** (6 Oct 1646 – 26
         Aug 1727) suc. brother 1688, but baronetcy became
         extinct upon his death
         = ...; **Catherine ...** (... – ca.Dec 1688)
         no issue
      (III) **Catherine Coke** (...)
         = ...; **Cornelius Norton** (...)
         issue ?

4) **Anne Coke** (...)
= 11 Sep 1601; **Ralph Sadleir** (... – 12 Feb 1660) son of
Sir Thomas Sadleir & Gertrude Markham
no issue

5) **Bridget Coke** (...)
=1 ...; **William Barney** (...) son of Sir Thomas Barney
=2 ...; **William Skinner** (...) son of Sir Vincent Skinner
issue ?

6) **John Coke** (...)
= ...; **Meriel Wheatley** (...) daughter of Anthony Wheatley
   a) **Bridget Coke** (... – Oct 1700)
      =1 ...; ◆**Edmund D' Oyly** (... – 28 Sep 1638) son of Sir
      Henry D' Oyly & Susan Talamache
      =2 aft.1638; **Sir Isaac Astley, Baronet** (... – 7 Sep 1659) son of
      Thomas Astley & Frances Deane; =1st Rachel Messenger; cr.
      Baronet 21 Jan 1641/2, but the title became extinct upon his
      death
      no survivng issue
   b) **John Coke** (...) unm.
   c) **Mary Coke** (... – bef.Jun 1662)
      = ...; ◆**Sir Nicholas le Strange, 3rd Baronet** (1632 – 1669)
      Children are listed with other parent

7) **Sir Robert Coke** (1586 – 19 Jul 1653)

    = ...; ♦**Theophelia Berkeley** (...) daughter of Sir Thomas
    Berkeley & Hon. Elizabeth Carey
    no issue
  II) **William Paston** (...)
  III) **Elizabeth Paston** (...)
    = ... **Sir John Savile** (...)
  IV) **Anne Paston** (...)
    = ...; ♦**Sir Gilbert Talbot** (... – 1542)
    Children are listed with other parent
  V) **Mary Paston** (19 Jan 1469/70 – 25 Dec 1489 London)
    = ...; ♦**Ralph, Lord Neville** (... – 1498) son of Ralph Neville,
    3rd Earl of Westmorland & Isabel Booth; =2nd Edith Sandys
    no issue
f. **Edmund Beaufort, 3rd Duke of Somerset** etc. (ca.1439 – 6
  May 1471 Tewkesbury, Glos.) executed unm.; suc. brother 15 May 1454
g. **John Beaufort, Earl of Dorset** (... – 4 May 1471 Tewkesbury)
  killed in battle
h. **Lady Joan Beaufort** (... – 11 Aug 1518)
  =1 1478; **Robert St.Lawrence, 3rd Baron Howth** (ca.1435 –
  1486 London) son of Christopher St.Lawrence, 2nd Baron
  Howth & Anne Plunket; =1st Alice White; suc. father ca.1464
  =2 ...; **Sir Richard Fry** (...)
  no issue
issue by ...[47]:
1. **Jane Beaufort** (1402 – 1453)
  = 1423; **Sir Edward Stradling** (ca.1389 St. Donat's Castle, Glamorgan,
  Wales – 5 May 1453 Acre, Safad [present-day Israel]) son of Sir William
  Stradling & Isobel St.Barbe
  a. **Sir Henry Stradling** (ca.1424 St. Donat's Castle – ca.1450
    Famagusta, Cyprus)
    = ...; **Elizabeth Herbert** (ca.1427 Raglan, Monmouths. – ...) daughter
    of Sir William ap Thomas & Gwladus ...
    I) **Thomas Stradling** (1454 St. Donat's Castle – 9 Aug 1480 St. Donat's
      Castle)
      = ...; **Janet Matthew** (ca.1456 Radyr, Glamorgan – 5 Feb 1533
      Wales)
      A) **Sir Edward Stradling** (1474 St.Donat's Castle – 8 May 1535)
        = ...; **Elizabeth Arundell** (ca.1484 Lanherne, Cornwall – 20 Feb
        1512/3) daughter of Thomas Arundell & Catherine Dynham
        1) **Jane Stradling** (20 Feb 1504/5 St.Donat's Castle – 1555
        Huntsworth, Som.)

---

[47] Some have claimed the Cardinal's mistress was Alice FitzAlan, a descendant of King John, but research by several genealogists suggests this is not correct.

= ...; **Alexander Popham** (ca.1504 Huntsworth – 1555) son of
John Popham & Isabella Knoyle
a) **Sir John Popham** (1531 Huntsworth – 10 Jun 1607
   Wellington, Som.) Speaker of the House 1508-1583
   = ca.1548 Castleton, Glamorgan; **Amy Games** (ca.1522
   Castleton – ca.1604 Wellington) daughter of Robert Games
   (I) **Eleanor Popham** (1551 Huntsworth – aft.1607)
      = ...; **Roger Warre** (ca.1547 Hestercombe, Som. – Jan. 1616
      Hestercombe)
      (A) **Amy Warre** (ca.1588 Hestercombe – 1650 Wilts.)
         =1 bef.1603; **Robert Wingate** (ca.1576 Beds. – ca.1603)
         =2 ca.1608; **GIofford Long** (1580 Broughton Gifford,
         Wilts. – 15 Dec 1635 Wilts.) son of Edward Long & Anne
         Brouncker
      issue of 2nd (none by 1st):
         (1) **Roger Long** (1609 Wilts. – aft.1636 Wilts.)
         (2) **Thomas Long** (1611 Wilts. – aft.1646)
            = 10 Apr 1648 London; **Katherine Edwards** (...)
            (a) **Thomas Long** (ca.1649 Wilts. – 1692 Baltimore, MD)
               = ...
               Has further generations of issue
         (3) **Edward Long** (1607 Rood Ashton, Wilts. – 1644 Wilts.)
            = 2 Feb 1631/2 London; **Dorothy Jones** (ca.1615 London –
            ...)
            daughter of Isaac Jones
            (a) **Henry Long** (1631 Rood Ashton – 1672 Wilts.)
               = ...; **Dionysia Bassett** (ca.1643 – 1674)
               no issue
            (b) **Elizabeth Long** (ca.1637 Wilts. – ...)
               = 9 Apr 1657 Wilts.; **Richard Long** (ca.1633 Wilts. – 7 Sep
               1669 Collingborne, Wilts.) son of Thomas Long & ... Floyer
               Has further generations of issue
         (4) **Eleanor Long** (ca.1618 Wilts. – ca.1671)
            = ca.1638 Wilts.; **Morris Carent** (...)
            (a) **Mary Anne Carent** (25 Sep 1639 Steeple Ashton,
               Wilts. – ...)
   (II) **Sir Francis Popham KB** (1573 – 1644)
      = ...; **Ann Gardiner Dudley** (24 Feb 1575 London – ...)
      daughter of John Dudley & Elizabeth Gardiner
      (A) **Frances Popham** (ca.1597 – 7 May 1671)
         = 1621; ♦**Edward Conway, 2nd Viscount Conway** (1594–
         1655)
         Children are listed with other parent
      (B) **Laetitia Popham** (... – 1738)
         = ...; ♦**Sir Edward Seymour, 5th Baronet** (1663 – 1741)
         Beyond the 12th generation on the father's line

(C) **John Popham** (... – 1638)
(D) **Alexander Popham** (1605 – 1669)
  = ...; **Letitia Carre** (... – 1660)
  (1) **Letitia Popham** (... 16 Mar 1714)
  = 1674; ♦**Sir Edward Seymour, 4th Baronet** (1633 – 1708)
  Beyond the 12th generation on the father's line
  (2) **Anne Popham** (...)
  = ...; **William Ashe** (...) son of Edward Ashe
  (a) **Edward Ashe** (...)
  (b) **Elizabeth Ashe** (...)
  = 1705; **Pierce à Court** (...) son of John à Court & Mary Pierce
  Has further generations of issue
  (3) **Essex Popham** (...)
  = ...; ♦**John Poulett, 3rd Baron Poulett** (... – 1679)
  Children are listed with other parent
  (4) **Alexander Popham** (...)
  = ...
  (a) **Francis Popham** (...)
  = ...; ♦**Anne Popham** (...) daughter of Alexander Popham
  Has further generations of issue
  (5) **Francis Popham** (1636 – 1674)
(E) **Hugh Popham** (... – Apr 1643)
(F) **Edward Popham** (ca.1610 – 19 Aug 1651 Dover, Kent)
  = 15 Oct 1645; **Anne Kerr** (... – 13 Aug 1692) daughter of William Kerr; =2nd ♦Philip Wharton, 4th Baron Wharton
  (1) **Letitia Popham** (ca.1645 – ...)
  (2) **Alexander Popham** (ca.1646 – ...)
  = ...
  (a) **Anne Popham** (...)
  = ...; ♦**Francis Popham** (...)
  see: above
B) **Jane Stradling** (ca.1476 St.Donat's Castle – ca.1520)
  = ...; **Sir William Griffith** (ca.1480 Penrhyn Castle, Caernarvon – 1531 Penrhyn Castle)
  issue ?
G. **JOAN, COUNTESS OF WESTMORLAND** (1375 – 1440)
see: Chapter 13
H. **Thomas Beaufort, 1st Duke of Exeter** Earl of Dorset, Lord de Lillebonne, Count d'Harcourt, KG (ca.Jan 1376/7 – 27 Dec 1426 East Greenwich, Kent) KG 1400; cr. Earl 5 Jul 1411, Duke 18 Nov 1416, Lord and Count 1 Jul 1418
= bef.15 Feb 1403/4; **Margaret Neville** (ca.1384 – bet.1413/26) daughter of Sir Thomas Neville & Joan Furnivall
no surviving issue

221

issue by **Marie de St. Hilaire** (1340 – aft.1399):

I. **Blanche de St.Hilaire** (1359 – 1389)
= 1381; **Sir Thomas Morieux** (1355 – 1387)
no issue

CHAPTER 7
STEWART/STUART

Before we continue to follow the path of succession to the English Throne, we have to back up a bit and talk about the Scottish one. The two will be joined in 1603, but for our purposes, the descendants of Edward III, we have to begin in 1424. This is when King James I of Scotland married Lady Joan Beaufort, the granddaughter of John of Gaunt. Lady Joan actually married two men named James Stewart. After the death of King James I, she married his very distant cousin, James Stewart, the Black Knight of Lorn. The common male line ancestor of the two James lived in the 1200s. One note: care should be taken to not confuse James I of Scotland with James I of England, who was simultaneously James VI of Scotland. They lived approximately 200 years apart.

In Scotland, there are a few things to consider that were different from the English custom. While the Scots had their own peerage, it was a much more exclusive group. The English tended to hand out Baronies willy-nilly, but in Scotland barons were not part of the peerage. A Scottish barony was a collection of properties combined together under one individual and he was given a grant declaring these to be his property. While the land was called a barony, the person was called a Laird.

The titles Laird and Lord should not be confused with one another. In Scotland, Lairds were very numerous and designated that the titleholder was the proprietor of a parcel of land. A Scottish Lord was the term used for the lowest rank of the peerage and was equivalent to an English Baron. A Lord would have that word as part of his title, such as the 10th Lord Saltoun. But Lairds were designated by being of the land they held, such as Ramsay of Mar, or Carnegie of

Northesk. These Lairdships were hereditary and were typically numbered in order of who held the charter for the land. An example of how this was written would be Robert Bruce, 2nd of Kinnaird, signifying that Robert's father was the original grant holder for the land and Robert has since inherited it.

Also in Scotland, we have an extensive network of Clans. While there may be—and were—dozens of Lairds named Campbell, each one being Campbell of Someplace Different, together they make up the Clan Campbell and the genealogically senior most male was Chief of their Clan. The Chiefs were nominally responsible for all of the branches of their Clan and had a limited judicial role in settling petty disputes amongst their various Lairds. They were also numbered, and their Chieftain designation and their territorial designation would be different. They would have a surname something like Gordon of Gordon or Moncreiffe of that Ilk. But they might also hold a land of grant. That could be rendered as such: James MacGregor of that Ilk, 3rd of Ardkinglass, 10th Chief of Clan Gregor.

Now that we have an understanding of the Scottish hierarchy, time to focus on this specific chapter. It is devoted the Stewart family and their descendants. First, it should be noted that the descendants of James I were very numerous and to maintain some semblance of manageability for the chapters, the descendants of three of James' daughters or granddaughters had to broken out into chapters of their own and will appear later in the book as the Douglas, Gordon, and Hamilton chapters.

Second, the name Stewart has many variant spellings, the most commonly known one is Stuart. The name itself was derived from the title the family held beginning in the 10th century: Steward. The royal Steward was the person who essentially handled all of the day-to-day administrative details of running the kingdom, freeing the King to fight wars and bed mistresses. In Scotland, this position was hereditary. When a particularly bloody era of fighting for the Throne had ended in the late 1300s, Robert, Steward of Scotland, ended up on the Throne as King Robert II. He declared his dynasty to be the Stewarts, derived from his previous position. King James I was his grandson.

A few generations later, one junior branch of the family married into French royalty and resided mostly in France. There, they were called Stuart. In time, a man from this line would marry the reigning Queen Mary and the family has been known alternately as Stewart or Stuart ever since. Because spelling was never considered to have rules prior to the 18th century, I have tried to use my own rules for which spelling to use when. The base spelling is Stewart, and I use it when there is not a specific reason to use one of the variants. I use Stuart for the French line, which includes the descendants of Mary, Queen of Scots and her husband, Lord Darnley. The Steuart spelling seems to be restricted to very specific branches and was not widely used until the unification of England and Scotland under one crown. So, I use it only when speaking of those families who use that spelling today.

This chapter includes the remainder of the royal line of England until the ascension of King George I, the first of the Hanovers. However, this royal line is only a small portion of this rather lengthy chapter. As previously noted, it starts with James I of Scotland. From a genealogical perspective, there is nothing much to say of the first three Jameses except to point out that most of this chapter actually follows the descendants of their daughters. These numerous descendants married into all of the large clans that dominated Scottish history in the 15th through 17th centuries. If your ancestry has names like Stewart, Campbell, Carnegie, Drummond, Hamilton, Gordon, or Douglas, just to name a few, this book will definitely help you identify potential royal connections you may have in both Scotland and in England. Many of the lines that do not go back to one of the King Jameses might well take you one of their Stewart predecessors, Kings Robert II and III, the grandfather and father of James I.

James IV is where things start to get interesting for royalty fans. It is his marriage to Margaret Tudor, daughter of Henry VII of England, that lays the groundwork for the unification of the two thrones into one Great Britain. James IV is also interesting as a progenitor. While Margaret only produced one child who would live past the age of five, the future James V, her royal husband fathered a half-dozen healthy bastards from almost as many mistresses.

James V, on the other hand, died relatively young at age 30, leaving only one surviving child, a daughter named Mary. Although Mary was queen in her own right since infancy, her mother, the manipulative Marie of Guise, arranged her childhood marriage to King François II of France in an effort to join to the two Thrones. When this marriage was being arranged in the 1540s, Henry VIII had three living children and was seeking to have more, so there was no reasonable expectation of joining Scotland to England. Marie, being a relative of the French King, preferred a union with her homeland for Mary anyway.

As so often happens in these grand schemes, fate intervened. François died less than two years after his marriage, still only aged 16. Although it was expected of him to consummate his marriage to Mary, there is wide speculation that his life-long frailty and ongoing illness likely prevented this.

Once back in Scotland, Mary married her cousin, Lord Darnley. The political situation was going from bad to worse and Darnley soon ended up murdered, but not before fathering Mary's only child, yet another James. Before long, circumstances forced Mary to leave her son behind as she escaped to England seeking asylum from her cousin, Elizabeth Tudor. What she found was imprisonment and eventual execution when she was discovered to be plotting to overthrow her hostess.

It was the abandoned James who would join the thrones of England and Scotland upon Elizabeth's death in 1603, ruling Scotland as James VI and England as James I. His descendants continue to thrive in very large numbers and include nearly every 20th century monarch of Europe. Although he personally joined the British crowns in 1603, the governments of the two countries were not merged for over another hundred years.

James was succeeded by his son, Charles I, famous for his losing battles with Parliament, which ultimately also caused him to lose both the Throne and his head. After an eleven-year failed experiment as a republic from 1649–1660, the Crown was restored to his son, Charles II. The second Charles died without any legitimate issue, despite the dozens of children and grandchildren he left behind with his numerous mistresses.

James II, Charles' younger brother, succeeded him in 1685, and almost immediately was in trouble. His devotion to Catholicism was a major stumbling block in being accepted by his people and Parliament alike. They tried to get along though, since his children were being raised Protestant, but by the time his first wife died, he only had two surviving daughters. He quickly remarried to the Catholic Mary of Modena, and fathered sons, whom he was raising as Catholics.

Parliament essentially invited his eldest daughter, Mary, and her husband, William of Orange, to invade the country and take the Throne. They did, with very minimal bloodshed, and once James fled, Parliament declared him as abdicated, and further declared the children of his 2nd marriage to be ineligible to succeed, making Mary the heiress. She was crowned jointly with her husband.

But alas, William and Mary had no children. This led to the formation of the Act of Settlement, which declared the Throne could not go to any Catholic, nor to anyone married to a Catholic. It further established the immediate succession to any legitimate children that either Mary or William might have, even if it by a second spouse once one of them had died. Failing that (which is what happened), the Throne would pass to Mary's younger sister, Anne, and failing any issue on her part (again which is what happened), the next living Protestant relative following the rules of primogeniture.

By the time Queen Anne died in 1714, this law caused several people to be skipped, due to their religion, and the Throne fell to George, Elector of Hanover, who became King George I of Great Britain. This was the last time the Throne had to pass to a cousin. Since 1714, it has followed a mostly direct line from parent to child or grandchild with a few cases of passing from one childless brother to the next. As the current Queen is a great-grandmother now, with two remaining grandchildren yet to marry, there seems to be no reason to believe the direct inheritance won't continue.

As was discussed in Chapter 1, the likelihood of any John Q. Public being descended from James I and VI, and not already knowing it, is rather remote. This would also apply to his grandfather, James V, since he only had one surviving child, as did Mary, Queen of Scots.

While James V also had a few bastards, they all carried the Stewart name and the male line did not survive. Nearly all of the female members of these lines married men who were also descended from Edward III so their descendants will be found in other parts of the book. But once we get back to James IV (1473–1513), that all changes.

James IV's daughter by Lady Isabella Stewart (of the Earls of Buchan), Janet, is a good example of providing a whole line of descendants that are not intertwined with the royal line. Janet married the 3rd Lord Fleming (+1547) and provided hundreds of descendants included in these pages alone, not to mention those born after the 12th generation of descent. In addition to the numerous Flemings, this line also includes the Maitland Earls of Lauderdale, the early Crichtons who later became Marquesses of Bute, and the Drummond Earls of Perth. From James' next illegitimate daughter, Margaret, we get the Elphinstones, the Forbes family, and the senior branch of the Innes clan.

Backing up a generation, to James III, his younger sons provide our path to the Campbells of Ardkinglass. The Campbell clan is one of those families whose branches are so numerous that it is rather common for two people, both named Campbell, to marry and each be the child of a couple who were both born Campbell, and yet none of the couples involved be particularly close akin to the others. Many of the branches of the Campbell family are represented in the four chapters that cover the descendants of Joan Beaufort and King James I.

James II's descendants do not provide much more information in this chapter. But he is the father of Princess Mary Stewart, whose marriage to a Lord Hamilton kicks off that chapter later in this book. James I's eldest two daughters remain in this chapter and provide another early connection foreign royalty. The firstborn, Margaret, was married to the Dauphin of France, the title given to the heir of that Throne. However she died prematurely and never got to be queen to King Louis XI and did not leave any surviving issue.

The second daughter, Isabella, married François I, Duke of Brittany. The male line of Brittany continues through the descendants of another wife of François, but will show up in another chapter. Isabella was the mother of two daughters, Marguerite and Marie. The elder died childless, but the younger became the ancestress of the House of Rohan, an influential noble family that saw itself at the top of French society several times over the centuries. Even in the present day, some of its members have married into the royal houses.

Queen Joan Beaufort, once a widow, remarried to one of the junior-most lines of the House of Stewart, the Stewarts of Lorn. Despite their genealogical position, this branch was particularly closely allied with the Stewart Kings and the Earls of Douglas. When James I was murdered, it was the Earl of Douglas who was made Regent for his young son. Sir James of Lorn, was one of the closest protectors of both the boy-king and his Regent. The Earls of Douglas were called the Black Douglases for their dark hair and features. Because of his close association with the family, Sir James was often called the Black Knight of Lorn.

Queen Joan had three more children with Sir James, all sons, the youngest of whom became a priest, and later a bishop. The elder two, the Earls of Atholl and Buchan, left behind extensive descendants, who will be included in later chapters.

Edward III

|

John of Gaunt, Duke of Lancaster

|

1st Marquess of Somerset

|

Lady Joan Beaufort (ca.1404 – 15 Jul 1445 Dunbar Castle, East Lothian)
=1 1423/4; **James I, King of Scotland** (Jul 1394 Dunfermline Palace,
Fife – 21 Feb 1436/7 Blackfriars, Perth) son of Robert III, King of Scotland &
Lady Annabella Drummond
=2 Sep 1439; **Sir James Stewart, the Black Knight of Lorn**[48] (ca.
1399 – at sea 1451) killed by pirates; son of Sir John Stewart & Isabell
MacDougall
issue of 1st:
a. **Princess Margaret Stuart** (1424 Perth – 16 Aug 1445 Châlon-sur-
Marne, France)
= 25 Jun 1436; **Louis, Dauphin** (later **King Louis XI) of France**
(3 Jul 1423 Bourges – 30 Aug 1483 Plessis-les-Tours) son of
Charles VII, King of France & Marie of Anjou
no issue
b. **Princess Isabella Stuart** (1426 – 13 Oct 1494 Vannes, Brittany)
= 30 Oct 1442 Chateau d'Aurey; **François I, Duke of Brittany** (14
May 1414 Vannes – 18 Jul 1450 Vannes) son of Jean VI, Duke of
Brittany & Joan of France; =1st Yolande of Anjou
I) **Marguerite of Brittany** (ca.1443 – 25 Sep 1469 Nantes)
= 16 Nov 1455 Vannes; (her first cousin) **François II, Duke of
Brittany** (23 Jun 1433 Clisson – 9 Sep 1488 Couëron) son of
Richard, Count d'Étampes & Marguerite of Orleans; =2nd
Marguerite de Foix
no surviving issue
II) **Marie of Brittany** (1444 – 1506)
= 1462; **Jean II, Vicomte de Rohan et Leon, Count de
Porhoët** (16 Nov 1452 – 1516) son of Alain IX, Vicomte de
Rohan & Marie de Lorraine-Vaudémont
A) **François de Rohan** (10 Jul 1469 – 1488) killed in action
B) **Jean de Rohan** (2 Oct 1476 – 2 Jun 1505)
C) **Jacques, 16th Vicomte de Rohan** etc. (1478 – 16 Oct 1527)
=1 ...; **Françoise de Rohan** (...)
=2 ...; **Françoise de Daillon** (...) daughter of Jean de Daillon;
she =2nd Joachim de Goyon de Matignon, Count de Thorigny

---

[48] The common male-line ancestor of James I and the Black Night was James Stewart, the 4th
Great Steward of Scotland (+1283).

229

no issue

D) **Georges de Rohan** (1479 – 1502)

E) **Claude, Bishop of Leon, 17ᵗʰ Vicomte de Rohan**, etc.
(1480 – 15 Jul 1540) suc. brother 1527

F) **Anne, Vicomtesse de Rohan**, etc. (1485 – 5 Apr 1529)
= 27 Sep 1515; **Pierre de Rohan, Lord de Frontenay** (... –
1525) killed in action

1) **René I, 18ᵗʰ Vicomte de Rohan**. etc. (1516 – 1552) suc. uncle 1540
= ...; **Isabella d'Albret, Princess of Navarre** (1512 – 1555)
daughter of Jean d'Albret (King Jean III of Navarre) & Catherine I,
Queen of Navarre

a) **Françoise de Rohan** (1540 – ...) unm.

b) **Henri I, 19ᵗʰ Vicomte de Rohan** etc. (...) unm.

c) **Rene II, 20ᵗʰ Vicomte de Rohan** etc. (1550 – 1586)
= ...; **Catherine de Partenay** (...)

(I) **Henri II, Duke of Rohan** (21 Aug 1579 Blain – 13 Apr
1638 Bern) suc. father 1586; cr. Duke 1603
= 1603; **Marguerite de Béthune** (1595 – 21 Oct 1660)
daughter of Maximilien de Béthune, Duke of Sully &
Rachel de Cochefilet

(A) **Marguerite, Duchess of Rohan** etc. (1617 – 9 Apr
1684 Paris) suc. father 1638
= 6 Jun 1645 Paris; **Henri Chabot** (1616 – 27 Feb 1655)
son of Charles Chabot & Henriette de Lur-Saluces

(1) **Marguerite** Gabrielle Charlotte **de Rohan-Chabot**
(... – 1720)
= 1662; ◆**Malo, Marquis de Coëtquen** (ca.1637 – 1679) son
of Malo, Marquis de Coëtquen & Françoise de la Marzelière
Children are listed with other parent

(2) **Anne** Julie **de Rohan-Chabot** (1648 – 7 Feb 1709)
= 17 Apr 1663 Paris; **François de Rohan, Prince of
Soubise** (1630 – 24 Aug 1712 Paris) son of Hercule de
Rohan, Duke of Rohan & Marie de Bretagne
d'Avaugour; =1ˢᵗ Catherine Lyonne

(a) **Anne** Marguerite **de Rohan** (4 Aug 1664 – 26 Jun 1721) a
nun

(b) **Prince Louis de Rohan** (11 Mar 1666 – 5 Nov 1689) unm.

(c) **Constance** Émilie **de Rohan** (1667 – ...)
= 1684; **José Diogo da Câmara, 2ⁿᵈ Count da
Ribeira Grande** (1665 – 1724 Lisbon) son of Manuel
Luiz da Câmara, 1ˢᵗ Count da Ribeira Grande
Has further generations of issue

(d) **Hercule Mériadec, Duke of Rohan-Rohan** etc. (8
Jul 1669 Paris – 26 Jan 1749 Paris) suc. 1717
=1 15 Feb 1694 Paris; **Anne Geneviève de Lévis** (Feb
1673 – 20 Mar 1727 Paris) daughter of Louis Charles

de Lévis & Charlotte de la Motte Houdancourt; =1st
Louis Charles de La Tour d'Auvergne
=2 2 Sep 1732; **Marie Sophie de Courcillon** (6 Aug
1713 – 4 Apr 1756 Paris) daughter of Philippe Egon
de Courcillon & Françoise de Pompadour; =1st
Charles François d'Albert d'Ailly
Has further generations of issue

(e) **Cardinal Armand** Gaston Maximilien **de Rohan**
(26 Jun 1674 – 19 Jul 1749) cr. Cardinal 1712

(f) **Sophronie-Pélagie de Rohan** (2 Jul 1678 – ...)
= ...; **Alfonso Francisco de Vasconcellos** (...)
no issue

(g) **Éléonore de Rohan** (25 Aug 1679 – 2 Nov 1753) a nun

(h) **Maximilien** Gaston **de Rohan** (1680 – 23 May
1706) killed in action; unm.

(3) **Louis, Duke of Rohan**, etc. (1652 – 1727) suc. father 1655
= 1678; **Marie Elisabeth du Bec-Crespin de Grimaldi**
(1661 – 1743)

(a) **Louis** Bretagne Alain, **Duke of Rohan**, etc. (1679 –
1738) suc. father 1727
= 1708; **Françoise de Roquelaure** (1683 – 1741)
Has further generations of issue

(b) **Marie Marguerite** Françoise **de Rohan** (1680 – 1706)
= 1700; **Ludwig** Peter Engelbert **von der Marck,
Count von Schleiden** (... – 1750)
issue ?

(c) **Anne** Henriette Charlotte **de Rohan** (18 Jun 1682
Paris – 12 May 1751 Paris)
= 19 Jun 1710; **Alfons** Franz Dominikus **de Berghes,
Prince of Berghes** (3 Aug 1679 – 4 Apr 1720) son of
Philipp. Prince de Berghes & Marie Jacquline de Lalaing
no issue

(d) **Guy Auguste, Count de Chabot** (1683 – 1760)
=1 1729; **Yvonne** Sylvie **du Breil de Rays** (1712 – 1740)
=2 1744; ♦**Lady Mary Howard** (1721 – 1769)
Has further generations of issue

(e) **Françoise Gabrielle de Rohan** (1685 – ...) a nun

(f) **Charlotte de Rohan** (... – 1710)

(g) **Charles Annibal de Rohan** (1687 – 1762)
= 1715; **Henriette** Charlotte **de Chabot, Countess
de Jarnac** (...)
no issue

(h) **Julie Victoire de Rohan** (1688 – 1730) a nun

(i) **Constance** Éleonore **de Rohan** (1691 – 1733) a nun

(j) **Marie Armande de Rohan** (1692 – 1742) a nun

(k) **Marie Louise de Rohan** (1681 – 1781) a nun

231

(4) **Jeanne Pélagie de Rohan** (ca.1659 – 18 Aug 1698 Versailles)
= 1668; **Alexandre de Melun, Prince de Epinoy** (1619 – 16 Feb 1679)
  (a) **Louis I de Melun, Prince de Epinoy** (27 Oct 1673 – 24 Sep 1704 Strassbourg)
    = ...; **Marie Elisabeth de Lorraine** (6 Mar 1664 Nancy – 1748) daughter of François de Lorraine, Prince de Lillebonne & Anne Elisabeth de Lorraine
    Has further generations of issue
(II) **Catherine de Rohan** (20 Jun 1578 – 10 May 1607 Zweibrücken)
= 28 Aug 1604; **Johann II, Duke of Zweibrücken** (1591 – 1635) son of Johann I Duke of Zweibrücken & Countess Magdalena of Jülich-Kleve-Berg; =2nd Countess Luise von Simmern; suc. father 1604
(A) **Countess Magdalena** Catharina **von Zweibrücken** (24 Apr 1607 Zweibrücken – 20 Jan 1648 Strassbourg)
  = 14 Nov 1630 Zweibrücken; **Christian I, Count von Birkenfeld** (3 Sep 1598 Birkenfeld – 6 Sep 1654 Neuenstein) son of Karl I, Count of the Palatine & Dorothea of Brunswick-Lüneburg; =2nd Countess Marie Johanna von Helfenstein-Wiesensteig
  (1) **Countess Dorothea** Catharina **von Birkenfeld** (3 Jul 1634 Bischweiler – 7 Dec 1715 Neukirchen)
    = 1649 Bischweiler; **Johann Ludwig, Count von Nassau-Ottweiler** (24 May 1625 Saarbrücken – 9 Feb 1690 Reichelsheim) son of Ludwig Wilhelm, Count von Nassau-Ottweiler & Margravine Anna Amalie of Baden-Durlach
    (a) **Friedrich Ludwig, Count von Nassau-Ottweiler** (3 Nov 1551 Ottweiler – 25 May 1728 Saarbrücken) suc. father 1690
      =1 28 Jul 1680 Gravenstein; **Countess Christiane von Ahlefeld** (11 Apr 1659 Glückstadt – 2 Feb 1695 Ottweiler)
      =2 27 Sep 1697 Dhaun; **Countess Luise Sofie von Hanau-Lichtenberg** (11 Apr 1662 – 9 Apr 1751 Ottweiler)
      Has further generations of issue
    (b) **Countess Anna Katharina von Nassau-Ottweiler** (20 Jan 1653 Ottweiler – 15 Feb 1731 Dhaun)
      = Nov 1671 Ottweiler; **Johann Philipp, Count von Dhaun** (... – 1693)
      issue ?
    (c) **Count Walrad von Nassau-Ottweiler** (7 Nov 1656

Saarbrücken – 15 Jan 1705 Ottweiler) unm.
- (d) **Count Karl Siegfried von Nassau-Ottweiler** (3 Sep 1659 Ottweiler – 3 Feb 1679 Butzbach)
- (e) **Count Ludwig von Nassau-Ottweiler** (16 Feb 1661 Ottweiler – 19 Dec 1699 The Hague) = 9 Apr 1694 The Hague; **Countess Amalie Luise von Hornes** (19 Aug 1665 – Jan 1728) daughter of Count Willem Adriaan von Hornes & Anna van Nassau no issue
- (f) **Countess Luise von Nassau-Ottweiler** (27 Oct 1662 Ottweiler – 10 Oct 1741 Ottweiler) unm.
- (III) **Benjamin de Rohan, Duke of Soubise** (21 Aug 1579 Blain – 13 Apr 1638 Bern)

G) **Marie de Rohan** (... – 9 Jun 1542)
= 17 Nov 1511; **Louis IV de Rohan, Lord de Guéméne** (... – 14 Jun 1527) son of Louis III de Rohan, Lord de Guéméne & Renée de Four

1) **Louis V de Rohan, Lord de Guéméne** (ca.1513 – 14 May 1557)
= ca.1529; **Marguerite de Laval** (...)

a) **Renée de Rohan** (... – aft.Sep 1573)
=1 ...; **François de Rohan, Lord de Gie et de Verger** (... – 1559)
=2 ...; **Rene de Laval, Baron de Maille** (... – 1562) son of Gilles II de Laval, Lord de Loue & Louise de Sainte-Maure
=3 ...; (her brother-in-law) **Jean de Laval, Marquis de Nesle** (... – 1576) son of Gilles II de Laval, Lord de Loue & Louise de Sainte-Maure
issue of 3rd (none by others):

(I) **Guy de Laval, Marquis de Nesle** (1565 – 1590 Esclimont)
= ...; **Marguerite Huralt** (... – 1614)
no issue

b) **Louis VI de Rohan, Prince of Guéméne** (3 Apr 1540 – 4 Jun 1611)
=1 22 Jul 1561; **Eleonore de Rohan, Countess de Rochefort** (10 Jan 1539 – 20 Sep 1583) daughter of François de Rohan, Vicomte de Fronsac & Catherine de Silly, Countess de Rochefort
=2 1 Feb 1586; **Françoise de Laval** (... – 16 Dec 1615) daughter of Rene II de Laval, Vicomte de Bresteau & Catherine de Baif; =1st Henri II de Lenoncourt, Baron de Vignory
issue of 1st:

(I) **Renée de Rohan** (1558 – ...)
= 1578; **Jean V de Coëtquen, Count de Combourg** (... – 1602) son of Jean IV de Coëtquen, Count de Combourg & Philippe d'Alcigny

(A) **Louis de Coëtquen, Marquis de Coëtquen** (... – 5 Oct 1628)
= 10 Mar 1609; **Henriette d'Orleans-Rothelin** (...) daughter

of François d'Orleans, Baron de Varangebec & Catherine
du Val de Fontenay
(1) **Malo I de Coëtquen, Marquis de Coëtquen** (...)
= ...; **Françoise de la Marzlière** (...)
(a) **Malo II de Coëtquen, Marquis de Coëtquen** (
= 1662; ♦**Marguerite** Gabrielle Charlotte **de Rohan-
Chabot** (... – 1720) daughter of Henri de Chabot &
Marguerite de Rohan, Duchess of Rohan
Has further generations of issue
(b) **Françoise de Coëtquen** (...)
= ...; ♦**Hercule, Lord de Boiséon** (...)
see: below
(II) **Lucrece de Rohan** (1560 – ...)
= 1574; **Jacques de Tournemine, Marquis de Coetmure**
(... – 1584)
(A) **Jeanne de Tournemine** (...)
= ...; **Odet de Saint Denis, Baron du Hertray** (...)
(1) **Marthe de Saint Denis** (...)
= ...; **Claude de Boiséon, Count de Boiséon** (...)
(a) **Hercule, Lord de Boiséon** (...)
= ...; ♦**Françoise de Coëtquen** (...)
Has further generations of issue
(III) **Isabelle de Rohan** (1561 – ...)
= 1593; **Nicolas de Pellevé, Count de Piers** (...) son of Henri de
Pellevé, Baron de Piers & Jeanne de Grosparmy de Flers
(A) **Louis de Pellevé, Count de Piers** (...) suc. father
(B) **Pierre de Pellevé, Count de Piers** (...) suc. brother
= ...; **Henriette de Refruge** (...)
(1) **Louis de Pellevé, Count de Piers** (...) suc. father
(2) **Antoine de Pellevé, Count de Piers** (8 Jun 1642 – 7
Oct 1701) suc. brother
= ...; **Marie Fauvel** (... – 2 Jul 1680)
(a) **Louis de Pellevé, Count de Piers** (... – 23 Apr
1722) suc. father 1701
= ...; **Madeleine de Gauréault du Mont** (...)
no issue
(IV) **Louis VII de Rohan, Duke of Montbazon** (1562 – 1
Nov 1589)
= 1581; (his step-sister) **Madeleine de Lenoncourt** (1576 – 28
Aug 1602 Coupvray) daughter of Henri II de Lenoncourt, Baron de
Vignory & Françoise de Laval; =2nd ♦Hercule de Rohan, Duke of
Brazon
no issue by marriage
issue by ...:
(A) **François de Boistoneau** (...) legitimated 1634
= ...

(1) **Samuel de Boistoneau** (... – aft.1689)
(V) **Pierre de Rohan, Prince of Guémène** (... – 1622)
=1 ...; **Madeleine de Rieux** (...)
=2 ...; **Antoinette de Bretagne** (... – 1681) daughter of Count
Charles de Bretagne & Philippine, Vicomtesse de Guigen
issue of 1st (none by 2nd):
   (A) **Anne de Rohan, Princess of Guémène** (1604 – 14
     Mar 1685) suc. father 1622
     = 1616; ♦**Louis VIII de Rohan, Duke of Montbrazon**
     (1598 – 1667)
     see: below
(VI) **Hercule de Rohan, Duke of Montbazon** (27 Aug
1568 – 16 Oct 1654 Touraine) suc. brother 1589
=1 1594; (his step-sister and sister-in-law) **Madeleine de
Lenoncourt** (1576 – 28 Aug 1602 Coupvray) daughter of Henri
II de Lenoncourt, Baron de Vignory & Françoise de Laval;
she =1st ♦Louis VII de Rohan, Duke of Montbrazon
=2 5 Mar 1628 Champtocé; **Marie de Bretagne** (1610 –
18 Aug 1657) daughter of Count Claude de Bretagne & Cather
Fouquet de La Varenne
issue of 1st:
   (A) **Louis VIII de Rohan, Duke of Montbazon** (5 Aug
     1598 – 28 Feb 1667) suc. father 1654
     = 1619; ♦**Anne de Rohan, Princess of Guémène**
     (1604 – 14 Mar 1685) daughter of Pierre de Rohan, Prince de
     Guémène & Madeline de Rieux; suc. father 1622
     (1) **Charles II de Rohan, Duke of Montbazon, Prince
       of Guémène** (7 Jul 1633 Couvpray – 3 Jul 1699 near
       Liège) suc. father 1667 and mother 1685
       = ca.1653; **Jeanne Armande de Schomberg** (5 Mar
       1633 – 10 Jul 1706) daughter of Henri de Schomberg, Duke
       of Alluyn & Anne de La Guiche
       (a) **Charles III de Rohan, Duke of Montbazon** (30
         Sep 1655 – 10 Oct 1727 Yveline) suc. father 1699
         =1 19 Feb 1678; ♦**Marie Anne d'Albret de Luynes**
         (7 Mar 1663 – 20 Aug 1679 Paris) daughter of Louis
         Charles d'Albret, Duke of Luynes & Anne de Rohan
         =2 1679; **Charlotte Elisabeth de Cochefilet** (1657 – 1619)
         Has further generations of issue
       (b) **Jean Baptist** Armand **de Rohan, Prince of
         Montaubon** (1657 – 1704)
         = 1682; **Charlotte de Bautru-Nogent** (1641 – 1725)
         Has further generations of issue
       (c) **Charlotte Armande de Rohan** (ca.1661 – 1754)
         =1 1688; **Gui Henri Chabot, Count de Jarnac**
         (1648 – 1691) son of Luis Chabot, Count de Jarnac &

Catherine de Rochechouart; =1st Marie Claire de Créqui
=2 1691; **Pons IV de Pons, Count de Rocquefort**
(... – 17 Mar 1705)
Has further generations of issue
(d) **Elisabeth de Rohan** (25 Mar 1663 – 27 Sep 1707)
= 1691; **Count Alexandre de Melun, Burggrave of
Ghent** (...) son of Count Charles de Melun, Burggrave
of Ghent & Renée de Rupierre; suc. father 1664
Has further generations of issue
(e) **Jeanne Thérèse de Rohan** (... – 1728) unm.
(2) **Chevalier Louis de Rohan** (ca.1635 – 27 Nov 1674
the Bastaille) executed
(B) **Marie Aimée de Rohan, Duchess of Chevreuse** (Dec
1600 Paris – 12 Aug 1679 Gagny)
= 11 Sep 1617 Paris; **Charles d'Albret, Duke of Luynes**
(1578 Pont-St.Espirit – 15 Dec 1721 Longueville) son of
Honore d'Albert, Lord de Luynes & Anne de Rodolf
=2 21 Apr 1622; **Claude of Guise** (5 Jun 1578 – 24 Jan
1457) son of Henri I, Duke of Guise & Catherine of Cleves
issue of 1st:
(1) **Louis Charles d'Albret, Duke of Luynes** (25 Dec
1620 Paris – 20 Oct 1699 Paris) suc. father 1721
=1 23 Apr 1641; **Louise** Marie **Seguier** (1624 – 13 Sep 1651)
=2 4 Sep 1661; ♦**Anne de Rohan** (1644 – 29 Oct 1684)
daughter of Hercule de Rohan, Duke of Monbrazon & Marie
de Bretagne
issue of 1st:
(a) **Charles Honoré d'Albret, Duke of Luynes and
Chevreuse** (7 Oct 1646 Paris – 5 Nov 1712 Paris) suc.
grandmother in Chevreuse 1667 and father in Luynes 1699
= 3 Feb 1667 Paris; **Jeanne** Marie **Colbert** (14 Feb
1650 Paris – 26 Jun 1732 Paris) daughter of Jean Baptiste
Colbert, Marquis de Seignelay
Has further generations of issue
(b) **Françoise** Paule Charlotte **d'Albret de Luynes** (... –
1670)
= 3 Mar 1667; **Henri Charles de Beaumanoir,
Marquis de Lavarin** (1664 – 1701) =2nd Louise de
Noailles
no issue
issue of 2nd:
(c) **Marie Anne d'Albret de Luynes** (7 Mar 1663 – 20
Aug 1679 Paris)
= 19 Feb 1678; ♦**Charles III de Rohan, Duke of
Montbrazon** (30 Sep 1655 – 10 Oct 1727 Yvelines)
son of Charles II de Rohan, Duke of Montbrazon &

Jeanne de Schomberg; =2nd Charlotte de Cochefilet
no issue
(d) **Charlotte** Victoire **d'Albret de Luynes** (6 Oct
1667 – 22 May 1701 Paris)
= 1682; ♦**Alexandre de Henin, Duke of
Bournonville** (1662 – 1705)
Children are listed with other parent
(e) **Catherine** Angélique **d'Albret de Luynes** (9 Nov
1668 – 17 Sep 1746 Paris)
= 23 Nov 1694; **Charles** Antoine **Goffier, Marquis
d'Heilly** (1672 – 23 May 1706) died from wounds
received in battle; son of Honoré Louis Goffier,
Marquis d'Heilly
Has further generations of issue
(f) **Jeanne** Genviève **d'Albret de Luynes** (18 Jan
1670 – 18 Nov 1736 Paris)
= 22 Aug 1683; **Giuseppe** Ignacio **Scaglia, Count de
Verua** (... – 1704 Hochstädt) killed in battle
no issue from marriage
Has issue by ♦**Vittorio Amedeo II, King of Sardinia**
(1666 – 1732)
Children are listed with other parent
(g) **Louis Joseph, Prince of Grimbergen** (1 Apr
1672 – 8 Nov 1758 Paris)
= 17 Mar 1715 Compeigne; **Princess Honorine** Charlotte **of
Berghes** (7 Dec 1680 – 3 Nov 1744 Paris) daughter of Philipp
Franz, Prince of Berghes & Jacqueline de Lalaing
Has further generations of issue
(h) **Chevalier Charles Hercules d'Albret de Luynes**
(8 Mar 1674 – 30 Jan 1734 Paris) unm.
(i) Jeanne **Thérèse d'Albret de Luynes** (8 Oct 1675 –
14 Jan 1756 Paris)
= 16 Mar 1698; **Louis de Castelnau** (... – 24 May 1705)
no issue
issue of 2nd:
(C) **Marie Eleonore de Rohan** (1629 – 1681) a nun
(D) **François de Rohan, Prince de Soubise** (1630 – 24 Aug
1712)
=1 ...; **Catherine de Lyonne** (... – 1660)
=2 16 Apr 1663; **Anne-Julie de Rohan-Chabot** (1648 –
4 Feb 1709) son of Henri Chabot, Duke of Rohan &
Margueite de Rohan
issue of 2nd (none by 1st):
(1) **Anne** Margueirte **de Rohan** (1664 – 1721) a nun
(2) **Louis de Rohan** (1666 – 1689) killed in battle; unm.
(3) **Constance** Emilie **de Rohan** (1667 – ...)

= 1683; **Jose Rodrigo da Camara, 2ⁿᵈ Count de Ribeira-Grande** (1665 – 1724 Lisbon) son of Manuel da Camara, 1ˢᵗ Count de Ribeira-Grande; suc father 1673, passed title to son 1720

(a) **Luís Manuel da Camara, 3ʳᵈ Count de Ribeira-Grande** (1685 – 1723 Lisbon) suc. father 1720
= 11 Mar 1711; **Leonor** Teresa Maria **da Ataide** (...) daughter of Don Jerónimo de Ataide, 9ᵗʰ Count de Atouguia
Has further generations of issue

(4) **Hercule de Rohan, Duke of Rohan-Rohan** (8 May 1669 – 26 Jan 1749) suc. as Duke 1714
=1 15 Feb 1694; **Anne Geneviève de Levis-Ventadour** (1623 – 1727)
=2 1732; **Marie Sophie de Courcillion** (1713 – 1756) issue of 1ˢᵗ (none by 2ⁿᵈ):

(a) **Louise-Françoise de Rohan** (4 Jan 1695 Paris – 7 Jul 1755 Paris)
= 5 May 1716 Paris; **Guy** Paul Jules **de La Porte-Mazarin, Duke of Rethel and Mazarin** (12 Sep 1701 – 30 Jan 1738) son of Paul-Jules de La Porte & Félice de Durfort
Has further generations of issue

(b) **Charlotte Armande de Rohan** (1696 – 1733) a nun

(c) **Jules** François Louis **de Rohan, Prince of Soubise** (16 Jan 1697 – 6 Apr 1724)
= 26 Sep 1714 Paris; **Anne** Julie Adelaide **de Melun** (1698 – 18 May 1724) daughter of Louis de Melun, 9ᵗʰ Prince de Epinoy & Elisabeth of Lorraine
Has further generations of issue

(d) **Marie Isabelle de Rohan** (1699 – 1754)
= 15 Mar 1713 Versailles; **Joseph de La Baum, Duke of Hostun** (7 Sep 1684 – 6 Sep 1755) son of Camille de La Baum, Duke of Hostun & Marie Catherine de Grolée-Viriville
Has further generations of issue

(e) **Louise** Gabrielle Julie **de Rohan** (1704 – aft.11 Mar 1741)
= 1718; ♦**Hercule Meriadec de Rohan, Duke of Montbazon** (... – 1757)
Beyond the 12ᵗʰ generation on the father's line

(5) **Henri Louis de Rohan** (1672 – 1693) unm.

(6) **Cardinal Armand** Gaston Maximilien **de Rohan-Soubise** (26 Jun 1674 Paris – 19 Jul 1749)

(7) **Emilie** Sophronie Pelagie **de Rohan** (1678 – ...)
= 1694; **Alfonso Francisco Vasconcelos, 7ᵗʰ Count de Calheta** (17 Jan 1664 – 2 Feb 1734 Lisbon) son of Luis de Vasconcelos, 3ʳᵈ Count de Calheta & Mariana de

Noronha
Has issue
(8) **Eleonore de Rohan** (1679 – 1753) a nun
(9) **Maximilien** Gaston Guy **de Rohan** (1680 – 1706
Ramillies) killed in battle; unm.
(E) **Anne de Rohan** (1644 – 29 Oct 1684)
= 1661; ◆**Louis Charles d'Albert, Duke of Luynes**
(1620 – 1699)
Children are listed with other parent
(VII) **Sylvie de Rohan** (16 Oct 1570 – 17 Oct 1651)
=1 23 Jan 1594; **François d'Éspinay, Marquis de Broons**
(1568 – 1598)
=2 1602; **Antoine II de Sillans, Baron de Breuilly** (... – 1641)
issue of 1st (none by 2nd):
(A) **Philippe Emmanuel d'Éspinay, Marquis de Broons**
(... – 1673)
= ...; **Madeleine de Warignies** (...)
(1) **Louis d'Éspinay, Marquis de Broons** (ca.1625 – 28 Feb
1708)
= ...; **Marie Françoise de Cousin** (...)
(a) **Marie-Madeleine d'Éspinay** (... – 12 Dec 1714 Paris)
= 23 Dec 1689; **Henri of Lorraine, Count de Brionne**
(15 Nov 1661 – 3 Apr 1712 Versailles) son of Louis de Lorraine,
Count d'Armagnac & Catherine de Neuville
Has further generations of issue
(VIII) **Marguerite de Rohan** (1574 – ca.1618)
=1 1605; **Charles d'Éspinay, Marquis d'Espinay** (... –1601)
=2 1612; **Leonard Philibert de Pompadour, Vicomte de
Pompadour** (... – 1634)
issue ?
(IX) **Alexandre de Rohan, Marquis de Marigny** (1578 – 1638)
= 1624; **Lucette Tarneau** (...)
no issue by marriage
issue by **Charlotte Fachon** (...):
(A) **Charlotte de Rohan** (... – 1703) legitimated 1619
= 1634; **Charles de l'Hopital, Count de Cordoux** (... – 1697)
issue ?
c. **Princess Mary Stewart, Countess of Buchan** (aft.1427 – 20 Mar
1465) cr. Countess ca.1444, but the title became extinct upon her death
= 1444 ter Veere, Netherlands; **Wolfert VI van Borselen, Count
de Grandpré** (1430 – 29 Apr 1487 Ghent) son of Hendrik II van
Borselen, Count de Grandpré & Johanna van Halewyn van
Hemsrode; =2nd Charlotte de Bourbon
no issue
d. **PRINCESS JOAN, COUNTESS OF MORTON** (1428 – 1486)
see: Chapter 20

e. **Princess Eleanor Stewart** (26 Oct 1427 – 20 Nov 1480)
= 12 Feb 1449; **Sigismund, Archduke of Austria** (26 Oct 1427 –
26 Oct 1496) son of Friedrich IV, Archduke of Austria & Anna of
Brunswick; =2nd Katherine of Saxony; suc. father 1439
no issue

f. **PRINCESS ANNABELLA, COUNTESS OF HUNTLY** (...) –
see: Chapter 21

g. **James II, King of Scotland** (16 Oct 1430 Edinburgh – 3 Aug 1460
Roxburgh Castle, Kelso) killed by gun misfire during a siege; suc. father
1437
= 3 Jul 1449 Edinburgh; **Marie of Guelders** (1433 – 16 Nov 1463
Edinburgh) daughter of Arnold van Egmont, Duke of Guelders &
Catrina of Cleves

I) **Princess Margaret Stewart** (aft.1449 – ...)
has issue by **William Crichton, 3rd Lord Crichton** (... – bef.22
Nov 1493) son of James Crichton, 2nd Lord Crichton & Lady
Janet Dunbar; = Hon. Marion Livingston

A) **Margaret Crichton** (bef.1493 – bef.1546)
=1 bef.1505; **William Todrik** (... – bef.27 Jul 1507)
=2 bef.4 Jul 1510; **George Halkerstoun** (... – 1513)
=3 1517 (dv.1520); **George Leslie, 4th Earl of Rothes**, Lord
Leslie (... – 28 Nov 1558) son of William Leslie, 3rd Earl of Rothes &
Margaret Balfour; =2nd Elizabeth Gray; =3rd Agnes Somverville; =4th his
first wife; =5th Isobel Lundie; suc. father Sep 1513
=4 aft.1530; her 3rd husband
issue of 2nd (none by 1st):
1) **James Halkerstoun** (...)
issue of 3rd:
2) **Norman, Master of Rothes** (... – 12 Aug 1554 Renty, nr.
Calais) killed in battle
= ...; ♦**Hon. Isabel Lindsay** (...) daughter of John Lindsay, 5th
Lord Lindsay & Lady Helen Stewart; =2nd Wiliam Christisson;
she =3rd John Innes of Leuchers
no issue
3) **Lady Margaret Leslie** (...)
= 25 Dec 1575 (dv.1587); ♦**Archibald Douglas, 8th Earl of
Angus**, etc. (ca.1555 – 4 Aug 1588 Smeaton, East Lothian)
son of David Douglas, 7th Earl of Angus & Margaret
Hamilton; =1st ♦Lady Mary Erskine; =3rd ♦Hon. Jean Lyon;
suc. father 1557
no issue

II) **PRINCESS MARY, COUNTESS OF ARRAN, LADY
HAMILTON** (1452 – 1488)
see: Chapter 22

III) **James III, King of Scotland**, etc. (10 Jul 1452 Stirling
Castle – 11 Jun 1488 Milltown, Bannockburn, Stirlings.)

murdered; suc. father 1460

= 13 Jul 1469 Edinburgh; **Princess Margaret of Denmark** (23 Jun 1456 – 14 Jul 1486 Stirling Castle) daughter of Christian I, King of Denmark & Margravine Dorothea of Brandenburg-Kulmbach

A) **James IV, King of Scotland**, etc. (17 Mar 1742/3 Stirling Castle – 9 Sep 1513 Flodden Field, Northumb.) killed in battle; suc. father 1488

= 8 Aug 1503 Edinburgh; ♦**Princess Margaret Tudor** (28 Nov 1489 London – 18 Oct 1541 Methven, Perths.) daughter of Henry VII, King of England & Princess Elizabeth of York; =2nd Archibald Douglas, 6th Earl of Angus; =3rd Henry Stewart, 1st Lord Methven

1) **James V, King of Scotland**, etc. (15 Apr 1512 Linlithgow Palace, W. Lothian – 14 Dec 1542 Falklland Palace, Fife) suc. father 1513

=1 1 Jan 1537 Paris; **Madeleine de Valois** (10 Aug 1520 Saint-Germain-en-Laye, France – 7 Jul 1737 Edinburgh) daughter of François I, King of France & Claude de Valois, Duchess of Brittany

=2 12 Jun 1538 St. Andrews, Fife; ♦**Marie de Lorraine de Guise** (22 Nov 1515 Bar-le-Duc, France – 10 Jun 1560 Edinburgh) daughter of Claude de Lorraine, Duke of Guise & Antoinette de Bourbon; =1st Louis II d'Orleans, Duke of Longueville

issue of 2nd (none by 1st):

a) **Mary, Queen of Scots**, etc. (7 Dec 1542 Linlithgow Palace – 8 Feb 1587 Fotheringhay Castle, Northants.) executed; suc. father 1542 (at age 6 days); abdicated (under duress) 24 Jul 1567

=1 24 Apr 1558 Paris; **François II, King of France**, etc. (16 Jan 1544 Fontainbleau Palace – 5 Dec 1560 Orléans, France) son of Henri II, King of France & Catherine de'Medici; suc. father 6 Jul 1559

=2 29 Jul 1565 Edinburgh; ♦**Henry Stuart, Duke of Albany** Earl of Ross, Lord Ardmannoch (7 Dec 1545 Temple Newsham, Yorks. – 10 Feb 1567 Edinburgh) murdered; son of Matthew Stuart, 4th Earl of Lennox & Lady Margaret Douglas; cr. Duke etc. upon marriage

=3 (forcibly) 15 May 1567 Edinburgh; **James Hepburn, Duke of Orkney**, Marquess of Fife, 4th Earl Bothwell, 5th Lord Hailes[49] (ca.1535 – 14 Apr 1578 Dragsholm Castle, Denmark) son of Patrick Hepburn, 3rd Earl Bothwell & Agnes Sinclair; =1st Lady Jean Gordon; suc. father Sep 1556; cr. Duke and Marquess 12 May 1567; all of his titles were forfeited 29 Dec 1567

issue of 2nd (none surviving by the others):

(I) **James I** Charles, **King of England**, etc. and (as **James VI**) **King of Scotland**, etc. (19 Jun 1566 Edinburgh – 27 Mar 1625 Theobalds Park, Herts.) suc. mother 1567; suc. cousin, Elizabeth I,

---

[49] He is generally known to history by his inherited title, Earl Bothwell.

1603
= 23 Nov 1589 Oslo & 21 Jan 1590 Copenhagen; **Princess Anne of Denmark** (14 Oct 1574 Skanderborg Castle, Denmark – 4 Mar 1619 Hampton Court Palace, London) daughter of Frederik II, King of Denmark & Sophie of Mecklenburg-Güstrow

(A) **Prince Henry** Frederick, **Prince of Wales** (19 Feb 1593/4 Stirling Castle – 6 Nov 1612 London) unm.; cr. Prince of Wales 4 Jun 1610

(B) **Princess Elizabeth of England and Scotland** (19 Aug 1596 Dunfermline Palace, Fife – 13 Feb 1661/2 London)
= 14 Feb 1612/3 London; ♦**Friedrich V, Elector of the Palatine, King of Bohemia**, etc. (26 Aug 1596 Amberg, Bavaria – 29 Nov 1632 Mainz, Baden) son of Friedrich IV, Elector of the Palatine & Luise Juliana of Orange-Nassau; suc. father 1610; proclaimed King 1619; deposed as King 1620 and as Elector 1623

(1) **Count Heinrich Friedrich of the Palatine** (1 Jan 1614 – 7 Jan 1629 Haarlemmermeer, the Netherlands) drowned

(2) **Karl I** Ludwig, **Elector of the Palatine**, etc. (12 Dec 1617 – 28 Aug 1680 Edinger) suc. father 1648
=1 12 Feb 1650 (dv.1657); **Landgravine Charlotte of Hesse-Cassel** (20 Nov 1627 – 16 Mar 1686) daughter of Wilhelm V, Landgrave of Hesse-Cassel & Countess Amalie Elisabeth von Hanau-Münzenberg
=2 6 Jan 1658 Schwetzingen, nr. Heidelberg; **Countess Marie** Susanne Louise **von Degenfeld** (28 Nov 1634 Strassburg, Austria – 18 Mar 1677) daughter of Martin, Baron von Degenfeld
issue of 1st:

(a) **Karl II, Elector of the Palatine** (31 Mar 1651 – 26 May 1685) suc. father 1680
= 20 Sep 1671; **Princess Wilhelmina of Denmark** (20 Jun 1650 Copenhagen – 22 Apr 1706 Lichtenberg, Bavaria) daughter of Frederik III, King of Denmark & Duchess Sophie Amalie of Brunswick-Lüneburg
no issue

(b) **Countess Elisabeth Charlotte of the Palatine** (27 May 1652 Heidelberg – 8 Dec 1722 Saint-Cloud, France)
= 1671; ♦**Philippe I, Duke of Orleans** (1640 – 1701)
Children are listed with other parent
issue of 2nd:

(c) **Count Karl Ludwig of the Palatine** (15 Oct 1658 – 12 Aug 1688) killed in battle

(d) **Countess Caroline Elisabeth of the Palatine** (19 Nov 1659 – 7 Jul 1696 London)
= 4 Jun 1683; **Meinhardt von Schönberg, Duke of**

Schomberg (in Germany) **Duke of Leinster**, Marquess of Harwich, Earl of Brentford, Earl of Bangor, and Baron Teyes (in Britain) (30 Jun 1641 Cologne – 5 Jul 1619 London) son of Friedrich von Schönburg, Duke of Schomberg & Johann Schönberg auf Wessel; naturalized a British subject with the surname Schomberg 1690; suc. brother in Schomberg Oct 1693; cr. Duke of Leinster, etc. 1690, but all of the titles became extinct upon his death
Has further generations of issue
(e) **Countess Luise of the Palatine** (25 Jan 1661 – 6 Feb 1733) unm.
(f) **Countess Amalie Elisabeth of the Palatine** (1 Apr 1663 – 13 Jul 1709) unm.
(g) **Count Karl Edward of the Palatine** (19 May 1668 – 2 Jan 1690) unm.
(h) **Count Karl Moritz of the Palatine** (9 Jan 1671 – 13 Jun 1702) unm.
(i) **Count Karl August of the Palatine** (19 Oct 1672 – 20 Sep 1691)
(j) **Count Karl Casimir of the Palatine** (1 May 1675 – 28 Apr 1691) unm.
(3) **Countess Elisabeth of the Palatine** (26 Dec 1618 – 8 Feb 1680) a nun
(4) **Count Rupert of the Palatine, Duke of Cumberland**, Earl of Holderness **KG** (17 Dec 1619 Prague – 29 Nov 1682 London) cr. Duke 1644; KG 1642; unm.
issue by **Hon. Frances Bard** (ca.1646 – 1708 Karlsruhe, Baden) daughter of Henry Bard, 1st Viscount Bellomont & Ann Gardiner:
(a) **Dudley Bard** (ca.1666 – 13 Jul 1686 Buda, Hungary) killed in battle; unm.
issue by **Margaret Hughes** (1630 – 1685):
(b) **Ruperta Hughes** (1671 – 24 Jul 1741)
= ...; ◆**Emanuel Scrope Howe** (... – 26 Sep 1709) son of John Howe & Lady Annabella Scrope
Beyond the 12th generation on the father's line
(5) **Count Moritz of the Palatine** (16 Jan 1620/1 – Sep 1652 near the Virgin Islands) drowned
(6) **Countess Luisa** Hollandine **of the Palatine** (18 Apr 1622 – 11 Feb 1709) a nun
(7) **Eduard, Count von Simmern** (5 Oct 1625 – 10 Mar 1663) cr. Count von Simmern
= 4 May 1645 Paris; ◆**Anna de Gonzaga** (1616 Mantua, Italy – 6 Jul 1684 Paris) daughter of Carlo I de Gonzaga, 8th Duke of Mantua & Catherine de Mayenne
(a) **Countess Luise Marie von Simmern** (23 Jul

1647 – 11 Mar 1679)
= 20 Mar 1671; **Prince Karl Theodor of Salm**
(1645 – 1710)
Has further generations of issue
(b) **Countess Anne** Henriette Julie **von Simmern** (23
Jul 1648 – 23 Feb 1723)
= 1663; ♦**Henri Jules de Bourbon, Prince of Condé**
(1643 – 1709)
Children are listed with other parent
(c) **Countess Benedicte** Henriette **von Simmern** (14
Mar 1652 Paris – 12 Aug 1730)
= 30 Nov 1668; **Johann Friedrich, Duke of Brunswick-
Lüneburg-Kalenberg** (25 Apr 1625 – ca.18 Dec 1679) son of
Georg, Duke of Brunswick-Lüneburg & Landgravine Anne
Eleonore of Hesse-Darmstadt
Has further generations of issue
(8) **Countess Henriette** Maria **of the Palatine** (7 Jul
1626 – 18 Sep 1651)
= 16 Jun 1651; **Prince Sigismund von Siebenbürgen**
(ca.1923 – 11 Feb 1652)
no issue
(9) **Count Johnn** Philipp Friedrich **of the Palatine** (15
Sep 1629 – 15 Dec 1650 Rethel) killed in batte
(10) **Countess Sophia Dorothea of the Palatine** (13 Oct
1630 – 8 Jun 1714) heiress-presumtive to thrones of
England and Scotland at time of death[50]
= 30 Sep 1638 Heidelberg; **Ernst August, Elector of
Hanover,** Duke of Brunswick-Lüneburg (20 Nov 1629
Herzberg, Saxony – 23 Jan 1698) son of Georg, Duke
of Brunswick-Lüneburg & Landgravine Anne Eleonore
of Hesse-Darmstadt; suc. father 1679; cr. Elector 1692
(a) **George I** Louis, **King of Great Britain**, etc.,
Elector of Hanover, etc.[51] (28 May 1660 Osnabrück,
Saxony – 11 Jun 1727 Osnabrück) suc. father 1698;
suc. 2nd cousin, Queen Anne, 1714
= 21 Nov 1682 (dv.1694); **Duchess Sophia Dorothea
of Brunswick-Celle** (5 Sep 1666 – 2 Nov 1726
Ahlden) daughter of Georg Wilhelm, Duke of Brunswick-
Celle & Eleonore Desnier
Has further generations of issue

---

[50] Had she lived two more months, she would have been Queen Sophia of Great Britain, etc.
[51] His descendants are traced to the present day by this author in *The Descendants of King
George I of Great Britain* (2002).

(b) **Prince Friedrich August of Hanover**, etc. (3 Oct 1661 Hanover – 31 Dec 1690 Ardeal, Transylvania) killed in battle; unm.

(c) **Prince Maximilian** Wilhelm **of Hanover** (13 Dec 1666 Hanover – 16 Jul 1726 Vienna) unm.

(d) **Princess Sophie** Charlotte **of Hanover** (12 Oct 1668 Hanover – 21 Jan 1705 Hanover)
= 8 Sep 1684; **Friedrich I, King in Prussia**, etc. (11 Jul 1657 – 25 Feb 1713) son of Friedrich Wilhelm, Elector of Brandenburg & Princess Louise of Orange-Nassau; =1st Landgravine Elisabeth olf Hesse-Cassel; he =3rd Duches Sophie of Mecklenburg- Schwerin; suc. father 1688; declared King 18 Jan 1701
Has further generations of issue

(e) **Prince Karl Philipp of Hanover** (3 Oct 1669 Hanover – 31 Dec 1690 Pristina, Albania) killed in battle; unm.

(f) **Prince Christian Heinrich of Hanover** (19 Sp 1671 Hanover – 31 Jul 1703 Ulm, Württemberg) drowned in the Danube

(g) **Prince Ernst August of Hanover, Duke of York and Albany**, Earl of Ulster **KG** (7 Sep 1674 Osnabrück – 14 Aug 1728 Osnabrück) cr. Duke 5 Jul 1716; KG 1716

(C) **Charles I, King of England and Scotland**, etc. (19 Nov 1600 Dunfermline Palace – 30 Jan 1649 London) ex ecuted; suc. father 1625; deposed 27 Jan 1649
= 13 Jun 1625 Canterbury, Kent; ♦**Princess Henriette Marie of France** (26 Nov 1609 Paris – 31 Aug 1669 Colombe, France) daughter of Henri IV, King of France & Marie de'Medici

(1) **Charles II, King of England and France**, etc. (29 May 1630 London – 6 Feb 1685 London) suc. father as King *de jure* 30 Jan 1649 and *de facto* 29 May 1660
= 21 May 1662 Portsmouth; ♦**Catarina da Bragança, Infanta of Portugal** (25 Nov 1638 Lisbon – 30 Nov 1705 Lisbon) daughter of Dom João IV, King of Portugal & Dona Luisa Marisa Pérez de Guzman
no issue by marriage
issue by **Lucy Walter** (ca.1630 – 1658 Paris):

(a) **James Scott** (previously Crofts), **Duke of Monmouth**, Earl of Doncaster, Baron Scott of Tindale, 1st Duke of Buccleauch, Eaerl of Dalkeith, Baron Scott of Whitchester and Eskdale **KG** (9 Mar 1649 Rotterdam – 15 Jul 1685 London) executed; cr. Duke of Monmouth 4 Feb 1662/3 (forfeited and extinct upon hisa death); cr. Duke of Buccleuch jointly with wife 26 Apr 1663; KG 1663

= 20 Apr 1663 London; ♦**Anne Scott, 4ᵗʰ Countess Buccleuch**, Lady Scott of Whitchester and Eskdale, 5ᵗʰ Lady Scott of Buccleuch, 1ˢᵗ Duchess of Buccleuch, etc. (11 Feb 1651 Dundee – 6 Feb 1731/2 Dalkeith, Midlothian) daughter of Francis Scott, 2ⁿᵈ Earl of Buccleuch & Lady Margaret Leslie; she =2ⁿᵈ Charles Cornwallis, 3ʳᵈ Baron Cornwallis; suc. sister 12 Mar 1661; cr. Duchess 26 Apr 1663
Has further generations of issue
issue by **Elizabeth Killigrew** (16 May 1622 – Dec 1681 London) daughter of Sir Robert Killigrew & Mary Wodehouse; = ♦Francis Boyle, 1ˢᵗ Viscount Shannon:
(b) **Lady Charlotte** Jemima Henrietta Maria **Fitzroy** (1650 – 28 Jul 1684)
=1 ca.1667; ♦**James Howard** (1640 – 1669) son of Hon . Thomas Howard
=2 17 Jul 1672; **William Paston, 2ⁿᵈ Earl of Yarmouth** Viscount Yarmouth, Baron Paston, 3ʳᵈ Baronet (1653 – 25 Dec 1732) son of Robert Paston, 1ˢᵗ Earl of Yarmouth & Rebecca Clayton
Has further generations of issue by both
issue by **Catherine Pegge** (... – 1678) daughter of Thomas Pegge & Catherine Kniveton; = Sir Edward Green Baronet:
(c) **Charles FitzCharles, Earl of Plymouth**, Viscount Totnes, Baron Dartmouth (1657 Flanders – 17 Oct 1680 Tangier, Morocco) cr. Earl 29 Jul 1675, but titles became extinct upon his death
= 19 Sep 1678 Wimbledon; ♦**Lady Bridget Osborne** (... – 9 May 1718 Hereford) daughter of Thomas Osborne, 1ˢᵗ Duke of Leeds & Lady Bridget Bertie; =2ⁿᵈ Philip Bisse no issue
(d) **Lady Catherine FitzCharles** (... – 1759) a nun
issue by **Barbara Villiers, 1ˢᵗ Duchess of Cleveland**, Countess of Southampton, Boness Nonsuch (17 Nov 1649 London – 9 Oct 1709 London) daughter of William Villiers, 2ⁿᵈ Viscount Grandison & Hon. Mary Bayning; she = 14 Apr 1659; Roger Palmer, 1ˢᵗ Earl of Castlemaine; cr. Duchess 3 Aug 1670
(e) **Lady Anne Fitzroy** (25 Feb 1660/1 – 16 May 1722) surnamed Palmer until acknowledged by the King 1674
= 1674; ♦**Thomas Lennard, Earl of Essex** (1654 – 1715) Children are listed with other parent
(f) **Charles Fitzroy, 2ⁿᵈ Duke of Cleveland**, etc., 1ˢᵗ **Duke of Southampton**, Earl of Chichester, Baron of Newbury **KG** (18 Jun 1662 London – 9 Sep 1730 London) suc. mother 9 Oct 1709; cr. Duke of

Southampton 10 Sep 1675; KG 1673

=1 1671; **Mary Wood** (ca.1663 – 15 Nov 1680 London) daughter of Sir Henry Wood, 1st Baronet & Mary Gardiner =2 Oct/Nov 1694; **Anne Pulteney** (25 Nov 1663 – 20 Feb 1745/6) daughter of Sir William Pulteney & Grace Corbet; =2nd Philip Southcote

issue of 2nd (none by 1st):

Has further generations of issue

(g) **Henry Fitzroy, 1st Duke of Grafton**, Earl of Euston, Viscount Ipswich, Baron Sudbury **KG** (28 Feb 1663 – 9 Oct 1690) cr. Earl etc. 16 Aug 1672 and Duke 11 Sep 1675

= 1 Aug 1672; ♦**Isabella Bennet, 2nd Countess of Arlington**, Viscountess Thetford, Baroness Arlington (ca. 1668 – 7 Feb 1722/3) daughter of Henry Bennet, 1st Earl of Arlington & Isabella de Nassau; suc. father 28 Jul 1685

Has further generations of issue

(h) **Lady Charlotte Fitzroy** (5 Sep 1664 – 17 Feb 1717/8 London)

= 6 Feb 1677; **Edward** Henry **Lee, 1st Earl of Lichfield**, Viscount Quarendon, Baron Spelsbury, 5th Baronet (4 Feb 1663 – 14 Jul 1716) son of Sir Francis Lee, 4th Baronet & Lady Elizabeth Pope; suc. father 4 Dec 1667; cr. Earl 1674

Has further generations of issue

(i) **George Fitzroy, Duke of Northumberland**, Earl of Northumberland, Viscount Falmouth, Baron of Pontefract (28 Oct 1665 Oxford – 28 Jun 1716) cr. Earl, etc. 1 Oct 1674 and Duke 6 Apr 1683, but all titles became extinct upon his death

=1 bef.15 Mar 1686; **Catherine Wheatley** (... – 25 May 1714) daughter of Robert Wheatley; =1st Thomas Lucy =2 10 Mar 1715; **Mary Dutton** (... – 27 Aug 1738 Frogmore House, Windsor) daughter of Henry Dutton

no issue

issue by Eleanor (**Nell**) **Gwynne** (1650 – 14 Nov 1687) daughter of Thomas Gwynne & Eleanor ...

(j) **Charles Beauclerk, 1st Duke of Saint Albans**, Earl of Burford, Baron Heddington, Baron Vere **KG** (8 May 1670 London – 11 May 1726) cr. Earl etc. 21 Dec 1676 and Duke 5 Jan 1684

= 17 Apr 1694; ♦**Lady Diana de Vere** (... – 15 Jan 1741/2) daughter of Aubrey de Vere, 20th Earl of Oxford & Diana Kirke

Has further generations of issue

issue by Louise Renée **de Penancoet de Keroualle,**

Duchess of Portsmouth, Countess of Fareham, Baroness of Petersfield, Duchess d'Aubigny (Sep 1649 Keroualle – 14 Nov 1734 Paris) daughter of Guillaume de Penancoet, Lord de Keroualle & Msarie du Timeur et de Kergolay; cr. Duchess of Portsmouth, etc. (ad personam) 1673; cr. Duchess d'Aubigny (in France) Jan 1683/4:

(k) **Charles Lennox, 1ˢᵗ Duke of Richmond**, Earl of March, Baron of Settrington, **Duke of Lennox**, Earl of Darnley, Lord of Torbolton, **KG** (29 Jul 1672 London – 27 May 1723 Goodwood, Sussex) cr. Duke of Richmond, etc in England 9 Aug 1675; cr. Duke of Lennox, etc. in Scotland 9 Sep 1675; KG 1681
= 8 Jan 1692/3; ♦**Anne Brudenell** (1671 – 9 Dec 1722) daughter of Francis, Lord Brudenell & Lady Frances Savile; =1ˢᵗ ♦Henry Belasyse, 2ⁿᵈ Baron Belayse
Has further generations of issue
issue by **Mary Davies** (ca.1648 – 1708):

(l) **Lady Mary Tudor** (16 Oct 1673 – 5 Nov 1726 Paris)
=1 18 Aug 1687; **Edward Radclyffe, 2ⁿᵈ Earl of Derwentwater** (9 Dec 1655 – 29 Apr 1705) son of Francis Radclyffe, 1ˢᵗ Earl of Derwentwater & Catherine Fenwick
=2 23 May 1705; ♦**Henry Graham** (... – 7 Jan 1706/7) son of James Graham & Dorothy Howard
=3 26 Aug 1707; **James Rooke** (... – 16 Jun 1773) son of Heyman Rooke
Has further generations of issue by 1ˢᵗ and 3ʳᵈ

(2) **Princess Mary Henrietta Stuart, The Princess Royal** (4 Nov 1631 London – 24 Dec 1660 London) cr. Princess Royal (first to carry that title) 1642
= 12 May 1641; **Willem II, Prince of Orange**, etc. **KG** (27 May 1626 The Hague – 6 Nov 1650 The Hague) son of Fredrik, Prince of Orange & Countess Amalie zu Solms-Braunfels; suc. father 14 Mar 1647; KG 1645

(a) **William III** Henry, **King of England and Scotland**, etc., **Prince of Orange**, etc. (4 Nov 1650 – 8 Mar 1702 London) suc. father 1650; proclaimed King (jointly with wife) 13 Feb 1689
= 4 Nov 1677 London; ♦**Mary II, Queen of England and Scotland**, etc. (30 Apr 1662 London – 28 Dec 1694 London) daughter of James II, King of England and Scotland & Lady Anne Hyde; suc. father (jointly with husband) 13 Feb 1689
no issue

(3) **James II, King of England and** (as **James VII**) **Scotland**, etc. (14 Oct 1633 London – 16 Sept 1701

Saint-Germain-en-Laye) suc. brother as King 1685; was forced to flee country Dec 1688 and was declared by Parliament to have abdicated 12 Feb 1689, his daughter being declared Queen the following day jointly with her husband

=1 24 Nov 1659 Breda [Belgium] (privately) & 3 Sep 1660 London (publicly); ♦**Lady Anne Hyde** (12 Mar 1637/8 Windsor – 31 Mar 1671 London) daughter of Edward Hyde, 1st Earl of Clarendon & Frances Aylesbury

=2 21 Nov 1673 Dover, Kent; **Donna Maria** Beatrice Eleanora Anna Margherita Isabella **d'Este di Modena** (5 Oct 1658 Modena, Italy – 7 May 1718 Staint-Germain-en-Laye) daughter of Alfonso IV d'Este, Duke of Modena & Donna Laura Martinozzi

issue of 1st:

(a) **Mary II, Queen of England and Scotland,** etc. (30 Apr 1662 London – 28 Dec 1694 London) suc. father (jointly with husband) 13 Feb 1689

= 4 Nov 1677 London; ♦**William III** Henry, **King of England and Scotland**, etc., **Prince of Orange**, etc. (4 Nov 1650 – 8 Mar 1702 London) son of Wilem II, Prince of Orange & Princess Mary Henrietta The Princess Royal; suc. father 1650; proclaimed King (jointly with wife) 13 Feb 1689

no issue

(b) **Anne, Queen of Great Britain and Ireland**, etc. (6 Feb 1664/5 London – 1 Aug 1714 London) suc. brother-in-law 1702; initially titled Qeen of the England and Scotland, etc.; the title became Queen of Great Britain and Ireland 1708

= 28 Jul 1683 London; **Prince George of Denmark, Duke of Cumberland**, Earl of Kendal, Baron of Wokingham (2 Apr 1853 Copenhagen – 28 Oct 1708 London) son of Frederik III, King of Denmark & Duchess Sophie of Brunswick-Lüneburg; cr. Duke 6 Apr 1689

no surviving issue

issue of 2nd:

(c) **Prince James** Francis Edward, **Duke of Cornwall**, Duke of Rothesay **KG** (*de jure King James III of England and VIII of Scotland*)(10 Jun 1688 London – 1 Jan 1766 Rome) suc. as Duke at birth; suc. father as Stuart claimant to the Throne 16 Sep 1701; attainted and all titles forfeited; known historically as "the Old Pretender"

= 3 Sep 1719 Bologna, Italy; **Princess Maria**
Kazimiera Klementina **Sobiekska** (6 Jul 1702 – 18
Jan 1735 Rome) daughter of Jakub Sobieski, Prince of
Poland & Countess Hedwig von Neuburg
Has further generations of issue
(d) **Princess Louisa** Maria Theresa **Stuart** (18 Jun
   1692 Saint-Germain-en-Laye – 8 Apr 1712 Saint-
   Germain-en-Laye) unm.
issue by **Arabella Churchill** (23 Feb 1647 – 4 May
1730) daughter of Sir Winston Churchill & Elizabeth Drake;
she = Charles Godfrey:
(e) **Henrietta FitzJames** (1667 – 3 Apr 1730
   Navestock, Essex)
   =1 29 Nov 1683; **Henry Waldegrave, 1ˢᵗ Baron
   Waldegrave**, 4ᵗʰ Baronet (1661 – ca.14 Jan 1689/90)
   son of Sir Charles Waldegrave, 3ʳᵈ Baronet & Helen
   Englefield; suc. father 1684; cr. Baron 1686
   =2 3 Apr 1695; **Piers Butler, 3ʳᵈ Viscount of
   Galmoye** (21 Mar 1651/2 – 18 Jun 1740 Paris) son of
   Edward Butler, 2ⁿᵈ Viscount of Galmoye & Eleanor
   Whyte; =1ˢᵗ Anne Mathew
   Has further generations of issue
(f) **James FitzJames, 1ˢᵗ Duke of Berwick**, Earl of
   Tinmouth, Baron of Bosworth, (England) 1ˢᵗ Duke de
   Liria y Xerica (Spain) and Duke de FitzJames
   (France) (21 Aug 1670 – 12 Jun 1734 Philippsburg,
   Germany) died of wounds received in battle; cr. Duke
   of Berwick 19 Mar 1686/7, Duke de Liria y Xerica 16
   Oct 1707; Duke de FitzJames 23 Mar 1710; attainted
   and English titles were forfeited 1690
   =1 26 Mar 1695 Saint-Germain-en-Laye; **Lady
   Honora Burke** (16 Jan 1674 Languedoc, France – 16
   Jan 1697/8 Languedoc) daughter of William Bourke, 7ᵗʰ
   Earl of Clanricarde & Lady Helen MacCarty; =1ˢᵗ
   Patrick Sarsfield, 1ˢᵗ Earl of Lucan
   =2 18 Apr 1700 Paris; **Anne Bulkeley** (... – 12 Jun
   1751) daughter of Hon. Henry Bukleley & Sophia Stewart
   Has further generations of issue
(g) **Henry FitzJames** (*de jure Duke of Albemarle, Earl of
   Rochford, Baron of Romney*) (6 Aug 1673 – 16 Dec 1702
   Languedoc) cr. Duke, etc. by his after he was deposed, so they
   are not considered legal titles
   = 20 Jul 1700; **Countess Marie Gabrielle d'Audibert de
   Lussan** (1675 – 15 May 1741) daughter of Jean d'Audibert,
   Count de Lussan & Marie Françoise Raimond; =2ⁿᵈ ♦John
   Drummond, 1ˢᵗ Earl of Melfort

Issue is extinct[52]

(h) **Arabella FitzJames** (ca.1674 – 7 Nov 1704) a nun
issue by **Catherine Sedley, Countess of Dorchester**,
Baroness of Darlington (21 Dec 1657 – 26 Oct 1717)
daughter of Sir Charles Sedley, 5th Baronet & Lady
Catherine Savage; = David Colyear, 1st Earl of
Portmore; cr. Countess, etc. ad personam 20 Jan 1685/6:
    (i) **Lady Catherine Darnley** (ca.1681 – 13 Mar 1743)
      =1 1699; ♦**James Annesley, 3rd Earl of Anglesey**
      (1674 – 1702)
      =2 1706; ♦**John Sheffield, 1st Duke of Buckingham**
      (1647 – 1721)
      issue of 1st:
      Children are listed with other parent
      issue of 2nd:
      Children are listed with other parent
  (4) **Prince Henry Stuart, Duke of Gloucester**, Earl of
    Cambridge **KG** (8 Jul 1640 Weybridge, Surrey – 13
    Sep 1660 London) KG 1653; cr. Duke 13 May 1659
  (5) **Princess Henrietta Anne Stuart** (16 Jun 1644
    Exeter, Devon – 30. Jun 1670 Saint Cloud, France)
    = 1661; ♦**Philippe I de Bourbon, Duke of Orleans** (1640 –
    1701)
    Children are listed with other parent
issue by ♦**Lady Elizabeth Stuart** (aft.1512 – bef.25 Nov
1564) daughter of John Stuart, 3rd Earl of Lennox & Lady
Elizabeth Stewart; = John Gordon, 11th Earl of Sutherland:
b) **Adam Stewart** (aft.1528 – 1575)
    = ...; **Janet Ruthven** (bef.1550 – 20 Jan 1616) daughter of
    William Ruthven
    no issue
issue by **Elizabeth Bethune** (...) daughter of Sir John Bethune, 2nd
of Creich & Janet Hay; =1st John Stewart, 4th Lord
Innermeath; =2nd Hon. James Gray:
c) **Jean Stewart** (aft.1528 – 7 Jan 1587/8)
    = 1 Jul 1553 (dv.1573); ♦**Archibald Campbell, 5th Earl of**
    Argyll etc. (ca.1532 – 12 Sep 1573) son of Archibald Campbell, 4th
    Earl of Argyll & Lady Helen Hamilton; =2nd ♦Lady Janet
    Cuninghame
    no issue
issue by **Elizabeth Shaw** (...):

---

[52] An only daughter who became a nun.

d) **James Stewart** (ca.1529 – 25 Sep 1557) a priest
issue by **Elizabeth Carmichael** (...) daughter of Sir John
Carmichael:
e) **John Stewart, 1ˢᵗ Lord Darnley** (ca.1531 – Nov. 1563) cr.
   Lord 1562
   = 4 Jan 1561/2; ♦**Lady Jean Hepburn** (... – bef.27 Jul 1599)
   daughter of Patrick Hepburn, 3ʳᵈ Earl of Bothwell & Agnes Sinclair;
   she =2ⁿᵈ ♦John, Master of Caithness; =3ʳᵈ Rev. Archibald Douglas
   (I) **Francis Stewart, Earl of Bothwell**, Lord Hailes, 2ⁿᵈ
      Lord Darnley (ca.1563 – 4 Nov 1613) suc. father 1563; cr.
      Earl 16 Jun 1581; attainted and titles forfeited 25 Jun 1591
      for witchcraft; escaped to Europe
      = bef.1 Jul 1592; ♦**Lady Margaret Douglas** (... – 1640)
      daughter of David Douglas, 7ᵗʰ Earl of Angus & Margaret
      Hamilton; =1ˢᵗ Sir Walter Scott, 4ᵗʰ of Buccleuch
      (A) **Francis, Master of Bothwell** (1584 – 1639)
         = 2 Aug 1614; ♦**Lady Isabel Seton** (30 Nov 1593 – ...)
         daughter of Robert Seton, 1ˢᵗ Earl of Winton & Lady Margaret
         Montgomerie; =1ˢᵗ James Drummond, 1ˢᵗ Earl of Perth
         (1) **Charles Stewart** (15 Jan 1617/8 Tranent, East Lothian – ...)
            unm.
         (2) **Margaret Stewart** (4 Apr 1619 – ...)
      (B) **Lady Elizabeth Stewart** (1590 – ...)
         = 1616; **James, Master of Cranstoun** (... – 1633) son of
         William Cranstoun, 1ˢᵗ Lord Cranstoun & Sarah
         Cranstoun; =1ˢᵗ Elizabeth Makgill
         (1) **William Cranstoun, 3ʳᵈ Lord Cranstoun** (aft.1620 –
            aft.Jul 1664) suc. uncle ca.1648
            = 10 Jul 1643; **Lady Mary Leslie** (...) daughter of
            Alexander Leslie, 1ˢᵗ Earl of Leven & Agnes Renton
            (a) **James Cranstoun, 4ᵗʰ Lord Cranstoun** (... – aft.
               1685) suc. father 1664
               = ...; **Anne Don** (...) daughter of Sir Alexander Don, Baronet
               Has further generations of issue
            (b) **Hon. Helen Cranstoun** (...)
               = ...; **John Adam** (...)
               Has further generations of issue
         (2) **Isabella Cranstoun** (...)
            = ca.1649; **Sir Gilbert Eliott of Stobs, 1ˢᵗ Baronet** (... –
            Sep 1677) son of William Eliott & Elizabeth Douglas
            (a) **Sir William Eliott of Stobs, 2ⁿᵈ Baronet** (... – 19 Feb
               1699) suc. father 1677
               =1 ...; **Elizabeth Scott** (...) daughter of Sir John Scott of
               Ancrum
               =2 3 Feb 1680; **Margaret Murray** (...) daughter of Charles
               Murray of Hadden

Has further generations of issue by 1st
(b) **John Eliott of Lymiecleugh** (...)
(c) **James Eliott** (...)
(3) **Margaret Cranstoun** (...)
= ...; **Patrick Cockburn** (...) son of Sir Richard
Cockburn Clerkington
issue ?
(C) **Lady Margaret Stewart** (...)
= ca.Aug 1621; ♦**Alan Cathcart, 5th Lord Cathcart**
(ca.1600 – 18 Aug 1628) son of Alan, Master of Cathcart
& Isabel Kennedy; =2nd Jean Colquhoun; suc. grandfather 1618
no issue
(D) **Hon. John Stewart** (... – aft.1650)
= ...
(1) **Margaret Stewart** (...)
= ...; **Sir John Home** (... – 13 Jul 1671) son of Sir Alexander
Home & Margaret Cockburn; =1st Janet Home
(a) **Sir Alexander Home, 1st Baronet** (... – 28 May
1698) cr. Baronet ca.1678
= 27 Apr 1678; **Margaret Scott** (...) daughter of Sir
Wiliam Scott & Barbaran Dalmahoy
Has further generations of issue
(b) **Patrick Home** (... – aft.1673)
(E) **Lady Jean Stewart** (...)
= ...; **Robert Elliot, 17th of Redreugh** (ca.1583 – bef.1673) son
of Robert Elliot & Marion Hamilton
(1) **Margaret Elliot, 18th of Redreugh** (ca.1620 – 1697)
= 1637; **James Eliott** (... – ca.19 Jul 1661) son of Gilbert
Eliott of Stobs & Margaret Scott
(a) **Robert Eliot, 19th of Redheugh** (...)
= ...
Has further generations of issue
(2) **Esther Elliot** (... – 30 Sep 1664 Latheron, Caithness)
= 1653; **Andrew Clerk** (... – 13 Sep 1683 Latheron)
no issue
(F) **Lady Helen Stewart** (ca.1576 – bef.6 Jun 1590)
= ca.1589; **John MacFarlane, 15th of Arrochar** (ca.1564 –
aft.14 Aug 1627) son of Andrew MacFarlane, 14th of Arrochar &
Agnes Maxwell
(1) **Walter MacFarlane, 16th of Arrochar** (1589 Arrochar,
Dunbarton – 1664 Arrochar)
= ca.1608 Beltrees, Renfrew; **Margaret Semphill** (ca.1590
Beltrees – aft.1629 Arrochar) daughter of James Semphill,
2nd of Beltrees & Egida Elphinstone
(a) **John** Dow **MacFarlane, 17th of Arrochar** (ca.1629 –
1679)

= ...; **Grizel Lamont** (ca.1629 – ...) daughter of Collin
Lamont & Beatrix Semphill
Has further generations of issue
issue by ♦**Hon. Margaret Erskine** (... – 5 May 1572) daughter of
John Erskine, 5th Lord Erskine & Lady Margaret Campbell; = Sir
Robert Douglas of Lochleven:
f) **James Stewart, 1st Earl of Moray**, Earl of Mar, Lord
   Abernethy, Lord Strathdearn (1531 – 20 Jan 1569/70
   Linlithgow) murdered; cr. Earl of Moray 30 Jan 1561/2 and
   Earl of Mar 7 Feb 1561/2; the Earldom of Mar became
   extinct upon his death, the remaining titles were inheritable
   by his daughter
   = 8 Feb 1561/2; ♦**Lady Anne Keith** (... – 16 Jul 1588) daughter
   of William Keith, 3rd Earl Marischal & Margaret Keith; =2nd
   ♦Colin Campbell, 6th Earl of Argyll
   (I) **Elizabeth Stewart, 2nd Countess of Moray**, Lady
   Abernethy and Strathdearn (... – 18 Nov 1591) suc. father 1570
   = 1581; ♦**James Stewart, 2nd Lord Doune** (... – 1592)
   Children are listed with other parent
   (II) **Lady Margaret Stewart** (... – 1586)
   = 27 Jun 1584; ♦**Francis Hay, 9th Earl of Erroll**, etc. (... –
   16 Jul 1631) son of Andrew Hay, 8th Earl of Erroll & Lady
   Jean Hay; =2nd ♦Lady Mary Stewart; =3rd ♦Lady
   Elizabeth Douglas; suc. father 1585
   no issue
issue by **Christine Barclay** (...):
g) **James Stewart** (aft.1531 – ...) unm.
issue of **Hon. Euphemia Elphinstone** (...) daughter of Alexander
Elphinstone, 1st Lord Elphinstone & Elizabeth Barlow; = John
Bruce of Cutmalindie:
h) **Robert Stewart, 1st Earl of Orkney**, Lord of Zetland
   (1533 – 4 Feb 1592/3) cr. Earl 1581
   = 14 Dec 1461 Edinburgh; ♦**Lady Janet Kennedy** (... –
   1598) daughter of Gilbert Kennedy, 3rd Earl of Cassillis &
   Margaret Kennedy
   (I) **Lady Katherine Stewart** (...)
   = ...; ♦**John Sinclair of Ulbster** (bef.1598 – ...)
   Children are listed with other parent
   (II) **Lady Jean Stewart** (ca.1563 – ...)
   = ...; ♦**Patrick Leslie, 1st Lord Lindores** (... – 1608)
   Children are listed with other parent
   (III) **Lady Mary Stewart** (...)
   = 1585; ♦**Patrick Gray, 6th Lord Gray** (... – 1611)
   Children are listed with other parent
   (IV) **Patrick Stewart, 2nd Earl of Orkney**, etc. (aft.1568 – 6
   Feb 1615 Edinburgh) executed; suc. father 1593, but title

became extinct on his death

= ...; ◆**Margaret Livingston** (...) daughter of William Livingston, 6th Lord Livingston & Agnes Fleming; =1st Lewis Bellenden
no issue

(V) **John Stewart, Earl of Carrick**, Lord Kincleven (... – bef.3 Mar 1645/6) cr. Lord 10 Aug 1607 and Earl 22 Jul 1628, but titles became extinct upon his death

= 26 Oct 1604 London; ◆**Lady Elizabeth Howard** (1564 – ca.Jan 1646) daughter of Charles Howard, 1st Earl of Nottingham & Katherine Carey; =1st Sir Robert Southwell

(A) **Lady Margaret Stewart** (...)
= ...; **Sir Matthew Mennes KB** (... – 1648)
(1) **Margaret Mennes** (aft.1624 – 1676)
= ...; **Sir John Heath** (...)
(a) **Margaret Heath** (...)
= 2 Dec 1683; **George Verney, 12th Baron Willoughby de Broke** (... – 26 Dec 1728) son of Richard Verney, 11th Baron Willoughby de Broke & Mary Pretyman; suc. father 18 Jul 1711
Has further generations of issue (extinct 1755)

(VI) **Hon. Sir James Stewart** (...)
= ...; **Margaret Lyon** (...)
(A) **Robert Stewart** (ca.1610 – ...)

(VII) **Hon. Robert Stewart** (...)

issue by **Marion Boyd** (...) daughter of Archibald Boyd of Bonshaw & Christian Mure:

2) **Catherine Stewart** (... – aft.1554)
= 1507; ◆**James Douglas, 3rd Earl of Morton** (... – 1548)
Children are listed with other parent

3) **Alexander Stewart** (ca.1493 – 9 Sep 1513 Flodden Field)
killed in battle

issue by ◆**Isabella Stewart** (...) illegimate daughter of James Stewart, 1st Earl of Buchan & Margaret Murray:

4) **Janet Stewart** (... – aft.22 Aug 1560)
= ...; **Malcolm Fleming, 3rd Lord Fleming** (ca.1494 – 10 Sep 1547) son of John Fleming, 2nd Lord Fleming & Euphemia Drummond; suc. father 1 Nov 1524

a) **James Fleming, 4th Lord Fleming** (... – 15 Dec 1558) suc. father 1547
= bef.23 Dec 1553; ◆**Lady Barbara Hamilton** (...) daughter of James Hamilton, 2nd Earl of Arran & Lady Margaret Douglas; =1st Alexander, Lord Gordon

(I) **Hon. Jean Fleming** (ca.1554 – 23 Jun 1609)
=1 16 Jan 1582/3; **John Maitland, 1st Lord Maitland of Thirlestane** (ca.1545 – 3 Oct 1595) son of Sir Richard

Maitland of Thirlesane & Mary Cranston

=2 4 Nov 1597; ♦**John Kennedy, 5ᵗʰ Earl of Cassillis**, etc. (1575 – Oct 1615) son of Gilbert Kennedy, 4ᵗʰ Earl of Cassillis & Margaret Lyon

issue by 1ˢᵗ (none by 2ⁿᵈ):

(A) **John Maitland, 1ˢᵗ Earl of Lauderdale**, Viscount Maitland and of Lauderdale, Lord Thirleston and Boulton, 2ⁿᵈ Lord Maitland of Thirleston (... – 18 Jan 1544/5) suc. father 1595; cr. Viscount Lauderdale 2 Apr 1616; cr. Earl 14 Mar 1624

= bef.18 Jun 1610; ♦**Lady Isabel Seton** (1 Aug 1594 – 2 Nov 1638 Lethington Castle, E. Lothian) daughter of Alexander Seton. 1ˢᵗ Earl of Dumfermline & Lilias Drummond

(1) **John Maitland, Duke of Lauderdale**, Marquess of March, Earl of Lauderdale, Viscount Maitland, Lord Thurlestane, Musselburgh, and Bolton, 2ⁿᵈ Earl of Lauderdale, etc. (all in Scotland), 1ˢᵗ Earl of Guilford, Baron Petersham (in England) (24 May 1616 – 24 Aug 1682) suc. father 1645; cr. Duke, etc. 24 Mar 1672; cr. Earl of Guilford, etc. 25 Jun 1674, the new creations all becoming extinct upon his death

=1 Aug/Sep 1632; ♦**Lady Anne Home** (... – 1671) daughter of Alexander Home, 1ˢᵗ Earl Home & Mary Dudley

=2 17 Feb 1671; **Elizabeth Murray, 2ⁿᵈ Countess of Dysart**, Lady Huntingtower (1626 – 4 Jun 1698) daughter of William Murray, 1ˢᵗ Earl of Dysart & Catherine Bruce; she =1ˢᵗ ♦Sir Lionel Tollemache, 3ʳᵈ Baronet; suc. father Sep 1653

issue of 1ˢᵗ (none by 2ⁿᵈ):

(a) **Lady Mary Maitland** (1645 – 20 Mar 1702)
= 1666; ♦**John Hay, 2ⁿᵈ Marquess of Tweeddale** (1645 – 1713)
Beyond the 12ᵗʰ generation on the father's line

(2) **Charles Maitland, 3ʳᵈ Earl of Lauderdale**, etc. (... – 9 Jun 1691) suc. brother 1682

= 18 Nov 1652 Halton, Midlothian; **Elizabeth Lauder** (... – aft.Dec 1685) daughter of Richard Lauder & Mary Scott

(a) **Richard Maitland, 4ᵗʰ Earl of Lauderdale**, etc. (20 Jun 1653 – 1695) suc. father 1691
= 1 Jul 1678; ♦**Lady Anne Campbell** (... – 18 Sep 1734) daughter of Archibald Campbell, 9ᵗʰ Earl of Argyll & Lady Mary Stuart; =2ⁿᵈ ♦Charles Stuart 6ᵗʰ Earl of Moray
no issue

(b) **John Maitland, 5ᵗʰ Earl of Lauderdale**, etc.
(ca.1655 – 30 Aug 1710) suc. brother 1695
= ca.1680; ♦**Lady Margaret Cuninghame** (ca.
1662 – 12 May 1742) daughter of Alexander Cuninghame,
10ᵗʰ Earl of Glencairn & Nicola Stewart
Has further generations of issue
(c) **Lady Isabel Maitland** (1655 Thirlestane,
Berwicks. – 7 Oct 1706 Edinburgh)
= 1670; ♦**John Elphinstone, 8ᵗʰ Lord Elphinstone**
(1649 – 1718)
Children are listed with other parent
(d) **Hon. Charles Maitland** (...)
= ...; **Lilias Colquhoun** (ca.1650 – ...) daughter of Sir John
Colquhoun of Luss, 2ⁿᵈ Baronet & Margaret Baillie;
she =1ˢᵗ Sir John Stirling, 8ᵗʰ of Kier and 5ᵗʰ of
Cadder
no issue
(e) **Lady Mary Maitland** (...)
= 1691; ♦**Charles Carnegie, 4ᵗʰ Earl of Southesk**
(1661 – 1699)
Children are listed with other parent
(f) **Hon. William Maitland** (... – 1724)
=1 ...; **Christian Makgill** (16 Mar 1677 – 1707)
=2 aft.1707; **Margaret Walker** (...)
Has further generations of issue
(g) **Hon. Alexander Maitland** (...)
= ...
Has further generations of issue
(3) **Hon. Robert Maitland** (11 Mar 1623 – 15 Dec 1658
Lundin, Fife)
= 25 Apr 1648; **Margaret Lundie** (...) daughter of John
Lundie of that Ilk & Katharine Lindsay
(a) **Sophia Maitland** (...)
= 1670; ♦**John Drummond, 1ˢᵗ Earl of Melfort**
(1650 – 1715)
Children are listed with other parent
(b) **Anna Maitland** (... – 3 Sep 1694)
= 1674; ♦**Hon. James Carnegie** (aft.1643 – 1707)
Beyond the 12ᵗʰ generation on the father's line
(B) **Hon. Anne Maitland** (ca.1589 – 6 Jul 1609)
= 1 Feb 1602/3; ♦**Robert Seton, 2ⁿᵈ Earl of Winton**,
etc. (ca.1583 – ...) son of Robert Seton, 1ˢᵗ Earl of Winton
& Lady Margaret Montgomerie; suc. father 22 Mar 1603;
resigned title to brother 26 Jun 1606
no issue
b) **Hon. Elizabeth Fleming** (...)

= bef.24 May 1540; **William Crichton, 5th Lord Crichton of Sanquhar** (aft.1516 – 11 Jun 1550 Edinburgh) murdered; son of Robert Crichton, 3rd Lord Crichton of Sanquhar & Elizabeth Murray; suc. brother Jan 1535/6

(I) **Robert Crichton, 6th Lord Crichton of Sanquhar** (... – 1561) suc. father 1550

= 1537; **Margaret Cuninghame** (...) daughter of Sir John Cuninghame, 4th of Caprington & Annabella Campbell; she =1st Gilbert Kennedy, younger of Blairquhan

no issue

(II) **Edward Crichton, 7th Lord Crichton of Sanquhar** (... – 23 May 1569) suc. brother 1561

= 4 Jun 1561; **Margaret Douglas** (...) daughter of Sir James Douglas, 7th of Drumlanrig & Christian Montgomerie; =2nd ♦William Graham, 5th Earl of Menteith; =3rd Robert Wauchope of Niddrie Marischal

(A) **Robert Crichton, 8th Lord Crichton of Sanquhar** (ca.1568 – 29 Jun 1612 London) executed

= 16 Apr 1608; **Anne Fermor** (12 Mar 1591/2 Easton Neston, Northants. – ca.Apr 1675) daughter of Sir George Fermor & Mary Curson; =2nd ♦Barnabas O'Brien, 5th Earl of Thomond

(1) **William Crichton of Sanquhar** (bef.16 Apr 1608 – aft.1619) legitimated 1609; unm.

(III) **Hon. Andrew Crichton** (...)

(IV) **Hon. William Crichton** (...)

= ...; **Katherine Carmichael** (...)

(A) **William Crichton, 1st Earl of Dumfries**, Viscount of Air, Lord of Sanquhar, Lord Crichton of Sanquhar and Cumnock, 9th Lord Crichton of Sanquhar (ca.1578 – 1642/3) suc. cousin 1612; cr. Viscount 2 Feb 1622; cr. Earl 12 Jun 1633

=1; ...; **Euphemia Seton** (... – 1617) daughter of James Seton, 5th of Touch & Jean Edmonstone; =1st Patricia Hamilton of Peel =2 bef.16 Jul 1630; **Ursula Barnham** (... – 28 May 1632 Doncaster, Yorks.) daughter of Stephen Barnham; =1st Sir Robert Swift

issue of 1st (none by 2nd):

(1) **William Crichton, 2nd Earl of Dumfries**, etc. (aft.1605 – 1691) suc. father 1642/3

= 29 Aug 1618; (his step-sister) **Penelope Swift** (aft.1612 – ...) daughter of Sir Robert Swift & Ursula Barnham

(a) **Lady Elizabeth Crichton** (... – 5 Dec 1675)

= 1658; ♦**Alexander Montgomerie, 8th Earl of Eglinton** (... – 1701)

Children are listed with other parent

(b) **Charles, Lord Crichton** (aft.1641 – bef.11 Mar

1689/90)
= ca.1679; **Hon. Sarah Dalrymple** (...) daughter of James
Dalrymple, 1st Viscount Stair & Margaret Ross
Has further generations of issue
(2) **Lady Mary Crichton** (... – 24 Aug 1674)
= 29 Aug 1618; (her step-brother) **Barnham Swift, 1st
Viscount Carlingford** (7 Dec 1606 Denne, Sussex – 28
Jan 1634/5 abroad) son of Sir Robert Swift & Ursula
Barnham; cr. Viscount 26 Mar 1628, but the title
became extinct upon his death
(a) **Mary Swift** (...)
= ...; **Robert Feilding** (...)
issue?
(3) **Lady Catherine Crichton** (...)
= ...; **Sir John Charteris, 12th of Amisfield** (... –
bef.1654) son of Sir John Charteris, 11th of Amisfield
(a) **Agnes Charteris** (...)
= ...; ◆**Thomas Kirkpatrick of Closeburn** (...)
Children are listed with other parent
(V) **Hon. John Crichton** (aft.1528 – 26 Jul 1549) unm.
c) **Hon. Margaret Fleming** (... – aft.15 Aug 1584)
=1 ...; ◆**Robert, Lord Graham** (... – 1547)
=2 30 Jan 1548/9; ◆**Thomas, Master of Erskine** (... – aft.7
Oct 1551) son of John Erskine, 5th Lord Erskine & Lady
Margaret Campbell
=3 1557; ◆**John Stewart, 4th Earl of Atholl** (aft.1533 –
1579)
issue of 1st:
Children are listed with other parent
issue of 3rd (none by 2nd):
Children are listed with other parent
d) **John Fleming, 5th Lord Fleming** (... – 6 Sep 1572) suc.
brother 1558
= ...; **Elizabeth Ross** (...) daughter of Robert, Master of Ross
(I) **Hon. Mary Fleming** (...)
= ...; **James Douglas, 8th of Drumlanrig** (... – 16 Oct 1616) son
of Sir William Douglas, younger, of Drumlanrig & Margaret Gordon
(A) **William Douglas, 1st Earl of Queensberry** Viscount of
Drumlanrig, Lord Douglas of Hawick and Tibberis (... – 8 Mar
1639/40) cr. Earl 13 Jun 1633 with special remainder
= 20 Jul 1603; **Lady Isabel Kerr** (... – 1628) daughter of Mark
Kerr, 1st Earl of Lothian & Margaret Maxwell
(1) **James Douglas, 2nd Earl of Queensberry** etc. (bef.Jan
1622 – 1671) suc. father 1640
=1 4 Jun 1630; ◆**Lady Mary Hamilton** (aft.1606 – 29
Oct 1633) daughter of James Hamilton, 2nd Marquess of

Hamilton & Lady Anne Cunninghame

=2 26 Mar 1635; ♦**Lady Margaret Stewart** (...) daughter of John Dtewart, 1st Earl of Traquair & Lady Catherine Carnegie issue of 2nd (none by 1st):

(a) **William Douglas, 1st Duke of Queensberry** Marquess of Queensberry, Earl of Drumlanrig and Sanchar, Viscount of Noth, Torthorwald, and Ross, Lord Douglas of Kinmouth, Midlebie, and Dornock, 3rd Earl of Queensberry etc. (1637 – 28 Mar 1695) suc. father 1671; cr. Marquess etc. 11 Feb 1681/2; cr. Duke 3 Nov 1684

= 1657; ♦**Lady Isabel Douglas** (Apr 1642 – 2 Dec 1691) son of William Douglas, 1st Marquess of Douglas & Lady Mary Gordon

Has further generations of issue

(b) **Hon. James Douglas** (... – 1691)

= ...; **Anna Hamilton** (...)

Issue extinct 1712

(c) **Hon. John Douglas** (... – 8 Aug 1675 Trèves, France) killed in battle

(d) **Hon. Robert Douglas** (... – 1676 Maastricht, Netherlands) killed in battle

(e) **Lady Catherine Douglas** (...)

= 28 Oct 1667; **Sir James Douglas, 1st Baronet** (19 Sep 1639 – bef.Apr 1708) son of Hon. William Douglas & Agnes Fawside; cr. Baronet 26 Feb 1667/8

Has further generations of issue

(f) **Lady Mary Douglas** (...)

= ...; **Alexander Stewart, 3rd Earl of Galloway** Lord Garlies, 2nd Baronet (... – Sep 1690) son of James Stewart, 2nd Earl of Galloway & Nicola Grierson; suc. father Jun 1671

Has further generations of issue

(g) **Lady Isabel Douglas** (...)

= ...; **Sir William Lockhart of Carstairs, 1st Baronet** (...

1710) son of Sir William Lockhart of Carstairs & Hon. Mary Carmichael; cr. Baronet 28 Feb 1671/2

Has further generations of issue

(h) **Lady Margaret Douglas** (...)

=1 bef.1675; **Sir Alexander Jardine of Applegirth, 1st Baronet** (1645 – bef.1689) son of Alexander Jardin of Applegirth; cr. Baronet 25 May 1672

=2 5 Dec 1689; **Sir David Thoirs** (...)

Has further generations of issue by both

(i) **Lady Henrietta Douglas** (1657 Sanquhar Castle, Dumfries. – 15 Apr 1736 Dumfries)

= 21 Sep 1676; **Sir Robert Grierson of Lag, 1st Baronet**

(1657 Barquhar, Dumfries. – 31 Dec 1733 Dumfries) son of
William Grierson of Barquhar & Margaret Douglas; cr.
Baronet 25 Mar 1685
Has further generations of issue
(2) **Hon. Sir William Douglas** (... – 1673)
=1 ...; **Agnes Fawside** (...) daughter of George Fawside
=2 1649; **Jean Stuart** (...) daughter of Sir Robert Stuart; =1st
Andrew Riddell
issue of 1st (none by 2nd):
  (a) **Sir James Douglas, 1st Baronet** (19 WSep 1639 – bef.Apr
  1708) cr. Baronet 26 Feb 1667/8
    = 28 Oct 1667; ◆**Lady Catherine Douglas** (...) sdaughter of
    James Douglas, 2nd Earl of Queensberry & Lady Margaret
    Stewart
    Has further generations of issue
  (b) **Sarah Douglas** (17 Nov 1641 – ...)
    = ...; **John Irving of Woodhouse** (...) son of William Irving
    of Woodhouse & Janet Jardine
    Has further generations of issue
  (c) **George Douglas** (...)
    = aft.1684; **Hon. Elizabeth Livingstone** (...) daughter of
    James Livingstone, 1st Viscount Kilsyth & Euphemia
    Cuningham
    issue?
(3) **Lady Margaret Douglas** (... – aft.1640)
= 1622; ◆**James Johnstone, 1st Earl of Hartfell** (1602–
1653)
Children are listed with other parent
(4) **Lady Janet Douglas** (...)
= 28 Jul 1640; **Thomas Maclellan, 2nd Lord
Kirkcudbright** (... – 1647) son of William Maclellan & Rosina
Agnew; suc. 1641
  (a) **John Maclellan, 3rd Lord Kirkcudbright** (... – 1664)
  suc. father 1647
(5) **Hon. Sir Archibald Douglas** (...)
  = ...
  (a) **William Douglas** (...)
    = ...
    Has further generations of issue
  (b) **James Douglas** (1634 – aft.1663 Jamaica)
    = ...
    Has further generations of issue
(B) **Janet Douglas** (...)
= ...; **William Livingston of Jerviswood** (...)
issue ?
(C) **James Douglas** (...)

261

(D) **David Douglas** (...)

(E) **George Douglas** (... – 9 Sep 1587) executed; a priest

(F) **Helen Douglas** (...)

= ...; **John Menzies of Castlehill** (...)

issue ?

(II) **Hon. Jane Fleming** (...)

= 1582; **William Bruce, younger of Airth** (...) son of Sir Alexander Bruce of Airth & Janet Livingston

(A) **John Bruce of Airth** (...)

= 1601; **Hon. Margaret Elphinstone** (7 Jun 1588 – bef.1628) daughter of Alexander Elphinstone, 4th Lord Elphinstone

(1) **Alexander Bruce of Airth** (...)

= ...

  (a) (a son) **Bruce** (...)

  = ...

  Has further generations of issue

(B) **Sir William Bruce of Stenhouse, 1st Baronet** (... – Feb 1630) cr. Baronet 29 Sep 1628

=1 ...; **... Middleton** (...)

=2 bef.1621; **Rachel Johnston** (...) daughter of Hoseph Johnston

issue of 2nd (none by 1st):

  (1) **Sir William Bruce of Stenhouse, 2nd Baronet** (19 Aug 1621 – ...) suc. father 1630

  = ...; **Helen Douglas** (...) daughter of Sir William Douglas, 9th of Cavers & Ann Douglas

    (a) **Sir William Bruce of Stenhouse, 3rd Baronet** (... – Mar 1682) suc. father

    =1 16 Sep 1665; **Jean Fortune** (...)

    =2 17 Apr 1679; **Alison Turnbull** (...)

    Has further generations of issue

  (2) **Charles Bruce** (aft.1621 – ...)

(C) **Patrick Bruce** (...)

= ...

  (1) **Rev. Michael Bruce** (...)

  = 1659; **Jean Bruce** (...) daughter of Robert Bruce, 2nd of Kinnaird & Margaret Menteith

    (a) **Rev. James Bruce** (... – 1726)

    = 25 Sep 1685; **Margaret Trail** (4 Aug 1662 – May 1706) daughter of James Trail & Mary Hamilton

    Has further generations of issue

  (2) **William Bruce** (...)

  = ...

    (a) **Alexander Bruce of Newton** (...)

    = ...

Has further generations of issue

(III) **John Fleming, 1ˢᵗ Earl of Wigton**, Lord Fleming and Cumbernauld, 6ᵗʰ Lord Fleming (ca.1566/7 – Apr 1619) suc. father 1572; cr. Earl 1 Jul 1606

=1 ca.12 Jan 1585/6; ♦**Lady Lilias Graham** (... – bef.Oct 1611) daughter of John Graham, 3ʳᵈ Earl of Montrose & Hon. Jean Drummond

=2 bef.21 Oct 1611; **Sarah Maxwell** (ca.1566/7 – Apr 1619) daughter of Sir John Maxwell & Agnes Herries, 4ᵗʰ Lady Herries

issue of 1ˢᵗ:

(A) **Lady Jean Fleming** (...)

= ...; ♦**George, Master of Loudoun** (... – Mar 1611/2)

Children are listed with other parent

(B) **John Fleming, 2ⁿᵈ Earl of Wigton**, etc. (7 Dec 1589 – 7 May 1650) suc. father 1619

= ...; ♦**Lady Margaret Livingstone** (... – ca.10 Dec 1651) daughter of Alexander Livingstone, 1ˢᵗ Earl of Linlithgow & Lady Helen Hay

(1) **Lady Eleanor Fleming** (... – 20 Apr 1652)

= 4 Apr 1650; ♦**David Wemyss, 2ⁿᵈ Earl Wemyss**, etc. (6 Sep 1610 – Jul 1679) son of John Wemyss, 1ˢᵗ Earl Wemyss & Jane Gray; =1ˢᵗ Hon. Anna Balfour; =3ʳᵈ ♦Lady Mary Leslie

no issue

(2) **Lady Anne Fleming** (... – 20 Apr 1661)

=1 1639; ♦**Robert Boyd, 8ᵗʰ Lord Boyd of Kilmarnock** (1618 – 1640)

=2 10 Dec 1644; **George Ramsay, 2ⁿᵈ Earl of Dalhousie**, Lord Ramsay of Carrington, 3ʳᵈ Lord Ramsay of Dalhousie (... – 11 Feb 1673/4) son of William Ramsay, 1ˢᵗ Earl of Dalhousie & Lady Margaret Carnegie; suc. father Nov 1672

issue of 1ˢᵗ:

Children are listed with other parent

issue of 2ⁿᵈ:

(a) **William Ramsay, 3ʳᵈ Earl of Dalhousie**, etc. (... – aft.28 Feb 1682) suc. father 1674

= ...; **Lady Mary Moore** (... – 17 Mar 1725/6) daughter of Henry Moore, 1ˢᵗ Earl of Drogheda & Hon. Alice Spencer; =2ⁿᵈ John Bellenden, 2ⁿᵈ Lord Bellenden

Has further generations of issue

(b) **Lady Jean Ramsay** (...)

=1 ca.1665; **George Ross, 11ᵗʰ Lord Ross of Halkhead** (... – Apr 1682) son of William Ross, 10ᵗʰ Lord Ross of Halkhead & Margaret Forrester; =1ˢᵗ Lady Grizel Cochrane; suc. father 1656

=2 26 Dec 1684; ♦**Robert Makgill, 2ⁿᵈ Viscount of Oxfuird**, etc.(20 May 1651 – Dec 1705) son of James Makgill, 1ˢᵗ Viscount of Oxfuird & Christian Livingston; =1ˢᵗ Lady Henrietta Livingstone; suc. father 5 May 1663
Has further generations of issue (extinct 1732)
(c) **Hon. John Ramsay** (...)
(d) **Hon. George Ramsay** (... – ca.Sep 1705)
= ...; **... Buckson** (...)
no surviving issue
(e) **Hon. Robert Ramsay** (... – bef.Jan 1678)
(f) **Lady Anne Ramsay** (...)
= ...; ♦**James Home, 5ᵗʰ Earl of Home**, etc (... – 1687) son of James Home, 3ʳᵈ Earl of Home & Lady Jean Douglas; suc. brother 1674
no issue
(3) **John Fleming, 3ʳᵈ Earl of Wigton**, etc. (... – Feb 1664/5) suc. father 1650
= 10 Mar 1633; ♦**Lady Jean Drummond** (1623/4 – 12 Jan 1663) daughter of John Drummond, 2ⁿᵈ Earl of Perth & Lady Jean Kerr
(a) **John Fleming, 4ᵗʰ Earl of Wigton**, etc. (... – Apr 1668) suc. father 1665
= 5 Dec 1660; ♦**Hon. Anne Ker** (... – Nov 1673) daughter of Henry, Lord Ker & Lady Margaret Hay
Has further generations of issue (extinct 1683)
(b) **William Fleming, 5ᵗʰ Earl of Wigton**, etc. (... – 8 Apr 1681) suc. brother 1668
= 8 Sep 1670; ♦**Lady Henrietta Seton** (Jun 1652 – ...) daughter of Charles Seton, 2ⁿᵈ Earl of Dunfermline & Lady Mary Douglas; =2ⁿᵈ William Lindsay, 18ᵗʰ Earl of Crawford
Has further generations of issue
(C) **James Fleming of Boghall** (... – Oct 1623)
= 1612; **Janet Brisbane** (...) daughter of John Brisbane & Anna Blair
issue ?
(D) **Lady Mary Fleming** (...)
= 1634; **Archibald Stewart, younger of Castlemilk** (... – May 1643) son of Sir Archibald Stewart, 12ᵗʰ of Castlemilk & Anne Semphill
(1) **Sir Archibald Stewart of Castlemilk, 1ˢᵗ Baronet** (... – 1681) cr. Baronet 26 Feb 1668
= 2 Sep 1665; ♦**Mary Carmichael** (...) daughter of William, Master of Carmichael & Lady Grizel Douglas
(a) **Anne Stewart** (...)
= ...; **Sir William Ruthven of Cunninghamehead,**

4th Baronet (... – Oct 1722) son of Sir William
Ruthven of Cunninghamehead, 3rd Baronet & Anne
Ruthven; suc. father Apr 1671, but the baronetcy
became extinct upon his death
no issue

  (b) **Sir William Stewart of Castlemilk, 2nd Baronet**
(... – 1715) suc. father 1681
= ...; **Margaret Crawford** (... – 28 Mar 1737) daughter of
John Crawford of Milton
Has further generations of issue

issue of 2nd:

(E) **Lady Anna Fleming** (...)
= ...; **Sir William Livingston of Darchester** (... – bef.16
Feb 1615) son of Sir Wiliam Livingston of Kilsyth &
Antoinette de Bord

  (1) **Sir William Livingston of Kilsyth** (27 Jun 1609 – 13
Jun 1633)
= 16 Feb 1626; **Hon. Margaret Ramsay** (...) daughter of
Sir George Ramsay, 1st Lord Ramsay of Dalhousie &
Margaret Douglas

    (a) **William Livingston of Kilsyth** (... – Jan 1647)
unm.

    (b) **Margaret Livingston** (...)
= 4 Mar 1647; **Andrew Rutherford of Hunthill** (... –
Feb 1650)
no issue

    (c) **Christian Livingston** (... – Mar 1664)
= 8 Jul 1646; **James Makgill, 1st Viscount of
Oxfiurd**, Lord Makgill of Cousland, Baronet (... – 5
May 1663) son David Makhgill & Mary Sinclair; =1st
Catherine Cockburn
Has further generations of issue

    (d) **Anna Livingston** (... – bef.Jan 1654) unm.

e) **Hon. Agnes Fleming** (ca.1505 – ...)
= ...; ♦**William Livingston, 6th Lord Livingston** (... – 1592)
Children are listed with other parent

f) **Hon. Mary Fleming** (...)
= 6 Jan 1567; **William Maitland of Lethington** (ca.1528 –
9 Jun 1573 Leith, Midlothian) died an English prisoner; son
of Sir Richard Maitland & Mary Cranston; =1st Janet
Menteith

  (I) **Margaret Maitland** (...)
= 5 Dec 1587; **Robert Ker, 1st Earl of Roxburghe**, Lord
Ker of Cressford and Caverton, Lord Roxburghe (... – 18
Jan 1649/50) son of Sir William Ker of Cressford & Janet
Douglas; =2nd ♦Hon. Jane Drummond; =3rd ♦Lady Isabel

Douglas

(A) **Lady Jean Ker** (...)

= 28 Aug 1613; **John Drummond, 2nd Earl of Perth**, 6th Lord Drummond (ca.1584 – 11 Jun 1662) son of Patrick Drummond, 3rd Lord Drummond & Lady Elizabeth Lindsay; suc. brother 18 Dec 1611

(1) **James Drummond, 3rd Earl of Perth**, etc. (1615 – 2 Jun 1675) suc. father 1662

= 6 Nov 1639; ◆**Lady Anne Gordon** (... – 9 Jun 1656) daughter of George Gordon, 2nd Marquess of Huntly & Lady Anne Campbell

(a) **Lady Anne Drummond** (...)

= 1674; ◆**John Hay, 12th Earl of Erroll** (... – 1704) Children are listed with other parent

(b) **James Drummond, 4th Earl of Perth**, etc. **KT** (*de jure 1st Duke of Perth, Marquess of Drumond, Earl of Stobhall, Viscount of Cargill, Lord Concraig*) (ca.1649 – 11 May 1716 Saint-Germain-en-Laye) suc. father 1675; cr. Duke etc. in the Jacobite peerage 10 Mar 1689/90

=1 18 Jan 1670; ◆**Lady Jean Douglas** (aft.1843 – ...) daughter of William Douglas, 1st Marquess of Douglas & Lady Mary Gordon

=2 5 Oct 1676; **Lilias Drummond** (... – ca.Sep 1685) daughter of Sir James Drummond, 2nd of Machany & Anne Hay; =1st James Murray, 2nd Earl of Tullibardine

=3 ca.Jan 1685/6; ◆**Lady Mary Gordon** (... – 13 Mar 1726) daughter of Lewis Gordon, 3rd Marquess of Huntly & Mary Grant; =1st Adam Urquhart of Meldrum issue of 1st:

Has further generations of issue

(c) **John Drummond, 1st Earl of Melfort**, Viscount of Forth, Lord Drummond of Riccartoun, Castlemains, and Gilstain, 1st Viscount of Melfort, Lord Drummond of Gillestoun (*de jure 1st Duke of Melfort, Marquess of Forth, Earl of Isla and Burntizland, Viscount Rickerton, Lord castlemains and Galston, Baron of Clewer*), Duke de Mefort (in France) (8 Aug 1650 – 25 Jan 1714/5 Paris) cr. Viscount 14 Apr 1685, Earl 21 Aug 1686, and Jacobite Duke 17 Apr 1792, Duke in France

1701

=1 30 Sep 1670; **Sophia Maitland** (...) daughter of Robert Maitland & Margaret Lundie

=2 1680; **Euphemia Wallace** (...) daughter of Sir Timothy Wallace

Has further generations of issue

(2) **Hon. Robert Drummond** (1618 – ... France) unm.

(3) **Hon. Sir John Drummond, 1st of Logie Almond**

(1620 – Jun 1678)
= 18 Aug 1664; **Grizel Stewart** (...) daughter of Sir Thomas
Stewart, 12th of Grandtully & Grizel Menzies
(a) **Thomas Drummond, 2nd of Logie Almond** (... – 18
   Dec 1757)
   =1 3 Dec 1701; **Hon. Anne Kinnaird** (...) daughter of
   Patrick Kinnaird, 2nd Lord Kinnaird of Inchture &
   Hon. Anne Fraser
   =2 ...; **Hon. Grizel Leslie** (...) daughter of David Leslie,
   2nd Lord Newark & Elizabeth Stewart
   no issue
(b) **William Drummond** (... – Jun 1724)
   = aft.3 May 1703; **Elizabeth Oliphant** (...) daughter of
   George Oliphant, 2nd of Clashneny
   Has further generations of issue
(c) **Grizel Drummond** (...)
(4) **Lady Lilias Drummond** (ca.1622 – bef.12 Jan 1663/4)
   = 1643; ♦**James Murray, 2nd Earl of Tullibardine**
   (1617 – 1670)
   Children are listed with other parent
(5) **William Ker, 2nd Earl of Roxburghe**, etc. (1622 – 2 Jul
   1675) né Drummond, changed name when inheriting the
   Earldom, suc. grandfather under a special remainder 1650
   = 17 May 1655; ♦**Jean Ker** (...) daughter of Jenry, Lord
   Ker & Lady Margaret Hay
   (a) **Robert Ker, 3rd Earl of Roxburghe**, etc. (ca.1658 –
      8 May 1682 lost at sea off Yarmouth) suc. father 1675
      = 10 Oct 1675; ♦**Lady Margaret Hay** (1657 – 22 Jan 1753)
      daughter of John Hay, 1st Marquess of Tweeddale & Lady Jane
      Scott
      Has further generations of issue
   (b) **John Bellenden, 2nd Lord Bellenden** (... – bef.5
      Nov 1706 Edinburgh) né Ker, changed name upon
      receiving the Lordship; suc. cousin 23 Dec 1671
      = 10 Apr 1683; **Lady Mary Moore** (... – 17 Mar
      1725/6) daughter of Henry More, 1st Earl of Drogheda &
      Hon. Alice Spencer; =1 ♦William Ramsay, 3rd Earl
      Dalhousie; =3rd Samuel Collins
      Has further generations of issue
   (c) **Lady Jean Ker** (...)
      = aft.1680; ♦**Colin Lindsay, 3rd Earl of Balcarres**
      (1652 – 1722)
      Children are listed with other parent
(6) **Lady Jean Drummond** (1623/4 – 12 Jan 1663)
   = 1633; ♦**John Fleming, 3rd Earl of Wigton** (... – 1665)
   Children are listed with other parent

(B) **Lady Mary Ker** (... – Apr 1650)
=1 ...; **Sir James Haliburton of Pitcur** (... – bef.1629)
=2 21 Feb 1629; **James Carnegie, 2ⁿᵈ Earl of Southesk**,
Lord Carnegie of Kinnaird and Leuchars (... – Mar 1669)
son of David Carnegie, 1ˢᵗ Earl of Southesk & Margaret
Lindsay; =2ⁿᵈ Janet Adamson; suc. father Feb 1627/8
issue of 1ˢᵗ:
(1) **Mary Haliburton** (...)
= ...; **Sir James Drummond, 2ⁿᵈ of Machany** (aft.
1619 – 1675) son ofSir James Drummond, 1ˢᵗ of
Machany & Catherine Hamilton; =2ⁿᵈ Anne Hay
no surviving issue
issue of 2ⁿᵈ:
(2) **Lady Katherine Carnegie** (... – 1693)
= 7 Jan 1658; ♦**Gilbert Hay, 11ᵗʰ Earl of Erroll**, etc.
(... – Mar 1674) son of William Hay, 10ᵗʰ Earl of Erroll
& Lady Anne Lyon; suc. father 1637
no issue
(3) **Lady Jean Carnegie** (... – Mar 1671)
=1 26 Jun 1647; **James Johnstone Murray, 2ⁿᵈ Earl of
Annandale**, Viscount Annand, Lord Murray of
Tynningham and Lochmaben, 3ʳᵈ Viscount Stormont,
Lord Scone (... – 28 Dec 1658) son of John Murray, 1ˢᵗ
Earl of Annadale & Elizabeth Shaw; suc. father as Earl
22 Sep 1640, but those titles became extinct upon his
death; suc. cousin as Viscount Mar 1641/2
=2 9 Aug 1659 Kinnaird, Perths.; **David Murray, 4ᵗʰ
Viscount Stormont**, Lord Scone, 2ⁿᵈ Lord Balvaird
(... – 14 Jul 1668) son of John Murray, 1ˢᵗ Lord Balvaird
& Lady Elizabeth Carnegie; suc. father 24 Sep 1644;
suc. cousin (and wife's previous husband) as Viscount 1658
issue of 2ⁿᵈ (none by 1ˢᵗ):
(a) **Hon. Catherine Murray** (... – Jan 1726)
= 1687; ♦**William Keith, 2ⁿᵈ Earl of Kintore** (... – 1718)
Children are listed with other parent
(b) **David Murray, 5ᵗʰ Viscount Stormont**, etc. (... – 9
Nov 1731) suc. father 1668
= 31 Jan 1688; ♦**Marjory Scott** (...) daughter of David
Scott & Nicola Grierson
Has further generations of issue
(4) **Robert Carnegie, 3ʳᵈ Earl of Southesk**, etc. (... – 19
Feb 1687/8) suc. father 1669
= ca.1660; ♦**Lady Anne Hamilton** (aft.1639 – Oct
1695) daughter of William Hamilton, 2ⁿᵈ Duke of Hamilton
& Lady Elizabeth Maxwell
(a) **Charles Carnegie, 4ᵗʰ Earl of Southesk**, etc. (7 Apr

1661 – 9 Aug 1699) suc. father 1688
= 15 Jul 1691; ♦**Lady Mary Maitland** (...) daughter of
Charles Maitland, 3rd Earl of Lauderdale
Has further generations of issue (extinct 1730)
    (b) **Hon. William Carnegie** (... – 1681 Paris) killed in a duel
  (C) **Lady Isabella Ker** (...)
= 4 Aug 1618; **James Scrymgeour, 2nd Viscount Dudhope**,
2nd Lord Scrimgeour (... – 2 Jul 1644 Marston Moor, Yorks.)
killed in battle; son of John Scrymgeour, 1st Viscount Dudhope &
Margaret Seton; suc. father 7 Mar 1643
    (1) **John Scrymgeour, 1st Earl of Dundee**, Viscount of
    Dudhope, Lord Scrimgeour and Innerkeithing, 3rd Viscount
    Dudhope, etc. (... – 23 Jun 1668) suc. father 1644, but these
    titles became extinct upon his death; cr. Earl Sep 1660 with a
    special remainder to male heirs whatsoever
    no issue
 (II) **James Maitland** (... – 1625)
= ...; **Agnes Maxwell** (...)
  (A) **Richard Maitland** (...)
g) **Hon. Joanna Fleming** (...)
= ...; **David Crawford, 5th of Kerse** (... – 19 Jan 1596) son
of David Crawford, 4th of Kerse & Catherine Hamilton
 (I) **Margaret Crawford** (...)
= ...; **Patrick Maxwell, 5th of Newark** (... – ca.1593) son
of George Maxwell, 4th of Newark & Marion Cuninghame
  (A) **George Maxwell of Newark and Tealing** (...)
= ...; **Helen Maxwell** (...) daughter of Hugh Maxwell of
Tealing & Elizabeth Buttar
   (1) **George Maxwell of Newark** (...)
   = ...
    (a) **Margaret Maxwell** (ca.1603 – aft.1638)
    = ca.1626; **Rev. Dugald Campbell of Knapdale**
    (1599 Knapdale, Agylls. – 1673) son of Patrick
    Campbell of Stuck & Elizabeth Cameron
    Has further generations of issue
   (2) **Sir Patrick Maxwell of Newark** (...)
   = ...; ♦**Marion Campbell** (...) daughter of Sir Dugald
   Campbell Campbell of Auchinbreck, 1st Baronet &
   Isabella Boyd
    (a) **Helen Maxwell** (...)
    = ...; **Sir Colin Campbell of Ardkinglass, 1st**
    Baronet (ca.1640 – Apr 1709) son of Sir James
    Campbell, 9th of Ardkinglass & Isobel Campbell; cr.
    Baronet 23 Mar 1679
    Has further generations of issue
    (b) **George Maxwell of Newark** (...)

= ...; ♦**Elizabeth Semphill** (...) daughter of Robert
Semphill of Beltrees & Marie Lyon
Has further generations of issue
(B) **Margaret Maxwell** (...)
= ...; **Sir Ludovic Houston of Houston** (... – 1662)
son of John Houston of Houston & Margaret Stirling
(1) **Sir Patrick Houston of Houston, 1ˢᵗ Baronet**
(ca.1635 – 1696)
= ...; ♦**Hon. Ana Hamilton** (... – Apr 1669) daughter of
John Hamilton, 1ˢᵗ Lord Bargeny & Lady Jean Douglas
(a) **Sir John Houston, 2ⁿᵈ Baronet** (... – Dec 1717)
suc. father 1696
= ...; **Lady Anne Drummond** (3 Mar 1671 Largo –
Apr 1738) daughter of John Drummond, 1ˢᵗ Earl of Melfort
& Sophia Maitland
Has further generations of issue
(b) **Archibald Houston** (...)
= ...; **Margaret Barclay** (...) daughter of Sir Rober
Barclay of Pierston, 2ⁿᵈ Baronet & Bethia Baird
issue ?
(c) **Margaret Houston** (...)
= 4 Apr 1684; **Sir Humphrey Colquhoun of Luss, 5ᵗʰ
Baronet** (... – 1718) son of Sir James Colqhuoun, 4ᵗʰ Baronet
& Penuel Cunningham
has further generations of issue
(d) **Jean Houston** (...)
=1 30 Jul 1685 Dalmeny, Lothian; ♦**Walter Dundas
of Dundas** (...) son of Walter Dundas of Dundas &
Lady Christian Leslie
=2 5 Apr 1694 Edinburgh; **Richard Lockhart, 13ᵗʰ of
the Lee** (...) son of Sir William Lockhart, 11ᵗʰ of the
Lee & Robina Sewster
=3 2 Mar 1701 Edinburgh; ♦**Ludovic Grant, 8ᵗʰ of
Freuchie and 1ˢᵗ of Grant** (1641 – 1714) son of
James Grant, 7ᵗʰ of Freuchie & Lady Isabel Stewart;
he =1ˢᵗ Janet Brodie
no issue
(e) **Henrietta Houston** (...)
=1 ...; **Andrew Brown of Braid** (...)
=2 ...; **Sir Colin Mackenzie of Coul, 4ᵗʰ Baronet**
(1674 – 1740) son of Sir Alexander Mackenzie of
Coul, 2ⁿᵈ Baronet & Janet Johnston; suc. brother 1715
issue of 2ⁿᵈ (none by 1ˢᵗ):
Has further generations of issue
(f) **Anne Houston** (... – 18 Jan 1721)
=1 31 Oct 1682 Cramond, Lothian; **Sir James Inglis**

of Cramond, 1ˢᵗ Baronet (17 May 1660 Edinburgh –
6 Dec 1688) son of John Inglis; cr. Baronet 22 Mar 1687
=2 30 Sep 1700; **William Hamilton** (... – 14 Dec 1704)
=3 12 Sep 1706 Ormiston, E. Lothian; **Adam
Cockburn of Ormiston** (ca.1655 – 26 Apr 1725) son
of John Cockburn of Ormiston & Jonet Hepburn; =1ˢᵗ
♦Lady Susanna Hamilton
Has further generations of issue
(g) **William Houston** (...)
(h) **James Houston** (...)
(i) **Patrick Houston** (...)
= ...
Has further generations of issue
(2) **George Houston of Johnstone Castle** (...)
= ...; ♦**Elizabeth Cuninghame** (...) daughter of William
Cuninghame, 7ᵗʰ of Craigends & Janet Cuninghame
(a) **Ludovik Houston** (...)
= ...; **Agnes Walkinshaw** (...) daughter of James
Walkinshaw of Walkinshaw
Has further generations of issue
(3) **Elizabeth Houston** (...)
= 1659; **Wiliam Napier** (... – 1685) killed in battle; son
of Robert Napier & Anna Drummond
no issue
(4) **Marion Houston** (...)
= ...; **Alexander Napier** (... – 1702) son of Robert
Napier & Anna Drummond; =2ⁿᵈ Margaret Lennox of
Woodhead
no issue
(5) **Jean Houston** (...)
= ...; **Sir James Hamilton, 6ᵗʰ of Orbiston** (... – 1664)
son of Sir John Hamilton, 5ᵗʰ of Orbiston & Bethia
Henderson
(a) **Margaret Hamilton** (...)
= Oct 1657; **Sir John Henderson of Fordell, 1ˢᵗ
Baronet** (aft.1624 – 26 Jan 1683) son of Sir John
Henderson, 5ᵗʰ of Fordell & Margaret Monteith; cr.
Baronet 15 Jul 1664
Has further generations of issue
(b) **William Hamilton, 7ᵗʰ of Orbiston** (...)
= ...; ♦**Lady Elizabeth Cuninghame** (...) daughter of
William Cuninghame, 9ᵗʰ Earl of Glencairn & Lady
Anne Ogilvy
surviving issue ?
issue by **Henri II, King of France** (31 Mar 1519 Saint-
Germain-en-Laye – 10 Jul 1559 Paris) son of François I, King

Catherine de'Medici; suc. father 1547:

h) **Henry de Valois, Count d'Angoulême** (1535 Aix-la-
Chapelle – 1590 Aix-la-Chapelle) nick-named "Batard
d'Angoulême"; unm.

issue by **Hon. Margaret Drummond** (... – 1502) daughter of John
Drummond, 1st Lord Drummond & Lady Elizabeth Lindsay:

5) **Margaret Stewart** (ca.1497 – ...)
=1 1512; ♦**John, Lord Gordon** (... – 1517)
=2 20 Jan 1530/1; **Sir John Drummond, 2nd of Innerpeffray**
(ca.1486 Innerpeffray, Perths. – ...) son of John Drummond, 1st
of Innerpeffray & Eliza Douglas of Lochleven
=3 ...; ♦**Lord Alexander Stewart** (1477 – 1537)
issue of 1st:
Children are listed with other parent
issue of 2nd:

a) **Agnes Drummond** (ca.1531 – 21 Jan 1589/90)
=1 bef.1561; **Sir Hugh Campbell of Loudoun** (1502 – Feb
1560/1) son of Hugh Campbell of Loudoun & Isobel
Wallace; =1st ♦Lady Elizabeth Stuart
=2 1562; ♦**Hugh Montgomerie, 3rd Earl of Eglinton**
(1536 – 1585)
=3 1588; **Patrick Drummond, 3rd Lord Drummond**
(1550 – aft.1602) son of David Drummond, 2nd Lord
Drummond & Lilias Ruthven; =1st ♦Lady Elizabeth Lindsay
issue of 2nd (none by others):
Children are listed with other parent

b) **Isabel Drummond** (ca.1533 Innerperffray – ...)
= ...; ♦**Sir Matthew Campbell of Loudon** (...)
Children are listed with other parent

c) **Margaret Drummond** (...)
= 1546; **Robert Elphinstone, 3rd Lord Elphinstone** (9 Sep
1530 – 18 May 1602) son of Alexander Elphinstone, 2nd
Lord Elphinstone & Katherine Erskine; suc. father 10 Sep
1547

(I) **Hon. Janet Elphinstone** (...)
= ...; **Sir Patrick Barclay of Towie** (... – Jun 1589
Edinburgh) son of Walter Barclay of Towie & Elizabeth
Hay; = 2nd Elizabeth Forbes

(A) **Patrick Barclay of Towie** (... – bef.30 Apr 1624)
= 22 Jun 1602; **Hon. Anne Drummond** (1583 – 1640)
daughter of Patrick Drummond, 3rd Lord Drummond & Lady
Elizabeth Lindsay; =2nd Andrew Fraser, 1st Lord Fraser

(1) **Jean Barclay** (...)
= ...; **Hon. William Fraser** (...) son of Andrew Fraser,
1st Lord Fraser & Hon. Anne Drummond
issue ?

(2) **Francis Barclay, younger of Towie** (ca.1605 – Oct 1621) unm.

(3) **Walter Barclay of Towie** (aft.1605 – bef.1643)
= ...

(a) **Patrick Barclay of Towie** (... – 2 Aug 1668)
= ...; **... Douglas** (...) =2nd Sir Patrick Ogilvie
Has further generations of issue

(4) **George Barclay of Seggat** (...)
= ...; **... Urquhart** (...) daughter of Adam Urquhart

(a) **Adam Barclay** (... – 12 Aug 1695)
= ...; **Christine Chalmers** (... – 18 Apr 1696)
Has further generations of issue

(b) **John Barclay of Towie Hill** (...)
= ...; **... Stewart** (...) daughter of John Stewart of Ordley
Has further generations of issue

(c) **William Barclay** (...)
= ...
Has further generations of issue

(5) **Alexander Barclay** (...) unm.

(6) **Christian Barclay** (...)
= 1621; **William Ruthven** (...) son of Sir William Ruthven & Katherine Stewart

(a) **Sir John Ruthven** (...)
=1 ...; **Jean Ramsay** (...)
=2 ...; **Lady Barbara Leslie** (...) daughter of Alexander Leslie, 1st Earl of Leven & Agnes Renton
Has further generations of issue by 2nd

(b) **William Ruthven** (...)

(c) **Sir Francis Ruthven** (... – 1655)

(7) **Elizabeth Barclay** (...) unm.

(II) **Hon. Jean Elphinestone** (...)
= 1587; **Walter Barclay** (...)
issue ?

(III) **Alexander Elphinestone, 4th Lord Elphinstone** (28 May 1552 – 14 Jan 1637/8) suc. father 1602
= 20 Apr 1575; ♦**Jean Livingston** (... – 15 Sep 1621 Elphinstone) daughter of William Livingston, 6th Lord Livingstone & Hon. Agnes Fleming

(A) **Alexander Elphinstone, 5th Lord Elphinstone** (13 Nov 1577 – 27 Aug 1648) suc. father 1738
= 28 Apr 1607; **Hon. Elizabeth Drummond** (1581 – 1 Dec 1637) daughter of Patrick Drummond, 3rd Lord Drummond & Lady Elizabeth Lindsay

(1) **Hon. Lilias Elphinstone** (...)
= ...; ♦**Alexander Elphinstone, 6th Lord Elphinstone** (... – 1654)

Children are listed with other parent

(B) **Hon. Agnes Elphinstone** (27 Oct 1579 – 18 Sep 1617)
= 1600; ♦**John Gordon, 13th Earl of Sutherland**
(1576 – 1615)
Children are listed with other parent

(C) **Hon. James Elphinstone** (20 Nov 1580 – bef.6 May
1628)
= bef.15 Sep 1625; **Margaret Forbes** (...) daughter of John
Forbes of Brux

(1) **James Elphinstone, 6th Lord Elphinstone** (... – 26
Oct 1654) suc. uncle/father-in-law 1648
= ...; ♦**Hon. Lilias Elphinstone** (...) daughter of Alexander
Elphinstone, 5th Lord Elphinstone & Hon. Elizabeth Drummond

(a) **Alexander Elphinstone, 7th Lord Elphinstone**
(bef.1649 – May 1669) suc. father 1654
= 10 Sep 1667; **Anne Burnet** (...) daughter of Alexander
Burnet; =2nd ♦Patrick Murray, 3rd Lord Elibank
no issue

(b) **John Elphinstone, 8th Lord Elphinstone** (28 Aug 1649
Airth, Stirlings. – 24 Mar 1718 Elphinstone) suc. brother 1669
= 23 Apr 1670 Edinburgh; ♦**Lady Isabel Maitland**
(1655 Thirlestane, Berwicks. – 7 Oct 1706) daughter of
Charles Maitland, 3rd Earl of Lauderdale & Elizabeth Lauder
Has further generations of issue

(c) **Hon. Jean Elphinstone** (...)
= ...; ♦**Sir Alexander Urquhart of Cromarty** (1613 –
1667)
Children are listed with other parent

(d) **Hon. Anne Elphinstone** (...)
= 1671; **Walter Sandilands, 6th Lord Torphichen**
(12 May 1629 Mid-Calder, W. Lothian – May 1696)
son of John Sandilands, 4th Lord Torphichen & Isabel
Dundas; =1st Jean Lindsay; =2nd ♦Hon. Catherine
Alexander; =4th Christian Primrose; suc. brother Jul
1649
no survivng issue

(D) **Jean Elphinstone** (17 Feb 1582 – bef.1628)
= 1600; ♦**Arthur Forbes, 9th Lord Forbes** (1581–1641)
Children are listed with other parent

(E) **Hon. Margaret Elphinstone** (...)
= 1601; ♦**John Bruce of Airth** (...)
Children are listed with other parent

(F) **Hon. Helen Elphinstone** (27 Aug 1589 – 1 Feb 1675)
=1 ca.1600; **Sir William Cockburn of Langton, 1st
Baronet** (... – ca.Dec 1628) son of William Cockburn of
Langton & Janet Home; cr. Baronet 22 Nov 1622

=2 ...; **Henry Rollo** (...)
issue of 1st (none by 2nd):
(1) **Jean Cockburn** (...)
  =1 Jan 1632; **Alexander Dunbar of Grange** (... –
  bef.Mar 1642) son of Thomas Dunbar & Crissell
  Crichton; =1st Jean Campbell
  =2 1644; **Thomas Mackenzie of Pluscarden** (...)
  issue of 1st:
  (a) **Thomas Dunbar of West Grange and Burgie** (...)
    =1 15 Aug 1659; **Jean Robertson** (...)
    =2 1666; **Katherine Gordon** (...)
    =3 1684; **Katherine Melville** (...)
    Has further generations of issue
  (b) **William Dunbar** (... – 1649) unm.
  (c) **Lilias Dunbar** (...)
    = 1676; **Francis Brodie of Milton and Inverlochtie**
    (... – 1693) son of Francis Brodie of Milton and
    Inverlochtie; =1st Barbara Johnston; =3rd Margaret
    Hay
    no issue
  (d) **Anne Dunbar** (...)
    = ...; **John Forbes, 2nd of Culloden** (...)
    Has further generations of issue
  (e) **Jean Dunbar** (...)
    = ...; **Donald McIntosh of Kyllachy** (...)
    Has further generations of issue
  issue of 2nd:
  (f) **Alexander Mackenzie** (...)
  (g) **Thomas Mackenzie** (...)
  (h) **Kenneth Mackenzie** (...)
  (i) **Charles Mackenzie** (...)
(2) **Sir William Cockburn of Langton, 2nd Baronet**
  (... – ca. 1650) suc. father 1628
  = ...; **Margaret Acheson** (ca.1612 Markethill, co.
  Armagh – ...) daughter of Sir Archibald Acheson, 1st
  Baronet & Agnes Vernor
  (a) **Sir William Cockburn of Langton, 3rd Baronet**
    (... – bef Dec 1657) suc. father 1650l unm.
  (b) **Sir Archibald Cockburn of Langton, 4th Baronet**
    (... – 25 Jun 1705 Langton, Berwicks.) suc. brother
    1657
    =1 ...; **Marion Sinclair** (...) daughter of John Sinclair,
    younger of Stevenson & Isabel Boyd
    =2 ...; **Anna Stewart** (...) daughter of Sir Thomas Stewart
    & Margaret Elliot
    Has further generations of issue

(3) **Isabella Cockburn** (...)
= 10 Sep 1635; ♦**Hon. Sir John Rollo of Bannockburn** (22 Feb 1702 – 1666) son of Andrew Rollo, 1st Lord Rollo of Duncrub & Catherine Drummond; =2nd Annabel Buchanan; =3rd Helen Sinclair
no issue

(G) **Hon. Christian Elphinstone** (19 Dec 1590 – ...)
= 1606; ♦**Sir Thomas Urquhart** (1585 – 1642)
Children are listed with other parent

(H) **Hon. John Elphinstone** (2 Dec 1591 – Sep 1621)
= ...; **Barbara Gordon** (...) daughter of John Gordon, 3rd of Pitlurg & Isabel Forbes
no issue

(I) **Hon. Michael Elphinstone, 1st of Quarell** (23 Dec 1593 – 1 Nov 1640)
= aft.12 Jan 1618; **Mary Bruce** (...) daughter of Rev. Robert Bruce, 1st of Kinnaird & Martha Douglas
issue ?

(IV) **Hon. Father George Elphinstone** (...) a priest in Rome

(V) **Hon. Elizabeth Elphinstone** (... – 26 Feb 1613)
= 1 Oct 1582; **Robert Innes of that Ilk** (ca.Apr 1562 – 25 Sep 1596) son of Alexander Innes, 18th of that Ilk and 3rd of Cromey & Isobel Forbes

(A) **Rt.Hon. Sir Robert Innes of that Ilk, 1st Baronet** (ca.1583/4 – 17 Nov 1658) cr. Baronet 28 May 1625
= 18 Dec 1611; ♦**Hon. Grizel Stewart** (...) daughter of James Stewart, 2nd Lord Doune & Elizabeth Stewart, Countess of Moray

(1) **Sir Robert Innes of that Ilk, 2nd Baronet** (aft.1611 – Feb 1689) suc. father 1658
= ...; **Hon. Jean Ross** (...) daughter of James Ross, 6th Lord Ross of Halkhead & Margaret Scott

(a) **Elizabeth Innes** (...)
= 4 Sep 1681; **Arthur Forbes, 12th of Echt** (...) son of Thomas Forbes of Knockwarne & ... Forbes
Has further generations of issue

(b) **Marie Innes** (...)
= 1668; ♦**Duncan Forbes, 3rd of Culloden** (1644 – 1704)
Beyond the 12th generation on the father's line

(c) **Sir James Innes of that Ilk, 3rd Baronet** (...)
= 18 Jul 1666; **Hon. Margaret Ker** (... – 8 Jan 1681) daughter of Henry, Lord Ker & Lady Margaret Hay
Has further generations of issue

(d) **Jean Innes** (... – 11 Feb 1684)
= ...; **Alexander Rose of Clava** (...) son of Hugh Rose of Clava

Has further generations of issue
(e) **William Innes** (...)
= bef.1670; **... Durie** (...)
Has further generations of issue
(f) **Idonea Innes** (...)
= ...; **... Sutherland** (...)
issue ?
(g) **Grizel Innes** (20 Jul 1654 – 1742)
= 1673; **Sir James Calder, 1st Baronet** (19 Apr 1657
Mid Calder, W.Lothian – 1711) son of Thomas
Calder; cr. Baronet 5 Nov 1686
Has further generations of issue
issue by ...:
(g) **Margaret Innes** (... – 20 May 1676)
= ...; **Hugh Rose, 14th of Kilravock** (... – 1687) son of
Hugh Rose, 13th of Kilravock & Margaret Mowat;
he =2nd ◆Marie Forbes
Has further generations of issue
(2) **Elizabeth Innes** (... – 1640)
=1 ...; **John Urquhart of Craigston** (... – 30 Nov 1634)
=2 28 Oct 1635; **Alexander Brodie, 15th of Brodie** (25
Jul 1617 – 1679) son of David Brodie, 14th of Brodie &
Katharine Dunbar
issue of 2nd (none by 1st):
(a) **Grizel Brodie** (Oct 1636 – ...)
= 1654; **Sir Robert Dunbar** (...)
Has further generations of issue
(b) **James Brodie, 16th of Brodie** (15 Sep 1637 – Mar
1708)
= 28 Jul 1659; ◆**Lady Mary Kerr** (... – Mar 1708) daughter
of William Kerr, 1st Earl of Lothian & Lady Anne Kerr
Has further generations of issue
(3) **Grizel Innes** (... – 19 Aug 1694)
= ...; ◆**Sir Robert Innes, 1st of Muirton** (... – 1667)
Children are listed with other parent
(4) **James Innes of Lichnett** (...)
= 9 May 1659; **Isabella Ross** (...) daughter of DavidRoss of
Balnagowan; =1st John Sutherland
(a) **Robert Innes** (...)
(b) **Peter Innes** (...)
(5) **William Innes of Nether Dallachy** (...)
= ...
(a) **Andrew Innes** (1641 – 29 Dec 1723)
=1 ...; **Jean Randall** (...)
=2 ...; **Elizabeth Martin** (...) daughter of Jeremy Martin
Has further generations of issue

(6) Mary Innes (...)
  = ...; **Sir James Stewart of Rosyth** (...)
  issue ?
(7) Barbara Innes (... – 9 Dec 1681)
  =1 ...; **Robert Dunbar of Westfield** (... – 1661)
  =2 Sep 1663; **David Dunbar of Dunphail** (...)
  =3 31 Mar 1676; **Robert Dunbar of Burgie** (...)
  issue ?
(8) Anne Innes (22 Apr 1625 – ...)
(B) **Sir John Innes of Cromey** (...)
  = 1613; **Elizabeth Sinclair** (...) daughter of Sir James Sinclair
  of Murkle
  (1) Sir Robert Innes, 1ˢᵗ of Muirton (... – 6 Apr 1667)
  =1 ...; **Jean Cockburn** (...)
  =2 ...; ♦**Grizel Innes** (...) daughter of Rt.Hon. Sir Robert
  Innes of that Ilk, 1ˢᵗ Baronet & Lady Grizel Stewart
    (a) **Robert Innes, 2ⁿᵈ of Muirton** (... – Jan 1678) unm.
    (b) **James Innes, 3ʳᵈ of Muirton** (...)
    (c) **Alexander Innes** (...)
    (d) **John Innes** (...)
    (e) **Elizabeth Innes** (...)
      = ...; **Donald Campbell of Urchany** (...)
      issue ?
  (2) John Innes of Bonellie (... – Mar 1672) unm.
(C) **Marie Innes** (...)
  =1 ...; ♦**William Hay of Fetterletter** (...) son of Andrew
  Hay, 8ᵗʰ Earl of Erroll & Lady Agnes Sinclair; =1ˢᵗ Lilias Gordon
  =2 16 Oct 1624; **John Urquhart of Laithers and
  Craigfintry** (... – 11 Dec 1632)
  =3 21 Nov 1633; **Alexander Douglas** (... – 11 May 1623)
  issue ?
(D) **Anne Innes** (...)
  = ...; **Rev. John Guthrie, younger of that Ilk** (... – 1643)
  issue ?
(E) **Margaret Innes** (...)
  = ...; **George Munro of Miltoun** (...)
  issue ?
(VI) **Hon. Margaret Elphinstone** (...)
  = ...; **John Cuninghame of Drumquhassel** (...) son f John
  Cuninghame & Janet Cuninghame
  issue ?
(VII) **Sir James Elphinstone, 1ˢᵗ Lord Balmerinoch** (19 Aug
  1557 – May 1612 Balmerinoch, Roxburghes.) cr. Lord 11 Jul 1606
  =1 aft.10 Apr 1589; **Sarah Monteith** (... – aft.14 Dec
  1592) daughter of Sir John Monteith of Carse
  =2 bef.23 Dec 1597; **Marjory Maxwell** (1573 Tealing,

Angus – aft.2 Aug 1601) daughter of Hugh Maxwell
issue of 1st:
(A) **John Elphinstone, 2nd Lord Balmerinoch** (bef.1587 –
28 Feb 1648/9 Edinburgh) suc. father 1612
= 20 Aug 1613; **Ann Kerr** (... – 15 Feb 1649/50 Leith, Lothian)
daughter of Sir Thomas Kerr of Ferniehirst & Janet Scott
  (1) **John Elphinstone, 3rd Lord Balmerinoch**, 2nd Lord
  Coupar (18 Feb 1623 Edinburgh – 10 Jun 1704) suc.
  father 1649; suc. uncle 1669
  = 30 Oct 1649 Edinburgh; ◆**Lady Margaret Campbell**
  (... – Dec 1665) daughter of John Campbell, 1st Earl of
  Loudoun & Margaret Campbell, 2nd Baroness Campbell
  of Loudoun
    (a) **John Elphinstone, 4th Lord Balmerinoch**, etc. (26
    Dec 1652 Edinburgh – 13 May 1736 Leith) suc. father
    1704
    =1 15 Feb 1671/2 Edinburgh; ◆**Lady Christiana
    Montgomerie** (...) daughter of Hugh Montgomerie, 7th
    Earl of Eglinton & Lady Mary Leslie
    =2 12 Jun 1687 Edinburgh; **Anne Rose** (... – ca.Nov
    1712 London) daughter of Most Rev. Arthur Rose,
    Archbishop of St.Andrews & Barbara Barclay
    Has further generations of issue
issue of 2nd:
(B) **James Elphinstone, 1st Lord Coupar** (ca.1587 – Jan
1668/9) cr. Lord 20 Dec 1607
=1 ...; **Margaret Halyburton** (aft.1586 – ...) daughter of
James Halyburton of Thorngreen & Margaret Scrymgeour
=2 11 Oct 1666; **Lady Marion Ogilvy** (... – bef.Sep
1695) daughter of James Ogilvy, 2nd Earl of Airlie & Helen
Ogilvy; =2nd John Leslie, 4th Lord Lindores
no issue
(C) **Hon. Margaret Elphinstone** (1591 – ...)
= 1618; ◆**Andrew Fraser, 2nd Lord Fraser** (...)
Children are listed with other parent
issue by ...:
(D) **Marjory Elphinstone** (...)
= ...; ◆**Hon. Francis Fraser** (...) son of Andrew Fraser,
1st Lord Fraser & Lady Elizabeth Douglas
issue ?
(VIII) **Hon. Agnes Elphinstone** (3 Oct 1559 – ...)
= ...; **Walter Ogilvy, 1st Lord Ogilvy of Deskford** (... –
ca.1626) son of Alexander Ogilvy & Barbara Ogilvy; =2nd
◆Lady Mary Douglas
no issue
d) **Jean Drummond** (...)

= ...; **James Chisholm, 3rd of Cromlix** (...) son of James
Chisholm, 2nd of Cromlix

(I) **Sir James Chisholm, 4th of Cromlix** (10 Sep 1550 – ...)
= 17 Sep 1580; **Agnes Beaton** (...) daughter of David Beaton,
4th of Creich & Lady Beatrix Leslie

  (A) **Sir James Chisholm, 5th of Cromlix** (... – aft.Nov 1633)
= aft.Feb 1610; **Helen Stirling** (...) daughter of William
Stirling of Ardoch

    (1) **James Chisholm, 6th of Cromlix** (... – bef. 30 Apr
1642) unm.

    (2) **Sir John Chisholm, 7th of Cromlix** (...) unm.

(II) **William Chisholm** (11 Mar 1551 – 1621 Vaison,
France) a priest

(III) **Helen Chisholm** (...)
= bef.26 Jul 1586; **Henry Lindsay, 13th Earl of Crawford**
(aft.1557 – 1623) son of David, 10th Earl of Crawford &
Margaret Bethune; =2nd Elizabeth Shaw; suc. nephew Jun 1620

  (A) **George Lindsay, 14th Earl of Crawford** (... – 1633)
murdered; suc. father 1623
= 21 May 1621; ♦**Lady Elizabeth Sinclair** (...) daughter of
George Sinclair, 5th Earl of Caithness & Lady Jean Gordon

    (1) **Lady Margaret Lindsay** (... – 1655) unm.

  (B) **Sir John Lindsay KB** (... – 1615) KB 1603
= 8 Dec 1608; ♦**Hon. Jean Abernethy** (...) daughter of
George Abernethy, 7th Lord Saltoun & Lady Margaret Stewart
no surviving issue

(IV) **Jane Chisholm** (13 Jul 1555 – Nov 1589)
= ...; **James Drummond, 1st Lord Maderty** (1551 – Sep
1623) son of David Drummond, 2nd Lord Drummond,
Lilias Ruthven

  (A) **John Drummond, 2nd Lord Maderty** (... – ca.1650)
suc. father 1623
= 30 Apr 1609; ♦**Hon. Margaret Leslie** (...) daughter of
Patrick Leslie, 1st Lord Lindores

    (1) **Hon. Anne Drummond** (... – May 1689)
= 1639; ♦**David Rattray, 18th of Rattray** (...–1677)
Children are listed with other parent

    (2) **David Drummond, 3rd Lord Maderty** (... – 1684)
suc. father ca.1650
=1 6 Feb 1637/8; **Alison Creighton** (... – Mar 1639)
daughter of John Creighton of Haltoun
=2 10 Dec 1641; ♦**Lady Beatrix Graham** (...) daughter of
John Graham, 4th Earl of Montrose & Lady Margaret Ruthven
issue of 2nd (none surviving by 1st):

      (a) **Beatrix Drummond** (...)
= 1669; ♦**John Carmichael, 1st Earl of Hyndford**

(1638 – 1710)
Children are listed with other parent
(b) **Mary Drummond** (... – 1685)
= 22 Aug 1677; **John Haldane, 14ᵗʰ of Gleneagles**
(31 Mar 1660 – 26 Jun 1721) son of Hugo Haldane,
13ᵗʰ of Gleneagles & Anne Grant
Has further generations of issue (but extinct 1768)
(c) **Margaret Drummond** (...)
= ...; **John Graham** (...)
issue ?

(3) **William Drummond, 1ˢᵗ Viscount Strathallan**, Lord
Drummond of Cromlix (1617/8 – 23 Mar 1687/8) cr.
Viscount 16 Aug 1686
= 28 Feb 1667/8; **Elizabeth Johnston** (...) daughter of Sir
Archibald Johnston; =1ˢᵗ Thomas Hepburn
(a) **William Drummond, 2ⁿᵈ Vicount Strathallan**,
etc., 4ᵗʰ Lord Maderty (8 Aug 1670 – 7 Jul 1702) suc.
father 1688; suc. cousin 20 Jan 1691/2
= bef.14 Jan 1687/8; ♦**Lady Elizabeth Drummond**
(27 Jul 1672 Largo – ...) daughter of John Drummond, 1ˢᵗ
Earl of Melfort & Sophia Maitland
Has further generations of issue (extinct 1711)
(b) **Hon. Margaret Drummond** (... – 21 Mzar 1695/6)
= 20 Dec 1683; **Thomas Hay, 7ᵗʰ Earl of Kinnoull**
Viscount of Dupplin, Lord Hay (ca.1660 – 5 Jan 1718/9) son of
George Hay & Marion Nicolson; suc. distant cousin 31 Dec
1697
Has further generations of issue

(B) **Sir James Drummond, 1ˢᵗ of Machany** (...)
= ...; ♦**Catherine Hamilton** (...) daughter of Sir John
Hamilton & Jean Campbell
(1) **Katharine Drummond** (...)
= ...; **Alexander Robertson, 12ᵗʰ Chief of Clan
Donnachaidh** (... – Nov 1688) son of Alexander
Robertson, 11ᵗʰ Chief of Clan Donnachaidh & Margaret
Graeme; =2ⁿᵈ Mariota Baillie
(a) **Anne Robertson** (...)
= ...; **Hugh Macdonald of Glenmore** (...)
issue ?
(b) **Robert Robertson** (ca.1663 – 1688) unm.
(2) **Sir James Drummond, 2ⁿᵈ of Machany** (aft.1619 – 1675)
=1 ...; ♦**Mary Haliburton** (...) daughter of Sir James
Halibuton of Pitcur
=2 11 Feb 1645; ♦**Anne Hay** (...) daughter of George Hay,
1ˢᵗ of Kellour & Isabel Cheyne; =1ˢᵗ William Moray,
10ᵗʰ of Abercairny

issue of 2nd (none surviving by 1st):

(a) **Sir John Drummond, 3rd of Machany** (... – 1707)
= ...; **Margaret Stewart** (...) daughter of Sir William
Stewart of Innernytie
Has further generations of issue

(b) **Lilias Drummond** (... – ca.Sep 1685)
=1 bef.12 Jun 1668; ♦**James Murray, 2nd Earl of
Tullibardine**, etc. (22 Sep 1617 Cheshunt, Herts. –
Jan 1669/70 Tullibardine, Perths.) son of Patrick
Murray, 1st Earl of Tullibardine & Elizabeth Dent; =1st
♦Lady Lilias Drummond; =2nd ♦Lady Anne Murray
=2 5 Oct 1676; ♦**James Drummond, 4th Earl of
Perth**, etc. (ca.1649 – 11 May 1617 St.Germain-en-
Laye, France) son of James Drummond, 3rd Earl of
Perth & Lady Anne Gordon; =1st ♦Lady Jean
Douglas; =3rd ♦Lady Mary Gordon
no issue

(c) **Anne Drummond** (...)
= 1671; **Thomas Graham, 4th of Balgowan** (...) son
of John Graham, 2nd of Balgowan & Helen Blair; =2nd
Hon. Christian Leslie
Has further generations of issue

(C) **Hon. Catherine Drummond** (...)
= ...; **Andrew Rollo, 1st Lord Rollo of Duncrub** (1577 –
22 May 1659) son of James Rollo, 8th of Duncrub &
Agnes Collace; cr. Lord 10 Jan 1650/1

(1) **James Rollo, 2nd Lord Rollo of Duncrub** (11 Dec
1600 – 9 Jun 1669) suc. father 1659
=1 24 Apr 1628; ♦**Lady Dorothea Graham** (... – 16
May 1638) daughter of John Graham, 4th Earl of Montrose
& Lady Margaret Ruthven
=2 20 Mar 1641/2; ♦**Lady Mary Campbell** (ca.1622 – ...)
daughter of Archibald Campbell, 7th Earl of Argyll & Anne
Cornwallis

(a) **Andrew Rollo, 3rd Lord Rollo of Duncrub** (... – 4
Mar 1700/1) suc. father 1669
= Nov 1670; **Hon. Margaret Balfour** (aft.1648 – 20
Oct 1734) daughter of John Balfour, 3rd Lord Balfour of
Burleigh & Isabel Balfour
Has further generations of issue

(b) **Hon. Margaret Rollo** (...)
= 7 Sep 1682; **Sir George Oliphant of Newton** (...)
issue ?

(2) **Hon. Sir John Rollo of Bannockburn** (22 Jun 1602–
1666)
=1 10 Sep 1635; ♦**Isabella Cockburn** (...) daughter of Sir

William Cockburn of Langton, 1st Baronet & Helen Elphinstone

=2 ...; **Annabel Buchanan** (...) daughter of Sir John Buchanan of that Ilk

=3 27 Aug 1654; **Helen Sinclair** (...) daughter of Sir William Sinclair of Rosslyn

issue of 3rd (none by others):

(a) **Jean Rollo** (...)

= ca.1678; **Sir Alexander Innes of Coxton, 1st Baronet** (... – 28 Jan 1709) son of John Innes & Helen Gordon; cr. Baronet 20 Mar 1685/6
Has further generations of issue

(3) **Hon. Laurence Rollo** (15 Mar 1604 – ...)

= ...; **Catherine Peebles** (...) daughter of Alexander Peebles
issue ?

(4) **Hon. Andrew Rollo** (Mar 1605 – May 1668)

=1 ...; **Isabella Lindsay** (...) daughter of David Lindsay

=2 1654; **Helen Oliphant** (...) daughter of William Oliphant of Pitlochie; =1st Patrick Murray

=3 ...; **Helen Mercer** (...) =1st James Crichton of Wester Aldie
issue ?

(5) **Hon. Margaret Rollo** (...)

= ...; **Sir John Drummond of Carnock** (...)
issue ?

(6) **Hon. Jean Rollo** (...)

=1 1652; **John Rollo of Powhouse** (...)

=2 ...; **John Drummond of Pitkellony** (...)
issue ?

(7) **Hon. Anne Rollo** (... – 21 Oct 1658)

=1 1633; **William Mercer of Clavadge** (...)

=2 ...; **... Drummond of Pitcairns** (...)
issue ?

(8) **Hon. Isabel Rollo** (...)

= ...; **William Halliday of Tullibole** (...)
issue ?

(9) **Hon. Sir William Rollo** (Mar 1613 – 21 Oct 1645) executed

(V) **John Chisholm** (1557 – ...)

(VI) **Thomas Chisholm** (1559 – ...)

(VII) **Janet Chisholm** (1562 – ...)

(VIII) **Agnes Chisholm** (...)

=1 ...; **John Napier, 8th of Merchistoun** (1550 – 3 Apr 1617) son of Sir Archibald Napier, 7th of Merchistoun & Janet Bothwell; =1st Elizabeth Stirling

=2 ...; **William Cunningham of Craigends** (...)

issue of 1st (none by 2nd):

(A) **John Napier of Schambodie** (...)
  = 1613; **Mary Foulis** (...) daughter of Sir James Foulis
  (1) **John Napier** (1615 – ...)
  (2) **Anna Napier** (1616 – ...)
(B) **Robert Napier of Culcreuch** (1580 – 1655)
  =1 ...
  =2 ...; **Anna Drummond** (...) daughter of Sir William
  Drummond, 3rd Baronet
  issue of 1st:
  (1) **Archibald Napier** (...)
    has issue, but extinct in 1817
  (2) **John Napier** (...) unm.
  issue of 2nd:
  (3) **William Napier** (... – 1685) killed in battle
    = 1659; ♦**Elizabeth Houston** (...) daughter of Sir Ludovic
    Houston of Houston & Margaret Maxwell
    no issue
  (4) **Alexander Napier** (... – 1702)
    =1 ...; ♦**Marion Houston** (...) daughter of Sir Ludovic
    Houston of Houston & Margaret Maxwell
    =2 ...; **Margaret Lennox of Woodhead** (...)
    issue of 2nd (none by 1st):
    (a) **John Napier of Culcreuch** (1686 – 1735)
      = ...; **Margaret Lennox** (...)
      Has further generations of issue
  (5) **Marie Napier** (...)
    = ...; **Alexander Seton of Wester Spittaltown** (...)
    issue ?
  (6) **Anna Napier** (...)
    = ...; **Walter Leckie of Deshours** (...)
    issue ?
  (7) **Jean Napier** (...) unm.
(C) **Alexander Napier** (... – Oct 1652)
  = ...; **Anne Dunkeson** (...)
  (1) **Anne Napier** (2 Apr 1636 – ...)
(D) **William Napier of Ardmore** (...)
  = ...; **Margaret Cunningham** (...)
  (1) **Mary Napier** (...)
    = ...; **Evan MacGregor of Kilmanan** (...) son of Duncan
    MacGregor & Margaret Macfarlane
    (a) **Archibald MacGregor, 16th Chief of Clan Gregor**
      (... – aft.1714)
      = 31 May 1679; **Anna Cochrane** (...) daughter of John

Cochrane
Has further generations of issue
(b) **John MacGregor** (... – aft.1673) unm.[53]
(E) **Adam Napier** (...)
= ...; **Anna Buchanan** (...)
(1) **Alexander Napier of Blackstoun** (1644 – ...)
= ...; **Catherine Maxwell of Blackstoun** (...) daughter of
John Maxwell of Blackstoun
(a) **John Napier of Blackstoun** (...) unm.
(b) **Alexander Napier of Blackstoun** (... – ca.1751)
= ...; **Mary Anna Johnstone** (...)
Has further generations of issue
(c) **Anne Napier** (...)
(F) **Margaret Napier** (...)
= 1606; **James Stewart, 11th of Rosyth** (... – bef.1641) son
of Henry Stewart, 10th of Rosyth
(1) **James Stewart, 12th of Rosyth** (...)
=1 aft.18 Apr 1642; **Mary Innes** (...) daughter of Sir Robert
Innes of the Ilk, 1st Baronet
=2 aft.7 Jul 1649; **Agnes Buchanan** (...) daughter of Sir
George Buchanan, 18th of Buchanan
issue of 1st:
(a) **Grissell Stewart** (1642 – ...)
= ...; **George Stewart** (...) son of Archibald Stewart of
Scotston & Margaret Hutcheson
Has further generations of issue
(b) **Margaret Stewart** (1644 – ...)
issue of 2nd:
(c) **David Stewart, 13th of Rosyth** (... – bef. Sep 1675) unm.
(d) **James Stewart, 14th of Rosyth** (... – 1683)
= Dec 1674; **Marion Maxwell** (...) daughter of Sir George
Maxwell of Nether Pollock
no issue
(e) **William Stewart, 15th of Rosyth** (... – 1696) unm.
(2) **Alexander Stewart** (... – Apr 1667)
= aft.21 Dec 1663; ◆**Katharine Drummond** (...) daughter
of George Drummond, 6th of Balloch & Anne Napier
has unknown issue
(3) **Anna Stewart** (1611 – ...)
=1 26 Apr 1642; **William Ged of Baldrig** (...) son of Robert
Ged of Baldrig

---

[53] Believed to have left some illegitimate issue, but no details are known.

=2 17 Apr 1656; **John Ramsey** (...)
has unknown issue by 1st
  (4) **Margaret Stewart** (...)
= bef.10 Feb 1648; **Patrick Winton of Strathdighty** (...)
issue ?
  (5) **Jean Stewart** (...)
= aft.15 Jun 1651; **John Aytoun, 5th of Inchdairney** (... –
Aug 1683) son of Robert Aytoun, 4th of Inchdairney & Hellen
Hamilton of Kelbrachmont
    (a) **Alexander Aytoun, 6th of Inchdairney** (...)
= ...; **Margaret Hog** (...) daughter of Lord Harcus
Has further generations of issue
  (6) **Archibald Stewart** (...)
  (7) **Helen Stewart** (1609 – ...)
 (F) **Jean Napier** (...)
=1 1606; **John Gaw of Maw** (...)
=2 aft.17 Mar 1620; **George Hamilton, younger of
Kilbrachtmont** (... – bef.7 Sep 1669) son of James Hamilton of
Kilbrachtmont & Agnes Betoun
no issue
 (G) **Elizabeth Napier** (...)
= 1622; ♦**William Cuninghame** (... – 1637)
Children are listed with other parent
 (H) **Anne Napier** (...)
= 1620; ♦**George Drummond, 6th of Balloch** (... – 1646)
Children are listed with other parent
 (I) **Helen Napier** (...)
= aft.18 Jan 1629; **Matthew Brisbane** (...)
issue ?
(IX) **Margaret Chisholm** (1567 – Dec 1629)
= 1590; **Sir George Muschet of Burnbank** (... – aft.1626) son of
James Muschet of Burnbank & Marion Seton
 (A) **James Muschet, younger of Burnbank** (... – bef.Apr 1626)
= ...; **Margaret Bellenden** (...) daughter of Sir James Bellenden
of Broughton & Elizabeth Ker; =2nd Henry Erskine
  (1) **George Muschet** (...)
  (2) **Adam Muschet** (...)
  (3) **Janet Muschet** (...)
 (B) **Jean Muschet** (...)
= 1618; **Archibald Stirling, 1st of Kippendavie** (... – bef.17
Apr 1646) son of Sir Archibald Stirling, 5th of Keir & Grizel Ross
  (1) **John Stirling, 2nd of Kippendavie** (... – 1 Jun 1697)
= 1667; **Christian Doig** (...) daughter of David Doig of
Ballingrew & Marion Doig; =1st John Graham of Meiklewood
   (a) **Charles Stirling, 3rd of Kippendavie** (14 Dec 1680 –
Nov 1745)

=1 1703; **Katharine Arbuthnott** (...) daughter of Alexander
Arbuthnott of Knox & Jean Scott
  =2 1709; **Christian ...** (...) =1st ... Douglas of Garvald
  Has further generations of issue by 1st
  (b) **Archibald Stirling** (...) unm.
  (c) **George Stirling** (...) unm.
  (d) **James Stirling** (...) unm.
  (e) **Alexander Stirling** (...)
  (f) **Christian Stirling** (...)
(X) **Anna Chisholm** (4 May 1568 – ...)
e) **Elizabeth Drummond** (1532 – ...)
= 1559; **Malcolm Drummond, 3rd of Boreland** (1520 – 24 Feb
1588) son of John Drummond, 2nd of Boreland & ... Drummond
(I) **John Drummond, 4th of Boreland** (ca.1554 – 15 Dec 1582)
= ...; **Barbara Cunningham** (1560 – ...) daughter of John
Cunningham & Margaret Fleming
  (A) **Sir John Drummond, 5th of Boreland** (ca.1576 – ca.1630)
  unm.
  (B) **Malcolm Drummond** (ca.1580 – ...)
  = ...; **Marjory ...** (...)
  (1) **William Drummond** (ca.1600 – ...)
  = ...; **Anna Hamilton** (...)
  (a) **William Drummond** (ca.1630 – ...)
  (b) **Jean Drummond** (...)
  (c) **Robert Drummond** (...)
  (d) **Thomas Drummond** (...)
  (2) **John Drummond** (...)
  (3) **Mungo Drummond** (...)
  (II) **Maurice Drummond** (1555 – ...)
  = ...; **Agnes Drummond** (1559 – ...)
  (A) **Anabella Drummond** (1585 – ...)
  = ...; **James Murray** (ca.1587 – bef.1630)
  issue ?
  (B) **Jean Drummond** (1587 – ...)
  =1 ...; **Alexander Stewart** (1570 – ...)
  =2 ...; **William Pitcairn** (1575 – ...)
  issue ?
  (C) **James Drummond** (17 Jan 1590 Stirling – ...)
  (III) **Andrew Drummond of Drumduy** (1560 – ...)
  (IV) **Malcolm Drummond** (...)
  (V) **Isaac Drummond** (...)
  (VI) **David Drummond** (...)
  issue of 3rd:
Children are listed with other parent
issue by ♦**Hon. Janet Kennedy** (... – aft.Dec 1543) daughter of
John Kennedy, 2nd Lord Kennedy & Lady Elizabeth Gordon; =1st

Archibald Douglas, 5th Earl of Angus; =2nd Sir Alexander
Gordon of Lochinvar; =3rd John Ramsay, Lord Bothwell:

6) **James Stewart, Earl of Moray** (1501 – 12 Jun 1544) cr.
Earl but it became extinct upon his death
= Aug 1529; ♦**Lady Elizabeth Campbell** (... – ca.1544/5)
daughter of Colin Campbell, 3rd Earl of Argyll & Lady Jean
Gordon

   a) **Lady Mary Stewart** (...)
   = bef.1546; ♦**John, Master of Buchan** (... – 10 Sep 1547)
   son of John Stewart, 3rd Earl of Buchan & Margaret
   Scrimgeour; =2nd Margaret Ogilvy
   no issue

B) **Prince James Stewart, Duke of Ross**, Marquess of Ormonde,
Earl of Ardmannoch, Baron of Brechin and Nevar, **Archbishop
of St.Andrews** (Mar 1475/6 – 12 Jan 1504 Edinburgh) cr.
Marquess 1476, Duke 23 Jan 1481, Earl and Baron 29 Jan 1488,
Archbishop 20 Sep 1497; unm.

C) **Prince John Stewart, Earl of Mar and Garioch** (1479/80 –
11 Mar 1502/3) cr. Earl 2 Mar 1485/6; unm.

IV) **Prince Alexander Stewart, 1st Duke of Albany**, Earl of Mar,
Garioch, and March, Lord Annandale (ca.1454 – 7 Aug 1485
Paris) cr. Earl of March and Lord bef. 4 Aug 1455, Duke aft. 4
Aug 1455, Earl of Garioch and Mar Jan. 1482/3
=1 bef.1477 (ann.1478); **Lady Catherine Sinclair** (...) daughter of
William Sinclair, 1st Earl of Caithness & Marjory Sutherland
=2 1479; **Anne de La Tour** (... – 13 Oct 1512 Savoy) daughter of
Bernard VI, Count d'Auvergne & Louise de La Trémoille; =2nd
Louis, Count de la Chambre
issue of 1st:

A) **Alexander Stewart** (ca.1477 – 19 Dec 1537) murdered;
declared illegitimate 1513 by parliament
= ...; ♦**Margaret Stewart** (ca,1497 – ...) daughter of James IV,
King of Scotland & Margaret Drummond; =1st John, Lord
Gordon; =2nd Sir John Drummond, 2nd of Innerperffray

   1) **Margaret Stewart** (... – aft.1539)
   = 1535; **David Drummond, 2nd Lord Drummond** (ca.1516 –
   1571) son of Walter, Master of Drummond & Lady Elizabeth
   Graham; =2nd Lilias Ruthven; suc. great-grandfather 1519

      a) **Hon. Sybilla Drummond** (...)
      = ...; **Sir Gilbert Ogilvy** (...)
      issue ?

illegitimate by unknown women:

   2) **Alexander Stewart** (...)

   3) **Margaret Stewart** (...)
   =1 ...; **Patrick Graham, 1st of Inchbrakie and Aberuthven**
   (ca.1508 – 1536) son of William Graham, 1st Earl of Montrose

& Christian Wawane
=2 ...; ♦**Sir Colin Campbell of Glenorchy** (... – 1583)
issue of 1st:
a) **George Graham, 2nd of Inchbrakie** (... – 1575)
  = ...; **Marjory Rollo** (... – 24 Feb 1625) daughter of Andrew
  Rollo, 6th of Duncrub & Marion Rollo
  (I) **Lilias Graham** (...)
    = ...; **William Colville of Condie** (...)
    issue ?
  (II) **Patrick Graham, 3rd of Inchbrakie** (... – 1635)
  =1 ...; **Nicola Brown** (...) daughter of John Brown of Forbell &
  Elizabeth Adamson
  =2 1613; **Margaret Scott** (...) daughter of Patrick Scott, 4th of
  Monzie & Egidia Drummond
  issue of 2nd (none by 1st):
  (A) **Beatrix Graham** (...)
    =1 ...; **Alexander Robertson** (... – 1639) son of
    Alexander Robertson, 8th of Lude & Agnes Gordon
    =2 ...; **Donald Robertson** (... – aft.1660) son of Robert
    Robertson, 10th Chief of Clan Dionnachaidh
    issue of 1st (none by 2nd):
    (1) **Alexander** de Atholia **Robertson, 9th of Lude** (... –
      1673)
      =1 ...; **Jean Menzies** (...) daughter of Sir Alexander Menzie
      of that Ilk
      =2 aft.21 Oct 1652; **Marjory Graham** (...) daughter of John
      Graham, 2nd of Balgowan & Helen Blair
      =3 ...; ♦**Catherine Campbell** (...) daughter of Sir John
      Campbell of Glenorchy, 4th Baronet & Lady Mary
      Graham
      issue of 1st:
      (a) **Margaret Robertson** (...)
        = ...; **Alexander Robertson of Faskally** (...)
        issue ?
      issue of 3rd (none by 2nd):
      (b) **John Robertson, 10th of Lude** (... – ca.1729)
        = ...; **Margaret Farquharson** (...) daughter of Alexander
        Farquharson, 7th of Invercauld & Elizabeth
        Mackintosh
        Has further generations of issue
      (c) **Alexander Robertson** (...)
      (d) **Patrick Robertson** (...)
      (e) **Agnes Robertson** (...)
        = ...; **... Murray of Kincairney** (...)
        issue ?
    (2) **John Robertson** (...)

(3) **Margaret Robertson** (...)
= ...; **William Menzies** (...) son of Sir Alexander
Menzies of that Ilk
issue ?

(III) **Beatrice Graham** (...)
= aft.15 Jan 1590; **Henry Drummond, 5ᵗʰ of Balloch** (...)
son of George Drummond, 4ᵗʰ of Balloch & Margaret
Drummond

(A) **George Drummond, 6ᵗʰ of Balloch** (... – ca.1646)
=1 ca.Jul 1620; ♦**Anne Napier** (...) daughter of John Napier,
8ᵗʰ of Merchistoun & Agnes Chisholm
=2 ...; ♦**Marjory Graham** (...) daughter of Rev. George
Graham of Merseyside & Marion Crichton; =1ˢᵗ George
Drummond, 4ᵗʰ of Blair
issue of 1ˢᵗ:

(1) **Katherine Drummond** (...)
= aft.21 Dec 1663; ♦**Alexander Steward** (... – Apr
1667) son of James Steward, 11ᵗʰ of Rosyth & Margaret
Napier

(2) **John Drummond, 7ᵗʰ of Balloch** (... – 21 Oct 1657
Dunkirk, France) died in a siege

(3) **Henry Drummond, 8ᵗʰ of Balloch** (... – Feb 1690)

(4) **Robert Drummond, 9ᵗʰ of Balloch** (... – Mar 1722)
issue of 2ⁿᵈ:

(5) **David Drummond** (... – 20 Feb 1696)
= 18 Feb 1673; ♦**Christian Graham** (...) daughter of
Patrick Graham, 1ˢᵗ of Graemeshall & Anna Stewart
issue ?

(6) **Agnes Drummond** (...)
= 1638; ♦**John Graeme, 7ᵗʰ of Gavrock** (...) son of
Ninian Graeme, 6ᵗʰ of Gavrock & Elizabeth Oliphant
issue ?

(B) **Margaret Drummond** (...)
= ...; **Alexander Murray, 7ᵗʰ of Strowan** (... – bef.1 Dec
1654) son of James Murray, Fiar of Strowan & Annabella
Drummond

(1) **John Murray, 8ᵗʰ of Strowan** (... – 13 Feb 1725)
= aft.5 Sep 1668; **Margaret Dow** (...) daughter of John Dow
of Arnhall
isue ?

(IV) **Marjory Graham** (...)
= ...; **Patrick Maxtone, 6ᵗʰ of Cultoquhey** (...)
issue ?

(V) **Rev. George Graham of Merseyside** (ca.1565 – 19 Dec
1643)
= bef.29 Jan 1595; **Marion Crichton** (... – 10 Apr 1632)

daughter of Sir Robert Crichton of Eliock & Elizabeth Stewart

(A) **Marjory Graham** (...)

=1 ...; **George Drummond, 4ᵗʰ of Blair** (...)

=2 ...; ♦**George Drummond, 6ᵗʰ of Balloch** (... – 1646)

issue of 1ˢᵗ:

(1) **Marie Drummond** (...)

= ...; **Patrick Blair of Little Blair** (...) son of Patrick Blair, 1ˢᵗ of Pittenreich & Janet Gargill

(a) **Margaret Blair** (...)

= ...; **James Blair, 10ᵗʰ of Ardblair** (Jun 1656 – 1724) son of John Blair, 9ᵗʰ of Ardblair & Isobel Stewart

Has further generations of issue

(2) **George Drummond, 1ˢᵗ of Blair Drummond** (29 Nov 1638 – 4 Jun 1717)

= aft. 20 May 1672; **Elizabeth Ramsay** (...) daughter of Sir Gilbert Ramsay, 1ˢᵗ Baronet & Elizabeth Blair

(a) **James Drummond, 2ⁿᵈ of Blair Drummond** (12 Sep 1673 – ...)

= ...; **Jean Carre** (...)

Has further generations of issue

(b) **Mary Drummond** (21 Mar 1689 Edinburgh – ...)

= 25 Aug 1709; **James Halyburton of Pitcur** (bef. 1690 – 1738) son of Savid Halyburton of Pitcur

Has further generations of issue

issue of 2ⁿᵈ:

Children are listed with other parent

(B) **Catherine Graham** (...)

= 1618; **Patrick Smyth of Braco** (... – 25 Apr 1655) son of Alexander Smyth & Margret Oliver

(1) **Katherine Smyth** (...)

= ...; **John Campbell, 6ᵗʰ of Glenlyon** (... – 1746 son of Robert Campbell, 5ᵗʰ of Glenlyon & Helen Lindsay

issue ?

(2) **Parick Smith of Methven** (1627 – ...)

= 19 May 1682; **Janet Haldane** (... – 1725) daughter of Mungo Haldane, 13ᵗʰ of Gleneagles & Margaret Gray

(a) **David Smythe of Methven** (1683 – 1732)

= 1707; **Katherine Cochrane** (...)

Has further generations of issue

(C) **Patrick Graham, 1ˢᵗ of Graemeshall** (...)

= ...; **Anna Stewart** (...) daughter of William Stewart of Burray & Barbara Stewart

(1) **Christian Graham** (...)

= 18 Feb 1673; **David Drummond** (...) son of George Drummond, 6ᵗʰ of Balloch & Marjory Graham

issue ?

(2) **James Graeme, 2nd of Graemeshall** (ca.1652 – 11 Jun 1716)

= ...; **Mary Murray** (...) daughter of Patrick Murray, 7th of Ochtertyre & Mary Moray

  (a) **Patrick Graeme, 3rd of Graemeshall** (... – 13 May 1742)
= 1694; ♦**Euphemia Honyman** (... – 1763) daughter of Robert Honyman, 1st of Graemsay & Catherine Graham
Has further generations of issue

(D) **John Graham, 1st of Breckness** (... – 1664)

= 22 Sep 1645; **Barbara Stewart** (...) daughter of Harry Stewart of Graemsay

  (1) **Harry Graham, 2nd of Breckness** (2 Feb 1648 – 20 Jun 1718)

= 9 Apr 1669; **Euphemia Honyman** (...) daughter of Andrew Honeyman & Mary Stewart of Graemsay

    (a) **Catherine Graham** (...)
= ...; **Robert Honyman, 1st of Graemsey** (...)
Has further generations of issue

(E) **David Graham, 2nd of Gorthie** (... – 11 Jan 1661)

= 1632; **Catherine Myrton** (...) daughter of Thomas Myrton of Cambo & Anne Halket

  (1) **Mungo Graham, 3rd of Gorthie** (...)

  (2) **David Graham, 1st of Braco** (...)

= 5 Jul 1683 Fowlis Wester, Perths.; **Margaret Murray** (...) daughter of Patrick Murray, 2nd of Keilour

    (a) **James Graham, 2nd of Braco** (13 Jul 1686 Dalkeith – Feb 1736)
= 11 Oct 1713; **Catherine Stirling** (...) daughter of Sir William Stirling of Ardoch, 2nd Baronet & Mary Erskine
Has further generations of issue

  (3) **John Graham** (... – aft.1723)

= ...; **Catherne Dow** (...)

    (a) **Anna Graham** (...)
= Apr 1711 Killearn, Stirlings. (dv.); **Alexander Macfarlane, 7th of Gargartan** (ca.1685 – aft.1719) son of Andrew Macfarlane, 6th of Gargartan & Marion Baillie
no issue

b) **John Graham** (...)

= ...

  (I) **Catherine Graham** (... – 1607)

= 1602; ♦**Archibald Campbell of Lagvinshoch and Monzie** (... – 1640)

Children are listed with other parent

c) **Nicola Graham** (...)

= ...; **Patrick Murray, 5th of Ochtertyre** (... – 1589) son of David Murray, 4th of Ochtertyre & Agnes Hay

(I) **William Murray, 6ᵗʰ of Octertyre** (... – 1647)
= ...; **Bethia Murray** (...) daughter of ... Murray of Letterbannochy
(A) **Patrick Murray 7ᵗʰ of Ochtertyre** (ca.1591 – 2 Feb 1677)
= ...; **Mary Moray** (... – Aug 1667) daughter of Sir William
Moray, 9ᵗʰ of Abercairney & Christian Mercer
(1) **Mary Murray** (...)
= ...; ◆**James Graeme, 2ⁿᵈ of Graemeshall** (ca.1652 – 1716)
Children are listed with other parent
(2) **Sir William Murray of Octertyne, 1ˢᵗ Baronet** (30
Oct 1615 – 18 Feb 1681) cr. Baronet 7 Jun 1673
= 7 Jun 1649; **Isabel Oliphant** (... – 6 Apr 1683) daughter
of John Oliphant of Bachiltoun
(a) **Anne Murray** (...)
= 6 Apr 1675; **Henry Cheape, 2ⁿᵈ of Rossie** (...)
issue ?
(b) **Sir Patrick Murray of Ochtertyre, 2ⁿᵈ Baronet**
(21 Jan1656 – 25 Dec 1735) suc. father 1681
= 15 Feb 1681 Gleneagles, Perths.; **Margaret
Haldane** (22 Jul 1657 – 17 Feb 1722) daughter of Mungo
Haldane, 13ᵗʰ of Gleneagles & Anne Grant
Has further generations of issue
(c) **Mungo Murray** (1662 – 1719)
=1 ...; **Janet Arnott** (...)
=2 ...; **Martha Forester** (...) daughter of Andrew Forester
Has further generations of issue
(B) **Rev. John Murray of Leller Baudachie** (...)
= 1 Aug 1628; **Christian Haldane** (... – 30 Oct 1653)
daughter of Sir James Haldene, 10ᵗʰ of Gleeagles & Lady
Margaret Murray
no issue
d) **Janet Graham** (... – Aug 1575)
=1 ...; **Robert Buchanan, 7ᵗʰ of Leny** (...) son of Robert
Buchanan & Marion Graham
=2 ca.1518; ◆**Dougal Campbell of Ardaillour** (ca.1493 – 1550)
issue of 2ⁿᵈ (none by 1ˢᵗ):
Children are listed with other parent
e) **Margaret Graham** (...)
= ca.1490; **Sir Ian Campbell, 4ᵗʰ of Ardkinglass** (ca,1460 –
...) son of Colin Campbell, 3ʳᵈ of Ardkinglass & Marion Houston
(I) **Colin Campbell, 5ᵗʰ of Ardkinglass** (... – bef.23 Sep 1565)
= ...; **Lady Matilda Montgomerie** (...) daughter of Hugh
Montgomerie, 1ˢᵗ Earl of Eglinton & Lady Helen Campbell
(A) **Mary Campbell** (...)
= ...; ◆**Hon. John Campbell, 1ˢᵗ of Lochnell** (...)
Children are listed with other parent
(B) **Marion Campbell** (ca.1515 Ardkinglass, Argylls. –

aft.23 Jul 1564)

= ca.1536; **John Campbell, 6th of Dunstaffnage**
(ca.1501 Dunstaffnage, Argylls. – 6 Jan 1586) son of
Archibald Campbell, 5th of Dunstaffnage

(1) **Alexander Campbell, 7th of Dunstaffnage** (... – ca.1619)
= bef.21 Aug 1587; ♦**Anne Campbell** (ca.1564
Lochnell, Argylls. – ...) daughter of Archibald Campbell, 2nd
of Lochnell & & Janet Macdougall

(a) **Katherine Campbell** (...)
=1 bef.1615; **John Macdougall, younger of
Ardincapel** (...)
=2 1615; ♦**Allan Macdougall** (...)
Children are listed with other parent

(b) **Archibald Campbell, 8th of Dunstaffnage** (ca.
1589 – bef.1 Dec 1652)
= 29 Apr 1614; ♦**Beatrix Campbell** (...) daughter of Sir
Donald Campbell of Ardnamurchan and Airds, 1st
Baronet & Anne Campbell
Has further generations of issue

(c) **Donald Campbell of Achanard** (1591 – ...)

(d) **Annabel Campbell** (ca.1601 – ...)
= 1620; **Patrick Campbell, 1st of Barcaldine** (1592 –
25 Mar 1678) son of son of Sir Duncan Campbell of
Glenorchy, 1st Baronet
Has further generations of issue

(e) **Colin Campbell, 1st of Clenamacrie** (ca.1603 – ...)

(II) **Dougal Campbell of Ardaillour** (ca.1493 –
bef.10 May 1550)
= ca.1518; (his aunt) ♦**Janet Graham** (... – Aug 1575)
daughter of Patrick Graham, 1st of Inchbrakie and Aberuthven
& Margaret Stewart

(A) **Rev. Alexander Campbell** (... – Feb 1608)
= aft.1579; **Helen Clephane** (... – Feb 1608) daughter of
George Clephane of Carslogie & Christian Learmouth;
she =1st ♦Robert Abuthnott of that Ilk

(1) **Marjory Campbell** (...)
= 1604; ♦**Alexander Menzies, 11th of Weems** (ca.
1566 – 1644)
Children are listed with other parent

issue of 2nd:

issue of 2nd:

Children are listed with other parent

B) **John Stewart, 2nd Duke of Albany**, etc. (aft.1481 – 2 Jun
1536 Mirefleur Château, Auvergne, France) suc. father 1515,
but his titles became extinct upon his death
= 13 Jul 1505; ♦**Anne de La Tour, Countess d'Auvergne**

(aft.1495 – Jun 1624) daughter of Jean III de La Tour, Count
d'Auvergne & Jeanne de Bourbon
no issue by marriage
issue by **Jean Abernathy** (...):
1) **Eleanor Stewart** (...)
 = ...; **John de l'Hôpital, Count de Choisy** (...)
 issue ?
V) **Prince John Stewart, Earl of Mar and Garioch**, (aft.1546 – 9
 Jul 1479 Edinburgh) possibly murdered; unm.
issue by ...:
VI) **John Stewart of Sticks** (aft.1445 – 11 Sep 1523)
 = ...; **Muriel Sutherland** (...)
 A) **William Stewart** (...)
 B) **John Stewart of Sticks** (... – 1559)
 = ...; **Matilda Johnson** (...)
 no issue
 C) **Patrick Stewart of Ballechin** (...)
 = 1553; **Elizabeth Buttar** (... – May 1590) daughter of John Buttar
 & Beatrix Gordon
 1) **Sir James Stewart of Ballechin** (... – 1627)
 =1 2 Feb 1586; **Marie Crichton** (...) daughter of Sir Robert
 Crichton of Eliock & Elizabeth Stewart
 =2 aft.31 Jul 1598; **Elizabeth Rollo** (...) daughter of James Rollo, 8th
 of Dencrub & Agnes Collace
 issue of 1st:
 a) **Robert Steuart of Ballechin** (...)
 = 1624; **Margaret Campbell** (...) daughter of Duncan Campbell, 4th
 of Glenlyon & Margaret Ogilvy; =1st George Bruce, 6th of
 Cultmalundy
 (I) **John Steuart of Ballechin** (...) unm.
 (II) **Patrick Steuart of Ballechin** (ca.1630 – ...)
 = 13 Nov 1659 Kilspendie, Perths.; **Elizabeth Lindsay** (...)
 daughter of Alexander Lindsay & Marjorie Falconer
 (A) **Charles Steuart of Ballechin** (ca.1661 – 1733)
 =1 aft.Jul 1678; **Anne Dow of Arnhall** (...) daughter of John
 Dow of Arnhall
 =2 1703; **Jean ...** (...) =1st Adam Reid of Pitnacree
 issue of 1st (none by 2nd):
 (1) **Patrick Steuart, younger of Ballechin** (... – bef.1733)
 = 1713; **Christian Menzies** (...) daughter of Sir Robert
 Menzies of Wemyss & Anne Sandilands
 (a) **Jean Steuart** (... – 1733) unm.
 (2) **James Steuart** (... – 1716) unm.
 (3) **Charles Steuart of Ballechin** (... – 1764)
 = 1719; **Grizel Mercer** (...) daughter of Sir Laurence Mercer of
 Aldie & Helen Mercer

(a) **Robert Steuart of Ballechin** (1727 – 21 Sep 1783)
= 1759; **Isabella Hope** (... – 1784) daughter of John Hope of
Rankeillor & Isabel Bannerman
Has further generations of issue
(b) **Jean Steuart** (...)
= 1760; **Henry Stewart of Fincastle** (...)
issue ?
(c) **Clementina Steuart** (...)
= 1749; **Sir John Stewart of Grandtully, 4ᵗʰ Baronet**
(... – 1797) son of Sir John Stewart of Grandtully, 3ʳᵈ Baronet
& Elizabeth Mackenzie
Has further generations of issue
(d) **George Steuart** (... – 1770) unm.
(e) **James Steuart** (... – 1779) unm.
(4) **Elizabeth Steuart** (aft.1678 – ...)
= 1700; ♦**John Stewart, 4ᵗʰ of Ardsheal** (... – aft.1717)
Children are listed with other parent
(5) **Helen Steuart** (...)
= 1700; **Alexander Menzies of Woodend** (...)
issue ?
(6) **Margaret Steuart** (...)
= 1702; **John Campbell of Kinloch** (...)
issue ?
(7) **Emilia Steuart** (...)
= 1707; **John Stewart of Bonskeld** (...)
issue ?
(8) **Anne Steuart** (...)
= 1725; **David Rattray of Tullichurran** (...)
issue ?
(9) **Jean Steuart** (...)
= 1721; **Sir Laurence Mercer of Aldie** (...)
no issue
(B) **Alexander Steuart** (...)
=1 aft. 23 Feb 1686; **Christine Murray** (...) daughter of John
Murray of Malnabroich & Janet Maxwell
=2 ...; **Jean Stewart** (...) daughter of Gilbert Stewart of Dunkeld
issue of 1ˢᵗ:
(1) **John Steuart** (...)
(2) **Anne Steuart** (...)
= ...; **James Robertson of Balnacree** (...)
issue ?
(3) **Margaret Steuart** (...)
= ...; **Thomas Bisset of Glenalbert** (...) son of James Bisset
(a) **James Bisset of Glenalbert** (...) unm.
(b) **Charles Bisset of Glenalbert** (1717 – May 1791)
= ...

Has further generations of issue
(c) **Thomas Bisset** (Jun 1722 – ...)
  = ...
Has further generations of issue
(d) **Robert Bisset** (Jul 1729 – 27 Aug 1811)
  = ...
Issue extinct in next generation
(e) **Margaret Bisset** (...)
  =1 ...; **James Dick of Colluthie** (... – 1743) son of William
  Dick & Isabel Makgill of Rankeillour
  =2 ...; **... Duncan of Tippermalloch** (...)
Has further generations of issue by both
(f) **a daughter** (...)
  = ...; **Robert Stewart of Strath Tay** (...)
  issue ?
(g) **David Bisset** (...) unm.
issue of 2nd:
(4) **Alexander Steuart** (...)
(C) **Jean Steuart** (...)
  = 1698; **John McLaren of Easthaugh** (...)
  issue ?
(D) **John Steuart, 1st of Kynnachan** (... – May 1733)
  = 23 Apr 1702 Methven, Perths.; **Jane Omey** (...) daughter of
  Rev. John Omey
  no issue
(E) **Robert Steuart** (...) unm.
(F) **George Steuart** (...) unm.
(G) **Helen Steuart** (...) unm.
(H) **Anne Steuart** (...) unm.
(I) **Isabel Steuart** (...) unm.
(III) **Alexander Steuart** (...)
  = ...; **Grizell Stewart** (...)
(A) **Patrick Steuart** (...)
(B) **Robert Steuart** (...)
(C) **Neil Steuart** (...)
(D) **Alexander Steuart** (...)
  = ...;
  (1) **Margaret Steuart** (...)
    = ...; ♦**Archibald Butter** (...) son of John Butter of Pitlochrry
    & Jean Steuart
    no issue
b) **Elizabeth Stewart** (...)
  = 1607; **Duncan Robertson of Dalcabon** (...)
  issue ?
issue of 2nd:
c) **Isabel Stewart** (...)

= 1620; **Donald Robertson of Killiechangie** (...)
issue ?
d) **Jean Stewart** (aft.1598 – ...)
= 1626; **John Butter of Pitlochry** (...) son of John Butter of
Pitlochry & Janet Bryson
(I) **John Butter** (...)
(II) **Archibald Butter** (...)
=1 ...; **Jean Balneaves** (...) daughter of Henry Balneaves
=2 ...; ◆**Margaret Steuart** (...) daughter of Alexander Steuart
issue of 1st (none by 2nd):
(A) **Henry Butter of Pitlochry** (...)
= ...; **Katherine Hay** (...) daughter of Peter Hay of Leys &
Elizabeth Scott
(1) **Archibald Butter of Faskally** (1768 – 1805)
= 1803; **Vere Menzies** (... Jan 1847) daughter of Sir Robert
Menzies of Weem, 5th Baronet & Catherine Ochiltree
has unknown issue
e) **John Stewart of Killichassie** (...)
f) **George Stewart** (...)
g) **Francis Stewart** (...)
h) **Andrew Stewart** (...)
2) **John Stewart of Arnaguy** (...)
3) **George Stewart of Dumnacarff** (...)
= ...
has issue: Steuarts of Innervack
4) **Anne Stewart** (...)
= 1578; **George Leslie of Balgonie** (...) son of George Leslie of
Drummuir & Mary Stewart
a) **George Leslie** (...)
= ...
(I) a daughter ...
= 1642; **... of Newhall** (...)
issue ?
b) **John Leslie** (...)
5) **Isabel Stewart** (...)
= ...; **John Stewart of Foss** (...)
issue ?
6) **Margaret Stewart** (...)
= 1589; **Robert Stewart of Fincastle** (...)
issue ?
7) **Barbara Stewart** (
= 1597; **Andrew Hering of Glasclune** (...)
issue ?
8) **Sibilla Stewart** (...)
= ...; **Alexander Leslie of Urquhill** (...)
issue ?

issue of 2nd:
see: Chapter 23

CHAPTER 8
PERCY

Now that we followed the royal line of descent from Edward III to George I, we can turn our attention to some of the lines of descent started by various daughters of the previous houses. The senior-most of these lines is the House of Percy, descended from Lady Elizabeth Mortimer, the granddaughter of Lionel of Antwerp, Edward III's second son.

The Percy family traces their lineage to Normandy and were among those who followed William the Conqueror to England, the first "de Perci" arriving in late 1067. They initially established themselves in northern Yorkshire but faced imminent extinction only a little over a hundred years later. The male lines had come down to one heiress.

Agnes de Percy (+1203) was married to her step-mother's younger brother, Jocelin de Louvain, of the ruling family of the Duchy of Brabant, in modern-day Belgium. His position as a younger son of a younger son entitled him to inherit a whole lot of nothing. But, by marrying Agnes, he suddenly acquired all of the wealth and lands of the powerful Percy family. Changing his family name to Percy was a small price to pay.

The descendants of this new line of Percy purchased Alnwick Castle, in Northumberland, in 1309. It remains their seat of power to this day. Alnwick is actually well known to the people of the 21st century as well. This magnificent castle often doubled as Hogwarts School in the *Harry Potter* movies, as well as Brancaster Castle, the home of Lady Edith in the finale of *Downton Abbey*.

By the time of Edward III, the Percys had long served the Crown as Barons Percy, and essentially ruled the north of England in the name of the Throne. They also served as the King's first line of defense, or offense depending on the battle, against Scotland. Edward, as well as most of his predecessors, spent considerable amounts of time trying to force a union with Scotland, with England being the overlord of that arrangement. The coming battles between Edward's descendants would soon calm that border, only to ignite more fighting on the southern one in France.

Lady Elizabeth Mortimer, our point of entrance into the great north, married a Percy who was better known to history by his nickname, Sir Harry "Hotspur." The name was actually bestowed on him by the Scots in deference to the readiness and speed with which he launched attacks against them. Harry's father was the first member of the family to be titled Earl of Northumberland. However this Earl, after initially supporting Henry IV's usurpation of the Throne from Richard II, turned on his liege Lord in favor of Hotspur's brother-in-law, the Earl of March. This earned him the forfeiture of his title and estates, not to mention his life in the Battle of Bramham Moor (1408). Hotspur also fell in battle five years before his father did at Shrewsbury.

Hotspur's son, Henry, swore allegiance to the Lancaster King once again and was restored to his father's properties and was given a new creation of the Earldom of Northumberland. From then on, the Percys remained staunch Lancastrians, surviving several bouts of attainder and forgiveness during the York years.

When the childless 5th Earl died in 1537, his heir was to be his brother, Thomas. However, Thomas had risen up in rebellion against Henry VIII when the latter broke with Rome and established England as a Protestant country. The outcome was a forgone conclusion: Thomas was attainted and then executed as a commoner. This attainder prevented his son from inheriting the Earldom so it was declared extinct. By modern doctrine, the title would have been considered inherited by his son, also named Thomas. The younger Thomas instead received a recreation of the title, albeit some twenty years later, and is now reckoned as the 1st Earl of this creation. He, too, faced the executioner, but not until 1572 and on the orders of Queen Elizabeth for his part in a plot to free Mary, Queen of Scots and overthrow Elizabeth. He was beatified by the Vatican in 1865.

Blessed Thomas, having only daughters, was succeeded by his brother, whose grandson, the 4th Earl, would be the next Northumberland to oppose the King. In the English Civil War, he sided with Parliament, but opposed trying and executing King Charles I. This opposition earned him forgiveness from Charles II after the

Restoration. His son and heir, the 5th Earl would be the last of this creation. He was the last legitimate male-line descendant of the 1st earl of the 1557 creation. The title was re-created once more for his daughter's son, the Duke of Somerset (who was a Beaufort from a couple of chapters ago) and then elevated to a Dukedom in the next generation, with the new Duke and Duchess adopting the name Percy once again.

There were more male lines descended from the 1414 creation of the 1st Earl, but they were considered ineligible to succeed due to the attainder of 1537. These male lines have closer connections to the United States. One of them was a colonial Governor of Virginia and his grandsons, surnamed West, were Governors of New Jersey and Maryland. The Percys returned to England, but the Wests remained in the colonies and are gateway ancestors to many Americans today.

There also remains an unsolved genealogical puzzle within the descendants of Sir Richard Percy, a younger son the 1st Earl of the 1414 creation. Sir Richard had a grandson, also named Richard, who was the founder of Pearce Hall, a now-demolished estate in Yorkshire. Pearce and Pierce families of America have tried to prove he is their ancestor. However, the work that has been published thus far seems to be based on an 1880 publication that makes several connections from their family to Richard of Pearce Hall that are either biologically impossible, or that have no factual data to support them. There very well could be a legitimate connection there, but the facts to prove it have thus far been elusive.

There are also several lines of descent that lead to America through the daughters of the Northumberland Earls. For example, the Sir Richard previously mentioned had an eldest sister, Elizabeth, whose great-granddaughter, Elizabeth le Scrope, married Sir Brian Stapleton and became the ancestors of a prominent Colorado family of that name. One descendant was Denver's Mayor Ben Stapleton who served from the 1920s to the 40s. He himself is the great-grandfather of a recent Colorado state treasurer, Walker Stapleton, who is maternally closely related to the Presidents Bush.

Lady Elizabeth's younger sister, Lady Margaret, married Sir William Gascoigne, and became ancestress to several gateway colonial settlers, including the Butler family of Maryland, who are in turn ancestors to this author. The Percy-Gascoigne marriage is featured prominently in many genealogies tracing Americans of royal descent. But it is far from the only one. There are several first families of Long

Island, New York, as well as Boston, who can claim direct descent from Harry Hotspur & Lady Elizabeth Mortimer.

The lines descended from the Percy daughters have proved so robust, they had to be continued in the following three chapters.

Edward III

|

Lionel of Antwerp, Duke of Clarence

|

Philippa, Countess of Ulster

|

Lady Elizabeth Mortimer (12 Feb 1371 Usk – 20 Apr 1417)
=1 1 May 1380; **Sir Henry** ("Hotspur"), **Lord Percy KG** (20 May 1364 – 21 Jul 1403 Shrewsbury) killed in battle; son of Henry de Percy, Earl of Northumberland[54] & Margaret de Neville; KG 1388
=2 aft.1403; **Thomas de Camoys, 1st Baron Camoys KG** (... – 28 Mar 1419) son of Sir John de Camoys & Elizabeth Latimer; =1st Elizabeth Louches
issue of 1st:
a. **Elizabeth Percy** (ca.1390 – 26 Oct 1437)
=1 ca.1404; **Sir John Clifford KG, 7th Baron Clifford** (1389 – 13 Mar 1422 Meaux) died during a siege; son of Thomas de Clifford, 6th Baron Clifford & Elizabeth de Ros; suc. 1391; KG 1421
=2 1426; **Ralph Neville, 2nd Earl of Westmorland, 5th Baron Neville of Raby** (1408 – 3 Nov 1484) son of John, Lord Neville & Lady Elizabeth de Holland; suc. grandfather 21 Oct 1425
issue of 1st:
I) **THOMAS CLIFFORD, 8TH BARON CLIFFORD** (1414–1455)
see: Chapter 9
II) **MARY, LADY WENTWORTH** (...)
see: Chapter 10
III) **Blanche Clifford** (...)
issue of 2nd:
IV) **Sir John Neville** (... – bef.1451)
= ...; **Anne Holland** (...) daughter of John Holland, 2nd Duke of Exeter
no issue
b. **Henry Percy, 1st Earl of Northumberland** (3 Feb 1392/3 – 22 May 1455 St.Albans) killed in battle; cr. Earl 11 Nov 1414
= 1414 Berwick; ♦**Lady Eleanor Neville** (1398 – 1472) daughter of Ralph Neville, 1st Earl of Westmorland & Lady Joan Beaufort; she =1st Richard, Lord le Despencer,
I) **Sir Henry Percy, Kt, 2nd Earl of Northumberland** (25 Jul 1421 – 29 Mar 1461 Towton, Yorks.) killed in battle; suc. father 22 May 1455; Kt 1426
= 25 Jun 1435; **Eleanor Poynings, (5th) Baroness Poynings** (ca.1422 – Feb 1484) daughter of Sir Richard Poynings & Joan

---

[54] This was the only Earl of this creation. He was cr. Earl in 1377 and attainted in 1406.

Seamer ; suc.grandfather 2 Oct 1446
A) **Lady Elizabeth Percy** (... – aft.20 May 1512)
  = ...; **Henry le Scrope, 6th Baron Scrope** (ca.1648 – 1506) John
  le Scrope, 5th Baron Scrope & Joanne FitzHugh; suc. father 17 Aug 1498
  1) **Henry le Scrope, 7th Baron Scrope** (ca.1480 – ca..Dec
    1533) suc. father 1506
    =1 bef.20 Apr 1494; **Alice Scope, (7th) Baroness Scrope of
    Masham** (... – ca.1510) daughter of Thomas, 6th Baron Scrope
    of Masham & Lady Elizabeth Neville
    =2 ...; **Mabel Dacre** (... – aft.Jun 1520) daughter of Thomas
    Dacre, 2nd Baron Dacre & Elizabeth Greystroke, Baroness Greystoke
    issue of 1st:
    a) **Elizabeth le Scrope** (...
      = ...; **Sir Brian Stapleton** (... – 2 Apr 1550) son of Sir Brian
      Stapleton & Joan Lovel
      (I) **Sir Richard Stapleton** (... – 11 Jan 1584/5)
        = ...; **Thomasin Amandas** (...) daughter of Robert
        Amandas
        (A) **Brian Stapleton** (... – 13 Dec 1606)
          = ...; ◆**Lady Eleanor Neville** (...) daughter of Ralph
          Neville, 4th Earl of Westmorland & Lady Catherine Stafford
          (1) **Richard Stapleton** (... – ca.1614)
            = ...
            (a) **Gilbert Stapleton** (... – ca.11 Apr 1636)
              =1 ...; **Katherine Hungate** (...)
              =2 ...; ◆**Eleanor Gascoigne** (...) daughter of Sir John
              Gascoigne
              Has further generations of issue
    issue of 2nd:
    b) **John le Scrope, 8th Baron Scrope** (... – 22 Jun 1549) suc.
      mother ca.1510 and father 1533
      = ca.1530; ◆**Lady Catherine Clifford** (1513 – 1598)
      daughter of Henry Clifford, 1st Earl of Cumberland & Lady
      Margaret Percy; =2nd Sir Richard Cholmley
      (I) **Henry Scrope, 9 Baron Scrope** (ca.1534 – 13 Jun 1592
        Carlisle, Cumberland) suc. father 1549
        =1 ...; **Mary North** (... – Nov 1558) daughter of Edward
        North, Baron North & Alice Squire
        =2 bef.10 Sep 1565; ◆**Lady Margaret Howard** (30 Jan
        1543 Lambeth, Surrey – 17 Mar 1590/1 Carlisle) daughter
        of Henry, Earl of Surrey & Lady Frances de Vere
        issue of 1st:
        (A) **Mary Scrope** (...)

= ...; **Sir William Bowes** (...)

(1) **Catherine Bowes** *de jure (12th) Baroness Scrope*[55] (...)
   = ...; **Sir William Eure** (...)

  (a) **Thomas Eure** *de jure 13the Baron Scrope* (ca. 1607 – 20 Sep 1643 Newbury, Berks.) killed in battle; unm.

  (b) **William Eure** *de jure 14th Baron Scrope* (ca.1608 – Mar 1684/5) suc. brother 1643
   = ...; **Mary Forcer** (... – Feb 1669/70) daughter of Peter Forcer & Catherine Hodshorn
   Has further generations of issue

issue of 2nd:

(B) **Thomas Scrope, 10th Baron Scrope** (ca.1567 – 2 Sep 1609) suc. father 1592
= ca.1584; **Philadelphia Carey** (... – 3 Feb 1626/7) daughter of Henry Carey, 1st Baron Hunsdon

(1) **Emmanuel Scrope, 1st Earl of Sunderland**, 11th Baron Scrope (1 Aug 1584 – 30 May 1630) suc. father 1609; cr. Earl 19 Jun 1627 which became extinct upon his death
  = ...; ♦**Lady Elizabeth Manners** (... – ca.Mar 1654/4) daughter of John Manners, 4th Duke of Rutland & Elizabeth Charlton
  no issue by marriage
  had issue by **Martha Jeanes** (aka Martha Sandford):

  (a) **Lady Annabella Scrope** (1629 – 21 Mar 1703) legitimated in 1663 and granted rank of Earl's daughter
   = ...; **John** Grubham **Howe** (...) son of Sir John Howe, 1st Baronet & Bridget Rich
   Has further generations of issue

  (b) **Mary le Scrope** (bef.1630 – 1 Nov 1680 Moulins, France)
   =1 bef.1649; **Henry, Lord Leppington** (... – 1649) son of Henry Carey, 2nd Earl of Monmouth & Martha Cranfield
   =2 1655; ♦**Charles Powlett, 1st Duke of Bolton** (1630 – 1699)
   issue of 2nd (none surviving of 1st):
   Children are listed with other parent

---

[55] On the death of the Earl of Sunderland, she should have suc. as Baroness Scrope, but did not claim the title.

B) **Lady Anne Percy** (1444 – 1522)
=1 bef.16 Oct 1460; **Sir Thomas Hungerford** (... – 17 Jan
1468/9) executed; son of Robert Hungerford, 3rd Baron
Hungerford & Eleanor de Moleyns
=2 ...; **Sir Laurence Raysford** (...)
issue by 1st (none by 2nd):
1) **Mary Hungerford, (5th) Baroness Botreux**, Hungerford,
   and Moleyns (ca.1468 – bef.10 Jul 1533; suc. great-
   grandmother in Botreux Feb 1477, others restored 1485
   =1 1487/8; ♦**Edward Hastings, 2nd Baron Hastings** (1467 – 1506)
   =2 1 May 1509; **Sir Richard Sacheverell** (... – ca.1530)
   issue of 1st (none by 2nd):
   Children are listed with other parent
C) **Lady Margaret Percy** (ca.1447 – ...)
   = ...; ♦**Sir William Gascoigne** (ca.1450 – 1486)
   Children are listed with other parent
D) **Sir Henry Percy KG, 3rd Earl of Northumberland**, 6th
   Baron Poynings (ca.1449 – 28 Apr 1489 in Yorks.) killed by a
   mob; suc. father 1461 and mother 1484, but the titles were
   attainted until 1472; KG 1474
   = ca.1476; **Lady Maud Herbert** (1448 – bef.27 Jul 1485)
   daughter of William Herbert, 1st Earl of Pembroke & Anne Devereux
   1) **Lady Eleanor Percy** (1476/7 – 13 Feb 1530)
      = 1490; ♦**Edward Stafford, 3rd Duke of Buckingham**
      (1478 – 1521)
      Children are listed with other parent
   2) **Sir Henry Algernon Percy KG, 4th Earl of
      Northumberland**, etc. (14 Jan 1477/8 – 19 May 1527) suc.
      father 1489; KB 1489, KG 1499
      = bef. 1502; ♦**Catherine Spencer** (ca.1480 – Oct 1542)
      daughter of Sir Robert Spencer & Lady Eleanor Beaufort
      a) **Sir Henry Algernon Percy KG, 5th Earl of
         Northumberland**, etc. (ca.1502 – 30 Jun 1537) suc. father
         19 May 1527; KG 1531; titles was declared extinct due to
         attainder of brother and heir.
         = ca. Jan 1524; **Lady Mary Talbot** (... – ca. May 1572)
         daughter of George Talbot, 4th Earl of Shrewsbury and
         Waterford & Anne Hastings
         no issue[56]
      b) **Sir Thomas Percy** (ca.1504 – 2 Jun 1537 Tyburn) executed

---

[56] Under the law of the day, since his brother and heir, Sir Thomas, was under attainter, this creation of the Earldom of Northumberland was deemed expired. upon the 5th Earl's death.

= ca.1526; ♦**Eleanor Harbottle** (ca.1504 Beamish, Durham − Apr 1567 Kingston-upon-Thames, Surrey) daughter of Sir Guiscard Hatbottle & Jane Willoughby; =2ⁿᵈ Sir Richard Holland

(I) **Blessed Thomas Percy, 1ˢᵗ Earl of Northumberland**
  Baron Percy (1528 − 22 Aug 1572) executed; cr. Earl, etc.
  1 May 1557; beatified by Pope Leo XIII 1895
  = 12 Jun 1558; ♦**Lady Anne Somerset** (... − 8 Sep 1591)
  daughter of Henry Somerset, 2ⁿᵈ Earl of Worcester &
  Elizabeth Browne
  (A) **Lady Elizabeth Percy** (ca.1560 − ...)
    = ...; **Richard Woodroffe** (...) son of Francis Woodroffe
    no surviving issue
  (B) **Lady Jane Percy** (ca.1562 − ...)
    = ...; ♦**Lord Henry Seymour** (ca.1540 Wolf Hall,
    Wilts. − 1588) son of Edward Seymour, 1ˢᵗ Duke of
    Somerset & Anne Stanhope
    no issue
  (C) **Lady Lucy Percy** (ca. 1565 − ...)
    = ...; **Sir Edward Stanley KB** (...)
    (1) **Frances Stanley** (...)
      = ...; ♦**Sir John Fortescue, 1ˢᵗ Baronet** (1592 − 1656)
      Children are listed with other parent
    (2) **Venetia Stanley** (1600 − 30 Apr 1633)
      = 1625; **Sir Kenelm Digby** (1603 − 11 Jun 1665) son of
      Sir Everard Digby
      (a) **John Digby** (...)
        = ...; ♦**Lady Catherine Howard** (...) daughter of
        Henry Howard, 22ⁿᵈ Earl of Arundel & Lady
        Elizabeth Stuart
        Has further generations of issue
  (E) **Sister Mary Percy**[57] (ca.1568 − 1642 Brussels)
(II) **Mary Percy** (1532 − 1598)
  = ...; **Sir Francis Slingsby** (... − 1600)
  (A) **Sir Henry Slingsby** (1560 − 17 Dec 1634)
    = ...; **Frances Vavasour** (... − ca.1610) daughter of
    William Vavasour & Elizabeth Beckwith
    (1) **Frances Slingsby** (2 Jul 1584 Knaresborough,
    Yorks. − ...)
      = ...; **Brian Stapylton** (1582 − 1658) son of Sir Robert

---

[57] Founder of Benedictine Convent at Brussels, the progenitor of most Benedictine Convents in England.

Stapylton & Olive Sharington
- (a) **Sir Henry Stapylton, 1st Baronet** (ca.1617 – 26
  Mar 1679) cr. Baronet 1667
  = 18 Oct 1650; **Lady Elizabeth Darcy** (... – 1729)
  daughter of Conyers Darcy, 1st Earl of Holderness &
  Grace Rokeby
  Has further generations of issue
- (b) Olivia **Frances Stapylton** (...)
  =1 ...; **Sir William Vavasour, Baronet** (... – 1658/9)
  cr. Baronet 17 Jul 1643 which became extinct upon
  his death
  =2 ...; **John Hutton** (...)
  Has further generations of issue
- (c) **Myles Stapylgton** (...)
  = ...; **... Hynde** (...)
  Has further generations of issue
- (d) **Ursula Stapylton** (...)
  = ...; **Thomas Pepys** (...)
  issue ?
- (2) **Eleanor Slingsby** (ca.1600 Scriven, Yorks. – 25 May
  1657 Yorks.)
  = ...; **Sir Arthur Ingram** (1598 Notts. – Jul 1655
  Notts.) son of Sir Arthur Ingram & Susan Brown; =2nd
  Hon. Katherine Fairfax
  - (a) **Henry Ingram, 1st Viscount Irvine**, Lord Ingram
    (bap.8 Apr 1641 Whitkirk, Yorks. – 13 Aug 1666) cr.
    Viscount, etc. 23 May 1661
    = 7 Jun1661; **Lady Essex Montagu** (1643 – 1677)
    daughter of Edward Montague, 2nd Earl of Manchester
    & Essex Cheeke
    Has further generations of issue
  - (b) **Elizabeth Ingram** (1625 – 1661)
    =1 ...; **William Cathers** (...)
    =2 1641; ♦**Robert Rich, 5th Earl of Warwick** (... – 1675)
    Has further generations of issue
  - (c) **Thomas Ingram** (1630 – 1660)
    = ...; **Mary Paylor** (1632 – 1656) daughter of
    Watkinson Paylor & Margaret Fairfax
    no issue
  - (d) **Anne Ingram** (1638 – 1695)
    = ...; **Henry Stapleton** (ca.1600 – ...)
    Has further generations of issue
  - (e) **Arthur Ingram** (ca.1643 Barrowby, Lincs. – 13 Sep
    1713 Whitkirk, Yorks.)
    = ...; **Jane Mallory** (1638 Studley Roger, Yorks. –
    1693 Whitkirk) daughter of Sir John Mallory & Mary Mosley

Issue extinct 1830

(f) **Katherine Ingram** (1645 Yorks. – 4 Apr 1715) unm.

(3) **Maria Slingsby** (1582 – 1662)

= 1637; **Sir Walter Bethell** (... – 1622)

(a) **Walter Bethell** (... – 1 Nov 1686)

= ...; **Mary Poyntz** (24 Sep 1604 –...) daughter of Sor John Poyntz & Grissell Roberts; =1st John Walter
no issue

(b) **Mary Bethell** (...)

= ...; **Thomas Hesketh** (... – Mar 1730)
Has further generations of issue

(c) **Sir Hugh Bethell** (1605 – ...)

= 1625; **Frances Frankland** (ca.1607 Fewston, Yorks. – 23 Aug 1673) daughter of William Frankland & Lucy Boteler
Has further generations of issue

(d) **Frances Bethell** (... – 3 Jan 1683/4)

= 1625; **Sir George Marwood, 1st Baronet** (28 Apr 1601 – 19 Feb 1679/80) cr. Baronet 31 Dec 1660
Has further generations of issue

(e) **Henry Bethell** (ca.1606 – 1668) unm.

(f) **Rev. William Bethell** (1616 – 1685)

= ...; **Bridget Bourchier** (...) daughter of Sir John Bourchier & Anne Rolfe
Has further generations of issue

(g) **Slingsby Bethell** (1617 – Feb 1697)

= ...; **Mary Burell** (... – bef.1681)
no issue

(h) **Matilda Bethell** (...)

= ...; **Rev. Robert Goodwin** (...)
issue ?

(4) **Alice Slingsby** (...)

= ...; **Thomas Waterton** (1585 – 1641)

(a) **Robert Waterton** (...)

= ...; **Anne Markham** (...) daughter of Charles Markham
isue ?

(b) **Thomas Waterton** (...)

= ...; **Alice Wetherby** (...) =1st Edward Clarke
Has further generations of issue

(c) **Priscilla Waterton** (... – Sep 1638)

= ...; **Thomas Beckwith** (...)
issue ?

(d) **Elizabeth Waterton** (...)

= ...; **Francis Metham** (... – 22 May 1660)
Has further generations of issue

(e) **Mary Waterton** (...)

=1 ...; **William Ramsden** (... – Sep 1639)
=2 ...; **Sir Thomas Smith** (...)
Has further generations of issue
(f) **Anne Waterton** (...)
= ...; **Francis Middleton** (...)
(5) **Sir Henry Slingsby, 1st Baronet** (14 Jan 1601/2 – 8 Jun 1658 Tower of London) executed; cr. Baronet 2 Mar 1638
= 7 Jul 1631 London; ♦**Barbara Belasyse** (...) daughter of Thomas Belasyse, 1st Viscount Fauconberg & Barbara Cholmeley
(a) **Barbara Slingsby** (...)
= ...; ♦**Sir John Talbot** (1630 – 1714)
Children are listed with other parent
(b) **Sir Thomas Slingsby, 2nd Baronet** (15 Jun 1636 – 1 Mar 1687/8) suc. father 1685
= 1658; **Dorothy Cradock** (... – 1673) daughter of George Cradock
Has further generations of issue
(III) **Henry Percy, 2nd Earl of Northumberland**, etc. (aft.1532 – 20/21 Jun 1585 Petworth, W.Sussex) suicide, possibly murder; suc. brother 22 Aug 1572
= bef. 25 Jan 1561/2; ♦**Katherine Neville** (... – 28 Oct 1596) daughter of John Neville, 4th Baron Latimer & Lady Lucy Somerset; =2nd Francis Fitton
(A) **Sir Henry Percy, 3rd Earl of Northumberland KG** (Apr 1564 – 5 Nov 1632) suc. father 21 Jun 1585; KG 1593
= 1594; **Lady Dorothy Devereux** (1561 – 3 Aug 1619) daughter of Walter Devereux, 1st Earl of Essex & Lettice Knollys ; =1st Sir Thomas Perrott
(1) **Lady Dorothy Percy** (bap.20 Aug 1598 – 20 Aug 1650)
= 1615; ♦**Robert Sydney, 2nd Earl of Leicester** (1595 – 1677)
Children are listed with other parent
(2) **Lady Lucy Percy** (ca.1600 – 5 Nov 1660)
= 6 Nov 1617; **James Hay 1st Earl of Carlisle**, etc. (ca.1580 Scotland – 25 Apr 1636 London) son of Sir James Hay & Margaret Murray; =1st Lady Honora Denny; cr. Earl 1622
no issue
(3) **Sir Algernon Percy KG, 4th Earl of Northumberland**, etc. (29 Sep 1602 – 13 Oct 1668) suc. father 5 Nov 1632; KB 1616, KG 1635
=1 bef.1630; ♦**Lady Anne Cecil** (bap.23 Feb 1612 – 6 Dec 1637) daughter of William Cecil, 2nd Earl of Salisbury & Lady Catherine Howard

=2 1 Oct 1642; **Lady Elizabeth Howard** (... – 11 Mar 1704/5) daughter of Theophilius Howard, 2ⁿᵈ Earl of Suffolk & Lady Elizabeth Home
issue of 1ˢᵗ:

  (a) **Lady Anne Percy** (19 Dec 1633 – 29 Nov 1654)
= 21 Jun 1652; **Philip Stanhope, 2ⁿᵈ Earl of Chesterfield**, etc. (ca.1634 – 28 Jan 1713/4) son of Henry, Lord Stanhope & Catherine Wotten, Countess of Chesterfield; =2ⁿᵈ Lady Elizabeth Butler; =3ʳᵈ Lady Elizabeth Dormer
no surviving issue

  (b) **Lady Elizabeth Percy** (1 Dec 1636 – 6 Feb 1718)
= 1653; ♦**Arthur Capell, 1ˢᵗ Earl of Essex** (1632–1683)
Children are listed with other parent
issue of 2ⁿᵈ:

  (c) **Joceline Percy, 5ᵗʰ Earl of Northumberland** (4 Jul 1644 – 31 May 1670 Turin) suc. father 13 Oct 1668; title of the 1557 creation came extinct upon his death
= 23 Dec 1662; **Lady Elizabeth Wriothesley** (1646 – 19 Sep 1690) daughter of Thomas Wriothesley, 4ᵗʰ Earl of Southampton & Lady Elizabeth Leigh; =2ⁿᵈ Ralph Montagu, 1ˢᵗ Duke of Montagu
Has further generations of issue

 (4) **Henry Percy, Baron Percy of Alnwick** (ca.1604 – 26 Mar 1659 Paris) cr. Baron 28 Jun 1643; unm.
(B) **Sir Richard Percy** (1566 – 1648)
(C) **Lady Lucy Percy** (ca.1570 Petworth, Sussex – ca.1613)
=1 ...; **Sir John Wotton** (...)
=2 ...; **Sir Hugh Owen** (1550 – 8 Feb 1614 Pembrokeshire, Wales) son of Owen ap Hugh & Elizabeth Griffith; =1ˢᵗ Elizabeth Werriott
issue of 2ⁿᵈ (none by 1ˢᵗ):

 (1) **Sir Richard Owen** (...)
  = ...

  (a) **Ann Owen** (...)
= ...; **Humphrey Magan** (ca.1590 Emoe, co. Westmeath – ...)
Has further generations of issue

 (2) **Percy Owen** (...)
(D) **William Percy** (1575 – 1648) unm.
(E) **Sir Charles Percy** (... – 9 Jul 1628)
= ...; **Dorothy Cocks** (...) daughter of Thomas Cocks; she =1ˢᵗ Edmund Hutchens
no issue
(F) **Sir Alan Percy KB** (1577 – 1611) KB 1604

= ...; **Mary ...** (...)
no issue
(G) **Sir Jocelyn Percy** (... – 1631)
(H) **Hon. George Percy**[58] (4 Sep 1580 Petworth – Mar
1632) Govenor of Virginia Sep 1609–May1610 and Mar
1611–Apr 1612
= ...; **Anne Floyd** (...)
(1) **Ann Percy** (...)
= ...; ◆**Gov. John West** (1590 – ca.1659)
Children are listed with other parent
(I) **Lady Eleanor Percy** (1583 – 24 Dec 1650)
= bef.1600; **William Herbert, 1ˢᵗ Baron Powis KB**
(ca.1574 – 7 Mar 1655/6) son of Sir Edward Herbert &
Mary Stanley; KB 1603; cr. Baron 2 Apr 1629
(1) **Percy Herbert, 2ⁿᵈ Baron Powis**, 1ˢᵗ Baronet (1598 –
19 Jan 1666/7) suc. father 1656; cr. Baronet 16 Nov
1622
= 19 Nov 1622; **Elizabeth Craven** (bap.7 Jan 1599/
1600 – 8 Oct 1662) daughter of Sir William Craven &
Elizabeth Whitmore
(a) **Mary Herbert** (...)
= Jan 1639; **George, Lord Talbot** (ca.1620 – 7 Mar
1642) son of John Talbot, 10ᵗʰ Earl of Shrewsbury &
Mary Fortescue
no issue
(b) **William Herbert, 1ˢᵗ Marquess of Powis**, Earl of
Powis, Viscount Montgomery, 3ʳᵈ Baron Powis, etc.
(ca.1626 – 2 Jun 1696) suc. father 1667; cr. Earl 4 Apr
1674; cr. Marquess and Viscount 24 Mar 1686/7; he
was further cr. Duke of Powis and Viscount
Montgomery in the Jacobite Peerage 12 Jan 1688/9
= 2 Aug 1654; ◆**Lady Elizabeth Somerset** (ca.
1634 – 16 Mar 1690/1) daughter of Edward Somerset,
2ⁿᵈ Marquess of Worcester & Elizabeth Dormer
Has further generations of issue
(IV) **Lady Catherine Percy** (...)
= ...; **Ralph Rethers** (...)
issue ?
e) **Sir Ingelram Percy** (ca.1506 – 1538) unm.
issue by ...:
(I) **Isabelle Percy** (...)

---

[58] One of first settlers of Virginia in 1600, but returned to Europe 1612.

= 1543; **Henry Tempest** (1520 – 1605)
Children are listed with other parent
f) **Lady Margaret Percy** (ca.1508 – 1540)
= aft.1515; ◆**Henry Clifford, 1ˢᵗ Earl of Cumberland**
(1493 – 1542)
Children are listed with other parent
g) **Lady Maud Percy** (...)
= ...; ◆**William Conyers, 1ˢᵗ Baron Conyers** (1468 – 1524)
Children are listed with other parent
3) **Sir William Percy** (... – 15 Sep 1540)
4) **Alan Percy** (1479 – May 1560) a priest
5) **Josceline Percy** (1480 – 8 Sep 1532)
= ...; **Margaret Frost** (... – 15 Nov 1530) daughter of Walter
Frost
a) **Edward Percy** (ca.1524 – 1590)
= ...; **Elizabeth Waterton** (... – Dec 1607) daughter of Sir
Thomas Waterton & Joanne Tempest
(I) **Alan Percy** (1560 – 1632)
= 1589; **Mary Moore** (...) daughter of Ralph Moore
(A) **Joscelyn Percy** *de jure 11ᵗʰ Earl of Northumberland*[59]
(... – 1653)
= ...; **Elizabeth Fitzwilliam** (...) daughter of William
Fitzwilliam
(1) **Alan Percy** *de jure 12ᵗʰ Earl of Northumberland* (21
May 1670 – 1688) suc. father 1653; unm.
(2) **John Percy** (...)
(3) **Charles Percy** (...)[60]
(4) **Eleanor Percy** (...)
= ...; **William Ferrand** (...)
issue ?
(B) **Edward Percy** (1594 – 27 Aug 1630)
(C) **Frances Percy** (...)
= ...; **Ralph Elleker** (...)
has issue
(II) **Thomas Percy** (1560 – 10 Nov 1605 Holbeach, Lincs.)

---

[59] Joscelyn would have succeeded to the 1414 creation of the title had it not been declared extinct due to attainder. The 1557 creation of the title was unusual in that the normal practice was to restore the previous title if the person getting it was the heir, as was the case in 1557.

[60] Since dates of death are not known for John nor Charles, it can only be assumed they would have succeeded in turn to the Northumberland claim. Nothing is known of John, suggesting he +young, but Charles is known to have lived to adulthood, but whether he married and has issue is still unknown. If they both died childless, the claim would pass to the descendants of Francis Percy (+1660).

died of wounds received when arrested[61]
= ...; **... Wright** (...)
(A) **Robert Percy** (...)
  = 22 Oct 1615; **Emma Mead** (...)
  (1) **Francis Percy** (ca.1616 – 1660)
    = ...
    (a) **Francis Percy** (ca.1650 – 1717)
      = ...
      Has further generations of issue[62]
(B) a daughter (...)
  = ...; **Robert Catesby** (...)
  issue ?
(III) **Ellen Percy** (...)
  = ...; **Ralph Moore** (...)
  has issue
(IV) **... Percy** (a daughter) (...)
  = ...; **John Birney** (...)
  issue?
6) **Hon. Arundel Percy** (1483 – 1544)
7) **Lady Anne Percy** (bef. 27 Jul 1485 – 1552)
  = 1501; ♦**William, 18ᵗʰ Earl of Arundel** (ca.1476 – 1544)
  Children are listed with other parent
II) **Sir Thomas Percy, 1ˢᵗ Baron of Egremont** (29 Nov 1422 Leconfield – 10 Jul 1460 Northampton) killed in battle; cr. Baron 20 Nov 1449
= ...
A) **John Percy, 2ⁿᵈ Baron of Egremont** (ca.1459 – bef.21 Mar 1497) suc. father 10 Jul 1460
III) **Lady Katherine Percy** (28 May 1423 Leconfield, Yorks. – aft.1475)
  = 1459; ♦**Edmund Grey, 1ˢᵗ Earl of Kent** (1416 – 1490)
  Children are listed with other parent
IV) **Sir Ralph Percy**[63] (11 Aug 1425 Leconfield – 25 Apr 1464 Hegeley Moor, Northumberland) killed in battle
=1 ...; **Eleanor de Acton** (1429 – aft.22 Aug 1498) daughter of Laurence de Acton & Matilda ...
=2 ...; **Jane Teye** (1427 – 1445) daughter of John Teye
issue of 1ˢᵗ:

---

[61] Thomas Percy was one of the principal conspirators in the Gunpowder Plot of 1605.
[62] Rev. Percy's male line endes with him. His descendants are through his three daughters.
[63] The Peerages traditionally list him as unmarried, however Ruvigny showed his married to Acton. Several online sites build upon their descendants.

A) **Catherine Percy** (bef.1445 Bursted, Essex – ...)
= ...; **Sir Simon le Graunt** (ca.1445 – ...) son of Simon le Gaunt
and Chenow ...
1) **William Graunt** (ca.1465 – ...)
  = ...;
  a) **Elizabeth Graunt** (ca.1485 – 1528)
    = ...; **William Servington** (ca.1475 – 1522) son of Sir
    Walter Servington & Mary Tropenell
    (I) **Nicholas Servington** (ca.1522 Langford, Wilts. – 16 Dec
    1553)
      = ...; **Jane Hungerford** (1526 Down Ampney, Glos. –
      1561 Longford) daughter of Sir Anthony Hungerford &
      Jane Darrell; =2nd Thomas South
      (A) **Nicholas Servington** (ca.1542 Langford – ...)
        = ...
        (1) **Margaret Servington** (ca.1580 Ewell, Surrey – 1660
        Egham)
          = ...; **John Thomas Foster** (8 Oct 1577 Hunsden,
          Herts. – 18 May 1612 Ewell) son of Thomas Foster &
          Margaret Browning
          (a) **Christopher Foster** (17 Aug 1603 Ewell – 24 Dec
          1687 Southampton, NY) emigrated ca.1635
            = ...; **Frances Stevens** (1 Jul 1610 Ewell – 1644
            Southampton, NY) daughter of Jerome Stevens &
            Alice ...
            Has further generations of issue
          (b) **Thomas Foster** (...)
          (c) **Margaret Foster** (...)
            = ...; **Thomas Harding** (...)
            issue ?
      (B) **John Servington** (1553 – ...)
2) **Edward Graunt** (1475 – ...)
  = ...
  a) **Edward Graunt** (1500 Northbrook, Warks. – 1589)
    = ...; **Anna Somerville** (1510 Arden, Warks. – ca.1534
    Bucks.) daughter of Robert Somerville & Mary Greville
    (I) **Mary Graunt** (ca.1535 Northbrook – 1630 ...)
      = ...; **Michael Colles** (ca.1530 Bradwell, Bucks. – 1606)
      son of William Colles & Margaret ...
      (A) **Elizabeth Colles** (ca.1565 London – Oct 1603
      Fifeshire, Scotland)

= ...; **Gratian Patton** (ca.1565 London – Oct 1603 Fife)[64]
(1) **Rev. William Patton** (ca.1595 Ferrochie, Fifes. – 31
    Jan 1642 Clondevadock, co Donegal, Ireland)
    = ...; **Margaret Johnstone** (1593 Suffolk – 1659 co
    Donegal) daughter of Henry Johnstone & Sarah Stewart
    (a) **Henry Patton** (31 Jan 1627 Ramoigh Parish, co.
        Donegal – ca.1689 Clondevadock)
        = ...; **Jean Guthree** (1620 Edinburgh – 1641 co.
        Donegal) daughter of Alexander Guthree of Guthrie &
        ... Christian
        Has further generations of issue
    (b) **John Patton** (...)
    (c) **William Patton** (...)
        = ...; **Margaret Skoech** (...)
        Has further generations of issue
issue of 2ⁿᵈ:
B) **Peter Percy** (1447 Leconfield – 1517 Norfolk)
   =1 ...; **Ann James** (...)
   =2 ...; **Catherine James** (1480 York – ...)
   issue of 1ˢᵗ:
   1) **Peter Percy** (...)
   issue of 2ⁿᵈ:
   2) **Richard Percy**[65] (1500 Norwich, Norfolk – 1553 Pearse
      Hall, Yorks.)
      = ...; **Anna James** (1525 Yorks. – 1552)
      a) **Richard Percy**[66] (ca.1553 Pearse Hall – 21 Mar 1632
         Sheffield, Yorks.)
      b) **Joanne Percy** (1539 – 1597)
C) **Sir Ralph Percy** (1451 Leconfield, Yorks. – 1510 Yorks.)
D) **Sir George Percy** (1453 Leconfield – 1500)
   = ..; **Eleanor Hylton** (1450 Hilton, Durham – 1 Jul 1513 Ogle
   Castle, Northumb.) daughter ofWilliam Hylton, *de jure* 6ᵗʰ Baron
   Hylton & Mary Stapleton; =1ˢᵗ Owen Ogle, 2ⁿᵈ Baron Ogle, =3ʳᵈ

---

[64] Geni.com gives the same dates/places for both husband and wife. One is likely incorrect, but I have no way of knowing which.
[65] Richard was the founder of Pearce Hall in Yorks. Pearce and Pierce family descendants have tried to make a connection, but there are problems with the information they provide, see the next footnote.
[66] On-line genealogies, quoting "Pierce Genealogy" by Col. Frederick Pierce (1880) list several children for Richard. However some of them are biologically impossible to be his children, and others do not seem to have any connection to Pearce Hall or even Yorkshire. They are being left out of this work for lack of verification of their family connection. A few of these siblings that are discounted emigrated to New England and became founders of several lines of descent in the US.

Raynfforth
no issue
E) **John Percy** (ca.1455 Newton by the Sea, Northumb. – ...)
= ...; **Margaret Harbottle** (1462 Dalton Travers, Yorks. – ...)
daughter of Bertram Harbottle & Joan Lumley
issue ?
F) **Sir Henry Percy** (1456 Yorks. – 1486 Thirsk, Yorks.)
= ...; **Catherine ...** (1454 Bambrough, Northumb. – ...)
1) **Margaret Percy** (1475 Acton, Northumb. – 25 Nov 1540
Skipton, Yorks.)
=1 ...; **Sir Henry Widdrington** (1470 Morpeth, Northumb. –
26 Aug 1518 Northumb.) son of Sir Ralph Widdrington &
Felice Claxton
=2 ...; **Sir William Ellerker** (1480 Brantingham, Yorks. –
1526 Brantingham, Yorks.) son of Sir Ralph Ellerker & Anne
Gower; =1st Agnes ...
issue of 1st:
a) **Dorothy Widdrington** (ca.1495 Widdrinton, Northumb. –
1 Mar 1527 Bothel, Northumb.)
= ...; **Robert Ogle, 5th Baron Ogle** (... – 6 Mar 1644/5) son
of Robert Ogle, 4th Baron Ogle & Anne Lumley; =2nd ♦Jane
Radcliffe; suc. father bef.1532
(I) **Robert Ogle, 6th Baron Ogle** (30 May 1529 Bothal – 1
Aug 1562 Allerton, Yorks.) suc. father 1645
= ...; **Jane Mauleverer** (1530 Allerton – 15 Jan 1595)
no issue
(II) **Margery Ogle** (ca.1532 – ...)
c) **Constance Widdrington** (ca.1497 Widdrington – ...)
= ...: **Valentine Fenwick** (bap.9 Jun 1475 Berwick-upon-
Tweed, Northumb. – ...) son of John Fenwick & Isabel ..;
he =2nd Elizabeth Muschamp
issue?
d) Margaret **Jane Widdrington** (ca. 1501 Widdrington – ...)
e) **Margery Widdrington** (1508 Seghill, Northumb. –
bef.1546)
= 1529; **John Mitford** (1506 Seghill – 1 Oct 1556 Seghill)
son of Robert Mitford & Anne Musgrave; =2nd Magdalen
Fenwick
(I) **John Mitford** (1530 – 6 Nov 1571)
= Dec 1550; **Barbara Lawson** (...) daughter of Thomas
Lawson
(A) **Robert Mitford** (1551 – 1611)
= 19 Sep 1594 Newcastle-upon-Tyne; **Alice Anderson**
(... – Jan 1616) daughter of Bertram Anderson
(1) **John Mitford** (...)
(2) **Michael Mitford** (1583 – 22 Nov 1637)

=1 1612; **Elizabeth Whittingham** (... – Nov 1613)
daugther of Sir Timothy Whittingham
=2 6 Sep 1615; **Jane de Laval** (...) daughter of Sir
Robert de Laval & Barbara Selby
issue of 1st:
(a) **Robert Mitford** (1613 – 1640)
  = 1637; **Mary de Laval** (... – Feb 1649) daughter of
  Robert de Laval
  no surviving issue
issue of 2nd:
(b) **Ralph Mitford** (1616 – Feb 1661)
  = ca.1644; **Barbara Heron** (...) daughter of Richard
  Heron & Ann Barnes
  Has further generations of issue
(c) **Dorothy Mitford** (1616 – ...)
  = 1 Jan 1652/3; **John** Humphrey **Proctor** (...)
  issue ?
(d) **Jane Mitford** (1620 – ...)
  =1 9 Feb 1643; **George Milbourne** (...)
  =2 1 Jan 1652/3; **Ralph Fenwick** (...)
  issue ?
(e) **Alison Mitford** (1622 – Jul 1662) unm.
(f) **Thomas Mitford** (1625 – 1672)
  = 10 Mar 1653/4; **Mary Anderson** (...)
  issue ?
(3) **Bertram Mitford** (... – Jul 1623)
(4) **Robert Mitford** (... – 29 Nov 1661)
(5) **Henry Mitford** (... – aft.5 Jul 1623)
(6) **Oswald Mitford** (... – aft.26 Nov 1634)
(7) **Isabel Mitford** (...)
  = 1601; **John Hull** (...)
  issue ?
(8) **Jane Mitford** (...)
  = 5 Feb 1626 Newcastle-upon-Tyne; **Oliver
Killingworth** (...)
  issue ?
(9) **Anne Mitford** (...) unm. in 1623
(10) **Barbara Mitford** (...) unm. un 1623
(B) **Henry Mitford** (... – 1592) unm.
(C) **Oswald Mitford** (... – aft.Mar 1592/3)
(D) **Gabriel Mitford** (... – aft. Mar 1592/3)
(E) **Philip Mitford** (... – aft.Mar 1592/3)
(F) **George Mitford** (... – aft.Mar 1592/3)
(G) **Magdalen Mitford** (... – ca.1554)
  = ...; **Oliver Ogle** (...)
  issue ?

(H) **Anne Mitford** (... – adt.Mar 1592/3)
(I) **Margery Mitford** (...)
  = 6 Feb 1595; **John Strangways** (...)
  issue ?
 (II) **Oswald Mitford** (1532 – 1589)
  = 1561; **Jane de Laval** (... – 21 Sep 1566) daughter of Sir
  John de Laval & Anne Ogle
  (A) **John Mitford** (... – 1598)
  (B) **Oswin Mitford** (... – aft. Mar 1588/9)
  (C) **Thomas Mitford** (... – aft.Mar 1588/9)
  (D) **Dorothy Mitford** (...)
  (E) **Margaret Mitford** (...)
    = ...; **William Shafto** (...)
    issue ?
  (F) **Ursula Mitford** (...)
  (G) **Grace Mitford** (...)
  (H) **William Mitford** (ca.1577 Stanfordham, Northumb. – ...)
    = 21 Jul 1601 Ryton, Durham; **Anna Watson** (...)
    (1) **William Mitford** (1602 – 1658) twin
      = 30 Sep 1639 Whickham, Durham; **Margaret
      Dagleish** (1617 – ...)
      (a) **John Mitford** (1655 – ...)
        = 15 Nov 1680; **Anne Bainbridge** (1642 – ...)
        Has further generations of issue
    (2) **Robert Mitford** (1602 – ...) twin
      = 14 Dec 1647 Morpeth, Northumb.; **Margaret Watt** (...)
      issue ?
issue of 2nd:
f) **Anne Ellerker** (1524 Widdrington – ...)
 = ...; **John Shafto** (1524 Bavington, Northumb. – 1560)
 son of Cuthbert Shafto & Isabel Bertram
 (I) **John Shafto** (1546 Bavington – ...)
 (II) **Edward Shafto** (1548 – 1593)
  = ...; **Margery Heron** (1550 Washington, Tyne nd Wear –
  ...) daughter of Sir George Heron & Margaret Forster
  (A) **William Shafto** (1576 Bavington – 1657 Bavington)
    = ...; **Frances ...** (1580 Carlisle, Cumbria – ...)
    (1) **Dalston Shafto** (1607 Bavington – ...)
    (2) **Jane Shafto** (1609 Bavington – ...)
    (3) **George Shafto** (1611 Bavington – 1679)
    (4) **Edward Shafto** (1613 Baviongton – 1645)
      = ...; **Margaret ...** (1618 High Warden, Northumb. – ...)
      (a) **John Shafto** (1641 Bavington – 1709 Throckringen,
        Northumb.)
        = ...; **Frances Fenwick** (1640 – 1704) daughter of
        Edward Fenwick & Frances Neville

Has further generations of issue
    (5) **Margery Shafto** (1615 Bavington – ...)
    (6) **John Shafto** (1617 Bavington – 1696)
    (7) **Grace Shafto** (1619 Bavington – ...)
    (8) **Charles Shafto** (1622 Bavington – 1697)
    (B) **Mary Shafto** (1602 Bavington – ...)
    (C) **Catherine Shafto** (1604 Bavington – ...)
    (D) **Frances Shafto** (1605 Bavington – ...)
   (III) **William Shafto** (1558 – 6 Oct 1599)
    = ...; **Ann Swinburne** (1546 Edlingham, Northumb. – ...)
    daughter of Roger Swinburne & Isabel Errington
   (IV) **Jane Shafto** (1550 Bavington – ...)
   (V) **Mary Shafto** (1552 Bavington – ...)
   (VI) **Dorothy Shafto** (1554 Bavington – ...)
   (VII) **Luke Shafto** (1556 – ...)
   (VIII) **Grace Shafto** (1561 Bavington – ...)
  g) **Sir Robert Ellerker** (...)
2) **John Percy** (ca.1477 – ca.1540)
G) **Margaret Percy** (ca.1462 – ca.1506
= ...; **Sir Ralph Harbottle** (1465 Horton, Northumb. – 1504)
son of Bertram Harbottle & Joan Lumley
1) **Guiscard Harbottle** (6 Jan 1485 Horton – 9 Sep 1513
  Flodden Field, Northumb.) killed in action
  = ...; **Jane Willoughby** (1485 Wollaton, Notts. – 26 Nov 1567
  Essex) daughter of Sir Henry Willoughby & Margaret Markham
  a) **Eleanor Harbottle** (ca.1504 Beamish, Durham – Apr 1567
    Kingston-upon-Thames, Surrey)
    =1 ...; ♦**Sir Thomas Percy** (1504 – 1537)
    =2 ...; **Richard Holland** (1493 – 1548)
    issue of 1st (none by 2nd):
    Children are listed with other parent
  b) **George Harbottle** (ca.1504 – 20 Jan 1527)
    = ...; **Margaret Ogle** (ca.1506 Horton – 25 Jul 1548) daughter of
    Ralph Ogle, 3rd Baron Ogle & Margaret Scargill; =2nd Thomas
    Middleton; =3rd John Dacre
    no issue
  c) **Mary Harbottle** (1507 Dalton Michael, Yorks. – 12 Dec
    1556 Gawsworth)
    = ...; **Sir Edward Fitton** (1500 Gawsworth, Ches. – 17 Feb
    1553) son of John Fitton & Ellen Brereton
    (I) **Sir Edward Fitton** (1527 Gawsworth – 3 Jul 1579 Dublin)
      = ...; **Anne Wharburton** (... – 9 Jan 1573) daughter of Sir
      Piers Wharburton & Elizabeth Winnington
     (A) **Sir Edward Fitton** (1548 Gawsworth – 1606 London)
      = ...; **Alice Holcroft** (... – 2 Feb 1626) daughter of John Holcroft
      (1) **Sir Edward Fitton** (3 Dec 1572 Gawsworth – 10

May 1619 Gawsworth)
= ...; **Anne Barrett** (1571 Tenby, Pembs. – 26 Mar
1644 Gawsworth) daughter of James Barrett
(a) **Penelope Fitton** (1595 Gawsworth – ...)
  = ...; **Sir Charles Gerard** (...) son of Ratcliffe Gerard
  & Elizabeth Somerset
  Has further generations of issue
(II) **Mary Fitton** (1529 Gawsworth – ...) (twin)
(III) **Margaret Fitton** (1529 Gawsworth – 29 Aug 1612) (twin)
=1 ...; **John Englefield** (ca.1526 Englefoeld, Berks. – 1
Apr 1567 Englefield) son of Sir Thomas Englefield &
Elizabeth Throckmorton
=2 ...; **Francis Warren** (1534 Poynton, Ches. – 1576) son
of Sir Edward Warren & Dorothy Booth
issue of 1st (none by 2nd):
(A) **Sir Francis Englefield, 1st Baronet** (30 Jun 1562
  Wootten Bassett, Wilts. – 6 Oct 1631 Englefield) cr.
  Baronet 25 Nov 1611
  = ...; **Jane Browne** (1575 Keinton, Wilts. – 17 Sep 1650
  Wales) daughter of Sir Anthony Browne & Mary Gerard
  (1) **Mary** Dorothy **Englefield** (ca.1595 Monmouthshire –
    ca.1678 Wales)
    = ...; ♦**Sir Edward Morgan, 1st Baronet** (1573 – 1653)
    Children are listed with other parent
  (2) **Sir Francis Englefield, 2nd Baronet** (1596
    Englefield – 1 May 1656 Wootton Bassett) suc. father
    1631
    = ...; **Winifred Brooksby** (1601 Shoby, Leics. – 25 Jun
    1672 Wootten Bassett)
    (a) **Helen Englefield** (1630 Wootten Bassett – 12 Jan 1694)
      = ...; ♦**Sir Charles Waldegrave, 3rd Baronet** (1626–1684)
      Children are listed with other parent
    (b) **Sir Francis Englefield, 3rd Baronet** (...)
      = ...; ♦**Lady Honora O'Brien** (...) daughter of Henry
      O'Brien, 4th Earl of Thomond & Mary Brereton= 2nd
      Sir Robert Howard
      no issue
    (c) **Mary Englefield** (...)
      = ...; **Sir G... Browne** (...)
      issue ?
    (d) **Catherine Englefield** (...)
      = ...; **W. Turvile** (...)
  (3) **Sir Thomas Englefield, 4th Baronet** (...)
    =1 ...; **Mary Winchcomb** (...) daughter of Sir Henry
    Winchcomb
    =2 ...; **Mary Huntly** (...) daughter of George Huntly

issue of 2nd (none by 1st):

    (a) **Sir Charles Englefield, 5th Baronet** (... – Apr 1728)
      = ...; **Susan Culpeper** (...) illegitimate daughter of
      John, Lord Culpeper & Mrs. Susan Willis
      no survivng issue

    (b) **Philadelphia Englefield** (...)
      = ...; **Henry Fossan** (...)
      no issue

  (4) **Anthony Englefield** (...)
    = ...; **... Ryley** (...)

    (a) **Anthony Englefield** (...)
      = ...; **Alice Stokes** (...) daughter o Thomas Stokes
      Has further generations of issue

  (5) **Henry Englefield** (...)
    =1 ...; **E. Pickford** (...)
    =2 ...; **Elizabeth Blount** (...)
    =3 ...; **Anne Hobard** (...)
    issue of 2nd (none by others):

    (a) **Elizabeth Englefield** (...)
      = ...; **Sir William Kennedy** (...)
      issue ?

    (b) **Mary Englefield** (...)
      = ...; **Thomas Havers** (...)
      issue ?

  (6) **Mary Englefield** (... – 21 Dec 1647)
    = 1640; **Christopher Roper, 4th Baron Teynham** (20 Apr
    1621 – 23 Oct 1673) son of John Roper & Hon. Mary Petre; =2nd
    Philadelphia Knollys; =3rd Hon. Margaret FitzMaurice
    no issue

  (7) **Margaret Englefield** (...)
    =1 ...; **Hatton Berners** (...)
    =2 ...; **Sir William Bradshaw** (...)
    issue ?

 2) **Eleanor Harbottle** (1488 Horton – ...)
 3) **Isabel Harbottle** (ca.1490 Horton – ...)
   = ...; **John Swinhoe** (1486 Horton – ...)
  issue ?

issue of 2nd:

c. **Sir Richard de Camoys** (ca.1406 – aft.9 Aug 1473) Kt 1426
  = 1448; **Isabel de Beauoy** (...)
  no issue

d. **ALICE, LADY HASTINGS** (1407 – 1455)
  see: Chapter 11

CHAPTER 9
CLIFFORD

While the Percys of Northumberland secured the western half of the Scottish border, it fell to the Clifford family of Westmorland to protect the eastern half. Unlike the Percys, though, the Cliffords did not come with the Norman Invasion. They were already here to meet it. Little is known of the family at that time except they were not yet called Clifford, but instead followed the older tradition of using a father's name as their surname. So John FitzAlan, was John, son of Alan. The first Clifford was Walter de Clifford (+1190) who is believed to have taken his surname from his birthplace, Clifford Castle, in present-day Herefordshire. Walter descended from the pre-Conquest Saxon Kings via his mother, Maud of Gloucester.

While the family remained closely associated with the Throne, they become important for our purposes in the early 1420s when the 7th Baron de Clifford married one of the daughters of Sir Harry "Hotspur" Percy and Lady Elizabeth Mortimer.

The Barony de Clifford is reckoned to have been created in 1274, and remains in existence to this day, the present holder being the 28th Baron. The title owes its longevity to the principle that the ancient baronies were created "by writ," which means a person was summoned to sit in Parliament, thus creating them a Baron. Since the creation itself was not spelled out in writing, neither were the rules of its succession, which is called the remainder. Therefore the succession was governed by Common Law, which held that daughters could succeed in the absence of any brothers or brothers' children. There are a lot of ifs and buts to this, but the general principle has kept titles like de Clifford alive for over eight centuries.

During the Wars of the Roses, the Cliffords remained loyal to the Lancastrians, often to the detriment to their lives. After that conflict was settled and Tudors were comfortably on the Throne, the 11th Baron was elevated to the Earldom of Cumberland. The Earldom lasted for five Earls before becoming extinct in 1643. Unlike the Barony, the Earldom was created by Letters Patent from the King. Such a creation spells out the remainder in detail. The standard remainder for these creations was for the male-line descendants of the original grantee of the title and did not allow female succession. Anything that varied from that was called a "special remainder."

Because the Barony could be inherited by a daughter, the title split from the Earldom on the death of the 3rd Earl. His younger brother became the 4th Earl, but it was his daughter who became the 14th Baroness, and that title continued through her descendants.

The female lines of descent are the ones of import to Americans looking for their connections to royalty. Among these descendants of daughters and granddaughters we can find colonial families such as the Fenwicks of Long Island, the Fosters of Boston, and the Fairfaxes of Virginia.

Edward III
|
Lionel of Antwerp, Duke of Clarence
|
Philippa, Countess of Ulster
|
Elizabeth, Lady Percy (later Baroness Camoys)
|
Elizabeth, Baroness de Clifford (later Countess of Westmorland)
|
Thomas Clifford, 8th Baron de Clifford (25 Mar 1414 – 22 May 1455 St.Albans, Herts.) killed in battle[67]; suc. father 13 Mar 1421/2
= Mar 1424; ♦**Joan Dacre** (...) daughter of Thomas Dacre, 6th Baron Dacre & Lady Philippa Neville
A) **Maud Clifford** (1430 – 1485)
=1 ...; **Sir John Harrington** (... – 30 Dec 1460 Wakefield) killed in battle[68]
=2 ...; **Sir Edmund Sutton** (1425 Dudley Castle, West Midlands– ca.1485) son of John Dudley, 1st Baron Dudley & Elizabeth Berkeley
issue of 1st:
1) **Anne Harrington** (ca.1455 – 5 Aug 1481)
= ...; ♦**Sir Edward Stanley, 1st Baron Monteagle**, Baronet **KG**
cr. Baronet 1482, Baron 21 May 1514; KG 1514; =2nd Elizabeth Vaughan
no issue
issue of 2nd:
2) **Thomas Sutton** (...)
B) **Joan Clifford** (1432 – 1504)
= ...; **Richard Musgrave** (1431 – 10 Aug 1491) son of Sir Thomas Musgrave & Joan Stapleton
1) **Sir Edward Musgrave** (ca.1461 – 23 May 1542) Kt. 1513
=1 ca.10 Jan 1483/4; **Alice Radcliffe** (...) daughter of Thomas Radcliffe
=2 ca.27 Oct 1496; **Joan Ward** (...) daughter of Sir Christopher Ward
issue of 1st:
a) **Mary Musgrave** (aft.1483 Edenhall, Cumberland – ...)
= ...; **John Martindale** (..)
issue ?
b) **Margaret Musgrave** (1487 Edenhall – 1540 London)
= ...; **John Heron** (1471 Chipchase Castle, Northumb. – ...)
(I) **Sir John Heron** (aft.1499 Chipchase Castle – 1562 London)
= ...; **Joan Ridley** (1500 – 1562) daughter of Sir Nicholas Ridley

---

[67] The Cliffords fought for the side of the Lancasters.
[68] Fought for the Yorks.

327

& Mary Musgrave
(A) **Sir George Heron** (bef.1515 Chipchase Castle – 7 Jul
1575 Redesdale, Northumb.)
=1 ...; **Marion Swinburne** (...) daughter of George Swinburne &
Marian Fenwick
=2 ca.1522; **Margaret Forster** (ca.1505 Etherstone,
Northumb. – 7 Feb 1588 Berwick on Tweed, Northumb.)
daughter of Sir Thomas Forster & Dorothy Ogle
issue of 1st:
(1) **John Heron** (... – Jun 1591)
= ...; **Margery Grey** (ca.1535 Horton, Northumb. –
ca.1613 Horton) daughter of Sir Thomas Grey & Dorothy Ogle
  (a) **Cuthbert Heron** (...)
    = ...; **Ann Carnaby** (...)
    Has further generations of issue
  (b) **Barbara Heron** (...)
    = ...; ♦**Sir Hugh Ridley** (1558 – ...)
    Children are listed with other parent
(2) **Isabel Heron** (...)
  = ...; **John Fenwick** (... – 1581)
  issue ?
issue of 2nd:
(3) **Margery Heron** (1550 – ...)
  = ...; **Edward Shafto** (1548 – 1593) son of John Shafto &
  Anne Elleker
  (a) **William Shafto** (1576 Bavington, Northumb. – 1657
    Bavington)
    = ...; **Frances ...** (1580 Carlisle, Cumbria – ...)
    Has further generations of issue
  (b) **Mary Shafto** (1602 Bavington – ...)
  (c) **Catherine Shafto** (1604 Bavington – ...)
  (d) **Frances Shafto** (1605 Bavington – ...)
(B) **Ursula Heron** (1530 Chipchase Castle – 1625 Doncaster, Yorks.)
  = ...; **Sir Roger Fenwick** (1528 – ...) son of Sir John
  Fenwick & Margery Harbottle
  (1) **George Fenwick** (ca.1550 Bitchfield, Lincs. – 12 Feb
    1612 Doncaster)
    = ...; **Isabel ...** (...)
    (a) **John Fenwick** (1590 – 1620)
      = ...; **Janetta Pye** (1590 – 1630) daughter of William Pye &
      Grace Harrison
      Has further generations of issue
    (b) **Jane Fenwick** (1604 Bitchfield – 1663 Hempstead, NY
      = bef.1620; ♦**John Strickland** (1584 – 1672)
      Children are listed with other parent
    (c) **George Fenwick** (1590 – 1657 Berwick Castle, Northumb.)

    (d) **Elizabeth Fenwick** (1595 – ... Boston, MA)
    (2) **Anthony Fenwick** (...)
(C) **Nicholas Heron** (...)
(D) **Isabel Heron** (...)
    = ...; **Sir Hugh Ridley** (...) son of Sir Nicholas Ridley &
    Mary Musgrave
    (1) **Nicholas Ridley** (...)
    = ...; **Mabel Dacre** (...) daughter of Sir Philip Dacre & Anne Grey
    (a) **Nicholas Ridley** (1550 – 16 Jan 1585)
        = ...; **Margaret Forster** (... – 1626) daughter of Sir Thomas
        Forster & Florence Wharton
        Has further generations of issue
    (b) **Sir Hugh Ridley** (1558 – ...)
        = ...; ◆**Barbara Heron** (...) daughter of John Heron &
        Margery Grey
        issue ?
    (c) **Alexander Ridley** (...)
        = ...; **Barbara Crane** (...)
        issue ?
    (d) **Thomas Ridley** (...)
        = ...; **Mary Ridley** (...) daughter of John Ridley & Anne
        Charlton
        issue ?
    (2) **John Ridley** (...)
    (3) **Cuthbert Ridley** (...)
    (4) **Thomas Ridley** (...)
    (5) **Dororthy Ridley** (...)
    = ...; **Henry Jackson** (...)
    issue ?
(II) **Giles Heron** (1519 Chipchase Castle – 28 Mar 1557)
(III) **Thomasine Heron** (ca.1523 – ...)
= ...; **Christopher Mapes** (ca.1518 Feltham, Norfolk – 1539
Feltham) son of John Mapes & Jane Higham
(A) **John Mapes** (ca.1536 Feltham – 1590 in France)
=1 ...; **Anna Moore** (...)
=2 ...; **Alice Wolmer** (ca.1536 Norwich – 30 Apr 1596
Norwich) daughter of Robert Wiolmer & Ann Cresacre
issue of 2nd (none by 1st):
    (1) **Leonard Mapes** (1558 Feltham – 4 Feb 1619 Norwich)
    = ...; **Catherine Southwell** (ca.1566 Horsham, Norfolk –
    1618 Norwich) daughter of Sir Richard Southwell & Bridget Copley
    (a) **Francis Mapes** (ca.1588 Feltham – 19 Mar 1638
        Rollesby, Norfolk)
        = ...; **Anna Laveday** (ca.1592 Rollesby – 13 Jun 1657
        Rollesby) daughter of Richard Loveday & Susan ...
        Has further generations of issue

            (b) **Robert Mapes** (...)
  issue of 2nd:
  c) **Elizabeth Musgrave** (...)
    = 20 Jul 1526 Snape, Yorks.; ♦**John Neville, 3rd Baron
    Latymer** (17 Nov 1493 – 2 Mar 1542/3 London) son of Richard
    Neville, 2nd Baron Latymer & Anne Stafford; =1st Dorothea de
    Vere; =3rd ♦Catherine Parr
    no issue
  d) **Sir Simon Musgrave** (... – 30 Jan 1596/7)
    = ...; **Julianne Ellerker** (...) daughter of William Ellerker
    (I) **Christopher Musgrave** (...)
      = ...; **Jane Curwen** (...) daughter of Sir Henry Curwen
     (A) **Sir Richard Musgrave, 1st Baronet KB** (... – 1615) cr.
      Baronet 29 Jun 1611; KB 1603
      = ...; ♦**Frances Wharton** (...) daughter of Philip Wharton,
      3rd Baron Wharton & Lady Frances Clifford
      (1) **Sir Philip Musgrave, 2nd Baronet** (21 May 1607 – 7
      Feb 1677/8) suc. father 1615
        = ...; **Julianne Hutton** (...) daughter of Sir Richard Hutton
       (a) **Sir Richard Musgrave, 3rd Baronet** (Jun 1635 – 27
       Dec 1687) suc. father 1678
       = 20 Jun 1655; **Margaret Harrison** (...) daughter of Sir
       Thomas Harrison & Margaret Darcy
       Has further generations of issue
       (b) **Sir Christopher Musgrave, 4th Baronet** (aft. 1635 –
       1704)
       =1 ...; **Mary Cogan** (...) daughter of Sir Andrew Cogan, 1st
       Baronet
       =2 15 Apr 1671; **Elizabeth Franklin** (...) daughter of Sir John
       Franklin
       issue of 1st:
       Has further generations of issue
  e) **Sir William Musgrave** (ca.1509 – 18 Oct 1544) Kt. 1523
    = ...; **Elizabeth Curwen** (...) daughter of Sir Thomas Curwen &
    Ann Huddlestone
    (I) **Sir Richard Musgrave** (Aug 1524 – 10/11 Sep 1555)
      = ...; **Anne Wharton** (...) daughter of Thomas Wharton, 1st
      Baron Wharton & Eleanore Stapleton
     (A) **Eleanor Musgrave** (ca.1546 – 25 Jul 1623)
      = ca.1566; **Robert Bowes** (1535 – 1597)
      no issue
     (B) **Thomas Musgrave** (ca.1547 – ca.1567) unm.
C) **Elizabeth Clifford** (1432 – 1461 Clifford, Heresfords.)
  =1 ...; **John Hamerton** (...)
  =2 ca.1450; **Sir William Plumpton** (28 Feb 1436 Plumpton,
York. – 29 Mar 1461 Towton) killed in battle; son of Sir William

Plumpton & Elizabeth Stapleton
issue of 2ⁿᵈ (none by 1ˢᵗ):
1) **Elizabeth Plumpton** (ca.1451 Plumpton – 21 Sep 1507
London)
= ...; **John Sothill** (ca.1440 Stockfaston, Leics. – 7 Oct 1494
Stockfaston) son of Henry Sothill & Anne Boyville
a) **Christina Sothill** (1465 Stockfaston – 8 Apr 1540 London)
=1 ...; **William Babthorpe** (1463 Osgoody, Yorks. – 10 Feb
1501) son of Robert Babthorpe & Elizabeth Ryther
=2 ...; **William Bedell** (...)
issue of 1ˢᵗ (none by 2ⁿᵈ):
(I) **Sir William Babthorpe KB** (1489/90 – 27 Feb 1555) KB 1547
= bef.1529; **Agnes Palmes** (1493 Naburn, Yorks. – ...) daughter of
Brian Palmes & Anne Markenfield
(A) **Sir William Babthorpe** (1528 Yorks. – 1581)
=1 ...; ♦**Barbara Constable** (ca.1525 – 1558) daughter of Sir
Robert Constable & Hon. Catherine Manners
=2 aft.1558; **Frances Dawnay** (1550 Yorks. – 1605
Wetherden, Suffolk) daughter of Sir Thomas Dawnay & Edith
Darcy; =2ⁿᵈ Edward Sulyard
issue of 1ˢᵗ:
(1) **Margaret Babthorpe** (ca.1550 Osgoody – 15 Apr 1628
York)
=1 ...; ♦**Sir William Cholmeley** (1556 – 1616)
=2 ...; **Thomas Meynell** (...)
issue of 1ˢᵗ (none by 2ⁿᵈ):
Children are listed with other parent
(2) **Ralph Babthorpe** (... – 1617)
= ...; **Grace Byrand** (... – 10 Nov 1623) daughter of William
Byrand & Grace Ingleby
(a) **Sir William Babthorpe** (ca.1580 – ...)
= ...; **Ursula Tyrwhitt** (...) daughter of William Tyrwhitt &
Frescheville
Has further generations of issue
(b) **Catherine Babthorpe** (...)
= ...; **Sir George Palmes** (...) son of James Palmes &
Jane Dawnay
Has further generations of issue (possibly extinct now)
(3) **Catherine Babthorpe** (...)
=1 ...; **John Ingleby** (ca.1544 Ripley, Yorks. – ...) son of
Sir William Ingleby & Mary Anne Mallory
=2 ...; **George Vavasour** (1521 – ...) son of Sir Peter
Vavasour & Anne Skipwith
issue of 1ˢᵗ (none by 2ⁿᵈ)
(a) **Catherine Ingleby** (...)
(b) **Anne Ingleby** (...)

= ...; **Thomas Dalton** (1583 – 1639) son of Robert
Dalton & Elizabeth Constable
Has further generations of issue
(c) **Mary Ingleby** (...)
(d) **Grace Ingleby** (...)
issue of 2ⁿᵈ:
(4) **Christiana Babthorpe** (1568 Osgoody – ...)
= ...; **Sir John Girlington** (1561 – 28 Feb 1613 Thurland
Castle, Lancs.) son of Nicholas Girlington & Dorothy
Meignell
(a) **Nicholas Girlington** (1582 Thurland Castle – 7 Feb
1627 Thurland Castle)
= 1609; **Jane Lambert** (...) daughter of Josias Lambert &
Ann Heber
Has further generations of issue
(b) **William Girlington** (1579 Thurland Castle – 21 Jul
1617 South Cave, Yorks.)
(c) **John Girlington** (1580 Thurland Castle – ...)
(d) **Anthony Girlington** (1581 Thurland Castle – ...)
(e) **Frances Girlington** (1582 Thurland Castle – ...)
(B) **Agnes Babthorpe** (...)
= ...; **William Hussey** (1524 – 22 Mar 1570) son of George
Hussey & Anne Constable
no surviving issue
(C) **Frances Babthorpe** (ca.1535 Morton – ...)
= ...; **William Creyke** (ca.1533 East Riding, Yorks. – ...) son
of Richard Creyke & Margaret Constable
(1) **Agnes Creyke** (1564 – ...)
= ...; **George St.Quintin** (1564 Harpham, Yorks. – 1584)
son of Gabriel St.Quintin & Dorothy Griffith
(a) **Sir William St.Quintin, 1ˢᵗ Baronet** (1579 Harpham –
Oct 1649 Beverely, Yorks.) cr. Baronet 8 Mar 1642
= bef.1605; **Mary Lacy** (1583 Folkestone, Kent – 4 May
1649 Beverely) daughter of Robert Lacy & Katherine Threlkeld
Has further generations of issue
(D) **Leonard Babthorpe** (...)
= ...; **Jane Redman** (...) daughter of Sir William Redman
(1) **Christiana Babthorpe** (...)
(2) **Elizabeth Babthorpe** (...)
b) **Henry Sothill** (1470 Stokerstone, Suffolk – 16 May 1506
London)
= ...; **Joan Empson** (ca.1480 Towcester, Northants. – 12 May
1510 Essex) daughter of Sir Richard Empson & Jane Hill; =1ˢᵗ
Thomas Lacy; =2ⁿᵈ Sir William Pierrepont
(I) **Jane Sothill** (1505 Stokefaston, Leics. – ...) (twin)
= ...; ◆**Sir John Constable** (ca.1489 – ca.1554)

Children are listed with other parent

(II) **Elizabeth Sothill** (1505 Stokefaston – 19 May 1575 Hawstead, Suffolk) (twin)

= ...; **Sir William Drury** (... – 1557) son of Sir Robert Drury & Anne Calthorpe; =1st Joan More

(A) **Anne Drury** (19 Aug 1523 Hawstead – 5 Sep 1561)

= bef.1540; **Sir Christopher Heydon** (ca.1517 Baconsthorpe, Norfolk – 10 Dec 1579 Baconsthorpe) son of Sir Christopher Heydon & Anne Crane; = 2nd Temperance Carew; =3rd Agnes Crane

(1) **Sir William Heydon** (1540 – 1594)

= ...; **Anne Wodehouse** (1542 Hickling, Norfolk – ...) daughter of Sir William Wodehouse & Anne Repps

(a) **Sir Christopher Heydon** (14 Aug 1561 – 1 Jan 1623)

=1 ...; **Mirabel Rivett** (1561 – 15 Jul 1593) daughter of Sir Thomas Rivett & Alice Cotton

=2 ...; **Anne Dodge** (ca.1567 – 1642) daughter of John Dodge; =1st Sir John Potts, 1st Baronet

Has further generations of issue

(2) **Elizabeth Heydon** (1543 Baconsthorpe – 1573 Baconsthorpe)

= ...; ♦**John Wentworth** (1525 – 1588)

Children are listed with other parent

(3) **Robert Heydon** (...)

= ...

(a) **John Heydon** (...)

(4) **Ursula Heydon** (...)

= ...; **Sir Roger Townsend** (1542 Eyam, Yorks. – 30 Jun 1590 London) son of Richard Townsend & Katherine Browne; =2nd Jane Stanhope

no issue

(5) **Christopher Heydon** (...)

(B) **Robert Drury** (31 Feb 1524 Halstead, Suffolk – 7 Dec 1557 Halstead)

= 20 Jan 1541; **Hon. Audrey Rich** (ca.1543 Essex – 1567) daughter of Richard Rich, 1st Baron Rich & Elizabeth Jenkes

(1) **Sir William Drury** (8 Mar 1550 Bobbing Court, Kent – 1590 the Netherlands) killed in a duel; Kt.1576

= ...; ♦**Elizabeth Stafford** (1550 Bobbing Court – 6 Feb 1596) daughter of Sir William Stafford & Dorothy Stafford; she =2nd Sir John Scott

(a) **Robert Drury** (ca.1575 – 2 Apr 1615)

= ...; **Ann Bacon** (1572 – 5 Jun 1624) daughter of Sir Nicholas Bacon, 1st Baronet & Anne Butts

no surviving issue

(b) **Frances Drury** (8 Jun 1576 Blatherwick, Northants. –

1642 Ashby, Lincs.)
=1 bef.1600; ♦**Sir Nicholas Clifford** (... – bef.1600)
=2 ca.1600; ♦**Sir William Wray, 1st Baronet** (1555 –
1617)
issue of 1st:
Children are listed with other parent
issue of 2nd:
Children are listed with other parent
(c) **Elizabeth Drury** (1578 – 26 Feb 1654)
= ...; ♦**William Cecil, 2nd Earl of Exeter** (1566 – 1640)
Children are listed with other parent
(d) **Mary Drury** (...)
(e) **Charles Drury** (...)
(f) **Susannah Drury** (...) unm.
(g) **Dorothy Drury** (...)
(h) **Diana Drury** (... – May 1631)
= 1617; ♦**Edward Cecil, Viscount Wimbledon** (1572 – 1638)
Children are listed with other parent
(2) **Dorothy Drury** (ca.1556 Hawstead – 5 Aug 1615 Soham,
Cambs.)
= ...; **Edward Barnes** (ca.1550 Salem, Cambs. – 1615 East
Winch, Norfolk) son of Thomas Barnes & Anne Themelthorpe
(a) **Alice Barnes** (...)
(b) **Bethany Barnes** (...)
(c) **Dorothy Barnes** (...)
(d) **Drurye Barnes** (...)
(e) **Edward Barnes** (...)
(f) **Mary Barnes** (1578 Soham, Cambs. – ...)
(g) **Thomas Barnes** (ca.1579 – ...)
(h) **William Barnes** (12 May 1580 Eastwick, Suffolk –
1657 Eastwich, Norfolk)
=1 ...; **Thomasine Shepherd** (ca.1580 – 15 Nov 1613
Kirby Bedon, Norfolk) daughter of Owen Shepherd &
Elizabeth Osborne
=2 1630 (dv.1648)[69]; **Sarah Evans** (... – 13 Oct 1648)
Has further generations of issue
(i) **Ann Barnes** (Jan 1580/1 Soham – ...)
(j) **Winifryd Barnes** (...)
(k) **Robert Barnes** (25 Nov 1585 Soham – ...)

---

[69] William immigrated to Salem, MA after marrying Sarah. Their divorce is a very rare example from colonial Massachusetts. After the divorce, and Sarah's subsequent death a short time later, William returned to England with his children.

(l) **Edmund Barnes** (...)
(m) **Charles Barnes** (...)
(C) **Mary Drury** (30 Jun 1526 Hawstead – ...)
=1 ...; **Sir Richard Corbet** (... – bef.1565)
=2 1565; **Sir John Tyrell** (... – 1591) =1ˢᵗ Anne Sulyard
issue of 1ˢᵗ (none by 2ⁿᵈ):
(1) **Elizabeth Corbet** (...)
= ...; ◆**Philip Wentworth** (ca.1533 – 1614)
Children are listed with other parent
(D) **Frances Drury** (9 Jun 1532 Halsted, Suffolk – 1621
Church Lodden, Norfolk)
= ...; **James Hobart** (1524 Hayles, Suffolk – 6 Feb 1615
Church Lodden) son of Henry Hobart & Anne Fineux
(1) **Mary Hobart** (1595 Hayles – ...)
= ...; **John Sherwood** (1595 – ...)
  (a) **Francis Sherwood** (ca.1620 Berks. – 1 Dec 1639
  Speen, Berks.)
  = ...; **Bridget Head** (1 Mar 1615 Beenham, Berks. – 1655
  Rappahannock Co. VA) daughter of William Head & Susan
  Alsbrook
  Has further generations of issue
(2) **Henry Hobart** (ca.1561 – ...)
= ...; **Margaret ...** (...)
  (a) **Edward Hobart** (...)
  = ...; **Alice Codde** (...)
  Has further generations of issue
  (b) **Anthony Hobart** (... – 1651)
  = ...; **Anne Breton** (...)
  Has further generations of issue
(3) **Robert Hobart** (ca.1572 – ca.1650 Norwich)
= ...; **Elizabeth Hord** (ca.1576 Ewell, Surrey – ...) daughter of
Alan Hord & Barbara Blount
  (a) **Elizabeth Hobart** (ca.1610 – ca.1681)
  = ...; **Abraham Hasnett** (...)
  issue ?
  (b) **Barbara Hobart** (ca.1614 – ca.1628)
  (c) **Thomas Hobart** (ca.1617 – ca.1645)
  (d) **Frances Hobart** (ca.1608 – ca.1681)
  = ...; **Robert Cornwallys** (... – ca.1658)
  issue ?
  (e) **Dorothy Hobart** (... – ca.1641)
  = ...; **Sir John Peyton, 3ʳᵈ Baronet** (1607 – 1666) son of
  Sir Edward Peyton, 2ⁿᵈ Baronet & Martha Liveset; suc.
  father Apr 1657
  Has further generations of issue
(4) **Elizabeth Hobart** (...)

= ...; **... Barney** (...)
issue ?
(5) **William Hobart** (...)
(6) **Sir John Hobart** (...)
(7) **Edward Hobart** (...)
(8) **Ann Hobart** (...)
= ...; **... Duke** (...)
issue ?
(9) **James Hobart** (...)
(10) **Edmond Hobart** (...)
(11) **Prudence Hobart** (...)
(12) **Catherine Hobart** (...)
(13) **Audrey Hobart** (...)
(E) **Bridget Drury** (11 Sep 1534 Hawstead – ...)
= ...; **Henry Yelverton** (ca.1533 Rougham, Norfolk – 26
Apr 1601 Rougham) son of William Yelverton & Anne Fermor
(1) **Anne Yelverton** (ca.1557 Bury St.Edmonds, Suffolk – ...)
= ...; **William Barsham** (7 Jun 1558 Fakenham, Norfolk – ...)
issue ?
(2) **Sir William Yelverton** (ca.1558 King's Lynn, Norfolk –
30 Oct 1631 King's Lynn)
=1 ...; **Ursula Richardson** (...)
=2 ...; **Dionysia Stubbe** (ca.1572 Sedgefield, Norfolk –
Rougham) daughter of Richard Stubbe & Elizabeth Gurney
issue of 1st:
(a) **Elizabeth Yelverton** (... – 3 Jun 1668 Rougham)
= ...; **Thomas Peyton** (bap.29 Mar 1617 Isleham,
Cambs. – 12 Oct 1683) son of Sir Edward Peyton, 2nd
Baronet & Jane Calthorpe
Has further generations of issue
(F) **Dorothy Drury** (4 Mar 1537 Hawstead – 1602)
= ...; **Robert Rookwood** (... – 1600)
(1) **Ambrose Rookwood** (ca.1578 – 31 Jan 1605/6 London)
executed[70]
= ...; **Elizabeth Tyrwhitt** (ca.1567 Kettleby, Lincs. – ...)
daughter ofWilliam Tyrwhitt & Elizabeth Frescheville
(a) **Sir Robert Rookwood** (... – Jun 1679) Kt. 1624
= ...; **Mary Townsend** (...) daughter of Sir Robert Townsend
Has further generations of issue
(b) **Henry Rookwood** (...)

---

[70] Was convicted of plotting to assassinate the King (and many others) in the Gun Powder Plot.

        (c) **Elizabeth Rookwood** (...)
        = ...; **Henry Calverly** (...)
        issue ?
      (2) **Christopher Rookwood** (...)
      (3) **Robert Rookwood** (...)
      (4) **Elizabeth Rookwood** (...)
        = ...; **Christopher Forster** (...)
        issue ?
      (5) **Anne Rookwood** (...)
      (6) **Dorothy Rookwood** (...)
      (7) **Henry Rookwood** (...)
    (G) **Henry Drury** (6 Apr 1539 Hawstead – ...)
    (H) **Roger Drury** (24 Mar 1540 Hawstead – ...)
    (I) **Elizabeth Drury** (1556 Hawstead – ...)
    = ...; **John Wallis** (ca.1655 – ...)
2) **Margaret Plumpton** (...)
  = ...; **John Rowcliffe** (ca.1413 – ...)
  a) **Joan** Elizabeth **Rowcliffe** (ca.1439 BIckerton, Yorks. – ...)
  = ...; **Robert Stokes** (ca.1435 Bickerton – ...) son of Robert
  Stokes & ... Malyverer
  (I) **Robert Stokes** (ca.1466 Bickerton – ...)
  = ...; **Bridget Carleton** (ca.1470 Gawthorpe, Yorks, –
  ca.1556) =2nd Sir William Gascoigne
  (A) **Margaret Stokes** (ca.1499 Bickerton – ...)
  = ...; **Richard Yaxley** (ca.1495 – ...)
  issue ?
  (B) **Elizabeh Stokes** (ca.1510 Brandsby, Yorks. – 1560
  Wassand, Yorks.)
  = ...; **Marmaduke Constable** (1509 Drox Abbey, Yorks. –
  11 Jul 1568 Barrow-upon-Humber, Lincs.) son of Sir
  William Constable & Joan Fulthrope
  (1) **William Constable** (ca.1531 Waltham, Yorks. – ...)
    = ...; **Everilda ...** (...)
    no issue
  (2) **Margaret Constable** (ca.1535 Wassand – ...)
  (3) **Marmaduke Constable** (1536 Wassand – 11 Jul 1568
    Goxhill, Yorks.)
    = ...; ♦**Catherine Holme** (1544 Holmfirth – 8 Jun 1634
    Barrow-upon-Humber) daughter of John Holme & Ann
    Ainsley; =2nd John Moore
    (a) **Marmaduke Constable** (... – 12 Oct 1607
      Yorkminster, Yorks.)
      = ...; **Elizabeth Strelley** (ca.1569 – ca.1591) daughter of John
      Strelley; =2nd Thomas Charleton
      Has further generations of issue
    (b) **Frances Constable** (12 Sep 1568 Holderness, Yorks. –

2 Sep 1628)
=1 ...; **Henry Cheek** (... – bef.1584)
=2 1584; **Sir John Rhodes**[71] (1562 Staveley
Woodthorpe, Derbys. – 16 Sep 1639 Barlborough,
Derbys.) son of Francis Rhodes & Elizabeth Sandford;
he =1st Dorothy Savile; =3rd Ursula Mallory
Has further generations of issue
    (4) **Edward Constable** (1539 Wassand – 23 Aug 1613 Wassand)
    (5) **John Constable** (1541 Wassand – ...)
    (6) **Robert Constable** (ca.1546 Wassand – ...)
  (II) **Anthony Stokes** (ca.1468 Bickerton, Yorks. – ...)
  (III) **Leonard Stokes** (ca.1470 Bickerton – ...)
  (IV) **Margaret Stokes** (ca.14721 Bickerton – ...)
D) **Sir John Clifford, 9th Baron de Clifford** (8 Apr 1435
Conisburgh Castle, Yorks. – 28 Mar 1461 Dintingdale, nr.
Tadcaster, Yorks.) suc. father 1455; Kt. 1460
= ...; **Margaret Bromflete** (1443 – 12 Apr 1493) daughter of
Henry Bromflete, 1st Baron Vessy & Eleanor FitzHugh; =2nd Sir
Lancelot Threlkeld
  1) **Henry Clifford, 10th Baron de Clifford KB** (ca.1454 – 23 Apr
    1523) suc. father 1461; KB 1509
    = bef.1493; **Anne St.John** (...) daughter of Sir John St.John &
    Alice Bradshaigh
    a) **Henry Clifford, 1st Earl of Cumberland**, 11th Baron de
      Clifford, **KG** (1493 Skipton Castle, Yorks. – 22 Apr 1542) suc.
      father 1523; cr. Earl 18 Jun 1525; KG 1537
      =1 ...; ◆**Lady Margaret Talbot** (... – bef.1516) daughter of
      George Talbot, 4th Earl of Shrewsbury & Anne Hastings
      =2 aft.1515; ◆**Lady Margaret Percy** (... – ca.22 Nov 1540)
      daughter of Henry Percy, 5th Earl of Northumberland &
      Catherine Spencer
      issue of 2nd (none by 1st):
      (I) **Henry Clifford, 2nd Earl of Cumberland**, etc. **KB** (1517 –
        2 Jan 1569/70 Brougham Castle, Umbria) suc. father 1542;
        KB 1523
        =1 June 1537; ◆**Lady Eleanor Brandon** (1520 – 27 Dec
        1547 Brougham Castle) daughter of Charles Brandon, 1st
        Duke of Suffolk & Princess Mary Tudor
        =2 1553; ◆**Anne Dacre** (ca.1521 – Jul 1581) daughter of
        William Dacre. 3rd Baron Dacre & Elizabeth Talbot
        issue of 1st:

---

[71] This family spelled the name Rhodes, Rodes, Roads, Roades interchangably.

(A) **Lady Margaret Clifford** (1540 – 28 Sep 1596)
= 7 Feb 1554/5; **Henry Stanley, 4th Earl of Derby**, 5th
Baron Stanley, 8th Baron de Mohun, 12th Baron Strange **KG
KB** (Sep 1531 Lathom, Lancs. – 25 Sep 1593 Lathom) son
of Edward Stanley, 3rd Earl of Derby & Lady Dorothy
Howard; suc. father 24 Oct 1572; suc. as Baron Strange 12
Jan 1558/9
  (1) **Ferdinando Stanley, 5th Earl of Derby**, etc. (1559 – 16
  Apr 1594) suc. father 1593; his baronies fell into abeyance
  among his daughters
  = ca.1580; **Alice Spencer** (ca.1556 – 23 Jan 1637)
  daughter of Sir John Spencer & Katherine Kitson; =2nd
  Thomas Egerton, 1st Viscount Brackley
    (a) **Lady Anne Stanley** (May 1580 – Oct 1647 London)
    =1 1608; ♦**Grey Brydges, 5th Baron Chandos**
    (bef.1581–1621)
    Children are listed with other parent
    (b) **Lady Frances Stanley** (May 1583 – 11 Mar 1635/6)
    = 27 Jun 1602; **John Egerton, 1st Earl of Bridgwater**,
    2nd Viscount Brackley, Baron Ellesmere **KB** (1579 – 4
    Dec 1649) son of Thomas Egerton, 1st Viscount Brackley
    & Elizabeth Ravenscroft; suc. father 15 Mar 1616/7; cr.
    Earl 27 May 1617; KB 1603
    Has further generations of issue
    (a) **Lady Elizabeth Stanley** (6 Jan 1587/8 – 20 Jan
    1632/3)
    = 1600/1; ♦**Henry Hastings, 5th Earl of Huntingdon**
    (1586–1643)
    Children are listed with other parent
issue of 2nd:
(B) **George Clifford, 3rd Earl of Cumberland**, etc. **KG** (8
  Aug 1558 Brougham Castle – 30 Oct 1605 London) suc.
  father 1569/70; KG 1592
  = 24 Jun 1577; ♦**Lady Margaret Russell** (7 Jul 1560
  Exeter – 24 May 1616) daughter of Francis Russell, 2nd Earl
  of Bedford & Margaret St.John
  (1) **Lady Anne Clifford, 14th Baroness de Clifford** (30 Jan
  1590 – 22 Mar 1676 Brougham Castle) suc. father 1605
  =1 1609; ♦**Richard Sackville, 3rd Earl of Dorset** (1589–1624)
  =2 1 Jun 1630; ♦**Philip Herbert, 4th Earl of Pembroke**,
  etc. **KG, KB** (10 Oct 1584 Wilton House, Salisbury – 23
  Jan 1650 London) son of Henry Herbert, 2nd Earl of
  Pembroke & Mary Sydney; suc. father 1601
  issue of 1st (none by 2nd):
  Children are listed with other parent
(C) **Francis Clifford, 4th Earl of Cumberland**, etc. **KB**

(1559 – 21 Jan 1640/1) suc brother 1605; KB 1605
= ca. Mar 1589; **Grisolda Hughes** (... – 15 Jun 1613)
daughter of Thomas Hughes & Elizabeth Dwnn
(1) **Lady Frances Clifford** (... – 1627)
  = ca.1615; **Sir Gervase Clifton, 1st Baronet KB** (25 Nov
  1587 – 28 Jun 1666) son of Sir George Clifton & Lady
  Anne Thorold; cr. Baronet 1611; KB 1603; =1st Lady
  Penelope Rich; =3rd Mark Egioke; =4th Isobel Meek; =5th
  Anne South; =6th Jane Eyre; =7th ◆Lady Elizabeth
  Hastings
  (a) **Margaret Clifton** (1627 – Feb 1697/8)
    =1 bef.1648; **Sir John South** (... – Nov 1648)
    =2 bef.1657; **Sir William Whichcote** (... – ca.1657)
    =3 aft. 1659; **Robert Carey, 6th Baron Hunsdon**
    (bef.1652 – 1692 La Hogue, Normandy) son of Sir
    Horatio Carey & Pernel Harrington
    issue of 1st:
    Has further generations of issue
  (b) **Frances Clifton** (...)
    =1 ...; **Richard Tempest** (...) son of Sir Richard Tempest
    & Elizabeth Rodes
    =2 ...; **Anthony Eyre** (...) son of Anthony Eyre
    Has further generations of issue
  (c) **Anne Clifton** (...)
    = ...; **Sir Francis Rodes, 2nd Baronet** (... – 1651) son of
    Sir Francis Rodes, 1st Baronet; suc. father 1646
    Has further generations of issue
  (d) **Lettice Clifton** (... – 1659)
    = ...; **Clifton Rodes** (...) son of Sir Francis Rodes, 1st
    Baronet
    issue ?
  (e) **Elizabeth Clifton** (...)
  (f) **Clifford Clifton** (1626 – Jun 1670)
    = 4 Jul 1650 London; **Frances Finch** (...) daughter of Sir
    Heneage Finch (Speaker of the House of Commons)
    Has further generations of issue
(2) **Lady Margaret Clifford** (– 1622)
  = ...; **Thomas Wentworth, 1st Earl of Strafford KG** (13
  Apr 1593 London – 12 May 1641 London) executed; son
  of Sir William Wentworth & Anne Atkins; =2nd Lady
  Arabella Holles; =3rd Elizabeth Rodes; cr. Earl 1640; KG
  1640; titles forfeited prior to death
  no issue
(3) **Henry Clifford, 5th Earl of Cumberland, 1st Baron
  Clifford** (28 Feb 1591/2 – 11 Deb 1643) cr. Baron 1628;
  suc. father 1641; Earldom became extinct upon his death,

the Barony was inheried by his daughter

= 25 Jul 1610; ◆**Frances Cecil** (1593 – 14 Feb 1643/4)
daughter of Robert Cecil, 1st Marquess of Salisbury &
Elizabeth Brooke

(a) **Elizabeth Clifford, 2nd Baroness Clifford** (18 Sep
1613 Skipton Castle – 6 Jan 1690/1) suc. father 1643
= 5 Jul 1635 Skipton Castle; **Richard Boyle, 1st Earl of
Burlington,** Baron Clifford of Lanesborough, 2nd Earl of
Cork, 2nd Viscount Boyle (20 Oct 1612 Youghal, co.
Cork – 15 Jan 1698) son of Richard Boyle, 1st Earl of
Cork & Catherine Fenton; suc. brother as Viscount 2 Sep
1642; cr. Baron 4 Nov 1644; suc. father as Earl of Cork
15 Sep 1643; cr. Earl of Burlington 20 Mar 1664
Has further generations of issue

(D) **Lady Frances Clifford** (... – 1592)
= 1577; ◆**Philip Wharton, 3rd Baron Wharton** (1555–1625)
Children are listed with other parent

(II) **Lady Maud Clifford** (...)
= 1539; ◆**Sir John Conyers, 3rd Baron Conyers** (...–1557)
Children are listed with other parent

(III) **Sir Ingelram Clifford** (...)
= ...; **Anne Ratcliff** (...) daughter of Sir Henry Ratcliff
no issue

(IV) **Lady Catherine Clifford** (ca.1513 Skipton – 1598
Whitby, Yorks.)
=1 ca.1530; ◆**John le Scrope, 8th Baron Scrope** (1510 – 1549)
=2 ...; **Sir Richard Cholmeley**[72] (1516 – 17 May 1583) son
of Sir Roger Cholmondeley & Katherine Constable
issue of 1st:
Children are listed with other parent
issue of 2nd:

(A) **Sir Henry Cholmeley** (1556 Whitby – Jan 1616 York)
= ...; ◆**Margaret Babthorpe** (ca.1550 Osgoodby, Yorks. –
15 Apr 1628 York) daughter of Sir William Babthorpe & Barbara
Constable; =2nd Thomas Meynell

(1) **Sir Richard Cholmeley** (Oct 1580 Whitby – 23 Sep 1631
Whitby)
=1 1590; **Susannah Legard** (1578 Ganton, Yorks. – 1611
Scorborough, Yorks.) daughter of John Legard & Alice Alsop
=2 1613; **Margaret Cobb** (1590 Addersbury, Oxon. – ...)
daughter of William Cobb & Alice Wild

---

[72] This names, pronounced Chumley, has a very wide range of spellings.

issue od 1st (none by 2nd)

- (a) **Sir Hugh Cholmeley, 1st Baronet** (22 Jul 1600 Thornton-le-Dale, Yorks. – 30 Nov 1657) cr. Baronet 1641 = 10 Dec 1622 London; **Elizabeth Twysden** (18 Aug 1600– 17 Apr 1655 London) daughter of Sir William Twysden & Lady Anne Finch
  Has further generations of issue
- (2) **Barbara Cholmeley** (ca.1581 Whitby – 28 Feb 1619 Coxwold, Yorks.)
  = ca.1600; ♦**Thomas Belasyse, 1st Viscount Fauconberg**, (1577–1653)
  Children are listed with other parent
- (3) **Dorothy Cholmeley** (bap.15 Apr 1587 – ...)
  = ...; **Nicholas Bushell** (1567 – ...)
  - (a) **Hester Bushell** (ca.1606 – ...)
    = ...; **Isaac Newton**[73] (...)
    Has further generations of issue
  - (b) **Mary Bushell** (...)
    = ...; **Henry Tempest** (Sep 1621 – 1657) son of John Tempest & Katherine Duckenfield
    Has further generations of issue
- (4) **Mary Cholmeley** (ca.1593 Whitby – 5 Jan 1650)
  = 4 Feb 1626/7; **Rev. Hon. Henry** Aske **Fairfax** (aft. 1585 – 6 Apr 1665) son of Thomas Fairfax, 1st Lord Fairfax & Ellen Aske; =1st Katherine Dukenfield
  - (a) **Henry** Cholmeley **Fairfax, 4th Lord Fairfax** (20 Dec 1631 Fairfax Co. VA – 9 Apr 1688) suc. first cousin 12 Nov 1671
    = ...; **Frances Barwick** (... – 14 Feb 1683) daughter of Sir Robert Barwick & Ursula Strickland
    Has further generations of issue
  - (b) **Brian Fairfax** (6 Oct 1633 – 20 Sep 1711)
    = 22 Apr 1675; **Charlotte Cary** (... – 14 Nov 1709) daughter of Sir Edmund Cary
    issue ?
  - (c) **Dorothy Fairfax** (... – 1744)
    =1 ...; **Robert Stapleton** (...)
    =2 ...; **Bennet Sherard** (...)
    issue ?
  - (d) **Frances Fairfax** (... – 1723)
    = 26 Oct 1686; **Rev. Nicholas Rymer** (...)
    issue ?

---

[73] Not the famous scientist.

(e) **Anne Fairfax** (...)
= 2 Sep 1690; **Ralph Carr** (...)
issue ?
(5) **Margaret Cholmeley** (...)
= ...; **Timothy Comyn** (...)
issue ?
(B) **Katherine Cholmeley** (1550 – ...)
= ...; **Richard Dutton** (1535 – ...) son of Robert Dutton &
Isabel Lambert
(1) **Barbara Dutton** (1583 – ...)
= ...; **Francis Gale** (1579 – ...) son of Robert Gale &
Thomasine Stapleton
(a) **Robert Gale** (1603 – ...)
= ...; **Elizabeth Langdale** (1601 – ...) daughter of William
Langdale & Elizabeth Constable
Has further generations of issue
(b) **Matthew Gale** (1606 – ...)
= ...; **Anne Thweng** (...)
issue ?
(c) **George Gale** (1609 – ...)
(IV) **Lady Elizabeth Clifford** (1515 Skipton – ...)
= ...; **Sir Christopher Metcalf** (1 Aug 1513 Nappa, Yorks. –
9 May 1574) son of James Metcalf & Margaret Pigott
(1) **James Metcalf** (1551 – 8 May 1580)
= ...; **Joan Savile** (... – 1617) daughter of John Savile &
Elizabeth Coxon; =2nd Sir Mauger Vavasour
no issue
(V) **Lady Jane Clifford** (ca.1525 Skipton – ...)
= ...; **Sir John Hudleston KB** (1488 Warleston, Cumb. – 12
Jan 1547 Millom, Cumb.) son of Sir John Hudleston & Joan
Stapleton; =2nd Joan Seymour; =3rd Joyce Prickley KB 1533
no issue
b) **Margaret Clifford** (...)
= ...; **Sir Cuthbert Ratcliffe** (...)
(I) **Jane Ratcliffe** (...)
= aft.8 Jul 1537; **Robert Ogle, 5th Baron Ogle** (... – 6 Mar
1544/5) son of Robert Ogle, 4th Baron Ogle & Anne Lumley;
he =1st ◆Dorothy Widdrington; suc. father 1532
(A) **Cuthbert Ogle, 7th Baron Ogle** (ca.1540 – 1597 Cockle
Park) suc. brother 1562; title fell into abeyance between his
daughters
= ca.1565; **Catherine Carnaby** (... – 10 Jan 1622/3) daughter of
Sir Reynold Carnaby & Dorothy Forster
(1) **Joane Ogle** (... – ca.1626)
= ca.1584; ◆**Edward Talbot, 8th Earl of Shrewsbury**, etc.
(bef.25 Feb 1561 – 8 Feb 1617) son of George Talbot, 6th Earl of

Shrewsbury & Gertrude Manners; suc. brother 8 May 1616
no issue
  (2) **Catherine Ogle, (8th) Baroness Ogle** (ca.1570 – 18 Apr
    1629 Bothal) suc. when abeyance was terminated 4 Dec 1628
    = 11 Jul 1591; **Sir Charles Cavendish** (ca.1553 – 4 Apr
    1617) son of Rt.Hon. Sir William Cavendish & Elizabeth Hardwicke
    (a) **William Cavendish, 1st Duke of Newcastle-upon-
      Tyne**, Marquess of Newscatle-upon-Tyne, Earl of Newcastle-
      upon-Tyne, Earl of Ogle, Viscount Mansfield, Baron Cavendish,
      9th Baron Ogle **KG** (bap.15 Dec 1593 – 25 Dec 1676) suc. mother
      1629; cr. Viscount 29 Oct 1620, Earl of Newcastle and Baron
      Cavendish 7 Mar 1627/8, Marquess 27 Oct 1643, Earl of Ogle and
      Duke 16 Mar 1664/5; KG 1650
      =1 ca.1618; **Elizabeth Basset** (... – 17 Apr 1646 Bolsover)
      daughter of William Basset & Judith Austen; =1st Henry Howard
      =2 ca.Dec 1645; **Margaret Lucas** (1623 Colchester, Essex – 15
      Dec 1673) daughter of Sir Thomas Lucas & Elizabeth Leighton
      Has further generations of issue
    (b) **Sir Charles Cavendish** (ca.1594 – 1654) Kt. 1619; unm?
2) **Richard Clifford** (...) killed in action in the Netherlands
3) **Elizabeth Clifford** (... – 21 Feb 1531)
  = ...; **Sir Robert Aske** (...)
  a) **Anne Aske** (...)
  = ...; **William Monckton** (... – 4 Jul 1584) son of Robert
  Monckton & Janet Lucas
  (I) **Christopher Monckton** (...)
    = ...; **Frances Hussey** (...) daughter of George Hussey
    (A) **Marmaduke Monckton** (...)
      = 1571; **Elizabeth Wentworth** (...) daughter of Matthew
      Wentworth
      (1) **John Monckton** (... – 1622)
        = ...; **Susanna Berrie** (...) daughter of William Berrie
        (a) **John Monckton** (...)
          = ...; **Mary Oldfield** (...) daughter of Samuel Oldfield
          Has further generations of issue
        (b) **Sir Edmund Monckton** (...)
          = ...; **Anne Hammerton** (...)
          issue ?
        (c) **Marmaduke Berrie** (...) né Monck
          = ...; **Mary Berrie** (...) daughter of Richard Berrie
          no issue
      (2) **Sir Philip Monckton** (1574 – 1646) Kt.1617
        = ...; **Martha Sutton** (...) daughter of Francis Sutton
        (a) **Sir Francis Monckton** (...) Kt. 1641
          = ...; **Margaret Saville** (...) daughter of Thomas Saville
          Has further generations of issue

(I) **Thomas Monckton** (... – 4 Jul 1584)
   = ...; **Marjery St.Quintin** (...) daughter of John St.Quintin
   (A) a son
   (B) a daughter
   (C) **Rev. Christopher Monckton** (28 Mar 1578 – 26 Jun 1652) ordained (Anglican) 1604
      =1 ...; **Ann ...** (... – bef.Sep 1641)
      =2 18 Sep 1641; **Sarah Stearle** (... – Mar 1654)
      issue of 1st (any by 2nd?):
      (1) **Rev. John Monckton** (... – 1708)
         =1 ...; **Sarah Fisher** (...) daughter of Rev. Samuel Fisher
         =2 ...; **Eleanor Kitchenham** (...)
         =3 ...; **Joan Kitchenham** (... – Feb 1730)
         issue of 1st (any by others?):
         (a) **Timothy Monckton** (11 Jan 1684 – 18 Aug 1751)
            = ...; **Ann Hooker** (... – 13 Dec 1751) daughter of John Hooker
            Has further generations of issue
   (D) a son
   (III) **Robert Monckton** (...)
 4) **Sir Thomas Clifford** (...)
   = ..; **Ellen Swarby** (...) daughter of John Swarby
   issue ?
E) **Sir Roger Clifford** (ca.1437 Conisborough, Yorks. – 2 May 1485 London) executed
   = ca.1462; ♦**Lady Joan Courtenay** (ca.1441 – aft.12 Sep 1498) daughter of Thomas Courtenay, 13th Earl of Devon & Lady Margaret Beaufort; =2nd Sir William Knyvet
   no issue
F) **Thomas Clifford** (1441 – 1520) unm,
G) **Sir Robert Clifford** (bef.1448 – 15 Mar 1508 Aspeden, Herts.)
   = ca.1479 Aspeden; **Elizabeth Barley** (...) daughter of William Barley & Elizabeth Darcy; =1st Sir Ralph Jocelyn
   surviving issue ?[74]
H) **Anne Clifford** (1448 – 1472)
   =1 ...; **Sir Richard Tempest** (...)
   =2 ...; **William Conyers** (...)
   no surviving issue
I) **Margaret Clifford** (1541 – 1567)

---

[74] At the church in Aspeden, there is a brass plate showing Elizabeth Barley with her 4 children by Clifford, 2 sons and 2 daughters. These children are all show as young, indicated they likely did not survive to adulthood.

= 12 Apr 1467; **Robert Carre** (...)
1) **Anne Carre** (1473 – 1518)
  = ca.1499; **Roger Tempest** (1471 – bef.Nov 1537) son of John
  Tempest & Agnes Banastre; =2nd Elizabeth Huddleston
  a) **Stephen Tempest** (1500 – 14 Aug 1549)
    =1 ca.1525; **Agnes Lister** (...) daughter of William Lister
    =2 ...; **Anne Preston** (...)
    issue of 1st (none by 2nd):
    (I) **Henry Tempest** (1527 – 17 Feb 1604/5)
      = 7 Jul 1543; ♦**Isabel Percy** (...) illegitimate daughter of Sir
      Ingelram Percy
      (A) **Thomas Tempest** (...)
      (B) **Mary Tempest** (...)
        = ...; **John Pulleyne** (...)
        issue ?
      (C) **Anne Tempest** (...)
        =1 ...; **William Burton** (...)
        =2 ...; **William Lambton** (...)
        issue ?
      (D) **Sir Stephen Tempest** (1553 – 30 Sep 1625)
        =1 ...; **Anne Eltofts** (...) daughter of Anthony Eltofts &
        Maud Stapleton
        =2 Oct 1591; **Catherine Lawson** (...) daughter of Henry
        Lawson
        issue of 1st:
        (1) **Anne Tempest** (...)
          = ...; **Henry Young** (...)
          issue ?
        (2) **Isabel Tempest** (...)
          = ...; **Francis Malham** (...)
          (a) **Francis Malham** (1606 – 22 May 1660 Grantham, Lincs.)
            = ...; **Jane Foster** (...)
            issue ?
        (3) **Maude Tempest** (...)
          = ...; **Michael Shawe** (... – ca.1621)
          (a) **James Shawe** (ca.1616 – ...)
          (b) **Stephen Shawe** (ca.1617 – ...)
          (c) **Elizabeth Shawe** (...)
        (4) **Robert Tempest** (... – 1646)
          = ...; **Thomazine ...** (...) =1st ... Mitchell
          issue ?
        (5) **Frances Tempest** (...)
          = ...; **Simon Blakey** (...)
          issue ?
        issue of 2nd:
        (6) **Stephen Tempest** (1593 – 1651)

=1 1612; **Susan Oglethorpe** (... – 1628) daughter of
William Oglethorpe
=2 1629; **Frances Gargrave** (1588 – 1662) daughter of
Sir Cotton Gargrave & Agnes Waterton
issue of 1st (none by 2nd):
  (a) **Stephen Tempest** (1617 – 1673)
    = ...; ♦**Anne Gascoigne** (... – 1684) daughter of
    Thomas Gascoigne, 2nd Baronet & Anne Symion
    no issue
  (b) **Mary Euphemia Tempest** (1619 – 1689) a nun
  (c) **Elizabeth** Juniper **Tempest** (1620 – 1670 Brugge) a nun
  (d) **William Tempest** (... – 1665)
  (e) **Thomas Tempest** (1625 – 24 Jun 1697)
    = 1653; **Anne Scrope** (... – 1692) daughter of Henry Scrope
    Has further generations of issue
  (h) **Frances Tempest** (ca.1628 – ...)
    = ...; **Thomas Aslaby** (bap. 13 Oct 1633 Norton,
    York – ...) son of Francis Aslaby & Dorothy...
    Has further generations of issue
  (f) **Catherine Tempest** (...)
  (g) **Anne Tempest** (...)
    = ...; **Richard Grimshaw** (...)
    issue ?
  (i) **Elizabeth** Frances Claire **Tempest** (1639 – 1694) a nun
(7) **Roger Tempest** (...)
(8) **Mary Euprasia Tempest** (1622 – 1689) a nun
(9) **Richard Tempest** (1596 – 1669)
  = ...; **Elizabeth Grimshaw** (...)
  (a) **Stephen Tempest** (...)
  (b) **Richard Tempest** (...)
    = ...
    Has further generations of issue
  (c) **John Tempest** (...)
    = ...; **Jane ...** (...) =1st ... Meriall
    Has further generations of issue
  (d) **Robert Tempest** (...)
    = ...; **Isabel ...** (...)
    issue ?
  (e) **Katherine Tempest** (...)
    = ...; **John Yorke** (...)
    issue ?
  (f) **Ellen Tempest** (...)
  (g) **Elizabeth Tempest** (...)
(10) **George Tempest** (...)
  = ...; **Frances Baildon** (...)
  (a) **George Tempest** (...)

    (b) **Francis Tempest** (...) a priest
    (c) **Frances Tempest** (...)
    = ...; **William Langdale** (...)
    Has further generations of issue
    (d) **Mary Tempest** (...)
    (11) **John Tempest** (... – 1649)
    (12) **Thomas Tempest** (... – 1647)
    (13) **James Tempest** (...)
    (14) **Katherine Tempest** (...)
 (E) **Dorothy Tempest** (...)
 = ...; **Edward Rudd** (...)
 issue ?
(F) **Frances Tempest** (... – ca.1605)
 = ...; **Oliver Breares** (...)
 issue ?
(G) **Henry Tempest** (... – 1612)
(H) **George Tempest** (ca.1582 Broughton – ca.1647 Broughton)
= ...; **Jane Parker** (ca.1574 Entwistle, Lancs. – 1642)daughter of
John Parker & Margaret Towneley; =1st ♦Thomas Tempest; =3rd
♦Edward Tempest
 (1) **Ellen Tempest** (1604 Broughton – ...)
  =1 ...; **John Wilson** (...)
  =2 ...; **Thomas Wilson** (...)
  issue of 2nd (any by 1st?):
  (a) **Tempest Wilson** (1640 – ...)
 (2) **Isabel Tempest** (1606 Broughton – ...)
  = ...; **Henry Butler** (ca.1600 Hales, Lancs. – ...) son of Nicholas
  Butler & Anne Clifton
  (a) **Sir Nicholas Butler** (ca.1623 – 1700 London)
  (b) **Elizabeth Butler** (...)
   = ...; **George MacCartney** (...) =1st Jane Calterwood
   issue ?
 (3) **Elizabeth Tempest** (28 Aug 1608 Broughton – ...)
  ...; **Edmund Fleetwood** (ca.1578 Rossall, Lancs. – 17
  Apr 1648) son of Edmund Fleetwood & Elizabeth Cheyne
  (a) **George Fleetwood** (ca.1633 – ...)
  (b) **Elizabeth Fleetwood** (ca.1635 – ...)
   = ...; **John Brekell** (...)
   issue ?
 (4) **Mary Tempest** (1614 Broughton – ...)
  = ...; **Rev. John Waite** (...)
  (a) **John Waite** (...)
b) **Katherine Tempest** (1503 – 1576)
= ...; **Thomas Maude** (1500 – 1576) son of Arthur Maude &
Jane Townley
 (I) **Arthur Maude** (... – 26 Dec 1587 Biongley, Yorks.)

= ...; **Jane Eltoft** (...) daughter of Anthony Eltoft
(A) **Agnes Maude** (...)
  =1 ...; **John Barstow** (...)
  =2 ...; **Thomas Hall** (...)
  no issue
(B) **Isabella Maude** (...)
  = ...; **Thomas Wade** (... − 1597)
  no issue
(C) **Jane Maude** (...)
(D) **Margaret Maude** (...)
(E) **Elizabeth Maude** (...)
(F) **Mary Maude** (...)
(II) **Thomas Maude** (... − aft.1585) unm.
(III) **Christopher Maude** (...)
  = ...; **Grace ...** (...)
  (A) **Thomas Maude** (... − 3 Jan 1633)
    = ...
     (1) a daughter (...)
     had issue by ...:
     (a) **Robert Maude** (... − 1685)
      = ...; **Frances Wandesford** (...) daughter of Sir Christopher Wandesford, 1st Baronet
      Has further generations of issue
  (B) **John Maude** (...)
  (C) **Isabel Maude** (...)
    = ...; **William Currer** (...)
    issue ?
(IV) **Anne Maude** (...)
  = ...; **Thomas Hall** (...)
  issue ?
(V) **Isabel Maude** (...)
  = ...; **Robert Bayldon** (...)
  issue ?
(VI) **Margaret Maude** (1552 − ...)
  = aft.1563; ♦**Thomas Tempest** (1545 − 1595)
  Children are listed with other parent

CHAPTER 10
WENTWORTH

Baroness de Clifford's younger sister, Mary, married Sir Philip Wentworth. It would take three more generations, but the Wentworths were eventually raised to the peerage as Barons in 1536. Little is known of the earlier Wentworths except they can be traced to the early 1300s in Yorkshire. Despite their origin, they also fought for the Lancasters in the 1400s. Once ennobled they typically married into other noble families.

The 4th Baron particularly stands out, as he fought valiantly for the cause of Charles I and was created Earl of Cleveland. However, that title became extinct upon his death. The Barony passed to his daughter.

For the most part, this family's contribution to history is limited to providing brides for more prominent families. One prime example is the 1494 marriage of Margaret Wentworth to Sir John Seymour. Their eldest son would become the first Seymour Duke of Somerset, and one of their daughters, Elizabeth, would capture the heart of Henry VIII and become his 3rd wife and mother of the male heir he sought most of his life.

The only connection to the New World to be found in this chapter is the Farrar Family of Virginia, descended through a path of non-nobles descended from one Elizabeth Wentworth (+1480). However, there are several lines that could have more descendants than we know.

Edward III
|
Lionel of Antwerp, Duke of Clarence
|
Philippa, Countess of Ulster
|
Elizabeth, Lady Percy (later Baroness Camoys)
|
Elizabeth, Baroness de Clifford (later Countess of Westmorland)
|

Mary Clifford (...)
= ...; **Sir Philip Wentworth** (ca.1424 – 18 May 1464) executed; son of Roger Wentworth & Marjery le Despencer
A) **Sir Henry Wentworth KB** (ca.1448 – ca.1500) KB 1489
=1 ...; **Anne Say** (... – bef.22 Oct 1494) daughter of Sr John Say & Elizabeth Cheyney
=2 22 Oct 1494 Savernake Forest, Wilts.; ♦**Elizabeth Neville** (... – Sep 1517) daughter of John Neville, 1st Marquess of Montagu & Isabel Ingaldsthorpe; =1st Thomas Scrope, 6th Baron Scrope
issue of 1st (none by 2nd):
1) **Sir Richard Wentworth** (...)
   = ...; **Anne Tyrell** (...) daughter of Sir James Tyrell[75]
   a) **Sir Thomas Wentworth, 1st Baron Wentworth** (1501 Nettlestead, Suffolk – 3 Mar 1551) Kt. 1523; cr. Baron 1536
      = ca.1520; **Margaret Fortescue** (...) daughter of Sir Adrian Fortescue & Anne Stonor
      (I) **Thomas Wenworth, 2nd Baron Wentworth** (1525 – 13 Jan 1583/4) suc. father 1551
         =1 9 Feb 1545/6; **Mary Wentworth**[76] (... – ca.1554) daughter of Sir John Wentworth
         =2 1556; **Anne Wentworth**[77] (... 2 Sep 1571) daughter of Henry Wentworth
         issue of 2nd (none known by 1st):
         (A) **William Wentworth** (... – 7 Nov 1582)
            = ...; ♦**Elizabeth Cecil** (...) daughter of William Cecil, 1st Baron Burghley & Mildred Cooke
            no issue
         (B) **Henry Wentworth, 3rd Baron Wentworth** (bef.20 Aug 1558 – 16 Aug 1593 Burley, Rutland) suc. father 1584
            = ca.1585; **Anne Hopton** (1561 – 7 May 1625) daughter of

---

[75] Sir James Tyrell has been named as the supposed murderer of the Princes in the Tower.
[76] Mary is descended in the male line from Philip Wentworth's (1424-1464) brother, Henry.
[77] Anne was Mary's first cousin (Henry and Sir John were brothers)

Sir Owen Hopton; =2nd William Pope, 1st Earl of Downe

(1) **Thomas Wentworth, Earl of Cleveland**, 4th Baron Wentworth **KB** (1591 – 25 Mar 1667) suc. father 1593; cr. Earl 1626, but title became extinct upon his death; KB 1610
=1 1611; ♦**Anne Crofts** (... – 16 Jan 1637/8) daughter of Sir John Crofts & Mary Shirley
=2 25 Oct 1638; ♦**Lucy Wentworth** (... – 23 Nov 1651) daughter of Sir John Wentworth, 1st Baronet
issue of 1st:

  (a) **Thomas Wentworth, 5th Baron Wentworth KB** (2 Feb 1612/3 – 1 Mar 1664/5) KB 1626; deemed to have suc. father (during his lifetime) in the Barony 3 Nov 1640
  = bef. 11 Mar 1657/8; **Philadelphia Carey** (... – 4 May 1696) daughter of Ferdinand Carey & Philippa Throckmorton
  Has further generations of issue

  (b) **Lady Anne Wentworth, (7th) Baroness Wentworth** (bef.29 Jul 1623 – 7 May 1697) suc. niece 1686
  = 11 Jul 1638; **John Lovelace, 2nd Baron Lovelace** (... – 14 Nov 1670) son of Richard Lovelace, 1st Baron Lovelace; suc. father
  Has further generations of issue
  issue of 2nd:

  (c) **Lady Catherine Wentworth** (...)

(C) **Cecily Wentworth** (...)
  = ...; **Sir Robert Wingfield** (...)

  (1) **Thomas Wingfield** (...)
  = ...

  (a) **Cecily Wingfield** (...)
  = ...; **William Blois** (bef.1625 – 1672)
  Has further generations of issue

(II) **Elizabeth Wentworth** (...)
=1 ...; **Richard Tempest** (...)
=2 ...; **Sir John Savile** (1545 – 2 Feb 1606/7) son of Henry Savile & Elizabeth Ramsden; =1st Jane Garth; =3rd ♦Dorothy Wentworth; =4th Margery Peake
issue of 2nd (none known by 1st):

(A) **John Savile** (... – 1651)
=1 ...; **Mary Robinson** (...) daughter of John Robinson
=2 ...; **Margaret Garraway** (...) daughter of Sir Henry Garraway
issue of 2nd (none known by 1st):

  (1) **Katherine Savile** (... – 1710)
  =1 Apr 1657; **Sir William Cholmley, 2nd Baronet** (Dec 1625 – 11 Oct 1663 Mitcham, Surrey) son of Sir Hugh Cholmley, 1st Baronet & Elizabeth Twysden; =1st Katherine Hotham; suc. father 20 Nov 1657

=2 aft.Jul 1665; **Sir Nicholas Strode** (...)
issue of 1st (none known by 2nd):
  (a) **Sir Hugh Cholmley, 3rd Baronet** (ca.1662 – 2 Jul
    1665) suc. father 1663; unm.
(2) **Margaret Savile** (... – 9 Nov 1697)
  = ...; **Sir William Ingleby, 2nd Baronet** (1621 – 1682) son
  of Sir William Ingleby, 1st Baronet & Annr Bellingham;
  suc. father 1652
  (a) **Sir John Ingleby, 3rd Baronet** (1664 – 1742) suc.
    father 1682
    = ...; **Mary Johnson** (1699 – 1733)
    Has further generations of issue (extinct 1772)
  (b) **Margaret Ingleby** (bef.21 Mar 1662 – 12 Sep 1715)
    = 23 Oct 1683 Ripley, Yorks.; **Mark Shaftoe** (8 Apr
    1662 – 28 Dec 1723) son of Sir Robert Shaftoe &
    Catherine Widdrington
    Has further generations of issue
  (c) **Anne Ingleby** (...)
    = 7 May 1685 Ripley; **John Arderne** (1663 – 1701) son
    of Sir John Arderne & Mary Leigh
    no surviving issue
(3) **Elizabeth Savile** (...)
  = ...; **Leonard Wastell** (...)
  issue ?
(4) **John Savile** (1644 – aft.1717)
  = ...; **Sarah Tryon** (...) daughter of Peter Tryon
  (a) **John Savile** (... – 1717)
    = ...; **Mary Banks** (... – Sep 1740) daughter of Sir JOhn
    Banks, Baronet & Elizabeth Dethick
    Has further generations of issue
  (b) **James Savile** (...)
    = ...
    [I] **Sarah Savile** (...)
      = ...; **Rev. Joseph Leech** (...)
      issue?
  (c) **Samuel Savile** (...)
    = ...
    [I] **Sarah Savile** (...)
      = ...; **William Sotherton** (...)
      issue ?
  (d) **Sarah Savile** (...)
    = 12 Apr 1692; **Sir Thomas Slingsby, 4th Baronet**
    (1668 – 1726) son of Sir Thomas Slingsby, 2nd Baronet;
    suc. brother 1691
    Has further generations of issue
  (e) **Charles Savile** (1676 – 5 Jun 1741)

= ...; **Alathea Millington** (... – 24 Jun 1759) daughter of
Gilbert Millington
Has further generations of issue[78]
  (5) **Dorothy Savile** (1 May 1647 – ...)
  = 15 Sep 1663; **John Clavering** (ca.1641 – 26 Feb 1687/8)
  son of Sir James Clavering, 1st Baronet & Jane Madison
    (a) **Sir James Clavering, 2nd Baronet** (bef.8 Apr 1668 –
    Jul 1707) suc. grandfather Mar 1701/2
    = ...; **Elizabeth Middleton** (... – May 1708) daughter of
    Sir William Middleton, 1st Baronet & Elizabeth Mundy
    no surviving issue
    (b) **Sir John Clavering, 3rd Baronet** (9 Apr 1672 Ryton –
    May 1714) suc. brother 1707
    = 17 Dec 1702 Newcastle-upon-Tyne; **Jane Mallabar**
    (bef.7 Feb 1668/9 Newcastle-upon-Tyne – 22 Feb
    1734/5) daughter of Robert Mallabar & Alice Swinborne
    Has further generations of issue
    (c) **Sir Francis Clavering, 5th Baronet** (9 Sep 1673
    Ryton – 31 Dec 1738) suc. nephew 18 May 1726;
    = ...; **Susan Sells** (...)
    no issue
(III) **Dorothy Wentworth** (...)
  =1 ...; **Sir Paul Widmerpool** (...)
  =2 ...; **Martin Frobisher** (...)
  =3 ...; **Sir John Savile** (1545 – 2 Feb 1606/7) son of Henry
Savile & Elizabeth Ramsden; =1st Jane Garth; =2nd ♦Elizabeth
Wentworth; =4th Margery Peake
no known issue
(IV) **Joan Wentworth** (... – 16 Apr 1614)
= bef.1581; **Sir Henry Cheney, Baron Cheney** (... – Aug/Sep
1587) son of Sir Thomas Cheney & Anne Houghton; cr. Baron
8 May 1572; title became extinct upon his death
  (A) **Frances Cheney** (...)
  = ...; **Nicholas Crispe** (...)
  no issue
(V) **Anne Wentworth** (...)
= ...; **Sir John Poley** (...)
  (A) **Susan Poley** (... – 13 Sep 1603)
  = ...; **Thomas Crofts** (12 Jun 1540 – 3 Apr 1612) son of
  Edmund Crofts & Elizabeth Kytson
    (1) **Sir John Crofts** (1563 – 29 Mar 1628) Kt.1599

---

[78] Their son became the 1st Earl of Mexborough.

= ...; **Mary Shirley** (... – Mar1648/9) daughter of Sir
Thomas Shirley
(a) **Cecilia Crofts** (... – 1 Jun 1638)
   = ...; **Thomas Killigrew** (...)
   issue ?
(b) **Anne Crofts** (... – 16 Jan 1637/8)
   = 1611; ◆**Thomas Wentworth, Earl of Cleveland**
   (1591–1667)
   Children are listed with other parent
(c) **Frances Crofts** (1589 – Mar 1661)
   =1 ...; **Sir John Crompton** (...)
   =2 ...; **Edmund Poley** (...)
   issue ?
(d) **Sir Henry Crofts** (ca.1590 – Mar 1667) Kt 1611
   =1 1 Nov 1610; **Elizabeth Wortley** (... – Sep 1642)
   daughter of Sir Richard Wortley & Elizabeth Boughton
   =2 ...; **Margaret ...** (... – 26 Mar 1674)
   Has further generations of issue
(e) **Samuel Crofts** (...)
(f) **Anthony Crofts** (ca.1593 – 1 Oct 1657)
   = 16 Jul 1633; **Mary Franklin** (... – 1678) daughter of
   Richard Franklin
   has issue: 3 sons
(g) **Edmund Crofts** (...)
(h) **Jane Crofts** (...)
   = Jul 1616; **Sir Humphrey Mildmay** (...)
   issue ?
(i) **Mary Crofts** (bef.Oct 1597 – ...)
   = Dec 1629; **Sir Christopher Abdy** (...)
   issue ?
(j) **John Crofts** (Dec 1598 – 1664)
(l) **Dorothea Crofts** (... – 1659)
   = ca.1615; **Sir John Bennett** (...)
   Has further generations of issue
(l) **Arabella Crofts** (...)
   = ...; **Sir William Bryers** (...)
   issue ?
(m) **Alice Crofts** (1608 – 7 Oct 1678)
   = 1629; **Sir Owen Smith** (...)
   issue ?
(2) **Sir Henry Crofts** (25 Apr 1565 – 1609) Kt. 1603
   = ...; **Angel Guest** (...)
   issue ?
(3) **Francis Crofts** (30 Mar 1567 – Nov 1638)
   = 27 Feb 1594; **Margaret Rampley** (... – Apr 1642)
   daughter of Reynold Rampley

(a) **Thomas Crofts** (bef.16 Jun 1597 – aft. 1634)
(b) **Anthony Crofts** (bef.24 Aug 1598 – ...)
(c) **Francis Crofts** (bef.22 Jul 1599 – ...)
    = ...; **Ann Suthey** (...)
    issue ?
(d) **Susan Crofts** (bef.14 May 1602 – ...)
(e) **Ann Crofts** (bef.23 Oct 1604 – 1653)
    = 26 May 1636; **Lionel Bacon** (...)
    issue ?
(f) **John Crofts** (bef.14 Nov 1605 – aft. 4 Jan 1665)
(g) **William Crofts** (bef.21 Dec 1606 – Feb 1663/4)
    = ...
    Has further generations of issue
(h) **Elizabeth Crofts** (bef.25 Aug 1608 – ...)
(i) **Charles Crofts** (bef.10 Oct 1610 – ...)
(j) **Mary Crofts** (bef.29 Sep 1611 – ...)
(k) **Edmund Crofts** (bef.7 Nov 1615 – 1666)
    = ...; **Margaret ...** (...)
    issue ?
(l) **Benjamin Crofts** (1 Nov 1617 – aft.1666)
    = ...; **Rebecca Hurleston** (...)
    issue ?
(4) **William Crofts** (bef.21 Apr 1568 – bef.1612)
= 19 Dec 1599; **Jane Poley** (...) daughter of William Poley;
she =1st ... Powell
(a) **William Crofts** (bef.28 Sep 1600 – ...)
(b) **Jane Crofts** (bef.17 Jan1600/1 – 1632)
(c) **John Crofts** (bef.21 Oct 1604 – May 1676)
(5) **Anne Crofts** (bef.18 Jun 1569 – 1634)
= 22 Apr 1588; **Sir Richard Gresham** (...)
issue ?
(6) **Robert Crofts** (bef.4 Jan 1571/2 – 22 Apr 1623)
(7) **Edmund Crofts** (bef.10 Jan 1572/3 – ...)
(8) **Elizabeth Crofts** (bef.25 Apr 1575 – ...)
= 1594; **Anthony Penning** (...)
issue ?
(9) **Susan Crofts** (bef.9 Feb 1576/7 – ...)
= 27 Sep 1597; **Sir Robert Barker KB** (...)
issue ?
(10) **Dorothea Crofts** (bef.4 Feb 1580/1 – ...)
b) **Richard Wentworth** (...)
c) **Philip Wentworth** (...)
d) **Anne Wentworth** (...)
e) **Elizabeth Wentworth** (...)
f) **Margery Wentworth** (...)
    = ...; **Christopher Glemham** (...)

(I) **Sir Thomas Glemham** (... – 1571)
  = ...; **Amy Parker** (1534 – Oct 1571) daughter of Sir Henry
  Parker & Grace Newport
  (A) **Sir Henry Glemham** (... – 30 Aug 1632) Kt 1591
    = ...; ◆**Lady Anne Sackville** (...) daughter of Thomas
    Sackville, 1ˢᵗ Earl of Dorset & Cecily Baker
    (1) **Anne Glemham** (... – 10 Jan 1638/9)
      =1 bef.1613; **Sir Paul Bayning, 1ˢᵗ Viscount Bayning of
      Sudbury**, Baron Bayning, 1ˢᵗ Baronet (bef.28 Apr 1588
      London – 29 Jul 1629 London) son of Paul Bayning &
      Susanna Norden; cr.Baronet 24 Sep 1611 and Viscount,
      etc. 8 May 1627/8
      =2 14 Jun 1630; **Dudley Carleton, Viscount Dorchester
      and Carleton** (1573 – 15 Feb 1631/2) son of Anthony
      Carleton; cr. Viscount Carleton 22 May 1626 and Viscount
      Dorchster 25 Jul 1628; both beame extinct upon his death
      issue of 1ˢᵗ (none by 2ⁿᵈ):
      (a) **Sir Paul Bayning, 2ⁿᵈ Viscount Bayning**, etc. (ca.
        1616 – 11 Jun 1638 Little Bentley Hall, Essex) suc. father
        1629; titles became extinct upon his death
        = 25 Aug 1624 Hitcham, Suffolk; **Penelope Naunton**
        (bef.2 Oct 1620 London – bef.1647 London) daughter of
        Sir Robert Naunton & Penelope Perrot; =2ⁿᵈ ◆Philip
        Herbert, 5ᵗʰ Earl of Pembroke
        Has further generations of issue (extinct 1659)
      (b) **Anne Bayning, (life) Viscountess Bayning of Foxley**
        (bef.23 Apr 1619 London – Oct 1678) cr. Viscountess 17
        Mar 1673/4
        =1 26 Nov 1635 London; **Henry Murray** (... – bef.May 1673)
        =2 1 Aug 1674; **Sir John Baber** (ca.1625 – Mar 1704)
      (c) **Hon. Cecilia Bayning** (...)
        = bef.1630; ◆**Henry Pierrepont, Marquess of
        Dorchester** (1607–1980)
        Children are listed with other parent
      (d) **Hon. Mary Bayning** (ca.1623 – bef.20 Jan 1671/2)
        =1 1639; ◆**William Villiers, 2ⁿᵈ Viscount Grandison**
        (1614–1643)
        =2 25 Apr 1648; **Charles Villiers, 2ⁿᵈ Earl of Anglesey**,
        Baron Daventree (ca.1627 – Feb 1660/1) son of
        Christopher Villers, 1ˢᵗ Earl of Anglesey & Elizbaeth
        Sheldon; suc. father 3 Apr 1630; titles sbecamew extinct
        upon his death
        =3 aft.1661; **Arthur Gorges** (... – 18 Apr 1668) son of
        Sir Arthur Gorges
        issue of 1ˢᵗ (none by others):
        Children are listed with other parent

(e) **Elizabeth Bayning, (life) Countess of Shepley** (1624 –
1686) cr. Countess 6 Sep 1680
=1 1641; ♦**Francis Lennard, 14th Baron Dacre** (1619–1662)
=2 ...; **David Walter** (...)
issue of 1st (none by 2nd):
Children are listed with other parent
(2) **Elizabeth Glemham** (...)
= ...; **Thomas Cressy** (...)
(a) **Anne Cressy** (ca.1644 – 11 Jan 1725/6)
= 1662; **Sir Thomas Parkyns, 1st Baronet** (bef.7 Jul
1639 – 15 Jul 1684) son of Isham Parkyns & Katherine
Cave; cr. Baronet 18 May 1681
[I] **Sir Thomas Parkyns, 2nd Baronet** (bef.10 Nov
1662 – 29 Mar 1741) suc. father 1684
=1 ...; **Elizabeth Sampson** (... – Dec 1727) daughter of
John Sampson
=2 7 Feb 1727/8; **Jane Barnat** (1707 – 27 Aug 1740)
Has issue by both born after 1700
(3) **Sir Thomas Glemham** (... – 1649 in the Netherlands)
= ...; **Catherine Vanlore** (... – ca.1627) daughter of Sir Peter
Vanlore
(a) **Thomas Glemham** (...)
= ...; **Elizabeth Knyvett** (bef.1658 – bef.1711) daughter
of Sir John Knyvett & Mary Bedingfield
Has further generations of issue
(4) **Henry Glemham** (1603 – 1670)
g) **Dorothy Wentworth** (...)
h) **Thomasine Wentworth** (...)
2) **Elizabeth Wentworth** (... – aft.22 Sep 1545)
=1 ...; **Sir Roger Darcy** (... – 30 Sep 1508)
=2 ...; ♦**Sir Thomas Wyndham** (... – 1522)
=3 ...; **John Bourchier, 1st Earl of Bath**, 11th Lord FitzWarin (20
Jul 1470 – 30 Apr 1639) son of Fulk Bourchier, 10th Lord
FitzWarin & Elizabeth Dinham; =1st Cicely Daubenay; =2nd
Florence Bonville; suc. father 16 Sep 1479; cr. Earl 9 Jul 1536
issue of 2nd (none by others):
Children are listed with other parent
3) **Margaret Wentworth** (ca.1478 – 18 Oct 1550)
= 22 Oct 1494 Savernake Forest, Wilts.; **Sir John Seymour** (1476 – 21
Dec 1536) son of John Seymour & Elizabeth Darell; Kt. 1497
a) **John Seymour** (... – 15 Jul 1510) unm.
b) **Edward Seymour, 1st Duke of Somerset**, Earl of Hereford,
Viscount Beauchamp **KG** (ca.1500 – 22 Jan 1552 London)
executed; cr. Viscount 5 Jun 1536. Earl 18 Oct 1537, and Duke
16 Feb 1547; KG 1541; titles were forfeited 1552
=1 1527; **Catherine Fillol** (ca.1507 – 1535) daughter of Sir William

Fillol
=2 bef.9 Mar 1535; ◆**Anne Stanhope** (ca.1510 – 1587)
daughter of Sir Edward Stanhope & Elizabeth Bourchier
issue of 1st:79
(I) **Lord John Seymour** (1527 – 19 Dec 1552 London)
  died in prison; unm.
(II) **Lord Edward Seymour, Kt.** (ca.1528 – 2 May 1593) Kt. 1547
  = 1563; **Margaret Walshe** (...) daughter of John Walshe
  (A) **Sir Edward Seymour, 1st Baronet** (ca.1563 Berry
    Pomeroy Castle, Devon. – 10 Apr 1613) cr. Baronet 29 Jun 1611
    = 19 Sep 1576; **Elizabeth Champernowne** (...) daughter of
    Sir Arthur Champernowne
    (1) **Bridget Seymour** (ca.1577 – ...)
      = ...; **Sir John Bruen** (ca.1577 – 28 Mar 1639) son of
      Henry Bruen & Elizabeth Martin
      no issue
    (2) **Sir Edward Seymour, 2nd Baronet** (bef.1580 – 5 Oct
      1659) suc. father 1613
      = 15 Dec 1600 London; **Dorothy Killigrew** (... – 1643)
      (a) **Sir Edward Seymour, 3rd Baronet** (10 Sep 1610 – 7
        Dec 1688) suc. father 1659
        = ca.1630; **Anne Portman** (1609 – 1695) daughter of Sir
        John Portman, 1st Baronet & Ann Gifford
        Has further generations of issue
      (b) **Henry Seymour** (1612 – 9 Mar 1686)
      (c) **Thomas Seymour** (...)
      (d) **Elizabeth Seymour** (... – bef.6 Feb 1664)
        =1 ...; ◆**Francis Courtenay** (1576 – 1638)
        =2 ...; **Sir Amos Meredith, 1st Baronet** (ca.1600 – 3 Sep
        1669) cr. Baronet 13 Aug 1622
        issue of 1st (none by 2nd):
        Children are listed with other parent
      (e) **Mary Seymour** (...)
        = ...; **Sir Jonathan Trelawny, 2nd Baronet** (ca.1623 – 5
        Mar 1681) son of Sir John Trelawny, 1st Baronet &
        Elizabeth Mohun; suc. father 24 Apr 1592
        Has further generations of issue
      (f) **Margaret Seymour** (...)

---

79 Seymour doubted the paternity of his two elder children after discovering his wife had an ongoing affair. When the Dukedom was created, the remainder was to his children by his 2nd wife, and could only be inherited by the issue of the Catherine if Anne's issue became extinct in the male line, which happened in 1750.

(3) **Mary Seymour** (ca.1580 – 1661 Bishops Hull, Som.)
= ...; **Sir George Farewell** (1579 Taunton, Som. – 12 May
1647 Bishops Hull) son of George Farewell & Philippa Parker
(a) **John Farewell** (... – 5 Sep 1637 Boston, Lincs.)
= ...; **Dorothy Routh** (...)
Has further generations of issue[80]
(b) **Margaret Farewell** (...)
= ...; **John Relf** (...)
Has further generations of issue
(4) **Elizabeth Seymour** (1588 – 1643)
= ...; **George Carey** (1587 – Jul 1643) son of John Carey
(a) **Rev. Robert Cary** (1614 – 1688)
(b) **Sir Henry Cary** (bef.1616 – ...)
= ...; **Amy Bagg** (1 Jan 1616 Plymouth, Devon – bef.16
Jun 1652) daughter of Sir James Bagg & Grace Fortescue
Has further generations of issue
(c) **Theodore Cary** (... – 1683)
= ...; **Dorothy Wade** (...)
issue ?
(5) **Amy Seymour** (... – ca.1639)
= ...; ◆**Edmund Parker** (ca.1593 – 1649)
Children are listed with other parent
(6) **John Seymour** (...)
(7) **Walter Seymour** (... – 1622)
(8) **Richard Seymour** (... – 1665)
issue of 2nd:
(III) **Edward Seymour, 1st Earl of Hertford**, 1st Baron
Beauchamp (22 May 1539 – 6 Apr 1621) cr. Earl 13 Jan 1558/9
=1 ca.Nov 1560 (ann.1561); ◆**Lady Catherine Grey** (Aug
1540 London – 26 Jan 1568 Yocford, Sussex) daughter of Henry
Grey, 1st Duke of Suffolk & Lady Frances Brandon; =1st
◆Henry Herbert, 2nd Earl of Pembroke
=2 ...; ◆**Hon. Frances Howard** (27 Jul 1578 – 8 Oct 1639
London) daughter of Thomas Howard, 1st Viscount Howard &
Mabel Burton; =1st Henry Parnell; =3rd ◆Ludovic Stuart, 2nd
Duke of Lennox
issue of 1st (none by 2nd):
(A) **Edward, Lord Beauchamp** (21 Sep 1561 London – 13
Jul 1612 Wick, Wilts.)

---

[80] Jonathan's only known son went the American colonies and his descendants settled in
Ontario, Canada. There may also be one more generation missing between the Jonathan
shown and the one who went to America.

= bef.1 Jul 1582; **Honora Rogers** (... – aft.28 Feb 1608) daughter of Sir Richard Rogers & Cecilia Luttrel

(1) **Hon. Honora Seymour** (... – Mar 1620)
   = 1610; ♦**Hon. Sir Ferdinando Dudley KB** (1588 – 1621) Children are listed with other parent

(2) **Hon. Edward** Beauchamp **Seymour** (12 Jun 1586 – Sep 1618)

(3) **William Seymour, 2ⁿᵈ Duke of Somerset**, etc., 1ˢᵗ Marquess of Marquess, 2ⁿᵈ Earl of Hertford, etc. (1588 – 24 Oct 1660 London) suc. grandfather 1621; cr. Marquess 3 Jun 1641; restored to the forfeited Dukedom, etc. 1660
   =1 (secretly) 22 Jun 1610; ♦**Lady Arabella Stuart** (ca.1577 – 27 Sep 1615 London[81]) daughter of Charles Stuart, 1ˢᵗ Earl of Lennox & Elizabeth Cavendish
   =2 3 Mar 1616/7 Drayton Bassett, Staffs.; ♦**Lady Frances Devereux** (20 Sep 1599 London – 23 Nov 1679) daughter of Robert Devereux, 2ⁿᵈ Earl of Essex & Frances Walsingham issue by 2ⁿᵈ (none by 1ˢᵗ):
   (a) **Lady Frances Seymour** (... – bef.1685)
      =1 28 Oct 1652; ♦**Richard Molyneux, 2ⁿᵈ Viscount Molyneux** (... – 1654) son of Richard, 1ˢᵗ Viscount Molyneux; suc. father 8 May 1636
      =2 7 May 1659; ♦**Thomas Wriothesley, 4ᵗʰ Earl of Southampton**, etc. (1607 – 16 May 1667) son of Henry Wriothesely, 3ʳᵈ Earl of Southampton & Elizabeth Vernon; =1ˢᵗ Rachel de Massue; =2ⁿᵈ Lady Elizabeth Leigh; suc. father 10 Nov 1625
      =3 1676; ♦**Conyers Darcy 2ⁿᵈ Earl of Holderness**, etc. (3 Mar 1621/2 – 13 Dec 1692) son of Conyers Darcy, 1ˢᵗ Earl of Holderness & Grace Rokesby; =1ˢᵗ ♦Lady Catherine Fane; =2ⁿᵈ ♦Lady Frances Howard; =4ᵗʰ Elizabeth Frescheville; suc. father 14 Jun 1689 no issue
   (b) **William, Lord Beauchamp** (1621 – 16 Jun 1642)
   (c) **Robert, Lord Beauchamp** (1622 – 1645/6)
   (d) **Henry, Lord Beauchamp** (1626 – 30 Mar 1654/5)
      = 28 Jun 1648; ♦**Hon. Mary Capell** (16 Dec 1630 Hadham Parva, Herts. – 7 Jan 1714/5 London) daughter of Arthur Capell, 1ˢᵗ Baron Capell & Elizabeth Morrison;

---

[81] She died imprisoned in the Tower of London since 1610, where she was driven mad. She was imprisoned with her husband for entering into a secret marriage against the King's wishes. They had escaped independently in 1611 and planned to meet up, but she was captured. He got away and was eventually pardoned.

she =2nd ♦Henry Somerset, 1st Duke of Beaufort
Has further generations of issue

  (e) **John Seymour, 4th Duke of Somerset**, etc. (... – 29
     Apr 1675) suc. nephew 1671
     = 1656; **Sarah Alston** (1642 – 2 Nov 1692) dasu. of Sir
     Edward Alston; =2nd Henry Hare, 2nd Baron Coleraine
     no issue

  (f) **Lady Mary Seymour** (6 Jul 1637 – bef.10 Apr 1673) (twin)
     = bef.1649; ♦**Heneage Finch, 3rd Earl of Winchilsea**
     (1627 – 1689)
     Children are listed with other parent

  (g) **Lady Jane Seymour** (6 Jul 1637 – 23 Nov 1679) (twin)
     = 7 May 1661; ♦**Charles Boyle, 2nd Baron Clifford of
     Lanesborough** (1639 – 1694)
     Children are listed with other parent

  (4) **Francis Seymour, 1st Baron Seymour** (ca.1590 – 12 Jul
     1664) cr. Baron 19 Feb 1641
     =1 1620; **Frances Prinne** (... – bef.1635) daughter of Sir
     Gilbert Prinne
     =2 1635; **Catherine Lee** (... – 1700/1 daughter of Sir Robert
     Lee & Anne Lowe
     issue of 1st (none by 2nd):

    (a) **Charles Seymour, 2nd Baron Seymour** (ca.1621 – 25
      Aug 1665) suc. father 1664
      =1 4 Aug 1632; **Mary Smith** (... – bef.1654) daughter of
      Thomas Smith
      =2 1654; **Hon. Elizabeth Alington** (1632 – 1691) daughter of
      William Alington, 1st Baron Alington & Elizabeth Tollemache
      Has further generations of issue

    (b) **Hon. Frances Seymour** (1652 – ca.Sep 1679)
      = 23 Jun 1662; **William Ducie, Viscount Downe**, Baron
      of Cloney, 3rd Baronet **KB** (... – 9 Sep 1679) son of Sir
      Robert Ducie, 1st Baronet & Frances Prinne; suc. brother
      as Baronet 7 Mar 1756/7; cr. Viscount and Baron 19 Jul
      1675 but they becamwe extinct upon his death; KB 1661
      no issue

 (B) **Hon. Thomas Seymour** (Feb 1563 London – 20 Aug
   1619)
   = ...; **Isabella Onley** (...) daughter of Edward Onley
   no issue

(IV) **Lady Anne Seymour** (... – 1588)
   =1 3 Jun 1550; ♦**John, Earl of Warwick** (... – 21 Oct 1554)
   son of John Dudley, 1st Duke of Northumberland & Jane Guilford
   =2 1555; ♦**Sir Edward Unton KB** (...)
   issue of 2nd (none by 1st):
   Children are listed with other parent

(V) **Lord Henry Seymour** (ca.1540 Wulfhall, Wilts. – 1588)
  = ...; ♦**Lady Jane Percy** (...) daughter of Thomas Percy, 1ˢᵗ Earl of
  Northumberland & Lady Jane Somerset
  no issue
(VI) **Lady Margaret Seymour** (1543 Wulfhall – ...) unm.
(VII) **Lady Jane Seymour** (1541 – 22 Oct 1605
  Sawbridgeworth, Herts.) unm.
(VIII) **Lady Mary Seymour** (...)
(X) **Lady Elizabeth Seymour** (ca.1552 – 3 Jun 1602)
  = aft.1573; **Sir Richard Knightley** (1534 – 1615) son of Sir
  Valentine Knightley & Anne Ferrers; =1ˢᵗ Mary Fermor;
  Kt.1565
  (A) **Sir Seymour Knightley** (1580 – 1640)[82]
    = ...; **Dorothy Bedell** (1584 Hamerton, Huntingdons. –
    1635) daughter of Sir John Bedell & Mathilda Lane
    (1) **Robert Knightley** (1602 – ...)
      = ...; **Ellen York** (...)
      (a) **Mary Knightley** (1665 – ...)
        = ...; **Pierce Manaton** (... – 1678)
        Has further generations of issue
    (2) **Elizabeth Knightley** (...)
      = ...; **... Chamberlin** (...)
      (a) **Elizabeth Chamberlin** (1625 – ...)
        = ...; **Thomas Ford** (1606 – ...)
        Has further generations of issue
c) **Sir Henry Seymour** (ca.1501 Machen, Monmouths. – 5 Apr
  1578 Winchester, Hants.)
  = ...; **Barbara Wolfe** (ca.1515 – ...) daughter of Morgan Wolfe
  (I) **John Seymour** (1540 Machen – ...)
    = ...; ♦**Susan Paulett** (1542 Monmouths. – ...) daughter of Lord
    Chidlock Paulett & Elizabeth White
    (A) **Edward Seymour** (1566 Monmouths. – ...)
      = ...
      (1) **Edward Seymour** (...)
        = ...
        (a) **John Seymour** (... – aft.1720 co. Limerick)
          = ...; **Jane Wroughton** (...) daughter of Seymour Wroughton
          Has further generations of issue
        (b) **William Seymour** (...)
          = ...

---

[82] Sir Seymour reportedly has 13 brothers and sisters, but appears to be the only one to leave issue and is the only child by Elizabeth to be named in any source the author has found.

Has further generations of issue
(B) **John Seymour** (1568 Monmouths. – ...)
(C) **Thomas Seymour** (1570 Monmouths. – ...)
(D) **Elizabeth Seymour** (1572 Mnmouths. – ...)
= ...; ♦**William Paulett** (1570 – ...)
Children are listed with other parent
(II) **Jane Seymour** (ca.1542 Machen – 15 Feb 1634)
= ...; **Sir John Rodney** (ca.1540 Rodney Stoke, Som. – 6 Aug
1612 Morelinch, Som.) son of Sir George Rodney & Elizabeth
Kirton; Kt.1603
(A) **Sir Edward Rodney** (29 Jun 1590 – 25 May 1657)
Kt.1614
= 29 May 1614; ♦**Frances Southwell** (... – 3 Aug 1659)
daughter of Sir Robert Southwell & Lady Elizabeth Howard
(1) **Elizabeth Rodney** (...)
(2) **Anna** Frances **Rodney** (1620 – ...)
= ...; **Thomas Brydges** (1617 Keynsham, Som. – 20 Feb
1705) son of Edward Brydges & Philippa Speke
(a) **Harry Brydges** (...)
=1 ...; ♦**Lady Diana Holles** (...) daughter of John Holles, 2nd
Earl of Clare & Hon. Elizabeth de Vere; =1st John
Mitchell
=2 ...; **... Freeman** (...)
issue of 1st:
Has further generations of issue
(b) **George** Rodney **Brydges** (...)
= 24 Jun 1677; ♦**Lady Anna Maria Brudenell** (1664 –
1702) daughter of Robert Brudenell, 2nd Earl of Cadigan &
Anne Savage; =1st ♦Francis Talbot, 11th Earl of
Shrewsbury
(3) **Penelope Rodney** (... – 17 Feb 1689)
= ca.1650; **Sir Peter Gleane, 1st Baronet** (1619 – 1695) son of
Thomas Gleane & Elizabeth Brewse; cr. Baronet 6 Mar 1665/6
(a) **Sir Thomas Gleane, 2nd Baronet** (1652 – ca.1700)
suc. father 1695
=1 24 Oct 1671 Oby, Norfolk; **Anne Mapes** (... – 6 Jan 1680/1)
=2 11 Dec 1683; **Frances Chamberlayne** (...)
Has further generations of issue
(b) **Rodney Gleane** (aft.1652 – ...) unm.
(c) **Frances Cleane** (...)
= 1684 Great Belings, Suffolk; **John Pullin** (...)
Has further generations of issue
(B) **George Rodney** (1608 – 1630)
= ...; **Ann Lake** (...) daughter of Sir Thomas Lake & Mary
Ryder; =1st ♦William Cecil, 16th Lord de Ros
(1) **Anthony Rodney** (...)

= ...; **Constantia Clark** (...)

(a) **Henry Rodney** (1681 – 1737)
= ...; **Mary Newton** (...) daughter of Sir Henry Newton
Has further generations of issue

(C) **William Rodney** (1610 Moorlich – 12 Jun 1669 Huntspill)
= ...; **Alice Caesar** (ca. 1611 – ...) daughter of Sir Thomas Caesar
& Susan Ryder

(1) **William Rodney** (21 Jun 1637 Catcott, Som. – Jan 1679
Huntsfield, Som.)
= ...; **Rachel ...** (1630 – May 1708 Bristol, Som.)

(a) **William Rodney** (ca.4 Mar 1652 Bristol – 8 Apr 1708 PA)
=1 ...; **Mary Hollyman** (ca.1671 Bristol – 20 Dec 1692
Kent Co. Delaware) daughter of Thomas Hollyman & Sarah Pease
=2 ...; **Sarah Jones** (1654 – 1709)
Has further generations of issue[83]

(D) **Jane Rodney** (1584 – ...)
= 1612; **John Trenchard** (ca.1586 Warmwell, Dorset – 11
Oct 1662) son of Sir George Trechard & Anne Speke

(1) **Frances Trenchard** (ca.1613 Warwell – ...)
= ...; **John Bingham** (1610 Melcombe, Dorset – ca.1675)
son of Richard Bingham & Jane Hopton
issue ?

(E) **Elizabeth Rodney** (... – aft.1649)
= ...; **James Kirton** (1555 – ...)

(1) **Seymour Kirton** (1607 – 15 Oct 1661)
= ...; **Lucy Southcott** (1618 – ...)

(a) **Jane Kirton** (1652 – ...)
= ...; **Edward Collins** (1650 – 1714)
Has further generations of issue

d) **Thomas Seymour, Baron Seymour of Sudeley KG** (1508
Wulfhall – 20 Mar 1549 London) executed; cr. Baron 1547 but
the title went extenct up on his death
= ca.May 1547 (secretly); ◆**Katherine Parr** (then **Dowager
Queen of England** (1512 – 5 Sep 1548 Winchcombe, Glos.)
daughter of Sir Thomas Parr & Maud Green; =1st Sir Edward Burgh;
she =2nd ◆John Neville, 3rd Baron Latymer; =3rd ◆Henry VIII,
King of England
no surviving issue

e) **Jane Seymour** (1509/10 Wulfhall – 24 Oct 1537 Whatehall
Palace, London)

---

[83] Including Caesar Rodney (1728-1784), who was a signer of the Declaration of
Independence.

= 1536; ♦**Henry VIII, King of England** (1491– 1547)
Children are listed with other parent
f) **Elizabeth Seymour** (ca.1518 – 19 Mar 1568)
=1 1531; **Sir Anthony Ughtred** (ca.1478 Kexby, Yorks. – 6 Oct 1534
Jersey) son of Sir Robert Ughtred & Katherine Eure; =1st Eleanor ...
=2 bef.1538; **Gregory Cromwell, 1st Baron Cromwell**
(ca.1520 – 4 Jul 1551 Launde, Leics.) son of Thomas Cromwell,
Earl of Essex & Elizabeth Wykes; cr. Baron 15 Dec 1540
=3 1554; ♦**John, Lord St.John** (ca.1510 – 4 Nov 1576
London) son of William Paulet, 1st Marquess of Winchester &
Elizabeth Capel; =1st Elizabeth Willoughby
issue of 1st:
(I) **Sir Henry Ughtred** (1533 Jersey – Oct 1598 Munster,
   Ireland[84]) Kt 1593
   =1 ca.1558; ♦**Lady Elizabeth Paulet** (ca.1536 – 4 Nov 1576)
   daughter of John Paulet, 2nd Marquess of Winchester & Elizabeth
   Willoughby; =1st ♦Sir William Courtney
   =2 ...
   no issue
(II) **Margery Ughtred** (ca.1534 – ...)
   = ...; **William Hungate** (...)
   (A) **William Hungate** (...)
   (B) **Leonard Hungate** (...)
issue of 2nd (none by 3rd):
(III) **Henry Cromwell, 2nd Baron Cromwell** (... – 20 Nov
   1592) suc. father 1551
   = bef.1560; ♦**Lady Mary Paulet** (... – 10 Oct 1592) daughter of
   John Paulet, 2nd Marquess of Winchester & Elizabeth Willoughby
   (A) **Edward Cromwell, 3rd Baron Cromwell** (ca.1560 Launde
      Abbey, Leics. – 27 Apr 1607 Downpatrick, co. Down) suc. father 1592
      =1 1581; **Elizabeth Umpton** (... – 5 Jan 1592/3) daughter of
      William Umpton & Mary Kirkham
      =2 ca.1593; **Frances Rugge** (... – bef.30 Nov 1631) daughter of
      William Rugge & Thomasine Townshend
      issue of 1st:
      (1) **Hon. Elizabeth Cromwell** (...)
         =1 ca.1597; **Sir John Shelton** (21 Dec 1559 – bef. 1606)
         son of Sir Ralph Shelton & Mary Wodehouse; =1st Joan Maleverer
         =2 ...; **Thomas FitzHughes** (...)
         issue ?

---

[84] Sir Henry and Lady Ughtred fled their home from appraching rebels 5 Oct 1598 and were
never heard from again. It is believed they died in their flight.

issue of 2nd:

(2) **Thomas Cromwell, 1st Earl of Ardglass**, Viscount
Lecale, 4th Baron Cromwell (11 Jun 1594 – 20 Nov 1653
Tickencote, Rutland) suc. father 1607; cr. Viscount 22
Nov 1624, and Earl 15 Apr 1645
= ...; **Elizabeth Meverell** (... – 1563) daughter of Robert
Meverell & Elizabeth Fleming

  (a) **Lady Mary Cromwell** (... – 8 Apr 1676)
    = ...; **William FitzHerbert** (ca.1626 – 24 Jun 1697) son
    of Sir John FitzHerbert & Elizabeth FitzHerbert; =2nd
    Anne Breton
    no issue

  (b) **Wingfield Cromwell, 2nd Earl of Ardglass**, etc. (12
    Sep 1624 Throwleigh, Staffs.– 3 Oct 1668) suc. father 1653
    = ...; **Mary Russell** (bef.1634 – aft.12 Sep 1687) daughter of
    William Russell, 1st Baronet & Frances Reade
    Has further generations of issue

  (c) **Vere** Essex **Cromwell, 4th Earl of Ardglass**, etc. (2
    Oct 1625 Ilam, Staffs. – 26 Nov 1687 Booncastle, co.
    Down) suc. nephew 1682; upon his death, all titles
    became extinct
    = 1672; **Catherine Hamilton** (...) daughter of James
    Hamilton & Margaret Kynaston; =1st Richard Price
    Has further generations of issue

(3) **Hon. Frances Cromwell** (1595 – 25 Jun 1662)
= 30 Jan 1619; **Sir John Wingfield** (ca.1595 – 25 Dec
1631) son of John Wingfield & Elizabeth Gresham; =1st Jane Turpin

  (a) **John Wingfield** (25 Jun 1623 – 30 Dec 1678 London)
    = ...; **Mary Owen** (1645 London – 31 Jan 1714 London)
    daughter of George Owen & Rebecca Darrell
    Has further generations of issue

  (b) **Francis Wingfield** (1628 – 1677)
    =1 bef.1660; **Anne Palmer** (...) daughter of Anthony Palmer
    =2 bef.1668; **Lucy ...** (...)
    Has further generations of issue

  (c) **Elizabeth Wingfield** (1626 – ...)
    = ...; **Thomas Chybnall** (...)
    issue ?

  (d) **Richard Wingfield** (1619 – 1663)
    =1 ...; ♦**Elizabeth Thorold** (...) daughter of Sir William
    Thorold, 1st Baronet &Anne Blythe
    =2 ...; **Elizabeth Lee** (... – 1686)
    Has further generations of issue

  (e) **Charles Wingfield** (...)

(4) **Hon. Anne Cromwell** (... – 11 Jul 1636)
= ...; **Sir Edward Wingfield** (... – 22 Ape 1638) son of

Richard Wingfield & Honora O'Brien
- (a) **Lewis Wingfield** (1620 – aft.1 Sep 1673 Sligo, Ireland)
  = ...; **Sydney Gore** (... – 1677) daughter of Sir Paul Gore, 1st
  Baronet (of Magherabegg) & Isabella Wycliffe
  Has further generations of issue
- (b) **Richard Wingfield** (... – 1644/5)
  = 7 May 1640; **Hon. Elizabeth Folliott** (...) daughter of
  Henry Folliott, 1st Baron Folliott & Anne Strode; =2nd
  Edward Trevor; =3rd Sir John Ponsonby
  Has further generations of issue (extinct 1717)
- (c) **Frances Wingfield** (...) unm.
- (B) **Hon. Sir Gregory Cromwell** (ca.1561 – ...)
  = ...; **Frances Griffin** (...)
  no issue
- (C) **Hon. Katherine Cromwell** (ca.1562 – 24 Mar 1620)
  = 10 Feb 1580/1 North Elmham, Norfolk; **Sir Lionel
  Tollemache, 1st Baronet** (bap.14 Dec 1562 Helmingham,
  Suffolk – aft.1617) son of Lionel Tollemache & Susanna
  Jermyn; cr. Baronet 22 May 1611
  - (1) **Sir Lionel Tollemache, 2nd Baronet** (1 Aug 1591
    Helmingham – 6 Sep 1640 Tilbury, Essex) suc. father
    aft.1617
    = 16 Dec 1612 London; **Hon. Elizabeth Stanhope** (... –
    ca.1661) daughter of John Stanhope, 1st Baron Stanhope &
    Margaret MacWilliams
    - (a) **Bridget Tollemache** (... – 1674)
      = 10 Sep 1650 Great Fakenham; **Sir Nicholas Bacon**
      (ca.1630 Shrubland, Suffolk – ...)
      Has further generations of issue
    - (b) **Jane Tollemache** (...)
      = ...; **Thomas Cholmondeley** (1627 – ...) son of Thomas
      Cholmondeley & Elizabeth Minshull; =2nd Anne St.John
      Has further generations of issue
    - (c) **Anne Tollemache** (... – bef.1685)
      = ...; **Sir Robert Brooke, Baronet** (ca.1630 – 25 Feb
      1693/4) son of Sir Richard Brooke & Mary Pakington;
      he =2nd Martha Thomlinson; cr. Baronet 21 May 1661 but
      it became extinct upon his death
      Has further generations of issue
    - (d) **Susannah Tollemache** (Sep 1621 Helmingham – ...)
      = ...; **Sir Henry Felton, 2nd Baronet** (27 Jul 1619 –
      1690) son of Sir Henry Felton, 1st Baronet & Dorothy
      Bacon; suc. father 18 Sep 1624
      Has further generations of issue
    - (e) **Sir Lionel Tollemache, 3rd Baronet** (ca.1623
      Helmingham – Mar 1669 Helmingham) suc. father 1640

= ca.1647; **Elizabeth Murray, (2ⁿᵈ) Countess of Dysart**, Lady Huntingtower (1626 Petersham, Surrey – 4 Jun 1698 Petersham) daughter of William Murray, 1ˢᵗ Earl of Dysart & Catherine Bruce; =2ⁿᵈ John Maitland, Duke of Lauderdale; suc. father Sep 1653
Has further generations of issue
 (f) **John Tollemache** (...)
 (2) **Elizabeth Tollemache** (1593 – 1662)
 = ...; **William Davenly** (1585 – 1641) son of William Davenly
 (a) **Sir William Davenly** (1616 – 1689) Kt 1662
 = ...; **Mary Appleton** (...) daughter of Sir Henry Appleton, 2ⁿᵈ Baronet & Joan Sheldon
Has further generations of issue
 (3) **Susan Tollemache** (...)
 = ...; ♦**Sir Henry d'Oyly** (...)
Children are listed with other parent
(IV) **Hon. Thomas Cromwell** (... – 1592)
(V) **Hon. Catherine Cromwell** (1546 – ...)
= ...; **Sir John Strode** (1524 – 8 Sep 1581) son of Sir Robert Strode & Elizabeth Hody; =2 Margaret Hadley
 (A) **Sir John Strode** (1561 – 1642)
 = ...; **Anne Wyndham** (...) daughter of Sir John Wyndham & Joan Portman
 (1) **Joan Strode** (1622 – ...)
 (2) **Sir John Strode** (1624 – 1679)
 =1 ...; **Anne Hewet** (...) daughter of William Hewet
 =2 ...; ♦**Anne Browne** (10 Jul 1635 – 1711) daughter of Sir Thomas Browne, 2ⁿᵈ Baronet & Anne Palmer; =2ⁿᵈ John Poulett, 2ⁿᵈ Baron Poulett
 issue of 1ˢᵗ (none by 2ⁿᵈ):
 (a) **Elizabeth Strode** (...)
 = ...; **Sir William Oglander, 3ʳᵈ Baronet** (1680 – 1734) son of Sir John Oglander, 2ⁿᵈ Baronet & Mary Webb; suc. father 1683
Has further generations of issue
 (3) **Sir George Strode** (...)
 = ...; **Grace FitzJames** (...) daughter of Sir John FitzJames
 (a) **Grace Strode** (... – 3 Apr 1725)
 = 1695; ♦**Hon. Henry Thynne** (1640 – 1714)
Children are listed with other parent
 (4) **Thomas Strode** (1628 – 1698)
 (5) **Hugh Strode** (... – 1727)
 = ...; **Grace Rauston** (
 (a) **Grace Strode** (ca.1679 – ...)
 = ...; **Richard March** (...)

Has further generations of issue

(B) **Sir Robert Strode** (1568 – ...)
=1 ...; **Margaret Luttrell** (...)
=2 ...; **Margaret Wyndham** (ca.1574 – ...) daughter of Edmund Wyndham & Margaret Chamberlaine
issue of 1st:
 (1) **Catherine Strode** (26 Oct 1585 Beeminster, Dorset – 1608)
  = ca.1604; **Sir Richard Strode** (25 Jun 1684 Plympton, Devon – Oct 1669 Plymouth) son of Sir William Strode & Mary Southcote; =2nd Elizabeth Earle
  no surviving issue
issue of 2nd:
 (2) **Margaret Strode** (ca.1614 – 24 Dec 1647 London)
  = ...; **George Trevelyan** (ca.1614 – 1653 Som.) son of Sir John Trevillian & Margaret Luttrell
  (a) **Sir George Trevelyan, 1st Baronet** (ca.1635 – 1671)
   cr. Baronet 24 Jan 1661/2
   = 8 Jan 1655; **Mary Willoughby** (... – 28 Nov 1689) daughter of John Willoughby
   Has further generations of issue
  (b) **Francis Trevelyan** (18 Feb 1642 Nettlecombe, Som. – ...)
   = ...; **Anne Bampfield** (ca.1647 – ...) daughter of Amias Bampfield & Ann ...
   Has further generations of issue
(C) **George Strode** (ca1565 – 1648)
 = ...; **Mary Fleet** (...)
 issue ?
(D) **Edward Strode** (...)
(E) **Thomas Strode** (...)
(VI) **Hon. Frances Cromwell** (ca.1544 Putney, Surrey – 7 Feb 1562 Plymouth)
 = ...; ♦**Richard Strode** (1528 – 1581)
 Children are listed with other parent
g) **Dorothy Seymour** (ca.1516 Wulfhall – 1566 Little Baddow, Essex)
=1 ...; **Sir Clement Smith** (1507 Little Baddow – 26 Aug 1552 Little Baddow) son of Thomas Smith & Isabelle Foster
=2 ...; **Thomas Levinthorpe** (...)
issue of 1st (none by 2nd):
(I) **Dorothy Smith** (ca.1552 Little Baddow – ...)
 = ...; **Edmund Parker** (ca.1546 North Molton, Devon – 29 Aug 1635) son of John Parker & Elizabeth Ellicott
 (A) **John Parker** (... – 1610)
  = ...; **Frances Mayhew** (...) daughter of Jeronimy Mayhew
  (1) **Edmund Parker** (ca.1593 – 1649)
   = ...; ♦**Amy Seymour** (... – 1639) daughter of Sir Edward

Seymour, 1ˢᵗ Baronet & Elizabeth Champernon
(a) **William Parker** (1615 – ...)
  = ...
Has further generations of issue
(b) **Edmond Parker** (... – Oct 1691)
  = ...
  [I] **George Parker** (... – 1743)
  =1 ...; **Elizabeth Fowell** (...) daughter of Sir John Fowell,
  2ⁿᵈ Baronet & Elizabeth Chichester
  =2 ...; **Anne Buller** (...) daughter of John Buller
  Has further generations of issue
  [II] **Edmund Parker** (...)
 (2) **Thomas Parker** (ca.1594 – ...)
 (3) **John Parker** (ca.1599 – ...)
 (4) **Anne Parker** (...)
(B) **Frances Parker** (...)
(C) **Jane Parker** (...)
  = ...; **John Norleigh** (...)
  issue ?
(D) **Elizabeth Parker** (...)
  = ...; **Walter Harlewin** (...)
  issue ?
(E) **Mary Parker** (...)
  = ...; **George Drake** (...)
  issue ?
 (II) **Sir John Smith** (ca.1534 – Aug 1607 Little Baddow)
 = ...; **Mary ...** (... – 1604)
 issue ?
4) **Dorothy Wentworth** (ca.1478 Nettlestead, Suffolk – ...)
= ...; **Sir Robert Broughton KB** (ca.1466 – 17 Aug 1506
Denston, Suffolk) son of John Broughton & Anne Denston; =2ⁿᵈ
♦Katherione de Vere; KB 1478
no issue
B) **Margaret Wentworth** (ca.1446 – 28 Apr 1479 Landwade, Cambs.)
= ...; **Sir Thomas Cotton** (ca.1439 Landwade – 30 Jul 1499
Landwade) son of Sir William Cotton & Alixce Abbott; =1ˢᵗ Joan Sharpe
1) **Anne Cotton** (ca.1465 Landwade – 1525 Pondhall, Suffolk)
= ...; **Edward d'Oyly** (1465 Pondhall – 25 Jan 1535 Pondhall)
son of John d'Oyly & Elizabeth Southwell
a) **Sir Henry d'Oyley** (ca.1493 Pondhall – 13 Feb 1563 Pondhall)
=1 ...; **Margaret Howard** (1500 Norfolk – 1554 Norfolk) =1ˢᵗ
Edmund White
=2 ...; **Jane Elwyn** (ca.1509 Wigenhall, Norfolk – 1570
Shottisham, Norfolk) au. of John Elwyn & Catherine ...
issue of 1ˢᵗ:
(I) **Mary d'Oyly** (1546 Norfolk – 9 Feb 1573 Norfolk)

= ...; **Sir Robert Bedingfield** (1528 Norfolk – 5 Nov 1600 Norfolk) son of Philip Bedingfield & Agnes Yaxley; =2ⁿᵈ Elizabeth Heydon

(A) **Henry Bedingfield** (...)
  = ...; **Mary Darcy** (...) daughter of Thomas Darcy
  (1) **Sir Philip Bedingfield** (...)
    = ...; **Frances Peyton** (...)
    (a) **Mary Bedingfield** (...)
    (b) **Martha Bedingfield** (...)
      = ...; **Robert Morse** (...)
      issue ?

issue of 2ⁿᵈ:

(II) **Henry d'Oyly** (1530 Shiottisham – May 1597 Shottisham)
  = ...; (his step-sister) **Anne White** (1534 Shottisham – 6 Dec 1592 Shottisham) daughter of Edmund White & Margaret Howard
  (A) **Edmund d'Oyly** (May 1555 – 12 Oct 1612 Shottisham)
    =1 ca.1581; **Anne Goodwin** (ca.1560 Winchendon, Bucks. – bef.1585) daughter of Sir John Goodwin & Elizabeth Throckmorton
    =2 Jun 1585 Waltham, Berks.; ♦**Catherine Neville** (ca. 1565 – ...) daughter of Sir Henry Neville & Elizabeth Gresham
    issue of 2ⁿᵈ (none by 1ˢᵗ):
    (1) **William d'Oyly** (1590 Shottisham – 1637)
      = ...; **Elizabeth Stocks** (...) daughter of Ven. Richard Stocks & Anne Wodehouse
      (a) **Sir William d'Oyly, 1ˢᵗ Baronet** (1616 – 1677)
        Kt.1641; cr. Baronet 29 Jul 1663
        = 1637; **Margaret Randall** (... – May 1679)
        Has further generations of issue
    (2) **Sir Henry d'Oyly** (...)
      = ...; **Susan Tollemache** (...) daughter of Sir Lionel Tollemache, 1ˢᵗ Baronet & Katherine Cromwell
      (a) **Edmund d'Oyly** (... – 28 Sep 1638)
        = ...; ♦**Bridget Coke** (... – Oct 1700) daughter of John Coke; she =2ⁿᵈ Sir Isaac Astley, Baronet
        no surviving issue

(III) **Thomas d'Oyly** (1530 – 1585)
  = ...; **Elizabeth Bendish** (ca.1532 – ...)
  (A) **Edward d'Oyly** (1552 – ...)
    = ...; **Audrey Stanhow** (...) daughter of John Stanhow
    (1) **Anne d'Oyly** (ca,1592 Elstow, Beds. – ...)
      = ...; **William James** (ca.1588 – ...)
      (a) **William James** (ca.1614 Elstow – 13 Oct 1695 Bedford)
        = ...; **Joan Connaway** (ca.1617 – 1 Jul 1671) daughter of Leonard Connaway & Anne Wilson
        Has further generations of issue
2) **Joan Cotton** (...)

= ...; **Nicholas Sharpe** (...)
issue ?
3) **... Cotton** (a daughter) (...)
= ...; **... Crockett** (...)
issue ?
C) **Elizabeth Wentworth** (ca.1427 Nettlestead – 1480)
= ...; **Sir Martin de la See** (1420 Barnston, Yorks. – 14 Dec 1494
Barnston) son of Brian de la See & Maud Monceaux; =1st Margaret Spencer
1) **Elizabeth de la See** (ca.1442 Yorks. – ...)
= ...; **Roger Kelke** (ca.1435 Barnetby, Lincs. – ...)
a) **Christopher Kelke** (1491 Barnetby – 1 Feb 1524 Yorks.)
= ...; **Isabelle Girlington** (1495 Frodingham, Lincs. – 1 Feb
1560 Scotter, Lincs.) daughter of William Girlington & Katherine
Hildyard; =1st Sir William Tyrwhitt
(I) **Christopher Kelke** (1517 Barnetby – 11 Aug 1557)
= ...; **Jane St.Paul** (...) daughter of John St.Paul & Mary Lee
(A) **Christopher Kelke** (ca.1536 Grimsby, Lincs. – ...)
= ...; **Elizabeth Carr** (...) daughter of Robert Carr & Elizabeth
Cawdron; =2nd William Fairfax
(1) **Anne Kelke** (...)
= ...; **Roger Leming** (...)
(a) **Anne Leming** (1583 Barnetby – 1614 Lincs.)
= ...; **William Wolley** (8 Sep 1568 Alford, Lincs. – 1638
Lincs.) son of William Wolley & Isabelle Hooker
Has further generations of issue
(II) **Francis Kelke** (bef.1519 Barnetby – 1590 Welton, Cumb.)
(III) **Roger Kelke** (3 Apr 1519 Barnetby – 6 Jan 1576 Barnetby)
(IV) **William Kelke** (1523 Barnetby – 1552 Barnetby)
= ...; **Thomasine Skerme** (ca.1535 Yorks. – 1557 London)
daughter of Percival Skerme
(A) **Elizabeth Kelke** (...)
(B) **Cecily Kelke** (...)
= 26 Aug 1574 London; **John Farrer** (2 Dec 1550 Halifax,
Yorks. – 28 May 1628 Mytholmroyd, Yorks.) son of
William Farrer & Margaret Lacy
(1) **John Farrer** (... – 1628 Cronton, Lincs.)
=1 ...; **Susanna Hanson** (...)
=2 ...; **Dorothy Hanson** (...)
issue of 1st:
(a) **William Farrer** (ca.1610 – Oct 1684 Wakefield, Yorks.)
= ...; **Frances James** (...) daughter of Richard James
Has further generations of issue
(b) **Edward Farrer** (...)
(c) **Susan Farrer** (...)
issue of 2nd:
(d) **John Farrer** (...)

(e) **Henry Farrer** (...)

(f) **Mary Farrer** (...)

(2) **Humphrey Farrer** (1579 Lincs. – ...)

(3) **Henry Farrer** (...)

= ...; **Martha Woodward** (...) daughter of John Woodward

(a) **Robert Farrer** (... – Jan 1667 Ormskirk, Lancs.)

= ...; **Alicia Burscough** (ca.1606 – Jul 1669 Ormskirk)
Has further generations of issue

(b) **Henry Farrer** (...)

(c) **John Farrer** (...)

(d) **Elizabeth Farrer** (...)

(4) **William Farrar** (bef.28 Apr 1583 Croxton – 11 Jun 1637 Henrico, VA) immigrated to VA 1618 aboard the *Neptune* = 1625 VA; **Cecily Reynolds** (ca.1601 Dorset – 12 Sep 1660 Charles City, VA) daughter of Thomas Reynolds & Cecily Phippen; =1st Thomas Bailey; =2nd Samuel Jordan

(a) **William Farrar** (1627 Jamestown, VA – 11 Feb 1677 Charles City)

= ...; **Mary Williams** (1627 Henrico Co. – 1682 Henrico Co.) daughter of John Williams & Mary Womack
Has further generations of issue

(b) **John Farrar** (1632 Henrico Co. – Mar 1684 Henrico Co.)

(c) **Cecily Farrar** (ca.1637 Henrico Co. – 1 Feb 1703 Henrico Co.)

=1 ...; **Isaac Hutchins** (... – 1657)

=2 ...; **Henry Sherman** (ca.1630 Henrico Co. – 1 Oct 1695 Henrico Co.) son of Henry Sherman & Cecilia Hutchins
Has further generations of issue

(5) **Elline Farrer** (...)

(6) **Mary Farrer** (...)

= ...; **Richard Wade** (ca.1561 – ...)

issue ?

2) **Joan de la See** (ca.1445 Humberside, Yorks. – 7 Apr 1528)

= ...; **Piers Hildyard** (... – 20 Mar 1503 Linc.) son of Robert Hildyard & Elizabeth Hastings

a) **Katherine Hildyard** (ca.1485 – ...)

= ...; **William Holme** (...)

(I) **John Holme** (1526 – 1564)

= ...; **Ann Ainsley** (15298 Beverley, Yorks. – ...)

(A) **Catherine Holme** (1544 Holmfirth, Yorks. – 8 Jun 1634 Barrow-upon-Humber, Lincs.)

=1 ...; ♦**Marmaduke Constable** (1536 – 1568)

=2 ...; **John Moore** (1552 – ...)

issue of 1st (none by 2nd):

Children are listed with other parent

b) **Christopher Hildyard** (1491 Holderness, Yorks. – 1538 Terrouaine, Artois, France)

= ...; **Margaret Coningsby** (1490 Halsham, Yorks. – 1548) daughter of Sir Humphrey Coningsby & Alice Fereby

(I) **Martin Hildyard** (1509 Holderness – 1545 Holdernes)

= ...; **Emma Rudston** (1512 Monchelsea, Kent – 1570)

(A) **Richard Hildyard** (1532 Holderness – 1602)

= ...; **Jane Thwenge** (ca.1536 Weatherthorpe, Yorks,. – 1602) daughter of Marmaduke Thwenge & Thomasine ...

(1) **Sir Christopher Hildyard** (ca.1560 – 3 Nov 1634)

= ...; **Elizabeth Welby** (1577 Coxhill, Lincs. – 28 Nov 1638) daughter of Henry Welby & Alice White

(a) **Elizabeth Hildyard** (1615 – 1672)

(2) **Ursula Hildyard** (... – 1607 Yorks.)

= ...; **Richard Jackson** (ca.1569 Killingswold Grove, Yorks. – Jun 1613) son of Anthony Jackson & Margaret Frobisher

(a) **Sir Anthony Jackson** (3 Sep 1599 Killingswold Grove – 16 Oct 1666 London)

= ...; **Mabel** Ann **Keate** (1602 – 1705 Ireland)

Has further generations of issue

(b) **Frances Jackson** (5 Jan 1600/1 Eccleston – 1667)

(c) **Elizabeth Jackson** (1601 Eccleston – ...)

(d) **Christopher Jackson** (...)

(e) **Jane Jackson** (ca.5 Feb 1605 London – 6 Jun 1667 Clapham, Yorks.)

= ...; **Thomas Squire** (ca.31 Dec 1603 Escrick, Yorks. – 19 Mar 1663 Escrick) son of William Squire & Patronella Rooke

Has further generations of issue

(f) **Margaret Jackson** (ca.1607 Eccleston – ...)

= ...; **John Vance** (...)

Has further generations of issue

(g) **James Jackson** (...)

(h) **William Jackson** (...)

(B) **Christopher Hildyard** (...)

= ...; ♦**Frances Constable** (...) daughter of Sir John Constable & Katherine Neville

(1) **William Hildyard** (...)

(2) **Elizabeth Hildyard** (...)

(C) **William Hildyard** (...)

(D) **John Hildyard** (...)

(E) **Anne Hildyard** (...)

(F) **Jane Hildyard** (...)

(II) **Leonard Hildyard** (...)

= ...

(A) **Leonard Hildyard** (...)

= ...; **Ellen ...** (...)

(1) **William Hildyard** (...)

= ...; **Jemyma Clarke** (...)
(a) **Leonard Hildyard** (...)
=1 ...; **Anne ...** (...)
=2 ...; **Barbar Swaine** (...)
Has further generations of issue
(B) **William Hildyard** (...)
(III) **John Hildyard** (...)
= ...; **Margaret Thorpe** (...)
issue ?
(IV) **Richard Hildyard** (...)
(V) **Ralph Hildyard** (...)
(VI) **Peter Hildyard** (...)
(VII) **Humphrey Hildyard** (...)
(VIII) **William Hildyard** (...)
(IX) **Sylvester Hildyard** (...)
(X) **Elizabeth Hildyard** (...)
(XI) **Margaret Hildyard** (...)
(XII) **Cecily Hildyard** (...)
(XIII) **Eleanor Hildyard** (...)
(XIV) **Anne Hildyard** (...)
c) **Isabel Hildyard** (1498 – 10 Jul 1540)
= ...; **Ralph Legard** (ca.1490 – 30 Jun 1540)
(I) **John Legard** (...)
= ...; **Margaret Franke** (...) daughter of Robert Franke
(A) **John Legard** (... – 1643)
= ...; **Elizabeth Mallory** (... – 21 Jun 1627) daughter of Sir
William Mallory & Jane Norton
(1) **John Legard** (1606 – bef.1643)
= ...; **Mary Dawnay** (...) daughter of Sir John Dawnay &
Elizabeth Tunstall
(a) **Sir John Legard, 1ˢᵗ Baronet** (1631 – 1678) cr.
Baronet 29 Dec 1660
=1 18 Oct 1655; ◆**Hon. Grace Darcy** (... – 1658) daughter of
Conyers Darcy, 1ˢᵗ Earl of Holderness & Grace Rokeby
=2 12 Aug 1658; **Frances Widdrington** (...) daughter of Sir
Thomas Widdrington
Has further generations of issue
d) **Peter Hildyard** (...)
e) **Anne Hildyard** (...)
f) **Richard Hildyard** (...)
g) **Elizabeth Hildyard** (...)
h) **Margaret Hildyard** (...)
i) **Eleanor Hildyard** (...)
3) **John de la See** (...)
4) **Martin de la See** (...)

377

CHAPTER 11
HASTINGS

The Hastings family trace their line back to the early 1200s when Sir Henry, a soldier, captured enough honor and glory to be raised to the knighthood and was married to Ada Huntington, a descendant of King David of Scotland. It was this connection that made the Hastings contenders for the throne of Scotland when it ultimately went to the Stewarts.

This chapter begins with the youngest daughter of Lady Elizabeth Mortimer, Alice. But Alice's father was Elizabeth's second husband, Lord Camoys. Alice married Sir Leonard Hastings in 1425. He was from a junior branch of the family, but his descendants would become the more prominent line.

Leonard and Alice's son, William, fought for the Yorks, and at one point was even chancellor to King Edward IV. He was raised to the peerage as a Baron, and is the Hastings featured in Shakespeare's play, *Richard III*. His fall came abruptly, and apparently at no fault of his own. When Edward IV died, his widow, Elizabeth Woodville, knew she was hated by most of the court and moved quickly to take control of the government in the name of her young son, Edward V. This included replacing Hastings, and several other court officials, with her numerous brothers and brothers-in-law.

The late King's brother, Richard of Gloucester (later Richard III), who was the rightful regent for Edward V according to his brother's will, kept Hastings as one of his chief advisors. For reasons that have never been completely understood by historians, Richard accused Hastings and a few other nobles of conspiring with the Woodvilles to kill him. The others were taken to the Tower, but Hastings went straight to the courtyard to be beheaded, without a trial.

Because William Hastings did not get a trial, there had not been an opportunity to declare his titles forfeited, so they were inherited by his son, Edward. Edward also made an advantageous marriage to the heiress of the Baronies of Beautreaux, Moleyns, and Hungerford. When all of these titles, and their respective lands, were combined in the following generation, the 3rd Baron Hastings was elevated to become the 1st Earl of Huntingdon.

The Huntingdons were loyal friends to the Tudor monarchs, even with the Crown's passage back and forth between Catholicism and Protestantism. However, his Yorkish ancestry caused those opposed to Elizabeth I to put the 3rd Earl forward as a possible replacement. Although Huntingdon did everything in his power to assure the queen of his faithfulness to her, she kept him at arm's length. This also might have had more to do with Huntingdon's sister being the wife of Elizabeth's beloved Robert Dudley.

The Earldom remains extant to this day and is currently held by the 17th Earl, a male-line descendant of the 2nd Earl through his younger son, Sir Edward. Sir Edward was also the ancestor of several other junior lines, causing the Hastings name to be widespread throughout the middle counties of England.

One notable line of descent begins with the marriage of the 2nd Earl and Catherine Pole, granddaughter and heiress of Margaret, Countess of Salisbury. This marriage brought the "Yorkist Claim" to the Throne to the Hastings family. It continued with them until the 10th Earl died without legitimate issue in 1789. While his earldom went to a cousin, the Hastings Barony, and the "Yorkist Claim" went to his only surviving sister, Elizabeth, already Countess of Moira by marriage. The Claim continued thru her descendants, who are outside the scope of this book, but now rests with the Earl of Loudon, a farmer in Australia.

As with most noble families, there are plenty of connections to their fellow peers through the marriages of their daughters. One notable marriage was the 1556 union of Lady Catherine Hastings, a daughter of the 2nd Earl, to Henry Clinton, 2nd Earl of Lincoln. Their granddaughter, Arabella Clinton, married Isaac Johnson, who is regarded as one of the founders of Boston, Massachusetts. Most of Arabella's siblings also made their way to America, but not all stayed.

Another family descended through a female line is the Ferrer family. Not only do they have numerous members who came to America in the colonial period and shortly after, they also have branches presented in this chapter who went first to Ireland for a few generations before crossing the ocean to America and Canada. One line went to the Caribbean and today is represented by an acting family, the most famous member likely being the late Miguel Ferrer, son of Jose Ferrer and Rosemary Clooney.

While much of this chapter bounces from one family to another of non-titled English folk, there are a few other American families included here, such as the Dean/Deanes of Dorchester County, Maryland. For many commoner families on both sides of the Atlantic, this chapter may prove very useful in proving their royal connections.

Edward III

|

Lionel of Antwerp, Duke of Clarence

|

Philippa, Countess of Ulster

|

Elizabeth, Baroness Camoys (formerly Lady Percy)

|

Alice de Camoys (1407 – 1455)
= 1425; **Sir Leonard Hastings** (ca.1397 – 20 Oct 1455) son of Sir
Ralph Hastings & Maud de St.John
I) **Joan Hastings** (...)
  = ...; **John Brokesby** (...)
  issue ?
II) **Elizabeth Hastings** (ca.1429 – 1508 Carmarthenshire, Wales)
  = 1462; **John Dun** (ca.1430 Kidwell, Wales – 1469 Edgcote,
  Oxon.) son of Gwyff ap Gwn
  A) **Ann Dun** (...)
  B) **Margaret Dun** (ca.1468 – ...)
    = ca.1489 Cubleston, Staffs.; **Edward Trussel** (ca.1464
    Kibbleston, Staffs. – 1499)
    1) **John Trussel** (ca.1494 Kibbleston – ...)
    2) **Elizabeth Trussel** (1496 Kibbleston – bef. Jul 1527)
      = 1509; ♦**John de Vere, 1th Earl of Oxford** (1488 – 1540)
      Children are listed with other parent
III) **Sir William Hastings, 1st Baron Hastings KG** (ca.1431 – 13
  Jun 1483 London) executed; KG 1461/2; cr. Baron 26 Jul 1461
  = Feb 1462; ♦**Lady Katharine Neville** (1442 – 1504) daughter of
  Richard Neville & Alice Montacute, 5th Countess of Salisbury;
  she =1st William Bonville, 6th Baron Harington of Aldingham
  A) **Sir Edward Hastings, 2nd Baron Hastings KB** (26 Nov 1466
    Kirby Muxlow Castle, Leicestershire – 8 Nov 1506) suc. father
    13 Jun 1483; KB 1475
    = 23 Jan 1488; ♦**Mary Hungerford, 5th Baroness Botreaux,
    4th Baroness Hungerford, and 7th Baroness Moleyns** (ca.
    1468 – bef.10 Jul 1533) daughter of Sir Thomas Hungerford &
    Lady Anne Percy; suc. grandmother in Moleyns 1476; great-
    grandmother in Botreaux 1477; and grandfather in Hungerford
    1485
    1) **Anne Hastings** (1485 – 17 Nov 1550)
      =1 bef.1503; ♦**Thomas Stanley, 2nd Earl of Derby** (bef.
      1485 – 1521)
      =2 ...; **John Radcliffe** (...)
      issue of 1st (none by 2nd):
      Children are listed with other parent
    2) **George Hastings, 1st Earl of Huntingdon**, Baron Hastings,

Hungerford, Botreaux, and Moleyns (1488 Ashby-de-la-Zouch, Leics. – 24 Mar 1544) suc. father 1506 and mother 1533; cr. Earl 3 Nov 1529

= Dec 1509; ♦**Lady Anne Stafford** (ca.1483 – 1544) daughter of Henry Stafford, 2nd Duke of Buckingham & Catherine Woodville; =1st Sir William Herbert

a) **Mary Hastings** (ca.1510 – Mar 1532/3 Huntingdon, Berwick)

  = 1526; **Thomas Berkeley, 6th Baron Berkeley KG** (1505 Hovingham, Yorks. – 19 Sep 1534) son of Thomas Berkeley, 5th Baron Berkeley & Eleanor Constable; KG 1533; suc. father 22 Jan 1632/3; =2nd Anne Savage

  no issue

b) **Sir Francis Hastings KG, 2nd Earl of Huntingdon**, etc. (1514 Ashby-de-la-Zouch – 20 Jun 1561) suc. father 1544

  = 25 Jun 1532; **Catherine Pole** (1511 – 23 Sep 1576) daughter of Henry Pole, 11th Baron Montacute & Jane Neville

  (I) **Lady Frances Hastings** (...)

    = ...; ♦**Henry Compton, 1st Baron Compton** (1538 – 1589) Children are listed with other parent

  (II) **Lady Mary Hastings** (...) unm.[85]

  (III) **Henry Hastings, 3rd Earl of Huntingdon**, etc. **KG** (ca. 1536 – 14 Dec 1595) suc. father 1561; KG 1570

    = 25 May 1553; ♦**Lady Catherine Dudley** (Nov 1544 – 4 Aug 1620) daughter of John Dudley, 1st Duke of Northumberland & Jan Guilford

    no issue

  (IV) **George Hastings, 4th Earl of Huntingdon**, etc. (ca. 1540 – 31 Dec 1604) suc. brother 1595

    = Jul 1557; **Dorothy Port** (... 2 Dec 1607) daughter of Sir John Port

    (A) **Francis, Lord Hastings** (... – 17 Dec 1595)

      = bef.1586; **Sarah Harington** (ca.1566 – 3 Oct 1629) daughter of Sir James Harington & Lucy Sydney; =2nd Sir George Kingsmille; =3rd Edward La Zouche, 11th Baron Zouche; =4th Sir Thomas Edmonds

      (1) **Henry Hastings, 5th Earl of Huntingdon**, etc. (24 Apr 1586 – 14 Nov 1643) suc. grandfather 1604

        = 15 Jan 1601; ♦**Lady Elizabeth Stanley** (6 Jan

---

[85] Was the object of affection of Ivan the Terrible of Russia. She turned down his marriage proposal, choosing to remain a spinster.

1587/8 – 20 Jan 1633) daughter of Ferdinando Stanley, 5th Earl of Derby & Alice Spencer
  (a) **Lady Alice Hastings** (... – 1666)
    = 17 Dec 1656 London; ◆**Sir Gervase Clifton, 1st Baronet KB** (25 Nov 1587 – 28 Jun 1666) son of Sir George Clifton & Lady Anne Thorold; =1st Lady Penelope Rich; =2nd ◆Lady Frances Clifford; =3rd Mary Egioke; =4th Isobel Meek; =5th Anne South; =6th Jane Eyre; KB 1603; cr. Baronet 1611
    no issue
  (b) **Lady Elizabeth Hastings** (...)
    = ...; **Sir Hugh Calverley** (...)
    issue ?
  (c) **Ferdinando Hastings, 6th Earl of Huntingdon**, etc. (15 Jan 1608/9 – 13 Feb 1655/6) suc. father 1643
    = 7 Aug 1623; ◆**Lucy Davies** (20 Jan 1623 Dublin – 14 Nov 1679) daughter of Sir John Davies & Eleanor Tuchet
    Has further generations of issue
  (d) **Henry Hastings, Baron Loughborough** (28 Sep 1610 – 10 Jan 1666/7) cr. Baron 23 Oct 1643, but it went extinct upon his death; unm.
  (2) **Catherine Hastings** (... – 26 Aug 1636)
    = 1605; ◆**Philip Stanhope, 1st Earl of Chesterfield** (1584 – 12 Sep 1656)
    Children are listed with other parent
  (3) **Sir George Hastings** (...)
    = ...; **Seymour Pryn** (...) daughter of Sir Gilbert Pryn
    issue ?
  (4) **Theodosia Hastings** (...)
    = ...; **Sir Francis Bodenham** (...)
    issue ?
  (5) **Edward Hastings** (... – 1617)
(B) **Sir Edward Hastings** (...) unm.
(C) **Hon. Henry Hastings** (20 Jan 1552 Lubbesthorpe Manor, Leics. – 1650)
  =1 1587 Wollaton, Northants.; **Dorothy Willoughby** (1574 Wollaton – 1 Dec 1638 Horton, Dorset) daughter of Sir Francis Willoughby & Elizabeth Lyttelton
  =2 3 Sep 1639 Pimperne, Dorset; **Anna Langton** (...)
  issue of 1st:
  issue of 1st:
  (1) **George Hastings** (1588 Horton – 25 Oct 1651 Horton)
    = 27 Jun 1614 Iwerne Courtney, Dorset; **Alice Freke** (...) daughter of Sir Thomas Freke & Elizabeth Taylor

(a) **George Hastings** (... – 1672 North Hinton, Hants.) unm.

(b) **John Hastings** (ca.1616 Horton – May 1658 Burnham, Bucks.)
= ...; **Elizabeth ...** (... – Sep 1667) =2nd Sir Francis Clarke
issue ?

(c) **Edward Hastings** (... – bef.13 Jun 1654 Horton) unm.

(d) **Mabel Hastings** (ca.1619 Horton – ...)
= 6 Apr 1659 London; **Edward Bennet** (...)
issue ?

(e) **Ann Hastings** (1620 Horton – ...)
= 1 Nov 1641 Horton; **John Wigmore** (...)
issue ?

(f) **Dorothy Hastings** (... – 1670) unm.

(g) **Frances Hastings** (... – 1670 Gussidge, Dorset)
= ...; **John Roy** (... – 1684)
Has further generations of issue

(2) **Frances Hastings** (...)

(3) **Ralph Hastings** (1592 Horton – 1648 Hinton, Hants.)
= 16 Sep 1620; **Joan Skeet** (1593 Warminster, Wilts. – ...) daughter of Edmund Skeet & Christian Stokes

(a) **Henry Hastings** (22 Aug 1619[86] Warminster – bef.1672) unm.

(b) **Ferdinando Hastings** (...)
= 31 Oct 1666 London; **Denorah Flavet** (... – aft.1682 Kennington, Surrey)
issue ?

(c) **Ralph Hastings** (30 Sep1623 Warminster – bef.14 Jun 1695 Hinton)
=1 ...; **Sarah More** (...)
=2 bef.1676 Ashly, Hants.; **Sarah Tulse** (... – 1702)
Has further generations of issue

(d) **George Hastings** (16 Oct 1625 Warminster – 8 Apr 1672 Hinton) unm.

(4) **Sir Henry Hastings** (bap.14 Sep 1594 – 21 Oct 1668 Newington Butts, Surrey)
=1 10 Dec 1623 London; **Susanna Offley** (16 Oct 1600

---

[86] This date makes him appear to be born prior to his parents' marriage, but this dae is documented (by his baptism) and the marriage date is not. I suspect the marriage date is incorrect.

London – 1650 London) daughter of Robert Offley &
Ann Osborne
=2 ...; **Catherine Wadsworth** (... – 1691 Leicester)
daughter of Thomas Wadsworth
issue of 1st (none by 2nd):
(a) **Anne Hastings** (ca.1625 – ...)
   = ...; **John Alway** (...)
   Has further generations of issue
(5) **Rev. William Hastings** (1596 Horton – 1666
Winfrith Newton, Dorset)
= ...; **Anne Cracknell** (... – 1672 London)
daughter of Gabriel Cracknell
(a) **Edward Hastings** (... – 1671 Puddletown, Dorset)
   unm.
(b) **Benjamin Hastings** (... – bef. 22 Oct 1680)
   = ...; **Ann Brown** (...) daughter of Henry Brown
   issue ?
(c) **Dorothea Hastings** (...)
   = ...; **... Hooper** (...)
   issue ?
(d) **Anna Hastings** (... – aft.1682)
(e) **Catherine Hastings** (1636 Puddletown – 1704
   Loders, Dorset)
   = 16 Oct 1656 Puddletown; **John Wray** (... – 1708 Loders)
   issue ?
(f) **Francis Hastings** (ca.1638 Puddletown – bef.1672 London)
   = 7 Sep 1658 Puddletown; **Ann Arnold** (21 Sep 1628
   Puddletown – 1 Apr 1670 London) daughter of Henry
   Arnold & Judith Squibb
   issue ?
(g) **Henry Hastings** (aft.1639 Puddletown – aft.1682 Dublin)
   = ca. 1664; **Frances Squibb** (...)
   issue ?
(h) **William Hastings** (ca.1642 Winfrith – ...)
   = ...; **Rebecca Pitfield** (1630 Allington, Dorset – ...)
   daughter of Sebastian Pitfield & Rebecca Beaton
   Has further generations of issue
(6) **Francis Hastings** (1600 Horton – 1625 Hinton)
   = ...; **Ellin Langton** (...) daughter of John Langton &
   Jane Raylestone
   no issue
(7) **Dorothy Hastings** (1601 Horton – ...)
   =1 1617 Horton; **John Ryves** (... – bef.1625) son of
   John Ryves & Elisabeth Maurin de Fountell
   =2 1625; **Thomas Tegonwell** (1603 Anderson, Dorset –
   1655 Dorset)

=3 ...; **Richard Wiseman** (...)
issue ?
issue of 2ⁿᵈ:
(8) **Henry Hastings** (1626 – aft.1641)
= ...; **Anne Arney** (...) daughter of Alexander Arney &
Jane Lambert
issue ?
(D) **Lady Catherine Hastings** (...)
=1 1581; ♦**Sir Edward Unton** (... – 1589) slain abroad;
son of Sir Edward Unton & Anne Seymour; =1ˢᵗ Dorothy
Knightley
=2 1605; ♦**Sir Walter Chetwynd** (... –1638)
issue of 2ⁿᵈ (none by 1ˢᵗ):
Children are listed with other parent
(E) **Lady Dorothy Hastings** (
=1 ...; **Sir James Stewart, Master of Blantyre** (... – 8
Nov 1609 London) killed in a duel; son of Walter
Stewart, 1ˢᵗ of Blantyre & Nicholas Somerville
=2 aft.1609; **Robert Dillon, 2ⁿᵈ Earl of Roscommon**,
Baron Dillon (... – 27 Aug 1642) son of James Dillon, 1ˢᵗ
Earl of Roscommon & Elinore Barnewell; =1ˢᵗ Margaret
Barry; =3ʳᵈ Anne Strode
no issue
(F) **Lady Margaret Hastings** (... – 17 Aug 1654) unm.
(V) **Sir Edward Hastings** (1542 Ashby de La Zouche,
Leics. – 1603 Abbey Gate, Leics.)
= 1567; ♦**Barbara Devereux** (... – aft.1618) daughter of
Sir William Devereux & Jane Scudamore
(A) **Sir Henry Hastings** (... – 1640)
= ...; **Mabel Faunt** (ca.1582 – 1618) daughter of
Antony Faunt & Elizabeth Noell
(1) **Henry Hastings** (1605 – ...)
= 19 Jul 1641 Belgrave, Leics,; **Jane Goodall** (... – 1655)
(a) **Jane Hastings** (bap.21 Jan 1640/1 Humberstone, Leics. – ...)
= ...; **Joseph Cradock** (...)
issue ?
(b) **Henry Hastings** (bap.22 Mar 1641/2 – ...)
=1 1671; **Elizabeth Warren** (...)
=2 16 Feb 1672 Humberstone; **Pentecost Smalley** (... – 1705)
no issue
(c) **Anne Hastings** (bap.16 Mar 1642/3 Humberstone – ...)
(d) **Walter Hastings** (bap.19 Mar 1643/4
Humberstone – 1681 Remptson, Notts.)
= ...; **Hannah Cradock** (...) daughter of Edmund Cradock
Has further generations of issue
(e) **Richard Hastings** (5 May 1645 Humberstone –

Oct 1714 Welford, Notts.)
=1 1 Oct 1697 Frolesworth, Leics.; **Sarah Sleath**
(1650 Frolesworth – Dec 1707)
=2 10 Nov 1709 Welford; **Goodith Smith** (1659
Welford – 13 Jul 1731 Welford) daughter of William
Smith & Susan Ragg; =1st Nicholas Bell
Has further generations of issue [87]
(f) **Lucy Hastings** (bap.28 Apr 1646 Humberstone – ...)
= ...; **Thomas Dyson** (...)
issue ?
(g) **Ferdinando Hastings** (15 Mar 1646/7
Humberstone – 28 Nov 1688) unm.
(h) **Edmund Hastings** (1648 Humberstone – ...)
(i) **Mabel Hastings** (bap.15 Dec 1650 Humberstone – ...)
(j) **Sarah Hastings** (...)
= ...; **John Browne** (...) son of John Browne & Mary Quarles
issue ?
(k) **Dorothy Hastings** (ca.1655 Humberstone – ...)
(2) **Barbara Hastings** (...)
= 24 Apr 1639; **Charles Blythe** (... – 1645)
issue ?
(3) **Walter Hastings** (1608 – 1672)
(4) **Sir Richard Hastings, Baronet** (1610 London – Aug
1668) cr. Baronet 7 May 1667 which became extinct on his death
= 16 Feb 1646/7; **Margaret Poyntz** (...) daughter of Sir
Robert Poyntz & Frances Gibbons; =1st Thomas Gorges; =3rd
Samuel Gorges
no issue
(5) **Mabel Hastings** (22 May 1611 – ...)
= ...; **Nicholas Herbert** (...)
issue ?
(6) **Antony Hastings** (1612 Humberstone – Jun 1667 Windsor)
=1 1638; **Anne Watkinson** (1616 London – ca.Feb
1653) daughter of Stephen Watkinson & Elizabeth Morris
=2 aft.1653; **Anna ...** (...)
isue of 1st:
(a) **Henry Hastings** (26 Mar 1640 – ...)
(b) **George Hastings** (1642 – 1704)
= 1665; **Elizabeth Fleming** (...)
no issue
(c) **Edward Hastings** (1647 – 1719/20)

---

[87] The Earldom of Huntingdon passed to this line in 1819.

= ...; **Catherine Dale** (...)
issue
(d) **Antony Hastings** (1649 – 1692)
= 11 Sep 1686 Churchill, Som.; **Caroletta Churchill**
(1666 – 22 Sep 1698 Backwell, Som.) daughter of Sir
John Churchill & Susan Prideaux; =2nd Robert Nettles
Has further generations of issue
issue of 2nd:
(e) **Lucy Hastings** (...)
(f) **Anna Hastings** (bap.26 Dec 1657 – ...)
(g) **Frances Hastings** (...)
(h) **Hussey Hastings** (...)
(i) **Jane Hastings** (...)
(7) **Elizabeth Hastings** (...)
= ...; **Robert Tirwhit** (...)
issue ?
(8) **Jane Hastings** (...)
= ...; **... Tomkins** (...)
issue ?
(9) **Lucy Hastings** (...)
= ...; **Ferdinand Sacheverell** (1599 Hopwell, Derbys. –
10 Jan 1628 Old Hays, Leics.) son of Henry Sacheverell
& Elizabeth Keies
issue ?
(B) **Walter Hastings** (...) unm.
(C) **Dorothy Hastings** (...)
= ...; **Samuel Aylmer** (... – 12 Jan 1634 Suffolk) son of
John Aylmer & Judith King; =2nd Ann Brabazon
no issue
(D) **Ann Hastings** (...)
(E) **Edward Hastings** (...) unm.
(VI) **Lady Catherine Hastings** (11 Aug 1542 London –
bef.20 Oct 1586)
= ca.1556; **Henry Clinton** (or **Fiennes**)[88], **2nd Earl of
Lincoln**, 10th **Baron Clinton** (1540 – 29 Sep 1616) son of
Edward Clinton, 1st Earl of Lincoln & Hon. Ursula
Stourton; =2nd Elizabeth Morrison; suc. father 16 Jan
1584/5
(A) **Thomas Clinton, 3rd Earl of Lincoln**, etc. (ca.1568 –

---

[88] The 5th Baron had married an heiress of the Fiennes family and adopted the surname
Fiennes. Their descendants used Clinton and Fiennes interchangably for centuries. For
consistency, the family members here will be called Clinton since that is the name that
prevailed in the end and is what the current living family members are called.

15 Jan 1618/9)[89] suc. father 1616
= 21 Sep 1584; **Elizabeth Knyvett** (...) daughter of Sir
Henry Knyvett & Elizabeth Stumpe
(1) **Lady Frances Clinton** (...)
(2) **Lady Arbella Clinton** (... – Aug 1630 Salem Mass.)
   = ...; **Isaac Johnson**[90] (... – 30 Sep 1630 Boston, Mass.)
   no issue
(3) **Lady Susan Clinton** (...)
   = ...; **John Humphrey**[91] (ca.1596 Chaldron, Dorset –
   1651 England) =1st Elizabeth Pelham
   (a) **Anne Humphrey** (17 Dec 1625 Fordingham,
      Dorset – 17 Dec 1693)
      =1 ..., Mass.; **William Palmer** (..., Ardfinan, Ireland –
      ..., Mass.)
      =2 ca.1668, MA; **Rev. John Myles**[92] (1621 Newton-
      Clifford, Herts. – 3 Feb 1683/4 Barrington, RI) son
      of Walter Myles
      Has further generations of issue
(4) **Lady Dorcas Clinton** (...)
(5) **Lady Sara Clinton** (...)
(6) **Theophilius Clinton, 4th Earl of Lincoln**, etc. **KB**
   (ca.1600 – 21 May 1667) suc. father 1619; KB 1616
   =1 ca.1622; **Bridget Fiennes** (...) daughter of William
   Fiennes, 1st Viscount of Say and Sele & Elizabeth Temple
   =2 ...; ◆**Elizabeth Gorges** (... – May 1675) daughter of
   Sir Arthur Gorges & Lady Elizabeth Clinton; =1st ◆Sir
   Robert Stanley
   issue of 1st (none by 2nd):
   (a) **Lady Catherine Clinton** (... – Jul 1643)
      = 30 Nov 1639; **George Booth, 1st Baron Delamer**
      (18 Dec 1622 – 8 Aug 1684) son of William Booth &
      Vere Egerton; =2nd ◆Lady Elizabeth Grey; cr. Baron
      24 Oct 1652

---

[89] In additon to the children listed, Lord Lincoln had a daughter Ann who died young. Several on-line sources (including Wikipedia) confuse this Ann with another Ann who married John Harrington and moved to Watertown, Massachusetts, leaving numerous descendants.
[90] Isaac and Arbella were one of the earliest settlers of present day Massachussets. Issac is regarded as a founder of the city of Boston, and one of the 12 signers of the Cambridge Agreement with established Mass. as a self-controlling colony.
[91] Also a signer of the Cambridge Agreement and arrived in Mass. in 1634. He and Susan returned to England 1641 leaving their children behind. The children were subjected to physical and sexual abuse with only one daughter out of 7 children surviving to adulthood.
[92] Went to Massachusetts 1662, founding the first Baptist church there, as well as the town of Swansea, Mass.

Has further generations of issue
    (b) **Edward, Lord Clinton** (30 Dec 1624 – bef.21 Apr 1657 London)
       = 30 Mar 1652; **Lady Anne Holles** (... – Oct 1707) daughter of John Holles, 2nd Earl of Clare; =2nd Charles Bates
       Has further generations of issue
    (c) **Lady Arabella Clinton** (...)
       = ...; **Robert Rolle** (...)
       Has further generations of issue
    (d) **Lady Margaret Clinton** (... – Oct 1688)
       = ...; **Hugh Boscawen** (bap.21 Aug 1625 Penkivel, Cornwall – Jun 1701) son of Hugh Boscawen & Margaret Rolle
       Has further generations of issue
(B) **Sir Edward Clinton** (...)
   = ..; **Mary Dighton** (...) daughter of Thomas Dighton
   (1) **Francis Clinton** (...)
      = ...; **Priscilla Hill** (...) daughter of John Hill
    (a) **Francis Clinton, 6th Earl of Lincoln** (ca.1635 – Aug 1693) suc. cousin 1692
       =1 ...; **Elizabeth Killigrew** (... – 1677) daughter of Sir William Killigrew & Mary Hill
       =2 ca.1683; **Susannah Penyston** (... – 23 Sep 1720
       Has further generations of issue (extinct 1754)
    (2) **Henry Clinton** (... – aft.1634) unm.
    (3) **Robert Clinton** (... – aft.1634) unm.
    (4) **Charles Clinton** (... – bef.1634)
    (5) **Jermyn Clinton** (... – bef.1634)
(VII) **Walter Hastings** (1544 Braunston, Leics. – Aug 1616 Muxloe, Leics.)
 = 22 May 1574 London; **Joyce Roper** (1548 – 1619 Leicester) daughter of Christopher Roper & Elizabeth Blore
 (A) **Sir Henry Hastings** (ca.1578 – 1649 Brampton, Cumb.)
   =1 ca.1606 Sawston, Cambs.; **Dorothy Huddleston** (... – bef.1640)
   =2 ...; **Eleanor Knyvett** (...) daughter of Sir Philip Knyvett, 1st Baronet & Katherine Ford; =2nd Thomas Waldron
   issue of 1st:
   (1) **Sir Walter Hastings** (1607 – bef.1682 Plumtree, Notts.)
   (2) **Edmund Hastings** (1611 – 1682 Plumtree)
     = 27 Jan 1625; **Mary Copley** (... – 5 Aug 1661) daughter of Averley Copley & Joan Gunby
     issue ?
   (3) **Dorothy Hastings** (...)
     = ...; **William Hammerson** (...)
     issue ?
   (4) **Henry Hastings** (1615 – ca.1670)

= aft.1628; **Hon. Elizabeth Beaumont** (...) daughter of
Thomas Beaumont, 1ˢᵗ Viscount Beaumont & Elizabeth
Sapcote; =1ˢᵗ Sir Thomas Waldron
  (a) **Henry Hastings** (... – Apr 1665 London) murdered
  (b) **Beaumont Hastings** (... – 1672 at sea) killed in naval battle
  (c) **Dorothy Hastings** (...)
  (d) **Elizabeth Hastings** (...)
  (e) **Catherine Hastings** (...)
  (f) **Walter Hastings** (1638 – aft.1682)
(5) **Ferdinando Hastings** (1617 Draunton, Devon – ...)
= ...; **Mary St.George** (...)
  (a) **Ferdinando Hastings** (...)
  = ...; **Mary Coote** (...) daughter of Richard Coote, 1ˢᵗ
  Baron Coote & Mary St.George
  issue ?
(6) **Federick Hastings** (5 Apr 1618 – bef.1682)
(7) **Joyce Hastings** (1619 Kirby, Lancs. – ...)
= ...; **John Butler** (...)
issue ?
issue of 2ⁿᵈ:
(8) **Knevet Hastings** (1644 Leics. – 1701)
= ...; **... Byron** (...) daughter of Sir Robert Byron
issue ?
(9) **Henry Hastings** (1645 – 1666) unm.
(10) **Charles Hastings** (15 May 1648 Braunston – 1734
Tombland, Norfolk)
= ...; **Hannah Russell** (1651 – Jul 1679) daughter of
Thomas Russell
  (a) **Knevet Hastings** (4 Mar 1674 – aft.1734)
  (b) **Charles Hastings** (26 Jun 1677 – aft.1724)
(VIII) **Sir Francis Hastings** (ca.1545 – Sep 1610)
=1 1567; **Maud Longford** (... – 14 Jun 1596 North Cadbury, Som.)
daughter of Sir Ralph Longford; =1ˢᵗ Sir George Vernon
=2 aft.1597; **Mary Watkins** (ca.1550 Holwell, Dorset – ...)
daughter of Richad Watkins & Mary Coker; =1ˢᵗ James Hannam
no issue
(IX) **Lady Elizabeth Hastings** (1546 – 24 Aug 1621 London)
= 1571; ♦**Edward Somerset, 4ᵗʰ Earl of Worcester** (1550–1628)
Children are listed with other parent
c) **Sir Thomas Hastings** (1515 – 1558)
= ...; ♦**Winifred Pole** (aft.1521 – ...) daughter of Henry
Pole, 1ˢᵗ Baron Montagu & Jane Neville; =2ⁿᵈ Sir Thomas Barrington
no issue
d) **William Hastings** (1518 Kirby, Lancs. – 1556)
e) **Dorothy Hastings** (1519 Kirby – ...)
= 1536; ♦**Sir Richard Devereux** (... – 1547)

Children are listed with other parent

f) **Edward Hastings, Baron Hastings of Loughborough** (ca.1520 – 5 Mar 1571/2) cr. Baron 19 Jan 1557/8 which became extinct upon his death

= ca.1544; **Joan Harrington** (... – aft.1573) daughter of John Harrington

Has further generations of issue

B) **Richard Hastings** (1468 – ...)

= ...; **Ann ...** (...)

1) **Mary Hastings** (...)

C) **Sir William Hastings** (1470 – aft.1541)

= 1500 Chelwell; **Jane Sheffield** (1474 – ...) daughter of Sir Robert Sheffield & Jane Lounde; =1st Sir Robert Staunton; =3rd Ralph Shirley

1) **Elizabeth Hastings** (... – aft.1574)

= ...; **John Beaumont** (... – 1557) son of Thomas Beaumont & Ann Harcourt

a) **Francis Beaumont** (... – 22 Apr 1598)

= ...; **Ann Pierrepont** (...) daughter of Sir George Pierrepont; =1st Thomas Thorold

(I) **Sir Henry Beaumont** (ca.1581 – 13 Jul 1605 Gracedieu, Leics.)

= ca.1604; **Barbara Faunt** (...) daughter of Antony Faunt & Elizabeth Noell; =2nd Sir Henry Harpur, 1st Baronet

(A) **Barbara Beaumont** (ph.Sep 1605 – 28 Dec 1666)

=1 ...; **John Harpur** (...) son of Sir Richard Harpur

=2 1629; **Sir Wolstan Dixie, 1st Baronet** (... – 13 Feb 1681/2) son of Sir Wolstan Dixie & Frances Beaumont; he =2nd Frances Haslerig; cr. Baronet 14 Jul 1660

issue of 2nd (none by 1st):

(1) **Sir Beaumont Dixie, 2nd Baronet** (... – May 1692) suc. father 1682

= ...; **Mary Willoughby** (... – 30 Nov 1710)

(a) **Sir Wolstan Dixie, 3rd Baronet** (25 Mar 1657 – 10 Dec 1713) suc. father 1692

= 10 Dec 1685; **Rebecca Atkins** (... – 19 Dec 1744) daughter of Sir Richard Atkins, 1st Baronet & Rebecca Wright

Has further generations of issue

(b) **Rev. John Dixie** (...)

(c) **Mary Dixie** (16 Mar 1660 – bef.1716)

=1 ...; **Charles Willoughby, 10th Baron Willoughby** (6 Oct 1650 – 9 Dec 1679 Knaith Lincs.) son of William Willoughby, 6th Baron Willoughby & Anne Cary; suc. brother Sep 1678

=2 aft.24 Apr 1683; ◆**Hon. George Cokayne** (ca. 1666 – 22 Jul 1722 Northampton) son of Brien Cokayne, 2nd Viscount Cullen & Elizabeth Trentham

no issue

(d) **Beaumont Dixie** (...)
    = 9 Jul 1693 Headon, Notts.; **Jane Eyre** (...) daughter
    of Antony Eyre
    issue ?
(2) **Henry Dixie** (...)
    = ...; **Anne Stringer** (...)
    issue ?
(II) **Sir John Beaumont, 1st Baronet** (ca.1582 – Apr 1627)
cr. Baronet 31 Jan 1626/7
= ...; **Elizabeth Fortescue** (... – aft.16 Apr 1652) daughter
of John Fortescue
(A) **Sir John Beaumont, 2nd Baronet** (24 Jun 1607 – Sep
    1643) killed in battle; suc. father 1627; unm.
(B) **Francis Beaumont** (13 Jan 1608 – ...) a priest
(C) **Henry Beaumont** (13 Apr 1610 – ...) unm.
(D) **Helen Beaumont** (5 Jun 1611 – ...) unm.
(E) **Anne Beaumont** (26 Sep 1612 – ...) unm.
(F) **Catherine Beaumont** (31 Jul 1615 – ...)
(G) **George Beaumont** (23 Nov 1616 – ...) unm.
(H) **Mary Beaumont** (7 Jul 1617 – ...)
    =1 ...; **Sir Edmond Williams** (...)
    =2 ...; **John Tasborough** (...)
    issue ?
(I) **Sir Thomas Beaumont, 3rd Baronet** (29 Apr 1620 – 17
Jul 1686) suc. brother 1643, tile became extinct upon his death
= ...; **Vere Tufton** (...) daughter of Sir William Tufton, 1st
Baronet & Anne Cave
(1) **Cicely Beaumont** (... – 1697)
    = ...; **Robert Beaumont** (...)
    issue ?
(2) **Vere Beaumont** (...)
    = ...; **Sir John Rayney, 3rd Baronet** (1660 – Feb 1704)
    son of Sir John Rayney, 2nd Baronet; suc. father 1680
    (a) **Catherine Rayney** (...)
        = ...; **Edward Betenson** (... – 1700) son of Sir Richard
        Betenson, 1st Baronet & Anne Monins
        Has further generations of issue (extinct 1786)
    (b) **Sir John** Beaumont **Rayney, 4th Baronet** (1688 –
        1716) suc. father 1704
        = ...
        Has further generations of issue (extinct 1721)
(3) **Mary Beaumont** (...)
    = ...; **George Morton** (...)
    issue ?
(4) **Jane Beaumont** (...)
    = ...; **Charles Byerly** (...)

issue ?
    (5) **Anne Beaumont** (...)
    = ...; **Robert Pawley** (...)
    issue ?
    (J) **Charles Beaumont** (6 Feb 1622 – ...) unm.
  (III) **Francis Beaumont** (1584 – 6 Mar 1615/6)
  = ...; **Ursula Isley** (...) daughter of Henry Isley
  (A) **Elizabeth Beaumont** (... – aft.1682)[93]
  (B) **Frances Beaumont** (... – aft.1700) unm.
b) **Elizabeth Beaumont** (... – Aug 1562)
= bef.1 Jun 1557; **William Vaux, 3rd Baron Vaux** (14 Aug
1535 – 20 Aug 1595) son of Thomas Vaux, 2nd Baron Vaux
& Elizabeth Cheney; =2nd Mary Tresham
  (I) **Henry Vaux** (1558 – Nov 1587) unm.
  (II) **Eleanor Vaux** (ca.1560 – ca.1625)
  (III) **Elizabeth Vaux** (ca.1561 – ...)
  (IV) **Anne Vaux** (Jul 1562 – 1635) unm.
c) **Henry Beaumont** (ca.1543 – 1585)
2) **Mary Hastings** (...)
= ...; **Thomas Saunders** (...)
issue ?
D) **Anne Hastings** (ca.1471 – 1520)
= 1481; ♦**George Talbot, 4th Earl of Shrewsbury** (1468 – 1538)
Children are listed with other parent
IV) **Thomas Hastings** (ca.1433 – ...)
V) **Sir Richard Hastings** (1433 York – Sep 1510)
= 12 Mar 1468; **Joan de Welles, (9th) Baroness Willoughby de
Eresby** (... – 1505) daughter of Richard de Welles & John
Willoughby, (7th) Baroness Willoughby de Eresby; suc. brother
19 Mar 1469/70
A) **Antony Hastings** (1469 – 1500) unm.
VI) **Sir Ralph Hastings** (ca.1435 – bef.1 Dec 1495 Wanstead, Essex)
= ...; **Ann Tattershall** (ca.1439 Woolwich, Kent – ...)
A) **Florence Hastings** (...)
= 1505; ♦**Edmund Grey, 9th Baron Grey** (1469 – 1511)
Children are listed with other parent
B) **Isabel Hastings** (...)
C) **Elizabeth Maud Hastings** (...)
D) **Catherine Hastings** (...)
E) **Emma Hastings** (...)
F) **Cecilia Hastings** (...)

---

[93] Is believed to have married a Scottish Colonel.

G) **Alice Hastings** (...)
VII) **Ann Hastings** (1438 – ...)
= 1468; **Sir Thomas Ferrers** (ca.1438 Tamworth Castle, Staffs. –
22 Aug 1499 Tamworth Castle) son of Thomas Ferrers &
Elizabeth Freville
A) **John Ferrers** (1452 Tamworth – 1485)
= ...; **Maud Stanley** (1464 Elford, Staffs. – ...) daughter of John
Stanley & Ann...
1) **John Ferrers** (1471 Tamworth – 16 Jul 1512 Tamworth)
= ...; **Dorothy Harpur** (1470 Rushall, Staffs. – 1532) daughter
of William Harpur & Margaret Cock
a) **Sir Humphrey Ferrers** (1493 Tamworth, Staffs – 1553
Tamworth)
= ...; **Margaret Pigot** (1487 Tamworth – 1576) daughter of
Sir Thomas Pigot & Agnes Forster
(I) **Sir John Ferrers** (1514 Tamworth – 1576 Ashbourne,
Derbys.)
= ...; **Barbara Cokayne** (1517 Ashbourne – 1595) daughter
of Francis Cokayne & Dorothy Marrow
(A) **Dorothy Ferrers** (... – 1594)
= ...; **Edward Holte** (1541 – 3 Feb 1593) son of Thomas
Holte & Margery Willington
(1) **Sir Thomas Holte, 1ˢᵗ Baronet** (1571 – 14 Dec 1654
Aston, Warks.) cr. Baronet 26 Nov 1611
=1 ...; **Grace Bradbourne** (...) daughter of Willam
Bradbourne
=2 1641; **Anne Littleton** (...) daughter of Sir Edward
Littleton & Mary Fisher
issue of 1ˢᵗ (none surviving by 2ⁿᵈ):
(a) **Grace Holte** (1598 Aston – 12 Apr 1677 Dublin)
=1 ...; **Sir Richard Shuckburgh** (ca.1596 – 27 Oct
1656) son of John Shuckburgh & Margery ...
=2 ...; **Sir John Keating** (1630 – 1691) son of Edmund
Keating & Elizabeth Eustace
Has further generations of issue
(b) **Elizabeth Holte** (... – 15 Apr 1647) unm.
(c) **Anne Holte** (...)
= ...; **Walter Giffard** (1611 – 1688) son of Peter
Giffard & Frances Fowler
Has further generations of issue
(d) **George Holte** (... – 1641)
(e) **Edward Holte** (1600 – 28 Aug 1643 Oxford)
= ...; **Elizabeth King** (...) daughter of Rt.Rev. John
King, Bishop of London & Joan ...
Has further generations of issue
(2) **Robert Holte** (...)

(3) **Francis Holte** (...)
(4) **Margaret Holte** (...)
(5) **Mary Holte** (...)
(6) **Dorothy Holte** (...)
(7) **Frances Holte** (...)
(8) **Anne Holte** (...)
  = ...; **Edward West** (...)
  issue ?
(9) **Lucy Holte** (...)
  = ...; **John Higford** (...)
  issue ?
(10) **Katherine Holte** (...)
  = ...; **Humphrey Wirley** (...)
  issue ?
(B) **Humphrey Ferrers** (1558 Tamworth – 1608 Tamworth)
= ...; **Ann Bradbourne** (1563 Derbys. – 1 Jan 1599 Tamworth)
daughter of Sir Humphrey Bradbourne & Elizabeth Turvile
(1) **Sir John Ferrers** (1566 – 1633 Tamworth)
  =1 ...; **Elizabeth Burdett** (...) daughter of Sir Thomas
  Burdett, 1st Baronet & Jane Francis
  =2 ...; **Dorothy Puckering** (... – 1616) daughter of Sir John
  Puckering & Jane Chowne
  issue of 2nd (none by 1st):
  (a) **Anna Ferrers** (...)
    = ...; **Sir Simon Archer** (21 Sep 1581 – 1662) son of
    Andrew Archer & Margaret ...
    Has further generations of issue
  (b) **Frances Ferrers** (...)
    =1 ...; **Sir John Pakington, 1st Baronet** (ca.1600 – Oct
    1624 Aylesbury, Bucks.) son of Sir John Pakington &
    Dorothy Smith; cr. Baronet Jun 1620
    =2 29 Dec 1626 London; **Robert Leasly** (...)
    Has further generations of issue
  (c) **Sir Humphrey Ferrers** (... – 1633 Tamworth)
    = ...; **Anne Pakington** (... – 1667) daughter of Sir John
    Pakington & Dorothy Smith; =2nd ♦Philip Stanhope, 1st
    Earl of Chesterfield
    Has further generations of issue
  (d) **Jane Ferrers** (...)
    = ...; **Sir Thomas Rouse, 1st Baronet** (1608 – 27 May
    1676) son of John Rouse & Ethel Temple; cr. Baronet
    23 Jul 1641; =2nd Frances Murray
    Has further generations of issue

(2) **Richard Ferrers**[94] (1585 Tamworth – 1614 Leics.)

(3) **Susan Ferrers** (... – 1624)

= ...; ◆**Sir George Gresley, 1st Baronet** (ca.1580 – 1651)
Children are listed with other parent

b) **Mary Ferrers** (ca.1482 Tamworth – aft.1544 Sibbertoft, Northants.)

=1 1516; ◆**Sir William Smythe** (ca.1480 – 1526)
=2 bef.1531; ◆**Walter Smythe** (1501 – ...)
issue of 1st:
Children are listed with other parent
issue of 2nd:

2) **Helen Ferrers** (ca.1484 Tamworth – 1508)

= ...; **William Turvile** (ca.1483 Newhall, Leics. – 3 Sep 1549)
son of John Turvile & Katharine Staunton; =2nd Jane Wharburton

a) **John Turvile** (ca.1498 Aston Flamville, Leics. – 2 Oct 1561 Thurlaston, Leics.)

= ...; **Mary Findern** (ca.1502 Derby – ...) daughter of Thomas Findern

(I) **Richard Turvile** (1530 – 1563)

= ...; **Jane Babington** (...)

(A) **Anne Turvile** (1565 – 1643)

= ...; **Charles Gunther** (2 Nov 1562 – ca.1643) son of John Gunther & Alice Kibblewhite

(1) **John Gunter** (9 Feb 1590 – ca.1579 Coaley, Glos.)

= ...; **Judith ...** (1590 – 1670)

(a) **John Gunter** (27 Dec 1624 – ca.1696 Henrico Co. VA) emigrated 1644

= ...;
Has further generations of issue

(b) **Geoffrey Gunter** (1626 – ...)

= ...
Has further generations of issue

(c) **Anne Gunter** (24 Nov 1627 – ...)

(d) **William Gunter** (1629 – 1675)

(2) **Ursula Gunter** (6 Feb 1591 – ...)

(3) **Alice Gunter** (15 Jun 1600 – ...)

(4) **Anthony Gunter** (24 Jul 1602 – ...)

(5) **Anne Gunter** (18 Sep 1603 – ...)

(6) **Pardingando Gunter** (10 Feb 1605 – ...)

= ...; **Mary Elgar** (1615 – ...)

---

[94] On-line sources (undocumented) list his children as people that have since been proven to be from another family. It is unknown therefore if this Richard ever married.

(a) **Anne Gunter** (1646 – ...)
(b) **Elizabeth Gunter** (1648 – ...)
(c) **Ferdinand Gunter** (1650 – ...)
(7) **Temperance Gunter** (16 Oct 1608 – ...)
(8) **Charles Gunter** (14 Oct 1610 – ...)
(9) **Jane Gunter** (2 Jun 1612 – ...)
(10) **Robert Gunter** (25 Sep 1614 – ...)
(B) **Edward Turvile** (...)
(II) **Geoffrey Turvile** (ca.1524 Thurlaston – ...)
= ...
(A) **Maria Turvile** (ca.1540 Tulson, Leics. – ...)
= ...; **John Marston** (ca.1533 Slawston, Leics. – ...) son of
William Marston
(1) **Thomas Marston** (9 May 1564 Medbourne, Leics. –
25 May 1606 Medbourne)
= ...; **Alicia Payne** (ca.1564 Medbourne – 1600) daughter of
Thomas Payne
(a) **Katherina Marston** (1591 Medbourne – 29 Oct 1651
Medbourne)
= ...; **Jacobus Barratt** (ca.1585 Medbourne – 8 Apr
1646 Medbourne) son of Richardus Barratt & Isabel ...
Has further generations of issue
3) **Elizabeth Ferrers** (1479 – ...)
= ...; **Sir William Chetwynd** (1477 – 1547) son of Sir William
Chetwynd & Alice Egerton
a) **Thomas Chetwynd** (... – 1555)
= ...; **Jane Salter** (...) daughter of Sir John Salter & Eliabeth ...
(I) **Mary Chetwynd** (...)
= ...; **Ralph Sneyd** (1527 – 15 Aug 1620) son of Sir William
Sneyd & Anne Barrow
(A) **Ralph Sneyd** (1564 – 1644)
= ...; **Felicia Archbold** (... – 1659) daughter of Nicholas Archbold
(1) **William Sneyd** (1612 – 17 Jan 1695 Newcastle-under-Lyme,
Staffs.)
= ...; **Elizabeth Audley** (...) daughter of Eobert Audley
(a) **William** Generosus **Sneyd** (1642 – 25 May 1708 Keele,
Staffs.)
= ...; **Sarah Wettenhall** (1631 – 1718) daughter of Edward
Wettenhall
Has further generations of issue
(2) **Ralph Sneyd** (... – 1650)
= ...; **Jane Downes** (... – 1670) daughter of Roger Downes
(a) **Phyllis Sneyd** (...)

= ...; **Robert Hyde** (1642 – 1670 Manchester) daughter
of Edward Hyde & Anne Brooke
Has further generations of issue[95]
(B) **Anne Sneyd** (1580 – 1656)
= ...; **Thomas Skrymsher** (1576 – 1633) son of Thomas
Skrymsher & Alice Starkey
(1) **Mary Skrymsher** (1601 – ...)
= ...; **Richard Walsh** (...)
issue ?
(2) **Gerard Skrymsher** (ca.1605 – ca.1665)
= ...; **Catherine Sandys** (...) daughter of Sir Edwin Sandys &
Catherine Bulkeley
(a) **Edwin Skrymsher** (ca.1633 – 1689)
=1 1659; **Joyce Aubrey** (...) daughter of William Aubrey
=2 29 Aug 1686; **Susanna ...** (...) =1st ♦Hon. John
Grey; =2nd ... Ball
no issue
(b) **Mary Skrymsher** (...)
=1 ...; **Sir Timothy Baldwyn** (...) son of Charles Baldwyn &
Mary ...
=2 ...; **Nicholas Acton** (ca.1620 – ...)
Has further generations of issue
(3) **Anne Skrymsher** (1612 – ...)
= ...; **George Brown** (...)
issue ?
(4) **Ralph Skrymsher** (...)
(5) **Elizabeth Skrymsher** (...)
(6) **John Skrymsher** (...)
(7) **Robert Skrymsher** (...)
(8) **Edwin Skrymsher** (...)
(C) **Mary Sneyd** (...)
= ...; **Walter Minors** (...)
issue ?
(D) **Jane Sneyd** (...)
= ...; **Gilbert Rolleston** (... – 1618)
issue ?
(II) **John Chetwynd** (... – 1592)
=1 ...; **Margery Middlemore** (ca.1547 Edgbaston, Warks. –
20 Dec 1602 Litchfield, Staffs.) daughter of Robert Middlemore

---

[95] Although George Clarke was a colonial Gov. of New York, his descendants in North America were through an illegitimate grandchild in Jamaica. The legitimate lines of descent remained in England. He was the founder of Hyde Park in NY.

=2 ...; **Mary Meverill** (...)

issue of 1st:

(A) **Sir Walter Chetwynd** (... – 31 May 1638)

=1 ...; **Mary Mullins** (...) daughter of John Mullins

=2 1605; ◆**Catherine Hastings** (...) daughter of George Hastings, 4th Earl of Huntingdon & Dorothy Port

issue of 1st:

(1) **Walter Chetwynd** (... – 1670)

= ...; **Frances Haslerig** (bef.1632 – ca.1686) =2nd ◆Sir Wolstan Dixie, 1st Baronet

(a) **Walter Chetwynd** (... – 21 Mar 1693)

= ...; **Anna Bagot** (bef. 14 Sep 1565 – ...) daughter of Edward Bagot

issue ?

issue of 2nd:

(2) **Mary Chetwynd** (...)

= ...; **George Digby** (...)

(a) **Jane Digby** (ca.1637 – Nov 1703)

= 1660; ◆**Charles Gerard, 4th Baron Gerard** (1634 – 1667)

Children are listed with other parent

(B) **Thomas Chetwynd** (– ca.1633)

= ...; **Dorothy Colman** (...) daughter of Walter Colman

(1) **William Chetwynd** (... – ca.1651)

(2) **Ralph Chetwynd** (... – 1653)

= ...; **Dorothy Twysden** (...) daughter of Sir William Twysden

(a) **Richard Chetwynd** (... – ca.1693)

= ...; **Ann Launder** (...) daughter of William Launder; =2nd William Sprott

Has further generations of issue

(b) **Charles Chetwynd** (... – ca.1719)

= ...; **Sarah Purefoy** (...) daughter of Gamaliel Purefoy

issue ?

(c) **John Chetwynd** (... – ca.1692)

= ...; ...

Has further generations of issue

(3) **Thomas Chetwynd** (... – Sep 1641)

=1 ...; **Mary Congreve** (...) daughter of Francis Congreve

=2 ...; **Dorothy Harcourt** (...) daughter of Robert Harcourt

issue of 1st:

(a) **Anne Chetwynd** (...)

= ...; **Thomas Melward** (...)

issue ?

issue of 2nd:

(b) **Mary Chetwynd** (...)

(c) **William Chetwynd** (...)

issue of 2nd:

(C) **Sir William Chetwynd** (... – 14 Jan 1613/4)
=1 ...; **Atalanta Huick** (... – 20 Dec 1602)
=2 ...; **Catherine Aston** (1566 – 1646) daughter of Sir Walter
Aston & Elizabeth Leveson; =1st Sir Esward Cope; =3rd Stephen
Slaney
no issue

B) **Isabel Ferrers** (ca.1445 – ...)
= ...; **Ralph Longford** (ca.1440 Ashbourne, Derbys. – 1513) son
of Ralph Longford & Margaret Melton

1) **Sir Ralph Longford** (ca.1478 London – ca.1544)
= ...; **Dorothy Fitzherbert** (ca.1472 Derby – ...) daughter of Sir
Richard Fitzherbert

a) **Elizabeth Longford** (ca.1515 Trafford near Manchester – 27
Jan 1578)
= ...; **Edmund Trafford** (...)

(I) **Alice Trafford** (ca.1537 Trafford – 16 Jun 1578 Cheadle, Lancs.)
= ...; **Urian Brereton** (1530 Cheshire – 1576 Cheshire) son
of Sir Urian Brereton & Margaret Handforth

(A) **Urian Brereton** (ca.1550 Stockport, Ches. – 1619) unm.

(B) **Margaret Brereton** (ca.1552 Stockport – ...) unm.

(C) **Dorothy Brereton** (ca.1554 Stockport – ca.1624
= ...; **George Redych** (...)
issue ?

(D) **Jane Brereton** (ca.1556 Stockport – ...)

(E) **Mary Brereton** (1559 Chester – 10 Jul 1627
Manchester)
= ...; **Sir Alexander Barlow** (1557 Chorlton, Lancs. – 20
Apr 1620 Manchester) son of Alexander Barlow &
Elizabeth Leigh

(1) **Sir Alexander Barlow** (1580 Chorlton – 1642)
=1 ...; **Mantreux Brereton** (...)
=2 ...; **Elizabeth Parker** (ca.1583 Manchester – ...)
=3 ...; ♦**Dorothy Gresley** (28 Apr 1584 Draklowe,
Derbys. – aft.Apr 1635) daughter of Sir Thomas Gresley &
Katherine Walsingham
issue of 3rd (none by others):

(a) **Thomas Barlow** (9 Sep 1618 Chorlton – 1 Sep 1684)

(b) **Anne Barlow** (ca.1620 Chorlton – ...)

(c) **Mary Barlow** (ca.1622 Chorlton – 6 Feb 1691
Lancs.)
= ...; **Caryll Molyneix, 3rd Viscount Molyneux** 4th
Baronet (1623/4 Leinster, Ireland – 2 Feb 1699/1700
Croxteth, Merseyside) son of Richard Molyneux, 1st
Viscount Molyneux & Mary Caryll; suc. brother J Jul 1654
Has further generations of issue

(d) **Elizabeth Barlow** (ca.1624 Chorlton – ...)

(e) **Henry Barlow** (ca.1626 Chorlton – ...)

(2) **Margaret Barlow** (16 Sep 1581 Manchester – ...)
= ...; **John Talbot** (1582 Blackburn, Lancs. – 22 Feb 1659)
issue ?

(3) **Dom Rudesind Barlow** (1585 Chorlton – 1656 Douai,
France) a monk, né William Barlow

(4) **George Barlow** (4 Mar 1583/4 Didsbury, Lancs. –
1684 Conn.) emigrated ca.1640
= 1606 Manchester; **Anne Howe** (1604 – Feb. 1684/5
Fairfield, Conn.)

(a) **Thomas Barlow** (1623 Manchester – 8 Sep 1659 Fairfield)
= ca.1650 Fairfield; **Rose Sherwood** (1623 Ipswich,
Suffolk – ca.1699 Norwalk, CT) daughter of Thomas
Sherwood & Alice Seabrook; =1st Edward Nash
Has further generations of issue

(5) **William Barlow** (ca.1584 Manchester – ...)

(6) **St. Ambrose Edward Barlow** (1585 Chorlton – 10 Sep
1641 Manchester) executed; a priest; canonized 25 Oct 1970

(7) **Katherine Barlow** (1594 Chorlton – ...)

(8) **Mary Barlow** (1596 Chorlton – ...)

(F) **Sybil Brereton** (ca.1561 Hanford, Ches. – ...)

(II) **Helen Trafford** (ca.1539 Trafford – ...)

(III) **Elizabeth Trafford** (ca.1541 Trafford – ...)

(IV) **Margaret Traffard** (ca.1543 Tafford – ...)
= ...; ♦**Sir William Radclyffe** (...)
Children are listed with other parent

b) **Maud Longford** (... – 14 Jun 1596 North Cadbury, Som.)
=1 ...; **George Vernon, Baron Haddon KB** (ca.1521 – 31 Aug 1565)
son of Richard Vernon & Margaret Manners; =1st Margaret Talboys
=2 1567; ♦**Sir Francis Hastings** (ca.1545 – Sep 1610) son of Francis
Hastings, 2nd Earl of Huntingdon & Catherine Pole; =2nd Mary Watkins
no issue

c) **Ralph Longford** (...)
= ...;

(I) **Richard Longford** (...)
= ...

(A) **Richard Longford** (...)

2) **Margaret Longford** (1480 Ashbourne, Derbys. – 1495)

3) **Elizabeth Longford** (1487 Derby – 27 Jan 1548)
= ...; **Sir Edmund Trafford** (ca.1485 Manchester – 28 Jun
1533 son of Sir Edmund Trafford & Margaret Savage

a) **Sir Edmund Trafford** (1498 Manchester – 10 Dec1563)
=1 ...; **Anne Radcliffe** (ca.1510 Manchester – ...) daughter of
Sir Alexander Radcliffe & Alice Booth
=2 ...; **Elizabeth Dutton** (...) daughter of Piers Dutton

issue of 1st (none by 2nd):

(I) **Sir Edmund Trafford** (3 Jun 1526 – 14 Jan 1590)
=1 ...; **Elizabeth Leycester** (...) Sir Ralph Leycester & Ellen House
=2 ...; ◆**Mary Howard** (1519 London – ...) daughter of Edmund Howard & Jocasta Leigh
issue of 1st (none by 2nd)

(A) **Sir Edmund Trafford** (ca.1560 – 8 May 1620)
=1 ...; **Mary Booth** (...) daughter of John Booth
=2 ...; (his sister-in-law) **Margaret Booth** (...) daughter of John Booth
=3 ...; ◆**Lady Mildred Cecil** (... – 23 Dec 1611) daughter of Thomas Cecil, 1st Earl of Exeter & Dorothy Neville
issue of 1st (none by others):

(1) **Sir Cecil Trafford** (15 Aug 1599 – ...)
= ...; **Penelope Davenport** (...) daughter of Sir Humphrey Davenport

(a) **Humphrey Trafford** (...)
=1 ...; **... Holland** (...)
=2 ...; **Katherine Warburton** (...) daughter of Sir George Warburton, 1st Baronet & Diana Bishopp
Has further generations of issue

(b) **John Trafford** (... – 1686)
= ...; **Anne Ashton** (...) daughter of Richard Aston
Has further generations of issue

(2) **Elizabeth Trafford** (...)
= ...; **Richard Fleetwood** (1592 Penwortham, Lancs. – ...) son of Richard Fleetwood & Margery Legh
issue ?

(B) **Margaret Trafford** (...)
= ...; **Sir Urian Leigh** (...)
issue ?

(C) **Elizabeth Trafford** (...)
= ...; **Sir John Michel** (...)
issue ?

b) **Margaret Trafford** (ca.1512 Lancs. – ...)
= ...; **Sir William Radcliffe** (1502 Manchester – 12 Oct 1568 Lancs.)
issue ?

c) **Elizabeth Trafford** (1515 Manchester – 1548 Trentham, Staffs.)
= ...; ◆**Sir George Booth** (1515 – 1543)
Children are listed with other parent

d) **Helen Trafford** (ca.1539 – ...)

e) **Cicely Trafford** (...)
= ...; **Sir Robert Langley** (1529 Agecroft, Lancs. – 1561) son of Thomas Langley & Cicely Davenport

(I) **Margaret Langley** (1555 Agecroft – 25 Sep 1616 Prestwich, Lancs.)

=1 ...; **John Reddish** (1539 – Aug 1569)
=2 ...; **Richard Holland** (1542 Denton, Lancs. – 2 Mar 1619 Heaton, Lancs.) son of Edward Holland & Jane Carrington
issue of 1st:
(A) **Grace Reddish** (...)
  = ...; **Sir Robert Darcy** (...) son of Sir Edward Darcy & Astley
  (1) **Edward Darcy** (...)
    = ...; ♦**Elizabeth Stanhope** (...) daughter of Philip Stanhope, 1st Earl of Chesterfield & Catherine Hastings
    Has further generations of issue
issue of 2nd:
(B) **Mary Holland** (ca.1571 Denton – ...)
(C) **Elizabeth Holland** (1574 Denton – ...)
  = ...; **John Preston** (ca.1563 Furness, Lancs. – 4 Sep 1642) son of Thomas Preston & Anne Westby
  (1) **Margaret Preston** (1598 Furness – 7 Sep 1625)
    = ...; ♦**Sir Francis Howard** (1588 – 1660)
    Children are listed with other parent
  (2) **Agnes Preston** (ca.1600 Furness – ...)
    = ...; **Christopher Anderton** (...)
    (a) **Anne Anderton** (...)
    (b) **Alice Anderton** (...)
      = ...; **John Orrell** (...) son of William Orrell & Mary Ireland
      issue ?
  (3) **Frances Preston** (ca.1602 Furness – ...)
  (4) **Sir John Preston, 1st Baronet** (1617 Furness – 1645) cr. Baronet 1 Apr 1644
    = ...; **Jane Morgan** (1620 Heyford Hails, Northants. – ...) daughter of Thomas Morgan & Jane Fermor
    (a) **Sir John Preston, 2nd Baronet** (ca.1638 Furness – Apr 1663) suc. father 1645; unm.
    (b) **Thomas Preston, 3rd Baronet** (1640 Furness – 27 Mar 1709 Flanders [Belgium]) suc. brother 1663; title became extinct upon his death
      = ...; **Mary Molyneux** (ca.1642 Lancs. – 6 Jun 1673 Barrow-in-Furness, Lancs.) daughter of Caryll Molyneux, 3rd Viscount Molyneux & Mary Barlow
      Has further generations of issue
    (c) **Anne Preston** (1642 Furness – ...)
      = 1662; ♦**Sir William Gerard, 4th Baronet** (1638 – 1702)
      Children are listed with other parent
    (d) **Elizabeth Preston** (1644 Furness – Apr 1688)
      = ...; **William Stourton, 12th Baron Stourton** (1644 – 1685)
      Children are listed with other parent
(D) **Jane Holland** (ca.1577 Denton – ...)

(E) **Margaret Holland** (ca.1585 Denton – 1609)
  = ...; **William Brereton** (1584 – 1610)
  (1) **Sir William Brereton, 1ˢᵗ Baronet** (13 Sep 1604
    Ches. – 7 Apr 1661) cr. Baronet 10 Mar 1627
    =1 ...; **Susanna Booth** (1600 Bowden, Ches. – 31 May
    1637) daughter of Sir George Booth, 1ˢᵗ Baronet & Catherine
    Anderson
    =2 ...; **Cicely Skeffington** (...) daughter of Sir William
    Skeffington
    issue of 1ˢᵗ:
    (a) **Sir Thomas Brereton, 2ⁿᵈ Baronet** (1632 – 17 Jan
      1673/4) suc. father 1661; title became extinct upon his
      death
      = bef.1664; ♦**Theodosia Ward** (15 May 1642 – ...)
      daughter of Humble Ward, 1ˢᵗ Baron Ward & Frances
      Dudley, (6ᵗʰ) Baroness Dudley; =2ⁿᵈ Charles Brereton
      no issue
    (b) **Frances Brereton** (1635 – 1676)
      = ...; ♦**Edward Ward, 7ᵗʰ Baron Dudley** (1631 – 1701)
      Children are listed with other parent
    (c) **Susanna Brereton** (...)
      = ...; **Edmund Lenthall** (...) son of Sir John Lenthall
      Has further generations of issue
    (d) **Catherine Brereton** (...)
    issue of 2ⁿᵈ:
    (e) **Cicely Brereton** (... – 12 Jul 1704)
      = bef.1677; ♦**Edward Brabazon, 4ᵗʰ Earl of Meath**,
      etc. (1638 – 1707) son of Edward Brabazon, 2ⁿᵈ Earl of
      Meath & Mary Chambré; suc. brother 28 Feb 1684/5;
      he =2ⁿᵈ Dorothy Stopford
      no issue
  f) **George Trafford** (...)
  g) **Thomas Trafford** (...)
  h) **Henry Trafford** (...)
  i) **Richard Trafford** (...)
C) **Anne Ferrers** (1453 Tamworth, Staffs. – 1516 Colton, Staffs.)
  = ...; **Sir Thomas Gresley** (ca.1445 Colton – 1503 Colton)
  1) **Sir William Gresley** (ca.1479 Colton – 10 Mar 1520) unm.
  2) **John Gresley** (1481 Colton – ...) unm.
  3) **Elizabeth Gresley** (ca.1483 Colton – 1584 Chillington, Staffs.)
    =1 ...; **John Montgomery** (... – 1513) son of Nicholas
    Montgomery & Isabella Vernon
    =2 ...; **Sir John Giffard, 12ᵗʰ of Chillington** (Apr 1466
    Chillington – 13 Nov 1556 Bridgworth, Salop.) son of Robert
    Giffard, 11ᵗʰ of Chillington & Cassandra Humphrestone; =1ˢᵗ
    Jane Hord

issue of 1ˢᵗ:

a) **Ellen Montgomery** (ca.1504 Cubley, Derbys. – 26 Mar 1549
Haddon Hall, Derbys.)
= ...; **Sir John Vernon** (1478 Haddon – ca.1545) son of Sir
Henry Vernon & Anne Shirley
(I) **Henry Vernon** (ca.1521 – 29 Sep 1569)
= ...; ♦**Margaret Swinnerton** (1520 – ...) daughter of Humphrey
Swinnerton & Cassandra Giffard
(A) **Henry Vernon** (1548 – 1592)
= ...; **Dorothy Heveningham** (1550 – 1635) daughter of Sir
Anthony Heveringham & Mary Shelton; =2ⁿᵈ Sir Henry
Townshend
(1) **Margaret Vernon** (1592 – Jan 1656/7)
= ...; **Sir Edward Vernon** (ca.1580 Houndshill, Staffs. –
1657) son of Walter Vernon & Mary Littleton
(a) **Dorothy Vernon** (ca.1611 – ...)
(b) **Henry Vernon** (1615 Houndshill – 1658)
= ...; **Muriel Vernon** (...) daughter of Sir George Vernon &
Jane Corbet
Has further generations of issue
(c) **John Vernon** (14 Aug 1649 – 13 Mar 1670)
=1 ...; **Anne Huish** (...)
=2 ...; **Elizabeth Walwyn** (...)
Has further generations of issue
(d) **Anne Vernon** (...)
(B) **John Vernon** (... – 8 Jun 1600)
= ...; **Mary Littleton** (1555 – ...)
issue ?
b) **Dorothy Montgomery** (ca.1493 Chillington – bef.1529)
= ...; (her step-brother) **Sir Thomas Giffard** (ca.1490 – 27
May 1560 Chillington) son of Sir John Giffard, 12ᵗʰ of
Chillington & Jane Hord; =1ˢᵗ Ursula Throckmorton
(I) **Elizabeth Giffard** (1515 Chillington – 1563)
= ...; **Sir John Port KB** (ca.1513 Derbys. – 1557) son of Sir
John Port & Jane Fitzherbert
(A) **Elizabeth Port** (1535 Etwell, Derbys. – 1632 Lancs.)
= ...; **Sir Thomas Gerard** (ca.1535 Lancs. – Sep 1601
Manchester) son of Sir Thomas Gerard & Jane Legh
(1) **Sir Thomas Gerard, 1ˢᵗ Baronet** (1560 Manchester –
Feb 1620/1 Lancs.) cr. Baronet 22 May 1611
=1 ca.1580; **Cecily Manney** (ca.1542 – ...) daughter of Sir
Walter Manney
=2 aft.1606; **Mary Hawes** (...) daughter of Sir James Hawes
& Audrey Copwood; =1ˢᵗ Sir John Smythe; =2ⁿᵈ Sir
Robert Lee
=3 ...; **Mary Margaret Dormer** (1555 Bucks. – Jul 1637

Midhurst, Sussex) daughter of Sir William Dormer & Dorothy
Pelham; =1st John Caryll; =2nd Sir Anthony Browne; =3rd
Sir Edwin Uvedale
issue of 1st (none by others):
  (a) **Sir Thomas Gerard, 2nd Baronet** (ca.1584 Bryn,
    Lancs. – 15 May 1630 New Hall, Lancs.) suc. father 1621
    = ca.1610; **Frances Molyneux** (... – Feb 1613/4) daughter
    of Sir Richard Molyneux, 1st Baronet & Frances Gerard
    Has further generations of issue
  (b) **Frances Gerard** (...)
    = ...; **Ralph Standish** (...)
    issue ?
  (c) **John Gerard** (...) unm.
(2) **Nicholas Gerard** (...)
  = ...
  (a) **Margery Gerard** (...)
    = ...; **Robert Arrowsmith** (...)
    Has further generations of issue
(3) **Mary Gerard** (...)
(4) **Dorothy Gerard** (...)
(5) **Martha Gerard** (...)
(6) **John Gerard** (1564 – 1637)[96]
(B) **Dorothy Port** (1536 Etwell, Derbys. – 2 Sep 1607
  Ashby, Leics.)
  = ...; ♦**George Hastings, 4th Earl of Huntingdon**
  (1540 – 1604)
  Children are listed with other parent
(C) **Margaret Anne Port** (14 Oct 1542 Etwell – 132
  Shelford, Notts.)
  = ...; **Sir Thomas Stanhope** (ca.1540 Shelford – 3 Aug
  1596 Shelford) son of Sir Michael Stanhope & Annr
  Rawson
  (1) **Sir John Stanhope** (1559 Nottingham – 1610 Derbys.)
    =1 ...; **Cordell Allington** (ca.1574 Sudbury, Suffolk –
    ...) daughter of Richard Allington & Joan Cordell
    =2 ...; **Catherine Trentham** (1566 Waterhouses,
    Staffs. – 1623) daughter of Thomas Trentham & Jane Sneyd
    issue of 1st:
    (a) **Philip Stanhope, 1st Earl of Chesterfield**, Baron
      Stanhope (1584 – 12 Sep 1656) Kt. 1605; cr. Earl etc. 4 Aug 1628

---

[96] A Jesuit priest who was assigned to covertly minister to Catholics in England during the
Elizabethan period. Wrote a autobiography of his efforts.

=1 1605; **Catherine Hastings** (... – 26 Aug 1636)
=2 aft.1636; **Anne Pakington** (... – Nov 1667) daughter of
Sir John Pakington & Dorothy Smith; =1st □Sir
Humphrey Ferrers
Has further generations of issue
issue of 2nd:
(b) **Cordelia Stanhope** (ca.1585 Shelford – Oct 1639
Sandford, Dorset)
=1 ...; **Sir Roger Aston** (... – 23 May 1612) illegitimate
son of Thomas Aston; =1st Marjory Stuart
=2 ...; **John Mohun, 1st Baron Mohun of
Okehampton**, 2nd Baronet (1595 Boconnoc, Cornwall –
28 Mar 1641) son of Sir Reginald Mohun, 1st Baronet &
Philippa Hele; suc. father 1642; cr. Baron 15 Apr 1628
Has further generations of issue
(c) **Sir John Stanhope** (ca.1590 Shelford – 29 May 1638)
=1 ...; **Olive Beresford** (1591 – 1614) daughter of Edward
Beresford & Dorothy ...
=2 ...; **Mary Radcyffe** (1605 – 1675)
Has further generations of issue
(d) **Jane Stanhope** (2 Jan 1585 Elvaston – 12 Mar 1683
Nottingham)
=1 bef.1624; **Sir Peter Courtene, Baronet** (... – ca.1623) son
of Sir William Courtene & Margaret Cromling; cr. Baronet 1622
which became extinct upon his death
=2 1629; **Francis Annesley, 1st Viscount of Valentia**,
Baron Mountnorris, 1st Baronet (bef.1 Feb 1583/4 – 22
Nov 1660) son of Robert Annesley & Beatrix Cornwall;
he =1st Dorothy Phillips; cr. Baronet 7 Aug 1620,
Viscount 11 Mar 1621, and Baron 8 Feb 1628/9
Has further generations of issue
(e) **Catherine Stanhope** (1610 Shelford – 1694 London)
= ...; **Sir Thomas Hutchinson** (ca.1587 Owthorpe,
Notts. – Aug 1643 London) son of Thomas Hutchinson
& Jane Sacheverell; =1st Alice Ingoldesby; =2nd
Margaret Byron
Has further generations of issue
(f) **Olive Stanhope** (...)
= ...; **Charles Cotton** (...)
Has further generations of issue
(g) **Dorothy Stanhope** (...)
(2) **Anne Stanhope** (18 Feb 1575 Shelford – 15 Nov 1651
London)
= ...; ♦**John Holles, 1st Earl of Clare** (1565 – 1637)
Children are listed with other parent
(3) **Edward Stanhope** (...)

(4) **Thomas Stanhope** (...)
issue of 2nd:
c) **Frances Giffard** (ca.1490 Chillington – 1570 Grafton
Northants.)
= ...; **Sir John Talbot** (ca.1500 – 6 Jun 1555) son of Sir John
Talbot & Margaret Troutbeck
(I) **Jane Talbot** (ca.1531 Durham – 1565)
= ...; **Sir John Bowes** (1527 Streatlam, Durham – 20 Aug
1580 Shetland Islands, Scotland) son of Richard Bowes &
Elizabeth Aske; =1st Dorothy Mallory
(A) **Francis Bowes** (...)
= ...; **Jane Hedlam** (...)
issue ?
(B) **Anne Bowes** (ca.1563 Durham – ca.1608)
= ...; **Thomas Hylton** (... – 1598) son of William Hylton,
de jure 11th Baron Hylton & Ann Yorke
(1) **Mary Hylton** (ca.1575 – ca.1636)
(2) **Jane Hylton** (1581 – ...)
= ...; ◆**Sir Ralph de Laval** (ca.1577 – ca.1628)
Children are listed with other parent
(3) **Henry Hylton**, *de jure 12th Baron Hylton* (1586 – 30 Mar
1641) suc. grandfather 1600
= ...; **Mary Whortley** (...) daughter of Richard Whortley; =2nd
Sir Thomas Smith
no issue
(4) **Robert Hylton**, *de jure 13th Baron Hylton* (... – 1641) suc.
brother 1641
= ...;
(a) **John Hylton**, *de jure 14th Baron Hylton* (... – 1655)
suc. father 1641
= ...;
Has further generations of issue
(5) **Edward Hylton** (1603 London – 1671 NH, America)
= ...; **Catherine Shapleigh** (1600 Devon – 30 May 1676 NH)
(a) **William Hilton** (1620 NH – 1690 Devon)
= ...;
Has further generations of issue
(C) **Sir Talbot Bowes** (1560 Streatlam – 14 Mar 1638)
= ...; **Agnes Warcop** (...) daughter of Thomas Warcop & Anne
Thornborough
issue ?
(D) **Thomas Bowes** (1577 Streatlam – ...)
= ...; **Anne Warcop** (ca.1579 – ...) daughter of Thomas Warcop
& Anne Thornborough
(1) **Thomas Bowes** (Dec 1607 Gibside, Durham – 9 Sep 1661
Gibside)

= ...; **Anne Maxton** (1629 Cultoquhey, Perths.
(Scotland) – 31 Dec 1705 Durham)
(a) **Eleanor Bowes** (1649 – ...)
(e) **Maxton Bowes** (a daughter) (1651 – ...)
(c) **Thomas Bowes** (1653 – 1673) (twin?) unm.
(f) **Jane Bowes** (1653 – ...) (twin?)
(g) **Dorothy Bowes** (2 Oct 1654 Barnard Castle,
   Durham – ...)
(h) **Sir William Bowes** (bap.6 Jan 1656/7 Barnard
   Castle – 7 Feb 1707) Kt 1684
   = 17 Aug 1691; **Elizabeth Blakiston** (1651 Gibside – Jul 1736)
   daughter of Sir Francis Blakiston, 3rd Baronet & Anne Bowes
   Has further generations of issue
(i) **John Bowes** (17 Aug 1658 Barnard Castle – 1721 Durham)
(j) **George Bowes** (6 May 1659 Barnard Bastle – 1724)
   = ...; **Anne Salvin** (...)
   issue?
(E) **Richard Bowes** (...)
(F) **John Bowes** (...)
  = ...; **Ursula Davel** (...)
  issue ?
(G) **Jane Bowes** (... – 1637)
  = ...; **... Chatterton** (...)
  issue ?
(II) **Sir John Talbot** (1545 Grafton, Worcs. – 29 Jan 1611
  Albrighton, Salop.)
=1 ...; **Catherine Petre** (28 Apr 1545 Longford, Salop. – 27
Feb 1596 Albrighton) daughter of William Petre & Anne Brown
=2 ...
issue of 1st:
(A) **George Talbot, 9th Earl of Shrewsbury and
  Waterford**, 14th Baron Furnivalle (19 Dec 1566 – 2 Apr
  1630) suc. distant cousin 1617; unm.
(B) **John Talbot** (ca.1575 Longford – ca.1607 London)
  = ...; **Eleanor Baskerville** (ca.1570 Banwell, Som. – ...)
  daughter of Sir Thomas Baskerville & Eleanor Abington
  (1) **John Talbot, 10th Earl of Shrewsbury**, etc. (ca.1601
    Longford – 8 Feb 1653/4 Wardour, Wilts.) suc. uncle 1630
    =1 ...; ◆**Mary Fortescue** (...) daughter of Sir Francis
    Fortescue & Grace Manners
    =2 ...; ◆**Hon. Frances Arundell** (ca.1614 Wardour –
    ca.1652 Wardour) daughter of Thomas Arundell, 1st Baron of
    Wardour & Anne Philipson
    issue of 1st:
    (a) **George, Lord Talbot** (ca.1620 – 7 Mar 1742)
      = Jan. 1639; ◆**Hon. Mary Herbert** (...) daughter of Percy

Herbert, 2nd Baron Powis & Elizabeth Craven
no issue
(b) **Francis Talbot, 11th Earl of Shrewsbury**, etc.
(ca.1623 – 16 Mar 1667/8) killed in a duel[97]; suc. father 1654
=1 ...; **Anne Conyers** (...) daughter of William Conyers &
Elizabeth Simeon
=2 10 Jan 1658/9; ♦**Lady Anna Maria Brudenell** (25
Mar 1642 Paris – 20 Apr 1702) daughter of Robert
Brudenell, 2nd Earl of Cardingan & Hon. Anne Savage
Has further generations of issue
(c) **Hon. Gilbert Talbot** (ca.1631 – 1711)
= ...; **Jane Flatsburg** (...)
Has further generations of issue
(d) **Lady Frances Talbot** (... – 17 Jul 1641)
= ...; **Sir George Wintour, Baronet** (1622 – 1658) cr.
Baronet 29 Apr 1642, which became extinct upon his
death
no surviving issue
(e) **Lady Mary Talbot** (... – Mar 1710/1)
=1 ...; ♦**Charles Arundell** (...)
=2 ...; ♦**Mervyn Tuchet, 4th Earl of Castlehaven** (...–1686)
issue of 1st:
Children are listed with other parent
issue of 2nd:
Children are listed with other parent
issue of 2nd:
(f) **Hon. John Talbot** (...)
(g) **Hon. Bruno Talbot** (...)
(2) **George Talbot** (...)
(3) **Gilbert Talbot** (...)
(4) **Mary Talbot** (...)
(5) **Katherine Talbot** (...)
issue of 2nd:
(C) **Anne Talbot** (..)
= 1585; ♦**Sir Thomas Hanmer** (... – 1619)
Children are listed with other parent
(III) **Margaret Talbot** (...)
(IV) **George Talbot** (1545 Dorset – 2 Apr 1630 Dorset)
= ...; **Joan Selwoode** (1522 Chard, Som. – 10 May 1597)
(A) **Alice Talbot** (ca.1556 Dorchester, Dorset – 1650

---

[97] He was killed by the 2nd Duke of Buckingham, his 2nd wife's lover by who she had several additional children..

Dorchester)
= ...; **William** Gilbert **Deane** (ca.1550 Dorchester – 11 Oct 1634 Dorchester)

(1) **William** Henry **Deane**[98] (ca.1600 Dorchester, Dorset[99] – 1699 Dorchester, Dorset[100]) emigratred to Maryand bef.1650
= ...; **Elizabeth Dampier** (1604 Som. – 1690 Dorchester Co.) daughter of William Dampier & Margaret Giles

  (a) **Robert** Edward **Deane** (1620 Dorchester, Dorset – 1690 Wingate)
    = ...; **Eleanor Hammon** (...)
    issue ?

  (b) **William** Richard **Deane** (1627 Dorchester, Dorset – 8 Feb 1699 Dorchester Co. MD)
    = ...; **Elizabeth Meredith** (ca.1651 Som. – ...) daughter of John Meredith
    Has further generations of issue

  (c) **Thomas** James **Deane** (1631 Dorchester, Dorset – ...)
    = ...; **Elizabeth Price** (...)
    issue ?

  (d) **Ralph** Edmund **Deane** (1634 Dorchester, Dorset – ...)
    = ...; **Alice Basset** (...)

  (e) **Anthony** Gilbert **Deane** (1637 Dorchester, Dorset – ...)

  (f) **Michael** Matthew **Deane** (1639 Dorchester, Dorset – 1724 Dorchester Co.)
    = ...; **Elizabeth Roper** (1683 MD – 1750 Dorchester Co.)
    Has further generations of issue

  (g) **Elizabeth** Ann **Deane** (1643 Dorchester, Dorset – ...)

  (h) **John** Charles **Deane** (1645 Dorchester, Dorset – ...)
    = ...; **Sarah Nicholas** (...)
    issue ?

  (i) **Francis** Henry **Deane** (1651 Dorchester Co. – 1746 Dorchester Co.)
    = ...; **Mary Ann Chilcott** (...)

---

[98] No two sources seem to agree on the number of children that William Gilbert & Alice (Talbot) Deane/Dean had. William Henry is the only child that seems to be universally accepted as theirs. Some sources give as many as eleven, but many of those do not appear to be part of the same family. I believe William Henry is likely the only child to have issue. Furthermore, the name is spelled Deane/Dean interchangably during this period.

[99] There is a good chance that sources have gotten confused between Dorchester, the town in Dorset, England and Dorchester County, Maryland as this family immigrated from one to the other. I have attempted to sort them out and clarify them as best I can.

[100] He was a sea captain and contnued to travel back and forth from England to America, but died in England. He seems to have taken his family to America in late 1640s.

issue ?

(V) **Thomas Talbot** (...)

d) **William Giffard** (1492 Bridgworth, Salop. – ...)

e) **Dorothy Giffard** (...)

f) **Cassandra Giffard** (...)

4) **Ellen Gresley** (1486 Strelley, Notts. – ...)

= ...; **Sir Nicholas Strelley** (ca.1480 Strelley – 25 Aug 1560)
son of Sir Nicholas Strelley & Margaret West; =1st Sarah
Digby; =3rd Elizabeth Spencer
no issue

5) **Sir George Gresley** (1494 – 21 Apr 1548 Dudley, Worcs.)

=1 ...; **Margaret Mulsho** (ca.1502 Finedon, Northants. – ...)
daughter of John Mulsho & Eleanor Stukeley

=2 ...; **Katherine Sutton** (ca.1490 – 22 Apr 1572 Lichfield, Staffs.)
daughter of Edward Sutton, 2nd Baron Dudley & Cecily Willoughby
issue of 1st:

a) **Sir William Gresley** (bap.12 May 1525 – 24 May 1573)

= ...; **Catherine Aston** (...) daughter of Sir Edward Aston & Joan
Bowles

(I) **Sir Thomas Gresley** (3 Nov 1552 Drakelow, Derbys. – 5
Sep 1610 Drakelow)

=1 ...; **Elizabeth Harvey** (1555 – ...) daughter of James Harvey

=2 ...; **Katherine Walsingham** (bef.1568 Swanton Morley,
Norfolk – 1637) daughter of Sir Thomas Walsingham & Dorothy
Guilford
issue 1st:

(A) **Catherine Gresley** (ca.1577 – 10 Apr 1635) unm.
issue of 2nd:

(B) **Dorothy Gresley** (28 Aug 1584 Drakelow – aft.Apr
1635)

= ...; ♦**Sir Alexander Barlow** (1580 – 1642)
Children are listed with other parent

(C) **Sir George Gresley, 1st Baronet** (ca.1580 Drakelow –
1651 London) cr.Baronet 29 Jun 1611

= ...; **Susan Ferrers** (... – 1624) daughter of Sir Humphrey

(1) **Sir Thomas Gresley** (ca.1605 – 16 Dec 1642)

= ...; **Bridget Burdett** (ca.1605 Foremark, Derbys. – 1685)
daughter of Sir Thomas Burdett, 1st Baronet & Jane Francis

(a) **Sir Thomas Gresley, 2nd Baronet** (ca.1628 –
1699) suc. grandfather 1651

= ...; **Frances Morewood** (...) daughter of Gilbert
Moorwood
Has further generations of issue

(b) **Frances Gresley** (ca.1631 – 1685)

= ...; **John Whitehall** (ca.1624 – 7 Aug 1684) =2nd
Frances Aston

414

Has further generations of issue
  (c) **Bridget Gresley** (... – 1713)
  = ...; **Thomas Brome** (ca.1613 – ...)
  Has further generations of issue (extinct by 1800)
  (d) **George Gresley** (... – 1704)
  = ...; **Jane Nelson** (...) daughter of Thomas Nelson
  issue ?
  (e) **Catherine Gresley** (...)
  (f) **Mary Gresley** (...)
  (2) **Dorothy Gresley** (1608 – 25 Mar 1649)
  = ...; **Rev. Edward Wilmot** (1605 – ...) son of Robert
  Wilmot & Dorothea Shrigley
  (a) **Dorothy Wilmot** (ca.1634 – Nov 1980)
  = ...; **Thomas Robey** (1598 – 1679)
  Has further generations of issue
  (b) **Edward Wilmot** (1640 – ...)
  = ...; **Susanna Coke** (1648 – ...)
  Has further generations of issue
  (3) **Elizabeth Gresley** (
 (D) **John Gresley** (... – aft. Jan 1597/8)
 (E) **Walsingham Gresley** (... – 28 Oct 1633)
 (F) **William Gresley** (... – aft. Jan 1603/4)
 (G) **Henry Gresley** (...)
(II) **Jane Gresley** (ca.1554 Drakelow – ...)
(III) **Mary Gresley** (ca.1556 – ...)
(IV) **Simon Gresley** (1560 Appleton, Cheshire – 4 Jan
1637)
= ...; **Anne Dixwell** (1565 – 1591) daughter of Humphrey
Dixwell
 (A) **George Gresley** (ca.1593 Appleton – 30 Sep 1647)
 (B) **William Gresley** (ca.1595 Appleton – 14 Jun 1637)
 (C) **Marian Gresley** (ca.1597 Appleton – ...)
 (D) **Katherine Gresley** (ca.1599 Appleton – 5 Jul 1689)
 (E) **Mary Gresley** (ca.1601 Appleton – 30 Sep 1647)
 (F) **Letitia Gresley** (1603 Appleton – 2 Dec 1689)
 (G) **Elizabeth Gresley** (ca.1605 Appleton – ...)
(V) **Elizabeth Gresley** (ca.1563 Drakelow – ...)
(VI) **Hastings Gresley** (1566 Drakelow – ...)
(VII) **Grace Gresley** (ca.1568 Drakelow – ...)
b) **Catherine Gresley** (ca.1528 Drakelow – aft.22 Apr 1572)
= ...; **Edward Winter** (1525 Worthington, Leics. – ...)
issue ?
issue of 2nd:
c) **Edward Gresley** (1531 Drakelow – 4 Apr 1594 Alrewas,
Staffs.)
= ...; **Ann Corbet** (1536 Drakelow – ...)

(I) **Charles Gresley** (1557 Drakelow – ...)
(II) **Arthur Gresley** (1559 Drakelow – ...)
(III) **William Gresley** (1561 Drakelow – 1585)
   = ...
   (A) **William Greasley**[101] (1579 Loughborough, Leics. – ...)
     = ...; **Joan Armstrong** (1593 – 1614)
     (1) **William Greasley** (1605 – ...)
       = ...; **Sarah Jarrett** (1611 – ...) daughter of John Jarrett
       (a) **John Greasley** (1636 – ...)
       (b) **Sarah Greasley** (1639 – ...)
         = ...; **Thomas Everard** (1635 – ...)
         issue ?
   (B) **Elizabeth Gresley** (1581 – ...)
   (C) **Humphrey Gresley** (1583 – ...)
   (D) **Richard Gresley** (1585 – ...)
     = ...; **Agnes Chamberlin** (1585 – ...)
     (1) **William Gresley** (1618 – ...)
     (2) **Richard Gresley** (1622 – ...)
       = ...
       (a) **Richard Gresley** (1646 – ...)
         = ...
       Has further generations of issue
(IV) **Thomas Gresley** (1563 Drakelow – ...)
d) **Thomas Gresley** (1533 Lullington, Derbys. – 1572)
= ...; **Margaret ...** (1538 Drakelow – aft. 1572)
(I) **Edward Gresley** (1559 Lullington – ...)
(II) **Charles Gresley** (1565 Lullington – ...)
(III) **Arthur Gresley** (1568 Lullington – ...)
   = ...; **Isabella ...** (1573 Lullington – 19 Feb 1645 Lullington)
   (A) **Sarah Gresley** (1594 Lullington – ...)
   (B) **Judith Gresley** (1596 Lullington – ...)
   (C) **Katherine Gresley** (1599 Lullington – ...)
   (D) **Thomas Gresley** (1603 Lullington – ...)
     = ...; **Mary ...** (...)
     (1) **Frances Gresley** (1630 – ...)
     (2) **Anne Gresley** (1632 – ...)
     (3) **Thomas Gresley** (1635 – ...)
     (4) **Mary Gresley** (1637 – ...)
     (5) **George Gresley** (1639 – ...)
     (6) **William Gresley** (1644 – ...)

---

[101] At some point this line of the family changed the spelling to Greasley. William appears with this spelling on some land records, so I started using it here.

e) **Elizabeth Gresley** (1535 Drakelow – ...)
  = ...; **Charles Somerset** (1530 Drakelow – ...)
  (I) **Susan Somerset** (... – 1618 Suffolk)
    = ...; **Stephen Wilterton** (... – 1622 Suffolk)
    (A) **Susannah Wilterton** (1585 Whersted, Suffolk – 25 Jan 1673)
    = ...; **Thomas Rice** (1588 Cavenham, Suffolk – 1638 Suffolk)
    (1) **Bridget Rice** (1614 Northants. – 1677 Northants.)
      = ...; **Walter Moulton** (1612 Long Bucky, Northants. – 1678 Northants.) son of John Moulton & Mary Hallewell
      (a) **Thomas Moulton** (23 Sep 1638 Great Yarmouth, Norfolk – 17 Jul 1711 Norfolk)
        = ...; **Hannah Levinge** (1641 Norfolk – 1698 Norfolk)
        Has further generations of issue
f) **Eleanor Gresley** (1537 Drakelow – ...)
6) **Robert Gresley** (ca.1496 – aft.1509)
7) **James Gresley** (ca.1498 Colton, Staffs. – ...)

CHAPTER 12
HOLLAND

The Holland family descends from John of Gaunt's second daughter, Elizabeth. She married three times, but only has continuing issue by her second husband, John Holland, Duke of Exeter. John was a son of Joan, the "Fair Maid of Kent" and her first husband. Joan would later marry Edward the Black Prince and by him become the mother of Richard II, making Richard and the Duke of Exeter half-brothers.

The Holland family's first recorded ancestor lived in the mid-1100s, but it is believed they were a Norman family who came to England in, or shortly after, the Conquest. Their rise to prominence began in the 1280s, when a Sir Robert Holland became a favorite of the 2nd Earl of Lancaster and fought with him during the uprising against Edward II. Thomas Holland, who would become the father of the Duke of Exeter, was one of the founding knights of the Order of the Garter.

John Holland received the Dukedom of Exeter from his half-brother, King Richard II, as a reward for successfully arresting the King's uncle, Thomas, Duke of Gloucester and capturing Arundel Castle at the King's request. These actions, and his continued support of his brother, would lead to Exeter's downfall. Once Richard was deposed, Exeter was executed.

Elizabeth's marriage to John Holland was not without its scandal. While she was married to her first husband, nine years her junior and still not reached puberty, she was seduced by Holland. Elizabeth had a bit of a reputation so the rumors of the day questioned who seduced whom, but either way, Elizabeth ended up pregnant, forcing her father, who was on the Regency Council, to have her marriage annulled, after which she quickly married Holland. They would go on to have six surviving children, though only one son, John, and two daughters Constance and Elizabeth, would give their mother grandchildren.

Elizabeth's son, John, dedicated himself to the service of Henrys IV through VI and was rewarded by being restored to his father's titles and estates. One of his last positions was Governor of Aquitaine. Like his mother, he married three times but only has surviving issue from one of the wives, that of his cousin Lady Anne Stafford. He also acknowledged several illegitimate children, but none of them seem to have had children of their own.

John's descendants are all from his daughter, as his son's line became extinct by 1474. This daughter, Lady Anne, continued the tradition of marrying three times and only have children from one of the husbands. In her case, it was the middle one, Baron Neville. Neville was a grandson of the 1st Earl of Westmorland who we will meet in a later chapter. This Baron was descended from the Earl's first wife, but it was the second wife who was Edward III's descendant. The title Earl of Westmorland would be inherited by Anne's and the Baron's son, Ralph, and continue on through his descendants. Some other prominent names to descend from various Neville daughters in this line are branches of the Pelhams, the Stapletons, and Inglebys.

Elizabeth, Duchess of Exeter's elder daughter, Constance, married into one branch of the very large Grey family tree. This branch was the Earls of Kent, which would eventually become extinct in the male line in 1740. Several lines of female descent still exist, the most prominent being the Tufton family who were the Earls of Thanet, and the Cavendish-Bentincks, who would later be Dukes and Earls of Portland.

Constance's younger sister was named Elizabeth for their mother, and she married into the Fiennes family. It was her son, Sir Richard who brought the Dacre Barony into the family when he married the 7th Baroness. Their descendants continue to carry this title, and since it is permitted to go through female lines, has changed the family name a few times. One point of prominence for the family was when the 15th Baron married one of the illegitimate daughters of Charles II. Their daughter ultimately succeeded to the barony and her descendants, the Barrett-Lennards, have large numbers living in England, Canada, the United States and Australia.

Other prominent families descended from Lady Elizabeth Fiennes are the Clintons, who are still the Earls of Lincoln; the Barons Willoughby, who emigrated to Virginia in 1676; and the acting brothers Joseph and Ralph Fiennes. The former played Shakespeare in *Shakespeare in Love* and the latter is famously known as Lord Voldemort from the *Harry Potter* movies.

Edward III

|

John of Gaunt, Duke of Lancaster

|

Elizabeth of Lancaster (bef.21 Feb 1363 Burford, Salop. – 24 Nov 1426 Burford)
=1 24 Jun 1380 Kenilworth Castle, Warks. (ann.1386); **John Hastings, 3ʳᵈ Earl of Pembroke** Baron Abergavenny, Baron Manny (Oct 1372 – 30 Dec 1389) son of John Hastings, 2ⁿᵈ Earl of Pembroke & Anne Manny, 2ⁿᵈ Baroness Manny; =2ⁿᵈ ♦Philippa Mortimer
=2 24 Jun 1386 Plymouth; **John Holland, 1ˢᵗ Duke Exeter**, Earl of Huntingdon, KG (ca.1352 – 16 Jan 1400 Pleshy Castle, Essex) executed; son of Thomas Holland, 1ˢᵗ Earl of Kent & Joan of Kent[102]; KG 1381; cr. Earl 2 Jun 1388 and Duke 29 Sep 1397
=3 1400; **John Cornwall, 1ˢᵗ Baron Fanhope and Milbroke** KG (ca.1364 – 11 Dec 1443) son of John Cornouayl; KG 1409; cr. Baron Fanhope 17 Jul 1433 and Baron Milbroke 30 Jan 1442
issue of 2ⁿᵈ (none by 1ˢᵗ):
1. **Lady Constance Holland** (1387 – 1437)
=1 bef.Jun 1402; **Thomas Mowbray, 4ᵗʰ Earl of Norfolk**, 2ⁿᵈ Earl of Nottingham, 8ᵗʰ Baron Segrave, 7ᵗʰ Baron Mowbray (1385 – 8 Jun 1405) son of Thomas Mowbray, 1ˢᵗ Duke of Norfolk & Lady Elizabeth FitzAlan; suc. father 22 Sep 1399 but not as Duke (which was attainted)
=2 1410; **Sir John Grey KG** (ca.1387 – 27 Aug 1439) son of Reginald Grey, 3ʳᵈ Baron Grey de Ruthyn & Margaret Roos; KG 4 May 1436; =2ⁿᵈ Lady Margaret Mowbray (Thomas' sister)
has issue of 2ⁿᵈ (none by 1ˢᵗ):
a. **Sir Edmund Grey, 1ˢᵗ Earl of Kent**, 4ᵗʰ Baron Grey de Ruthyn (26 Oct 1416 – 22 May 1490) suc. grandfather as Baron 1440; cr. Earl 30 May 1465
= bef.Jan 1459; ♦**Lady Katherine Percy** (28 May 1423 – ...) daughter of Henry Percy, 1ˢᵗ Earl of Northumberland & Lady Eleanor Neville
I) **Anthony Grey** (...)
= **Joan Woodville** (...) daughter of Richard Woodville, 1ˢᵗ Earl Rivers & Jacquetta of Luxembourg
no issue
II) **Sir George Grey, 2ⁿᵈ Earl of Kent**, etc. KT (1454 – 25 Dec 1505 Ampthill) suc. father 2 May 1490; KT 1483

---

[102] Joan was the "Fair Maid of Kent" whose 2ⁿᵈ husband was ♦Edward, Prince of Wales, the "Black Prince."

=1 ...; **Lady Anne Woodville** (... – 30 Jul 1489) daughter of
Richard Woodville, 1st Earl Rivers & Jacquetta of Luxembourg;
she =1st Henry Bouchier, Viscunt Bouchier
=2 1490; **Lady Catherine Herbert** (... – Nov 1506) daughter of
William Herbert, 1st Earl of Pembroke & Anne Devereux
issue of 1st:
A) **Sir Richard Grey, 3rd Earl of Kent**, etc. **KG** (1481 – 3
  May 1524) suc. father 25 Dec 1505; KG 1505
  =1 ...; **Elizabeth Hussey** (... – 19 Nov 1516 Ampthil) daughter
  of Sr William Hussey & Elizabeth Berkeley
  =2 ...; **Margaret Fynche** (...) daughter of James Fynche
  no issue
issue of 2nd:
B) **Lady Anne Grey** (1490 Denbigh – bef.11 Feb 1545/6)
  = ca.1509; **Sir John Hussey, 1st Baron Hussey of Sleaford**
  (1466 – 1537) son of Sir William Hussey & Elizabeth
  Berkeley; =1st Margaret Blount
  1) **Hon. Ann Hussey** (...)
    = ...; **Sir Humphrey Browne** (... – aft.1562)
    a) **Christian Browne** (...)
      = 10 Dec 1575; **Sir John Tufton, 1st Baronet** (1544 – 2 Apr 1624)
      son of John Tufton & Mary Baker; =1st Olympia Blore; cr. Baronet
      of Hothfeld, Kent 29 Jun 1611
      (I) **Nicholas Tufton, 1st Earl of Thanet**, 2nd Baronet (of
        Hothfeld) (19 Jan 1577/8 Terling, Essex – 1 Jul 1631 Sapcote,
        Leics.) suc. father 1624, cr. Earl 5 Aug 1628
        = bef.3 Sep 1602; ♦**Lady France Cecil** (28 Feb 1580/1
        London – 12 Jun 1653 Rainham, Kent) daughter of Thomas Cecil,
        1st Earl of Exeter & Dorothy Neville
        (A) **Elizabeth Tufton** (... – 24 Jan 1622)
          = 29 Nov 1619; **Sir Edward Dering, 1st Baronet** (28 Jan
          1598 – 22 Jun 1644) =2nd Anne Ashburnham
          no issue
        (B) **Lady Dorothy Tufton** (ca.1606 – 28 Jan 1635 Downham.
          Lancs.)
          = aft.17 Apr 1630; **Sir Ralph Assheton**, (later **2nd Baronet**)
          (ca.1605 – 30 Jan 1679/80 London) son of Sir Ralph Assheton,
          1st Baronet & Dorothy Bellingham; =2nd Elizabeth Harington;
          suc. father 18 Oct 1644
          no issue
        (C) **Lady Mary Tufton** (... – 1663)
          = ca.1626; **Sir Edward Bishopp, 2nd Baronet** (ca.1601 – Apr
          1649) son of Sir Thomas Bishopp, 2nd Baronet & Jane Weston;
          suc. father 1626
          (1) **Sir Thomas Bishopp, 3rd Baronet** (3 Dec 1627 Parham,
            Sussex – 1652) unm. suc. father 1649

(2) **France Bisopp** (... – 14 Dec 1694)
   = 2 May 1642 London; **Sir Henry Goring, 2nd Baronet** (22
   May 1622 Washsington, Sussex – 3 Apr 1702) son of Henry
   Goring & Mary Eversfield; suc. Feb 1679/80 under special
   remainder
   (a) **Henry Goring** (ca.1647 – 1687) slain by Sir Edward
      Dering, 3rd Baronet
      =1 3 Oct 1667; **Elizabeth Morewood** (ca.1651 – Jun 1673)
      daughter of Anthony Morewood
      =2 2 Feb 1675; **Mary Covert** (...) daughter of Sir John
      Covert, 1st Baronet; =2nd Nicholas Best
      Has additional generations of issue by both
   (3) **Sir Cecil Bishopp, 4th Baronet** (ca.1635 – 3 Jun 1705
   Parham)
   = 7 Jun 1666 Culham, Oxon; **Sarah Bury** (11 Sep 1650 –
   ca.Mar 1679 Culham) daughter of George Bury
   (a) **Sir Cecil Bishopp, 5th Baronet** (... – 25 Oct 1725
      Parham) suc. father 1705
      = 13 Aug 1698; **Elizabeth Dunch** (1684 – bef.1751)
      daughter of Henry Dunch
      Has additional generations of issue
   (b) **Christian Bishopp** (... – 30 Aug 1765)
      = ...; **Sir Robert Fagge, 3rd Baronet** (... – 22 Jun 1736)
      son of Sir Robert Fagge, 2nd Baronet & Elizabeth Culpepper;
      suc. father 26 Aug 1715
      Has additional generations of issue
(D) **John Tufton, 2nd Earl of Thanet**, etc. (1609 – 6 May
   1664) suc. father 1631
   = 21 Apr 1629; ♦**Lady Margaret Sackville** (2 Jul 1614 – 14
   Aug 1676) daughter of Richard Sackville, 3rd Earl of Dorset &
   Anne Clifford, 14th Baroness Clifford
   (1) **Nicholas Tufton, 3rd Earl of Thanet**, etc. (7 Aug 1631 –
      24 Nov 1679) suc. father 1664
      = 11 Apr 1664; ♦**Lady Elizabeth Boyle** (... – 1 Sep 1725)
      daughter of Richard Boyle, 2nd Earl of Cork & Elizabeth
      Clifford, 2nd Baroness Clifford
      no issue
   (2) **Lady Mary Tufton** (... – Feb 1673/4)
      = 1671; **Sir William Walter, 2nd Baronet** (... – 5 Mar 1693)
      son of Sir William Walter, 1st Baronet & Elizabeth Lucas; =1st
      Lady Mary Bruce; suc. father 23 Mar 1675
      (a) **Sir John Walter, 3rd Baronet** (ca.1673 – 11 Jun 1722)
         suc. father 1693
         = ...; **Elizabeth Vernon** (1678 – 12 Jul 1748) daughter of
         Sir Thomas Vernon; =2nd Simon Harcourt, 1st Viscount
         Harcourt

no issue

(3) **Lady Cecilia Tufton** (... − 1672 Castle Cornet, Guernsey) killed in an explosion

= ...; **Christopher Hatton, 2nd Baron Hatton** (later 1st Viscount Hatton) (1632 − 1706) son of Christopher Fatton, 1st Baron Hatton; =2nd Frances Yelverton; =3rd Elizabeth Haslewood; suc. father 1670, cr. Viscount 1682

(a) **Hon. Anne Hatton** (... − 26 Sep 1743)

= 29 Dec 1685; **Daniel Finch, 7th Earl of Winchilsea**, Viscount of Maidstone, 2nd Earl of Nottingham, Baron Finch, 2nd & 8th Baronet (2 Jul 1647 − 1 Jan 1729/30) son of Heneage Finch, 1st Earl of Nottingham & Elizabeth Harvey; suc. father 18 Feb 1679/80; suc. cousin in Winchilsea 9 Sep 1729

Has additional generations of issue

(4) **Lady Margaret Tufton** (13 Jul 1636 − aft.1687 Canterbury, Kent)

= 18 Jul 1653 London; **George Coventry, 3rd Baron Coventry** (ca.1628 − 15 Dec 1680 London) son of Thomas Coventry, 2nd Baron Coventry & Mary Craven; suc. father 27 Oct 1661

(a) **John Coventry, 4th Baron Coventry** (2 Sep 1654 Croome Dabitot, Worcs. − 25 Jul 1687) unm. suc. father 1680

(b) **Hon. Margaret Coventry** (14 Sep 1657 Hothfield, Kent − 7 Feb 1681/2)

= 10 Jul 1679 London; ◆**Charles, Marquess of Winchester** (later **2nd Duke of Bolton**, etc.) (1661 − 21 Jan 1721/2 London) son of Charles Powlett, 1st Duke of Bolton & Mary le Scrope; suc. father 27 Feb 1698/9 no issue

(5) **John Tufton, 4th Earl of Thanet**, etc. (7 Aug 1638 − 27 Apr 1680) unm. suc. father 1679

(6) **Richard Tufton, 5th Earl of Thanet**, etc. (30 May 1640 − 8 Mar 1683/4) unm. suc brother 1680

(7) **Thomas Tufton, 6th Earl of Thanet**, etc. **18th Baron Clifford** (30 Aug 1644 − 30 Jul 1729) suc. brother 1683/4; suc. distant cousin as Baron Clifford 12 Dec 1691 which fell into abeyance among his daughters at this death

(a) **Lady Katherine Tufton** (24 Ap 1693 − 13 Feb 1733/4)

= 1709; ◆**Edward, Viscount Sondes** (...−1722)

Children are listed with other parent

(b) **Lady Anne Tufton** (9 Aug 1693 − 22 Apr 1750)

= 1708/9; ◆**James Cecil, 5th Earl of Salisbury** (1691 − 1728)

Children are listed with other parent

(c) **Lady Isabella Tufton** (... – 10 Jan 1764)
=1 1731; ◆**Lord Sir Nassau Powlett** (1698 – 1741)
=2 ...; **Sir Francis** Blake **Delaval KB** (1727 – 1771) son of
Francis Delaval & Rhoda Apreece
issue of 1st (none by 2nd):
Children are listed with other parent

(d) **Margaret Tufton, 19th Baroness Clifford** (16 Jun
1700 – 28 Feb 1775 Holkham, Norfolk) suc. when abeyance
was terminated in her favor 3 Aug 1734
= 3 Jul 1718; **Thomas Coke, Earl of Leicester**, Viscount
Coke, Baron Lovel **KB** (17 Jun 1697 – 20 Apr 1759) son of
Edward Coke & Cary Newton cr. Earl 9 May 1744, which
became extinct upon his death; KB 1725
Issue extinct 1753

(e) **Lady Mary Tufton** (6 Jul 1701 – 19 Feb 1785)
=1 17 Feb 1718; ◆**Anthony Grey, 3rd Baron Lucas** (21 Feb
1695/6 – 21 Jul 1723) son of Henry Grey, Duke of Kent &
Hon. Jemima Crew; suc. cousin 8 Nov 1718
=2 16 May 1736; **John Leveson-Gower, 1st Earl Gower,**
Viscount Tentham, 2nd Baron Gower, 6th Baronet (10 Aug
1694 – 25 Dec 1754) son of John Leveson-Gower, 1st Baron
Gower & Lady Catherine Manners; =1st Lady Evelyn
Pierrepont; =2nd Penelope Stonhouse; suc. father 31 Aug
1709
Has additional generations of issue by 2nd

(8) **Sackville Tufton** (ca.1647 – 30 Mar 1721)
= ...; ◆**Elizabeth Wilbraham** (...) daughter of Ralph
Wilbraham & Christiana Leigh

(a) **Sackville Tufton, 7th Earl of Thanet** etc. (11 May
1688 – 4 Dec 1753) suc. uncle 1729
= 11 Jun 1722; **Lady Mary Saville** (1700 – 30 Jul 1751)
daughter of William Saville, 2nd Marquess of Halifax & Lady
Mary Finch
Has additional generations of issue

(9) **Lady Anne Tufton** (ca.1654 – 22 Nov 1713)
= bef.1674; **Sir Samuel Grimston, 3rd Baronet** (74 jan
1643 – Oct 1700) son of Sir Harbottle Grimston, 2nd Baronet &
Mary Croke; =1st Lady Elizabeth Finch; suc. father 2 Jan 1685
no issue

(II) **Mary Tufton** (... – 1659)
= ca.1612; **Henry Constable, 1st Viscount Dunbar** (ca.1588 –
1645) son of Sir Henry Constable & Margaret Dormer; cr.
Viscount 14 Nov 1620

(A) **John Constable, 2nd Viscount Dunbar** (1615 – ca.1668)
suc. father 1645
= ...

(1) **Robert Constable, 3rd Viscount Dunbar** (1651 – 1714)
suc. father 1668
(2) **William Constable, 4th Viscount Dunbar** (1654 – 1718)
suc. brother 1714; became extinct upon his death
(B) **Hon. Mary Constable** (...)
= ...; **Robert Brudenell, 2nd Earl of Cardigan** Baron
Brudenell, 2nd Baronet (5 Mar 1607 – 16 Jul 1703) son of
Thomas Brudenell, 1st Earl of Cardigan & Mary Tresham; suc.
father 16 Sep 1663
no surviving issue
(III) **Sir Humphrey Tufton, 1st Baronet** (of the Mote, Kent)
(... –1659)
= ...; **Margaret Morley** (ca.1586 – ca.1667) daughter of Herbert
Morley
(A) **Olimpia Tufton** (...)
= ...; ♦**Sir William Wray, 1st Baronet** (1625 – 1669)
Children are listed with other parent
(IV) **Richard Tufton** (... – ca.3 Oct 1631)
= ...; **Chrysogon Morley** (...) daughter of Herbert Morley & Ann
Lennard
(A) **Christian Tufton** (...)
= ...; **Sir Richard Huddleston** (...) son of Henry Huddleston
& Dorothy Dormer
issue ?
(V) **Cecily Tufton** (1587 – 19 Sep 1653)
=1 bef.1607; **Sir Edward Hungerford** (... – 1607) son of Walter
Hungerford, 1st Baron Hungerford & Alice Sandys; =1st Jane ...
=2 aft. 26 Oct 1608; ♦**Francis Manners, 6th Earl of Rutland**,
etc. (1578 – 17 Dec 1632) son of John Manners, 4th Earl of
Rutland & Elizabeth Charlton; suc. brother 26 Jun 1612
no issue
(VI) **Sir William Tufton, 1st Baronet** (of Vinters, Kent) (1589 –
1650 Barbados) cr. Baronet 1622, but it went extinct upon his
death; was Gov. of Barbados
= 30 Jan 1620 Greenwich, Kent; **Anne Cave** (... – 31 Mar 1649)
daughter of Cecil Cave
(A) **Vere Tufton** (...)
=1 ...; ♦**Sir Thomas Beaumont, 3rd Baronet** (1620 – 1686)
=2 aft.1686; **George Lane** (...)
issue of 1st:
Children are listed with other parent
2) **Hon. Bridget Hussey** (ca.1526 – 12 Jan 1600/1)
=1 ...; **Sir Richard Morrison** (... – 17 Mar 1556 Strasbourg,
France) son of Thomas Morrison & ... Merry
=2 1560; ♦**Henry Manners, 2nd Earl of Rutland**, etc. (... – 17
Sep 1563) son of Thomas Manners, 1st Earl of Rutland & Eleanor

Paston; =1st ♦Lady Margaret Neville

=3 25 Jun 1566; ♦**Francis Russell, 2nd Earl of Bedford**, etc.
(1527 – 28 Jul 1585 London) son of John Rusasell, 1st Earl of Bedford
& Anne Sapcote; =1st Margaret St.John
issue of 1st (none by others):
a) **Jane** Sibella **Morrison** (... – Jul 1615)
   =1 ca.1571; ♦**Edward, Lord Russell** (... – bef.Jun 1572) son of
   Francis Russell, 2nd Earl of Bedford & Margaret St.John
   =2 aft.1572; ♦**Arthur Grey, 14th Baron Grey** (1536 – 1593)
   issue of 2nd (none by 1st):
   Children are listed with other parent
b) **Elizabeth Morrison** (... – 4 Jul 1611)
   =1 ca.1576; ♦**William Norris** (ca.1548 – 1579)
   =2 1586; ♦**Henry Clinton, 2nd Earl of Lincoln** (1540 – 1616)
   issue of 1st:
   Children are listed with other parent
   issue of 2nd:
   Children are listed with other parent
C) **Henry Grey, 4th Earl of Kent**, etc. (ca.1495 – 24 Sep 1562)
suc. half-brother 3 May 1524
= ...; **Anne Blennerhasset** (...)
1) **Henry Grey** (1520 – 1545)
= ...; **Margaret St.John** (...)
a) **Reginald Grey, 5th Earl of Kent**, etc. (bef.1541 – 17 Mar
   1573) suc. grandfather 24 Sep 1562
   = ...; **Susan Bertie** (...) daughter of Bertie Bertie &
   Catherine Willoughby, 12th Baroness Willoughby of
   Eresby
   no issue
b) **Henry Grey, 6th Earl of Kent**, etc. (1541 – 31 Jan
   1615/6) suc. brother 17 Mar 1573
   = ...; **Mary Cotton** (...) daughter of Sir George Cotton &
   Mary Onley
   no issue
c) **Charles Grey, 7th Earl of Kent**, etc. (aft.1541 – 26 Sep
   1623) suc. brother 31 Jan 1516/6
   = ...; **Susan Cotton** (...) daughter of Sir Richard Cotton
   (I) **Sir Henry Grey, 8th Earl of Kent**, etc. (ca.1583 – 21
     Nov 1639) suc. father 26 Sep 1623; Kt.1603
     = 16 Nov 1601 London; ♦**Lady Elizabeth Talbot** (1582 – 7 Dec
     1651) daughter of Gilbert Talbot, 7th Earl of Shrewsbury & Mary
     Cavendish
     no issue
   (II) **Lady Susan Grey** (... – Dec 1620)
     = ...; **Sir Michael Longueville** (...)
     (A) **Charles Longueville, 12th Baron Grey de Ruthyn**

(...) suc. uncle (Earl of the Kent) as Baron 21 Nov 1639

2) **Katherine Grey** (...)
=1 ...; **... Slayton** (...)
=2 ...; **... Spencer** (...)
issue ?

D) **George Grey** (...)

E) **Anthony Grey** (...)
= ...

1) **George Grey** (...)
= ...; **Margery Salvaine** (...) daughter of Gerard Salvain

a) **Rev. Anthony Grey, 9th Earl of Kent** (1557 – 9 Nov 1643) suc 2nd cousin 21 Nov 1639
= ...; **Magdalene Purfoy** (...) daughter of William Purfoy & Katherine Wigston

(I) **Lady Grace Grey** (1593 Burbage, Leics. – ...)
= ...; **James Ward** (...)
issue ?

(II) **Henry Grey, 10th Earl of Kent** (24 Nov 1594 Burbage – 28 May 1651) suc. father 9 Nov 1643
=1 ...; **Mary Courteen** (... – 9 Mar 1644/5) daughter of Sir William Courteen
=2 1 Aug 1644; **Annabel Benn** (...) daughter of Sir Anthony Benn; =1st Anthony Fane
issue of 1st:

(A) **Henry Grey** (+young)
issue of 2nd:

(B) **Anthony Grey, 11th Earl of Kent** (1645 – 19 Aug 1702) suc. father 28 May 1651
= ...; ♦**Mary Lucas, Baroness Lucas of Crudwell**[103] (... – 1 Nov 1702) daughter of John Lucas, 1st Baron Lucas of Crudwell

(1) **Sir Henry Grey, 1st Duke of Kent**, Marquess of Kent, Earl of Harold, Viscount Goderich; 1st Marquess Grey; 12th Earl of Kent, 2nd Baron Lucas of Crudwell **KG** (1671 – 5 Jun 1740) suc father 19 Aug 1702; suc. mother 1 Nov 1702; cr. Marquess etc. 1706; cr. Duke 1710; KG 1712; all titled except Marquess of Grey and Baron Lucas became extinct upon his death[104]

---

[103] Lady Lucas was cr. Baroness in her own right with a unique remainder: it will not fall in abeyance between female co-heirs. The senior female automatically inherits.

[104] The Marquess of Grey was cr. with a special remainder for the heirs male of Lady Jemina Campbel, the 1st Marquess' granddaughter.

=1 ..; **Jemima Crew** (... – 2 Jul 1728) daughter of
Thomas Crew, 2nd Baron Crew & Anne Armine
=2 24 Mar 1729; **Lady Sophia Bentinck** (... – 5 Jun
1741) daughter of William Bentinck, 1st Earl of
Portland & Jane Temple
issue of 1st:
(a) **Anthony, Earl of Harold** (21 Feb 1695 – 21 Jul
   1723)
   = 17 Feb 1718; **Lady Mary Tufton** (...) daughter of
   Thomas Tufton, 6th Earl of Thanet & Lady Catherine
   Cavendish; =2nd John Levenson-Gower, 1st Earl
   Gower
   no issue
(b) **Henry Grey** (1696 – 1717)
(c) **Lady Amabel Grey** (... – 2 Mar 1726)
   = 20 Feb 1717; **John Campbell, 3rd Earl of
   Breadalbane and Holland,** Lord Glenorchy, **KB**
   (10 Mar 1696/7 – 26 Jan 1782) son of John
   Campbell, 2nd Earl of Breadalbane and Holland &
   Henriette Villiers; suc. father 1752; =2nd Arabella
   Pershall
   Has further generations of issue
(d) **Lady Jemima Grey** (1699 – 7 Jul 1731)
   = aft.1718; **John Ashburnham, 1st Earl of
   Ashburnham,** Viscount St. Aspagh, 3rd Baron
   Ashburnham (13 Mar 1687/8 – 10 Mar 1737) son of
   John Ashburnham, 1st Baron Ashburnham & Bridget
   Vaughan; =1st Lady Mary Butler; =2nd Henrietta
   Stanley, 4th Baroness Strange; suc. brother as Baron
   1710; cr. Earl and Viscount 14 May 1730
   Has further generations of issue
(e) **Lady Anne Grey** (... – 20 Sep 1733)
   = 9 Jan 1727; **Lord Charles Cavendish** (17 Mar
   1704 – 28 Apr 1783) son of William Cavendish, 2nd
   Duke of Devonshire & Rachel Russell
   Has further generations of issue
(f) **Lady Mary Grey** (...)
   = ...; **Rev. David Gregory** (1696 – 16 Sep 1767) son
   of David Gregory
   issue ?
issue of 2nd:
(g) **George, Earl of Harold** (1732–1733)
(h) **Lady Anne** Sophia **Grey** (... – 24 Mar 1780)
   = 21 Nov 1748; **Rt.Rev. John Egerton, Bishop of
   Durham** (30 Nov 1721 – 18 Jun 1787) son of
   Rt.Rev. Henry Egerton; =2nd Mary Boughton

Has further generations of issue
(2) **Lady Anabel Grey** (... – 1762)
(C) **Lady Elizabeth Grey** (...)
= ...; **Banastre Maynard, 3rd Baron Maynard** (ca.1642 – 3
Mar 1718) son of William Maynard, 2nd Baron Maynard &
Dorothy Banastre; suc. father 3 Feb 1699/1700
(1) **Hon. Annabella Maynard** (... – 8 Aug 1734)
= 1691; **Sir William Lowther, 1st Baronet** (... – 6 Mar
1728/9) daughter of Sir William Lowther & Catherine
Harrison
(a) **Sir William Lowther, 2nd Baronet** (... – 22 Dec 1763)
suc. father 1728/9, but title became extinct upon his death
=1 1719; **Diana Condon** (... – 1 Jan 1736) daughter of
Thomas Condon
=2 17 Aug 1736; **Catherine Ramsden** (... – 5 Jan 1778)
daughter of Sir William Ramsden, 2nd Baronet & Hon.
Elizabeth Lowther
no issue
(b) **Henry Lowther** (... – 1743) unm.
(c) **John Lowther** (...) unm. Gov. of Surat
(III) **Lady Magdalene Grey** (14 Nov 1596 Burbage – Sep 1668)
= ...; **John Browne** (...)
issue ?
(IV) **Lady Christian Grey** (8 May 1598 Burbage – 5 Jan 1681)
= ...; **Theophilus Burdett** (...)
issue ?
(V) **Faithmyjoye Grey** (1599 Burbage – 1602)
(VI) **Lady Patience Grey** (1603 Burbage – ...)
= ...; **... Wood** (...)
issue ?
(VII) **John Grey** (Apr – Sep 1605 Burbage)
(VIII) **Job Grey** (1606 Burbage – ...)
(IX) **Theophilus Grey** (1608 Burbage – 30 Mar 1679)
(X) **Lady Priscilla Grey** (1609 Burbage – 1644)
(XI) **Nathaniel Grey** (1613 Burbage – ...)
(XII) **Lady Presela Grey** (1615 Burbage – ...)
III) **Lady Elizabeth Grey** (...)
= ...; **Sir Robert Greystock** (...)
issue ?
IV) **Lady Anne Grey** (...)
= ...; **John Grey, Baron Grey of Wilton** (...)
issue ?
b. **Sir Thomas Grey, Baron Richemount Grey** (... – 1461)
executed; cr. Baron 25 Jun 1450
c. **Lady Constance Grey** (...)
= ...; **Sir Richard Herbert** (...)

2. **Lady Elizabeth Holland** (ca.1389 – 18 Nov 1449)
= ...; **Sir Roger Fiennes, Kt.** (ca.1384 – ca.1449) son of William
Fiennes & Elizabeth Battisford; Kt. 1422
a. **Robert Fiennes** (...)
b. **James Fiennes** (...)
c. **Margaret Fiennes** (...)
  = ...; **Sir Nicholas Carew** (...)
  issue ?
d. **Sir Richard Fiennes** (1415 – 25 Nov 1483)
= Jun 1446; **Joan Dacre, 7ᵗʰ Baroness Dacre** (ca.1433 – 8 Mar
1486) daughter of Sit Thomas Dacre & Elizabeth Bowett; suc.
grandfather 5 Jan 1458
  I) **Sir John Fiennes** (ca.1447 Herstmonceux Castle, Sussex –
    8 Mar 1485/6)
  = ...; **Alice FitzHugh** (ca.1448 – 10 Jul 1516) daughter of
  Henry FitzHugh, 5ᵗʰ Baron FitzHugh & Lady Alice Neville
    A) **Sir Thomas Fiennes KB, 8ᵗʰ Baron Dacre** (... – 9 Sep
      1533) KB1484; suc. father 8 Mar 1485/6
    = ca.1492; **Anne Bourchier** (...) daughter of Sir Humphrey
    Bourchier & Elizabeth Tylney
      1) **Sir Thomas Fiennes** (... – 26 Oct 1528)
      = 1514; **Joan Sutton** (... – Aug 1539) daughter of Edward
      Sutton, 2ⁿᵈ Baron Dudley & Cicely Willoughby
        a) **Thomas Fiennes, 9ᵗʰ Baron Dacre** (ca.1516 – 29 Jun
          1541) executed for murder; suc. grandfather 9 Sep 1533;
          titled was attainted 1541
          = 1536; ♦**Mary Neville** (aft.1523 – ca.1576) daughter of
          George Neville, 3ʳᵈ Baron Abergavenny & Lady Mary
          Stafford; =2ⁿᵈ ... Wooten; =3ʳᵈ Sir Thomas Thursby
          (I) **Gregory Fiennes, 10ᵗʰ Baron Dacre** (bap.25 Jun
            1539 – 25 Sep 1594) restored in titles 1558
            = bef.1558; **Ann Sackville** (... – 14 May 1595) daughter
            of Sir Robert Sackville & Winifred Brydges
            no issue
          (II) **Margaret Fiennes, (11ᵗʰ) Baroness Dacre** (1541 – 16
            Mar 1611/2) suc. brother 25 Sep 1594
            = 10 Nov 1564; **Sampson Lennard** (... – 20 Sep 1615)
            (A) **Elizabeth Lennard** (...)
              = 3 Jan 1589/9 Sevenoaks, Kent; **Sir Francis Barnham**
              (...)
              (1) **Dacre Barnham** (ca.1604 – ...)
              (2) **Sir Robert Barnham, Baronet** (ca.1606 – May/Jun
                1685) cr. Baronet 15 Aug 1663; title became extinct
                upon his death
                =1 ...; **Elizbaeth Henley** (...) daughter of Robert Henley
                =2 1663; **Hannah Nichols** (ca.1625 – 1685)

issue of 1st:

(a) **Mary Barnham** (...)
= ...; **Sir Nathaniel Powell, 2nd Baronet** (ca.1640 –
ca.1707) son of Sir Nathaniel Powell, 1st Baronet;
suc. father 1675
Has further generations of issue

(b) **Elizabeth Barnham** (...)

(c) **Ann Barnham** (...)

(d) **Francis Barnham** (ca.1637 – 1668)
= 12 Sep 1667; **Anne Parker** (...) daughter of Sir
Thomas Parker; =1st John Shirley
no issue

issue of 2nd:

(e) **Philadelphia Barnham** (1664 – ...)
= ...; **Thomas Rider** (...)
issue ?

(B) **Ann Lennard** (...)
= ...; **Herbert Morley** (...)

(1) **Christian Morley** (...)
= ...; **Richard Tufton** (...) son of Sir John Tufton, 1st
Baronet & Christian Browne
issue ?

(2) **Margaret Morley** (ca.1586 – ca.1667)
= ...; **Sir Humfrey Tufton, 1st Baronet** (1584 – Oct
1659 Bobbing, Kent) son of Sir John Tufton, 1st
Baronet (of Hothfield) & Christian Browne; cr. 1st
Baronet (of the Mote) 24 Dec 1641

(a) **Sir John Tufton, 2nd Baronet** (ca.1623 – 11 Oct
1685) suc. father Oct 1659; baronetcy became
extinct upon his death
=1 ...; **Margaret Wotton** (...) daughter of Thomas
Wotton, 2nd Baron Wotton
=2 bef.1657; **Mary Altham** (...) daughter of Sir
James Altham
no issue

(b) **Olimpia Tufton** (...)
= ...; **Sir William Wray, 1st Baronet** (1625–1669)
son of Sir Christopher Wray & Albinia Cecil
Has further generations of issue

(C) **Sir Henry Lennard, 12th Baron Dacre** (bap.25 Mar
1570 – 8 Aug 1616) Ktr. 1596; suc. mother 16 Mar
1611/2
= 1589; **Chrysogona Baker** (... – ca.Sep 1616)
daughter of Sir Richard Baker & Mary Giffard

(1) **Pembroke Lennard** (... – 1643)
= ...; **Sir William Brooke** (*de jure* 12th Baron

Cobham) (bap.1 Dec 1601 – 20 Sep 1643 Newbury,
Berks.) died of wounds received in action; son of Rev.
George Brooke & Elizabeth Burgh; =2nd Penelope
Hill; suc. uncle, but for attainder, 1619; upon his death
the claim to the Barony fell into abeyance between his
four daughters

(a) **Pembroke Brooke** (bap.1 Oct 1626 – 10 Jun
1683)
= ...; **Sir Matthew Tomlinson** (... – 5 Nov 1681)
son of John Tomlinson & Eleanor Dodsworth
no surviving issue

(2) **Philadelphia Lennard** (...)
= ...; **Sir Thomas Parker** (...)

(a) **Mary Parker** (bap.15 May 1637 Willingdon,
Sussex – ...)
= aft.1658; ♦**Thomas Howard, 3rd Earl of
Berkshire** (1619 – 1702)
Children listed with other parent

(3) **Margaret Lennard** (...)
= ...; **Sir Anthony Wildgoose** (...)
issue ?

(4) **Richard Lennard, 13th Baron Dacre** (Apr 1596 –
18 Aug 1630) suc. father 8 Aug 1616
=1 14 Jul 1617; **Elizabeth Throckmorton** (... – Feb
1621/2) daughter of Sir Arthur Throckmorton
=2 4 Jan 1624/5; **Dorothy North** (ca.1605 – 21 Apr
1698) daughter of Dudley North, 3rd Baron North &
Frances Brocket; =2nd Challoner Chute
issue of 1st:

(a) **Francis Lennard, 14th Baron Dacre** (11 May
1619 – 12 May 1662) suc. father 18 Aug 1630
= 1641; **Elizabeth Bayning, Countess of Shepey**
(1624 – 1686) daughter of Paul Bayning, 1st
Viscount of Sudbury & Anne Glemham; cr.
Countess (*ad personam*) 6 Sep 1680
Has further generations of issue
issue of 2nd:

(b) **Richard Barrett** (... – 1696) né Lennard, changed
as heir to estates of kinsman, 1st Baron Barrett
= ...; **Anne Loftus** (...) daughter of Sir Robert Loftus
& Elinor Rishe
Has further generations of issue

(5) **Fynes Lennard** (...)
= ...; **... Prude** (...)
issue ?

(6) **Edward Lennard** (...) unm.

(7) **Barbara Lennard** (...)
= ...; **Sir Philip Stapleton** (...)
issue ?
(D) **Mary Lennard** (...)
= ...; **Sir Ralph Bosville** (...)
issue ?
(E) **Margaret Lennard** (...)
= ...; **Sir Thomas Waller** (...)
(1) **Gen. Sir William Waller** (1598 – 19 Sep 1668)
=1 ...; **Jane Reynell** (...)
=2 ...; **Lady Anne Finch** (... – 1652) daughter of
Thomas Finch, 2nd Earl Winchilsea
=3 ...; **Hon. Anne Paget** (...) daughter of Sir William
Paget, 5th Baron Paget & Lady Frances Rich; =1st Sir
Simon Harcourt
issue of 1st:
(a) **Anne Waller** (... – 23 Aug 1664)
= ...; (her step-brother) **Philip Harcourt** (... – 20
Mar 1687) son of Sir Simon Harcourt & Hon. Anne
Paget
Has further generations of issue
issue of 2nd (none by 3rd):
(b) **Margaret Waller** (... – Jan 1693/4)
= ...; **Sir William Courtenay, 1st Baronet** (bap.7
Sep 1628 – 4 Aug 1702) son of Francis Courtenay &
Elizabeth Seymour
Has further generations of issue
(F) **Frances Lennard** (...)
= ...; **Sir Robert More** (...)
issue ?
(G) **Gregory Lennard** (... – 1620)
= 1614; **Maud Llewellyn** (...) daughter of Richard
Llewellyn
no surviving issue
2) **Mary Fiennes** (...)
= ...; **Sir Henry Norreys** (... – 17 May 1536) son of Sir Edward
Norreys & Frideswide Lovel
a) **Mary Norreys** (...)
= ...; **Sir Arthur Champernowne** (...)
(I) **Elizabeth Champernowne** (...)
= 1576; ♦**Sir Edward Seymour, 1st Baronet** (1556–1613)
Children are listed with other parent
(II) **Gawen Champernowne** (...)
= ...
(A) **Arthur Champernowne** (1579 – ...)
= ...

435

(1) **Elizabeth Champernowne** (...)
= ...; **John Giffard** (1612 – aft.1666) son of John Giffard &
Elizbaeth Tremaine
no issue
(2) **Amias Champernowne** (1605 – 1661)
= ...
  (a) **Arthur Champernowne** (... – 1697)
  = ...
  Has further generations of issue
b) **Henry Norreys, 1ˢᵗ Baron Norris** (ca.1525 – 27 Jun 1601)
cr. Baron 6 May 1572
= ...; **Margaret Williams** (...) daughter of John Williams
(I) **Hon. William Norris** (bef.1550 – 25 Dec 1579)
= 1576; ♦**Elizabeth Morrison** (... – 4 Jul 1611) daughter of Sir
Richard Morrison & Bridget Hussey; =2ⁿᵈ ♦Henry Clinton, 2ⁿᵈ
Earl of Lincoln
(A) **Francis Norris, Earl of Berkshire** Viscount Thame, 2ⁿᵈ
Baron Norris **KB** (6 Jul 1579 – 29 Jan 1621/2) suc.
grandfather 1601; cr. Earl etc. 28 Jan 1620/1, but those titles
became extinct upon his death; KB 1605
= 28 Apr 1599; ♦**Lady Bridget de Vere** (6 Apr 1584 – 1631)
daughter of Edward de Vere, 17ᵗʰ Earl of Oxford & Hon. Anne
Cecil
(1) **Elizabeth Norris, 3ʳᵈ Baroness Norris** (... – Nov
1645) suc. father 1622
= 27 May 1622; **Edward Wray** (...) son of Sir William
Wray, 1ˢᵗ Baronet & Lucy Montagu
(a) **Bridget Wray, 4ᵗʰ Baroness Norris** (12 May 1627 –
Mar 1656/7) suc. mother 1645
=1 bef.1646; ♦**Hon. Edward Sackville** (6 Jan 1623 –
1646) son of Edward Sackville, 4ᵗʰ Earl of Dorset & Mary
Curzon
=2 aft.1646; ♦**Montagu Bertie, 2ⁿᵈ Earl of Lindsey**
(1608–1666)
issue of 2ⁿᵈ (none by 1ˢᵗ):
Children are listed with other parent
has issue by **Sarah Rose** (...) = Samuel Hayward:
(2) **Francis Rose** (...)
(II) **Hon. Thomas Norris** (...)
= ...
(A) **Elizabeth Norris** (...)
= ...; **Sir John Jephson** (... – 16 May 1638) son of William
Jephson & Mary Dannett
(1) **William Jephson** (1609 – 1658)
= ...; **Alicia Denham** (...)
(a) **John Jephson** (ca.1638 – ...)

= 1661; ♦**Hon. Elizabeth Boyle** (...) daughter of Francis
Boyle, 1st Viscount Shannon & Elizabeth Killigrew
Has further generations of issue
(b) **Alicia Jephson** (...)
= Feb 1664; **Bartholomew Purdon** (ca.1635
Ballyclough, co. Cork – 19 Sep 1689 Galway) son of Sir
Nicholas Purdon & Ellis Stephens
Has further generations of issue
(c) **William Jephson** (... – 1692)
= ...; **Mary Lewis** (...) daughter of William Lewis & Mary
Denham
no issue
(d) **Denham Jephson** (... – bef.1677) unm.
(e) **Anthony Jephson** (...)
(f) **Mary Jephson** (...)
(g) **Penelope Jephson** (...)
(h) **Frances Jephson** (...)
(2) **John Jephson** (...)
=1 ...; ♦**Bridget Boyle** (ca.1604 – ...) daughter of Rt.Hon.
Most Rev. Richard Boyle, Archbishop of Tuam & Martha
Wright
=2 ...; ♦**Philippa Neville** (...) dsaughter of Sir Henry
Nevielle & Elizabeth Smythe
issue of 1st (none by 2nd):
(a) **John Jephson** (...)
= ...; **... Maguire** (...) daughter of Richard Maguire
Has further generations of issue
(b) **Michael Jephson** (...)
(c) **Very Rev. William Jephson** (ca.1655 – 11 Apr 1720)
= ...; **Anne Barry** (...) daughter of Redmond Barry
Has further generations of issue
(3) **Norris Jephson** (...)
= ...; **Eleanor Colley** (...) daughter of Sir Henry Colley &
Anne Peyton
issue ?
(4) **Thomas Jephson** (... – 1646) killed in battle; unm.
(5) **Mary Jephson** (...)
= ...; **Richard Kyrle** (... – Aug 1684)
issue ?
(6) **Elizabeth Jephson** (...)
= Oct 1636; **Sir John Gifford** (... – 24 Apr 1657) son of
Richard Gifford & Mary Duke
issue ?
(7) **Francesca Jephson** (...)
= 1641; **John Wolveridge** (...)
issue ?

(III) **Hon. Catherine Norris** (...)
　= 1583; **Sir Anthony Poulett** (... – 22 Jul 1600) son of Sir
　Amyas Paulet & Margaret Harvey
　(A) **Elizabeth Poulett** (...)
　　= ...; **Sir Henry Hawley** (...)
　　(1) **Catherine Hawley** (...)
　　　= ...; **Robert Napier** (... – 1686) son of Sir Nathaniel
　　　Napier & Elizabeth Gerard; =1st Anna Corrance; =3rd Mary
　　　Evelyn
　　　no issue
　　(2) **Francis Hawley, 1st Baron Hawley** 1st Baronet
　　　(ca.1608 – 22 Dec 1684) cr. Baronet 1644, and Baron 8 Jul
　　　1646
　　　= ...; **Jane Gibbes** (... – bef.1684) daughter of Sir Ralph
　　　Gibbes & Gertrude Wroughton
　　　(a) **Unton Hawley** (...)
　　　　= ...; **John Malet** (... – 1656) son of John Malet & Anne
　　　　Tracy
　　　　Has further generations of issue
　　　(b) (a son) **Hawley** (... – bef.Dec 1684)
　　　　= ...
　　　　Has further generations of issue
　(B) **John Poulett, 1st Baron Poulett** (1586 – 20 Mar 1648/9)
　　cr. Baron 23 Jun 1627
　　= ...; **Elizabeth Kenn** (1593 – 1663) daughter of Christopher
　　Kenn; =2nd ◆John Ashburnham
　　(1) **John Poulett, 2nd Baron Poulett** (1615 – 15 Sep 1665)
　　　suc. father 1649
　　　=1 Mar 1640; ◆**Hon. Catherine de Vere** (ca.1613 Brielle,
　　　the Netherlands – aft.27 Mar 1648) daughter of Horatio de
　　　Vere, Baron Vedre & Mary Tracy; =1st ◆Oliver St.John
　　　=2 ca.1660; ◆**Anne Browne** (10 Jul 1635 – 1711) daughter
　　　of Sir Thomas Browne, 2nd Baronet & Anne Palmes; =2nd Sir
　　　John Strode
　　　issue of 1st:
　　　(a) **John Poulett, 3rd Baron Poulett** (... – Jul 1679) suc.
　　　　father 1665
　　　　=1 ...; ◆**Lady Susan Herbert** (...) daughter of Philip
　　　　Herbert, 5th Earl of Pembroke & Catherine Villiers
　　　　=2 ...; ◆**Essex Popham** (...) daughter o Alexander
　　　　Popham & Latitia Carre
　　　　Has further generations of issue by both
　　　(b) **Hon. Horatio Poulett** (...)
　　　issue of 2nd:
　　　(c) **Hon. Amias Poulett** (...)
　　　(d) **Hon. Charles Poulett** (...)

(e) **Hon. Catherine Poulett** (1665 – bef.1716)
= 1696; **James Johnston** (1655 – 1744)
i8ssue ?

(2) **Hon. Margaret Poulett** (...)
= ...; **Dennis Rolle** (...) son of Sir Henry Rolle & Anne Dennis

(a) **Margaret Rolle** (... – ca.1673)
=1 1654; ◆**Sir John Acland, 3ʳᵈ Baronet** (1636–1655)
=2 aft. 1655; **Henry Ayshford** (...)
issue of 1ˢᵗ (any by 2ⁿᵈ?):
Children are listed with other parent

(b) **Florence Rolle** (...)
= ...; **Sir John Rolle** (...) son of Andrew Rolle
Has further generations of issue

(3) **Hon. Florence Poulett** (...)
= ...; **Thomas Smith** (...)

(a) **Sir Hugh Smith, 1ˢᵗ Baronet** (... – 28 Jul 1680) cr. Baronet 16 May 1661
=...; ◆**Elizabeth Ashburnham** (...) daughter of John Ashburnham & Frances Holland
Has further generations of issue

(4) **Hon. Susannah Poulett** (...)
= ...; **Michael Warton** (1623 – 9 Aug 1688 London) son of Michael Warton & Catherine Maltby

(a) **Mary Warton** (...)
= ...; **Sir James Pennyman, 3ʳᵈ Baronet** (...) son of Sir Thomas Pennyman, 2ⁿᵈ Baronet & Frances Lowther
Has further generations of issue

(b) **Sir Michael Warton** (ca.1648 – 25 Mar 1725) unm.

(5) **Hon. Elizabeth Poulett** (1628 – 1690)
=1 ...; ◆**William Ashburnham** (...–1665)
=2 ...; **Sir William Hartopp** (... – ca.1700) son of Sir Thomas Hartopp & Dorothy Bendish; =1ˢᵗ Agnes Lister
issue of 1ˢᵗ (none by 2ⁿᵈ):
Children are listed with other parent

B) **Anne Fiennes** (... – 10 Sep 1497)
=1 ca.1486; **Sir William Berkeley, 1ˢᵗ Marquess of Berkeley**, Earl of Nottingham, Viscount and Berkeley, 2ⁿᵈ Baron Berkeley (1426 Berkeley Castle, Glos. – 14 Feb 1491/2 London) son of James Berkeley, 1ˢᵗ Baron Berkeley & Lady Isabel Mowbray; =1ˢᵗ Elizabeth West; =2ⁿᵈ Joan Strangways; Kt. 1438; suc. father Nov 1463; cr. Viscount ca.1482, Earl 1483, and Marquess 24 Jan 1488/9. The titles we was created became extinct upon his death.
=2 bef.14 May 1496; **Sir Thomas Brandon KG** (... – 1510)
no issue

II) **Sir Thomas Fiennes** (...)
III) **Elizabeth Fiennes** (ca.1455 – ...)
  = ca.1463 Herstmonceux; **John Clinton, 6ᵗʰ Baron Clinton** (ca. 1429 – 29 Feb 1487/8) son of John Clinton, 5ᵗʰ baron Clinton & Joan Ferrers; =2ⁿᵈ ♦Anne Stafford
  A) **John Clinton, 7ᵗʰ Baron Clinton KB** (ca.1471 – 4 Jun 1514) suc. father 1487/8; KB 1501
    = bef.1490; **Elizabeth Morgan** (... – bef.1501) daughter of Sir John Morgan
    1) **Thomas Clinton, 8ᵗʰ Lord Clinton** (ca.1490 – 7 Aug 1517) suc. father 1514
      = 4 may 1510; **John Poynings** (...) daughter of Sir Edward Poynings; =2ⁿᵈ Sir Robert Wingfield
      a) **Edward Clinton, 1ˢᵗ Earl of Lincoln** 9ᵗʰ Baron Clinton, **KG** (1512 – 16 Jan 1584/5) suc. father 1517; cr. Earl 4 May 1572; KG 1551
        =1 15 Apr 1530 (dv.1534/5); **Elizabeth Blount**[105] (ca.1502 – ca.1540) daughter of Sir John Blount; =1ˢᵗ Gilbert Tailboys, 1ˢᵗ Baron Tailboys
        =2 bef.15 Jun 1541; **Hon. Ursula Stourton** (... – 4 Sep 1551) daughter of William Stourton, 7ᵗʰ Baron Stourton & Elizabeth Dudley
        =3 1 Oct 1552; **Lady Elizabeth FitzGerald** (1528 – Mar 1589/90) daughter of Gerald FitzGerald, 9ᵗʰ Earl of Kildare & Lady Elizabeth Grey; =1ˢᵗ ♦Sir Anthony Browne
        issue of 1ˢᵗ:
        (I) **Lady Katharine Clinton** (... – ca.Aug 1621 Lingfield, Surrey)
          = 1621; ♦**William Burgh, 2ⁿᵈ Baron Burgh** (1522 – 1584)
          Children are listed with other parent
        (II) **Lady Margaret Clinton** (...)
          = ...; **Charles Willoughby, 2ⁿᵈ Baron Willoughby** (1536–1612)
          Children are listed with other parent
        issue of 2ⁿᵈ:
        (III) **Henry Clinton, 2ⁿᵈ Earl of Lincoln**, etc. **KB** (1540 – 29 Sep 1616) suc. father 1584/5; KB 1553
          =1 ca.1556; ♦**Lady Catherine Hastings** (11 Aug 1542 London – bef.20 Oct 1586) daughter of Francis hastings, 2ⁿᵈ Earl of Huntingdon & Catherine Pole
          =2 aft.20 Oct 1586; **Elizabeth Morrison** (... – 4 Jul 1611)

---

[105] Elizabeth Blount was also a mistress of King Henry VIII and was the mother of his only acknowledged illegitimate child, Henry FitzRoy, Duke of Richmond (1519–1536).

daughter of Sir Richard Morrison & Bridget Hussey; =1st ◆Hon. William Norris

issue of 1st:

(A) **Thomas Clinton, 3rd Earl of Lincoln**, etc. (ca.1568 – 15 Jan 1618/9) suc. father 1616

= 21 Sep 1584; **Elizabeth Knyvett** (...) daughter of Sir Henry Knyvett & Elizabeth Stumpe

(1) **Lady Frances Clinton** (...)

= ...; ◆**John Gorges** (...)

Children are listed with other parent

(2) **Lady Arabella Clinton** (1597 – Aug 1630 Salem, MA)

= 15 Apr 1623; **Rev. Isaac Johnson** (1601 – 30 Sep 1630 Salem) son of Abraham Johnson; emigrated to USA 1629

no issue

(3) **Lady Susan Clinton** (...)

= ...; **John Humphrey** (...) emigrated to USA 1635, but returned 1641

issue ?

(4) **Theophilius Clinton, 4th Earl of Clinton** etc. **KB** (1599 – 21 May 1667) suc. father 1618/9; KB 1616

=1 ca.1622; ◆**Hon. Bridget Fiennes** (...) daughter of William Fiennes, 1st Viscount Saye and Sele & Elizabeth Temple

=2 ...; ◆**Elizabeth Gorges** (... – ca.May 1675) daughter of Sir Arthur Gorges & Lady Elizabeth Clinton; =1st ◆Sir Robert Stanley

issue of 1st (none by 2nd):

(a) **Edward, Lord Clinton** (Dec 1624 – bef.21 Apr 1657 London)

= 30 Mar 1652; ◆**Lady Anne Holles** (... – Oct 1707) daughter of John Holles, 2nd Earl of Clare; =2nd Charles Bates

Issue extinct 1692

(b) **Lady Catherine Clinton** (... – ca.Jul 1643 Bowden, Ches.)

= 30 Nov 1639 London; **George Booth, 1st Baron Delamer** 2nd Baronet (18 Dec 1622 – 8 Aug 1684) son of William Booth, 1st Baronet & Vere Egerton; suc. father 24 Oct 1652; cr. Baron 20 Apr 1661

Has further generations of issue

(c) **Lady Arabella Clinton** (...)

= ...; **Robert Rolle** (... – 1663)

Has further generations of issue

(d) **Lady Margaret Clinton** (... – Oct 1688)

= ...; **Hugh Boscawen** (Aug 1625 Penkivel, Cornwall – Jun 1701) son of Hugh Boscawen & Margaret Rolle

Has further generations of issue

441

(5) **Hon. Edward Clinton** (1600 – ...)
(6) **Lady Ann Clinton** (1602 – ...)
(7) **Hon. Charles Clinton** (1604 – ...)
(8) **Hon. Knyvett Clinton** (1605 – ...)
(9) **Lady Dorcas Clinton** (1614 – ...)
(10) **Lady Sara Clinton** (1615 – ...)
(B) **Hon. Sir Edward Clinton** (...)
= ...; **Mary Dighton** (...) daughter of Thomas Dighton
(1) **Francis Clinton** (...)
    = ...; **Priscilla Hill** (...) daughter of John Hill
    (a) **Francis Clinton, 6th Earl of Clinton** (ca.1635 – Aug
      1693) suc. cousin 25 Nov 1692, the Barony Clinton fell into
    abeyance among the daughters of the 4th Baron
    =1 ...; **Elizabeth Killigrew** (... – 1677) daughter of Sir
    William Killigrew & Mary Hill
    =2 ca.1683; **Susanna Penyston** (... – 23 Sep 1720 London)
    daughter of Anthony Penyston
    issue of 2nd (none surviving by 1st):
    (a) **Henry Clinton, 7th Earl of Clinton KG** (1684 – 7 Sep
      1728) suc. father 1693; KG1721
    = 16 May 1717; ♦**Hon. Lucy Pelham** (... – 20 Jul 1736)
    daughter of Thomas Pelham, 1st Baron Pelham & Lady Grace
    Holles
    Has further generations of issue
    (b) **Hon. George Clinton** (1686 – 10 Jul 1761)
    = ...; **Anne Carle** (... – 5 Aug 1761) daughter of Peter Carle
    Has further generations of issue
    (c) **Lady Susannah Clinton** (...)
    = ...; **Robert Booth** (...) son of Thomas Booth & Elizabeth
    Middlemore
    Issue extinct 1754
(2) **Henry Clinton** (...) unm.
(3) **Robert Clinton** (...) unm.
(4) **Charles Clinton** (...)
(5) **Jermyn Clinton** (...)
issue of 2nd:
(C) **Lady Elizabeth Clinton** (...)[106]
    = ca.1597; **Sir Arthur Gorges** (ca.1569 Charlton, Som. – 10
    Oct 1625) son of Sir William Gorges & Winifred Budockshed;
    KT. 1597; =1st Douglas Howard
    (1) **Elizabeth Gorges** (... – May 1675)
      =1 ...; ♦**Sir Robert Stanley** (...)

---

[106] Lady Elizabeth had 12 children. I don't know the names or fates of the other 10.

=2 ...; ♦**Theophilius Clinton, 4ᵗʰ Earl of Lincoln** (1599 – 21 May 1667) son of Thomas Clinton, 3ʳᵈ Earl of Clinton & Elizabeth Knyvett
issue of 1ˢᵗ (none by 2ⁿᵈ):
Children are listed with other parent
(2) **Sir Arthur Gorges** (... – 1661)
= ...
(a) **Arthur Gorges** (... – 18 Apr 1668)
= aft.1661; ♦**Hon. Mary Bayning** (ca.1623 – bef.20 Jan 1671/2) daughter of Paul Bayning, 1ˢᵗ Viscount Bayning & Anne Glemham; =1ˢᵗ ♦William Villiers, 2ⁿᵈ Viscount Grandison[107]; =2ⁿᵈ Charles Villiers, 2ⁿᵈ Earl of Anglesey
no issue
(b) **Carew Gorges** (...)
= ...; **John Crewe** (1626 – 1684) son of Sir Clippesby Crewe & Joan Pultney
Has further generations of issue
(D) **Hon. Kendal Clinton** (...)
(E) **Hon. Sir Henry Clinton** (1587 – 1641)
=1 ...; **Eleanor Harrington** (...) daughter of Sir James Harrington
=2 1624; **Elizabeth Hickman** (...) daughter of Henry Hickman & Anne Wallop
issue of 1ˢᵗ (none by 2ⁿᵈ):
(1) **Harrington Clinton** (...) unm.
(2) **Norreys Clinton** (... – 1693)
= ...; **Margaret Raines** (... – 1707)
(a) **Norreys Clinton** (1651 – 1736)
= 1685; **Elizabeth Kendall** (... – 1730)
Has further generations of issue
(3) **Henry Clinton** (... – 1674)
= ...
(a) **Catherine Clinton** (...)
= 1674; **Daniel Disney** (...)
issue ?
(4) **Elizabeth Clinton** (... – ca.1666)
= ...; **Sir Michael Livesey, Baronet** (1614 Eastchurch, Kent – 1665 Rotterdam, Netherlands) son of Gabriel Livesey & Anne Sondes; cr. Baronet 1627 which was forfeited in 1660[108]

---

[107] By whom she was mother of Barbara Villiers, Duchess of Cleveland, one of Charles II's official mistresses.
[108] Livesey was one of the judges at Charles I's trial and voted in favor of execution. After the Restoration he was condemned as a regicide and fled to the Netherlands.

(a) **Deborah Livesey** (...)

(b) **Anne Livesey** (1634 – ...)

= ...; **Sir Robert Sprignell** (1622 – 1688)

issue ?

(IV) **Lady Frances Clinton** (... – 12 Sep 1623 Woburn Abbey, Beds.)

= 1573; ◆**Giles Brydges, 3rd Baron Chandos** (1548–1594)

Children are listed with other parent

IV) **Richard Fiennes** (...)

V) **Roger Fiennes** (...)

VI) a daughter (...)

= ...; **Sir Walter Denys** (... – 1505)

no issue

e. **Eleanor Fiennes** (...)

= ...; **Sir Hugh Fenne** (...)

3. **Lady Alice Holland** (ca.1392 – ca.1406)

= bef.1400; **Richard de Vere, 11th Earl of Oxford** KG (15 Aug 1385 – 15 Feb 1417) son of Aubrey de Vere, 10th Earl of Oxford & Alice FitzWalter; he =2nd Alice Sergeaux; KG 1416; suc. father 15 Feb 1400

no issue

4. **John Holland, 2nd Duke of Exeter**, etc. KG (18 Mar 1395 Dartington, Devon – 5 Aug 1447 London) suc. father 16 Jan 1400; KG 1416

=1 6 Mar 1427; ◆**Lady Anne Stafford** (... – 20 Sep 1432) daughter of Edmund Stafford, 5th Earl of Stafford & Anne of Gloucester

=2 20 Jan 1433; **Dona Beatriz de Portugal** (ca.1386 – 1439) illegitimate daughter of João I, King of Portugal & Inês Pires; =1st Thomas FitzAlan, 12th Earl of Arundel

=3 ...; **Lady Anne Montagu** (... – 28 Nov 1457) daughter of John Montagu, 3rd Earl of Salisbury & Maud Francis; =1st Sir Riochard Hankford; =2nd Sir John FitzLewis

issue of 1st (none by others):

a. **Henry Holland, 3rd Duke of Exeter**, etc. (27 Jun 1430 – Sep 1475) drowned in the Channel

= bef.30 Jul 1447; ◆**Anne of York** (10 Aug 1439 Fotheringhay, Northants – 14 Feb 1476) daughter of Richard, 3rd Duke of York 1 & Lady Cecilie Neville; =2nd Thomas St.Leger

I) **Lady Anne Holland** (ca.1455 – btw.1467/74)

= Oct 1466 Greenwich; **Thomas Grey, 1st Marquess of Dorset**, Earl of Huntingdon, 7th Baron Ferrers of Groby, KG (1455 Gorby, Leics. – 20 Sep 1501 London) suc. as Baron 23 Jan 1483; cr. Marquess and Earl bef.1467; =2nd Cecily Bonville, 7th Baroness Harington

no issue

b. **Lady Anne Holland** (bef.1432 – 26 Dec 1486)

=1 bef.18 Feb 1440/1; **Sir John Neville** (... – bef.16 Mar 1450/1) son of Ralph Neville, 2nd Earl of Westmorland & Hon. Elizabeth Percy

=2 bef.5 Feb 1442; (her uncle-in-law) **John Neville, Baron Neville**[109]
(ca.1410 – 29 Mar 1461 Towton) killed in battle; son of Sir John Neville &
Lady Elizabeth Holland; cr. Baron 20 Nov 1459
=3 ca.1462; **James Douglas, 9th Earl of Douglas** (1426 Scotland –
1488 Lindores Abbey, Fife) son of James Douglas, 7th Earl of Douglas &
Beatrice Sinclair; suc. brother 22 Feb 1452; =1st Margaret Douglas
has issue of 2nd (none by others):

I) **Ralph Neville, 3rd Earl of Westmorland** 6th Baron Neville of Raby,
   2nd Baron Neville **KB** (1456 – 6 Feb 1498/9 Hornby Castle, Yorks.) suc.
   father 1461; suc. uncle 3 Nov 1484; KB 1475
   = bef.20 Feb 1472/3; **Isabel Booth** (...) daughter of Sir Roger Booth &
   Catherine Hatton
   A) **Ralph, Lord Neville** (... – 1498)
      =1 bef.1489; ♦**Mary Paston** (19 Jan 1469/70 – 25 Dec 1489 London)
      daughter of Sir William Paston & Lady Anne Beaufort
      =2 aft.1489; **Edith Sandys** (... – 22 Aug 1529 London) daughter of Sir
      William Sandys & Margaret Cheney; =2nd Thomas Darcy, 1st Baron
      Darcy
      issue of 2nd (none by 1st):
      1) **Ralph Neville, 4th Earl of Westmorland**, etc. **KG** (21 Feb
         1497/8 – 24 Apr 1549) suc. grandfather 1498/9; KG 1525
         = bef. Jun 1520; ♦**Lady Catherine Stafford** (... – 14 May 1555
         London) daughter of Edward Stafford, 3rd Duke of Buckingham &
         Lady Eleanor Percy
         a) **Lady Margaret Neville** (... – 13 Oct 1559)
            = 1536; ♦**Henry Manners, 2nd Earl of Rutland** (... – 1563)
            Children are listed with other parent
         b) **Henry Neville, 5th Earl of Westmorland** etc. **KG** (ca.1524 –
            10 Feb 1563/4 Kelvedon, Essex) suc. father 1549; KG 1552
            =1 3 Jul 1536; ♦**Lady Anne Manners** (... – aft. 27 Jun 1549)
            daughter of Thomas Manners, 1st Earl of Rutland & Eleanor Paston
            =2 aft.1549; **Jane Cholmley** (... – bef.Dec 1558) daughter of Sir
            Roger Cholmley & Katherine Constable
            =3 bef.21 Jun 1560; (his sister-in-law) **Margaret Cholmley** (... –
            ca.Mar 1570) daughter of Sir Roger Cholmley & Katherine
            Constable; =1st Sir Henry Gascoigne
            issue of 1st (none by others):
            (I) **Lady Eleanor Neville** (... – 1574)
               = ...; **Sir William Pelham** (ca.1530 – 24 Nov 1587) son of Sir
               William Pelham & Mary Sandys; =2nd Dorothy Catesby

---

[109] John was the grandson of the 1st Earl of Westmorland by his fist wife. The Earl's second
wife was tLady Margaret Beaufort and they are the progenitoprs of Chapter 16: The Nevilles.

(A) **Sir William Pelham** (...)

= ...; ♦**Hon. Anne Willoughby** (...) daughter of Charles Willoughby, 2nd Baron Willoughby & Lady Margaret Clinton

(1) **Sir William Pelham** (...)

= ...; ♦**Hon. Frances Conway** (...) daughter of Edward Conway, 1st Viscount Conway & Dorothy Tracy

(a) **Anne Pelham** (... – 15 Jan 1701/2)

= 16 Apr 1654; **Sir George Wynne, 1st Baronet** (ca.1607 – 18 Jul 1667) son of Edmund Wynne & Mary Berkeley; =1st Rachel Turner; =2nd Elizabeth Jeffreys; cr. Baronet 3 Dec 1660

issue ?

(b) **Charles Pelham** (...)

=1 ...; **Anne Hussey** (...) daughter of Sir Edward Hussey, 1st Baronet & Elizabeth Anton

=2 ...; **Elizabeth Pelham** (...) daughter of Sir Thomas Pelham, 2nd Baronet & Margaret Vane

=3 ...; **Elizabeth Wharton** (...) daughter of Michael Wharton

Has further generations of issue by 1st and 3rd

(c) **Elizabeth Pelham** (...)

= aft.11 Dec 1668; (her sister's step-son) **Sir Edmund Wynne, 2nd Baronet** (ca.1644 – 27 Aug 1694) son of Sir George Wynne, 1st Baronet & Elizabeth Jeffreys; =2nd Catherine Jackson; suc. father 18 Jul 1667

Issue extinct in the next generation

(II) **Charles Neville, 6th Earl of Westmorland**, etc.[110] (ca. 1543 – 16 Nov 1601 Nieuport, Belgium)

= ca.1564; ♦**Lady Jane Howard** (... – 27 Jun 1593 Kenninghall, Norfolk) daughter of Henry, Earl of Surrey & Lady Frances de Vere

(A) **Lady Margaret Neville** (...)

= ...; **Nicholas Pudsey** (...)

issue ?

(B) **Lady Catherine Neville** (...)

= ...; **Sir Thomas Grey** (...)

issue ?

(C) **Lady Anne Neville** (...)

= ...; **David Ingleby** (...) son of Sir William Inglesby

(1) **Mary Ingleby** (...)

= ...; **Sir Peter Middleton** (...)

---

[110] Spent much of his adult live plotting in favor of Mary, Queen of Scots

issue ?
(2) **Frances Ingleby** (...)
= ...; **Sir Robert Hodgson** (...)
issue ?
(3) **Ursula Ingleby** (...)
= ...; **Robert Widdrington** (...)
issue ?
(D) **Lady Eleanor Neville** (... – bef.25 Jun 1604) unm.
c) **Lady Dorothy Neville** (... – ca.1546)
= 3 Jul 1536; **John de Vere, 16th Earl of Oxford** (1516 Castle
Hedingham, Essex – 3 Aug 1562) son of John de Vere, 15th Earl
of Oxford & Elizabeth Trussel; suc. father 21 Mar 1539/40
(I) **Lady Katherine de Vere** (... – 17 Jan 1599)
= ca. 1556; **Edward Windsor, 3rd Baron Windsor KB**
(... – 24 Jan 1574) son of William Windsor, 2nd Baron Windsor
& Margaret Sambourne; suc. father 20 Aug 1558; KB 1553
(A) **Frederick Windsor, 4th Baron Windsor** (2 Feb
1558/9 – 24 Dec 1585) suc. father 1574; unm.
(B) **Henry Windsor, 5th Baron Windsor** (10 Aug 1562 – 6
Apr 1605) suc. brother 1585
= bef.1586; **Anne Rivett** (... – 27 Nov 1615) daughter of Sir
Thomas Rivett & Hon. Griselda Paget
(1) **Hon. Margaret Windsor** (...)
= ...; ♦**Sir John Talbot** (...) son of Sir John Talbot &
Frances Gifford; =1st ♦Catherine Petre
no issue
(2) **Hon. Elizabeth Windsor** (...)
= 24 Jul 1616; **Dixie Hickman** (...) son of Walter Hickman
& Elizabeth Staines
(a) **Mariana Hickman** (...)
= ...; **Sir Henry Hunloke, 1st Baronet** (1616 – 1648) cr.
Baronet 28 Feb 1643
Has further generations of issue
(b) **Catherine Hickman** (...)
= ...; **John Columbine** (...)
issue ?
(c) **Anne Hickman** (...)
= 13 Dec 1643 Gainsborough, Lincs.; **John Chaworth,
2nd Viscount Chaworth** Baron Chaworth (bef.1619 –
Jun 1644) son of George Chaworth, 1st Viscount Chaworth
& Mary Knyveton; =1st Hon. Elizabeth Noel; suc. father 3
Jul 1639
no issue
(d) **Elizabeth Hickman** (... – 4 Nov 1667)
= 11 Feb 1650; **James Ware** (9 Aug 1622 – 6 May 1689
Chester) son of Sir James ware & Elizabeth Newman; =2nd

Barbara Stone
Has further generations of issue

(e) **Thomas Windsor, 1ˢᵗ Earl of Plymouth** 7ᵗʰ Baron
Windsor (ca.1627 – 3 Nov 1687) suc. uncle as Baron 16 Jun
1660; cr. Earl 6 Dec 1682
=1 12 May 1656; ♦**Anne Savile** (... – 22 Mar 1666)
daughter of Sir William Savile, 3ʳᵈ Baronet & Hon. Anne
Coventry
=2 9 Apr 1668; ♦**Ursula Widdrington** (... – 22 Apr 1717)
daughter of Sir Thomas Widdrington & Hon. Frances
Fairfax
Has further generations of issue by both

(3) **Thomas Windsor, 6ᵗʰ Baron Windsor** (29 Sep 1591 –
6 Dec 1642) suc father 1605
= bef.14 Jan 1607/8; ♦**Lady Katherine Somerset**
(ca.1585 – ...) daughter of Edward Somerset, 4ᵗʰ Earl of
Worcester & Lady Elizabeth Hastings
no issue

d) **Lady Mary Neville** (...)
= ...; ♦**Sir Thomas Danby** (...) son of Sir Christopher Danby
issue ?

e) **Lady Elizabeth Neville** (...)
= bef.1546; **Thomas Dacre, 4ᵗʰ Baron Dacre** (ca.1526 –
ca.1566) son of William Dacre, 3ʳᵈ Baron Dacre & Lady Elizabeth
Talbot; =2ⁿᵈ Elizabeth Leyburne
no issue

f) **Lady Eleanor Neville** (...)
= ...; **Brian Stapleton** (... – 13 Dec 1606) son of Sir Richard
Stapleton & Thomasin Amandas

(I) **Richard Stapleton** (... – ca.1614)
= ...

   (A) **Gilbert Stapleton** (... – ca.11 Apr 1636)
   =1 ...; **Katherine Hungate** (...)
   =2 ...; **Eleanor Gascoigne** (...) daughter of Sir John Gascoigne
   issue of 2ⁿᵈ 9none by 1ˢᵗ):

   (1) **Anne Stapleton** (...)
      = ...; **Mark Errington** (...)
      (a) **Nicholas Stapleton** (... – 1715) né Errington, legally
         changed to Stapleton
         = ...
      Has further generations of issue

   (2) **Sir Miles Stapleton, Baronet** (19 Oct 1626 – 16 Feb
   1706/7) cr. Baronet 20 Mar 1661/2, but it went extinct upon
   his death
   =1 1661; **Lady Elizabeth Bertie** (... – 28 Feb 1683/4)

daughter of Robert Bertie, 1st Earl of Lindsey & Hon. Elizabeth
Montagu
=2 ...; **Elizabeth Longueville** (...) daughter of Sit Thomas
Longueville, 2nd Baronet
no issue
  g) **Lady Anne Neville** (...)
= ca.1553; ♦**Fulke Greville, 4th Baron Willoughby** (1536 –
1606)
Children are listed with other parent
  h) **Hon. Christopher Neville** (bef. 1540 – ...)
= ...; **Anne Fulthorpe** (...) daughter of John Fulthorpe; =1st
Francis Wandisford
no issue
  i) **Hon. Cuthbert Neville** (bef.1541 – aft.1569) unm.
 B) **Lady Anne Neville** (...)
=1 ...; ♦**William Conyers, 1st Baron Conyers** (1468 – 1524)
=2 aft.29 Apr 1525; **Anthony Saltmarsh** (...)
issue of 1st (none by 2nd):
Children are listed with other parent
issue by ...[111]:
c. **William of Exeter** (... – 29 Mar 1461 Towton) killed in battle
d. **Thomas of Exeter** (... – 29 Mar 1461 Towton) killed in battle
e. **Robert of Exeter** (...)
issue of 3rd:
5. **Constance Cornwall** (ca.1401 – ca.1427)
= ...; **John FitzAlan, 14th Earl of Arundel** Baron Maltravers Duke
of Touraine KG (14 Feb 1408 Lychett Maltravers, Dorset – 12 Jun
1435 Beauvais, France) son of John FitzAlan, 13th Earl of Arundel
& Eleanor Berkeley; suc. father as Baron 1429; had his claim to Earldom
approved by parliament 1433; KG 1432; cr. Duke 1434; =2nd Maud Lovell
no issue
6. **Sir John Cornwall** (ca.1404 – 2 May 1422 Meaux) killed in
battle unm.

---

[111] There is no record of these sons getting married or leaving issue.

CHAPTER 13
NEVILLE

The Neville family was a politically significant family in the north of England well before Edward III's time. They appear to be one of the few Anglo-Saxon families to retain their property and position after the Norman Conquest of 1066, but their exact origins prior to that time period are simply not known.

When they do pop up in history, they are already well-established in County Durham in the northeast portion of the country, nestled between Yorkshire and Northumbria. One Ralph Neville was among the founding members of the Peerage of England being summoned to Parliament at its very establishment in 1295 as the 1st Baron Neville.

They established themselves in the present-day town of Staindrop and, by Edward III's day, had built the formidable Raby Castle, which continues to stand and be lived in until the present day. The castle was removed from the Nevilles' possession in 1569, and later bought by the Vane family, who still own it.

It is Ralph, the 4th Baron Neville, who brings this family into the descendants of Edward III, but it should be noted that Ralph was himself descended from earlier Plantagenet kings, notably Henry III. He married, as his second wife, Joan Beaufort, one of the legitimated daughters of John of Gaunt. Joan was married previously to Baron Ferrers, and her descendants from that marriage are featured in the next chapter. Shortly after Neville's marriage to Lady Joan, he was elevated to Earl of Westmorland. This title would continue through his son by his first marriage and be inherited by a grandson, also named Ralph. Ralph the 2nd Earl married a Percy daughter and their family continues on that chapter.

Although the Earldom passed to Ralph's first family, Lady's Joan's fourteen children did not go without. Of this large brood, four sons and four daughters are known to have married and had children of their own. Most of the others also lived to adulthood but fell into obscurity or joined a religious order.

All four sons obtained a title for themselves, two by being summoned to Parliament as a Baron, called receiving a title by Writ, one by a direct grant of the King, but his title became extinct upon his death, and the eldest by marrying an heiress and inheriting her title jointly with her. He was Richard Neville, who married the last Montagu Countess of Salisbury. Their son, and eventual heir, Richard would inherit this title, but be created his own by which he is known to history, the Earl of Warwick.

Warwick is likely the most prominent name from the Wars of the Roses aside from the royals themselves who were fighting for the Crown. He earned the nickname 'Kingmaker' by supporting the York claim and using his immense resources to secure not only the north of England for Edward IV, but also foreign assistance as well. His ultimate goal was to make the young king his son-in-law, by marrying one of his daughters off to him. Other advisors were lobbying hard for Edward to marry the fabulously wealthy Mary of Burgundy. The king made enemies of the lot of them by running off and marrying Elizabeth Woodville instead.

Warwick did manage to get nice consolation prizes for his surviving daughters though. Each married a brother of King Edward, the younger, Anne, reaching the Throne as the wife of Richard III. The elder, Isabel, was the ancestress of the Pole family, who later caused grief for Henry VIII, as well as the living descendants whose DNA was used to confirm the remains of Richard III when they were found in the 21st century.

Warwick considered the King's elopement as nothing short of a complete slap in his face after all he done to get him on the Throne. He soon taught Edward that which the Kingmaker gives, he also can take away. Warwick joined forces with Margaret Beaufort, the leading force behind the Lancastrians, and soon Edward and Henry VI were trading the Throne back forth until they were both dead. Warwick himself fell in those battles, after which the Yorks got the upper hand briefly, until Henry Tudor came to town.

The 2nd son of Joan, Countess of Westmorland, another Edward, was created Baron Abergavenny in 1450. This title still exists and is held by the 24th Baron, though he is now known by his higher title, the Marquess of Abergavenny. One of the hallmarks of this line of the Neville family is that each generation had numerous daughters in their efforts to have an heir and a spare for the titles. These daughters have often married back into the nobility, but a few married commoners and everyday folks on the street might be able to find a Neville or two in their family tree. If they do, it is likely from this branch.

Lady Joan's third son became the Earl of Kent but died without surviving sons to leave the title to. His youngest daughter, Lady Alice, is the only of his children to have continuing generations of descendants via her marriage to John Conyers. Her son, William, was called to Parliament as the 1st Baron Conyers. But upon the death of the 3rd Baron without sons, the title fell into an abeyance among his several daughters.

This is an odd but common situation unique to English titles. Those that were created by Writ do not have written rules dictating their succession. Therefore, the rules of Common Law take over, and under this principle, an eldest son automatically has claim to his father's property, with younger sons only having a claim if the elder son dies without heirs. But women are treated differently than their brothers. A set of sisters collectively have the same rights as one son if no son is present. Therefore, they each have an equal claim to a noble title if they have no brother. This is called an abeyance, it will remain until either the lines of all sisters but one fails, leaving a sole heir, or the House of Lords makes a decision in favor of one of the claimants.

The latter is what happened to the Conyers barony in 1642, when the Lords ended the abeyance in favor of one of the 3rd Baron's grandsons, Baron Darcy. Darcy's descendants continued to hold the title until 2013 when it became abeyant for the fourth time in its existence. The male line of the Darcys were better known by their higher title, Earls of Holderness, until that title became extinct in 1778, the properties and lower titles by Writ going to the Dukes of Leeds for a couple of generations. Along the way there are families of younger daughters who are traced out that could prove a fertile ground for genealogical researchers.

The fourth and youngest son of Lady Joan, Countess of Westmorland was a periodic lunatic named George, who was called to Parliament during his more lucid periods as Baron Latymer. The Latymer properties had been held by the Nevilles for a few generations from previous marital inheritances, and eventually were bestowed on George, but maintained by his much more level-headed wife, Lady Elizabeth Beauchamp.

The Latymer barony is another that fell into abeyance among four sisters when their father died without sons in 1577. As a good example of how long these abeyances can last, this one went until 1913. The Lords found in favor of one claimant due to his military knowledge which was needed with a potential war looming over Europe. Of the four sisters who started the abeyance, all but one married back into the descendants of Edward III. The remaining one, Lady Elizabeth Danvers, has numerous descendants among the commoners of both Great Britain and America.

Of Lady Joan's four daughters with descendants, three have their own chapters coming up soon, and the fourth married back to the royal family when she married the 3rd Duke of York, becoming the mother of King Edward IV.

Edward III

|

John of Gaunt, Duke of Lancaster

|

Lady Joan Beaufort (ca.1375 château de Beaufort – 13 Nov 1440 Howden, Yorks.)

=1 1391 château de Beaufort; **Robert de Ferrers, 3rd Baron Ferrers of Wem** (ca.1373 Willisham, Suffolk – bef. 29 Nov 1396) son of Robert Ferrers, 2nd Baron Ferrers of Wem & Elizabeth, 4th Baroness le Boteler; suc. father Dec. 1380

=2 bef.29 Nov 1396 château de Beaufort; **Ralph Neville, 1st Earl of Westmorland, 4th Baron Neville, KG** (ca.1364 Raby Castle, Durham – 21 Oct 1425 Raby Castle) son of John Neville, 3rd Baron Neville & Maud Percy; sc. father 17 Oct 1388; cr. Earl 29 Sep 1397; KG ca.1403; =1st ♦Lady Margaret Stafford

issue of 1st:

1. **ELIZABETH, BARONESS DE BOTELER AND GREYSTOKE**
   (1393 – 1434 York)
   see: Chapter 16

2. **Mary Ferrers** (1394 – 25 Jan 1527/8)
   = ca.1413 Oversley, Warks.; (her step-brother) **Sir Ralph Neville** (ca.1392 Raby Castle, Durham – 25 Feb 1458) son of Ralph Neville, 1st Earl of Westmorland & Lady Margaret Stafford
   a. **Mary Neville** (ca.1414 Oversley – ...)
   b. **John Neville** (ca.1416 Oversley – 17 Mar 1482)
      = ca.1442 Oversley; **Elizabeth Newmarch** (ca.1420 Oversley – ...) daughter of Robert Newmarch
      I) **JOAN, LADY GASCOIGNE** (ca.1443 – ...)
         see: Chapter 14

issue of 2nd:

3. **Lady Eleanor Neville** (ca.1397 Raby Castle – 1472)
   =1 1412; ♦**Richard le Despencer, 4th Baron Burghersh** KB (30 Nov 1396 – 7 Oct 1414 Merton, Surrey) son of Thomas le Despencer, Earl of Gloucester & Constance of Clarence; suc. father 1409; KB 1413
   =2 aft.1414; ♦**Henry Percy, 2nd Earl of Northumberland** (1393–1455)
   has issue by 2nd (none by 1st):
   Children are listed with other parent

4. **Lady Katherine Neville** (ca.1399 – aft.1483)
   =1 12 Jan 1412/3; **John Mowbray, 2nd Duke of Norfolk** 5th Earl of Norfolk, 3rd Earl of Nottingham, 9th Baron Segrave, 8th Baron Mowbray KG **Earl Marshal of England** (1392 – 19 Oct 1432 Epworth, Lincs.) son of Thomas Mowbray, 1st Duke of Norfolk & Elizabeth FitzAlan; suc. brother, Thomas, in the earldoms 1405; received remaining titles from father's attaintment and appointed Earl Marshal 1413
   =2 bef.27 Jan 1441/2; **Sir Thomas Strangways** (...)

=3 aft.1442; **John Beaumont, 1ˢᵗ Viscount Beaumont**, 6ᵗʰ Baron Beaumont, Count de Boulogne, KG (16 Aug 1410 – 10 Jul 1460 Northants.) killed in battle; son of Henry Beaumont, 5ᵗʰ Baron Beaumont & Elizabeth Willoughby; =1ˢᵗ Elizabeth Phelip; suc father as Baron Jun 1413; cr. Count 27 Jul 1436; cr. Viscount 18 Jan 1440/1; KG 1441

=4 ca.1465; **Sir John Woodville/Wydevill**[112] (ca.1445 – 12 Aug 1469 Edgecote, Oxon.) executed; son of Richard Wydevill, 1ˢᵗ Earl Rivers & Jacquetta of Luxemburg

issue of 1ˢᵗ:

a. **John Mowbray, 3ʳᵈ Duke of Norfolk** etc. KG (1415 – 6 Nov 1461)
   suc. father 1432; KG1451
   = 1444; ♦**Eleanor Bourchier** (ca.1417 – Nov 1474) daughter of Sir
   William Bourchier, Count d'Eu & Anne Plantagenet, Countess of
   Buckingham
   I) **John Mowbray, 4ᵗʰ Duke of Norfolk**, etc. 1ˢᵗ Earl of Surrey and
      Warenne **KG** (18 Oct 1444 – 16 Jan 1475/6) suc. father 1461; cr. Earl 24
      Mar 1450/1; KG1472; upon his death, the Dukedom of Norfolk and
      Earldom of Nottingham became extinct
      = bef.27 Nov 1448; **Lady Elizabeth Talbot** (,,,) daughter of John
      Talbot, 1ˢᵗ Earl of Shrewsbury & Lady Margaret Beauchamp
      A) **Anne Mowbray, 8ᵗʰ Countess of Norfolk** 12ᵗʰ Baroness
         Seagrave, 11ᵗʰ Baroness Mowbray (10 Dec 1472 Framlingham,
         Suffolk – 10 Nov 1481 London) suc. father 1476; upon her death the
         Earldon of Norfolk went dormant and the Baronies into abeyance
         = 15 Jan 1477/8 London; ♦**Prince Richard, Duke of York** Earl of
         Nottingham, Earl Warren, Duke of Norfolk **KG** (17 Aug 1473
         Shrewsbury, Salop – Nov 1483 London) murdered in the Tower; son of
         Edward IV, King of England & Elizabeth Wydeville; titles all became
         extinct upon his death
         no issue
issue of 2ⁿᵈ:

b. **Joan Strangways** (... – 24 Feb 1484/5)
   =1 bef.1468; **Sir William Willoughby** (... – bef.1468)
   =2 Nov 1468; **William Berkeley, Marquess of Berkeley** Earl of
   Nottingham, Viscount Berkeley, 2ⁿᵈ Baron Berkeley (1426 Berkeleey,
   Glos. – 14 Feb 1491/2 London) son of James Berkeley, 1ˢᵗ Baron Berkeley
   &
   Lady Isabel Mowbray; =1ˢᵗ Hon. Elizabeth West; =3ʳᵈ Anne Fiennes; suc.
   father Nov 1463; cr. Viscount 21 Apr 1481, Earl 28 Jun 1483, and
   Marquess 28 Jan 1488/9, all by the Barony became extinct upon his

---

[112] Throughout the Plantagenet era, the name was alternately spelled Woodville and Wydevill.

death
no surviving issue
  c. **Catherine Strangways** (...)
    = aft.31 Aug 1454; **Henry Grey, 4th Baron Grey** (ca.1435 – 8 Apr 1496)
    son of Henry Grey, 3rd Baron Grey & Margaret Percy; =2nd Margaret ...;
    he =3rd Hon. Catherine Stourton; suc. father 14 Jul 1444, but upon his
    death the title fell into abeyance among his aunts.
    no issue
5. **Sir Richard Neville KG** (1400 Raby Castle – 31 Dec 1460
  Wakefield, Yorks.) executed; shared wife's titles; KG 1436
  = bef. Feb 1421/2 Salisbury, Wilts.; **Alice Montagu, 5th Countess
  of Salisbury**, 7th Baroness Montacute (1407 Salisbury – 9 Dec
  1462 Bidham, Berks. daughter of Thomas Montagu, 4th Earl of
  Salisbury & Eleanor Holand; suc. father 3 Nov 1428
  a. **Lady Cecily Neville** (ca.1425 – 26 Jul 1450)
    =1 1434; ♦**Henry Beauchamp, 1st Duke of Warwick** (1425 – 1446)
    =2 3 Apr 1449; **John Tiptoft, 1st Earl of Worcester** 2nd Baron
    Tiptoft, KG (8 May 1427 – 18 Oct 1470 Tower of London)
    executed; son of John Tiptoft, 1st Baron Tiptoft & Joyce
    Cherleton; suc. father 27 Jan 1442/3; cr. Earl 16 Jul 1449; KG
    Mar 1461/2; =2nd Elizabeth Greyndour; =3rd Elizabeth Hopkin
    issue of 1st (none by 2nd):
    Children are listed with other parent
  b. **Richard Neville, 16th Earl of Warwick**[113] 6th Earl of Salisbury,
    KG (22 Nov 1428 – 14 Apr 1471 Barnet, Herts.) killed in battle;
    suc. niece in Warwick 23 Jul 1449, and mother in Salisbury 9 Dec
    1462 (upon his death this last title reverted to the Crown); KG 1460
    = 1434; ♦**Lady Anne Beauchamp** (ca.Sep 1426 – ca.20 Sep
    1492) daughter of Richard Beauchamp, 13th Earl of Warwick &
    Lady Isabel le Despencer
    I) **Lady Isabel Neville** (5 Sep 1451 Warwick Castle – 22 Dec
      1476 Warwick Castle) murdered
      = 1469; ♦**George Plantagenet, 1st Duke of Clarence** (1449 – 1478)
      see:
    II) **Lady Anne Neville** (11 Jun 1456 Warwick Castle – 16 Mar
      1485 Westminster Palace)
      =1 13 Dec 1470 Amboise, Burgundy; ♦**Prince Edward, Prince
      of Wales** (13 Oct 1453 Westminster Palace – 4 May 1471
      Tewkesbury, Glos.) killed in battle; son of Henry VI, King of
      England & Margaret of Anjou

---

[113] Known to history as Warwick the Kingmaker for is ability to maneuver situations to his will
in support of whichever King he was supporting at the moment.

=2 1472; ♦**Richard III, King of England** (1452 – 1485)
issue of 2nd (none by 1st):
see:

c. **John Neville, 1st Marquess of Montagu** Earl of
Northumberland, Baron Montagu, KG (ca.1431 – 14 Apr 1471
Barnet) killed in action; cr. Baron 23 May 1461, Earl 27 May
1464, and Marquess (ad personam) 25 Mar 1470; relinquished
Earldom in favor of Percy family 25 Mar 1470; KG Mar 1461/2
= 25 Apr 1457; **Isabel Ingaldesthorpe** (ca.1441 – 20 May
1476) daughter of Sir Edmundf Ingaldsthorpe & Joan Tiptoft;
she =2nd Sir William Norreys

I) **George Neville, 1st Duke of Bedford**, 2nd Baron Montagu
(ca.1461 – 4 May 1483) suc. father 14 Apr 1471; cr. Duke 5 Jan
1469/70; deprived of titles by Parliament 1478; unm.[114]

II) **Lady Anne Neville** (bef.1464 – bef. 1486)
= bef.1482; **Sir William Stonor, KB** (1449 – 1494) son of
Thomas Stonor & Jeanne de la Pole; =1st Elizabeth Croke; =2nd
Alice Winnard

A) **John Stonor** (1482 – 1499) unm.
B) **Anne Stonor** (...)
= ...; **Sir Adrian Fortescue** (...) son of Sir John Fortescue &
Elizabeth Boleyn
1) **Margaret Fortescue** (...)
= 1520; ♦**Thomas Wentworth, 1st Baron Wentworth** (1501–
1551)
Children are listed with other parent

III) **Lady Elizabeth Neville** (ca.1464 – Sep 1517)
=1 bef.1477; ♦**Thomas le Scrope, 6th Baron Scrope of
Masham** (ca.1459 –1493)
=2 ca.Oct 1494; **Sir Henry Wentworth** (...)
issue of 1st (none by 2nd):
see:

IV) **Lady Margaret Neville** (1466 – 31 Jan 1527/8)
=1 bef.1504; **Thomas Horne** (...)
=2 bef.12 Nov 1504; **Sir John Mortimer** (bef.1494 – ...)
=3 bef.Feb 1560/7 (dv.1507, ann.1528); **Charles Brandon, 1st
Duke of Suffolk** KG (ca.1484 – 1545 Guilford, Surrey) son of
Sir William Brandon & Elizabeth Bruyn; =2nd Anne Browne;
he =3rd ♦Princess Mary of England; =4th Catherine Willoughby,
12th Baroness Willoughby de Eresby
=4 ca.Feb 1521/2; **Robert Downes** (...)

---

[114] Was engaged to Princess Elizabeth, daughter of Edward IV, at time of death.

no issue

V) **Lady Lucy Neville** (aft.1466 – ca.1534)
=1 bef.1490; **Sir Thomas FitzWilliam** (bef.1474 – bef.1506)
=2 bef.1506; **Sir Anthony Browne** (29 Jun 1443 Bettesworth
Castle, Surrey – 19 Nov 1506 Calais) son of Sir Thomas
Browne & Eleanor FitzAlan
issue of 1st:

A) **William FitzWilliam, Earl of Southampton KG** (ca.1490 – 15
Oct 1542) cr. Earl 18 Oct 1537, but it became extinct upon his death
= Nov 1513; ♦**Hon. Mabel Clifford** (... – Aug 1550) daughter of
Henry Clifford, 10th Baron Clifford & Anne St.John
no issue

B) **Thomas FitzWilliam** (... – 9 Sep 1513 Flodden Field, Northumb.)
killed in battle
= ...

1) **Alice FitzWilliam** (...)
= ...; **Sir James Foljambe** (...)
issue ?

2) **Margaret FitzWilliam** (...)
= ...; **Godfrey Foljambe** (...)
issue ?

C) **John FitzWilliam** (bef.1498 – 9 Sep 1513 Flodden Field) killed in
battle
issue of 2nd:

D) **Sir Anthony Browne** (1500 – 1548 Byfleet, Surrey)
=1 ...; **Alice Gage** (... – ca.1540) daughter of Rt.Hon. Sir John Gage &
Philippa Guildford
=2 ..; **Lady Elizabeth FitzGerald** (1528 – Mar 1589/90) daughter
of Gerald FitzGerald, 9th Earl of Kildare & Lady Elizabeth Grey; =2nd
♦Edward Clinton, 1st Earl of Lincoln
issue of 1st (none by 2nd):

1) **Anthony Browne, 1st Viscount Montagu** (ca.1527 – 1592) cr.
Viscount 2 Sep 1554
=1 ca.1551; ♦**Lady Jane Radcliffe** (1533 – 1553) daughter of
Robert Radcliffe, 1st Earl of Sussex – Lady Margaret Stanley
=2 bef.10 Dec 1558; ♦**Hon. Magdalen Dacre** (1538 Naworth
Castle, Cumb. – ca.1608) daughter of William Dacre, 3rd Baron Dacre
& Lady Elizabeth Talbot
issue of 1st:

a) **Hon. Anthony Browne** (... – 29 Jun 1592 Cowdray Park,
Sussex)
= ...; **Mary Dormer** (...) daughter of Sir William Dormer &
Dorothy Catesby; =2nd Sir Edward Uvedale; =3rd Sir Thomas
Gerard, 1st Baronet

(I) **Anthony Maria Browne, 2nd Viscount Montagu** (1 Feb
1573/4 – 23 Oct 1629) suc. grandfather 1592

= Feb 1591; **Lady Jane Sackville** (...) daughter of Thomas
Sackville, 1st Earl of Dorset & Cecily Baker
(A) **Hon. Mary Browne** (ca.1593 – 13 Nov 1692)
=1 bef.17 Feb 1614; ♦**William, Earl of Wiltshire** (1588 – Aug
1621) son of William Paulet, 4th Marquess of Winchester & Lady
Lucy Cecil
=2 1627; ♦**Hon. William Arundell** (...)
issue of 2nd (none by 1st):
Children are listed with other parent
(B) **Hon. Catherine Browne** (...)
= ...; ♦**William Tyrwhitt** (...)
Children are listed with other parent
(C) **Hon. Anne Browne** (...) a nun
(D) **Hon. Lucy Browne** (...)
(E) **Hon. Maria Brown** (ca.1603 – 13 Jan 1684/5)
= 1620; ♦**Robert Petre, 3rd Baron Petre** (1599 – 1638)
Children are listed with other parent
(F) **Francis Browne, 3rd Viscount Montagu** (2 Jul 1610 – Oct
1682) suc. father 1629
= aft.6 Jul 1637; ♦**Lady Elizabeth Somerset** (ca.1618 – 1684)
daughter of Henry Somerset, 1st Marquess of Worcester & Hon.
Anne Russell
(1) **Francis Browne, 4th Viscount Montagu** (1638 – Apr
1708) suc. father 1682
= ca.1690; ♦**Lady Mary Herbert** (... – 30 Oct 1744)
daughter of William Herbert, 1st Marquess of Powis & Lady
Elizabeth Somerset; =1st Hon. Richard Molyneux; =3rd Sir
George Maxwell, 3rd Baronet
no issue
(2) **Henry Browne, 5th Viscount Montagu** (ca.1640 – 25
Jun 1717) suc. brother 1708
= bef.1685; ♦**Barbara Walsingham** (...) daughter of
Thomas Walsingham & Lady Anne Howard
(a) **Anthony Browne, 6th Viscount Montagu** (1686 –
1767) suc. father 1717
= ...; **Barbara Webb** (...) daughter of Sir John Webb, 1st
Baronet & Barbara Belasyse
Has further generations of issue
(3) **Hon. Elizabeth Browne** (... – aft.1686)
= 1674; ♦**Christopher Roper, 5th Baron Teynham** (... –
1689)
Children are listed with other parent
(II) **Jane Browne** (... – ca.1650)
= ...; ♦**Sir Francis Englefield, 1st Baronet** (1561–1631)
Children are listed with other parent
(III) **John Browne** (...)

= ...
(A) **Stanislaus Browne** (...)
  = ...
  (a) **Stanislaus Browne** (...)
    = ...
    Has further generations of issue
(IV) **Dorothy Browne** (...)
  = ...; **Edmund Lee** (...)
  (A) **Dorothy Lee** (...)
    = ...; **Sir John Temple** (10 Nov 1593 – 1632) son of Sir
Thomas Temple, 1st Baronet & Hester Sandys
    (1) **Sir Peter Temple** (1613 – 22 Jan 1659/60) Kt. 1641
      = ...; **Eleanor Tyrrell** (... – 1671) daughter of Sir Timothy
Tyrrell; =2nd Richard Grenville
      (a) **Eleanor Temple** (... – 22 Mar 1729)
        = ...; **Richard Grenville** (14 Jan 1646/7 – 1 Jul 1719) son of
Richard Grenville & Annr Borlase
        Has further generations of issue
      (b) **William Temple** (... – Aug 1706)
        = ... **Mary Green** (...)
        Has further generations of issue
    (2) **Sir Thomas Temple, Baronet** (bef.10 Jun 1614 – 27 Mar
1674) unm. cr. Baronet 7 Jul 1662, which became extinct upon
his death; Gov. of Noca Scotia 1656-1670
    (3) **Sir Purbeck Temple** (... – Aug 1695) Kt.1660
      = ...; **Sarah Draper** (...) daughter of Robert Draper
no issue
    (4) **Dorothy Temple** (...)
      = ...; **John Alson** (...)
issue ?
    (5) **Hester Temple** (...)
      = ...; **Edward Paschal** (...)
issue ?
    (6) **Edmund Temple** (6 Jun 1622 – 6 Mar 1667/8)
      = 1647; **Eleanor Harvey** (...) daughter of Sir Stephen Harvey
      (a) **Stephen Temple** (... – 23 Oct 1672) unm.
      (b) **John Temple** (... – 19 Feb 1702)
        = ...; **Martha ...** (... – 1723)
        Has further generations of issue
      (c) **Edmund Temple** (.. – aft.1690)
        = ...; **Ellen ...** (...)
        Has further generations of issue
    (7) **Mary Temple** (1623 – ...)
      = ...; **Robert Nelson** (...)
      (a) **John Nelson** (... – 1734)
        = ...; **Elizabeth Teller** (...) daughter of William Teller

Has further generations of issue

b) **Hon. Mary Browne** (22 Jul 1552 – 1607)
=1 19 Feb 1565/6 London; **Henry Wriothesley, 2ⁿᵈ Earl of
Southampton** (bef.24 Apr 1545 – 4 Oct 1581) son of Thomas
Wriothesley, 1ˢᵗ Earl of Southampton & Jane Cheney; suc. father 30
Jul 1550
=2 ...; **Sir Thomas Heneage** (... – 17 Oct 1595) son of Robert
Heneage; =2ⁿᵈ Anne Poyntz
=3 May 1597; **Henry Hervey, Baron Hervey** 1ˢᵗ Baronet (... –
Jul 1642) son of Henry Hervey & Jane Thomas; =2ⁿᵈ Cordell
Annesley; Kt. 1596; cr. Baronet 31 May 1619 and baron 27 Feb
1627/8, both of which became extinct upon his death
issue of 1ˢᵗ (none by others):
(I) **Mary Wriothesley** (... – Jun 1607)
   = 1585; ♦**Thomas Arundell, 1ˢᵗ Baron Arundell** (ca.1560 –
   1639)
   Children are listed with other parent
(II) **Henry Wriothesley, 3ʳᵈ Earl of Southampton** (6 Oct 1573
   Cowdray, Som. – 10 Nov 1624 Bergen-op-Zoom, Brabant) suc.
   father 1581
   = bef.30 Aug 1598; **Elizabeth Vernon** (1573 – 1655) daughter of
   John Vernon & Elizabeth Devereux
   (A) **Lady Penelope Wriothesley** (bef.8 Nov 1598 – 16 Jul 1667
      Brington, Northants.)
      = 1615; ♦**William Spencer, 2ⁿᵈ Baron Spencer** (1592 –
      1636)
      Children are listed with other parent
   (B) **Lady Anne Wriothesley** (... – 1662)
      = ...; **Robert Wallop** (20 Jul 1601 – 19 Nov 1667 London) son
      of Sir Henry Wallop & Elizabeth Corbet; =2ⁿᵈ Elizabeth ...
      issue ?
   (C) **James, Lord Wriothesley** (1 Mar 1604/5 – 5 Nov 1624)
      unm.
   (D) **Thomas Wriothesley, 4ᵗʰ Earl of Southampton** (1607 –
      16 May 1667) suc. father 1624
      =1 18 Aug 1634; **Rachel de Massue** (1603 – 16 Feb 1639/40)
      daughter of Daniel de Massue, Seigneur de Ruvigny
      =2 24 Apr 1642; **Lady Elizabeth Leigh** (... – 1655) daughter
      Francis Leigh, 1ˢᵗ Earl of Chichester & Hon. Audrey Boteler
      =3 7 May 1659; ♦**Lady Frances Seymour** (... – 2 Jan 1680/1)
      daughter of William Seymour, 2ⁿᵈ Duke of Somerset & Lady
      Frances Devereux; =1ˢᵗ Richard Molyeux, 2ⁿᵈ Viscount
      Molyneux; =3ʳᵈ Conyers Darcy, 2ⁿᵈ Earl of Holderness
      issue of 1ˢᵗ:
      (1) **Lady Elizabeth Wriothesley** (... – 1680)
         = May 1661; **Edward Noel, 1ˢᵗ Earl of Gainsborough**

Baron Noel, 4th Viscount Campden, Baron Hicks, 3rd Baron
Noel, 3rd Baronet (bef.27 Jan 1640/1 Boughton Malherbe,
Kent – Jan 1688/9) son of Baptist Noel, 3rd Viscount Campden
& Hon. Hester Wotton; =2nd Mary Herbert; suc. father as
Viscount Campden and Baron Noel 1 Dec 1682; cr. Earl 1 Dec
1682

(a) **Wriothesley Baptist Noel, 2nd Earl of
Gainsborough**, etc. (bef.1665 – 21 Sep 1690) suc. father
1689
= 30 Dec 1687; **Hon. Catherine Greville** (... – 7 Feb
1703/4) daughter of Fulke Greville, 5th Baron Brooke Sarah
Dashwood; =2nd ♦John Sheffield, 1st Duke of Buckingham
Has further generations of issue

(b) **Lady Frances Noel** (... – 29 Sep 1684)
= 27 Aug 1683; **Simon Digby, 4th Baron Digby** (18 Jul
1657 – 19 Jan 1685) son of Kildare Digby, 2nd Baron Digby &
Mary Gardiner; suc. father 29 Jul 1677
Has further generations of issue

(c) **Lady Jane Noel** (... – Sep 1733)
= 1686; ♦**William Digby, 5th Baron Digby** (1661–1752)
Children are listed with other parent

(d) **Lady Elizabeth Noel** (... – 1705)
= ...; **Richard Norton** (...)
issue ?

(2) **Lady Rachel Wriothesley** (ca.1636 – 29 Sep 1723
London)
=1 ca.1653; **Francis, Lord Vaughan** (bef.1639 – 7 Mar
1666/7) son of Richard Vaughan, 2nd Earl of Carbery &

Frances

Altham
=2 1669; ♦**Rt.Hon. William, Lord Russell** (1639 – 1683)
issue of 2nd (none by 1st):
Children are listed with other parent
issue of 2nd (none by 3rd):

(3) **Lady Elizabeth Wriothesley** (1646 – 19 Sep 1690)
=1 1662; ♦**Joceline Percy, 5th Earl of Northumberland**
(1644 – 1670)
=2 24 Aug 1673; **Ralph Montagu, 1st Duke of Montagu**
Marquess of Monthermer, Earl of Montagu, Viscount
Monthermer, 3rd Baron Montagu (24 Dec 1638 – 19 Mar
1708/9) son of Edward Montagu, 2nd baron Montagu & Anne
Winwood; =2nd Lady Elizabeth Cavendish; suc. father 10 Jan
1683/4; cr. Duke etc. 14 Apr 1705
issue of 1st:
Children are listed with other parent
issue of 2nd:

463

(a) **Lady Anne Montagu** (1683 – 1761)
= 6 May 1707; **Daniel Harvey** (1664 – 1732) son of Daniel
Harvey & Elizabeth Montagu
issue ?

(b) **John Montagu, 2ⁿᵈ Duke of Montagu**, etc. **KG** (29
Mar 1690 – 5 Jul 1749) suc. father 1709; KG 1718
= 17 Mar 1705; **Lady Mary Churchill** (15 Jul 1689 – 14
May 1751) daughter of John Churchill, 1ˢᵗ Duke of
Marlborogh & Sarah Jenyns
Has further generations of issue

c) **Hon. Sir George Browne** (...)
= ...

(I) **George Browne** (... – Feb 1683/4)
= ...; **Ellinor Blount** (...) daughter of Sir Richard Blount

(A) **Sir John Browne, 1ˢᵗ Baronet** (ca.1631 – ca.1680) cr.
Baronet 10 May 1665
= 10 May 1666; **Elizabeth Bradley** (...)

(1) **Sir Anthony Browne, 2ⁿᵈ Baronet** (... – Dec 1688) suc.
father 1680; unm.

(2) **Sir John Browne, 3ʳᵈ Baronet** (... – ca.1692) suc. brother
1688; unm.

(3) **Sir George Browne, 4ᵗʰ Baronet** (... – 20 Feb 1729/30)
suc. brother 1692
=1 2 May 1699 London; **Gertrude Morley** (... – bef.Jul 1720)
=2 5 Feb 1721/2 London; **Prudence Torold** (... – 19 Dec
1725 London) daughter of Charles Thorold & Anne Clarke)
issue of 1ˢᵗ:

(a) **Sir John Browne, 5ᵗʰ Baronet** (... – 21 Jan 1775
Sunning, Berks.) suc. father 1730, but the baronetcy became
extinct upon his death; unm.

(B) **Sir George Browne KB** (... – Dec 1678) KB 1661
= ...

(1) **Winifred Browne** (...)
= ...; **Basil Brooke** (...)
issue ?

(2) **Helen Browne** (...)
= ...; **Henry Fermor** (...)

(a) **Arabella Fermor**[115] (1696 – 1737)
= ca.1715; **Francis Perkins** (... – 1736)
Has further generations of issue

issue of 2ⁿᵈ:

---

[115] She was "Belinda" in Alexander Pope's *Rape of the Lock*.

d) **Hon. Elizabeth Browne** (... – aft. 29 Sep 1623)
= ca.1590; **Robert Dormer, 1st Baron Dormer** 1st Baronet (26 Jan 1551 Wing, Bucks. – 8 Nov 1616) son of William Dormer & Elizabeth Catesby; cr. Baronet 10 Jun and Baron 30 Jun 1615
(I) **Hon. Sir William Dormer** (... – 19 Oct 1616 Wing)
= 21 Feb 1609/10; **Alice Molyneux** (...) daughter of Sir Richard Molyneux, 1st Baronet & Frances Gerard
  (A) **Robert Dormer, 1st Earl of Carnarvon** Viscount Ascott, 2nd Baron Dormer, etc. (ca.1610 – 20 Sep 1643 Newbury, Berks.) killed in battle; suc. grandfather 1616; cr. Earl 2 Aug 1628
  = 27 Feb 1624/5; ♦**Lady Anna Sophia Herbert** (... – Feb 1694/5) daughter of Philip Herbert, 4th Earl of Pembroke & Lady Susan de Vere
    (1) **Charles Dormer, 2nd Earl of Carnarvon** etc. (25 Oct 1632 – 29 Nov 1709 Wing) suc. father 1643, upon his death the Earldom and Viscountcy became extinct
    =1 bef.1652; ♦**Elizabeth Capell** (4 Jun 1633 Hadham Parva, Herts. – 30 Jul 1678) daughter of Arthur Capell, 1st Baron Capell & Elizabeth Morrison
    =2 aft. Jul 1678; **Lady Mary Bertie** (1 Sep 1655 London – 30 Jun 1709 London) daughter of Montagu Bertie, 2nd Earl of Lindsey & Bridget Wray, 4th Baroness Wray
    issue of 1st (none by 2nd):
      (a) **Charles, Viscount Dormer** (25 Jun 1652 Wing – bef.1673) unm.
      (b) **Lady Elizabeth Dormer** (1653 Wing – 24 Oct 1677)
      = aft.1665; ♦**Philip Stanhope, 2nd Earl of Chesterfield** (1634 – 1714)
      Children are listed with other parent
      (c) **Lady Isabella Dormer** (...)
      = 4 Aug 1679; **Charles Coote, 3rd Earl of Mountrath** Viscount Coote, Baron Coote (1656 – May 1709) son of Charles Coote, 2nd Earl of Mountrath & Alice Meredyth
      Has further generations of issue
      (d) **Lady Anna Sophia Dormer** (...)
  (B) **Elizabeth Dormer** (... – 31 May 1635 London)
  = ca.1628; ♦**Edward Somerset, 2nd Marquess of Worcester** (1603 – 1667)
  Children are listed with other parent
(II) **Hon. Anthony Dormer** (...)
= ...; **Margaret Terringham** (...) daughter of Sir Henry Terringham
  (A) **Robert Dormer** (...)
  = ...; **Anne Eyre** (...)
    (1) **Rowland Dormer, 4th Baron Dormer, 4th Baronet** (ca.1651 – 27 Sep 1712) unm. suc. 2nd Earl of Chesterfield 1709

(III) **Hon. Robert Dormer** (...)
 = ...; **Mary Banester** (...) daughter of Edward Banester
 (A) **Charles Dormer** (...)
  = ...; **Mary Cellier** (...)
  (1) **Charles Dormer, 5ᵗʰ Baron Dormer** (... – 2 Jul 1728)
   suc. 2nd cousin 1712
   =1 ...; **Catherine Fettiplace** (...) daughter of Edmond
   Fettiplace
   =2 7 Jun 1694; **Elizabeth Biddulph** (... – 29 OPct 1739)
   daughter of Richard Biddulph
   issue of 1ˢᵗ:
   (a) **Rev. Charles Dormer, 6ᵗʰ Baron Dormer** etc. (... – 7
    Mar 1761) a Catholic Priest; suc.father 1728
   (b) **John Dormer, 7ᵗʰ Baron Dormer** etc. (2 Jun 1691 – 7
    Oct 1785) suc. brother 1761
    = 1719; ◆**Mary Bishopp** (... – 29 Oct 1739) daughter of Sir
    Cecil Bishopp & Elizabeth Dunch
    Has further generations of issue
   issue of 2ⁿᵈ:
   (c) **Hon. Frances Dormer** (...)
    = 1726; **William Plowden** (... – 27 Aug 1754) son of
    William Plowden & Mary Stonor
    Has further generations of issue
   (d) **Hon. James Dormer** (...)
(IV) **Hon. Mary Dormer** (...)
 = ...; **Sir John Caryll** (...)
 (A) **Elizabeth Caryll** (... – Mar 1658)
  = ...; **Charles Smyth, 1ˢᵗ Viscount Carrington** Baron
  Carrington (ca.1598 – 22 Feb 1664/5 Pontoise, France)
  murdered; son of Sir Francis Smyth & Anne Markham; cr.
  Baron 31 Oct 1643 and Viscount 4 days later
  (1) **Francis Smith, 2ⁿᵈ Viscount Carrington** etc. (ca.1621 –
   Apr 1701) suc. father 1665
   =1 bef.1670; **Juliana Walmesley** (... – aft.5 Dec 1670)
   daughter of Sir Thomas Walmesley & Johanna Molyneux
   =2 23 May 1687; ◆**Lady Anne Herbert** (... – 11 May 1748
   London) daughter of William Herbert, 1ˢᵗ Marquess of Powis &
   Lady Elizabeth Somerset
   no issue
  (2) **Charles Smith, 3ʳᵈ Viscount Carrington** etc. (5 Jul
   1635 – 11 May 1706 Ashby Folville, Leics.) suc. brother 1701,
   but his titles became extinct upon his death
   = 11 Feb 1656/7 London; **Frances Pate** (... – 8 Juil 1693)
   daughter of Sir John Pate, Baronet & Elizabeth Skipwith
   no issue
(V) **Hon. Dorothy Dormer** (...)

= ...; ◆**Henry Huddleston** (...)
Children are listed with other parent
e) **Hon. Sir Henry Browne** (... – Jan 1628 Kidlington, Oxon)
= ...
  (I) **Sir Peter Browne** (ca.1615 – Jun 1645 Oxford) died of wounds
  received in battle ·
    = ...; **Margaret Knollys** (...) daughter of Sor Henry Knollys
    (A) **Sir Henry Browne, 1ˢᵗ Baronet** (ca.1639 – 1689
    Kidlington)
      = bef.1662; ◆**Frances Somerset** (...) daughter of Hon. Sir
      Charles Somerset & Elizabeth Powell
      (1) **Sir Charles Browne, 2ⁿᵈ Baronet** (ca.1667 – 20 Dec 1751
      Kidlington) suc. father 1689
        = bef.1694; ◆**Mary Pitt** (... – Aug 1739) daughter of George
        Pitt & Jane Savage
        (a) **Sir Charles Browne, 3ʳᵈ Baronet** (ca.1694 – 20 Jun
        1754 Kidlington) suc. father 171, but became extinct upon his
        death
          =1 May 1725; ◆**Lady Barbara Lee** (3 Mar 1694 London –
          ...) daughter of Edward Lee, 1ˢᵗ Earl of Lichfield & Lady
          Charlotte Fitzroy
          =2 ...; **Frances Sheldon** (... – 20 Mar 1790) daughter of
          Edward Sheldon & Elizabeth Shelley; =1ˢᵗ Henry Fermor
          Has further generations of issue by 1ˢᵗ
2) **Mabel Browne** (1528 – 25 Aug 1610)
  = 1554; ◆**Gerald FitzGerald, 11ᵗʰ Earl of Kildare** (1525–1585)
  Children are listed with other parent
3) **William Browne** (...)
  =1 ...; **Anne Hastings** (1528 – bef.1559) daughter of Sir Hugh
  Hastings & Katherine le Strange
  =2 aft.1558; **Elizabeth Noell** (... – 11 Apr 1620) =1ˢᵗ Antony Faunt
  and =3ʳᵈ Sir John Harpur
  issue ?
4) **Francis Browne** (...)
  = ...; **Anne Goring** (...) daughter of Sir William Goring & Elizabeth
  Covert; =1ˢᵗ Sir George Delalynde
  issue ?
5) **Lucia Browne** (... – 1606)
  = ...; **Thomas Roper** (1532 – 1567) son of William Roper &
  Margaret More
  a) **Sir William Roper** (1557 – 1628)
    = ...; **Catherine Browne** (... – 1616) daughter of Sir Anthony
    Browne
    (I) **Anthony Roper** (1583 – 1643)
      = ...; **Margaret Compton** (...) daughter of Sir Henry Compton
      (A) **Edward Roper** (1640 – 1723)

= 1668; **Catherine Butler** (...) daughter of James Butler
(1) **Elizabeth Roper** (... – 1722)
  = 1706; **Edward Henshaw** (1662 – 1726)
  (a) **Mary Henshaw** (... – Mar 1735)
    = 24 Feb 1728; **Sir Edward Dering, 5ᵗʰ Baronet** (... – 15
    Apr 1762) son of Sir Cholmely Dering, 4ᵗʰ Baronet & Mary
    Fisher; =2ⁿᵈ Mary Fotherby; suc. father 9 May 1711
    Has further generations of issue
  (b) **Susanna Henshaw** (... – ca.21 Mar 1741/2)
    = 29 Aug 1729; **Sir Rowland Winn, 4ᵗʰ Baronet** (ca.
    1706 – 23 Aug 1765) son of Sir Rowland Winn, 3ʳᵈ Baronet
    Laetitia Harbord; suc. father 3 Mar 1721/2
    Has further generations of issue
(II) **Anne Roper** (...)
= ...; ♦**Sir Philip Constable, 1ˢᵗ Baronet** (1595–...)
Children are listed with other parent
6) **Annabelle Browne** (... – 1603)
= ...; **Thomas Spring** (... – 1597) son of Thomas Spring
a) **Thomas Spring** (...)
= ...; **Avice Blennerhasset** (...) daughter of Robert Blennerhasset
& Avice Conway
(I) **Alice Spring** (...)
= ...; **Edward Conway** (...)
issue ?
(II) **Anne Spring** (...)
(III) **Annabelle Spring** (...)
(IV) **Mary Spring** (...)
(V) **Thomas Spring** (1705 – 6 Dec 1761)
= 1733; **Hannah Annesley** (...) daughter of Francis Annesley
issue ?
(VI) **Francis Spring** (1710 – 1752)
= ...; **Catherine Mason** (1696 – 12 Dec 1770) daughter of John
Mason & Avis McLoughlin
(A) **William** Cecil **Spring** (...) unm.
(B) **Francis Spring** (...)
= ...; **Catherine Fitzgerald** (...)
(1) **Rev. Edward Spring** (...)
= ...; **Arabella** Matilda **Rudkin** (...)
(a) **Sir Francis** Joseph Edward **Spring KCIE**¹¹⁶ (20 Jan
1849 Magourney, co Cork – 25 Mar 1933) KCIE 1911
= 1873; **Charlotte Townsend** (...) daughter of Samuel

---

¹¹⁶ Knight Commander, Order of the Indian Empire.

Townsend & Charlotte Becher
issue ?
(C) **John Spring** (23 Jun 1730 – 23 Sep 1786)
= ...; **Mary** Blennerhasset **Collis** (...) daughter of Rev. Thomas
Collis & Avice Blennerhasset
(1) **William** Collis **Spring** (1769 – 14 Aug 1825 Tralee, co
Kerry)
= ...; **Anne Carter** (ca.1787 – 19 Feb 1853 Cork) daughter of
Joseph Carter
(a) **Francis Spring** (3 Apr 1821 – 7 Jul 1857 Jhelum, India)
killed in battle
= 1853; **Sara** Ellen **Day** (...) daughter of Edward Day
no issue
b) **Walter Spring** (...)
= ...; **Alice Blannerhasset** (... – ca.1733) daughter of Robert
Blennerhasset & Avice Conway
(I) **Avice Spring** (...)
= ...; **Thomas Blennerhasset** (... – 1 Feb 1777) son of John
Blennerhasset & Margaret Crosbie
(A) **John Blennerhasset** (4 Aug 1728 – bef.1774) unm.
(B) **Arthur Blennerhasset** (5 Aug 1731 – 20 Nov 1810)
=1 ...; **Arabella Blennerhasset** (21 Dec 1726 – 27 Jan 1795)
daughter of John Blennerhasset & Jane Denny; =1st Richard
Ponsonby
=2 ...; **Margaret** Mary **Coghlan** (... – 6 Nov 1821) daughter of
James Coghlan; =1st George L'Estrange; =3rd Valentine Quin, 1st
Earl of Dunraven and Mount-Earl
issue of 1st (none by 2nd):
(1) **Edward Blennerhasset** (1755 – 4 Nov 1772) unm.
(C) **Thomas Blennerhasset** (18 Dec 1736 – ...)
= ...
(1) **Arthur Blennerhasset** (ca.1755 – Aug 1826 Ballyseedy, co
Kerry)
= ...
(a) **John Blennerhasset** (...) emigrated to NZ
(b) **William Blennerhasset** (...) emigrated to NZ
(c) **Arthur Blennerhasset** (...)
(d) **Thomas** Arthur **Blennerhasset** (1786 – 20 Mar 1868
Ballyseedy)
= 20 Jan 1820; **Susan Hill** (... – 1886)
Has further generations of issue
(D) **Margaret Blennerhasset** (1740 – 25 Nov 1827)
= ...; **Thomas Sheldon** (... – 1804)
no issue
(II) **Edward Spring** (...)
= ...; **Anne Browne** (...) daughter of Sir Nicholas Browne &

Sheela Beake
(A) **Walter Spring** (...)
  = ...; **Juliana Fitzgerald** (...) daughter of John Fitzgerald 12th Knight of Kerry & Katherine FitzMaurice
  (1) **Mary Spring** (...)
  (2) **Thomas Spring** (...)
    = ...
    (a) **Catherine Spring** (...)
      = 10 Aug 1785; **Stephen** Edward **Rice** (... – 1831) son of Thomas Rice & Mary FitzGerald
      Has further generations of issue
(B) **Thomasine Spring** (...)
  = ...; **Patrick Fitzgerald** (...) son of John Fitzgerald, 12th Knight of Kerry & Katherine FitzMaurice
  (1) **John Fitzgerald** (...)
  (2) **Katherine Fitzgerald** (...)
    = ...; **James Conway** (...) son of Edmund Conway & Alice Blennerhasset
    (a) **Alice Conway** (...)
      = ...; **John Colhurst** (... – 12 Jul 1756) son of John Colthurst & Eliza Purdon; =2nd Mahetabel Wallis
      Has further generations of issue
  (3) **Anne Fitzgerald** (...)
    = ...; **Thomas Conway** (...) son of Christopher Conway
    (a) **Christopher Conway** (...)
      = ...; **Ellen McCarthy** (... – bef.1765) daughter of Randall Maccarthy & Maria MacCarthy of Cloghroe
      issue ?
  (4) **Lucy Fitzgerald** (...)
    = ...; **Richard Ferriter** (...)
    issue ?
E) **Elizabeth Browne** (... – 1565)
  = bef.1527; ♦**Henry Somerset, 2nd Earl of Worcester** (ca.1496 – 1549)
  Children are listed with other parent
F) **Anne Browne** (...)
  = ...; **Charles Brandon, 1st Duke of Suffolk** (1484 – 21 Aug 1545) son of Sir William Brandon & Elizabeth Bruyn; =2nd ♦Lady Margaret Neville; =3rd ♦Princess Mary Tudor; =4th ♦Kathenrine Willoughby, 12th Baroness Willoughby
  1) **Lady Anne Brandon** (1510 – ca.1542)
    = ca.1528; ♦**Thomas Stanley, 2nd Baron Monteagle** (1507 – 1560)
  Children are listed with other parent
G) **Lucy Browne** (...)
  = ...; **Hon. Thomas Clifford** (...) son of Henry Clifford, 10th Baron

Clifford & Anne St.John
issue ?
VI) **Lady Isabella Neville** (aft.1467 – ...)
=1 ...; **Sir William Hodleston** (...) son of Sir John Hodleston & Jane Stapleton
=2 ...; **Sir William Smythe** (...)
issue of 1st (none by 2nd):
A) **Sir John Hudleston** (...)
  = ...
  1) **Sir John Hudleston** (...)
   = ...
   a) **Sir Edmund Hudleston** (...
    = ...
    (I) **Frances Hudleston** (...)
     = ...; **George Wylde** (...)
     (A) **Elizabeth Wylde** (... – 23 Apr 1656 Mawley Hall, Worcs.)
     = ...; **Sir Walter Blount, 1st Baronet** (ca.1594 – 27 Aug 1654 Blagdon, Devon) son of Sir George Blount & Eleanor Norwood; cr. Baronet 6 Oct 1642
     (1) **Sir George Blount, 2nd Baronet** (... – 12 Nov 1667 Mawley Hall)
      = ...; **Mary Kirkham** (... – bef.10 Feb 1667/8) daughter of Richard Kirkham & Mary Tichborne
      (a) **Sir Walter** Kirkham **Blount, 3rd Baronet** (... – 12 May 1717 Ghent, Belgium) suc. father 1667
       =1 ...; **Alicia Strickland** (... – 1 Dec 1680) daughter of Sir Thomas Strickland & Jane Moseley
       =2 18 Jun 1688; **Mary Wood** (1661 Loudham, Suffolk – ...) daughter of Sir Caesar Wood & Lelia Pelliott
       no issue
      (b) **George Blount** (... – 20 May 1702)
       =1 ...; ♦**Lady Mary O'Brien** (... – 1686) daughter of Henry O'Brien, 4th Earl of Thomond & Mary Brereton; =1st Charles Cokayne, 1st Viscount Cullen
       =2 ...; ♦**Constantia Cary** (...) daughter of Sir George Cary
       Has further generations of issue by 2nd
      (c) **Edward Blount** (... – 1726)
       = ...; **Anne Guise** (...) daughter of Sir John Guise, 2nd Baronet & Elizabeth Howe
       Has further generations of issue
      (d) **Anne Blount** (... – 13 Feb 1734/5)
       = 29 Jun 1675; **Sir Francis Jerningham, 3rd Baronet** (ca.1650 – 1730) son of Sir Henry Jerningham, 2nd Baronet & Mary Hall; suc. father 1680
       Has further generations of issue
     (2) **Eleanor Blount** (... – 3 Dec 1674)

=1 bef.1657; **Robert Knightley** (... – bef.1657)
=2 ca.1657; **Walter Aston, 3ʳᵈ Lord Aston** 3ʳᵈ Baronet
(1633 Tixall, Staffs. – 24 Nov 1714 Standon, Herts.) son of
Walter Aston, 2ⁿᵈ Lord Aston & Mary Weston; =2ⁿᵈ Catherine
Gage; suc. father 232 Apr 1678
issue of 2ⁿᵈ (none by 1ˢᵗ):
(a) **Hon. Edward** Walter **Aston** (1658 – 1678 Paris) unm.
(b) **Hon. Francis Aston** (ca.1659 – 1694 Standon) unm.
(c) **Walter Aston, 4ᵗʰ Lord Aston** etc. (1660 – 4 Apr 1748
Tixall) suc. father 1714
= 1 Oct 1698; ♦**Anne Howard** (... – 236 May 1723)
daughter of Lord Thomas Howard & Mary Savile
Has further generations of issue
(II) **Henry Huddleston** (...)
= ...; ♦**Hon. Dorothy Dormer** (...) daughter of Robert Dormer,
1ˢᵗ Baron Dormer & Hon. Elizabeth Browne
(A) **Sir Richard Huddleston** (...)
= ...; ♦**Christian Tufton** (...) daughter of Richard Tufton &
Chrysogon Morley
issue ?
d. **Most Rev. George Neville, Archbishop of York** (ca.1432 – 8
Jun 1476) appointed Archbishop 15 Mar 1464/5
e. **Lady Joan Neville** (1434 – bef.9 Sep 1462)
= aft.17 Aug 1438; **William FitzAlan, 16ᵗʰ Earl of Arundel** Earl of
Surrey, **KG** (23 Nov 1417 – 1487) son of John FitzAlan, 13ᵗʰ Earl of
Arundel & Eleanor Berkeley; suc nephew 24 Apr 1438; KG 1471
I) **Thomas FitzAlan, 17ᵗʰ Earl, of Arundel** etc. **KG** (ca.1450 – 25 Oct
1524 Singleton, Sussex) suc. father 1487; KG 1474
= Oct 1464; **Lady Margaret Woodville** (ca.1439 – bef.6 Mar 1490/1)
daughter of Richard Wydevill, 1ˢᵗ Earl Rivers & Jaquetta of Luxembourg
A) **Lady Margaret FitzAlan** (... – aft.1443)
= ...; ♦**John de la Pole, 1ˢᵗ Earl of Lincoln** etc. (ca.1463 – 16 Jun
1487 Stoke) killed in battle; son of John de la Pole, 2ⁿᵈ Duke of Suffolk
& Lady Elizabeth Plantagenet
no issue
B) **Lady Joan FitzAlan** (...)
= bef.1494; ♦**George Neville, 3ʳᵈ Baron Abergavenny** (ca.1469 –
ca.1535)
Children are listed with other parent
C) **William FitzAlan, 18ᵗʰ Earl of Arundel** etc. **KG** (ca.1476 – 23
Jan 1543/4) suc. father 1524; KG1525
=1 bef.1510; **Hon. Elizabeth Willoughby** (...) daughter of Robert
Willoughyby, 1ˢᵗ Baron Willoughby & Blanche Champernowne
=2 15 Feb 1510/1; ♦**Lady Anne Percy** (bef.27 Jul 1485 – 1552)
daughter of Henry Percy, 3ʳᵈ Earl of Northumberland & Lady Maud
Herbert

issue of 2nd (none by 1st):

1) **Henry Fitzalan, 19th Earl of Arundel** etc. **KG** (23 Apr 1512 – 24 Feb 1579/80 London) suc. father 1544; KG 1544
=1 aft.25 Jan 1524/5; ♦**Lady Catherine Grey** (1512 – 1 May 1542) daughter of Thomas Grey, 2nd Marquess of Dorset & Margaret Wotton
=2 19 Dec 1545; **Mary Arundell** (... – 20 Oct 1557 London) daughter of Sir John Arundell & Katherine Grenville; =1st Robert Radcliffe, 1st Earl of Sussex
issue of 1st (none by 2nd):

a) **Lady Mary Fitzalan** (... – 25 Aug 1557)
= 1555; ♦**Thomas Howard, 4th Duke of Norfolk** (1538 – 1572) Children are listed with other parent

b) **Lady Joan Fitzalan** (... – 1576)
= ...; **John Lumley, Baron Lumley KB** (ca.1533 – 11 Apr 1609) son of George Lumley & Jane Knightley; =2nd Hon. Elizabeth Darcy; cr. Baron 1547, but it became extinct upon his death; KB 1553
no issue

c) **Sir Henry, Lord Mautravers KB** (1538 – 30 Jun 1556 Brussels) KB 1547
= 12 Apr 1555; **Ann Wentworth** (... – Jan 1580/1) daughter of Sir John Wentworth; =1st Sir Hugh Rich; =3rd William Deane
no issue

f. **Lady Katherine Neville** (1442 – bef.22 Nov 1503)
=1 ca.1458; **William Bonville, 6th Baron Hartington** 2nd Baron Bonville (1442 – 31 Dec 1460 Wakefield, Yorks.) killed in battle; son of William Bonville & Elizabeth Hartington; suc. in Hartington Mar 1457/8; and in Bonville 18 Feb 1460/1
=2 1462; ♦**William Hastings, 1st Baron Hastings** (ca.1431 – 1483)
issue of 1st:

I) **Cecilia Bonville, 7th Baroness Hartington** 3rd Baroness Bonville (ca.1461 – 12 May 1529 Astley, Warks.) suc. father 1460
=1 18 Jul 1474; **Thomas Grey, 1st Marquess of Dorset** 7th Baron Ferrers, Baron Astley (1451 – 20 Apr 1501) son of Sir John Grey & Elizabeth Wydevill; =1st Lady Anne Holand; suc. to Astley 18 Dec 1457, Ferrers 23 Jan 1483; cr. Marquess 1475
=2 ca.1504; ♦**Henry Stafford, 1st Earl of Wiltshire KG** (ca.1479 – 6 Mar 1523) son of Henry Stafford, 2nd Duke of Buckingham & Katherine Woodville; cr. Earl 28 Jan 1509/10 but it became extinct upon his death; KG 1505
issue of 1st (none by 2nd):

A) **Lady Cicely Grey** (... – Apr 1554)
= aft.30 Oct 1519; **John Sutton, 3rd Baron Dudley** (ca.1495 – Sep 1553 London) son of Edward Sutton, 2nd Baron Dudley & Cicely Willoughby; suc. father 31 Jan 1508

1) **Edward Dudley, 4ᵗʰ Baron Dudley** (... – 8 Jul 1586) suc. father 1553; took Dudley as surname
=1 1556; ♦**Hon. Katherine Brydges** (1524 – Apr 1566) daughter of John Brydges, 1ˢᵗ Baron Chandos & Hon. Elizabeth Grey
=2 1566/7; ♦**Lady Jane Stanley** (... – Aug 1569) daughter of Edward Stanley, 3ʳᵈ Earl of Derby & Lady Dorothy Howard
issue of 1ˢᵗ:
a) **Hon. Agnes Dudley** (...)
=1 ...; **Francis Throckmorton** (...)
=2 ...; **Thomas Wylmer** (...)
issue ?
issue of 2ⁿᵈ:
b) **Edward Dudley, 5ᵗʰ Baron Dudley** (bef.17 Sep 1567 – 24 Jun 1643) suc. father 1586
= ca.1586 **Theodosia Harington** (... – Jan 1649/50) daughter of Sir James Harington & Lucy Sydney
(I) **Hon. Mary Dudley** (2 Oct 1586 – ...)
= 1607, ♦**Alexander Home, 1ˢᵗ Earl of Home** (1566–1619)
Children are listed with other parent
(II) **Hon. Sir Ferdinando Dudley KB** (4 Sep 1588 – 22 Nov 1621 London) KB 1610
= 9 Jul 1610; ♦**Lady Honora Seymour** (... – Mar 1620) daughter of Edward, Lord Beauchamp & Honora Rogers
(A) **Frances Dudley, 6ᵗʰ Baroness Dudley** (23 Jul 1611 – Aug 1697) suc. grandfather 1643
= 17 Feb 1628; **Humble Ward, 1ˢᵗ Baron Ward** (ca.1614 – 14 Oct 1670) son of William Ward & Elizabeth Humble; cr. Baron 23 Mar 1643/4
(1) **Hon. Anne Ward** (12 Feb 1629/30 – ...) unm.
(2) **Edward Ward, 7ᵗʰ Baron Dudley** 2ⁿᵈ Baron Ward (ca.1631 – 3 Aug 1701) suc. father 1670 and mother 1697
= ...; ♦**Frances Brereton** (... – Nov 1676) daughter of Sir William Brereton, 1ˢᵗ Baronet & Susan Boorth
(a) **Hon. John Ward** (16 Oct 1656 – Jun 1675) unm.
(b) **Hon. William Ward** (5 Jan 1659/60 – May 1692) (twin)
= ...; ♦**Frances Dilke** (ca.1664 – ...) daughter of William Dilke & Hon. Honor Ward
Has further generations of issue
(c) **Hon. Elizabeth Ward** (5 Jan 1659/60 – ...) (twin) unm.
(d) **Hon. Henreitta Ward** (...)
(e) **Hon. Humble Ward** (...) unm.
(f) **Hon. Catherine Ward** (ca.1663 – ...)
= 1683; ♦**Hon. John Grey** (...)
Children are listed with other parent
(g) **Hon. Ferdinando Ward** (... – Oct 1717) unm.
(h) **Hon. Lettice Ward** (...) unm.

(3) **Hon. William Ward** (...)
= 30 Dec 1672; **Anna Parkes** (ca.1646 – ...) daughter of
Thomas Parkes & Rebecca ...
(a) **William Ward** (... – 25 Oct 1720)
= ...; ◆**Mary Grey** (ca.1686 – ...) daughter of Hon. John
Grey & Mary Wollryche
Has further generations of issue
(b) **Dudley Ward** (...) unm.
(c) **Jane Ward** (...)
= ...; **Daniel Jevon** (...)
issue ?
(d) **Rebecca Ward** (...) unm.
(e) **Frances Ward** (...)
= 15 May 1695; **Robert Pigott** (... – 1 Jun 1764)
Has further generations of issue
(4) **Hon. Honor Ward** (ca.1636 – ...)
= ...; **William Dilke** (... – 31 Aug 1669)
(a) **Ward Dilke** (...)
(b) **Elizabeth Dilke** (...)
(c) **Thomas Dilke** (...)
(d) **Seymour Dilke** (...)
(e) **William Dilke** (...)
(f) **Frances Dilke** (... – 13 Mar 1698)
= ...; ◆**Hon. William Ward** (1660–1692)
Children are listed with other parent
(5) **Hon. Frances Ward** (
= 9 Jul 1672; **Sir William Noel, 2nd Baronet** (ca.1642 –
23 Apr 1675) son of Sir Varney Noel, 1st Baronet & Elizabeth
Dixie; =1st Margaret Lovelace; suc. father 1670
(a) **Frances Noel** (bef.14 Apr 1673 Himley Hall, Staffs. – Feb
1751)
=1 ...; **Ralph Sneyd** (22 Dec 1669 – ...) son of Ralph Sneyd
=2 bef.1714; **Sir Charles Skrimshire** (... – bef.1714)
=3 Apr 1714; **Sir John Chester, 4th Baronet** (24 Jun
1666 – 6 Feb 1725/6) son of Sir Anthony Chester, 3rd Baronet
& Mary Cranmer; =1st Anne Wolleaston; suc. father 15 Feb
1697/8
=4 aft.1726; **Charles Adderley** (28 Sep 1667 – 2 Feb
1746/7) son of Arden Adderley & Mary Draper; =1st Mary
Bowyer
Has further generations of issue by 1st
(b) **William Noel** (...)
(c) **Elizabeth Noel** (...)
(6) **Hon. Theodosia Ward** (bef.15 May 1642 Dudley, Staffs. –
Jan 1678/9)
=1 bef.1664; ◆**Sir Thomas Brereton, 2nd Baronet** (1632–

7 Jan 1673/4) son of Sir William Brereton, 1st Baronet & Susan Booth; suc. father 7 Apr 1661

=2 bef.Feb 1677; **Charles Brereton** (...)

issue of 2nd (none by 1st):

(a) **Charles Brereton** (23 Feb 1677/8 – ...)

(III) **Hon. Anne Dudley** (... – 8 Dec 1615 Heidelberg)

= 22 Mar 1615 London; **Count Hans Meinhardt von Schönberg auf Wesel** (28 Aug 1582 Bacharach, Germany – 3 Aug 1616 Heidelberg) son of Meinhard I Baron von Schönberg auf Wesel & Dorothea Riedesel zu Bellersheim

(A) **Count Frederic von Schönberg, 1st Duke of Schomberg** (6 Dec 1615 Heidelberg – 11 Jul 1690 Drogheda, co Louth) cr. Duke 1689

=1 30 Apr 1638; **Johanna Elisabeth Schönberg auf Wesel** (1617 – 21 Mar 1664 Geisenheim) daughter of Count Heirnich Dietrich von Schönberg auf Wesel & Baroness Elisabeth Kettler

=2 14 Apr 1669; **Suzanne d'Aumâle, Dame d'Aucourt** (... – Jul 1688) daughter of Daniel, Count d'Aumâle & Françoise de Conflans, Dame de Villiers-Outreaux

issue of 1st (none by 2nd):

(1) **Friedrich X, Count von Schönberg auf Wesel** (14 Mar 1640 Oberwesel – 5 Dec 1700 Geisenheim)

=1 1670 (dv.); **Baroness Katharina** Ernestina **von Bocholtz** (1650 – 30 Aug 1716)

=2 1684; **Baroness Amalia** Charlotta Veronica **von Spaen** (1661 – 1731) daughter of Baron Alexander von Spaen & Henrietta van Arnhem

issue of 1st (none by 2nd):

(a) **Countess Maria** Wilhelmine Elisabeth **von Schönberg** (bef.1684 – aft.1728)

= 1703; **Count Karl Friedrich zu Sayn-Wittgenstein-Homburg** (1674 – 27 Mar 1723 Homburg) son of Count Wilhelm Friedrich zu Sayn-Wittgenstein-Homburg & Countess Anna von Sayn und Wittgenstein

no issue

(2) **Meinhardt von Schönberg, 3rd Duke of Schomburg, 1st Duke of Leinster** Marquess of Harwich (30 Jun 1641 Cologne – 5 Jul 1719 London) suc. brother 1693; cr. Duke of Leinster etc. 30 Jun 1690

=4 Jun 1683; ♦**Countess Caroline Elisabeth of the Palatine** (19 Nov 1659 – 7 Jul 1696 London) daughter of Karl I, Elector of the Palatine & Countess Marie Susanne von Degenfeld

(a) **Charles Louis, Marquess of Harwich** (15 Dec 1683 – 14 Oct 1713) unm.

(b) **Lady Caroline Schomberg** (1687 – 18 Jun 1710) unm.

476

(c) **Lady Frederica Susanna Schomberg** (ca.1688 – 7 Aug 1751)
=1 1715; ◆**Robert Darcy, 3rd Earl of Holderness** (1681–1722)
=2 18 Jun 1724 London; ◆**Benjamin Mildmay, Earl FitzWalter** etc. (27 Dec 1672 – 29 Feb 1756 London) son of Benjamin Mildmay, 17th Baron FitzWalter & Hon. Catherine Fairfax
issue of 1st (none by 2nd):
see: pafge
(d) **Lady Maria Schomberg** (16 Mar 1692 – 29 Apr 1762)
= 1717; **Count Christoph Martin von Degenfeld-Schonburg** (... – 10 Aug 1762)
Has further generations of issue
(3) **Karl von Schönberg, 2nd Duke of Schomberg** (5 Aug 1645 's-Hertogenbosch, Netherlands – 17 Oct 1693 Turin) died of wounds received in battle; unm.
(IV) **Hon. Margaret Dudley** (ca.1597 – ...)
issue by **Elizabeth Tomlinson** (... – 1629) daughter of William Tomlinson:
(V) **Robert Dudley** (...)
(VI) **Edward Dudley** (... – bef.1638) unm.
(VII) **Dud Dudley** (...)
(VIII) **Elizabeth Dudley** (...)
= ca.1611; **Jeffrey Dudley** (...)
issue ?
(IX) **Jane Dudley** (...)
= ca.16096; **Richard Parkes** (...)
(A) **Margaret Parkes** (...)
= ...; **John Darby** (...)
(1) **John Darby** (1649 – 1725)
= ...
(a) **Abraham Darby** (1678 – 1717)
= ...
Has further generations of issue
(X) **Catherine Dudley** (...)
(XI) **Alice Dudley** (...)
(XII) **Dorothy Dudley** (...)
(XIII) **Martha Dudley** (...)
= ...; **Thomas Wilmer** (...)
(A) **Elizabeth Wilmer** (...)
(B) **Anne Wilmer** (...)
(C) **Martha Wilmer** (...)
c) **Hon. John Dudley** (bef.30 Nov 1569 – Feb 1644/5)
= ...; **Elizabeth Whorwood** (...) daughter of Thomas Whorwood & Magdalen Edwards

(I) **Anne Dudley** (...)
= ...; **Edward Gibson** (...)
issue ?
2) **Hon. Henry Dudley** (...)
= ...; **... Ashton** (...) daughter of Sir Christopher Ashton
issue ?
3) **Hon. George Dudley** (...) unm.
4) **Hon. Eleanor Sutton** (...) unm.
5) **Hon. Thomas Dudley** (ca.1539 – 1574)
= ...
a) **Elizabeth Dudley** (...)
B) **Lady Elizabeth Grey** (...)
= 1519; **Gerald FitzGerald, 9th Earl of Kildare** (1487 – 13 Dec
1534 London) died in prison; son of Gerald FitzGerald, 8th Earl of
Kildare & Alison Eustace; =1st Elizabeth Zouche; suc. father 3 Sep 1513
1) **Gerald FitzGerald, 11th Earl of Kildare** 1st Baron Offaly (25 Feb
1525 – 16 Nov 1585 London) suc. half-brother 23 Feb 1568/9; cr.
Baron 13 May 1554
= 28 May 1554; ♦**Mabel Browne** (1528 – 25 Aug 1610) daughter of
Sir Anthony Browne & Alice Gage
a) **Gerald, Lord Garratt** (28 Dec 1559 – Jun 1580)
= Oct 1578; ♦**Catherine Knollys** (1559 – ...) daughter of Sir
Francis Knollys & Katherine Carey; =2nd Philip Boteler
(I) **Lettice FitzGerald, 2nd Baroness Offaly** (ca.1580 – 1 Dec
1658) suc. grandfather 1585
= 1598; ♦**Sir Robert Digby** (...–1618)
Children are listed with other parent
b) **Henry FitzGerald, 12th Earl of Kildare** (1562 – 1 Aug 1597)
died from wonds received in battle; suc. father 1585
= bef.22 Feb 1589/90; **Lady Frances Howard** (bef.1572 – 7 Jul
1628) daughter of Charles Howard, 1st Earl of Nottingham &
Katherine Carey; =2nd Henry Brooke, 11th Lord Cobham
(I) **Lady Elizabeth FitzGerald** (...)
= bef.1611; **Lucas Plunkett, 1st Earl of Fingall** 9th Baron
Killeen (... – 29 Mar 1637) son of Christopher Plunkett, 8th Lord
Killeen & Genet Dillon; =2nd Hon. Susannah Brabazon; =3rd
Eleanor Bagenal; =4th Margaret St.Lawrence; suc. father 12 Oct
1613; cr. Earl 26 Sep 1628
no issue
(II) **Lady Bridget FitzGerald** (ca.1590 – ...)
=1 bef.1606; **Ruaidhri O'Donnell, 1st Earl of Tyrconnel**
(1575 – 30 Jul 1608) son of Air Aodh O'Donnell & Finola
Macdonald; cr. earl 1603
=2 bef.7 Jul 1617; **Nicholas Barnewall, 1st Viscount
Barnewall** Baron Turvey (1592 – 20 Aug 1663 Turvey, co
Dublin) son of Sir Patrick Barnewall & Mary Bagenal; cr. Viscount

etc. 29 Jun 1646

issue of 1st:

(A) **Albert, Baron O'Donnell** (1 Oct 1606 – 1 Jul 1642 at sea) killed in battle

= ...; **Anna Margaret de Hennin** (...) daughter of Maximilien de Hennin, Count du Boussu

no issue

(B) **Mary O'Donnell** (... – aft. 1632)

= ...; **John Edward O'Gallagher** (...)

issue ?

issue of 2nd:

(C) **Henry Barnewall, 2nd Viscount Barnewall** etc. (... – 1 Jun 1688) suc. father 1663

=1 1661; **Hon. Mary Netterville** (... – 28 Oct 1663) daughter of John Netterville, 2nd Vicount Netterville & Lady Elizabeth Weston

=2 29 Nov 1664; **Lady Mary Nugent** (21 Feb 1648 – 25 Jun 1680) daughter of Richard Nugent, 2nd Earl of Westmeath & Mary Nugent

issue of 1st:

(1) **Hon. Marianna Barnewall** (... – 16 Sep 1735)

= 1680; ◆**Thomas Nugent, 1st Baron Nugent** (...–1715) Children are listed with other parent

issue of 2nd:

(2) **Nicholas Barnewall, 3rd Viscount Barnewall** etc. (15 Apr 1668 – 14 Jun 1725) suc. father 1688

= 15 May 1688; **Mary Hamilton** (bef.1676 – 15 Feb 1735/6 Turvey, co Dublin) daughter of Sir George Hamilton, Count Hamilton[117] & Frances Jenyns

(a) **Hon. Frances Barnewall** (ca.1700 – 19 May 1735)

= ...; (Hon.) **Richard Barnewall** (...) son of John Barnewall, *de jour 11th Baron Trimlestown* & Mary Barnewall

Has further generations of issue

(b) **Henry** Benedict **Barnewall, 4th Viscount Barnewall** (1 Feb 1708 – 11 Mar 1774 Quansbury, co Galway) suc. father 1725

= 22 May 1735 Arbor Hill; **Honora Daly** (... – 1784) daughter of Peter Daly & Elizabeth Blake

no issue

(c) **Hon. George Barnewall** (ca.1711 – Jun 1771)

---

[117] Title was from the Kingdom of France.

= ...; ♦**Lady Barbara Belasyse** (...) daughter of Thomas
Belasyse, 1ˢᵗ Earl of Fauconberg & Catherine Betham
Issue extinct 1800
(3) **Hon. Henry Barnewall** (...)
= ...
  (a) **Christopher Barnewall** (22 Feb 1680 – ...) unm.
(4) **Hon. Mary Barnewall** (... – 16 Oct 1715)
= 23 Sep 1687; **Thomas St.Lawrence, 13ᵗʰ Baron Howth**
(1659 – 30 May 1727) son of William St.Lawrence, 12ᵗʰ Baron
Howth & Elizabeth St.Lawrence; suc. father 17 Jun 1671
  (a) **William St. Lawrence, 14ᵗʰ Baron Howth** (11 Jan
  1688 – 4 Apr 1748) suc. father 1727
  = 2 Aug 1728; ♦**Lucy Gorges** (ca.1711 – ...) daughter of
  Richard Gorges & Hon. Nichola Hamilton
  Has further generations of issue
(5) **Hon. Mabel Barnewall** (...)
= ...; **Oliver Plunkett, 8ᵗʰ Baron Louth** (1668 – 1707) son
of Matthew Plunkett, 7ᵗʰ Baron Louth & Jane FitzGerald; suc.
father Sep 1689
  (a) **Hon. Matthew Plunkett** *de jure 9ᵗʰ Baron Louth*
  (1698 – ...) suc. father 1707
  = 20 Apr 1716; **Susanna Mason** (... – 21 Feb 1767)
  Has further generations of issue
  (b) **Hon. Jane Plunkett** (...)
  = ...; **Draycott Talbot** (...) son of Henry Talbot
  Has further generations of issue
  (c) **Hon. Mabel Plunkett** (...)
(D) **Hon. Richard Barnewall** (...)
= ...
(1) **Nicholas Barnewall** (... – 1735)
= ...
  (a) **Matthew Barnewall** (... – 1773)
  = ...; **Anne McCan** (...) daughter of Thomas McCan
  Has further generations of issue
(E) **Hon. Mabel Barnewall** (... – Feb 1699)
=1 Jan 1636; **Christopher Plunkett, 2ⁿᵈ Earl of Fingall** etc.
(... – 16 Aug 1649 Dublin) died in prison; son of Lucas Plunkett,
1ˢᵗ Earl of Fingall & Hon. Susannah Brabazon; suc. father 29
Mar 1637
=2 1653; **James Barnewall** (1615 – bef.23 Jul 1661) son of Sir
Patrick Barnewall, 1ˢᵗ Baronet & Cecilia Fleming
issue of 1ˢᵗ:
(1) **Luke Plunkett, 3ʳᵈ Earl of Fingall** etc (1639 – ca.1684)
  suc. father 1649
  =...; **Lady Margaret MacCarty** (1646 – 4 Jan 1703)
  daughter of Donough MacCarty, 1ˢᵗ Earl of Clancarty & Hon.

Eleanor Butler
(a) **Lady Helen Plunkett** (...)
=1 1681; ◆**Sir FitzGerald Aylmer, 3ʳᵈ Baronet** (1663–1685)
=2 1694; **Michael Fleming** (...)
issue of 1ˢᵗ:
Children are listed with other parent
issue of 2ⁿᵈ:
Has further generations of issue
(b) **Lady Amelia Plunkett** (... – 4 Oct 1757 Brussels)
= bef.5 Feb 1696/7; **Theobald Taaffe, 4ᵗʰ Earl of Carlingford** 5ᵗʰ Viscount Taafrfe, Baron of Ballymote (... – 24 Nov 1738) son of Hon. John Taaffe & Lady Rose Lambart; suc. uncle Aug 1704
Has further generations of issue
(c) **Peter Plunkett, 4ᵗʰ Earl of Fingall** etc. (... – 24 Jan 1717) suc. father 1684
= 1698; **Frances Hales** (...) daughter of Sir Edward Hales, 3ʳᵈ Baronet; =2ⁿᵈ Stephen Taaffe; =3ʳᵈ Patrick Bellew
Has further generations of issue
(d) **Lady Elizabeth Plunkett** (...)
= ...; **Rowland Eyre** (...)
issue ?
(2) **Lady Mary Plunkett** (...)
=...; **Walter Butler** (... – 1700)
(a) **Thomas Butler** (... – 1738)
= ...; **Lady Margaret Bourke** (... – 19 Jul 1744) daughter of William Bouke, 7ᵗʰ Earl of Clanricarde & Lady Helen MacCarty; =1ˢᵗ Brian O'Iveaugh, 5ᵗʰ Viscount of Mogennis
Has further generations of issue
(b) **John Butler** (...)
= ...; **Frances Butler** (...) daughter of George Butler
Has further generations of issue
(c) **Lucy Butler** (... – 1703)
= Apr 1697; **Sir Walter Butler, 3ʳᵈ Baronet** (ca.1678 – 8 Oct 1723) son of Sir Richard Butler, 2ⁿᵈ Baronet & Elizabeth ...; suc. father 1680
Issue extinct by 1723
(d) **Christopher Butler, Archbishop of Cashel** (... – 4 Sep 1757) Catholic priest
(e) **Mary Butler** (...)
= ...; **James Tobin** (...)
issue ?
(f) **Frances Butler** (...)
= ...; **... Gould** (...)
issue ?

(g) **Helen Butler** (...)
  = ...; **Maurice FitzGerald** (...)
  Has further generations of issue
issue of 2nd:
(3) **Mabel Barnewall** (...)
  = ...; **Edward Hussey** (...)
  (a) **Catherine Hussey** (... – Mar 1746/7)
    = ...; ♦**Sir Andrew Aylmer, 4th Baronet** (...–1740)
    Children are listed with other parent
(4) **Eleanor Barnewall** (...) unm.
(5) **George Barnewall** (bef.1662 – ...)
  = ...; **... Dillon** (...)
  (a) **Bartholomew Barnewall** (... – 1736)
    = ...; **Jane Georghegan** (...) daughter of Kidagh
    Georghegan
    Has further generations of issue
(F) **Hon. James Barnewall** (...)
  = ...
  (1) **George Barnewall** (...)
    = ...
    (a) **Christopher Barnewall** (...)
      = ...
      Has further generations of issue
(G) **Hon. Mary Barnewall** (... – May 1642)
= ...; **Nicholas Preston, 6th Viscount Gormanston** 9th Lord
Preston (ca.1608 – 28 Jul 1643) son of Jenico Preston, 5th
Viscount Gormanston & Margaret St.Lawrence
(1) **Jenico Preston, 7th Viscount Gormanston** etc. (... – 17
  Mar 1690/1) suc. father 1643
  =1 ...; ♦**Lady Frances Leke** (... – 29 Jul 1682) daughter of
  Francis Leke, 1st Earl of Scarsdale & Anne Carey
  =2 Nov 1683; **Hon. Margaret Molyneux** (... – 2 Sep 1711)
  daughter of Caryll Molyneux, 3rd Viscount Molyneux & Mary
  Barlow; =2nd James Butler; =3rd Robert Casey
  issue of 2nd (none by 1st):
  (a) **Hon. Mary Preston** (... – 27 Dec 1750)
    = 1700; ♦**Anthony Preston** (...–1716)
    see: below
(2) **Hon. Nicholas Preston** (...)
  = ...; **Hon. Elizabeth Preston** (...) daughter of Anthony
  Preston, 2nd Viscount Taragh & Margaret Warren
  (a) **Jenico Preston, 8th Viscount Gormanston** etc. (... –
    1699) suc. uncle 1691; unm.
  (b) **Anthony Preston, 9th Viscount Gormanston** etc.
    (... – 25 Sep 1716)
    = 1700; ♦**Hon. Mary Preston** (... – 27 Dec 1750) daughter

of Jenico Preston, 7th Viscount Gormanston & Hon. Margaret Molyneux
Has further generations of issue
c) **Lady Elizabeth FitzGerald** (... – 12 Jan 1617)
= aft.6 Nov 1585; **Donough O'Brien, 3rd Earl of Thomond** Baron of Ibracken (... – 5 Sep 1624 Clonmel, co Tipperary) son of Conor O'Brien, 2nd Earl of Thomond & Una O'Brien; =1st Hon. Helen Roche; =3rd Hon. Joan FitzMaurice
(I) **Henry O'Brien, 4th Earl of Thomond** etc. (ca.1588 – bef.22 Apr 1639)
= 13 Jul 1608 Brereton, Ches.; ♦**Hon. Mary Brereton** (bef.28 Dec 1580 – Apr 1640) daughter of William Brereton, 1st Baron Brereton & Margaret Savage
(A) **Lady Margaret O'Brien** (... – 26 Jul 1681)
=1 Aug 1639; ♦**Edward Somerset, 2nd Marquess of Worcester** etc. (9 Mar 1602/3 Raglan, Monmouths – 3 Apr 1667 London) son of Henry Somerset, 1st Marquess of Worcester & Hon. Anne Russell; =1st Elizabeth Dormer; suc. father 1646
=2 Jun 1679; **Donogh Kearney** (ca.1650 – Apr 1718) son of Michael Kearney
no issue
(B) **Lady Mary O'Brien** (... – 1686)
=1 24 Jun 1627; **Charles Cokayne, 1st Viscount Cullen** Baron Cullen (4 Jul 1602 – 1661) son of Sir William Cokayne & Mary Morris; cr. Viscount etc. 11 Aug 1642
=2 ...; ♦**George Blount** (... – 20 May 1702) son of Sir George Blount, 2nd Baronet & Mary Kirkham; =2nd Constantia Carey
issue of 1st (none by 2nd):
(1) **Hon. Mary Cokayne** (...)
= ...; **Robert Pierson** (...)
issue ?
(2) **Brien Cokayne, 2nd Viscount Cullen** etc. (1631 – Jul 1687) suc. father 1661
= bef.1 Apr 1657; **Elizabeth Trentham** (1640 – 30 Nov 1713) daughter of Francis Trentham
(a) **Charles Cokayne, 3rd Viscount Cullen** etc. (15 Nov 1658 – 30 Dec 1688) suc. father 1687
= 26 Dec 1678; **Katherine Willoughby** (... – 11 Feb 1688/9) daughter of William Willoughby, 6th Baron Willoughby
Has further generations of issue
(C) **Lady Elizabeth O'Brien** (... – ca.1658)
=1 ...; **Dutton Gerard, 3rd Baron Gerard** (4 Mar 1613 – 22 Apr 1640) son of Gilbert Gerard, 2nd Baron Gerard & Eleanor Dutton; =1st Lady Mary Fane
=2 ...; **Philip Wenman, 3rd Viscount Wenman** (... – 29 Apr

1686) son of Sir Richard Wenman & Jane West; suc. nephew 25 Jan 1664

issue of 1st (none by 2nd):

(1) **Hon. Elizabeth Gerard** (...)

= ...; ◆**Hon. William Spencer** (aft.1622–...)

Children are listed with other parent

(D) **Lady Anne O'Brien** (... – 3 Sep 1644)

= 1641; ◆**Henry O'Brien, 6th Earl of Thomond** etc. (1620–1691)

Children are listed with other parent

(E) **Lady Honora O'Brien** (...)

=1 ...; ◆**Sir Thomas Englefield, 3rd Baronet** (...) son of Sir Francis Englefield, 2nd Baronet

=2 ...; ◆**Hon. Sir Robert Howard** (1622 – 1698) son of Thomas Howard, 1st Earl of Berkshire & Lady Elizabeth Cecil

no issue

(II) **Barnabas O'Brien, 5th Earl of Thomond** etc. (ca.1590 – 12 Nov 1657) suc. brother 1639

= 17 Jul 1615 Easton Neston, Northants.; **Anne Fermor** (12 Mar 1591/2 – Apr 1675) daughter of Sir George Fermor & Mary Curson; =1st Robert Crichton, 8th Lord crichton

(A) **Lady Penelope O'Brien** (...)

= 1644; ◆**Henry Mordaunt, 2nd Earl of Peterborough** 6th Baron Mordaunt **KG** (bef.18 Oct 1623 – 19 Jun 1697) son of John Mordaunt, 1st Earl of Peterborough & Elizabeth Howard; suc. father 19 Jun 1644

(1) **Mary Mordaunt, 7th Baroness Mordaunt** (... – 17 Nov 1705) suc. father 1697

=1 8 Aug 1677 (dv.1700); ◆**Henry Howard, 7th Duke of Norfolk** etc. (11 Jan 1654/5 – 2 Apr 1701) son of Henry Howard, 6th Duke of Norfolk & Lady Anne Somerset

=2 15 Sep 1701; **Sir John Germaine, Baronet** (...) =2nd Lady Elizabeth Berkeley; cr. Baronet, but the ntitle bewcame extinct upon his death

no issue

(B) **Henry O'Brien, 6th Earl of Thomond** etc. (ca.1620 – 2 May 1691) suc. father 1657

=1 1641; ◆**Lady Anne O'Brien** (... – 13 Sep 1644) daughter of Henry O'Brien, 4th Earl of Thomond & Mary Brereton

=2 1660; **Sarah Russell** (bef.19 Sep 1639 – 1715) daughter of Sir Francis Russell, 2nd Baronet & Catherine Wheatley; =1st Sir John Reynolds

issue of 1st:

(1) **Henry, Lord O'Brien** (... – 1 Sep 1678)

= bef.14 Dec 1661; ◆**Katherine Stuart, 7th Baroness Clifton** (bef.5 Dec 1640 – 2 Nov 1702) daughter of George

Stuart, 9th Siegneur d'Aubigny & Lady Katherine Howard; =2nd
Sir Joseph Williamson
  (a) **Hon. Mary O'Brien** (7 May 1662 – 24 Nov 1683)
     = ...; ♦**John FitzGerald, 18th Earl of Kildare** etc. (1661 –
     9 Nov 1707) son of Wentworth FitzGerald, 17th Earl of
     Kildare & Lady Elizabeth Holles; =2nd ♦Lady Elizabeth Jones
     no surviving issue
  (b) **Donogh, Lord Ibracken** (16 Sep 1663 – 5 May 1682)
     = 26 May 1679; **Lady Sophia Osborne** (1661 – 8 Dec 1746)
     daughter of Thomas Osborne, 1st Duke of Leeds & Lady
     Bridget Bertie; =2nd William Fermor, 1st Baron Leominster
     no issue
  (c) **George O'Brien** (...) unm.
  (d) **Katherine O'Brien, 8th Baroness Clifton** (29 Jan
     1673 – 11 Aug 1706 New York) suc. mother 1702
     = 1688; ♦**Edward Hyde, 3rd Earl of Clarendon** (1661–
     1723)
     Children are listed with other parent
issue of 2nd:
  (2) **Lady Auberie** Anne Penelope **O'Brien** (... – 2 Dec 1703)
     = 1691; ♦**Henry Howard, 6th Earl of Suffolk** (1670–1718)
     Children are listed with other parent
  (3) **Lady Elizabeth O'Brien** (... –3 Jun 1688) unm.
  (4) **Lady Mary O'Brien** (... – 9 Nov 1735)
     = ...; **Sir Matthew Dudley, 2nd Baronet** (...)
     no issue
  (5) **Henry** Horatio, **Lord O'Brien** (ca.1670 – 10 Jul 1690)
     = 24 Jun 1686; ♦**Lady Henrietta Somerset** (ca.1669 – 2
     Aug 1715 Audley End, Essex) daughter of Henry Somerset, 1st
     Duke of Beaufort & Mary Capell
     (a) **Henry O'Brien, 7th Earl of thomond** etc. **1st Viscount
        Tadcaster** (14 Aug 1688 – 20 Apr 1741 Dublin) suc.
        grandfather 1691; cr. Viscount 19 Oct 1714; ujpon his death
        the new title became extinct and the older ones fell to a
        cousin who was under attainder
        = 4 Jun 1707; ♦**Lady Elizabeth Seymour** (1685 – 2 Apr
        1734 London) daughter of Charles Seymour, 6th Duke of
        Somerset & Lady Elizabeth Percy
        no issue
     (b) **Hon. Mary O'Brien** (... – 30 Aug 1716) unm.
  (III) **Hon. Teige O'Brien** (...)
     = ...; **Slany O'Brien** (1575 – ...) daughter of Teige O'Brien &
     Móre O'Brien
     no issue
d) **Lady Mary FitzGerald** (... – 1 Oct 1610)
  = 6 May 1575; **Christopher Nugent, 5th Baron Delvin** (ca.
485

1544 – 26 Aug 1602 Dublin) died in prison; son of Richard Nugent, 4th Baron Delvin & Hon. Elizabeth Preston; suc. father 10 Dec 1559

(I) **Hon.Mabel Nugent** (...)

=1 ...; **Murrough O'Brien, 4th Baron Inchiquin** (1550 – 20 Apr 1573) son of Murrough O'Brien, 3rd Baron Inchiquin & Lady Margaret O'Brien; suc. father 20 Apr 1573

=2 ...; **Hon. John FitzPatrick** (...) son of Florence FitzPatrick, 3rd Baron of Upper Ossory

issue of 1st (none by 2nd):

(A) **Dermot O'Brien, 5th Baron of Inchiquin** (Oct 1594 – 29 Dec 1624) suc. father 1573

= bef.1614; **Ellen FitzGerald** (...) daughter of Sir Edmond FitzGerald & Honora FitzGerald

(1) **Morrogh O'Brien, 1st Earl of Iniquin** Baron O'Brien, 6th Baron of Inchiquin (Oct 1614 – 9 Sep 1674) suc. father 1624; cr. Earl etc. 21 Oct 1654

= 1 Oct 1635; **Elizabeth St.Leger** (... – 22 May 1685) daughter of Sir William St.Leger

(a) **William O'Brien, 2nd Earl of Inchiquin** etc (ca.1640 – Jan 1691/2) suc. father 1674

=1 1665; ♦**Lady Margaret Boyle** (... – 24 Dec 1683) daughter of Roger Boyle, 1st Earl of Orrey & Lady Margaret Howard

=2 aft.1684; ♦**Hon. Elizabeth Brydges** (25 Mar 1651 – 3 Feb 1718) daughter of George Brydges, 6th Baron Chandos & Lady Susan Montagu

Has further generations of issue by 1st

(b) **Lady Honora O'Brien** (... – aft.10 Oct 1718)

= ...; **Theobald Bourke, 3rd Baron of Brittas** (... – ca.1706) son of William Bourke & Elizabeth FitzPatrick; suc. cousin 6 Jan 1658/9

Has further generations of issue

(c) **Lady Elizabeth O'Brien** (... – Sep 1688)

=1 ...; **Richard Southwell** (... – bef.Feb 1679/80) son of Sir Thomas Southwell, 1st baronet & Elizabeth Starkey

=2 ...; **John MacNamara** (...)

Has further generations of issue by 1st

(d) **Lady Mary O'Brien** (...)

=1 ...; ♦**Hon. Henry Boyle** (1648–1693)

=2 ...; **Sir Thomas Dilkes** (1667 – 1707)

=3 ...; **John Irwin** (...)

issue of 1st (none by others):

Children are listed with other parent

(e) **Hon. Charles O'Brien** (...) killed at sea; unm.

(f) **Hon. John O'Brien** (... – ca.1699)

= ...; **Honora Georghegan** (...) daughter of Connla

Georghegan
no issue
(2) **Hon. Mary O'Brien** (...)
= ...; **Most Rev. Michael Boyle, Archbishop of Armagh**
(ca.1610 – 10 Dec 1702) son of Rt.Hon. Most Rev. Richard
Boyle, Archbishop of Tuam & Martha Wright; =1st Margaret
Synge
(a) **Eleanor Boyle** (...)
= ...; **Rt.Hon. William Hill** (... – ca.1693) son of Rt.Hon.
Arthur Hill & Mary Parsons; =2nd Hon. Mary Trevor
Has further generations of issue
(b) **Honora Boyle** (... – ca.Nov 1710)
=1 ...; **Thomas Cromwell, 3rd Earl of Ardglass** Viscount
Lecale, 6th Baron Cromwell (29 Nov 1653 Strensham,
Worcs. – 11 Apr 1682) son of Wingfield Cromnwell, 2nd Earl
of Ardglass & Mary Russel; suc. father 3 Oct 1668
=2 bef.1687; **Francis Cuffe** (12 Sep 1656 – 26 Dec 1694)
son of Sir James Cuffe & Alice Aungier
=3 ca.1700; **Sir Thomas Burdett, 1st Baronet** (14 Sep
1668 Garrahill, co Carlow – 14 Apr 1727) son of Thomas
Burdett & Catherine Kennedy; =2nd Martha Vigors; cr.
Baronet 11 Jul 1723
Has further generations of issue by 2nd
(c) **Murrough Boyle, 1st Viscount Blesington** Baron
Boyle (ca.1645 Cork – 26 Apr 1718 Dublin) cr. Viscount 23
Aug 1673
=1 ...; **Mary Parker** (... – 13 Sep 1668) daughter of Most
Rev. John Parker, Archbishop of Dublin & Mary Clarke
=2 Nov 1672; **Lady Anne Coote** (ca.1658 – 6 Apr 1725)
daughter of Charles Coote, 2nd Earl of Mountrath & Alice
Meredyth
Has further generations of issue by both
(3) **Hon. Honora O'Brien** (...)
= ...; **Anthony Stoughton** (...)
(a) **Ellen Stoughton** (...)
= ...; **Thomas Blennerhassett** (... – bef.1713) son of John
Blennerhassett & Martha Lynn
Has further generations of issue
(b) **Henry Stoughton** (...)
= ...; **Sarah Crosbie** (...) daughter of Sir Thomas crosbie &
Bridget Tynte
Has further generations of issue
(4) **Hon. Henry O'Brien** (... – 1645) unm.
(5) **Hon. Christopher O'Brien** (... – ca.1662)
= ...; **Honora MacMahon** (...) daughter of Turlough
MacMahon; =1st Baltius Clancy

no issue

(II) **Hon. Elizabeth Nugent** (...)

= aft.1600; ♦**Gerald FitzGerald, 14ᵗʰ Earl of Kildare** (...–1612)

Children are listed with other parent

(III) **Hon. Julia Nugent** (... – 12 Nov 1617)

= 1611; **Sir Gerald Aylmer, 1ˢᵗ Baronet** (... – 19 Aug 1634) son of Richard Aylmer & Elinor Fleming; =1ˢᵗ Mary Travers; cr. Baronet 25 Jan 1621/2

(A) **Sir Andrew Aylmer, 2ⁿᵈ Baronet** (aft.1610 – bef.1681) suc. father 1634

= 1634; ♦**Hon. Ellen Butler** (...) daughter of Thomas, Viscount Thurles & Elisabeth Poyntz

(1) **Garret Aylmer** (1635 – 20 Dec 1663)

= 1662; ♦**Jane FitzGerald** (...) daughter of Philip FitzGerald

(a) **Elizabeth Aylmer** (...)

(b) **Sir FitzGerald Aylmer, 3ʳᵈ Baronet** (1663 – 9 Jun 1685) suc. grandfather bef.1681

= Jun 1681; ♦**Lady Helen Plunkett** (...) daughter of Luke Plunkett, 3ʳᵈ Earl of Fingall & Lady Margaret MacCarty

Has further generations of issue

(B) **Julia** Lettice **Aylmer** (...)

= aft.1628; **Sir Richard Barnewall, 2ⁿᵈ Baronet** (21 Dec 1602 – 6 Jul 1679) son of Sir Patrick Barnewall, 1ˢᵗ Baronet & Cecilia Fleming; =1ˢᵗ Thomazine Dowdall; suc. father 21 Jun 1624

(1) **Elizabeth Barnewall** (...)

= ca.1660; **Sir Patrick Bellew, 1ˢᵗ Baronet** (... – Jan 1715/6) son of Sir John Bellew & Mary Dillon; cr. Baronet 11 Dec 1688

(a) **Sir John Bellew, 2ⁿᵈ Baronet** (ca.1660 – 23 Jul 1734) suc. father 1716

=1 1 Dec 1685; **Mary Margaret Taylor** (... – 1708) daughter of Edward Taylor & Clare Humphries

=2 aft.1708; **Elizabeth Curling** (... – 3 jan 1735) daughter of Edward Curling; =2ⁿᵈ St.Laurence Besford

Has further generations of issue by both

(b) **Juliana Bellew** (... – ca.1729)

= aft.1680; **John Browne** (bef.1664 – 11 Apr 1711) son of George Browne & Alicia Bingham; =1ˢᵗ ♦Hon. Anne Hamilton

Has further generations of issue

(2) **Sir Patrick Barnewall, 3ʳᵈ Baronet** (ca.1630 – bef.1702)

= ...; ♦**Frances Butler** (... – Jan 1709) daughter of Hon. Richard Butler & Lady Frances Tuchet

(a) **Sir George Barnewall, 4ᵗʰ Baronet** (... – 22 Oct 1735) suc. father bef.1702; unm.

(b) **Ellinor Barnewall** (...)
= 1703; **Hugh Montgomery, 4ᵗʰ Earl of Mount Alexander** (... – 27 Feb 1744/5) son of Henry Montgomery, 3ʳᵈ Earl of Mont Alexander & Mary St.Lawrence; suc. father
no issue

(c) **Frances Barnewall** (... – 23 May 1758) unm.

(d) **Elizabeth Barnewall** (... – bef.17 Sep 1728) unm.

(e) **Mary Barnewall** (... – 1750) unm.

(C) **Mabel Aylmer** (...)
= ...; **Sir Oliver Tuite, 1ˢᵗ Baronet** (ca.1588 – 1642) son of John Tuite & Margaret Nugent; cr. Baronet 16 Jun 1622

(1) **Mary Tuite** (...)
= ...; ♦**Hon. Patrick Plunkett** (...) son of Matthew plunkett, 5ᵗʰ Baron Louth & Mary Fitzwilliam
no issue

(2) **Thomas Tuite** (... – Oct 1624)
= ...; **Martha Luttrell** (...) daughter of Thomas Luttrell

(a) **Sir Oliver Tuite, 2ⁿᵈ Baronet** (... – Aug 1661) suc. grandfather 1642
= ...; **Elinor O'Ferrall** (...) daughter of Roger O'Ferrall; she =2ⁿᵈ Owen O'Conor
Issue extinct 1664

(b) **Sir Henry Tuite, 4ᵗʰ Baronet** (...) suc. nephew 1664
= ...; **Diana Mabbott** (...) daughter of Kympton Mabbott & Susan Hyde
Has further generations of issue

(IV) **Richard Nugent, 1ˢᵗ Earl of Westmeath** 6ᵗʰ Baron Devlin (1583 – aft.May 1642) suc. father 1602; cr. Earl 4 Sep 1621
= bef.1604; **Hon. Jane Plunkett** (... – aft.24 Jan 1626/7) daughter of Christopher Plunkett, 8ᵗʰ Baron Killeen & Genet Dillon

(A) **Christopher, Lord Delvin** (1604 – 10 Jul 1625)
= ...; **Lady Anne MacDonnell** (...) daughter of Randal MacDonnell, 1ˢᵗ Earl of Antrim & Alice O'Neill; =2ⁿᵈ William Fleming, 14ᵗʰ Baron Slane

(1) **Hon. Mary Nugent** (...)
= ...; **Hon. Owny O'Dempsey** (... – ca.1638) son of Terence O'Dempsey, 1ˢᵗ Viscount Clanmalier

(a) **Lewis O'Dempsey, 2ⁿᵈ Viscount Clanmalier** Baron of Philipstown (... – 1683) suc. grandfather 1638
=1 ...; **Martha Itchingham** (...) daughter of John Itchingham & Margaret Whitly
=2 7 Mar 1671; **Dorothy Molloy** (... – ca.1708) daughter of Charles Molloy; =2ⁿᵈ Kyran Molloy
Has further generations of issue by 1ˢᵗ

      (b) **Sir Christopher O'Dempsey** (... – bef.1683) unm.
    (2) **Richard Nugent, 2ⁿᵈ Earl of Westmeath** etc. (ca.1622 –
      bef.25 Feb 1683/4) suc. father 1642
      = bef.1641; ◆**Mary Nugent** (... – 19 May 1672) daughter of
      Sir Thomas Nugent, 1ˢᵗ Baronet; =1ˢᵗ Hon. Christopher
      Plunkett
      (a) **Lady Anne Nugent** (... – aft.14 Jul 1710)
        =1 1681; ◆**Lucas Dillon, 6ᵗʰ Viscount Dillon** (... – 1682)
        son of Theobald Dillon & Sarah Bourke; =1ˢᵗ Lady Ursula
        Dongan
        =2 1683; **Sir William Talbot, 3ʳᵈ Baronet** (... – 18 May
        1691) son of Sir Robert Talbot, 2ⁿᵈ Baronet & Grace Calvert;
        suc. father 21 Oct 1670
        no issue
      (b) **Christopher, Lord Delvin** (... – bef.1680)
        = ca.1665; ◆**Mary Butler** (... – 28 Mar 1737) daughter of
        Hon. Richard Butler & Lady Frances Tuchet
        Has further generations of issue
      (c) **Thomas Nugent,** *de jure 1ˢᵗ Baron Nugent* (... – 2 Apr
        1715) cr. Baron 3 Apr 1689 by James II after vacating the
        Throne and therefore not recognized
        = Sep 1680; ◆**Marianna Barnewall** (... – 16 Sep 1735)
        daughter of Henry Barnewall, 2ⁿᵈ Vicount Barnewall & Hon.
        Mary Netterville
        Has further generations of issue
      (d) **Lady Mary Nugent** (21 Feb 1648 – 25 Jun 1680)
        = 1664; ◆**Henry Barnewall, 2ⁿᵈ Vicount Barnewall**
        (...–1688)
        Children are listed with other parent
  (B) **Hon. Ignatius Nugent** (... – Feb 1671)
    = ...; **Hon. Jane Plunkett** (...) daughter of Matthew
    Plunkett, 5ᵗʰ Baron Louth & Mary Fitzwilliam
    (1) **Jane Nugent** (...)
      = ...; **Daniel Dunne** (...)
      issue ?
    (2) **Mary Nugent** (...)
      = ...; **Andrew Pallas** (...)
      issue ?
  (C) **Hon. Francis Nugent** (...) unm.
  (D) **Hon. John Nugent** (...)
    = ...
    has unknown issue
  (E) **Hon. Lawrence Nugent** (...)
 (V) **Hon. Christopher Nugent** (aft.1583 – 3 Jul 1626)
 (VI) **Hon. Eleanor Nugent** (... – 31 Aug 1636)
  = ...; **Christopher Chevers** (1580 – 7 Nov 1640) son of John

Chevers & Catherine Travers; =2nd Jane Bath

(A) **John Chevers** (... – 1688)
=1 ...; **Mary Bealings** (...) daughter of Sir Henry Bealings
=2 ...; **Joan Sutton** (...) daughter of Edward Sutton
issue of 2nd (none by 1st):
   (1) **Edward Chevers, Viscount Mount Leinster** Baron
   Bannow (... – 1709) cr. Viscount etc. 23 Aug 1689 but it
   became extinct upon his death
      = ...; **Anne Sarsfield** (...) daughter of Patrick Sarsfield
      no issue
   (2) **Andrew Chevers** (...)
      = ...
      (a) **Hyacinth Chevers** (... – ca.1758)
         = ...; **Helen Power** (... – 29 Jul 1757) daughter of John
         Power & Mary Power
         no issue
   (3) **John Chevers** (...)
      = ...; **Ellis Geoghegan** (...) daughter of Edward Geoghegan
      (a) **Michael Chevers** (... – bef.16 Oct 1779)
         = ...; **Margaret O'Flyn** (... – bef.21 Jul 1781) daughter of
         John O'Flyn
         Has further generations of issue
      (b) **Edward Chevers** (...)
         = ...; **Bridget Telberton** (...)
         Has further generations of issue
      (c) **Christopher Chevers** (...)
         = ...; **Barbara Smyth** (...) daughter of John Smyth
         Has further generations of issue
      (d) **Mathias Chevers** (... – Oct 1771) unm.
      (e) **Most Rev. Augustin Chevers, Bishop of Meath** (... –
      18 Aug 1778) Catholic priest
      (f) **Hyacinth Chevers** (... – 4 Nov 1758)
         =1 ..; **Clare Bellew** (...) daughter of Richard Bellew
         =2 ...; **Elizabeth Curling** (... – 3 Jan 1735) daughter of
         Edward Curling
         Has further generations of issue by 1st
(B) **Christopher Chevers** (...)
(C) **Garrett Chevers** (...
   = ...; **Katherine** Anne **Chevers** (...) daughter of Hamon
   Chevers
   issue ?
(D) **Anthony Chevers** (...)
(E) **Richard Chevers** (...)
(F) **Peter Chevers** (...)
(G) **Mary Chevers** (...)
   = ...; **Edward Dalton** (...)

issue ?

(H) **Bridget Chevers** (...)

(VII) **Hon. William Nugent** (...)

= ...; **Margaret Leigh** (...)

has unknown issue

e) **William FitzGerald, 13ᵗʰ Earl of Kildare** etc. (... – Apr 1599 lost at sea between England and Ireland) suc. brother 1597; unm.

2) **Lady Elizabeth FitzGerald** (1528 – Mar 1589/90) =1 1543; ♦**Sir Anthony Browne** (1500 – 1548 Byfleet, Surrey) son of Sir Anthopny Browne & Lady Lucy Neville; =1ˢᵗ Alice Gage =2 1 Oct 1552; ♦**Edward Clinton, 1ˢᵗ Earl of Lincoln** etc. KG (1512 – 16 Jan 1584/5) son of Thomas Clinton, 8ᵗʰ Baron Clinton & Joan Poynings; =1ˢᵗ Elizabeth Blount; =2ⁿᵈ Hon. Ursula Stourton; suc. father 7 Aug 1517; cr. Earl 4 may 1572; KG 1551 no issue

3) **Hon. Edward FitzGerald** (17 Jan 1528 – 1590) = ...; **Anne Leigh** (...) daughter of Sir John Leigh & Elizabeth Darcy

a) **Gerald FitzGerald, 14ᵗʰ Earl of Kildare** (... – 11 Feb 1611/2) suc. cousin 1599

= aft.1600; ♦**Elizabeth Nugent** (...) daughter of Christopher Nugent, 5ᵗʰ Baron Delvin & Lady Mary FitzGerald

(I) **Gerald FitzGerald, 15ᵗʰ Earl of Kildare** (ph.26 Dec 1611 – 11 Nov 1620) suc. father at birth, died age 8

b) **Thomas FitzGerald** (... – 1619) = ...; **Frances Randolph** (...) daughter of Thomas Randolph

(I) **George FitzGerald, 16ᵗʰ Earl of Kildare** (23 Jan 1611/2 – 1660) suc. cousin 1620

= 15 Aug 1630; ♦**Lady Joan Boyle** (1611 – 11 Mar 1656/7) daughter of Richard Boyle, 1ˢᵗ Earl of Cork & Catherine Fenton

(A) **Lady Elizabeth FitzGerald** (... – Feb 1697/8) =1 ...; **Callaghan MacCarty, 3ʳᵈ Earl of Clancarty** 3ʳᵈ Baronet, 4ᵗʰ Viscount Muskerry (... – 21 Nov 1676) son of Donough MacCarty, 1ˢᵗ Earl of Clancarty & Hon. Eleanor Butler; suc. nephew 22 Sep 1666

=2 17 Jun 1682 Dublin; **Sir William Davys** (... – 24 Sep 1687) son of Sir Paul Davys & Margaret Ussher

issue of 1ˢᵗ (none by 2ⁿᵈ):

(1) **Lady Catherine MacCarty** (... – Apr 1738) = ...; **Paul Davys, 1ˢᵗ Viscount Mountcashell** Baron Mountcahsell (... – 5 Aug 1716) son of Sir John Davys; cr. Viscount etc 31 Jan 1705/6

(a) **James Davys, 2ⁿᵈ Viscount Mountcashell** etc. (ca.1710 – 10 Mar 1718/9) suc. father 1716

(b) **Edward Davys, 3ʳᵈ Viscount Mountcashell** etc. (1711 – 1736) suc. brother 1719, but title became extinct upon his death

(c) **Hon. Margaret Davys** (... – 2 Dec 1788 Dublin)
= 1738; ♦**James Barry, 5th Earl of Barrymore** (1717–1751)
Children are listed with other parent
(2) **Donogh MacCarty, 4th Earl of Clancarty** etc. (ca.1668 – 1 Oct 1734 on the Elbe River, Germany) suc. father 1676 but titles were forfeited for fighting for the Jacobites
= 31 Dec 1684 London; **Lady Elizabeth Spencer** (ca.1673 – Jun 1704) daughter of Robert Spencer, 2nd Earl of Sunderland & Lady Anne Digby
  (a) **Robert, Viscount Muskerry** (1685 – 19 Sep 1769 in France)
  =1 14 Dec 1722; **Joanna Player** (17 Oct 1693 Alverstoke, Hants. – 13 Jan 1759 London) daughter of Henry Player & Joanna Benett
  =2 aft.1758; **Elizabeth Farnelly** (... – 1790) =2nd Charles Macarty-More
  Issue extinct by 1792
  (b) **Lady Charlotte MacCarty** (... – 7 Feb 1734/5)
  = 1721; ♦**John West, 1st Earl De La Ware** (1693–1766)
  Children are listed with other parent
(B) **Lady Eleanor FitzGerald** (... – 3 Aug 1681)
= 16 Feb 1656; **Sir Walter Borrowes, 2nd Baronet** (ca.1620 – 1685) son of Sir Erasmus Borrowes, 1st Baronet & Sarah Weldon; =2nd Margaret Loftus; suc. father 1650
(1) **Sir Kildare Borrowes, 3rd Baronet** (ca.1660 – May 1709) suc. father 1685
= ...; **Elizabeth Dixon** (... – 11 Mar 1745) daughter of Sir Richard Dixon & Mary Eustace
  (a) **Sir Walter Borrowes, 4th Baronet** (... – 9 Jun 1741 Colverstown, co Kildare) suc. father 1709
  = 18 Mar 1720; **Mary Pottinger** (... – 28 Sep 1763) daughter of Edward Pottinger
  Has further generations of issue
  (b) **Elizabeth Borrowes** (...)
  = ...; **John Short** (...)
  Has further generations of issue
(C) **Wentworth FitzGerald, 17th Earl of Kildare** (1634 – 5 Mar 1663/4) suc. father 1660
= ca.1655; ♦**Lady Elizabeth Holles** (...) daughter of John Holles, 2nd Earl of Clare & Hon. Elizabeth de Vere
(1) **Lady Anne FitzGerald** (...)
=1 ...; ♦**Hon. Francis Robartes** (1650–1718)
=2 ...; **Hugh Boscawen of Tregothnan** (...) son of Huigh Boscawen & Margaret Clinton
issue of 1st (none by 2nd):

Children are listed with other parent
(2) **John FitzGerald, 18th Earl of Kildare** (1661 – 9 Nov
1707) suc. father 1664
=1 ...; ♦**Hon. Mary O'Brien** (7 may 1662 – 24 Nov 1683)
daughter of Henry, Lord O'Brien & Katehrine Stuart, 7th
Baroness Clifton
=2 12 Jun 1684; ♦**Lady Elizabeth Jones** (ca.1665 – 10 Apr
1758) daughter of Richard Jones, Earl of Ranelagh & Hon.
Elizabeth Willoughby
no issue

(D) **Rt.Hon. Robert FitzGerald** (ca.1637 – 31 Jan 1697/8)
= 4 Aug 1663; **Mary Clotworthy** (...) daughter of James
Clotworthy

(1) **Lady Catherine FitzGerald** (...)
= ...; **Rt. Rev. Dive Downes** (16 Oct 1653 Tornby,
Northhants. – 13 Nov 1709) son of Rev. Lewis Downes; =1st
Sarah Dodwell; =2nd Anne Carlson; =3rd Elizabeth Becher
(a) **Robert Downes** (1708 – ...)
(b) **Anne Downes** (13 Nov 1709 – ...)
= 1731; **Thomas Burgh** (... – aft.15 Nov 1754)
Has further generations of issue

(2) **Lady Elizabeth FitzGerald** (...)
= ...; **Henry Sandford** (...)
(a) **Frances Sandford** (... – 1757)
= 1718; ♦**Michael Cuffe** (1694–1744)
Children are listed with other parent

(3) **Lady Margaret FitzGerald** (... – 8 Dec 1758)
= 1712; **Toby Hall** (... – 4 May 1734) son of Roger Hall &
Christian Poyntz
(a) **Roger Hall** (...)
= 10 Sep 1740; **Catherine Savage** (...) daughter of Rowland
Savage
has further generations of issue
(b) **Christian Hall** (...)
(c) **Elizabeth Hall** (...)

(4) **Lady Mary FitzGerald** (22 Aug 1666 – aft.19 Aug 1697)
= 23 Jul 1684; **John Allen, 1st Viscount Allen** Baron Allen
(13 Feb 1660/1 – 8 Nov 1726 London) son of Sir Joshua Allen
& Mary Wybrow; cr. Viscount 28 Aug 1717
(a) **Joshua Allen, 2nd Viscount Allen** etc. (17 Sep 1685
Dublin – 5 Dec 1742 Stillorgan, co Dublin) suc. father 1726
= 18 Nov 1707 London; **Margaret du Pass** (bef.1692 – 4
Mar 1758 London) daughter of Samuel du Pass & Dorothy
Ellis
Has further generations of issue
(b) **Hon. Robert Allen** (... – 1741)

= ...
Has further generations of issue
(c) **Hon. Richard Allen** (16 Jul 1696 – 14 Apr 1745)
= ...; **Dorothy Green** (...) daughter of Samuel Green
Has further generations of issue
(5) **Robert FitzGerald, 19ᵗʰ Earl of Kildare** (4 May 1675 –
20 Feb 1744) suc. cousin 1707
= 7 Mar 1708/9; ♦**Lady Mary O'Brien** (...) daughter of
William O'Brien, 3ʳᵈ Earl of Inchiquin & Mary Villiers
(a) **Lady Margaretta FitzGerald** (... – 19 Jan 1766)
= 1 Mar 1747; **Wills Hill, 1ˢᵗ Marquess of Downshire**
Earl of Hillsborough, Viscount Kilwarlin, Baron Harwich, 2ⁿᵈ
Viscount Hillsborough, Baron Hill (30 May 1718 – 7 Oct
1793) son of Trevor Hill, 1ˢᵗ Viscount Hillsborough & Mary
Rowe; =2ⁿᵈ Mary Stawell, 1ˢᵗ Baroness Stawell of Somerton;
suc. father 3 May 1742; cr. Earl 3 Oct 1751 and Marquess 20
Aug 1789
Has further generations of issue
(b) **James FitzGerald, 1ˢᵗ Duke of Leinster** Marquess of
Kildare, Earl of Offaly, Viscount Leinster, 20ᵗʰ Earl of Kildare
(29 May 1722 – 19 Nov 1773) suc. father 1744; cr. Viscount 21
Feb 1746/7, Marquess 3 Mar 1761, and Duke 26 Nov 1766
= 7 Feb 1747; ♦**Lady Emilia** Mary **Lennox** (6 Oct 1731 – 27
Mar 1814 London) daughter of Charles Lennox, 2ⁿᵈ Duke of
Richmond & Lady Sarah Cadogan; =2ⁿᵈ William Ogilvie
Has further generations of issue
(c) **Hon. Richard FitzGerald** (...)
= ...; **Hon. Margaret King** (... – 29 Jan 1763) daughter of
James King, 4ᵗʰ Baron Kingston & Elizabeth Meade
Has further generations of issue
C) **Thomas Grey, 2ⁿᵈ Marquess of Dorset** etc. (22 Jun 1477 – 10
Oct 1530) suc. aftehr 1501
=1 ...; **Eleanor St.John** (...) daughter of Oliver St.Johyn & Elizabeth
Scrope
=2 1509; **Margaret Wotton** (1487 – aft.6 Oct 1535) daughter of Sir
Richard Wotton & Anne Belknap; =1ˢᵗ William Medley
issue of 2ⁿᵈ (none by 1ˢᵗ):
1) **Lady Elizabeth Grey** (1510 – 1564)
=1 22 Apr 1538; **Thomas Audley, Baron Audley of Walden**
(ca.1488 Earls Colne, Essex – 30 Apr 1544 London) son of Geoffrey
Audley; =1ˢᵗ Margaret Bernardiston
=2 aft.1545; **George Norton** (...)
issue of 1ˢᵗ (none by 2ⁿᵈ):
a) **Hon. Margaret Audley** (1539 – 10 Jan 1563/4)
=1 bef.1557; **Lord Sir Henry Dudley** (... – 10 Aug 1557
St.Quentin de Baron, France) killed in battle; son of John Dudley,

1st Duke of Northumberland & Jane Guilford; =1st Winifred Rich
=2 ...; ♦**Thomas Howard, 4th Duke of Norfolk** (1538–1572)
issue of 2nd (none by 1st):
Children are listed with other parent
  b) **Hon. Mary Audley** (aft.1539 – ...) unm.
2) **Lady Catherine Grey** (1512 – 1 May 1542)
  = 1525; ♦**Henry FitzAlan, 12th Earl of Arundel** (1512–1580)
  Children are listed with other parent
3) **Lady Margaret Grey** (...)
  = ...; **Richard Wake** (... – 10 Aug 1558) son of Roger Wake &
  Elizabeth Catesby; =1st Dorothy Dyve
  no issue
4) **Lady Anne Grey** (... – 1548)
  = ...; **Sir Henry Willoughby** (... – 27 Aug 1549 Norfolk) killed
  while in a rebellion; son of Sir Edward Willoughby
  a) **Margaret Willoughby** (...)
    = ...; ♦**Sir Matthew Arundell** (...–1598)
    Children are listed with other parent
  b) **Thomas Willoughby** (... – 1559)
  c) **Sir Francis Willoughby** (1546/7 – 1596)
    = ca.1564; **Elizabeth Lyttleton** (...) daughter of Sir John
    Lyttleton
    (I) **Margaret Willoughby** (ca.1564 – 17 Aug 1597)
      = 15 Feb 1587/8 Brington, Northants; **Robert Spencer, 1st
      Baron Spencer KG** (1570 – 25 Oct 1627 Wormleighton,
      Warks.) son of Sir John Spencer & Mary Catlin; cr. Baron 21 Jul
      1603; KG 1601
      (A) **Hon. Mary Spencer** (ca.1588 – ...)
        = ...; **Sir Richard Anderson** (... – 3 Aug 1630) son of Sir
        Henry Anderson
        (1) **Robert Anderson** (...)
        (2) **Sir Henry Anderson, 1st Baronet** (ca.1608 – 7 Jul 1653)
          cr. Baronet 3 Jul 1643
          =1 18 Dec 1632; **Jacomina Caesar** (bef.10 Dec 1615
          Benington, Herts. – Oct 1639) daughter of Sir Charles Caesar
          & Anne Vanlore
          =2 aft.1639; **Mary Lytton** (... – aft.1653) daughter of Sir
          William Lytton
          issue of 1st:
          (a) **Sir Richard Anderson, 2nd Baronet** (ca.1635 – 16 Aug
            1699) suc. father 1653 but title became extinct upon his
            death
            =1 ...; **Elizabeth Hewett** (... – 25 Dec 1698) daughter of Sir
            Thomas Hewett, 1st Baronet & Margaret Lytton
            =2 aft.1698; **Mary Methuen** (...) daughter of Rt. Hon. John
            Methuen & Mary Chevers; =1st Humphrey Simpson; =3rd Sir

Brownlow Sherard, 3rd Baronet
Has further generations of issue by 1st
(B) **Hon. Elizabeth Spencer** (aft.1589 – ...)
= ...; **Sir George Fane** (... – 26 Jun 1640)
issue ?
(C) **Hon. John Spencer** (bef.6 Dec 1590 Wormleighton – 16
Aug 1610 Blois, France) unm.
(D) **William Spencer, 2nd Baron Spencer** (4 Jan 1591/2
Brington – 19 Dec 1636) suc. father 1627
= 1615; ♦**Lady Penelope Wriothesley** (bef.8 Nov 1598 – 16
Jul 1667 Brington) daughter of Henry Wriothesley, 3rd Earl of
Southampton & Elizabeth Vernon
　(1) **Hon. Elizabeth Spencer** (16 Feb 1617/8 – 11 Aug 1672)
　=1 4 Dec 1634 Brington; **John Craven, Baron Craven**
　(bef.10 Jun 1610 London – bef.26 Feb 1647/8) son of Sir
　William Craven & Elizabeth Whitmore; cr. Baron 21 Mar
　1642/3 but it became extinct upon his death
　=2 7 Jul 1648; ♦**Hon. Henry Howard** (ca.1620 – 1663) son
　of Thomas Howard, 1st Earl of Berkshire & Lady Elizabeth
　Cecil
　=3 aft.1663; **William Crofts, Baron Crofts**[118] (ca.1611 –
　1677) son of Sir Henry Crofts; cr. Baron 1658 but the title
　became extinct upon his death; =1st Dorothy Hobart
　no issue
　(2) **Henry Spencer, 1st Earl of Sunderland** 3rd Baron
　Spencer (Oct 1620 Althorp, Northants. – 20 Sep 1643) suc.
　father 1636; cr. Earl 8 Jun 1643
　= 20 Jul 1639 Penhurst, Kent; ♦**Lady Dorothy Sydney**
　(bef.5 Oct 1617 – 5 Feb 1683/4) daughter of Robert Sydney, 2nd
　Earl of Leicester & Lady Dorothy Percy; =2nd Robert Smythe
　　(a) **Lady Dorothy Spencer** (1640 – 16 Dec 1670 London)
　　= 1656; ♦**George Saville, 1st Marquess of Halifax**
　　(1633–1695)
　　Children are listed with other parent
　　(b) **Robert Spencer, 2nd Earl of Sunderland** etc (1641
　　Paris – 28 Sep 1702 Althorp) suc. father 1643
　　= 10 Jun 1665; ♦**Lady Anne Digby** (ca.1646 – 16 Apr 1715)
　　daughter of George Digby, 2nd Earl of Bristol & Lady Anne
　　Russell
　　Has further generations of issue[119]

---

[118] Was responsible for the upbring of the Duke of Monmouth, Charles II's eldest illegitimate
child. The Duke took his name prior to marriage to the heiress of Buccleuch.
[119] Direst male line ancestors of Diana, Princess of Wales

(c) **Lady Penelope Spencer** (1642 – 1667) unm.

(3) **Hon. William Spencer** (...)
= ...; ♦**Hon. Elizabeth Gerard** (...) daughter of Dutton
Gerard, 3rd Baron Gerard & Lady Elizabeth O'Brien

(a) **Elizabeth Spencer** (...)
= ...; **Robert Hesketh** (...) son of Thomas Hesketh & Sidney
Grosvenor
Has further generations of issue

(4) **Hon. Alice Spencer** (bef.29 Dec 1625 Brington – bef.1712)
= ...; **Henry Moore, 1st Earl of Drogheda** 3rd Viscount
Moore, Baron Moore (... – 12 Jan 1675/6) son of Charles
Moore, 2nd Vicount Moore & Hon. Alice Loftus; suc. father 7
Aug 1643; cr. Earl 14 Jun 1661

(a) **Lady Penelope Moore** (...)
= ...; **Randall Fleming, 16th Baron Slane** (... – 1676) son
of William Fleming, 14th Baron Slane & Lady Anne
MacDonnell; suc. brother 1661
Issue extinct 1748

(b) **Charles Moore, 2nd Earl of Drogheda** etc (... – 18 Jun
1679) suc. father 1676
= 1669; ♦**Lady Letitica** Isabella **Robartes** (... – 1714)
daughter of John Robartes, 1st Earl of Radnor & Letitita
Smythe; =2nd William Wycherley
no issue

(c) **Henry Hamilton-Moore, 3rd Earl of Drogheda** etc
(... – 7 Jun 1714) suc. brother 1679
= 3 Jul 1675; **Mary Cole** (... – 6 May 1726) daughter of Sir
John Cole, 1st Baronet
Has further generations of issue

(d) **Lady Mary Moore** (... – 17 Mar 1725/6)
=1 bef.1682; ♦**William Ramsay, 3rd Earl of Dalhousie**
(...–1682)
=2 10 Apr 1683; **John Bellenden, 2nd Lord Bellenden**
(... – bef.5 Nov 1706 Edinburgh) son of William Ker, 2nd Earl
of Roxburgh & Jean Ker
=3 aft.1707; **Samuel Collins** (...)
issue of 1st:
Children are listed with other parent
issue of 2nd (none by 3rd):
Has further generations of issue

(e) **Lady Alice Moore** (... – 25 Dec 1677 Dublin)
=1 May 1667; **Henry Hamilton, 2nd Earl of Clanbrassill**
3rd Viscount Claneboye (ca.1647 – 12 Jan 1675) son of James
Hamilton, 1st Earl of Clanbrassill & Lady Anne Carey; suc.
father 20 Jun 1659
=2 Sep 1677; **John Hamilton, 2nd Lord Bargany** (... – 15

May 1693) son of John Hamilton, 1st Lord Bargany & Lady
Jean Douglas; =1st Lady Margaret Cuninghame; suc. father
Apr 1658
no issue
(f) **Hon. William Moore** (...)
= 1686; ♦**Elizabeth Lennard** (... – 28 Dec 1701) daughter
of Francis Lennard, 14th Baron Dacre & Elizabeth Bayning,
Countess of Shepey; =1st William Brabazon, 3rd Earl of March
no issue
(5) **Hon. Margaret Spencer** (1627 – 1693)
= 30 Aug 1655; **Anthony Ashley-Cooper, 1st Earl of
Shaftesbury** Baron Ashley, Baron Cooper, 2nd Baronet (22
Jul 1621 – 22 Jan 1683 Amsterdam) son of Sir John Cooper, 1st
Baronet & Anne Ashley; =1st Hon. Margaret Coventry; =2nd
♦Lady Frances Cecil; suc. father 23 Mar 1631; cr. Baron
Cooper and Baron Ashley 20 Apr 1661, and Earl 23 Apr 1672
no issue
(6) **Robert Spencer, 1st Viscount Teviot** (bef.2 Feb 1629 –
20 May 1694) cr. Viscount 10 Oct 1685, but it became extinct
upon his death
= ...; **Jane Spencer** (...) daughter of Sir Thomas Spencer, 3rd
Baronet
no issue
(II) **Bridget Willoughby** (...)
= ..; **Sir Percival Willoughby** (... – ca.1642) son of Thomas
Willoughby & Catherine Hart
(A) **Sir Francis Willoughby** (1585 – 17 Dec 1665)
= ...; **Lady Cassandra Ridgeway** (...) daughter of Thomas
Ridgeway, 1st Earl of Londerry & Cicely MacWilliam
(1) **Catherine Willoughby** (...)
= ...; **Clement Winstanley** (...) son of James Winstanley
(a) **James Winstanley** (ca.1667 – 22 Jan 1719)
= ...; **Frances Holt** (...) daughter of James Holt & Dorothy
Grantham
Has further generations of issue
(2) **Francis Willoughby** (22 Nov 1635 Middleton Hall,
Warks. – 3 Jul 1672)
= 1667; **Emma Barnard** (... – 16 Oct 1725) daughter of Sir
Henry Barnard; =2nd Sir Josiah Child, 1st Baronet
(a) **Sir Francis Willoughby, 1st Baronet** (ca.1669 – 1688)
cr. Baronet 7 Apr 1677 with special remainder to brother;
unm.
(b) **Cassandra Willoughby** (... – 18 Jul 1735)
= 4 Aug 1713 London; ♦**James Brydges, 1st Duke of
Chandos** etc (6 Jan 1673/4 – 9 Aug 1744 London) son of
James Brydges, 8th Baron Chandos & Elizabeth Barnard; =1st

Marke Lake; =3rd Lydia van Hatten
no issue
  (c) **Thomas Willoughby, 1st Baron Middleton** 2nd
Baronet (9 Apr 1672 – 2 Apr 1729) suc. brother 1688; cr.
Baron 1 Jan 1711/2
= 9 Apr 1691 Stapleford, Lincs.; **Elizabeth Rothwell** (... –
bef.Feb 1735/6 Tong Castle, Salop.) daughter of Sir Richard
Rothwell, 1st Baronet & Elizabeth ...
Has further generations of issue
(B) **Bridget Willoughby** (...)
= 14 Oct 1610; **Henry Cavendish** (...) natural son of Henry
Cavendish
  (1) **Bridget Cavendish** (1613 – ...)
  = ...; **Samuel Mason** (...)
  issue ?
  (2) **Charles Cavendish** (...) unm.
  (3) **Grace Cavendish** (...) unm.
  (4) **Mary Cavendish** (...)
  = 20 Apr 1648; **John Broughton** (...)
  (a) **Susannah Broughton** (...)
  = ...; **John Chetwynd** (... – 1674) son of John Chetwynd &
Mary Welles
Has further generations of issue
  (5) **Francis Cavendish** (1618 – 17 Jun 1650)
  =1 13 Nov 1642; **Dorothy Bullock** (...) daughter of John
Bullock
  =2 ...; **Dorothy Broughton** (...) daughter of Thomas
Broughton & Frances Bagot
issue of 1st:
  (a) **Dorothy Cavendish** (...)
  = ...; **Gervase Nevill** (...)
  issue ?
issue of 2nd:
  (b) **Henry Cavendish** (1648 – 23 May 1698)
  = ...; **Mary Tyrrell** (...) daughter of Sir Timothy Tyrrell
Has further generations of issue
  (c) **Charles Cavendish** (1650 – ...) unm.
(C) **Theodosia Willoughby** (... – Nov 1630)
= 1610; **Rowland Mynors** (... – Apr 1651) son of Roger
Mynors & Jane Harley
  (1) **Robert Mynors** (23 Sep 1616 – 23 Aug 1672)
  = 21 Feb 1650 **Elizabeth Oswald** (... – 1727) daughter of
James Oswald
  (a) **Crompton Mynors** (1650 – Apr 1687)
  = 3 Mar 1678; **Anne Reed** (...) daughter of Richard Reed
  no surviving issue

(b) **Theodosia Mynors** (1652 – Dec 1700)
=1 16 Jun 1670; **Roger Boulcott** (...)
=2 ...; **Richard Witherston** (...)
Has further generations of issue by both
(c) **Robert Mynors** (1654 – Jun 1710)
= ...; **Elizabeth Adams** (...) daughter of William Adams
Has further generations of issue
(D) **Elizabeth Willoughby** (... – 1642)
= 1612; **Sir John Gell, 1st Baronet** (22 Jun 1593 Hopton,
Derbys – 26 Oct 1671) son of Thomas Gell & Millicent
Sachaverell; =2nd Mary Radclyffe; cr. Baronet Jan 1642
(1) **Sir John Gell, 2nd Baronet** (1612 – 8 Feb 1689 London)
suc. father 1671
= ...; **Katherine Packer** (... – 1668) daughter of John Packer
(a) **Catherine Gell** (...)
= ...; **William Eyre** (...)
Has further fgenerations of issue
(b) **Sir Philip Gell, 3rd Baronet** (1651 – 14 Jul 1719) suc.
father 1689 but title became extinct upon his death
= 26 Nov 1678; **Elizabeth Fagge** (...) daughter of Sir John
Fagge, 1st Baronet & Mary Morley
no issue
(E) **Percival Willoughby** (1596 – 1685) unm.
(III) **Dorothy Willoughby** (1574 – 1 Dec 1638 Horton, Dorset)
= 1587; ♦**Hon. Henry Hastings** (1552–1650)
Children are listed with other parent
5) **Henry Grey, 1st Duke of Suffolk** 3rd Marquess of Dorset etc. **KG**
(17 Jan 1517 – 23 Feb 1554 London) executed; suc. father 1530; cr.
Duke 11 Oct 1551; KG 1547
=1 bef.1530 (ann.); **Katherine FitzAlan** (... – aft.1553)
=2 Mar 1533 London; ♦**Lady Frances Brandon** (16 Jul 1517 – 20
Nov 1559 Godalming, Surrey) daughter of Charles Brandon, 1st Duke
of Suffolk & Princess Mary Tudor; =2nd Adrian Stokes
issue of 2nd (none by 1st):
a) **Jane, Queen of England** (Oct 1537 Bradgate, Leics. – 12 Feb
1554 12 feb 1554 London) executed; proclaimed Queen upon death
of Edward VI 10 Jul 1553 but deposed by Mary I 19 Jul 1553
= 21 May 1553; **Lord Guilford Dudley** (1536 – 12 Feb 1554)
executed; son of John Dudley, 1st Duke of Northumberland & Jane
Guilford
no issue
b) **Lady Catherine Grey** (Aug 1540 London – 27 Jan 1568 Yoxford,
Suffolk)
=1 21 May 1553 London (dv.1555); ♦**Henry Herbert, 2nd Earl of
Pembroke** etc. (aft.1538 – 19 Jan 1601 Wilton, Wilts.) son of
William Herbert, 1st Earl of Pembroke & Ann Parr; =2nd ♦**Lady**

Katherine Talbot; =3rd ◆Mary Sydney
=2 1560; ◆**Edward Seymour, 1st Earl of Hertford** (1537–1621)
issue of 2nd (none by 1st):
Children are listed with other parent
  c) **Lady Mary Grey** (1545 – 20 Apr 1578 London)
    = 10 Aug 1564 London; **Thomas Keyes** (1523 – 1571) son of
    Richard Keyes & Agnes Saunders
    no issue
6) **Lord Leonard Grey** (...)
7) **Lady Mary Grey** (...) unm.
8) **Lord John Grey** (1523 – 19 Nov 1569)
  = ...
  a) **Margaret Grey** (...)
    = ...; ◆**Sir Arthur Capell** (...–1632)
    Children are listed with other parent
9) **Lord Thomas Grey** (1526 – 1554) executed; unm.
D) **Lord Sir Richard Grey** (...)
= aft.1523; **Florence Pudsey** (...) daughter of Henry Pudsey &
Margaret Conyers; =1st Sir Thomas Talbot; =2nd ◆Henry Clifford, 10th
Baron Clifford
no issue
E) **Lady Dorothy Grey** (1480 – 1552)
=1 ...; **Robert Willoughby, 2nd Baron Willoughby de Broke**
(1472 – 10 Nov 1521) son of Robert Willoughby, 1st Baron Willoughby
de Broke & Blanche Champernowne; =1st ◆Hon. Elizabeth Beauchamp
=2 ...; **William Blount, 4th Baron Montjoy KG** (... – 8 Nov 1534)
son of John Blount, 3rd Baron Mountjoy & Lora Berkeley; =1st
Elizabeth Say; =2nd Alice Keble; suc. father 1485
issue of 1st:
1) **Hon. Elizabeth Willoughby** (...)
  = bef.20 Oct 1528; **John Paulet, 2nd Marquess of Winchester**
  Earl of Wiltshire, Baron St.John (ca.1510 – 4 Nov 1576) son of
  William Paulet, 1st Marquess of Winchester & Elizabeth Capell; =2nd
  ◆Elizabeth Seymour; =3rd Winifred Brydges; suc. father 10 Mar
  1571/2
  a) **Lady Elizabeth Paulet** (... – 4 Nov 1576)
    =1 28 Nov 1545; **Sir William Courtenay** (ca.1529 – 18 Aug 1557
    St. Quintin) killed in battle; son of George Courtenay & Catherine
    St.Leger
    =2 aft.1557; **Sir Henry Oughtred** (...)
    issue of 1st:
    (I) **Sir William Courtenay** (ca.1553 – 24 Jun 1630)
      =1 8 Jan 1572/3; ◆**Lady Elizabeth Manners** (...) daughter of

Henry Manners, 2nd Earl of Rutland & Lady Margaret Neville
=2 ...; **Elizabeth Sydenham** (... – 9 Jun 1598) daughter of Sir
George Sydenham; =1st Sir Francis Drake[120]
issue of 1st (none by 2nd):

(A) **Francis Courtenay** (ca.1576 – 3 Jun 1638)
=1 7 Nov 1606; ♦**Mary Pole** (bef. 26 Jun 1586 – ...) daughter of
Sir William Pole & Mary Perlam
=2 ...; **Elizabeth Seymour** (... – bef.6 Feb 1664) daughter of
Sir Edward Seymour, 2nd Baronet & Dorothy Killigrew; =2nd Sir
Amos Meredith, 1st Baronet
issue of 2nd:

(1) **Sir William Courtenay, 1st Baronet** (7 Sep 1628 – 4 Aug
1702) cr. Baronet Feb 1644/5 but never had patent enrolled so
it died with him
= ...; **Margaret Waller** (... – Jan 1693/4) daughter of Sir
William Waller & Jane Reynell
(a) **Isabella Courtneay** (...)
= ...; **Sir Thomas Lear, 2nd Baronet** (1672 – 1705) son of
Thomas Lear & Dorothy ...; suc. uncle 1684
no issue
(b) **Francis Courtenay** (ca.1651 – May 1699)
= ...; **Mary Boevey** (...) daughter of William Boevey
Has further generations of issue
(c) **Richard Courtenay** (... – 1696)
= ...; **Katherine Waller** (...)
Has further generations of issue
(2) **Edward Courtenay** (17 Jul 1632 – ...)
= ...; **Frances Moore** (...) daughter of John Moore &
Elizabeth Honeywood
(a) **Charles Courtenay of Archambaid** (1690 – 20 Aug
1763)
= ...; **Elizabeth Wyatt** (21 Mar 1698 – 1 Jun 1734) daughter
of Thomas Wyatt & Elizabeth ...
Has further generations of issue
(B) **Sir George** Oughtred **Courtenay, 1st Baronet** (bef.1585 –
...) cr. Baronet Jan 1621/2
= bef.1616; **Catherine Berkeley** (...) daughter of Francis
Berkeley
(1) **Sir William Courtenay, 2nd Baronet** (ca.1616 – ca.1651)
unm.; suc. father but titel became extinct upon his death
(2) **Francis Courtenay** (ca.1617 – ...)

---

[120] The explorer.

(3) **Morris Courtenbay** (...) unm.

(C) **Sir William Courtenay** (... – 1603) unm.

(D) **Elizabeth Courtenay** (...)

= 1600; **Sir William Wrey, 1st Baronet** (... – Jun 1636) son of John Wrey & Blanche Killigrew; cr. Baronet 20 Jun 1628

(1) **Sir William Wrey, 2nd Baronet** (... – Aug 1645) suc. father 1636

= 6 Oct 1624; ♦**Elizabeth Chichester** (...) daughter of Edward Chichester, 1st Viscount Chichester & Anne Coplestone

(a) **Sir Chichester Wrey, 3rd Baronet** (1628 – 14 Feb 1668) suc. father 1645

= 1653; ♦**Lady Anne Bourchier** (ca.1628 – 6 Sep 1662) daughter of Edward Bourchier, 4th Eatl of Bath & Hon. Dorothy St.John

Had further generations of issue

(2) **John Wrey** (...)

(3) **Philippa Wrey** (...)

issue of 2nd:

(II) **George Oughtred** (...)

b) **William Paulet, 3rd Marquess of Winchester** etc. **KB** (ca.1532 – 24 Nov 1598) suc. father 1592; KB 1553

= bef.10 Feb 1547/8; **Hon. Agnes Howard** (...) daughter of William Howard, 1st Baron Howard & Katherine Broughton

(I) **William Paulet, 4th Marquess of Winchester** etc. (... – 4 Feb 1628) suc. father 1598

= 28 Feb 1586/7; ♦**Lady Lucy Cecil** (... – Oct 1614) daughter of Thomas Cecil, 1st Earl of Exeter & Hon. Dorothy Neville

(A) **William, Earl of Wiltshire** (1587/8 – Aug 1621)

= bef.17 Feb 1613/4; ♦**Hon. Mary Browne** (ca.1593 – 13 Nov 1692) daughter of Anthony Browne, 2nd Viscount Montagu & Lady Jane Sackville; =2nd ♦Hon. William Arundell

no issue

(B) **John Paulet, 5th Marquess of Winchester** etc. (1598 – 5 Mar 1674/5) suc. father 1629

=1 18 Dec 1622; ♦**Hon. Jane Savage** (...) daughter of Thomas Savage, 1st Viscount Savage & Elizabeth Darcy, 2nd Countess Rivers

=2 4 Oct 1633; **Lady Honora de Burgh** (... – 10 Mar 1661) daughter of Richard Bourke, 4th Earl of Clanricade & Frances Walsingham; =1st Garrett McCoghlan

=3 1669; ♦**Hon. Isabella Howard** (... – 5 Sep 1691) daughter of William Howard, Viscount Stafford & Mary Stafford, Countess of Stafford

issue of 1st:

(1) **Charles Powlett, 1st Duke of Bolton** 6th Marquess of Winchester, etc. (ca.1630 – 27 Feb 1698/9 Amport, Hanrts.)

suc. father 1675; cr. Duke 9 Apr 1689

=1 28 Feb 1651/2; **Hon. Christian Frescheville** (13 Dec 1633 – 22 May 1653) daughter of John Frescheville, 1st Baron Frescheville & Sarah Harington

=2 12 Feb 1654/5 London; ♦**Mary le Scrope** (bef.1630 – 1

Nov

1680 Moulins, France) natural daughter of Emmanuel Scrope, 1st Earl of Sunderland & Martha Jeanes; =1st Henry, Lord Leppington

issue of 2nd (none by 1st):

(a) **Lady Jane Powlett** (ca.1655 – 23 May 1716)
= 1673; ♦**John Egerton, 3rd Earl of Bridgwater** (1646– 1701)
Children are listed with other parent

(b) **Lady Mary Powlett** (...)
= ...; **Tobias Jenkyns** (...)
Has further generations of issue

(c) **Charles Powlett, 2nd Duke of Bolton** etc (1661 – 21 Jan 1721/2 London) suc. father 1699
=1 10 Jul 1679 London; ♦**Hon. Margaret Coventry** (14 Sep 1657 Hothfield, Kent – 7 Feb 1681/2) daughter of George Covertry, 3rd Baron Coventry & Lady Margaret Tufton
=2 8 Feb 1682/3 London; **Frances Ramsden** (14 Jun 1661 Almondsbury, Glos. – 22 Nov 1696) daughter of William Ramsden & Elizabeth Palmes
=3 bef.15 Oct 1697 Dublin; ♦**Henrietta Crofts** (ca.1682 – 27 Feb 1729/30) natural daughter of James Scott, Duke of Monmouth & Eleanor Needham
Has further generations of issue by 2nd and 3rd

(d) **Lord William Powlett** (ca.1663 – 25 Sep 1729)
=1 ...; **Louisa de Caumont** (... – 1698) daughter of Arman de Caumont, Marquis de Monpouillon & Amelia van Brederode
=2 Oct 1699; **Anne Egerton** (... – 1737) daughter of Randolph Egerton & Hon. Elizabeth Murray
Has furtyher generations of issue by both

issue of 2nd (none by 3rd):

(2) **Lady Anne Paulet** (... – Sep 1694)
= aft.1622; ♦**John Belasyse, 1st Baron Belasyse** (1614– 1689)
Children are listed with other parent

(C) **Lord Henry Paulet** (... – 1672)
= ....; **Lucy Philpot** (...) daughter of Sir George Philpot

(1) **Francis Paulet** (ca.1645 – 25 Feb 1695/6)
= 20 May 1674; **Elizabeth Norton** (...) daughter of Sir Richard Norton, Baronet & Mabell Becher

(a) **Norton Paulet** (ca.1679 – 6 Jun 1741)
= ...; **Jane Morley** (...) daughter of Sir Charles Morley &
Hon. Magdalen Herbert
Has further generations of issue
(D) **Lord Charles Paulet** (...)
(II) **Lady Anne Paulet** (...)
= ...; **Sir Thomas Dennis** (...)
issue ?
(III) **Lady Katherine Paulet** (...)
= ...; **Sir Giles Wroughton** (...)
issue ?
(IV) **Lady Elizabeth Paulet** (...)
= ...; **Sir Edward Hoby** (...)
issue ?
has issue by ...:
(V) **Sir William Paulet** (...)
= ...
(A) **Elizabeth Paulet** (... – 1656)
=1 1631; ♦**Robert Devereux, 3rd Earl of Essex** (1591–1646)
=2 ...; **Sir Thomas Higgons** (1624 – 24 Nov 1691) son of
Thomas Higgons & Elizabeth Barker; =2nd Bridget Granville
issue of 1st:
Children are listed with other parent
issue of 2nd:
(1) **Elizabeth Higgons** (...)
(2) **Frances Higgons** (...)
c) **Lord Sir George Paulet** (... – May 1608 Londonderry)
murdered; unm.
d) **Lord Richard Paulet** (...)
e) **Lord Thomas Paulet** (...)
f) **Lady Mary Paulet** (... – 10 Oct 1592)
= bef.1560; ♦**Henry Cromwell, 2nd Baron Cromwell** (...–1592)
Children are listed with other parent
2) **Hon. Anne Willoughby** (...)
= ...; **Charles Blount, 5th Baron Montjoy** (28 Jun 1516 – 1545)
son of William Blount, 4th Baron Mountjoy & Alice Keble; suc. father
8 Nov 1534
a) **James Blount, 6th Baron Mountjoy KB** (ca.1533 – 1582) suc.
father 1545; KB 1553
= ...; **Catherine Leigh** (...) daughter of Sir Thomas Leigh &
Joanna Cotton
(I) **William Blount, 7th Baron Mountjoy** (ca.1561 – 1594) suc.
father 1582; unm.
(II) **Charles Blount, 1st Earl of Devonshire** 8th Baron
Mountjoy (1563 – 3 Apr 1606 London) suc. brother 1594; cr. Earl
21 Jul 1603, his titles all became extinct upon his death

= 20 Dec 1605; ♦**Lady Penelope Devereux** (adft.1561 – 7 Jul 1607) daughter of Walter Devereux, 1st Earl of Essex & Lettice Knollys; =1st ♦Robert Rich, 1st Earl of Warwick
Children were born before the marriage
(A) **Penelope Rich** (1592 – 26 Oct 1613)
    = ...; **Sir Gervase Clifton, 1st Baronet KB** (ca.1586 – 28 Jun 1666) son of George Clifton & Winifred Thorold; =2nd ♦Lady Frances Clifford; =3rd Mary Egioke; =4th Isobel Meek; =5th Anne South; =6th Jane Eyre; =7th ♦Lady Alice Hastings
    (1) **Sir Gervase Clifton, 2nd Baronet** (ca.1612 – 1676) suc. father 1666; unm.
(B) **Mountjoy Blount, 1st Earl of Newport** Baron Mountjoy (1597 – 1665) cr. Baron 2 Jan 1617/8 and Earl 27 Jul 1628
    = ...; **Hon. Anne Boteler** (1600 – 1669) daughter of John Boteler, 1st Baron Boteler & Elizabeth Villiers; =2nd Thomas Weston, 4th Earl of Portland
    (1) **Lady Isabella Blount** (... – Feb 1654/5)
        = ...; ♦**Nicholas Vaux, 3rd Earl of Banbury** etc. (3 jan 1630/1 Harrowden, Northants. – 14 Mar 1673/4 Boughton, Northants.) son of William Knollys, 1st Earl of banbury & Lady Elizabeth Howard; =2nd Anne Sherard; suc brother 1645 no issue
    (2) **George Blount, 2nd Earl of Newport** etc. (... – 1675) suc. father 1665; unm.
    (3) **Thomas Blount, 3rd Earl of Newport** etc. (... – 1675) suc. brother same year he died; unm.
    (4) **Henry Blount, 4th Earl of Newport** etc. (... – bef.1681) suc. brother 1675, and uppon his death titles became extinct; unm.
(C) **Sir St.John Blount KB** (...) KB 1626
(D) **Ruth Blount** (...)
(E) **Isabella Blount** (...)
(F) **Charles Blount** (...)
  b) **Hon. Francis Blount** (... – 1 Mar 1594/5) unm.
issue of 2nd:
3) **John Blount** (...) unm
4) **Dorothy Blount** (...)
5) **Mary Blount** (...)
F) **Lord John Grey** (...)
=1 ...; **Elizabeth Catesby** (...) daughter of Sir William Catesby; =1st Roger Wake
=2 ...; **Anne Barley** (... – 1557/8) =1st Sir Robert Sheffield
no issue
G) **Lord Edward Grey** (... – bef.1501)
= ...; **Anne Jerningham** (...) daughter of Sir Edward Jerningham & Margaret Bedingfield; =2nd Henry Barley; =3rd Sir Robert Drury; =4th

Sir Edmund Walsingham
no issue
H) **Lord Anthony Grey** (... – bef.1501)
I) **Lord George Grey** (...)
J) **Lady Bridget Grey** (...)
K) **Leonard Grey, 1ˢᵗ Viscount Grane** (ca.1490 – 28 Jun 1541) cr.
Viscount 2 Jan 1536, but itg became extict upon his death; unm.
L) **Lady Mary Grey** (bef.1502 – 22 Feb 1534)
= 1530; ♦**Walter Devereux, 1ˢᵗ Viscount Hereford** (1491–1558)
Children are listed with other parent
M) **Lady Eleanor Grey** (... – bef.Dec 1503)
= ...; **Sir John Arundell** (1474 – 1545) son of Thomas Arundell &
Catherine Dynham
1) **Sir John Arundell** (...)
has unknown issue
2) **Sir Thomas Arundell KB** (... – 26 Feb 1552) executed; KB 1533
= ...; **Margaret Howard** (...) daughter of Lord Edmund Howard &
Joyce Culpeper
a) **Sir Matthew Arundell** (... – Dec 1598)
= ...; ♦**Margaret Willoughby** (...) daughter of Sir Henry
Willoughby & Lady Anne Grey
(I) **Thomas Arundell, 1ˢᵗ Baron Arundell** (ca.1560 – 7 Nov
1639 Wardour Castle, Wilts.) cr. Baron 4 May 1605, cr. Count of
the Roman Empire 14 Dec 1595[121]
=1 18 Jun 1585; ♦**Lady Mary Wriothesley** (... – Jun 1607)
daughter of Henry Wriothesely, 2ⁿᵈ Earl of Southampton & Hon.
Mary Browne
=2 1 Jul 1608 London; **Anne Philipson** (... – 28 Jun 1637
London) daughter of Miles Philipson & Barbara Sandys
issue of 1ˢᵗ:
(A) **Thomas Arundell, 2ⁿᵈ Baron Arundell** (ca.1586 – 19
May 1643 Oxford) died of wounds received in battle; suc. father
1639
= 11 May 1607; ♦**Lady Blanche Somerset** (ca.1584 – 28 Oct
1649 Winchester, Hants.) daughter of Edward Somerset, 4ᵗʰ Earl
of Worcester & Lady Elizabeth Hastings
(1) **Henry Arundell, 3ʳᵈ Baron Arundell** (bef.23 Feb
1607/8 – 28 Dec 1694 Breamore, Hants.) suc. father 1643
= ...; ♦**Cicely Compton** (ca.1610 – 24 Mar 1675/6) daughter
of Hon. Sir Henry Compton & Lady Cicely Sackville; =1ˢᵗ Sir

---

[121] All male-line members of the Arundell family are technically title Count/Countess
Arundell, but as British subjects, do not use the title.

John Fermor
- (a) **Thomas Arundell, 4ᵗʰ Baron Arundell** (1633 – 10 Feb 1711/2 Breamore) suc. father 1694
  = ...; **Margaret Spencer** (... – 23 Dec 1704) daughter of Thomas Spencer; =1ˢᵗ Robert Lucy
  Has further generations of issue
- (b) **Hon. Henry Arundell** (...)
  = 10 Feb 1675; **Mary Scrope** (...) daughter of Edmund Scrope; =1ˢᵗ Thomas Kempe
  no issue
- (c) **Hon. Cicely Arundell** (... – 1717) a nun
- (2) **Hon. Anne Arundell** (...)
  = ...; **Roger Vaughan** (...)
  issue ?
- (3) **Hon. Katherine Arundell** (ca.1614 – ...)
  = ...; **Francis Cornwallis** (...) son of Sir Charles Cornwallis
  issue ?
- (B) **Hon. William Arundell** (...)
  = bef.22 Oct 1627; ◆**Hon. Mary Browne** (ca.1593 – 13 Nov 1692) daughter of Anthony Browne, 2ⁿᵈ Vicount Montagu & Lady Jane Sackville; =1ˢᵗ ◆William Paulet, Earl of Wiltshire
- (1) **Mark Arundell** (...) unm.
- (2) **Charles Arundell** (...)
  = ...; ◆**Lady Mary Talbot** (... – Mar 1710/1) daughter of John Talbot, 10ᵗʰ Earl of Shrewsbury & Mary Fortescue; =2ⁿᵈ Mervyn Tuchet, 4ᵗʰ Earl of Castlehaven
  - (a) **Charles Arundell** (...)
    = ...
    Has further generations of issue
- (3) **Mary Arundell** (... – 24 Dec 1698)
  = ...; **Sir Henry Tichborne, 3ʳᵈ Baronet** (... – Apr 1689) son of Sir Richard Tichborne, 2ⁿᵈ Baronet; suc. father 1657
  - (a) **Sir Henry** Joseph **Tichborne, 4ᵗʰ Baronet** (... – 15 Jul 1743) suc. father 1689
    = ...
    Has further gnerations of issue
  - (b) **Sir John** Hermengil **Tichborne, 5ᵗʰ Baronet** (... – 5 May 1748 Ghent, Belgium) a priest; suc. brother 1743
- (4) **Katherine Arundell** (... – 4 Mar 1642) unm.
- (C) **Hon. Elizabeth** Mary **Arundell** (...)
  = 14 Jun 1606; **Sir John Philpot** (...)
  issue ?
issue of 2ⁿᵈ:
- (D) **Hon. Matthew Arundell** (1609 – 1620) unm.
- (E) **Hon. Catherine Arundell** (bef.1612 – 1657)
  = 1627; ◆**Ralph Eure** (1606–1640)

Children are listed with other parent

(F) **Hon. Frances Arundell** (1614 – aft.2 May 1652)
= 1648; ♦**John Talbot, 10ᵗʰ Earl of Shrewsbury** (1601–1654)
Children are listed with other parent

(G) **Hon. Anne Arundell** (ca.1616 – 23 Jul 1649)
= 20 Mar 1627/8; **Cecil Calvert, 2ⁿᵈ Baron Baltimore** (bef.2 Mar 1605/6 – Dec 1675) son of George Calvert, 1ˢᵗ Baron Baltimore & Anne Minne; suc. father 15 Apr 1632

   (1) **Charles Clavert, 3ʳᵈ Baron Baltimore** (27 Aug 1637 – 21 Feb 1714/5) suc. father 1675
=1 bef.1666; **Mary Darnall** (... – bef.1667 MD) daughter of Ralph Darnall
=2 ca.1666; **Jane Lowe** (... – 19 Jan 1700/1) daughter of Vincent Lowe & Anne Cavendish; =1ˢᵗ Henry Sewell
=3 aft.1701; **Mary Bankes** (... – Mar 1710/11) =1ˢᵗ ... Thorpe
=4 1712; **Margaret Charleton** (... – 20 Jul 1731) daughter of Thomas Charleton; =2ⁿᵈ Laurence Elliott
issue of 2ⁿᵈ (none by others):

      (a) **Benedict** Leonard **Calvert, 4ᵗʰ Baron Baltimore** (21 Mar 1679 – 16 Apr 1715) suc. father Feb 1715
= 2 Jan 1698/9; ♦**Lady Charlotte Lee** (13 Mar 1678 London – 22 Jan 1721 Woodford, Essex) daughter of Edward Lee, 1ˢᵗ Earl of Lichfield & Lady Charlotte Fitzroy; =2ⁿᵈ Christopher Crowe
Has further generations of issue

   (2) **Hon. Mary Calvert** (...)
= ...; ♦**Sir William Blakistan, 2ⁿᵈ Baronet** (... – Feb 1692) son of Sir Ralph Blakistan, 1ˢᵗ Baronet & Margaret Fenwick; suc. father Dec 1650
no issue

(H) **Hon. Mary Arundell** (...)
= ...; ♦**Sir John Somerset** (aft.1604 – ...) son of Henry Somerset, 1ˢᵗ Marquess of Worcester & Hon. Anne Russell
no issue

(I) **Hon. Margaret Arundell** (1620 – ...)
= ...; **Sir John Fortescue, 2ⁿᵈ Baronet** (1614 – 1683) =2ⁿᵈ Margaret Thomas; =3ʳᵈ Mary Stonor; =4ᵗʰ Elizabeth Windour
no issue

(J) **Hon. Clara Arundell** (1620 – ...)
= 7 Jul 1638; **Humphrey Weld** (... – ca.1684) son of Sir John Weld & Frances Whitmore

   (1) **Mary Weld** (...)
= ...; ♦**Nicholas Taaffe, 2ⁿᵈ Earl of Carlingford** (... – 1 Jul 1690 Boyne) killed in battle; son of Theobald Taaffe, 1ˢᵗ Earl of Carlingford & Mary White; suc. father 31 Dec 1677

no issue
    (II) **William Arundell** (aft.1560 – 16 Feb 1592) unm.
  b) **Sir Charles Arundell** (... – 9 Dec 1587) unm.
  c) **Dorothy Arundell** (...)
    = ...; **Sir Henry Weston** (...)
    issue ?
  d) **Jane Arundell** (...)
    = ...; **Sir William Bevill** (ca.1548 – 1600) son of John Bevill &
    Elizabeth Milliton; =2nd Frances Knyvett
    no issue
 3) **Elizabeth Arundell** (...)
   = 1516; **Sir Richard Edgcombe** (...)
   issue ?
N) **Lady Margaret Grey** (...)
  = ...; **Richaerd Wake** (...)
  issue ?
issue of 2nd:
Children are listed with other parent
g. **Lady Eleanor Neville** (1447 – bef.Nov 1482)
= aft.10 May 1457; **Thomas Stanley, 1st Earl of Derby** 2nd
Baron Stanley, KG (ca. 1435 – 29 Jul 1504 Lathom, Lancs.) son
of Thomas Stanley, 1st Baron Stanley & Joan Gioushill; =2nd
♦Lady Margaret Beaufort; suc. father 20 Feb 1458/9; cr. Earl 27
Oct 1485; KG 1483
I) **George, Lord Stanley** (... – 5 Dec 1503) poisoned
= bef.26 Feb 1480/1; **Joan Lestrange, 9th Baroness Strange** 5th
Baroness Mohun (ca.1463 – 20 Mar 1513/4) daughter of John
Lestrange, 8th Baron Strange & Lady Jacquetta Woodville; suc. father 16
Oct 1479
  A) **Thomas Stanley, 2nd Earl of Derby** etc. 10th Baron Strange, etc.
    KB (bef.1485 – 23 May 1521) suc. grandfather 1504; suc. mother 1514;
    KB 1494
    = bef.1503; ♦**Hon. Anne Hastings** (1485 – Nov 1550) daughter of
    Sir Edward Hastings, 2nd Baron Hastings & Mary Hungerford, 5th
    Baroness Botreaux
    1) **Lady Margaret Stanley** (... – Jan 1534)
      = 1532; **Robert Radcliffe, 1st Earl of Sussex** Viscount FitzWalter,
      10th Baron FitzWalter **KG** (1483 – 27 Nov 1542) son of John
      Radcliffe, 9th Baron FitzWalter & Margaret ...; =1st ♦Lady Elizabeth
      Stafford; =3rd ♦Mary Arundell; suc. father 3 Nov 1505; cr. Viscount
      18 Jun 1525 and Earl 8 Dec 1529; KG aft.1524
      a) **Lady Anne Radcliffe** (... – 7 Jun 1561)
        = May 1547; **Thomas Wharton, 2nd Baron Wharton** (1520 –
        14 Jun 1572) son of Thomas Wharton, 1st Baron Wharton & Eleanor
        Stapleton; suc. father 24 Aug 1568
        (I) **Philip Wharton, 3rd Baron Wharton** (23 Jun 1555 – 26

Mar 1625) suc. father 1572

=1 24 Jun 1577 ; ♦**Lady Frances Clifford** (... – 1592) daughter of Henry Clifford, 2nd Earl of Cumberland & Anne Dacre

=2 1597; **Dorothy Colby** (... – 4 Apr 1621) daughter of Thomas Colby; =1st John Tamworth; =2nd Sir Francis Willoughby

issue of 1st (none by 2nd):

(A) **Hon. Frances Wharton** (...)
  = ...; ♦**Sir Richard Musgrave, 1st Baronet** (... – 1615)
  Children are listed with other parent

(B) **Hon. Eleanor Wharton** (...)
  = ...; **William Thwaytes** (...)
  issue ?

(C) **Hon. Margaret Wharton** (Jul 1581 – 10 Mar 1658/9)
  = Sep 1603; **Edward Wotton, 1st Baron Wotton** (1548 – 1625) son of Thomas Wotton & Elizabeth Rudston; =1st Hester Pickering; cr. Baron 13 May 1603
  no issue

(D) **Hon. Sir George Wharton KB** (1583 – 1609) killed ina duel; unm. KB 1603

(E) **Hon. Sir Thomas Wharton** (1588 – 17 Apr 1622)
  = 11 Apr 1611; ♦**Lady Philadelphia Carey** (...) daughter of Robert Carey, 1st Earl of Monmouth & Elizabeth Trevannion

  (1) **Philip Wharton, 4th Baron Wharton** (8 Apr 1613 – 5 Feb 1695/6) suc. grandfather 1625
    =1 23 Sep 1632; **Elizabeth Wandsford** (...) daughter of Sir Rowland Wandesford
    =2 7 Sep 1637; ♦**Jane Goodwin** (... – 21 Apr 1658) daughter of Arthur Goodwin
    =3 Aug 1661; **Anne Kerr** (... – 13 Aug 1692) daughter of William Kerr; =1st Sir Fancis Popham
    issue of 1st:

    (a) **Hon. Elizabeth Wharton** (... – 1669)
      = ...; ♦**Robert Bertie, 3rd Earl of Lindsey** (1630–1701)
      Children are listed with other parent
    issue of 2nd:

    (b) **Hon. Philadelphia Wharton** (... – bef.19 Nov 1703)
      =1 2 Sep 1679; **Sir George Lockhart, 1st of Carnwath** (ca.1630 – 31 Mar 1689 Edinburgh) son of James Lockhart, 10th of the Lee & Martha Douglas
      =2 ...; **John Ramsay** (...)
      Has further generations of issue by 1st

    (c) **Hon. Margaret Wharton** (...)
      =1 bef.1679 ...; **... Dunch** (...)
      =2 ...; **Thomas Sulyards, 2nd Baronet** (... – 1 May 1692)
      =3 bef.Sep 1695; **William Ross, 12th Lord Ross** (ca. 1656 – 15 Mar 1738) son of George Ross, 11th Lord Ross &

Lady Grizel Cochrane; =1ˢᵗ ♦Lady Anne Hay; =3ʳᵈ Agnes
Wilkie; =4ᵗʰ Henrietta Scott
Might have surviving issue by 1ˢᵗ

(d) **Hon. Hon. Anne Wharton** (1640 – 1689)
= ...; **William Carr** (...)
issue ?

(e) **Thomas Wharton, 1ˢᵗ Marquess of Wharton**
Marquess of Malmesbury, Earl of Wharton, Viscount
Winchesdon, Marquess of Catherlough, Earl of
Rathfurnham, Baron Trim, 5ᵗʰ Baron Wharton (Aug 1648 –
12 Apr 1716) suc. father 1696, cr. Earl of Wharton etc. 23 Dec
1706; Marquess of Catherlough etc. 12 Apr 1715; Marquess of
Wharton and Malmesbury 15 Feb 1714/5
=1 16 Sep 1673; **Anne Lee** (... – 29 Oct 1685) daughter of Sir
Henry Lee, 3ʳᵈ Baronet
=2 Jul 1692; ♦**Hon. Lucy Loftus** (1670 – 5 Feb 1716/7)
daughter of Adam Loftus, Viscount Lisburne & Lucy Brydges
Has further generations of issue by 2ⁿᵈ

(f) **Hon. Mary Wharton** (1649 – 1699)
=1 14 Feb 1672/3; **William Thomas** (1649 – 28 Apr 1677)
son of Edmond Thomas & Elizabeth Morgan
=2 1678; **Sir Charles Kemeys, 3ʳᵈ Baronet** (... – Dec
1702) =2ⁿᵈ Mary Lewis
Has further generations of issue by both
issue of 3ʳᵈ:

(g) **Hon. William Wharton** (Jun 1662 – 14 Dec 16857)
killed in a duel; unm.

(2) **Sir Thomas Wharton** (1615 – 1684)
= ...; ♦**Lady Mary Carey** (...) daughter of Henry Carey, 1ˢᵗ
Earl of Dover
issue ?

b) **Lady Jane Radcliffe** (1533 – 1553)
= ca.1551; **Anthony Browne, 1ˢᵗ Viscount Montagu** (1527–
1592)
Children are listed with other parent

2) **Edward Stanley, 3ʳᵈ Earl of Derby** etc. KG (10 May 1509 – 24
Oct 1572) suc. father 1521; KG 1547
=1 21 Feb 1530; ♦**Lady Dorothy Howard** (aft.1497 – ...) daughter
of Thomas Howard, 2ⁿᵈ Duke of Norfolk & Agnes Tylney
=2 ...; **Margaret Barlow** (... – 19 Jan 1558/9) daughter of Ellis
Barlow
=3 ...; **Mary Cotton** (... – 16 Nov 1580) daughter of Rt.Hon. Sir
George Cotton; =2ⁿᵈ ♦Henry Grey, 6ᵗʰ Earl of Kent
issue of 1ˢᵗ:

a) **Lady Jane Stanley** (... – Aug 1569)
= 1567; ♦**Edward Dudley, 4ᵗʰ Baron Dudley** (... – 1586)

Children are listed with other parent

b) **Henry Stanley, 4ᵗʰ Earl of Derby** etc. **KG** (... – 25 Sep 1593)
suc. father 1572; KG 1574
= 74 Feb 1555; ◆**Lady Margaret Clifford** (1540 – 29 Sep 1596)
daughter of Henry Clifford, 2ⁿᵈ Earl of Cumberland & Lady Eleanor
Brandon

(I) **Ferdinando Stanley, 5ᵗʰ Earl of Derby** etc. (1559 – 16 Apr
1594) suc. father 1593; upon his death the baronies of Stanley,
Strange, and Mohun fell into abeyance among his daughters
= ca.1580; **Alice Spencer** (ca.1556 – 23 Jan 1637) daughter of
Sir John Spencer & Katherine Kitson

(A) **Lady Anne Stanley** (May 1580 – 8 Oct 1647)
=1 1608; ◆**Grey Brydges, 5ᵗʰ Baron Chandos** (1578–1621)
=2 22 Jul 1624 London; **Mervyn Tuchet, 2ⁿᵈ Earl of
Castlehaven** Baron Audley of Orier, 12ᵗʰ Baron Audley of
Heleigh (ca.1593 – 14 May 1631 London) executed[122]; son of
George Tuchet, 1ˢᵗ Earl of Castlehaven & Lucy Mervyn; =1ˢᵗ
Elizabeth Barnham; his title Baron Audley of Heleigh was
forfeited
issue of 1ˢᵗ (none by 2ⁿᵈ):
Children are listed with other parent

(B) **Lady Frances Stanley** (May 1583 – 11 Mar 1635/6)
= 1602; **John Egerton, 1ˢᵗ Earl of Bridgwater** 2ⁿᵈ Viscount
Brackley, Baron of Ellesmere **KB** (1579 – 4 Dec 1649 Herts.) son
of Thomas Egerton, 1ˢᵗ Viscount Brackley & Elizabeth
Ravenscroft; suc. father 15 Mar 1616/7; cr. Earl 27 May 1617; KB
1603

(1) **Lady Elizabeth Egerton** (... – 20 Mar 1687/8)
= ...; ◆**David Cecil, 3ʳᵈ Earl of Exeter** (... – 18 Apr 1643)
see; page

(2) **Lady Mary Egerton** (... – 1659)
= 19 Nov 1627 London; **Richard Herbert, 2ⁿᵈ Baron
Herbert** (... – 13 May 1655) son od Edward Herbert, 1ˢᵗ Baron
Herbert & Mary Herbert; suc. father 5 Aug 1648

(a) **Hon. John Herbert** (ca.1627 – 1675 Norfolk Co, VA)
born prior to marriage so not eligible to succeed
= ...; **Mary Bennett** (bef.1640 – 1672 Norfolk Co)
issue ?

(b) **Hon. Florentina Herbert** (... – 1692)
= 21 Aug 1663 Llanerfyl, Wales; **Richard Herbert** (ca.
1629 – 1676) son of Francis Herbert & Abigail Garton

---

[122] Convicted of "unnatural acts" with his page.

Has further generations of issue
- (c) **Hon. Magdalen Herbert** (...)
  = ...; **Sir Charles Morley** (...)
  Has further generations of issue
- (d) **Edward Herbert, 3ʳᵈ Baron Herbert** (ca.1633 – 9 Dec 1678) suc. father 1655
  =1 bef.1660; **Anne Myddleton** (... – aft.1660) daughter of Sir Thomas Myddleton & Mary Napier
  =2 m20 Aug 1673; ♦**Hon. Elizabeth Brydges** (25 Mar 1651 – 3 Feb 1718) daughter of George Brydges, 6ᵗʰ Baron Chandos & Lady Susan Montagu; =2ⁿᵈ William O'Brien, 2ⁿᵈ Earl of Inchiquin; =3ʳᵈ ♦Charles Howard, 4ᵗʰ Baron Howard
  no issue
- (e) **Henry Herbert, 4ᵗʰ Baron Herbert** (ca.1640 – 21 Apr 1691) suc. brother 1678
  = Dec 1681; **Lady Katherine Newport** (...) daughter of Francis Earl of Bradford & Lady Diana Russell
  no issue
- (3) **Lady Penelope Egerton** (...)
  = ...; **Sir Robert Napier, 2ⁿᵈ Baronet** (... – 1660) son of Sir Robert Napier, 1ˢᵗ Baronet & Mary Robinson; suc. father Apr 1627; =1ˢᵗ Frances Thornhurst
  - (a) **Frances Napier** (... – Nov 1706 Norwich, Norfolk)
    =1 ...; **Sir Edward Barkham, 2ⁿᵈ Baronet** (1628 – 1688) son of Sir Edward Barkham, 1ˢᵗ Baronet Frances Berney; suc. father 2 Aug 1667; =1ˢᵗ Hon . Grace Watson
    =2 ...; **Henry Richardson, 3ʳᵈ Baron Cramond** (ca. 1651 – 5 Jan 1701) son of Thomas Richardson, 2ⁿᵈ Baron Cramond & Anne Guerney; suc. father 16 May 1674
    Has further generations of issue by 1ˢᵗ
  - (b) **Sir John Napier, 4ᵗʰ Baronet** (... – Aug 1711) suc. nephew 1675
    = ...; **Elizabeth Buddulph** (...) daughter of Simon Biddulph & Jane Birch
    Has further generations of issue
  - (c) **Alexander Napier** (...)
    = ...; **Mary Mason** (...) son of Richard Mason
    Has further generations of issue
- (4) **Lady Arabella Egerton** (... – ca.1669)
  = bef. Mar 1628; **Oliver St.John, 5ᵗʰ Baron Saint John** (... – 23 Oct 1642 Edgehill, Warks.) died opf wounds received in battle; son of Oliver St.John, 1ˢᵗ Earl of Bolingbroke & Elizabeth Paulet; suc. father 14 May 1641 during the latter's lifetime
  - (a) **Hon. Dorothy St.John** (...)
    = ...; **Francis Charlton** (...)

Has further generations of issue

(5) **Lady Frances Egerton** (... – 27 Nov 1664 Norwich)
= Feb 1621; **Sir John Hobart, 2nd Baronet** (19 Apr 1593
Norwich – 20 Apr 1647 Norwich) son of Sir Henry Hobart, 1st
Baronet & Dorothy Bell; =1st Lady Philippa Sydney; suc. father
29 Dec 1625
   (a) **Philippa Hobart** (12 Oct 1635 Blickling, Norfolk – Jan
   1654/5)
      = ...; **Sir John Hobart, 3rd Baronet** (bef.20 Mar 1627/8 –
      22 Aug 1683) son of Sir Miles Hobert & Frances Peyton; =2nd
      Mary Hampden; suc. cousin (and father-in-law) 1647
      no issue

(6) **Lady Alice Egerton** (... – Jul 1689)
= 20 Jul 1652; ♦**Richard Vaughan, 2nd Earl of Carbery**
etc. (... – 3 Dec 1686) son of John Vaughan, 1st Earl of Carbery
& Margaret Meyrick; =1st Bridget Lloyd; =2nd Frances Altham;
suc. father 25 Oct 1643
no issue

(7) **Lady Catherine Egerton** (...)
= ...; **William Courten** (... – 1655 Florence, Italy) son of Sir
William Courten & ... Tryon
   (a) **Katherine Courten** (...)
   (b) **William Courten** (28 Mar 1642 London – 29 Mar 1702
   London)

(8) **Lady Cecilia Egerton** (...) unm.

(9) **Lady Magdalen Egerton** (...)
= ...; **Sir Gervase Cutler** (...) =1st Elizabeth Bentley
issue ?

(10) **John Egerton, 2nd Earl of Bridgwater** etc. (Jun 1623 –
26 Oct 1686 London) suc. father 1649
= 22 Jul 1641 London; **Lady Elizabeth Cavendish** (ca.
1627 – 14 Jun 1663 London) daughter of William Cavendish,
1st Duke of Newcastle-upon-Tyne & Elizabeth Basset
   (a) **John Egerton, 3rd Earl of Bridgwater** etc. **KB** (9 Nov
   1646 – 19 Mar 1700/1 London) suc. father 1686; KB 1661
   =1 17 Nov 1664 London; **Lady Elizabeth Cranfield**
   (ca/1648 – 3 Mar 1669/70 Herts.) daughter of James
   Cranfield, 2nd Earl of Middlesex & Lady Anne Bourchier
   =2 2 Apr 1673 London; ♦**Lady Jane Powlett** (ca.1655 – 23
   May 1716 Herts.) daughter of Charles Powlett, 1st Duke of
   Bolton & Mary le Scrope
   Has further generations of issue by 2nd
   (b) **Hon. Sir William Egerton KB** (15 Aug 1649 – 1691)
   = 1674; **Honora Leigh** (17 May 1649 – 11 Sep 1730)
   daughter of Hon. Sir Thomas Leigh & Jane FitzMaurice;
   she =2nd ♦Hugh Willooughby, 2nd Baron Willoughby

Has further generations of issue
(c) **Hon. Thomas Egerton** (...)
= ...
Has further generations of issue
(d) **Lady Elizabeth Egerton** (1653 – 1709)
= 1672; ♦**Robert Sydney, 4ᵗʰ Earl of Leicester** (1649–1702)
Children are listed with other parent
(C) **Lady Elizabeth Stanley** (6 Jan 1587/8 – 20 Jan 1633)
= 1601; ♦**Henry Hastings, 5ᵗʰ Earl of Huntingdon** (1586–1643)
Children are listed with other parent
(II) **William Stanley, 6ᵗʰ Earl of Derby** etc. **KG** (1561 – 29 Sep 1642) suc. brother 1594; KG 1601
= 26 Jun 1594; ♦**Lady Elizabeth de Vere** (... – 10 Mar 1626/7) daughter of Edward de Vere, 17ᵗʰ Earl of Oxford & Hon. Anne Cecil
(A) **Lady Anne Stanley** (ca.1600 – 12 Feb 1656/7)
=1 20 Jul 1615; **Sir Henry Portman, 2ⁿᵈ Baronet** (ca.1595 – Feb 1623/4) son of Sir John Portman, 1ˢᵗ Baronet & Anne Gifford; suc. father 4 Dec 1612
=2 aft.6 Nov 1621; **Robert Kerr, 1ˢᵗ Earl of Ancrame** Lord Kerr **KB** (1578 – 9 Dec 1654 Amsterdam) son of William Kerr of Ancram & Margaret Dundas; =1ˢᵗ Elizabeth Murray; cr. Earl etc. 24 Jun 1633
issue of 2ⁿᵈ (none by 1ˢᵗ):
(1) **Charles Kerr, 2ⁿᵈ Earl of Ancrame** etc. (6 Aug 1624 Richmond, Surrey – bef.11 Sep 1690) suc. father 1654
= ...; **Frances ...** (...)
(a) **Lady Anne Kerr** (...)
= ...; **Nathaniel Rich** (... – 1701) son of Robert Rich; =1ˢᵗ Elizabeth Hampden
no issue
(2) **Hon. Stanley Kerr** (... – ca.1669)
(3) **Lady Vere Kerr** (...)
= ...; **... Wilkinson** (...)
issue ?
(4) **Lady Elizabeth Kerr** (...)
(B) **James Stanley, 7ᵗʰ Earl of Derby** etc. **KG** (31 Jan 1607 – 15 Oct 1651 Bolton, Lancs.) suc. father 1642; KG 1650
= 26 Jun 1626; **Charlotte de la Trémoille** (1599 – 21 Mar 1663/4) daughter of Claude de la Trémoille, Duke de Thouars & Charlotte of Nassau-Dillenburg
(1) **Charles Stanley, 8ᵗʰ Earl of Derby** etc. (19 Jan 1928 – 21 Dec 1672) suc. father 1651
= 1650; **Dorothea** Helena **van den Kerchhove** (... – 6 Apr

1673) daughter of Jan Polyander van der Kerchhove, Lord van
Henvliet & Catherine Wotton, (life) Countess of Chesterfield
- (a) **William** George Richard **Stanley, 9th Earl of Derby** etc.
  (18 Mar 1656 – 5 Nov 1702) suc. father 1672, upon his death
  the Baron Strange fell into abeyance between his daughters
  = 10 Jul 1673; ♦**Lady Elizabeth Butler** (... – 5 Jul 1717)
  daughter of Thomas Butler, 6th Earl of Ossory & Amelia de
  Nassau
  Issue became extinct in 1732
- (b) **James Stanley, 10th Earl of Derby** etc. 10th Baron
  Strange (3 Jul 1664 – 1 Feb 1735/6) suc. brother 1702, suc.
  grandniece as Baron Strange 1732
  = Feb 1705; **Mary Morley** (1667 – 29 Mar 1752) daughter of
  Sir William Morley & Ann Denham
  no surviving issue
- (2) **Lady Amelia** Anne Sophia **Stanley** (... – 22 Feb 1702/3)
  = 1659; ♦**John Murray, 1st Marquess of Atholl** (1631–
  1703)
  Children are listed with other parent
- (3) **Lady Henrietta** Maria **Stanley** (...)
  = ...; ♦**William Wentworth, 2nd Earl of Strafford** etc.
  (... – Oct 1695) son of Thomas Wentworth, 1st Earl of Strafford
  & Lady Arabella Holles; =2nd Henriette de la Rochefoucauld;
  suc. father 12 May 1641
  no issue
- (C) **Hon. Sir Robert Stanley** (...)
  = ...; ♦**Elizabeth Gorges** (... – May 1675) daughter of Sir
  Arthur Gorges & Lady Elizabeth Clinton; =2nd ♦Theophilius
  Clinton, 4th Earl of Clinton
- (1) **Sir Charles Stanley KB** (...)
  = ...; ♦**Hon. Jane Widdrington** (...) daughter of William
  Widdrington, 1st Baron Widdrington & Mary Torold
  Issue became extinct
- (2) **James Stanley** (...)
  = ...
  no surviving issue
- (III) **Hon. Francis Stanley** (...) unm.
- c) **Hon. Sir Thomas Stanley** (... – 1576)
  = ...; ♦**Margaret Vernon** (...) daughter of Sir George Vernon &
  Margaret Tailboys; =2nd William Mather
- (I) **Sir Edward Stanley KB** (...)
  = ...; ♦**Lady Lucy Percy** (...) daughter of Thomas Percy, 1st Earl
  of Northumberland & Lady Anne Someset
- (A) **Frances Stanley** (...)
  = ...; **Sir John Fortescue, 1st Baronet** (1592 – 1656) cr.
  Baronet 17 Feb 1636

(1) **Sir John Fortescue, 2nd Baronet** (1614 – 1683) suc. father 1656

= ...

(a) **Sir John Fortescue, 3rd Baronet** (1644 – 1717) suc. father 1683

= ...

Has further generations of issue

(B) **Venetia Stanley** (1600 – 30 Apr 1633)

= 1625; **Sir Kenelm Digby** (1603 – 11 Jun 1665) son of Sir Everard Digby

(1) **John Digby** (...)

=1 ...; ♦**Lady Catherine Howard** (...) daughter of Henry Howard, 22nd Earl of Arundel & Lady Elizabeth Stuart

=2 ...; **Margaret Longueville** (...) daughter of Sir Edward Longueville, 1st Baronet & Margaret Temple

issue of 2nd (none by 1st):

(a) **Margareta** Maria **Digby** (...)

= ...; **Sir John Conway, 2nd Baronet** (1663 Rhuddlan, Flints. – 27 Apr 1721) son of Sir Henry Conway, 1st Baronet & Mary Lloyd; =2nd ♦Penelope Grenville; suc. father 1669

Has further generations of issue

(b) **Charlotte** Theophile **Digby** (...)

= ...; ♦**Richard** Henry **Mostyn** (...)

Children are listed with other parent

d) **Lady Anne Stanley** (...)

=1 10 Feb 1548/9; **Charles Stourton, 8th Baron Stourton** (ca.1521 – Mar 1556/7) hanged[123]; son of William Stourton, 7th Baron Stourton & Elizabeth Dudley

=2 aft. 1557; **Sir John Arundell** (...)

issue of 1st (none by 2nd):

(I) **Hon. Mary Stourton** (1549 Stourton, Wilts. – 1608 Wilts.)

= ...; **Francis Tregian** (1548 Probus, Cornwall – 25 Sep 1608 Lisbon, Portugal)

issue ?

(II) **Hon. Anne Stourton** (...)

= ...; **Edward Rogers** (...)

issue ?

(III) **John Stourton, 9th Baron Stourton** (Jan 1552/3 – 13 Oct 1588) suc. father 1557

= ca.1580; **Hon. Frances Brooke** (...) daughter of William Brooke, 10th Baron Cobham & Frances Newton; =2nd Sir Edward Moore

----

[123] Convicted of murdering his father's steward and his son.

519

no issue

(IV) **Edward Stourton, 10th Baron Stourton**[124] (ca.1555 – 7
May 1633) suc. brother 1588
= bef.1588; **Frances Tresham** (...) daughter of Sir Thomas
Tresham

(A) **Hon. Margaret Stourton** (...)
= ...; **Sir Thomas Sulyard** (...)
issue ?

(B) **Hon. Mary Stourton** (...)
= ...; **Walter Norton** (...)
issue ?

(C) **Willliam Stourton, 11th Baron Stourton KB** (bef.1594 –
25 Apr 1672) suc. father 1633; KB 1616
= ca.1616; **Frances Moore** (... – 5 Jan 1662) daughter of Sir
Edward Moore & Mary Poynings

(1) **Hon. Edward Stourton** (1617 – Jan 1643/4)
= aft.28 Oct 1638; ♦**Hon. Mary Petre** (... – 1672) daughter
of Robert Petre, 3rd Baron Petre & Hon. Mary Browne

(a) **William Stourton, 12th Baron Stourton** (ca.1644 – 7
Aug 1685) suc. grandfather 1672
= 1665; **Elizabeth Preston** (... – Apr 1688) daughter of Sir
John Preston, 1st Baronet
Has further generations of issue

(b) **Mary Stourton** (ca.1646 – ...) unm.

(2) **Hon. William Stourton** (... – bef.1672) unm.

(3) **Hon. Thomas Stourton** (... – 1684 Paris) a monk

(4) **Hon. Mary Stourton** (... – 1650)
= 1649; **Sir John Weld** (... – 11 Jul 1674) son of Sir John
Weld & Frances Whitmore

(a) **William Weld** (... – 1698)
= ...
Has further generations of issue

(5) **Hon. Frances Stourton** (...) a nun

(D) **Hon. Francis Stourton** (1599 – 1638)
= ...; **Elizabeth Norton** (...) daughter of Henry Norton

(1) **Frances Stourton** (...)
= ...; **Francis Rockley** (...)
issue ?

(V) **Hon. Charles Stourton** (...)

(VI) **Hon. Katherine Stourton** (...)
= ...; **Richard Sherborne** (...)
issue ?

---

[124] Confined to the Tower 1605-1606 for suspected complicity ion the Gunpowder Plot

e) **Lady Mary Stanley** (... – 3 Sep 1609)
  = 1566; ♦**Edward Stafford, 3ʳᵈ Baron Stafford** (1536–1603)
  Children are listed with other parent
f) **Lady Elizabeth Stanley** (ca.1535 – 1591)
  = ...; **Henry Parker, 11 Baron Morley** (ca.1532 – 22 Oct 1577)
  son of Hon. Sir Henry Parker & Grace Newport; suc. grandfather
  20 Jan 1558
  (I) **Edward Parker, 12ᵗʰ Baron Morley** (ca.1550 – 1618) suc.
    father 1577
    =1 ...; ♦**Hon. Elizabeth Stanley** (1558 – 1585) daughter of
    William Stanley, 3ʳᵈ Baron Monteagle & Anne Leybourne
    =2 ...; **Gertrude Arundel** (...)
    issue of 1ˢᵗ (none by 2ⁿᵈ):
    (A) **William Parker, 13ᵗʰ Baron Morley** 4ᵗʰ Baron
      Monteagle[125] (1575 – 1 Jul 1622 Great Hallingtbury, Essex) suc.
      father 1618; suc. maternal grandfather in Monteagle 10 Nov
      1581
      = 1589; **Elizabeth Tresham** (1573 – 1648) daughter of Sir
      Thomas Tresham & Muriel Throckmorton
      (1) **Henry Parker, 14ᵗʰ Baron Morley** etc. KB (ca.1600 – 10
        May 1655) suc. father 1622
        = ca.1619; **Philippa Caryll** (5 Oct 1600 – ca.1660) daughter
        of Thomas Caryll & Mary Tufton
        (a) **Thomas Parker, 15ᵗʰ Baron Morley** etc. (ca.1636 –
          1686) suc. father 1655, upon his death the title fell into
          abeyancy among his aunts.
          = ...; **Mary Martin** (...) daughter of Henry Martin
          no issue
      (2) **Hon. Catherine Parker** (...)
        = ...; ♦**John Savage, 2ⁿᵈ Earl Rivers** (...–1654)
        Children are listed with other parent
      (3) **Hon. Elizabeth Parker** (...)
        = ...; **Edward Cranfield** (...)
        (a) **Mary Cranfield** (...)
          = bef.1711; **Sir John Becher** (1 Sep 1677 co Cork – ...) son
          of Thomas Becher & Elizabeth Turner; =1ˢᵗ Hester
          Duddlestone
          Has further generations of issue
        (b) **Edward Cranfield** (... – ca.1700) Gov. of NH 1682–1685
      (4) **Hon. William Parker** (...) unm.

---

[125] Responsible for exposing the Gunpowder Plot after recevinig an anonymous letter
warning him not to attend the targeted opening of Parliament.

(5) **Hon. Charles Parker** (...) unm.

(6) **Hon. Frances Parker** (...) a nun

(B) **Hon. Frances Parker** (...)

= ...; ♦**Christopher Danby** (...)

Children are listed with other parent

(C) **Hon. Henry Parker** (...)

(D) **Hon. Charles Parker** (...)

(E) **Hon. Mary Parker** (...)

= ...; **Thomas Abington** (...)

issue ?

(F) **Hon. Elizabeth Parker** (...)

= ...; **Sir Alexander Barlow** (...)

issue ?

(II) **Hon. Ann Parker** (... – May 1612)

= ...; **Sir Henry Brouncker** (... – 3 Jun 1607) son of Henry Brouncker & Ursula Yate

(A) **William Brouncker, 1ˢᵗ Viscount Brouncker** Baron Brouncker (1585 – Nov 1645) cr. Viscount etc 12 Sep 1645

= bef.1645; **Winifred Leigh** (... – 30 Jul 1649 London) daughter of Sir William Leigh & Frances Harington

(1) **William Brouncker, 2ⁿᵈ Viscount Brouncker** etc. (1620 – 5 Apr 1684 London) unm. suc. father 1645

(2) **Henry Brouncker, 3ʳᵈ Viscount Brouncker** etc. (ca.1627 – 4 Jan 1687/8 Sheen Abbey, Richmond) suc. brother 1684 but titles became extinct upon his death

= 1 May 1661; **Rebecca Rodway** (...) =1ˢᵗ Thomas Jermyn

no issue

(III) **Hon. Mary Parker** (... – 4 Nov 1566 Forehow, Norfolk)

= ...; **Sir Edward Leventhorpe** (... – 8 Oct 1556)

(A) **Sir John Leventhorpe, 1ˢᵗ Baronet** (ca.1560 – 23 Sep 1625) cr. Baronet 30 May 1622

= ...; **Joan Brograve** (... – 1 Mar 1627 Sawbridgeworth, Herts.) daughter of Sir John Brograve

(1) **Joan Leventhorpe** (...)

= ...; **Sir Edward Altham** (...)

(a) **Joan Altham** (... – 15 Jul 1658)

= bef.1633; **Sir Thomas Smith, 1ˢᵗ Baronet** (ca.1602 – 5 May 1668) son of Sir William Smith & Bridget Fleetwood

Has further generations of issue

(b) **Leventhorpe Altham** (...)

= ...

Has further generations of issue

(2) **Sir Thomas Leventhorpe, 2ⁿᵈ Baronet** (1592 – 1636) suc. father 1625

= ...

(a) **Sir John Leventhorpe, 3ʳᵈ Baronet** (1629 – 1649) suc.

father 1636

    (b) **Sir Thomas Leventhorpe, 4ᵗʰ Baronet** (1635 – 1679)
    suc. brother 1649
    = ...; **Mary Bedell** (...) daughter of Sir Capell Bedell,
    Baronet
    Has further generations of issue

    (3) **Sir Charles Leventhorpe, 5ᵗʰ Baronet** (1594 – 1680)
    suc. nephew 1679, but title became extinct upon his death

(IV) **Hon. Alice Parker** (...)
    = ...; **Sir Thomas Barrington** (ca.1530 – 1581)
    issue ?

issue of 2ⁿᵈ (none by 3ʳᵈ):

g) **Lady Margaret Stanley** (... – 1586)
= ...; **Sir Nicholas Poyntz** (ca.1535 – 1 Sep 1585) son of Sir
Nicholas Poyntz & Joan Berkeley; =1ˢᵗ Anne Verney

(I) **Edward Poyntz** (ca.1575 – 5 Oct 1613)
=1 ...; **Florence ...** (...)
=2 ...; **Mary ...** (...)
issue of 1ˢᵗ:

    (A) **Nicholas Poyntz** (ca.1597 – 1630)
    =1 ...; **Bridget Badger** (...) daughter of Talbot Badger
    =2 ...; **Jeannette ...** (...)
    issue of 1ˢᵗ (none by 2ⁿᵈ):

        (1) **Rowland Poyntz** (...)
        =1 ...; **Bridget Robnett** (...)
        =2 1650; **Margaret ...** (...) =2ⁿᵈ David Lloyd
        issue of 1ˢᵗ:
        (a) **Nicholas Poyntz** (... – bef.17 Dec 1701)
        issue of 2ⁿᵈ:
        (b) **Rowland Poyntz** (... – aft.1701)
        (2) **Nichoals Poyntz** (... – Nov 1624)
        (3) **John Poyntz** (...)
        = ...
        has unknown issue
    issue of 2ⁿᵈ:
    (B) **Mary Poyntz** (– 1651) unm.
    (C) **Ann Poyntz** (...)
    (D) **Rev. John Poyntz** (ca.1602 – 6 Mar 1671 Ghent) a Catholic
    priest

(II) **Hugh Poyntz** (ca.1579 – 1 Mar 1604/5) unm.
(III) **Robert Poyntz** (ca.1581 – ...)
=1 bef.1627; **Ann ...** (...)
=2 17 Dec 1627 **Elizabeth Walsh** (... – Jan 1631/2) daughter of
William Walsh
issue ?

B) **Hon. Sir James Stanley** (...)

= ...; **Anne Hart** (...) daughter of John Hart & Elizabeth Peache; =2nd Edmund Talbot de Bashall

1) **Sir George Stanley** (...)

   = ...;

   a) **Mary Stanley** (... – 21 Jul 1586)

   = ...; **Robert Hesketh** (20 Jan 1560 Whalley, Lancs. – 7 Nov 1620) son of Sir Thomas Hesketh & Alice Holcroft; =2nd Blanche Twyford; =3rd Jane Spencer

   (I) **Robert Hesketh** (... – Jan 1653)

   = ...; **Margaret Standish** (...) daughter of Alexander Standish & Elizabeth Hawarden

   (A) **Robert Hesketh** (... – Sep 1651)

   = ...; **Lucy Rigby** (...) daughter of Alexander Rigby; =2ns Sir John Molyneux, 3rd Baronet

   (1) **Thomas Hesketh** (...)

   = ...; **Sidney Grosvenor** (...) daughter of Sir Richard Grosvenor, 2nd Baronet & Sydney Mostyn; =2nd ... Spencer

   (a) **Thomas Hesketh** (...)

   = ...; **Ann Graham** (...) daughter of Sir Reginald Graham, 2nd Baronet

   Has further generations of issue

   (b) **Robert Hesketh** (...)

   = ...; ◆**Elizabeth Spencer** (aft.1640 – ...) daughter of Hon. William Spencer & Elizabeth Gerard

   Has further generations of issue

   (II) **Thomas Hesketh** (... – Nov 1646)

   =1 ...; **Susan Powys** (...) daughter of Thomas Powys

   =2 ...; **Jane Edmundsen** (...)

   =3 ...; **Katherine Briers** (...) daughter of Alexander Briers

   no issue

   (III) **Henry Hesketh** (...) unm.

   (IV) **George Hesketh** (...)

   = ...; **Jane ...** (...)

   issue ?

   (V) **John Hesketh** (...)

   = ...; **Mary Haydock** (...)

   (A) **Robert Hesketh** (...)

   (VI) **Holcroft Hesketh** (...)

   =1 ...; **Lawrence Rawstorne** (...)

   =2 ...; **Roger Dodsworth** (...)

   issue ?

   (VII) **Jane Hesketh** (...)

   =1 ...; **Edward Raynall** (...)

   =2 ...; **... Heneage** (...)

   issue ?

   (VII) **Mary Hesketh** (...)

=1 ...; **Richard Barton** (...)
=2 ...; **Thomas Stanley** (...)
issue ?

2) **Henry Stanley** (1515 – 23 Jul 1598)
= 26 Sep 1563; **Mary Stanley** (...) daughter of Peter Stanley

a) **Sir Edward Stanley, 1st Baronet** (... – Apr 1640) cr. Baronet 26 Jun 1627
=1 ...; **Catherine Wainwaring** (... – Nov 1613) daughter of Sir Randal Mainwaring & Margaret Fitton
=2 aft. Nov 1613; **Isabel Warburton** (...) daughter of Sir Peter Warburton
issue of 2nd: (issue of 1st was 3 unknown daughters):

(I) **Sir Thomas Stanley, 2nd Baronet** (bef.22 Oct 1616 – May 1653) suc. father 1640
= ...; **Mary Egerton** (...) daughter of Peter Egerton; =2nd Henry Hoghton

(A) **Sir Edward Stanley, 3rd Baronet** (... – 16 Oct 1671) suc. father 1653
= 25 Dec 1663; **Elizabeth Bosvile** (...) daughter of Thomas Bosvile

(1) **Barbara Stanley** (...)
= ...; **Rev. Zachary Taylor** (...)
issue ?

(2) **Sir Thomas Stanley, 4th Baronet** (27 Sep 1670 – 7 May 1714) suc. father 1671
=1 16 Aug 1688; **Elizabeth Patten** (... – 1694) daughter of Thomas Patten
=2 aft.1694; **Margaret Holcroft** (... – 14 Oct 1735) daughter of Thomas Holcroft; =1st Sir Richard Standish, 1st Baronet
issue of 1st (none by 2nd):

(a) **Edward Stanley, 11th Earl of Derby** 5th Baronet (17 Sep 1689 – 22 Feb 1776) suc. father 1714 and distant cousin as Earl 1 Feb 1735/6
= 14 Sep 1714; ♦**Elizabeth Hesketh** (... – 24 Feb 1776) daughter of Robert Hesketh & Elizabeth Spencer
Has further generations of issue

(b) **Rev. John Stanley** (aft.1690 – 1781)
=1 ...; **Alice Warren** (...) daughter of Edward Warren
=2 May 1753; **Sarah Earle** (... – Feb 1807) daughter of John Earle
no issue

(B) **Peter Stanley** (... – Jan 1686)
= 19 Apr 1683; **Catherine Rigby** (...) daughter of Alexander Rigby; =2nd Paul Amyas

(1) **Thomas Stanley** (... – Apr 1733)
= ...; **Catherine Parker** (...) daughter of Anthony Parker

(a) **Rev. Thomas Stanley** (bef.2 Jan 1717 – Jun 1764)
= ...; **Betty Shaw** (... – 4 Dec 1780) daughter of John Shaw
Has further generations of issue
(b) **Charles Stanley** (...)
= ...
Has unknown issue via a daughter
(c) **Margaret** Sarah **Stanley** (...)
= ...; ♦**John** Henry Grosvenot **Taylor**[126] (1726 Scale Hall,
Lancs. – ...) son of George Taylor & Mary Hesketh
Has further generations of issue
(C) **Mary Stanley** (...)
= ...; **John Bradshaw** (...)
issue ?
(II) **Henry Stanley** (3 Sep 1617 – ...)
=1 ...; **Eleanor Dutton** (...)
=2 ...; **Mary Cropper** (...) daughter of Hamlet Cropper
issue of 2nd:
(A) **Edward Stanley** (ca.1651 – Dec 1754)
= ...
(1) **Henry Stanley** (... – bef.17 Jan 1799 Jamaica) unm.
(2) **Charles Stanley** (16 Sep 1702 – ...)
= ...; **Elizabeth Parker** (...) daughter of Christopher Parker &
Katherine Stanley
(a) **Charles Stanley** (3 Apr 1745 – ...)
= ...
Has further generations of issue
b) **James Stanley** (...)
C) **Hon. Jane Stanley** (...)
= ...; **Sir Robert Sheffield** (bef.1505 – 15 Nov 1531) son of Sir Robert
Sheffield; =2nd Margaret la Zouche
1) **Edmund Sheffield, 1st Baron Sheffield** (22 Nov 1521 – 31 Jul
1549 Norwich) killed in battle
= bef.31 Jan 1537/8; ♦**Lady Anne de Vere** (ca.1522 Castle
Hedingham, Essex – 11 Feb 1571/2) daughter of John de Vere, 15th
Earl of Oxford & Elizabeth Trussel; =2nd John Brock
a) **John Sheffield, 2nd Baron Sheffield KB** (ca.1538 – 10 Dec
1568) suc. father 1549; KB 1559
= ca.1562; ♦**Hon. Douglas Howard** (aft.1537 – 8 Dec 1608)
daughter of William Howard, 1st Baron Howard & Margaret
Gamage; =2nd ♦Robert Dudley, 1st Earl of Leicester; ♦=3rd Sir

---

[126] Thru his mother, John is more than 12 generations descended from Edward III, therefoe
not listed, so he and the reference to his descendants are here.

Edward Stafford

(I) **Hon. Elizabeth Sheffield** (... – Nov 1600 co Kilkenny)
= ca.1582; **Thomas Butler, 10th Earl of Ormonde** 3rd Earl of
Ossory, 2nd Viscount Thurles, **KG** (1531 – 22 Nov 1614 co
Kilkenny) son of James Butler, 9th Earl of Ormonde & Lady Joan
FitzGerald; =1 Hon. Elizabeth Berkeley; =3rd Hon. Helen Barry;
suc. father 28 Oct 1546; KG 1588

(A) **James, Viscount Thurles** (1584 – bef.1614) unm.

(B) **Hon. Thomas Butler** (... – 12 Jan 1606) unm.

(C) **Lady Elizabeth Butler** (... – 10 Oct 1628 Wales)
=1 Feb 1602/3; **Theobald Butler, Viscount Butler** (... – Dec
1613) son of Sir Edmund Butler & Hon. Eleanor Eustace; cr.
Viscount 4 Aug 1603, but it became extinct upon his death
=2 aft.Dec 1613; **Richard Preston 1st Earl of Desmond** Lord
Dingwall, Baron Dunmore **KB** (... – 28 Oct 1628) cr. Lord 8 Jun
1609 (Scotland), Baron 11 Jul 1619 (Ireland), and Earl 24 Jul
1619.
issue of 2nd (none by 1st):

(1) **Elizabeth Preston, 2nd Baroness Dingwall** (25 Jul
1615 – 21 Jul 1684) suc. father 1628
= Sep 1629; **James Butler, 1st Duke of Ormond** Marquess
of Ormonde, Earl of Brecknock, Baron Butler, 12th Earl of
Ormonde, etc. **KB** (19 Oct 1610 – 21 Jul 1688) son of Thomas,
Viscount Thuries & Elizabeth Poyntz; suc. couisn as 12th Earl
24 Feb 1632/3; cr. Marquess 30 Aug 1642, Baron 20 Jul 1660,
Earl of Brecknock 30 Mar 1661; and Duke 9 Nov 1682; KB
1649

(a) **Thomas, Earl of Ossory** 1st Baron Butler (8 Jul 1634 –
30 Jul 1680) cr. Baron during father's lifetime 17 Sep 1666
= 17 Nov 1659; **Amelia de Nassau** (1635 – 24 Jan 1684)
daughter of Louis de Nassau, Lord can der Leer and
Beverwaerde
Has further generations of issue

(b) **John Butler, Earl of Gowran** Viscount Clonmore,
Baron of Aghrim (aft.1639 – 1677) cr. Earl etc. 13 Apr 1676,
but titles became extinct upon his death
= Jan 1674; **Lady Anne Chichester** (... – 14 Nov 1697)
daughter of Arthur Chichester, 1st Earl of Donegall & Letitia
Hicks; =2nd Francis Aungier, 1st Earl of Longford
no issue

(c) **Richard Butler, Earl of Arran** Viscount Tullogh, Baron
Butler of Cloughgrenan, Baron Butler of Weston (15 Jun
1639 – 25 Jan 1685/6 London) cr. Earl etc. 13 May 1662 and
Baron Butler of Weston 27 Aug 1673, but his titles became
extinct upon his death
=1 bef.16 Mar 1666/7; ♦**Mary Stuart, 5th Baroness**

Clifton (bef.10 Jul 1651 London – 4 Jul 1668 Kilkenny) daughter of James Stuart, 4th Duke of Lennox & Lady Mary Villiers; suc. father 10 Aug 1660

=2 Jun 1673; **Dorothy Ferrers** (... – 30 Nov 1716) daughter of John Ferrers & Anne Carleton

Has further generations of issue by 2nd

    (d) **Lady Elizabeth Butler** (29 Jun 1640 Kilkenny – Jul 1665 Buxton, Northants.)

    = 1660; ◆**Philip Stanhope, 2nd Earl of Chesterfield** (1634– 1714)

    Children are listed with other parent

    (e) **Lady Mary Butler** (1646 – 31 Jul 1710)

    = 26 Oct 1662; ◆**William Cavendish, 1st Duke of Devonshire** (1641–1707)

    Children are listed with other parent

(II) **Edmund Sheffield, 1st Earl of Mulgrave** 3rd Baron Sheffield (7 Dec 1565 – Oct 1646) suc. father 1568; cr. Earl 5 Feb 1625/6

=1 bef.13 Nov 1581; **Ursula Tyrwhitt** (... – bef.4 Aug 1618) daughter of Sir Robert Tyrwhitt

=2 4 Mar 1618/9; **Mariana Irwin** (...) daughter of Sir William Irwin

issue of 1st

    (A) **Sir John Sheffield** (... – Dec 1641) drowned

    = ...; **Grizel Anderson** (...) daughter of Sir Edmund Anderson

    (1) **Edmund Sheffield, 2nd Earl of Mulgrave** etc. (Dec 1611 – 24 Aug 1658) suc. father 1646

    = 13 Apr 1631; **Lady Elizabeth Cranfield** (...) daughter of Lionel Cranfield, 1st Earl of Middlesex & Elizabeth Shepherd; she =2nd John Bennet, 1st Baron Ossulston

    (a) **John Sheffield, 1st Duke of County of Buckingham** and of Normandy, Marquess of Normandy, 3rd Earl of Mulgrave etc. **KG** (8 Sep 1647 – 24 Feb 1721 Buckingham House[later Palace]) suc. father 1658, cr. Marquess 10 May 1694 and Duke 23 Mar 1702/3

    =1 18 Mar 1685/6 Ramsbury, Wilts.; **Ursula Stawel** (... – 13 Aug 1697) daughter of Sir John Stawel & Ursula Austen

    =2 12 Mar 1698/9 London; ◆**Hon. Catherine Greville** (... – 7 Feb 1703/4) daughter of Fulke Greville, 5th Baron Brooke & Sarah Dashwood; =1st Wriothesley Noel, 2nd Earl of Gainsborogh

    =3 16 Mar 1705/6; ◆**Lady Catherine Darnley** (ca. 1681 – 13 Mar 1743) natural daughter of James II, King of England & Catherine Sedley, Countess of Dorchester; =1st James Annesley, 3rd Earl of Anglesey

Has further generations of issue by 1st, 3rd and a mistress
(B) **Lady Mary Sheffield** (... – Jun 1619)
= 1607; **Ferdinando Fairfax, 2nd Baron Fairfax** (29 Mar
1584 – 14 Mar 1648/8) son of Thomas Fairfax, 1st Baron
Fairfax & Ellen Aske; =2nd Rhoda Chapman; suc. father 2 May
1640
   (1) **Thomas Fairfax, 3rd Baron Fairfax** (17 Jan 1611/2
   Ilkley, Yorks. – 12 Nov 1671) suc. father 1648
      = 20 Jun 1637; ♦**Hon. Anne de Vere** (1618 the
      Netherlands – 16 Oct 1665 Bolton Percy, Yorks.) daughter of
      Horatio de Vere, Baron Vere of Tilbury & Mary Tracy
      (a) **Hon. Mary Fairfax** (30 Jul 1638 – 20 Oct 1704)
         = 15 Sep 1657 Bolton Percy, Yorks.; ♦**George Villiers,
         2nd Duke of Buckingham**, etc. 19th Baron de Ros **KG**
         (30 Jan 1627/8 – 16 Apr 1687 Kirkby Moorside, Yorks.)
         son of George Villiers, 1st Duke of Buckingham & Catherine
         Manners, 18th Baroness de Ros; suc. father 1628 and
         mother 1649; KG 1661; all of his paternal titles became
         extinct upon his death
         no issue
   (2) **Hon. Charles Fairfax** (22 Mar 1614/5 – 7 Jul 1644
   Easton Moor) killed in battle; unm.
   (3) **Hon. Elizabeth Fairfax** (...)
   =1 30 Mar 1646; **Sir William Craven** (1610 – 12 Oct 1655)
   son of Robert Craven & Mary Shearwood
   =2 ...; **Thomas Prior** (... – 1690)
   issue of 1st:
      (a) **William Craven** (ca.1649 – 1665) unm.
   (4) **Hon. Ellen Fairfax** (... – 17 Mar 1671)
      = ...; **Sir William Selby** (...)
      issue ?
   (5) **Hon. Frances Fairfax** (... – 4 May 1649)
      = ...; **Sir Thomas Widdrington** (ca.1600 – 1664) son of
      Lewis Widdrington & Katherine Lawson
      (a) **Ursula Widdrington** (... – 22 Apr 1717)
         = 1668; ♦**Thomas Windsor, 1st Earl of Plymouth**
         (1627–1687)
         Children are listed with other parent
      (b) **Frances Widdrington** (...)
         = 12 Aug 1658; **Sir John Legard, 1st Baronet** (1631 –
         1678) son of John Legard & Mary Dawnay; cr. Baronet 29
         Dec 1660
         Has further generations of issue
   (6) **Hon. Mary Fairfax** (... – Dec 1678)
      = 24 May 1638; **Henry Arthington** (...)
      issue ?

(7) **Hon. Dorothy Fairfax** (... – 7 Jun 1687)
= ...; **Richard Hutton** (...) son of Sir Thomas Hutton; =2nd
♦Ursula Sheffield
(a) **Matthew Hutton** (...)
= ...; **Elizabeth Burgoyne** (...) Sir Roger Burgoyne, 2nd
Baronet & Anne Robinson
issue ?
(C) **Lady Elizabeth Sheffield** (...)
= ...; **Sir Edward Swift** (...) son of Sir Robert Swift
no issue
(D) **Hon. Sir Edmund Sheffield** (...)
= ...
(1) **Ursula Sheffield** (...)
= ...; **Richard Hutton** (...) son of Sir Thomas Hutton; =1st
♦Hon. Dorothy Fairfax
issue ?
b) **Hon. Eleanor Sheffield** (...)
= ...; **Denzill Holles** (... – 12 Apr 1590)
(I) **John Holles, 1st Earl of Clare** Baron Houghton (May 1564
Haughton, Notts. – 4 Oct 1637 Clare Palace, Notts.) cr. Baron 9
Jul 1616 and Earl 2 Nov 1624
= 23 May 1591 Shelford, Notts.; **Anne Stanhope** (Feb 1576 – 18
Nov 1651 London) daughter of Sir Thomas Stanhope & Margaret
Port
(A) **Lady Arabella Holles** (...)
= ...; **Thomas Wentworth, 1st Earl of Strafford** Viscount
Wentworth, Baron Wentworth, Baron Raby, 2nd Baronet (13 Apr
1593 – 12 May 1641 London) executed; son of Sir William
Wentworth, 1st Baronet & Anne Atkinson; cr. Viscount and
Baron Wentworth 1629 and Earl and Baron Raby 1640; =1st
♦Lady Margaret Clifford; =3rd Elizabeth Rodes
(1) **William Wentworth, 2nd Earl of Strafford** etc. (... – Oct
1695) suc. father 1641, but hisa titles became extinct upon his
death
=1 ...; ♦**Lady Henrietta** Maria **Stanley** (...) daughter of
James Stanley, 7th Earl of Derby & Charlotte de la Trémoille
=2 ...; **Henriette de la Rochefoucauld** (...) daughter of
Frédéric de la Rochefoucauld
no issue
(2) **Lady Anne Wentworth** (...)
= 1654; ♦**Edward Watson, 2nd Baron Rockingham**
(1630–1689)
Children are listed with other parent
(3) **Lady Arabella Wentworth** (1630 – 1689)
= ...; **Justin MacCarthy, Viscount Mountcashell**
(ca.1643 – 21 Jul 1694 Barèges, France) son of Donough

MacCarty, 1st Earl of Clancarty & Eleanor Butler; cr. Viscount 1689, but it became extinct upon his death
no issue
(B) **John Holles, 2nd Earl of Clare** etc. (13 Jun 1595 Haughton, Notts. – 2 Jan 1665/6 Haughton) suc. father 1637
= 4 Sep 1626 London; ♦**Hon. Elizabeth de Vere** (ca.1608 London – Dec 1683) daughter of Horatio de Vere, Baron Vere & Mary Tracy
(1) **Lady Elizabeth Holles** (...)
= ca.1655; ♦**Wentworth FitzGerald, 17th Earl of Kildare** (1634–1664)
Children are listed with other parent
(2) **Lady Penelope Holles** (...)
= 13 Apr 1667; **Sir James Langham, 2nd Baronet** (1620 – Aug 1699) son of Sir John Langham, 1st Baronet & Mary Bunce; =1st Mary Alston; =2nd ♦Lady Elizabeth Hastings; =4th Dorothy Pomeroy
no issue
(3) **Gilbert Holles, 3rd Earl of Clare** etc. (24 Apr 1633 – 16 Jan 1688/9 London) suc. father 1666
= 9 Jul 1655 London; **Grace Pierrepont** (... – Jul 1702) daughter of Hon. William Pierrepont & Elizabeth harries
(a) **Lady Grace Holles** (... – 13 Sep 1700)
= 21 May 1686; **Thomas Pelham, 1st Baron Pelham** 4th Baronet (ca.1653 – 23 Feb 1711/2) son of Sir John Pelham, 3rd Baronet & Lady Lucvy Sydney; =1st Elizabeth Jones; suc. father Jan 1702/3, cr. Baron 16 Dec 1706
Has further generations of issue
(b) **Lady Elizabeth Holles** (ca.1657 – 9 Nov 1725)
= aft.9 May 1676; **Christopher Vane, 1st Baron Barnard** (bef.21 May 1653 – 28 Oct 1723 Shipbourne, Kent) son of Sir Henry Vane & Frances Wray; cr. Baron 25 Jul 1698
Has further generations of issue
(c) **John Holles, Duke of Newscastle-upon-Tyne** Marquess of Clare, 4th Earl of Clare, etc. **KG** (9 Jan 1661/2 Edwinstow, Notts. – 15 Jul 1711 Welbeck, Notts.) suc. father 1689; cr. Duke and Marquess 14 May 1694; KG 1698; upon his death all of titles became extinct
= 1 Mar 1689/90; ♦**Lady Margaret Cavendish** (22 Oct 1661 – 24 Dec 1716 London) daughter of Henry Cavendish, 2nd Duke of Newcastle-upon-Tyne & Frances Pierrepont
Has further generations of issue
(4) **Lady Diana Holles** (...)
= ...; ♦**Henry Brydges** (...)
Children are listed with other parent
(5) **Lady Susan Holles** (...)

531

= ...; **Sir John Lort, 2ⁿᵈ Baronet** (ca.1637 – ca.1673) son of
Sir Roger Lord, 1ˢᵗ Baronet; suc. father 1663
  (a) **Elizabeth Lort** (... – 28 Sep 1714)
    = 1689; ♦**Sir Alexander Campbell, younger of Cawdor**
    (...–1697)
    Children are listed with other parent
  (b) **Sir Gilbert Lort, 3ʳᵈ Baronet** (ca.1670 – 1698) suc.
    father ca.1673
(C) **Lady Eleanor Holles** (...)
= ...; **Oliver Fitzwilliam, Earl of Tyrconnel** 2ⁿᵈ Viscount
Fitzwilliam (... – 11 Apr 1667) son of Thomas FitzWilliam, 1ˢᵗ
Viscount Fitzwilliam & Hon. Margaret Plunkett; =1ˢᵗ Dorothy
Brereton; suc. father 1650; cr. Earl 1660, but that title became
extinct upon his death
no issue
(D) **Denzil Holles, 1ˢᵗ Baron Holles** (31 Oct 1599 – 17 Feb
1679/80) cr. Baron 1661
=1 4 Jun 1626; **Dorothy Ashley** (... – 21 Jun 1640) son of Sir
Francis Ashley
=2 12 Mar 1641/2; **Jane Shirley** (... – Apr 1666) daughter of
Sir John Shirley
=3 14 Sep 1666; **Esther le Lou** (... – 1684) daughter opf
Gideon le Lou
issue of 1ˢᵗ (none by others):
  (1) **Francis Holles, 2ⁿᵈ Baron Holles** (1627 – 1 Mar 1690)
    suc. father 1660
    =1 ...; **Lucy Carr** (...) daughter of Sir Robert Carr, 2ⁿᵈ Baronet
    & Mary Gargrave
    =2 ...; **Anne Pile** (...) daughter of Sir Francis Pile, 2ⁿᵈ Baronet
    issue of 2ⁿᵈ (none by 1ˢᵗ):
    (a) **Denzil Holles, 3ʳᵈ Baron Holles** (... – 25 Jan 1693/4)
      unm. suc. father 1690, but title became extinct upon his
      death
(E) **Hon. Francis Holles** (... – 1622)
II) **Edward Stanley, 1ˢᵗ Baron Monteagle KG** (... – 7 Apr 1523) cr.
Baron 21 May 1514; KG 1514
=1 ...; **Anne Harington** (ca.1455 – 5 Aug 1481) daughter of Sir John
Harington & Maud de Clifford
=2 bef.25 Nov 1501; **Elizabeth Vaughan** (... – 15 Jan 1514/5) daughter
of Sir Thomas Vaughan; =2ⁿᵈ ♦John Grey, 8ᵗʰ Baron Grey
issue of 2ⁿᵈ:
A) **Thomas Stanley, 2ⁿᵈ Baron Monteagle KB** (25 May 1507 – 25
Aug 1560) suc. father 1523; KB 1533
=1 ca.1528; ♦**Lady Mary Brandon** (1510 – ca.1542) daughter of
Charles Brandon, 1ˢᵗ Duke Suffolk & Anne Browne
=2 aft.1542; **Helen Preston** (... – bef.14 Nov 1571) daughter of

Thomas Preston; =1ˢᵗ Sir James Leyburne
issue of 1ˢᵗ:

1) **William Stanley, 3ʳᵈ Baron Monteagle** (... – 10 Nov 1581) suc.
father 1560
=1 ...; (his step-sister) **Anne Leyburne** (...) daughter of Sir James
Leyburne
=2 15 Sep 1575; **Anne Spencer** (... – 22 Sep 1618) daughter of Sir
John Spencer & Katherine Kitson; =2ⁿᵈ Sir Henry Compton, 1ˢᵗ Baron
Compton; =3ʳᵈ ◆Robert Sackville, 2ⁿᵈ Earl of Dorset
issue of 1ˢᵗ:

a) **Elizabeth Stanley** (1558 – 1585)
= ...; ◆**Edward Parker. 12ᵗʰ Baron Morley** (ca.1550–1618)
Children are listed with other parent

2) **Hon. Anne Stanley** (...)
= ...; **Sir John Clifton** (...)

a) **Gervase Clifton, 1ˢᵗ Baron Clifton** (ca.1569 – 14 Oct 1618
London) committed suicide while a prisoner; cr. Baron 9 Jul 1608
= 25 Jun 1591; **Catherine Darcy** (...) daughter of Sir Henry Darcy
& Katherine Fermor

(I) **Katherine Clifton, 2ⁿᵈ Baroness Clifton** (ca.1592 – 21 Aug
1637 Paisley, Renfrews.) suc. father 1618
=1 1609; ◆**Esmé Stuart, 3ʳᵈ Duke of Lennox** (ca.1579–1624)
=2 ca.1632; ◆**James Hamilton, 2ⁿᵈ Earl of Abercorn**
(ca.1604–1670)
issue of 1ˢᵗ:
Children are listed with other parent
issue of 2ⁿᵈ:
Children are listed with other parent
illegitimate issue by ...:

B) **Edward Stanley** (... – aft.1514)
C) **Thomas Stanley** (... – aft.1523)
D) **Mary Stanley** (... – 7 Apr 1522)
= ...; ... **Radcliff** (...)
issue ?

III) **Hon. Rt.Rev. James Stanley, Bishop of Ely** (...) unm.

h. **ALICE, BARONESS FITZHUGH** (1430–1503)
see: Chapter 15

i. **Lady Margaret Neville** (ca.1450 – aft. 20 Nov 1506)
= ...; **John de Vere, 13ᵗʰ Earl of Oxford** KG, KB (8 Sep 1442 –
10 Mar 1512/3 Castle Hedingham, Essex) son of John de Vere,
12ᵗʰ Earl of Oxford & Elizabeth Howard; suc. father 26 Feb
1461/2; KB 1465; KG 1486
no issue

issue by ...:

j. **Sir Thomas Neville, Kt.**[127] (1429 – 22 Sep 1471 Middleham
Castle, Yorks.) executed; Kt.1449
= ca.Aug 1453; **Maud Stanhope, Baroness Cromwell** (... – 30
Aug 1497) daughter of Sir Richard Stanhope & Maud Cromwell;
suc. maternal grandfather; =1st Robert Willoughby, 6th Baron
Willoughby; =3rd Sir Vervase Clifton
no issue

6. **Robert Neville, Bishop of Durham** (1404 Raby Castle – 8 Jul
1457 Durham)

7. **William Neville, Earl of Kent** KG (ca.1405 Raby Castle – 9 Jan
14632/3) KG 1440; cr. Earl 1 Nov 1461 (title went extincgt upon
his death)
= bef. 28 Apr 1422; **Joan Fauconberg, 6th Baroness Fauconberg**
(ca.1406 – 1490) daughter of Thomas Fauconberg, 5th Baron
Fauconberg & Joan Brounflete; suc. father, after termination of
abeyance, 1422; became abeyant again upon her death

a. **Lady Alice Neville** (...)
= bef.1463; **John Conyers** (... – 26 Jul 1469) son of Sir John Conyers &
Margery Darcy

I) **Margery Conyers** (... – 10 May 1524)
= ...; **Sir William Bulmer** (23 Apr 1465 – 18 Oct 1531) son of Sir Ralph
Bulmer & Joan Bowes

A) **Sir John Bulmer** (bef.1446 – 25 May 1537) executed[128]
=1 ...; **Anne Bigod** (... – aft.6 Oct 1531) daughter of Sir Ralph Bigod &
Margaret Constable
=2 ...; **Margaret Stafford** (... – 25 May 1537) executed with husband
issue of 1st:

1) **Sir Ralph Bulmer** (... – 9 Oct 1558)
= ...; **Anne Tempest** (... – 28 Apr 1555) daughter of Sir Thomas
Tempest & Elizabeth Borough

a) **Joan Bulmer** (...)
=1 ...; ♦**Francis Cholmley** (... – Apr 1586) son of Sir Richard
Cholmley & Margaret Conyers
=2 ...; **Sir Francis Hildesley** (... – aft.1612)
no issue

b) **Frances Bulmer** (... – 10 Apr 1614 Borth Cliff, Yorks.)
= ...; **Marmaduke Constable** (...)
issue ?

c) **Millicent Bulmer** (...)
= ...; **Thomas Grey** (... – aft.1584)

---

[127] Often refered to as the Bastard of Fauconberg or as Thomas Fauconberg.
[128] For being a participant in Aske's Rebellion.

issue ?
    d) **Dorothy Bulmer** (...)
      = ...; **Ralph Williamson** (...)
      issue ?
    e) **Bridget Bulmer** (...)
      = ...; **... Farley** (...)
      issue ?
    f) **Mary Bulmer** (...)
      = ...; **... Morton** (...)
      issue ?
    g) **Anne Bulmer** (...)
      =1 ...; **Anthony Welbury** (... – 5 Nov 1596 Castle Eden, Durham)
      =2 ca.1598; **Sir Gerard Lowther** (11 Dec 1561 Lowther,
      Westmorland – 14 Oct 1624) son of Sir Richard Lowther & Frances
      Middleton; Kt. 1618
      issue ?
II) **John Conyers** (... – aft.4 Jul 1472)
III) **Anne Conyers** (...)
  = ...; ♦**Richard Lumley, 3ʳᵈ Baron Lumley** (1477–1510)
  Children are listed with other parent
IV) **William Conyers, 1ˢᵗ Baron Conyers** (21 Dec 1468 – 1524) cr.
  Baron 17 Oct 1509; Kt. 1497
  A) **Christopher Conyers, 2ⁿᵈ Baron Conyers** (... – 14 Jun 1538)
    suc. father 1524; Kt. 1523
    = 28 Sep 1514; ♦**Hon. Anne Dacre** (... – 1547/8) daughter of
    Thomas Dacre, 2ⁿᵈ baron Dacre & Elizabeth Greystoke, 6ᵗʰ Baroness
    Greystoke
    1) **John Conyers, 3ʳᵈ Baron Conyers** (... – 30 Jun 1557) suc. father
      1538 and upon his death the barony fell into abeyance among his
      daughters
      = bef.28 Oct 1539; ♦**Lady Maud Clifford** (...) daughter of Henry
      Clifford, 1ˢᵗ Earl of Cumberland & Lady Margaret Percy
      a) **Hon. Elizabeth Conyers** (... – 6 Jun 1572)
        = ...; ♦**Thomas Darcy** (... – 1605)
        Children are listed with other parent
      b) **Hon. Anne Conyers** (...)
        = ...; **Anthony Kempe** (...)
        (I) **Henry Kempe** (...) unm.
      c) **Hon. Katherine Conyers** (...)
        = ...; **John Atherton** (...)
        (I) **... Atherton** (a son) (...)
          = ...; **Anne Byron** (...) daughter of Sir John Byron
          (A) **Anne Atherton** (... – 13 Jul 1644)
            = ...; **Sir William Pennyman, Baronet** (1607 – 22 Aug 1643)
            natural son of William Pennyman; cr. Baron 6 May 1628, but it
            became extinct upon his death

no issue

    d) **Hon. Margaret Conyers** (... – bef.1557) unm.

  2) **Jane Conyers** (1522 – 1558)

    = 1547; ♦**Sir Marmaduke Constable** (...–1575)

    Children are listed with other parent

 B) **Hon. Margaret Conyers** (...)

  = ca.1537; **Sir Richard Cholmley** (ca.1516 – 17 May 1583) son of Sir Roger Cholmley & Katherine Constable;' =2ⁿᵈ ♦Lady Catherine Clifford

  1) **Francis Cholmley** (... – Apr 1586)

    = ...; ♦**Joan Bulmer** (...) daughter of Sir Ralph Bulmer & Anne Tempest

    no issue

  2) **Richard Cholmley** (...)

    = ...

    a) **Marmaduke Cholmley** (...)

b. **Lady Elizabeth Neville** (...)

  = ...; **Sir Richard Strangways** (... – 13 Apr 1488) son of Sir James Strangways & Elizabeth Darcy

  I) **Sir James Strangways** (...)

c. **Lady Joan Neville** (...)

  = ...; **Edward Bechom** (...)

  no issue

8. **Lady Anne Neville** (... – 20 Sep 1480)

=1 1424; ♦**Humphrey Stafford, 1ˢᵗ Duke of Buckingham** (1402 – 1460)

=2 bef.25 Nov 1467; **Walter Blount, 1ˢᵗ Baron Mountjoy** KG (ca.1420 – 1 Aug 1474 London) son of Thomas Blount & Margaret Gresley; =1ˢᵗ Helena Byron; cr. Baron 1465; KG 1472

issue of 1ˢᵗ (none by 2ⁿᵈ):

Children are listed with other parent

9. **Sir Edward Neville, 1ˢᵗ Baron Abergavenny** (bef.1414 – 18 Oct 1476) cr. Baron 5 Sep 1450

=1 bef.18 Oct 1424; **Elizabeth Beauchamp, 3ʳᵈ Baroness Bergavenny** (16 Sep 1415 – 18 Jun 1448) daughter of Richard Beauchamp, 1ˢᵗ Earl of Worcester & Lady Isabel le Despencer; suc. father 18 Mar 1421/2

=2 14 Oct 1448; **Katherine Howard** (... – aft.29 Jun 1478) daughter of Sir Robert Howard & Lady Margaret Mowbray

issue of 1ˢᵗ:

a. **Alice Neville** (aft.1435 Raby Castle – ...)

  = 4 Feb 1460 Raby Castle; **Sir Thomas Grey** (aft.1435 Chillingham Castle, Northumberland – ...) son of Sir Ralph Grey & Elizabeth FitzHugh

  issue ?

b. **Richard Neville** (bef.1439 – bef.1476)

c. **George Neville, 2ⁿᵈ Baron Abergavenny** 4ᵗʰ Baron Bergavenny (ca.1440 – 20 Sep 1492) suc. mother 18 Jun 1448 and father 18 Oct 1476
=1 bef.1469; **Margaret Fenne** (... – 28 Sep 1485) daughter of Hugh Fenne
=2 aft.1485; **Elizabeth ...** (...) =1ˢᵗ Richard Naylor; =2ⁿᵈ Sir Robert Bassett; =3ʳᵈ John Stokker
issue of 1ˢᵗ (none by 2ⁿᵈ):

I) **George Neville, 3ʳᵈ Baron Abergavenny** 5ᵗʰ Baron Bergavenny, KG, KB (ca.1469 – ca.1535) suc. father 20 Sep 1492; KB 1483; KG 1513
=1 bef.1494; **Lady Joan FitzAlan** (...) daughter of Thomas FitzAlan, 17ᵗʰ Earl of Arundel & Margaret Woodville
=2 bef.21 Dec 1495; **Margaret Brent** (... – aft.3 Aug 1516) daughter of William Brent & Anne Rosmoderes
=3 ca.Jun 1519; ◆**Lady Mary Stafford** (...) daughter of Edward Stafford, 3ʳᵈ Duke of Buckingham & Lady Eleanor Percy
issue of 1ˢᵗ:

A) **Lady Elizabeth Neville** (ca.1495 – ...)
= bef.16 Jul 1517; **Henry Daubeney, Earl of Bridgewater** 2ⁿᵈ Baron Daubeney **KB** (Dec 1493 – 12 Apr 1548) son of Giles Daubeney, 1ˢᵗ Baron Daubeney & Elizabeth Arundell; =2ⁿᵈ Lady ◆Katharine Howard; suc. father 22 May 1508; cr. Earl 19 Jul 1538, but all titles became extinct upon his death; KB 1509
no issue

B) **Lady Joan Neville** (...)
= May 1510; ◆**Henry Pole, 1ˢᵗ Baron Montagu** (1492–1539)
Children are listed with other parent
issue of 3ʳᵈ (none by 2ⁿᵈ):

C) **Lady Mary Neville** (... – ca.1576)
=1 1536; ◆**Thomas Fiennes, 9ᵗʰ Baron Dacre** (1516–1541)
=2 ...; **... Wooten** (...)
=3 ...; **Sir Francis Thursby** (...)
issue of 1ˢᵗ (none by others):
Children are listed with other parent

D) **Lady Catherine Neville** (aft.1519 – ...)
= ca.1540; ◆**John St.Leger** (ca.1520–1596)
Children are listed with other parent

E) **Lady Margaret Neville** (...)
= ...; **John Cheney** (...) son of Sir Thomas Cheney
issue ?

F) **Lady Dorothy Neville** (... – 22 Sep 1559 Cobham, Kent)
= bef.1559; **William Brooke, 10ᵗʰ Baron Cobham KG** (1 Nov 1527 – 6 Mar 1596/7) son of George Brooke, 9ᵗʰ Baron Cobham & Anne Bray; =2ⁿᵈ Frances Newton; suc. father Nov 1558; KG 1584

1) **Hon. Frances Brooke** (...)
  =1 ...; **Thomas Coppinger** (...)
  =2 ...; **Edward Becher** (...) son of Henry Becher & Alice Heron
  issue ?
G) **Lady Ursula Neville** (... – 1575)
  = ...; **Sir Warham St.Leger** (ca.1525 – 1597 Cork) son of Sir
Anthony St.Leger & Agnes Warham; =2nd Emmeline Goldwell
1) **Anne St.Leger** (...)
  = ...; **Thomas Digges** (1540 – 1595)
a) **Joan Digges** (...)
  = ...; **Sir John Bayntun** (1460 – 31 Oct 1516) son of Sir Robert
Bayntun & Elizabeth Haute
(I) **Sir Edward Bayntun** (1480 – 27 Nov 1544 France)
  =1 ca.1505; **Elizabeth Sulyard** (...) daughter of Sir John Sulyard
  & Anne Andrews
  =2 ...; **Isabel Leigh** (1510 – 1573) daughter of Ralph Leigh &
  Joyce Culpepper
  issue of 1st:
(A) **Anne Bayntun** (...)
(B) **Jane Bayntun** (...)
(C) **Ursula Bayntun** (...)
(D) **Bridget Bayntun** (...)
  = ...; **Sir james Stumpe** (1519 – 1563)
  issue ?
(E) **Sir Andrew Bayntun** (1515 – 21 Feb 1564)
  =1 ...; **Philippa Brulet** (...) daughter of Gwylliam Brulet
  =2 1550; **Frances Lee** (...)
  issue of 1st:
(1) **Anne Bayntun** (1552 – ...)
(F) **Sir Edward Bayntun** (1517 – 21 Mar 1593)
  =1 ...; ♦**Agnes Rice** (... – 19 Aug 1574) daughter of Rhys ap
  Griffith & Lady Katharin Howard
  =2 ...; **Anne Packington** (... – 1578)
  issue of 1st:
(1) **Sir Henry Bayntun** (1572 – 24 Sep 1616)
  = ...; ♦**Lucy Danvers** (... – 1621) daughter of Sir John
  Danvers & Hon. Elizabeth Neville
(a) **Sir Edward Bayntun** (1593 – 1657)
  =1 ...; **Elizabeth Maynard** (...) daughter of Sir Henry
  Maynard
  =2 ...; **Mary Bowell** (...)
  Has further generations of issue by 1st
(b) **Charles Bayntun** (1594 – ...)
(c) **Elizabeth Bayntun** (1596 – 1648)
  = ...; **John Dutton** (... – 14 Jan 1657) =2nd Anne King
  Has further generations of issue

(G) **Henry Bayntun** (1520 – ...)
= ...; **Dorothy Mantell** (...)
issue ?
issue of 2nd:
(H) **Henry Bayntun** (1536 – ...)
= ...; **Anne Cavendish** (...) daughter of Sir William Cavendish
& Margaret Bostock
issue ?
(I) **Francis Bayntun** (1537 – ...)
(II) **Richard Bayntun** (...)
(III) **John Bayntun** (...)
(IV) **Thomas Bayntun** (...)
(V) **Eleanor Bayntun** (...)
(VI) **Elizabeth Bayntun** (...)
(VII) **Margery Bayntun** (... – 1563)
b) **Sir Dudley Digges** (1583 – 1639)
= ...; **Mary Kempe** (1583 – 1631) daughter of Sir Thomas Digges
issue
H) **Henry Neville, 4th Baron Abergavenny** etc. **KB** (ca.1530 – 10
Feb 1586/7 Birling, Kent) suc. father 1535; KB 1553
=1 bef.31 Jan 1555/6; ♦**Lady Frances Manners** (... – Sep 1576)
daughter of Thomas Manners, 1st Earl of Rutland & Eleanor Paston
=2 bef.1586; **Elizabeth Darrell** (... – aft. Feb 1601/2) daughter of
Stephen Darrell & Philippa Weldon; =2nd Sir William Sedley, 1st
Baronet
issue of 1st (none by 2nd):
1) **Mary Neville, 3rd Baroness le Despencer** (25 Mar 1554 – 28
Jun 1626) suc. upon termination of abeyance 25 May 1604
= 12 Dec 1574; **Sir Thomas Fane** (... – 13 Mar 1588/9) son of
George Fane & Joan Waller; =1st Elizabeth Colepepper; Kt. 1573
a) **Francis Fane, 1st Earl of Westmorland** Baron Burghersh, 4th
Baron le Despencer, **KB** (Feb 1579/80 – 23 Mar 1628) suc. mother
1626; cr. Earl 29 Dec 1624; KB 1603
= 15 Feb 1598/9; **Mary Mildmay** (ca.1582 – 9 Apr 1640) daughter
of Sir Anthony Mildmay & Grace Sherington
(I) **Mildmay Fane, 2nd Earl of Westmorland** etc. **KB** (24 Jan
1601/2 Mereworth, Kent – 12 Feb 1665/6) suc. father 1628; KB
1626
=1 6 Jul 1626; ♦**Grace Thornhurst** (...) daughter of Sir William
Thornhurst & Hon. ... Howard
=2 21 Jun 1638 London; ♦**Hon. Mary de Vere** (1608 the
Netherlands – 15 Nov 1669 Mereworth) daughter of Horatio de
Vere, Baron Vere & Mary Tracy; =1st Sir Roger Townshend, 1st
Baronet
issue of 1st:
(A) **Lady Frances Fane** (...)
539

= ...; ◆**Sir Erasmus Harby, 2nd Baronet** (...) son of Sir Job
Harby, 1st Baronet (...) son of Thomas Harby & Katarine
Throckmorton
issue ?

(B) **Charles Fane, 3rd Earl of Westmorland** etc. (6 Jan
1634/5 – 18 Sep 1691) suc. father 1666
=1 15 Jun 1665; **Elizabeth Nodes** (1 Aug 1648 – ...) daughter
of Charles Nodes
=2 bef. 1691; ◆**Hon. Dorothy Brudenell** (1646 – 26 Jan
1739/40) daughter of Francis, Lord Brudenell & Lady Frances
Savile; =2nd ◆Robert Constable, 3rd Viscount Dunbar
no issue
issue of 2nd:

(C) **Lady Mary Fane** (1639 Mereworth – 16 Oct 1681)
=1 bef.1670; **Francis Palmes** (... – bef.1670) son of Sir Brian
Palmes
=2 24 Jan 17669/70; ◆**John Cecil, 4th Earl of Exeter**
(1628 – 18 Mar 1677/8) son of David Cecil, 3rd Earl of Exeter &
Lady Elizabeth Egerton; =1st ◆Lady Frances Manners
issue ?

(D) **Hon. Mildmay Fane** (1640 Mereworth – bef.1691)

(E) **Vere Fane, 4th Earl of Westmorland**, etc. **KB** (13 Feb
1644 Lamport, Northants. – 29 Dec 1693) suc. brother 1691; KB
1661
= 13 Jul 1671 London; **Rachel Bence** (... – 17 Feb 1710/1)
daughter of John Bence & Judith Andrews

(1) **Lady Rachel Fane** (...)

(2) **Lady Catherine Fane** (... – 1737)
= 1696; **William Paul** (1673 Braywick Berks. – May 1711) son
of James Paul & Martha Duppa

(a) **Catherine Paul** (... – 28 Jun 1753)
= 28 Apr 1724 London; **Sir William Stapleton, 4th
Baronet** (1698 – 12 Jan 1739/40 Bath) son of Sir William
Stapleton, 3rd Baronet & Frances Russell; suc father 6 Dec
1699
Has further generations of issue

(3) **Lady Mary Fane** (1676 – 19 Aug 1910)
= 30 May 1705; **Sir Francis Dashwood, 1st Baronet** (1658
West Wycombe, Bucks. – 4 Nov 1724 London) son of Francis
Dashwood & Alice Sleigh; =1st Mary Jennings; =3rd Mary King;
she =4th ◆Lady Elizabeth Windsor; cr. Baronet 28 Jun 1707

(a) **Rachael Dashwood** (ca.1706 West Wycombe – 16 May
1788)
= 4 Nov 1738 Mereworth; **Sir Robert Austen, 4th
Baronet** (6 Oct 1697 Bexley, Kent – 7 Oct 1743) son of Sir
Robert Austen, 3rd Baronet & Elizabeth Stawel; suc. father

Jul 1706
no issue

(b) **Sir Francis Dashwood, 11ᵗʰ Baron le Despencer**, 2ⁿᵈ
Baronet (Dec 1708 London – 11 Dec 1781) suc. father 1724;
suc. as Baron 1763 up termination of abeyancy
= 19 Dec 1745; **Sarah Gould** (... – 19 Jan 1769) daughter of
George Gould; =1ˢᵗ Sir Richard Ellys, 3ʳᵈ Baronet
no issue

(4) **Vere Fane, 5ᵗʰ Earl of Westmorland** etc. (25 May
1678 – 19 May 1698) unm.; suc. father 1693

(5) **Thomas Fane, 6ᵗʰ Earl of Westmorland** etc. (3 Oct
1681 – 4 Jun 1736) suc. brother 1698
= Jun 1707; **Catherine Stringer** (... – 4 Feb 1729/30)
daughter of Thomas Stringer; =1ˢᵗ Richard Beaumont
no issue

(6) **Lady Elizabeth Fane** (...)

(7) **John Fane, 7ᵗʰ Earl of Westmorland**, etc. (bef.24 Mar
1686/6 – 26 Aug 1762) suc. brother 1736; upon his death the
Barony of le Despencer fell into abeyancy among his sisters
= ...; ♦**Mary Cavendish** (... – 29 Jul 1778) daughter of Lord
Henry Cavendish & Rhoda Cartwright
no issue

(8) **Lady Susan Fane** (...)

(9) **Hon. Mildmay Fane** (1689 – 1715) unm.

(F) **Lady Rachel Fane** (ca.1646 Mereworth – ...)

(G) **Lady Catherine Fane** (15 Feb 1649 Mereworth – ...)

(H) **Lady Susan Fane** (21 Feb 1651 Mereworth – ...)

(I) **Lady Elizabeth Fane** (ca.1653 Mereworth – ...)

(II) **Hon. Sir Francis Fane** (... – ca.1681)
= ...; **Elizabeth West** (... – Jul 1669) daughter of William West;
she =1ˢᵗ ♦John Darcy, 4ᵗʰ Baron Darcy

(A) **Sir Francis Fane KB** (... – bef.Sep 1691)
= 16 Feb 1663/4; **Hannah Rushworth** (...) daughter of John
Rushworth

(1) **George Fane** (Jan 1666 – ...)

(2) **Henry Fane** (1669 – 19 Dec 1726)
= ...; **Anne Scrope** (... – 1720) daughter of Thomas Scrope

(a) **Francis Fane** (ca.1698 – 28 May 1757) unm.

(b) **Thomas Fane, 8ᵗʰ Earl of Westmorland**, etc. (8 Mar
1700/1 – 12 Nov 1771) suc. distant cousin 1762
= 8 Aug 1727; **Elizabeth Swymmer** (Aug 1708 – 17 Nov
1782) daughter of William Swymmer; =1ˢᵗ Samuel Kentish
Has further generations of issue

(c) **Henry Fane** (1703 – 31 May 1777)
=1 17 Jul 1735; **Charlotte Rowe** (... – 29 Sep 1739)
daughter of Nicholas Rowe

=2 20 May 1742; **Anne Wynn** (... – 1744) daughter of Rev. John Wynn & Anne Pugh

=3 Sep 1748; **Charlotte Luther** (... – Apr 1758)

Has further generations of issue by all three

  (3) **Sir Francis Fane** (... – 19 Dec 1726)

  (4) **Edward Fane** (... – 6 Feb 1736)

(III) **Lady Mary Fane** (3 Aug 1606 Mereworth – ca.1634)

= aft.18 May 1625; **Dutton Gerard, 3ʳᵈ Baron Gerard** (4 Mar 1613 – 22 Apr 1640) son of Gilbert Gerard, 2ⁿᵈ Baron Gerard & Eleanor Dutton; =2ⁿᵈ Lady Elizabeth O'Brien; suc. father 1622

  (A) **Hon. Mary Gerard** (...)

  = ...; ♦**Sir Anthony Cope, 4ᵗʰ Baronet** (16 Nov 1632 – 11 Jun 1675) son of Sir John Cope, 3ʳᵈ Baronet & Lady Elizabeth Fane

  issue ?

  (B) **Charles Gerard, 4ᵗʰ Baron Gerard** (ca.1634 – 28 Dec 1667 London) suc. father 1640

  = 28 Nov 1660; **Jane Digby** (ca.1637 – Nov 1703) daughter of George Digby & Mary Chetwynd; =2ⁿᵈ Sir Edward Hungerford

    (1) **Digby Gerard, 5ᵗʰ Baron Gerard** (17 Jul 1662 – 10 Oct 1684 London) died in a drinking match; suc. father 1667

    = 3 Sep 1678; **Lady Elizabeth Gerard** (ca.1659 – 11 Jan 1699/1700) daughter of Charles Gerard, 1ˢᵗ Earl of Macclesfield & Jeanne de Civelle

      (a) **Hon. Elizabeth Gerard** (ca.1680 – 13 Feb 1743/4 London)

      =1698; ♦**James Hamilton, 4ᵗʰ Duke of Hamilton** (1658–1712)

      Children are listed with other parent

(IV) **Lady Catherine Fane** (... – 27 Aug 1649)

= ...; ♦**Conyers Darcy, 2ⁿᵈ Earl of Holderness** etc. (bef.3 Mar 1621/2 – 13 Dec 1692) son of Conyers Darcy, 1ˢᵗ Earl of Holderness & Grace Rokeby; =2ⁿᵈ ♦Lady Frances Howard; =3ʳᵈ ♦Lady Frances Seymour; =4ᵗʰ Elizabeth Freschville; suc. father 1 Nov 1680

no issue

(V) **Hon. George Fane** (...)

= ...

  (A) **Sir Henry Fane** (... – Jan 1705/6)

  = ...; **Elizabeth Southcote** (1640 – ...) daughter of Thomas Southcote

    (1) **Charles Fane, 1ˢᵗ Viscount Fane** (bef.30 Jan 1675/6 – 7 Jul 1744) cr. Viscount 1718

    = 12 Dec 1707; ♦**Mary Stanhope** (...) daughter of Hon. Alexander Stahope & Catherine Burghill

      (a) **Hon. Dorothy Fane** (... – 17 Jul 1797)

      = 1741; ♦**John Montagu, 4ᵗʰ Earl of Sandwich** (1718–

1792)
Children are listed with other parent

(b) **Charles Fane, 2ⁿᵈ Viscount Fane** (ca.1708 – 24 Jan 1766) suc. father 1744, but his titles became extinct upon his death
= 7 Jun 1749; **Susanna Marriott** (1706 – 10 Apr 1792) daughter of John Marriott; =1ˢᵗ Sir William Juxon, 2ⁿᵈ Baronet
no issue

(c) **Hon. Mary Fane** (1710 – 31 Mar 1785)
= 7 Jan 1734/5; **Jerome de Salis, Count de Salis**[129] (8 Jul 1709 – Aug 1794) son of Peter de Salis, Count de Salis & Margaretha de Salis-Soglio
Has further generations of issue

(VI) **Lady Elizabeth Fane** (...)
=1 ...; ♦**Sir John Cope, 3ʳᵈ Baronet** (...)
=2 ...; **William Cope** (...)
issue of 1ˢᵗ (none by 2ⁿᵈ):
Children are listed with other parent

(VII) **Hon. Anthony Fane** (1613 – 1643)
= ...; **Anabel Benn** (3 Sep 1607 – 17 Aug 1698) daughter of Sir Anthony Benn; =2ⁿᵈ ♦Henry Grey, 10ᵗʰ Earl of Kent
(A) **Anthony Fane** (...)
(B) **Jane Fane** (...

(VIII) **Lady Rachael Fane** (28 Jan 1612/3 Mereworth – 11 Nov 1680 London)
=1 18 Dec 1638 London; ♦**Henry Bourchier, 5ᵗʰ Earl of Bath** (ca.1587 – 16 Aug 1654) son of Hon. Sir George Bourchier & Martha Howard; suc. cousin 2 Mar 1636/7
=2 1 May 1655 London; **Lionel Cranfield, 3ʳᵈ Earl of Middlesex** Baron Cranfield (1625 – 26 Oct 1674) son of Lionel Cranfield, 1ˢᵗ Earl of Middlesex & Anne Brett; suc. brother 16 Sep 1651
no issue

II) **John Neville** (...)
III) **William Neville** (...)
IV) **Sir Edward Neville, Kt.** (1471 – 8 Dec 1538 Tower of London) executed; Kt. 1513
= bef.6 Apr 1529; **Eleanor Windsor** (1479 – 25 Mar 1531) daughter of Andrew Windsor, 1ˢᵗ Baron Windsor & Elizabeth Blount
A) **Edward Neville, 5ᵗʰ Baron Abergavenny** (... – 10 Feb 1588/9)

---

[129] Naturalized british Subjecrt 1730. Count of the Holy Roman Empire.

suc. cousin 1587

=1 bef.1550; **Katherine Brome** (...) daughter of Sir John Brome & Margaret Rowse

=2 bef.1588; **Grisold Hughes** (... – 15 Jun 1613) daughter of Thomas Hughes & Elizabeth Dwnn; =2nd Francis Clifford, 4th Earl of Cumberland

issue of 1st (none by 2nd):

1) **Edward Neville, 6th Baron Abergavenny** (ca.1550 – 1 Dec 1622) suc. father 1589

= bef.1580; **Rachel Lennard** (... – ca.Oct 1616) daughter of John Lennard & Elizabeth Harman

  a) **Henry Neville, 7th Baron Abergavenny** (bef.1580 – Dec 1641) suc. father 1622

  =1 bef.1601; ◆**Lady Mary Sackville** (...) daughter of Thomas Sackville, 1st Earl of Dorset & Cecily Baker

  =2 bef.1616; ◆**Catherine Vaux** (aft.1592 – 7 Jul 1649) daughter of Hon. Vaux & Hon. Elizabeth Roper

  issue of 1st:

  (I) **Hon. Cecily Neville** (ca.1604 Birling, Kent – aft.1652)

  = 12 Jul 1617 London; **FitzWilliam Coningsby** (ca.1589 Hampton Court, Hereford – bef.23 Aug 1666) son of Sir Thomas Coningsby & Philippa FitzWilliam

    (A) **Cecilia** FitzWilliam **Coningsby** (1621 – 7 Oct 1689 Hereford)

    = 23 May 1654 London; **David Hyde** (...)

    (1) **Cecilia Hyde** (...)

      = 1676; **Richard Norbury** (...)

      issue ?

    (B) **Philippa Coningsby** (bef.24 Apr 1621 Docklow, Herefords – 1663) unm.

    (C) **Humphrey Coningsby** (bef.22 Sep 1622 Hampton Court – aft.1692)

    = ...; **Lettice Loftus** (... – aft.1674) daughter of Arthur Loftus

    (1) **Elizabeth** Philippa **Coningsby** (...)

    = 21 Oct 1680 London; **Michael Browne** (...)

    (a) **Elizabeth** Barbara **Browne** (... – bef.31 Jan 1763)

    = 15 Jan 1729/30 Bodenham, Herefords.; **George Coningsby** (aft.1686 – 15 Mar 1766) son of Thomas Coningsby & Chrysogen Emes

    no issue

    (2) **Thomas Coningsby, 1st Earl of Coningsby** Baron Coningsby (2 Nov 1656 Hampton Court – 1 May 1729 Hampton Court) cr. Baron 1693 and Earl 1719 with special remainder to youngest daughter

    =1 18 Feb 1674/5 Coningsby, Lincs.; **Barbara Georges** (ca.1657 Eve, Herefords. – bef.4 Nov 1697)

=2 23 Apr 1688; ♦**Lady Frances Jones** (1674 – 19 Feb 1714/5 Hampton Court) daughter of Richard Jones, Earl of Ranelagh & Hon. Elizabeth Willoughby
issue of 1st:
(a) **Lady Meliora Coningsby** (6 Sep 1675 London – 1735)
=1694; ♦**Thomas Southwell, 1st Baron Southwell** (1665–1720)
Children are listed with other parent
(b) **Lady Barbara Coningsby** (15 Apr 1677 Hampton Court

...)
= 8 Apr 1708 Galway; **George Eyre** (1680 – 1710) son of John Eyre & Margery Preston
Has further generations of issue
(c) **Lady Philippa Coningsby** (16 Apr 1708 Hope under Dinmore, Hereforsds. – ...)
(d) **Lady C. Coningsby**[130] (13 Apr 1679 – ...)
(e) **Thomas, Lord Coningsby** (bef.22 Apr 1679 Hope under Dinmore – bef.1717)
= ...; **... Carr** (...)
no surviving issue
(f) **Lady Letitia Coningsby** (bef.7 Apr 1680 – ...)
= 1700; **Edward Denny** (... – 1728) son of Edward Denny & Mary Maynard
Has further generations of issue
(g) **Hon. Humphrey Coningsby** (bef.16 Feb 1681/2 Bodenham – Oct 1697 London) unm.
(h) **Hon. Ferdinando Coningsby** (bef.16 May 1683 Bodenham – ca.1717)
(i) **Lady Mary Coningsby** (bef.14 Sep 1684 – ...)
= 24 Jun 1712 Hope under Dinmore; **Rev. ... Hathway** (...)
Has further generations of issue
(j) **Hon. William Coningsby** (bef.16 Nov 1695 – ...)
issue of 2nd:
(k) **Lady Frances Coningsby** (15 Jan 1707/8 Hampton Court – 31 Dec 1781)
= Jul 1732; **Sir Charles Hanbury-Williams** (8 Dec 1708 Coldbrook, Monmouths. – 2 Nov 1759) son of John Hanbury & Bridget Ayscough
Has further generations of issue

---

[130] Only referred to as C in Family Bible. With no further records, he/she likely died young.

(l) **Margaret Coningsby, 2ⁿᵈ Countess of Coningsby** etc (ca.1709 Hampton Court – bef.24 Jun 1761 London) suc. father by special remainder 1729

= 14 Apr 1730 London; **Sir Michael Newton KB, 4ᵗʰ Baronet** (... – 6 Apr 1743 London) son of Sir John Newton, 3ʳᵈ Baronet & Susanna Wharton; suc. father 12 Feb 1733/4

no surviving issue

(D) **Thomas Coningsby** (17 Apr 1628 – Masr 1682)

= ...

(1) **Philippa Coningsby** (...)

= 1713 Middleton, co Cork; **James Atkin** (...)

issue ?

(2) **Cecilia Coningsby** (...)

= 9 Dec 1691 Dublin; **Henry Owens** (...)

issue ?

(3) **Thomas Coningsby** (1671 Neen Solers, Salop – 9 Nov 1711) unm.

(4) **Ursula Coningsby** (bef.Mar 1674/5 Bayton, Worcs. – ...)

= 4 Dec 1703 Middleton; **Barry Maynard** (...) son of Sir Boyle Maynard

issue ?

(5) **Elizabeth Coningsby** (bef.1680 – 4 Nov 1715 Midldeton)

= 10 Dec 1699 Middleton; **Walter Atkin** (...)

(a) **John** Thomas **Atkin** (26 Feb 1700/1 – ...)

(b) **Mary Atkin** (Oct 1702 – ...)

(c) **Coningsby Atkin** (8 May 1705 – ...)

(d) **Catherine Atkin** (1706 – ...)

(e) **Barbara Atkin** (1708 – ...)

(f) **Walter Atkin** (7 Jul 1710 – ...)

(g) **Elizabeth Atkin** (1712 – ...)

(h) **William Atkin** (22 Feb 1713/4 – ...)

(E) **Henry Coningsby** (bef.21 Jun 1929 – aft.1692) unm.

(II) **Hon. Sir Thomas Neville KB** (... – May 1628)

= ...; ♦**Hon. Frances Mordaunt** (...) daughter of Henry Mordaunt, 4ᵗʰ Baron Mordaunt & Hon. Margaret Compton

(A) **Margaret Neville** (...)

= ...; **Thomas Brooke** (ca.1614 – aft.1663)

(1) (a son) **Brooke** (...)

= ...

(a) **Basil Brooke** (ca.1659 – ...)

(B) **Charles Neville** (... – 1637) unm.

(C) **Henry Neville** (... – 1639) unm.

(III) **Hon. Anne Neville** (...) a nun

(IV) **Hon. Mary Neville** (...) unm.

issue of 2ⁿᵈ:

(V) **John Neville, 8ᵗʰ Baron Abergavenny** (ca.1614 – 23 Oct

1662) suc. father 1641

= ...; **Elizabeth Chamberlaine** (... – ca.1691) daughter of John Chamberlaine & Katarine Plowden

no issue

(VI) **George Neville, 9th Abergavenny** (aft.1614 – 2 Jun 1666) suc. brother 1662

= ...; **Mary Gifford** (... – Nov 1669) daughter of Thomas Gifford & Anne Brooksby; =2nd Sir Charles Shelley, 2nd Baronet

(A) **Hon. Bridget Neville** (...)

= ...; **Sir John Shelley, 3rd Baronet** (... – 25 Apr 1703) son of Sir Charles Shelley, 2nd Baronet & Elizabeth Weston; =2nd Mary Gage; suc. father 1681

(1) **Frances Shelley** (ca.1672 – 15 Nov 1771)

= 1704; ◆**Richard Fitzwilliam, 5th Viscount FitzWilliam** (...)

Children are listed with other parent

(B) **George Neville, 10th Baron Abergavenny** (21 Apr 1665 – 26 Mar 1695) suc. father 1666

= ...; ◆**Hon. Honora Belasyse** (... – 1 Jan 1706/7) daughter of John Belasyse, 1st Baron Barlasyse & Lady Anne Paulet

no issue

(VII) **Hon. Frances Neville** (...) unm.

(VIII) **Hon. Catherine Neville** (...)

=1 ...; ◆**Hon. Sir Robert Howard** (...) son of Theophilius Howard, 2nd Earl of Suffolk & Lady Elizabeth Home

=2 ...; **Robert Berry** (...)

no issue

(IX) **Hon. Elizabeth Neville** (ca,1641 – ...)

= 1651; **Thomas Stonor** (1626 – 1683) son of Sir William Stonor & Elizabeth Lake

(A) **John Stonor** (22 Mar 1655/6 – 1687)

= 8 Jul 1675; ◆**Lady Mary Talbot** (...) daughter of Francis Talbot, 11th Earl of Shrewsbury & Anne Conyers

(1) **Thomas Stonor** (20 Jun 1677 – 10 Aug 1724)

=1 16 Mar 1696; ◆**Hon. Isabel Belasyse** (...) daughter of John Belasyse, 1st Baron Belasyse & Lady Anne Paulet

=2 14 Jul 1705; ◆**Hon. Winifred Roper** (...) daughter of Christopher Roper, 5th Baron Teynham & Hon. Elizabeth Browne

issue of 2nd:

(a) **Winifrede Stonor** (... – 3 Feb 1739)

= 1724; ◆**Philip Howard** (1688–1750)

Children are listed with other parent

(b) **Thomas Stonor** (18 Apr 1710 – 2 Feb 1772)

= 19 Apr 1732; ◆**Mary Biddulph** (1710 – 14 Jun 1778) daughter of John Biddulph & Mary Arundell

Has further generations of issue
(2) **John** Talbot **Stonor, Baron de Lard** (1678 – 1756) a priest, cr. Baron in France
(3) **Charles Stonor** (... – 1705)
(4) **Mary Stonor** (...)
= ...; **William Plowden** (1666 – 5 Mar 1740/1) son of Edmund Plowden & Penelope Drummond; =1st Mary Morley; and =3rd ♦Mary Lyttleton
  (a) **William Plowden** (... – 27 Aug 1754)
  = 1726; ♦**Hon. Frances Dormer** (...) daughter of Charles Dormer, 5th Baron Dormer & Elizabeth Biddulph
  Has further generations of issue
(5) **Anne Stonor** (... – Apr 1714)
= ...; **Charles Bodenham** (...) son of John Bodenham
  (a) **Charles** Stonor **Bodenham** (... – 1764)
  = ...
  Has further generations of issue
  (b) **Catherine Bodenham** (...)
  = ...; **John Berkeley** (...) son of Thomas Berkeley & Mary Davis; =2nd Jane Compton
  Has further generations of issue
b) **Hon. Sir Christopher Neville KB** (... – 1649)
= ...; **Mary d'Arcy** (...) daughter of Thomas d'Arcy & Camilla Guiccoardini
(I) **Richard Neville** (... – ca.1643)
  = ...; **Sophia Carew** (...) daughter of Sir George Carew
  (A) **George Neville** (... – 1665)
  = ...; **Mary Whitelock** (...) dasughter of Sir Bulstrode Whitelock
    (1) **George Neville, 11th Baron Abergavenny** (ca.1659 – 11 Mar 1720/1) suc. distant cousin 1695
    22 Oct 1698 London; **Anne Walker** (... – 26 Jun 1748 Balderwood Lodge, Hants.) daughter of Nehemiah Walker; =2 ♦John West, 1st Earl De La Warr
      (a) **George Neville, 12th Baron Abergavenny** (16 May 1702 – 15 Nov 1723 London) suc. father 1721
      = 21 Feb 1722/3 London; **Elizabeth Thornicroft** (ca. 1693 – 4 Mar 1778) daughter of Edward Thornicroft & Mary Delaune; =2nd Alured Pinke
      no issue
      (b) **Hon. Jane Neville** (8 Mar 1703 – 17 Mar 1786)
      = 27 Jan 1729 Godalming, Surrey; **Abel Walter** (ca.1701 Barbados – Oct 1767 Bath) son of John Walter & Lucy Alleyne
      Has further generations of issue
      (c) **Edward Neville, 13th Baron Abergavenny** (ca.1705 –

9 Oct 1724 London) suc. brother 1723

= 6 May 1724 London; **Katherine Tatton** (... – 4 Dec 1729) daughter of William Tatton; =2nd William Neville, 14th Baron Abergavenny

no issue

  (d) **Hon. Ann Neville** (ca.1715 – Mar 1736/7) unm.

  (2) **Edward Neville** (... – 12 Sep 1701)

= ...; **Hannah Thorp** (...) daughter of Jervoise Thorp

  (a) **William Neville, 14th Baron Abergavenny** (... – 21 Sep 1744 Bath) suc. cousin 1724

=1 20 May 1725; **Katherine Tatton** (... – 4 Dec 1729) daughter of William Tatton; =1st Edward Neville, 14th Baron Abergavenny

=2 20 May 1732; ♦**Lady Rebecca Herbert** (... – 20 Oct 1758) daughter of Thomas Herbert, 8th Earl of Pembrike & Margaret Sawyer

Has further generations of issue by both

  (b) **Mary Neville** (...)

= ...; **Charles** Chamberlain **Rebow** (...)

issue ?

 (II) **Anne Neville** (ca.1611 – 22 Aug 1660)

= 17 Dec 1628; **John Lucas, 1st Baron Lucas of Sheffield** (23 Oct 1606 – 2 Jul 1671) son of Sir Thomas Lucas & Elizabeth Leighton

  (A) **Mary Lucas, 1st Baroness Lucas of Crudwell** (... – 1 Nov 1700) cr. Baroness 7 May 1663

= 1663; ♦**Anthony Grey, 11th Earl of Kent** (1645–...)

Children are listed with other parent

c) **Hon. Edward Neville** (...) unm.

d) **Hon. Elizabeth Neville** (...)

=1 ...; **Sir John Grey** (...)

=2 ...; **Sir John Bingley** (...)

issue ?

e) **Hon. Mary Neville** (... – Jul 1648)

= bef.1608; ♦**George Goring, 1st Earl of Norwich** (1585–1663)

Children are listed with other parent

f) **Hon. Catherine Neville** (...)

= ...; **Sir Stephen Lessour** (...)

issue ?

g) **Hon. Frances Neville** (...) unm.

h) **Hon. Margaret Meville** (...) unm.

2) **Hon. Grisel Neville** (1561 – ...)

= ...; **Sir Henry Poole** (ca.1564 Chilworth, Wilts. – 1632) son of Edward Poole & Margaret Walton; =2nd Anne Bernard

a) **Neville Poole** (ca.1587 Oaksey, Wilts. – 1661)

= ...; **Frances Poole** (ca.1587 Sapperton, Glos. – 1657) daughter of

Sir Henry Poole
(I) **Edward** Neville **Poole** (1617 Oaksey – 1673)
= ...; **Dorothy Pye** (ca.1617 – 1687)
(A) **Grissel** Neville **Poole** (1630 Oaksey – 25 Feb 1677 Kemble, Wilts.)
(B) **Robert** Neville **Poole** (1644 Oaksey – ...)
(C) **Walton** Neville **Poole** (1645 Oaksey – ...)
(D) **Neville Poole** (1646 Oaksey – 1677)
= ...; **Elizabeth Bard** (ca.1646 – 1716)
(1) **Henry Poole** (ca.1673 Oaksey – 1726)
= ...; **Elizabeth Earl** (1673 Crudwell, Wilts. – 1743)
(a) **Finetta Poole** (bef.1700 Kemble – 27 Feb 1737/8)
= 1714; **Benjamin Bathurst** (1693 – 5 Nov 1767) son of Sir Benjamin Bathurst & Frances Apsley; =2nd Catherine Brodrick
Has further generations of issue
(b) (a son) **Poole** (...)
= ...
Has further generations of issue
(II) **Giles Poole** (ca.1621 – ...)
3) **Hon. Francis Neville** (bef.1589 – ...)
= ...; **Mary Lewkenor** (...) daughter of Thomas Lewkenor
issue ?
4) **Hon. George Neville** (...) unm.
5) **Hon. Henry Neville** (...)
= ...; **Eleanor Poole** (1567 Chilworth – ...) daughter of Edward Poole & Margaret Walton
a) **Catherine Neville** (ca.1603 – ...)
b) **Edward Neville** (1604 – 1622) unm.
c) **Henry Neville** (ca.1604 – ...)
d) **Frances Neville** (ca.1605 – ...)
e) **Thomas Neville** (ca.1606 – ...)
f) **William Neville** (ca.1610 – ...)
g) **George Neville** (ca.1612 – ...)
6) **Hon. Margaret Neville** (...)
= ...; **Sir Nicholas Lewkenor** (...)
issue ?
7) **Hon. Mary Neville** (...)
= ...; **Edward Blount** (...)
issue ?
B) **Sir Henry Neville** (... – 1593)
=1 ...; **Elizabeth Gresham** (...) daughter of Sir John Gresham
=2 **Elizabeth Bacon** (...) daughter of Sir Nicholas Bacon & Jane Fernley; =1st Sir Robert D'Oyly
issue of 1st (none by 2nd):
1) **Catherine Neville** (...)

= ...; **Edmond D'Oyly** (... – 1612) son of Henry D'Oyly & Anne Whyte

a) **Sir Henry D'Oyly** (...)

= ...; **Susan Talmache** (...) daughter of Sir Lionel Talmache

(I) **Edmond D'Oyly** (... – 28 Sep 1638)

= ...; **Bridget Coke** (... – Oct 1700) daughter of John Coke; =2nd Sir Isaac Astley, Baronet

(A) **Susan D'Oyly** (... – 1648) unm.

b) **William D'Oyly** (... – 1637)

= ...; **Elizabeth Stocks** (...) daughter of Ven. Richard Stocks & Anne Wodehouse

(I) **Sir William D'Oyly, 1st Baronet** (... – Nov 1677) cr. Baronet 29 Jul 1663

= 1637; **Margaret Randall** (... – May 1679)

(A) **Margaret D'Oyly** (...)

= ...; **Robert Suckling** (...) son of Charles Suckling & Mary Drury

(1) **Horatio Suckling** (ca.1665 – ...)

(2) **William Suckling** (ca.1668 – ...)

(B) **Sir William D'Oyly, 2nd Baronet** (ca.1637 – 1680) suc. father 1677

= 1666; **Mary Hadley** (...) daughter of John Hadley & Anne Hadley

(1) **Sir Edmund D'Oyly, 3rd Baronet** (ca.1666 – 1700) suc. father 1680

= 3 Nov 1684; **Dorothy Bedingfeld** (... – Dec 1718) daughter of Philip Bedingfeld & Ursula Potts

(a) **Sir Edmund D'Oyly, 4th Baronet** (... – 1763) suc. father 1700; unm.

(b) **William D'Oyly** (... – 1737) unm.

(2) **Hadley D'Oyly** (...)

= ...; **Elizabeth Yallop** (...) daughter of Charles Yallop

(a) **Rev. Sir Hadley D'Oyly, 5th Baronet** (... – 30 Jul 1764) suc. cousin 1763

= ...; **Henrietta** Maynard **Osborne** (... – Aug 1793) daughter
of Rev. Henry Osborne

Has further generations of issue

(b) **Thomas D'Oyly** (...)

= ...

Has further generations of issue

2) **Sir Henry Neville** (ca.1564 – 10 Jul 1615)

= ...; **Anne Killigrew** (...) daughter of Sir Henry Killigrew & Catherine Cooke; =2nd George Carleton

a) **Mary Neville** (aft/1586 – Oct 1642)

= 1610; **Sir Edward Lewknor** (4 Jan 1587 – 1 Mar 1618) son of

Sir Edward Lewknor & Susan Heigham
(I) **Anne Lewknor** (1612 – 15 Jul 1663)
= 1630; ♦**Sir Nicholas le Strange, 1ˢᵗ Baronet** (1604–1655)
Children are listed with other parent
(II) **Sir Edward Lewknor** (bef.11 feb 1614/5 – ...)
= 1633; **Elizabeth Russell** (...) daughter of Sir William Russell,
1ˢᵗ Baronet & Elizabeth Gerard
(A) **Mary Lewknor** (... – 1673)
= bef.13 Apr 1659; ♦**Horatio Townshend, 1ˢᵗ Viscount
Townshend** etc. (bef.16 Dec 1630 – 7 Dec 1687) son of Sir
Roger Townshend, 1ˢᵗ Baronet & Hon. Mary de Vere; =2ⁿᵈ Mary
Ashe; suc. brother 1648; cr. Viscount 1682
no issue
(III) **Susan Lewknor** (bef.21 Feb 1615/6 – ...)
(IV) **Katherine Lewknor** (11 May 1617 – ...)
= ...; **James Calthorpe** (...)
issue ?
b) **Elizabeth Neville** (ca.1588 – 1656)
=1 ...; **William Glover** (...)
=2 ca.1608; **Sir Henry Berkeley** (1579 – 1667) son of Sir Henry
Berkeley
=3 ...; **Thomas Dyke** (...)
issue of 2ⁿᵈ:
(I) **Dorothy Berkeley** (... – Nov 1668)
= ...; **Sir Francis Godolphin** (25 Dec 1605 – 22 Mar 1667) son
of Sir William Godolphin & Thomasin Sidney
(A) **Elizabeth Godolphin** (bef.8 Feb 1636 Breage, Cornwall –
1707)
= 1650; **Sir Arthur Northcote, 2ⁿᵈ Baronet** (bef. 25 Mar
1628 – 1688) son of Sir John Northcote, 1ˢᵗ Baronet & Grace
Halswell; =1ˢᵗ Elizabeth Welsh; suc. father Jun 1676
(1) **Sir Francis Northcote, 3ʳᵈ Baronet** (... – 1709) suc.
father 1688
= 26 Jul 1688; ♦**Anne Wrey** (...) daughter of Sir Chichester
Wrey, 3ʳᵈ Baronet & Lady Anne Bourchier
no issue
(2) **Sir Henry Northcote, 4ᵗʰ Baronet** (1655 – Feb 1729/30)
suc. brother 1709
= ...; **Penelope Lovett** (...) daughter of Edward Lovett
(a) **Sir Henry Northcote, 5ᵗʰ Baronet** (1710 – May 1743)
suc. father 1730
= 16 Aug 1732; **Bridget** Maria **Stafford** (21 Jan 1711/2 – 15
Aug 1773) daughter of Hugh Stafford; =2ⁿᵈ Richard Madan
Has further generations of issue
(b) **Elizabeth Northcote** (... – ca.1758)
=1 1734; **John Incledon** (... – 28 Jun 1746)

=2 aft.1746; **Rev. John Wright** (...)
issue ?
(3) **Charles Northcote** (...)
= ...; **Sarah Northcote** (...) daughter of John Northcote
(a) **Arthur Northcote** (...)
(b) **Charles Northcote** (...)
(4) **Elizabeth Northcote** (...) unm.
(5) **Dorothy Northcote** (...)
= 1685; **Andrew Quick** (...)
issue ?
(6) **Penelope Northcote** (...)
= ...; **John Hesket** (...)
issue ?
(B) **Dorothea Godolphin** (bef.16 Dec 1637 Breage – ...)
(C) **Sir William Godolphin, Baronet** (... – 17 Aug 1710) cr.
Baronet 29 Apr 1661 but it became extinct upon his death; unm.
(D) **Francis Godolphin** (... – 1675)
(E) **Sidney Godolphin, 1ˢᵗ Earl of Godolphin** Viscount
Rialton **KG** (bef.15 Jun 1645 Breage – 15 Sep 1712 St.Albans,
Herts.) cr.Earl Dec 1706; KG 1704
= 16 May 1675 London; **Margaret Blagge** (... – 9 Sep 1678)
daughter of Thomas Blagge
(1) **Francis Godolphin, 2ⁿᵈ Earl of Godolphin** etc. 1ˢᵗ
Baron Godolphin (3 Sep 1678 – 17 Jan 1766) suc. father 1712;
cr. Baron 1645 with special remainder to heirs whatsoever
= 23 Apr 1698; **Henrietta Churchill, 2ⁿᵈ Duchess of
Marlborough** Marchioness of Blanford, Countess of
Marlborough, Baroness Churchill (19 Jul 1681 – 24 Oct 1733)
daughter of John Churchill, 1ˢᵗ Duke of Marlborough & Saran
Jenyns; suc. father 9 Aug 1722
(a) **William, Marquess of Blandford** (ca.1700 – 24 Aug
1731 Oxford)
= 25 Apr 1729; **Maria Catherina Haeck de Jong** (12 Sep
1695 Utrecht, Netherlands – 7 Sep 1779 Mortlake, Surrey)
daughter of Peter Haeck de Jong & Anna Maria van Weede;
she =2ⁿᵈ Sir William Wyndham, 3ʳᵈ Baronet
no issue
(b) **Lady Henrietta Godolphin** (1701 – 17 Jul 1776)
= 2 Apr 1717; ♦**Thomas Pelham-Holles, 1ˢᵗ Duke of
Newcastle-upnder-Lyne** etc. (1 Jul 1693 – 17 Nov 1768)
son of Thomas Pelham, 1ˢᵗ Baron Pelham & Lady Grace
Holles; cr. Duke 17 Nov 1756
no issue
(c) **Lord Harry Godolphin** (...)
(d) **Lady Margaret Godolphin** (...)
(e) **Lady Mary Godolphin** (1705 – 3 Aug 1764)

= 1740; ♦**Thomas Osborne, 4ᵗʰ Duke of Leeds** (1713–1789)

Children are listed with other parent

(F) **Rev. Henry Godolphin** (15 Aug 1648 Breage – 29 Jan 1732/3 Windsor)

= ...; **Mary Godolphin** (...) daughter of Sidney Godolphin

(1) **Mary Godolphin** (...)

= ...; **William Owen** (ca.1688 – 14 Feb 1767) son of Sir Robert Owen & Margaret Wyn

(a) **Francis Owen** (... – 1774) unm.

(b) **Robert** Godolphin **Owen** (ca.1733 – 1792) unm.

(c) **Margaret Owen** (Jan 1738 – 2 Mar 1806)

= 1777; **Owen Ormsby** (...) son of Willliam Ormsby & Hannah Wynne

Has further generations of issue

(2) **Francis Godolphin, 2ⁿᵈ Baron Godolphin** (ca.1700 – 25 May 1785) suc. cousin 1712, but tityle became extinct upon his death

= 18 Feb 1733/4; ♦**Lady Barbara Bentinck** (... – 1 Apr 1736) daughter of Hans William Bentinck, 1ˢᵗ Earl of Portland & June Temple

no issue

(G) **Catheryn Godolphin** (bef.13 Jul 1655 Breage – ...)

(H) **Anne Godolphin** (bef.30 May 1657 Breage – ...)

(II) **Maurice Berkeley** (... – 1674) unm.

(III) **Frances Berkeley** (...)

= ...; **Peter Roynon** (...)

issue ?

(IV) **Janel Berkeley** (...)

c) **Sir Henry Neville** (10 Mar 1588 Mayfield, Sussex – 29 Jun 1629 Berkshire)

= 2 May 1609; **Elizabeth Smythe** (... – 1669) daughter of Sir John Smythe & Elizabeth Fineux; =2ⁿᵈ Sir John Thoroughgood; she =3ʳᵈ William Herbert

(I) **Katherine Neville** (...)

= ...; **Sir Thomas Lumsford** (...)

issue ?

(II) **Mary Neville** (...)

= ...; **... Borell** (...)

issue ?

(III) **Philippa Neville** (...)

= ...; **John Jephson** (...) son of Sir John Jephson & Elizabeth Norris; =1ˢᵗ ♦Bridget Boyle

no issue

(IV) **Richard Neville** (30 May 1615 – 1676)

= bef.1646; **Anne Heydon** (... – 1678) daughter of Sir John

Heydon
(A) **Anne Neville** (14 Feb 1647 – 1700)
   = ...; **Richard Raynsford** (... – 17 Mar 1702/3) son of Sir
   Richard Raynsford & Catherine Clerke
   (1) **Ann Raynsford** (... – 1707)
      = 1684; ♦**James Griffin, 2nd Baron Griffin** (1667–1715)
      Children are listed with other parent
(B) **Mirabell Neville** (...)
(C) **John Neville** (123 Jul 1652 – Dec 1678) unm.
(D) **Richard Neville** (12 Oct 1655 – 1 Jul 1723)
   = ...; **Hon. Katheirne Grey** (...) daughter of Ralph Grey, 2nd
   Baron Grey & Catherine Ford
   (1) **Catherine Neville** (...)
      = ...; **Richard Aldworth** (...)
      issue ?
   (2) **Grey Neville** (23 Sep 1681 – 24 Apr 1723)
      = bef.1723; **Elizabeth Boteler** (... – 16 Nov 1740) daughter of
      Sir John Boteler
      no issue
   (3) **Henry Grey** (17 Aug 1683 – 1740) legally changed name
      = bef.1740; ♦**Elizabeth Griffin** (bef.30 Nov 1691 – 13 Jul
      1762) daughter of James Griffin, 2nd Baron griffin & Ann
      Raynsford; =2nd John Wallop, 1st Earl of Portsmouth
      no issue
(E) **Elizabeth Neville** (6 May 1657 – ...)
(F) **Catherine Neville** (23 Jun 1659 – 1720)
   = ...; **Richard Aldworth** (... – 1738)
   (1) **Richard Neville** (3 Sep 1717 – 17 Jul 1793) né Aldworth
      = 1748; **Magdalen Calendrini** (... – ca.1750) daughter of
      Francis Calendrini
      (a) **Richard Griffin, 2nd Baron of Braybrooke** (3 Jun
         1750 London – 28 Feb 1825 Billingbeer, Berks.) né
         Aldworth-Neville, change to Griffin 27 Jul 1797 upon suc. to
         Griffin estates; suc. grand-uncle as Baron 25 May 1797
         =19 Jun 1780 Stowe, Bucks; **Catherine Grenville** (1761 – 6
         Nov 1796 London) daughter of Rt.Hon. George Grenville &
         Elizabeth Wyndham
         Has further generations of issue
      (b) **Frances Neville** (...)
         = ...; **Francis Jalabert** (...)
         issue ?
(G) **Frances Neville** (19 May 1664 – ...)
   = ...; **Sir Richard Cocks, 2nd Baronet** (ca.1659 – 1726) son of
   Richard Cocks & Mary Cooke; =2nd Mary Bethell; suc.
   grandfather 1684
   no issue

(V) **Anne Neville** (... – 1700)
(VI) **Frances Neville** (... – 1723)
(VII) **Dorothy Neville** (...)
(VIII) **Henry Neville** (1620 – 1694)
= ...; **Elizabeth Staverton** (...) daughter of Richard Staverton
no issue
d) **Anne Neville** (...) unm.
e) **Frances Neville** (ca.1592 – ca.1660)
=1 ca.1610; **Sir Richard Worsley, 1st Baronet** (ca.1570 – 27 Jun 1621)
=2 aft.1621; **Jerome Brett** (...)
issue of 1st:
(I) **Sir Henry Worsley, 2nd Baronet** (...)
= ...
(A) **Sir Robert Worsley, 3rd Baronet** (1669 – 1742)
= ...; ◆**Mary Herbert** (... – 6 Apr 1693) daughter of Hon.
James
Herbert & Jan Spiller; =2nd Edward Noel, 1st Earl of Gainsborough
(1) **Sir Robert Worsley, 4th Baronet** (...)
= 1690; ◆**Hon. Frances Thynne** (31 Oct 1673 – ...) daughter of Thomas Thynne, 1st Viscount Weymouth & Frances Finch
(a) **Frances Worsley** (6 Mar 1693/4 – 20 Jun 1743)
= 17 Oct 1710; **John Carteret, 2nd Earl Granville**
Viscount
Carteret, Baron Carteret, 3rd Baronet (22 Apr 1690 – 2 Jan 1763) son of George Carteret, 1st Baron Carteret & Grace Granville, 1st Countess Granville; =2nd Lady Sophia Fermor; suc. father 22 Sep 1695 and mother 18 Oct 1744
Has further generations of issue
(2) **Jane Worsley** (...)
= ...; **Sir Nathaniel Napier, 3rd Baronet** (ca.1668 – 24 Feb 1728) son of Sir Nathaniel Napier, 2nd Baronet & Blanch Wyndham; =2nd ◆Hon. Catherine Alington
no issue
(B) **Sir James Worsley** (...)
= ...; **Mary Stuart** (...) daughter of Sir Nicholas Stuart, 1st Baronet & Mary Sandys
(1) **Sir James Worsley, 5th Baronet** (...)
= ...
(a) **Sir Thomas Worsley, 6th Baronet** (22 Apr 1728 –
1768)
= 1749; ◆**Lady Elizabeth Boyle** (7 May 1731 – 16 Jan
1800)
daughter of John Boyle, 5th Earl of Cork & Lady Henrietta Hamilton

Has further generations of issue
(II) **Elizabeth Worsley** (...)
= ...; ♦**Sir John Meux, 1ˢᵗ Baronet** (...–1657)
Children are listed with other parent
(III) **Thomas Worsley** (...)
= ...
  (A) **George Worsley** (...)
  = ...
    (1) **Rev. John Worsley** (...)
    = ...
      (a) **Robert Worsley** (...)
      =
      Has furtyher generations of issue
f) **Katherine Neville** (2 Jan 1592 – 1650)
= ...; **Sir Richard Brooke** (bef.14 Mar 1571 – 10 Apr 1632) son of
Thomas Brooke & Anne Tuchet; =1ˢᵗ Jane Chaderton
(I) **Anne Brooke** (...)
= ...; **Edward Hyde** (...)
  (A) **Margaret Hyde** (... – 1661)
  = 1659; **Piers Legh** (...) son of Peter Legh & Anne Birkenhead;
  he =2ⁿᵈ Abigail Chetwode
    (1) **Piers Legh** (... – 1686) unm.
  (B) **Robert Hyde** (1642 – 1670)
  = ...; **Phillis Sneyd** (...)
    (1) **Anne Hyde** (...)
    =1 ...; **George Creston** (...)
    =2 ...; **John Brydges** (...)
    issue ?
    (2) **Penelope Hyde** (...)
    = ... **Rev. John Thane** (...)
    issue ?
    (3) **Edward Hyde** (1667 – 8 Sep 1712 Bertie Co, NC) Gov. of
NC

    1711-1712
    = ...; **Catherine Rigby** (...) daughter of Alexander Rigby
    (a) **Anne Hyde** (1693 – 19 May 1760 NY)
    = 1714; **George Clarke** (1676 – 12 Jan 1760 Chester, Ches.)
    son of George Clerke
    Has further generations of issue
(II) **Sir Henry Brooke, 1ˢᵗ Baronet** (1611 – 1664) cr. Baronet 12
Dec 1662
= ca.1635; **Mary Pusey** (...) daughter of Timothy Pusey
  (A) **Sir Richard Brooke, 2ⁿᵈ Baronet** (ca.1635 – Feb 1709/10)
  suc. father 1664
  = Apr 1656 Frodsham, Ches.; **Francisca** Posthuma **Legh** (...)
  daughter of Rev. Thomas Legh & Letticve Caverley

(1) **Mary Brooke** (...)
= ...; **Randle Wilbraham** (... – 1732) son of Roger
Wilbraham
& Alice Wilbraham
(a) **Randle Wilbraham** (... – 1770)
= 24 Aug 1722; **Dorothy Kenrick** (...) daughter of Ansdrew
Kenrick
Has further generations of issue
(b) **Roger Wilbraham** (...)
= ...
Has further generations of issue
(c) **Thomas Wilbraham** (...) unm.
(d) **Rev. Henry** William **Wilbraham** (...) unm.
(2) **Letitia Brooke** (... – 1756)
= 17 Oct 1701; **Henry Legh** (bef.6 Jun 1680 – Nov 1757) son
of
Richard Legh & Mary Legh
(a) **George Legh** (11 Jul 1703 – 26 Jan 1780)
= 26 Mar 1731; **Anna Maria Cornwall** (1711 – 7 Jul 1741)
daughter of Francis Cornwall & Mary Woodhouse
Has further generations of issue
(3) **Sir Thomas Brooke, 3rd Baronet** (ca.1664 – 1739) suc.
father 1710
= 12 Jul 1688; **Grace Wilbrham** (ca.1667 – 1739) daughter
of Roger Wilbraham & Alice Wilbraham
(a) **Richard Brooke** (ca.1692 – 1720)
= ...; **Margaret Hill** (...) daughter of John Hill
Has further generatidons of issue
(B) **Henry Brooke** (aft.1635 – ...)
g) **William Neville** (ca.1596 – 1640)
= ...; **Catherine Billingsley** (...) daughter of Sir Henru Billingsley
issue ?
h) **Dorothy Neville** (ca.1596 – 1644)
=1 ...; **Richard Catellyn** (...)
=2 ...; **Richard Billingsley** (...) son of Sir Henry Billingsley
issue of 1st:
(I) **Sir Nevil Catelyn** (1634 – Jul 1702)
=1 ...; **Dorothy Bedingfeld** (...) daughter of Sir Thomas
Bedingfeld
=2 ...; **Elizabeth Houghton** (... – 1681) daugher of Robert
Houghton
=3 ...; **Mary Blois** (...) daughter of Sir William Blois & Martha
Brooke; =1st Sir Charles Turner, 1st Baronet
no issue
i) **Edward Neville** (1602 – 1632)
= ...; **Alice Pryor** (...)

no issue
 j) **Charles Neville** (1607 – 1626)
 k) **Richard Neville** (1608 – 1644)
C) **Katherine Neville** (...)
 = ...; **Clement Throckmorton** (... – 1573) son of Sir George
Throckmorton & Katherine Vaux
 1) **Ursula Throckmorton** (...)
  = ...; **Sir Thomas Biggs** (...)
  a) **Sir Thomas Biggs, Baronet** (ca.1577 – 11 Jun 1621) cr.
   Baronet 26 May 1620 (extinct upon his death)
   = ...; **Anne Witham** (... – aft.Nov 1630) daughter of
   William Witham; =1st Sir John Walter
   no issue
D) **Elizabeth Neville** (...)
 = ...; **Thomaxs Eymes** (...)
 issue ?
E) **Mary Neville** (...)
 = ...; **Henry Dingley** (...)
 1) **Anne Dingley** (... – Jan 1620)
  = Jul 1575; **Edmund Lechmere** (... – 22 Mar 1568) son of
  Richard Lechmere & Margery Rocke
  a) **Edmund Lechmere** (19 Jun 1577 – 31 Jul 1650)
   =1 ...; **... Blackwall** (...)
   =2 Jun 1610; **Margaret Overbury** (... – 14 Mar 1634)
   daughter of Sir Nicholas Overbury
   issue of 2nd (none by 1st):
   (I) **Richard Lechmere** (Jun 1611 – 7 Aug 1632) unm.
   (II) **Mary Lechmere** (...)
    = ...; **Nicholas Short** (...)
    issue?
   (III) **Sir Nicholas Lechmere** (Sep 1613 – 30 Apr 1701)
    = 12 Nov 1642; **Penelope Sandys** (... – 3 Jun 1690)
    daughter of Sir Edwin Sandys & Penelope Bulkeley
    (A) **Letitia Lechmere** (19 Jan 1644/5 – 7 Oct 1669) unm.
    (B) **Edwin Lechmere** (1 Apr 1646 – ...) unm.
    (C) **Penelope Lechmere** (26 Jul 1647 – 29 May 1710)
     = 27 Sep 1664; **Ralph Taylor** (...)
     issue ?
    (D) **Edmund Lechmere** (5 Nov 1648 – 1703)
     = 7 Aug 1673; **Lucy Hungerford** (... – 9 Nov 1729)
     daughter of Anthony Hungerford & Rachel Jones
     (1) **Anthony Lechmere** (1674 – 8 Feb 1720) MP for
      Henley Castle
      = ...; **Anne Foley** (...) daughter of Thomas Foley & Anne
      Knightley
      (a) **Edmund Lechmere** (4 Apr 1710 – Apr 1805)

=1 12 Oct 1732; ♦**Elizabeth Charlton** (... – 13 Sep 1762) daughter of Sir Blunden Charlton, 3rd Baronet & Mary Foley
=2 4 Jun 1765; **Elizabeth Whitmore** (..._) daughter of Rev. John Whitmore
Has further generations of issue by both

(2) **Nicholas Lechmere, Baron Lechmere of Evesham** (5 Aug 1675 – 18 Jun 1727) cr. Baron 4 Sep 1721 (extinct upon his death)
= 1719; ♦**Lady Elizabeth Howard** (1701 – 1739) daughter of Charles Howard, 3rd Earl of Carlisle & Lady Anne Capell
no issue

(3) **Edmund Lechmere** (22 Apr 1677 – 15 Jan 1703) killed in battle (War of Spanish Succession) unm.

(4) **William Lechmere** (21 Jul 1678 – 26 Sep 1725) unm.

(5) **Lucy Lechmere** (11 Nov 1679 – 26 Jun 1758)
= 8 Jun 1699; **Henry Biggs** (...)
issue ?

(6) **Penelope Lechmere** (21 Dec 1680 – 1737)
= 20 Nov 1701; **William Scudamore** (...)
issue ?

(7) **Thomas Lechmere**[131] (18 Jun 1683 – 4 Jun 1765)
= ...; **Anne Winthrop** (...) daughter of John Winthrop
  (a) **Richard Lechmere** (...)
  = ...; **Mary Philipps** (...) daughter of Spencer Phipps
  Has further generations of issue

(8) **Richard Lechmere** (25 Jan 1686 – 7 Jan 1775)
= ...; **Elizabeth Corfield** (...)
  (a) **William Lechmere** (... – 12 Dec 1815)
  = 31 Oct 1787; **Elizabeth Dashwood-King** (... – 1827) daughter of Sir John Dashwood-King, 3rd Baronet & Sarah Moore
  Has further generations of issue
  (b) **Nicholas Lechmere** (...) lived in Jamaica
  (c) **Lucy Lechmere** (...)
  = ...; **... Thompkins** (...)
  issue ?
  (d) **Elizabeth Lechmere** (...)
  = ...; **Thomas Tudor** (...)

(E) **Sandys Lechmere** (23 Aug 1651 – 1694)
= ...; **Joanna Clarke** (...) daughter of Robert Clarke;

---

[131] Went to North America

she =1st John Holmes
issue ?
(F) **Isabella Lechmere** (21 Aug 1655 – ...)
= 9 Jul 1678; **Richard Barneby** (...)
issue ?
(G) **Mary Lechmere** (29 Nov 1656 – 21 Apr 1689)
= 23 Apr 1685; **Higham Coke** (...)
issue ?
(IV) **Elizabeth Lechmere** (... – 5 Jan 1686)
= 1643; **Gabriel Yonge** (...)
issue ?
(V) **Anne Lechmere** (27 Nov 1615 – ...)
= 8 Aug 1634; **Thomas Russell** (...) son of Sir Thomas Russell
issue ?
(VI) **Thomas Lechmere** (bap.25 Jan 1616/7 – 11 Mar 1669/70)
= ...
(A) **Thomas Lechmere** (...)
= Dec 1677; **Jane Blagrave** (...)
issue ?
(B) **Nicholas Lechmere** (...)
= ...; **Judith Corbett** (...)
(1) **Richard Lechmere** (... – aft.1738)
= ...
(a) **Rev. Nicholas Lechmere** (... – 1770)
(C) **Richard Lechmere** (...)
(VII) **Jane Lechmere** (... – 1694)
= 9 Apr 1654; **William Parsons** (...)
issue ?
(VIII) **Margaret Lechmere** (18 Jan 1620/1 – ...)
= ...; **Edmond Neale** (...)
issue ?
(IX) **Edmund Lechmere** (Aug 1623 – 4 Feb 1646/7)
killed in battle unm.
F) **Frances Neville** (1519 – 18 Oct 1599 Borley, Essex)
=1 ...; **Sir Edward Waldegrave** (1517 – 1 Sep 1561) son of
Edward Waldegrave & Elizabeth Cheney
=2 ...; **Lord Chidiock Paulet** (...) son of William Paulet, 1st
Marquess of Winchester & Elizabeth Capel
has issue of 1st (any by 2nd?):
1) **Charles Waldegrave** (... – 25 Jan 1580)
= ...; **Jermina Jerningham** (ca.1550 – 4 Feb 1627) daughter of Sir
Henry Jerningham & Frances Baynham
a) **Sir Edward Waldegrave, 1st Baronet** (ca.1568 – aft.1647) cr.
Baronet 1 Aug 1643
= 19 Jul 1598; **Eleanor Lovell** (... – 12 Dec 1604) daughgter of Sir
Thomas Lovell

(I) **Sir Henry Waldegrave, 2nd Baronet** (1598 - 1658) suc. father 1647

=1 ...; **Anne Paston** (...) daughter of Edward Paston

=2 ...; **Catherine Bacon** (... – bef.1695) daughter of Richard Bacon

  (A) **Sir Charles Waldegrave, 3rd Baronet** (... – aft.26 May 1684) suc. father 1658

  = ...; **Eleanor Englefield** (...) daughter of Sir Francis Englefield, 1st Baronet

    (1) **Henry Waldegrave, 1st Baron Waldegrave** 4th Baronet (1661 – 14 Jan 1689/90 Paris) suc. father 1684; cr. Baron 20 Jan 1685/6

    = 29 Nov 1683; ♦**Lady Henrietta FitzJames** (1667 – 3 Apr 1730) natural daughter of James II, King of England & Arabella Churchill; =2nd Piers Butler, 3rd Viscount of Galmoye

      (a) **James Waldegrave, 1st Earl of Waldegrave** Viscount Chewton, 2nd Baron Waldegrave, etc. **KG** (1684 – 11 Apr 1741) suc. father 1690; cr. Earl etc. 13 Sep 1729

      = 20 May 1714; ♦**Mary Webb** (... – 22 Jan 1718/9) daughter of Sir John Webb, 3rd Baronet & Hon. Barbara Belayse
Has further generations of issue

      (b) **Hon. Arabella Waldegrave** (10 May 1687 – 30 Apr 1740) a nun

      (c) **Hon. Henry Waldegrave** (15 Feb 1688 – 1 Mar 1726/7)

(II) **Charles Waldegrave** (...)

= ...

  (A) **Elizabeth Waldegrave** (... – 6 Sep 1681)

  = 1663; **Sir William Tancred, 2nd Baronet** (... – 19 Aug 1703) son of Sir Thomas Tancred, 1st Baronet & Frances Maltby

    (1) **Sir Thomas Tancred, 3rd Baronet** (1665 – 24 Au7g 1744) suc. father 1703

    = 1712; **Elizabeth Messenger** (... – 18 Dec 1753) daughter of William Messenger

      (a) **Sir Thomas Tancred, 4th Baronet** (... – 30 May 1759) suc. father 1744

      = 1740; **Judith Dalton** (... – 1781) daughter of Peter Dalton
Has further generations of issue

      (b) **Henrietta Maria Tancred** (...)

      =1 ...; **William Ingleby** (...)

      =2 ...; **Nicholas Wogan** (...)

      issue ?

    (2) **Charles Tancred** (...)

    = ...; **Mary Walpole** (...)

    issue ?

    (3) **Waldegrave Tancred** (...)

    = ...; **Alethia Blackett** (...) daughter of Sir Edward Blackett,

2nd Baronet & Mary Yorke
no issue
(4) **Elizabeth Tancred** (...)
= ...; **Christopher Percehay** (...)
issue ?
2) **Nicholas Waldegrave** (...)
3) **Magdalene Waldegrave** (...)
= ...; **Sir John Southcote** (...)
issue ?
4) **Catherine Waldegrave** (...)
= ...; **Thomas Gawen** (...)
issue ?
5) **Mary Waldegrave** (1549 – 29 Aug 1604)
= 1570; ♦**John Petre, 1st Baron Petre** (1549 – 1613)
Children are listed with other parent
V) **Sir Thomas Neville** (bef.1484 – 20 May 1542 Mereworth,
Kent) Speak of the House of Commons 1515–1518
=1 bef.1527; **Katherine Dacre** (... – 20 Aug 1527) daughter of
Humphrey Dacre, 1st Baron Dacre & Mabel Parr; =1st George
FitzHugh, 8th Lord FitzHugh
=2 28 Aug 1532; **Elizabeth Bryce** (... – bef.1542) =1st Robert Amadas
issue of 1st (none by 2nd):
A) **Margaret Neville** (...)
=1 1 May 1536; **Sir Robert Southwell** (ca.1506 Windham
Manor, Norfolk – 1559 Mwereworth) son of Francis Southwell
=2 ...; **William Plumbe** (...)
issue of 1st:
1) **Thomas Southwell** (24 May 1537 – 1568)
=1 ...; **Mary Jerningham** (...) daughter of Sir Henry
Jerningham
=2 ...; **Mary Mansell** (...) daughter of Sir Rice Mansell
=3 ...; **Nazareth Newton** (... – 1583) daughter of Sir John
Newton; =2nd Thomas Paget, 4th Baron Paget
issue of 2nd (none by 1st):
a) **Sir Robert Southwell** (...)
= bef.1599; ♦**Lady Elizabeth Howard** (... – Jan 1646) daughter
of Charles Howard, 1st Earl of Nottingham & Katherine Carey
Has further generations of issue
issue of 3rd:
b) **Elizabeth Southwell** (...)
= ...; **Barentyne Molyns** (...) son of Michael Molyns
issue ?
2) **Francis Southwell** (14 Dec 1538 – ...)
3) **Henry Southwell** (4 Sep 1543 – ...)
4) **Anne Southwell** (18 Mar 1540 – ...)
5) **Dorothy Southwell** (21 Sep 1542 – ...)

VI) **Sir Richard Neville** (bef.1485 – ca.1515)
VII) **Elizabeth Neville** (...)
  =1 ...; **Thomas Berkeley** (...)
  =2 ...; **Richard Covert** (...)
  issue ?
d. **Catherine Neville** (ca.1444 – ...)
  = ...; **Sir John Iwardby** (...)
  I) **Joan Iwardby** (...)
  = ...; **Sir John St.John** (1473 – 1 Sep 1512) son of Oliver
  St.John & Elizabeth Scrope
  A) **John St.John** (ca.1495 – 5 Apr 1576)
    =1 ...; ♦**Margaret Carew** (...) daughter of Sir Richard Carew & Malyn
    Oxenbridge
    =2 ...; **Elizabeth Whettle** (...) daughter of Sir Richard Whettle
    issue of 1st:
    1) **Nicholas St.John** (... – 1589)
      = ...; ♦**Elizabeth Blount** (...) daughter of Sir Richard Blount
      a) **Oliver St.John, 1st Viscount Grandison** Baron Tregoz
        (ca.1560 – 30 Dec 1630 Battersea, Surrey) cr. Viscount 3 Jan
        1620/1 with a special remainder to his niece, cr. Baron 21 May
        1626, but it became extinct upon his death
        = ...; **Joan Roydon** (... – Feb 1630/1) daughter of Henry Roydon;
        she =2nd Sir William Holcroft
        no issue
      b) **Richard St.John** (...)
      c) **Elizabeth St.John** (...)
        = ...; **Sir Richard St.George** (... – 17 May 1635) son of Francis
        St. George & Rose Hutton
        Has further generations of issue
      d) **Eleanor St.John** (...)
        = ...; **Sir Thomas Cave** (...) son of Roger Cave & Margaret Cecil
        Has further generations of issue
      e) **Sir John St.John** (ca.1552 Wilts. – 20 Sep 1594 Lydiard
        Tregoze, Wilts.)
        = ...; ♦**Lucy Hungerford** (1560 Farley, Berks. – 1627) daughter of
        Sir Walter Hungerford & Anne Dormer; =2nd Sir Anthony
        Hungerford
        Has further generations of issue
    issue of 2nd:
    2) **William St.John** (1 Aug 1538 – 18 Apr 1609)
      = ...; **Barbara Gore** (... – 31 Dec 1613) daughter of Thomas Gore;
      she =1st Thomas Twyne
      a) **Henry St.John** (1586 – bef.21 Jun 1621)
        = ...; **Ursula Stukeley** (...) daughter of Hugh Stukeley
        Has further generations of issue
  issue of 2nd:

e. **Margaret Neville** (aft.1448 – 30 Sep 1506)
= bef.1481; ♦**John Brook, 7ᵗʰ Baron Cobham** (aft.1446 – 1511/2)
see:
f. **Catherine Neville** (bef.1473 – ...)
= ...; **Robert Tanfield** (...)
I) **William Tanfield** (ca.1489 – ...)
g. **Anne Neville** (bef.1476 – aft.26 Feb 1480/1)
= ...; **John LeStrange, 8ᵗʰ Baron LeStrange** (ca.1444 – 16 Oct 1479) son of Richard LeStrange; =1ˢᵗ Jaquetta Woodville
no issue
10. **Lady Cecily Neville** (3 May 1415 Raby Castle – 31 May 1495 Berkhamsted Castle, Herts.)
= 1424; ♦**Richard Plantagenet, 3ʳᵈ Duke of York** (1411 – 1460)
Children are listed with other parent
11. **George Neville, 1ˢᵗ Baron Latymer** (ca.1407 –30 Dec 1469) cr. Baron 25 Feb 1431/2
= ca.Feb 1436/7; **Lady Elizabeth Beauchamp** (ca.1417 – bef.2 Oct 1480) daughter of Richard Beauchamp, 13ᵗʰ Earl of Warwick & Elizabeth Berkeley
a. **Katherine Neville** (...)
= ...; **Oliver Dudley** (...)
no issue
b. **Sir Henry Neville** (... – 26 Jul 1469 Edgcote, Oxon.) killed in battle
= ...; **Joanna Bourchier** (...) daughter of John Bourchier, 1ˢᵗ Baron Berners & Margaret Berners
I) **Joane Neville** (...)
= ...; **Sir James Ratcliffe** (...)
issue ?
II) **Richard Neville, 2ⁿᵈ Baron Latymer** (bef.1468 – Dec 1530) suc. grandfather 30 Dec 1469
=1 ca.1490; **Anne Stafford** (...)
=2 5 Jul 1502; **Margaret ...** (...) =1ˢᵗ Sir James Strangways
issue of 1ˢᵗ (none by 2ⁿᵈ):
A) **John Neville, 3ʳᵈ Baron Latymer** (17 Nov 1493 – 2 Mar 1543) suc. father Dec 1530
=1 bef.1520; **Dorothea de Vere** (... – 17 Feb 1526/7) daughter of Sir George de Vere & Margaret Stafford
=2 20 Jul 1526; **Elizabeth Musgrave** (...) daughter of Sir Edward Musgrave & Joan Ward
=3 1533; **Catherine Parr** (1512 London – 5 Sep 1548 Sudeley Castle, Glos.) daughter of Sir Thomas Parr & Maud Green; =1ˢᵗ Sir Edward Burgh; =3ʳᵈ ♦Henry VIII, King of England; =4ᵗʰ Thomas Seymour, 1ˢᵗ Baron Seymour of Sudeley
issue of 1ˢᵗ (none by others):

1) **John Neville, 4ᵗʰ Baron Latymer** (1520 – 22 Apr 1577)
suc. father 1543[132]
= ca.1545; ♦**Lady Lucy Somerset** (... – 23 Fenb 1582/3)
daughter of Henry Somerset, 2ⁿᵈ Earl of Worcester &
Elizabeth Browne
a) **Katherine Neville** (1545 – 28 Oct 1596)
=1 1561; ♦**Henry Percy, 2ⁿᵈ Earl of Northumberland** (+1585)
=2 1588; **Francis Fitton** (... – 17 Jun 1608)
issue of 1ˢᵗ (none by 2ⁿᵈ):
see:
b) **DOROTHY, COUNTESS OF EXETER** (1548 – 1608)
see: Chapter 17
c) **Lucy Neville** (ca.1549 – 30 Apr 1608)
= ...; **Sir William Cornwallis** (ca.1551 – 1611) son of Sir Thomas
Cornwallis & Anne Jerningham; =2ⁿᵈ Jane Meautys
(I) **Frances Cornwallis** (... – Sep 1625)
= ...; **Sir Edmond Withipole** (... – 6 Nov 1619)
(A) **Sir William Withipole** (... – 11 Aug 1645)
= 25 Apr 1621; ♦**Jane Stanhope** (...) daughter of Sir Michael
Stanhope & Anne Reade; =1ˢᵗ ♦Henry, Viscount Fitzwalter
(1) **Elizabeth Withipole** (... – Jan 1669)
= 1642; ♦**Leicester Devereux, 6ᵗʰ Viscount Hereford**
(1617–1676)
Children are listed with other parent
(II) **Elizabeth Cornwallis** (... – 31 Jan 1657/8)
=1 1592; **Sir William Sandys** (
=2 11 May 1630; **Richard Lumley, 1ˢᵗ Viscount Lumley** (bef.7
Apr 1589 – befg.12 Mar 1662/63) son of Roger Lumley & Anne
Kurtwich; =1ˢᵗ Frances Shelley; cr. Viscount 12 Jul 1628
no issue
(III) **Cornelia Cornwallis** (...)
= ...; **Sir Richard Fermor** (...)
issue ?
(IV) **Anne Cornwallis** (... – 12 Jan 1634/5 London)
= 1610; ♦**Archibald Campbell, 7ᵗʰ Earl of Argyll** (1575–1638)
Children are listed with other parent
(V) **Thomas Cornwallis** (... – 1626) unm.
d) **Elizabeth Neville** (1545 – 21 Jun 1630)
=1 ...; **Sir John Danvers** (1540 – 10 Dec 1594) son of Sylvester

---

[132] Upon his death the Barony fell into abeyance among his four daughters and remained abeyant until 1913 when a descendant of the 3ʳᵈ daughter of was summoned to Parliament as the 5ᵗʰ Baron Latymer.

Danvers & Elizabeth Mordaunt
=2 ...; ◆**Sir Edmund Carey** (1558 – 12 Sep 1637 Culham, Oxon.)
son of Henry Carey, 1st Baron Hunsdon of Hunsdon & Ann Morgan;
he =1st Mary Crocker; =3rd Judith Humphrey; Kt. 1587
has issue of 1st (none by 2nd):
(I) **Sir Charles Danvers** (ca.1568 – 18 Mar 1600/1 London)
    executed[133]
(II) **Eleanor Danvers** (... – Aug 1666)
  = ...; **Thomas Walmesley** (...)
  (A) **Anne Walmesley** (...)
    =1 ...; **William Middleton** (...)
    =2 bef.1630; **Sir Edward Osborne, 1st Baronet** (bef.12 Dec
    1596 London – 9 Sep 1647) son of Sir Hewett Osborne & Joyce
    Fleetwood; =1st ◆Hon. Margaret Belayse; cr. Baronet 13 Jul
    1620
    (1) **Thomas Osborn, 1st Duke of Leeds** Marquess of
        Carmarthen, Earl of Danby, Viscount Latimer, Viscount
        Oseborne, Baron Osborne, 2nd Baronet **KG** (20 Feb 1631/2 –
        26 Jul 1712) suc. father 1647; cr. Viscount Oseborne 2 Feb
        1672, Viscount Latimer and Baron 15 Aug 1673, Earl 27 Jun
        1674, Marquess 9 Apr 1689, and Duke 4 Mar 1694; KG 1675
        = 1651; ◆**Lady Bridget Bertie** (6 Jun 1629 – 7 Jan 1704)
        daughter of Montagu Bertie, 2nd Earl of Lindsey & Martha
        Cokayne
        (a) **Lady Catherine Osborne** (...)
            = ...; ◆**Hon. James Herbert** (1623–1677)
            Children are listed with other parent
        (b) **Lady Bridget Osborne** (... – 9 May 1718)
            =1 12 Sep 1678 London; ◆**Charles FitzCharles, Earl of
            Plymouth** (1657 the Netherlands – 17 Oct 1680 Tangier,
            Morocco) natural son of Charles II, King of England &
            Catherine Pegge
            =2 1705; **Rt.Rev. Philip Bisse, Bishop of Hereford** (...)
            no issue
        (c) **Edward, Viscount Latimer** (1655 – Jan 1688/9)
            = ...; **Elizabeth Bennett** (... – 1 May 1680) daughter of
            Simon Bennett & Grace Moorwood
            no surviving issue
        (d) **Lady Anne Osborne** (1657 – 1722)
            =1 ...; **Robert Coke** (... – 16 Jan 1678/9) son of Richard
            Coke & Mary Rous

---

[133] For participating in Essex' rebellion against Elizabeth I.

=2 ...; **Horatio Walpole** (... – 17 Oct 1717) son of Sir
Edward Walpole & Susan Crane
Has further generations of issue by 1st
(e) **Peregrine Osborne, 2nd Duke of Leeds** etc. (ca.1659 –
25 Jun 1729) suc. 1674
= 25 Apr 1682; **Bridget Hyde** (ca.1662 – 8 Mar 1733/4)
daughter of Sir Thomas Hyde, 2nd Baronet
Has further generations of issue
(f) **Lady Sophia Osborne** (1661 – 8 Dec 1746)
=1 26 May 1679; ◆**Hon. Donogh O'Brien** (16 Sep 1663 – 5
May 1682) drowned at sea; son of Henry, Lord O'Brien &
Katherine Stuart, 7th Baroness Clifton;
=2 5 Mar 1691/2; **William Fermor, 1st Baron
Leominster** 2nd Baronet (ca.1648 – 7 Dec 1711) son of Sir
William Fermor, 1st Baronet & Mary Perry; =1st Jane Barker;
he =2nd ◆Hon. Catherine Poulett; suc. father 14 May 1661; cr.
Baron 12 Apr 1692
Has further generations of issue by 2nd
(g) **Lady Martha Osborne** (ca.1664 – 11 Sep 1689)
= 22 May 1648 London; ◆**Charles Granville, 2nd Earl of
Bath** etc. (bef.31 Aug 1661 London – 4 Sep 1701 London)
suicide; son of John Granville, 1st Earl of Bath & Jane Wyche;
he =2nd Isabelle de Nassau; suc. father 22 Aug 1701
no issue
(III) **Catherine Danvers** (...)
= ...; **Sir Richard Gargrave** (...)
(A) **Mary Gargrave** (... – 1675)
= 30 Apr 1629 London; **Sir Robert Carr, 2nd Baronet** (... –
14 Aug 1667) son of Sir Edward Carr, 1st Baronet & Anne Dyer;
suc. father 1 Oct 1618
(1) **Rt.Hon. Sir Robert Carr, 3rd Baronet** (... – Nov 1682)
suc. father 1667
= ...; **Elizabeth Bennett** (... – 1696) daughter of Sir John
Bennett & Dorothy Crofts
(a) **Sir Edward Carr, 4th Baronet** (ca.1665 – 28 Dec 1683)
unm.; suc. father 1682
(b) **Isabella Carr** (20 Jan 1669/70 – 7 Mar 1692/3)
= 1 Nov 1688 London; **John Hervey, 1st Earl of Bristol**
Baron Hervey (27 Aug 1665 – 20 Jan 1750/1 Ickworth,
Suffolk) son of Sir Thomas Hervey & Isabella May; =2nd
Elizabeth Felton; cr. Baron 23 Mar 1702/3 and Earl 19 Oct
1714
Issue extinct in 1723
(c) **Elizabeth Carr** (... – Feb 1661)
=1 ...; **William Thorold** (...) son of Sir William Thorold, 1st
Baronet & Anne Blythe

=2 ...; **Sir William Trollope, 2ⁿᵈ Baronet** (3 Jan 1621 –
16 May 1678) son of Sir Thomas Trollope, 1ˢᵗ Baronet &
Hester Street; su7c. father 7 Mar 1754/55
Issue extinct in 1703

(2) **Lucy Carr** (...)
= ...; ♦**Francis Holles, 2ⁿᵈ Baron Holles** (1627 – 1 Mar
1690) son of Denzil Holles, 1ˢᵗ Baron Holles & Dorothy Ashley;
he =2ⁿᵈ Anne Pile; suc. father 17 Feb 1679/80
no issue

(3) **Mary Carr** (... – 1685)
= ...; **Sir Adrian Scrope KB** (... – 1667)
  (a) **Sir Carr Scrope, Baronet** (1649 – Nov 1680) unm. cr.
Baronet 16 Jan 1666/7, but it became extinct upon his death

(IV) **Henry Danvers, Earl of Danby** Baron Danvers **KG** (28
Jun 1573 Dauntsey, Wilts. – 20 Jan 1644 Cornbury Park, Oxon)
unm. cr. Baron 21 Jul 1603 and Earl 5 Feb 1626, but both went
extinct upon his death; KG 1633

(V) **Dorothy Danvers** (...)
= ...; **Sir Peter Osborne** (... – Mar 1653) son of Sir John
Osborne & Dorothy Barlee

(A) **Thomas Osborne** (1609 – 1637)

(B) **Elizabeth Osborne** (1610 – ...)
= 1631; **Edward Duncombe** (...)
issue ?

(C) **Ann Osborne** (1613 – ...)
= ...; **Sir Thomas Peyton, 2ⁿᵈ Baronet** (18 Aug 1613 – 11 Feb
1684) son of Sir Samuel Peyton, 1ˢᵗ Baronet & Mary Aston; =2ⁿᵈ
Cecilia Clerke; =3ʳᵈ Jane Monins; suc. father 1623
no issue

(D) **Henry Osborne** (1614 – 1645 Naseby, Northants.) killed in
battle

(E) **Sir John Osborne, 1ˢᵗ Baronet** (ca.1615 – 5 Feb 1698/9)
cr. Baronet 11 Feb 1661/2
= 22 Dec 1647; **Eleanor Danvers** (... – 16 Nov 1677) daughter
of Sir Charles Danvers

(1) **Sir John Osborne, 2ⁿᵈ Baronet** (1659 – 28 Apr 1720)
suc. father 1699
=1 ...; **Elizabeth Strode** (... – 27 Mar 1683) daughter of
William Strode
=2 1688; **Martha Kelynge** (... – 12 Nov 1713) daughter of
John Kelynge
issue of 1ˢᵗ:

(a) **John Osborn** (1 Apr 1683 – 11 Jan 1718/9) legally
changed spelling of name
= 8 Aug 1710; **Hon. Sarah Byng** (2 Oct 1695 – Nov 1775)
daughter of George Byng, 1ˢᵗ Viscount Torrington & Margaret

Master
Has further generations of issue
issue of 2nd:
(b) **Rev. Thomas Osborne** (... – 1790)
=1 ...; **Mary Willys** (...) daughter of Sir John Willys, 2nd
Baronet; =1st Edward Snagg
=2 ...; **Elizabeth Green** (...) daughter of Rt.Rev. Thomas
Green, Bishop of Ely (formerly of Norwich)
issue ?
(c) **Peter Osborne** (bef.4 Sep 1690 – 13 Feb 1754)
= 1718; **Mary Skelton** (... – 1 Apr 1765) daughter of Bevil
Skelton; =1st ◆William Molyneux, 4th Viscount Molyneux
Has further generations of issue
(d) **Henry Osborne** (bef.27 Aug 1694 – 4 Feb 1771)
= ...; **Mary Hughes** (...) daughter of Richard Hughes
Has further generations of issue
(e) **Robert Osborne** (Jun 1696 – ...)
= ...
Has further generations of issue
(F) **Sir Henry Osborne** (1619 – 1675)
(G) **Charles Osborne** (1620 – 1642) killed in battle
(H) **Robin Osborne** (1626 – ca.1653) unm.
(I) **Dorothy Osborne**[134] (1627 – ...)
= 31 Jan 1654/5; **Sir William Temple, Baronet** (bef.20 Apr
1626 London – 27 Jan 1698/9) son of Sir Jophn Temple & Mary
Hammond; cr. Baronet 31 Jan 1665/6, but it became exinct
upon his death
(1) **John Temple** (... – 1689)
= 1685 Paris; **Marie du Plessis-Rambouillet** (...) daughter
of Paul du Plessis-Rambouillet
(a) **Dorothy Temple** (...)
= ...; ◆**Nicholas Bacon** (...) son of Nicholas Bacon & Lady
Catherine Montagu
issue ?
(b) **Elizabeth Temple** (...)
= ...; **John Temple** (... – Feb 1742) son of Sir John Temple
& Jane Yarner
Has further generations of issue
(2) **Diana Temple** (ca.1665 – 1679)
(VI) **Lucy Danvers** (... – 1621)

---

[134] Prior to her marriage to Sir William, she was engaged to Henry Cromwell, son of Oliver,
Lord Protector of England. They broke it off and each married other people.

= ...; ♦**Sir Henry Baynton** (1572–1616)
Children are listed with other parent
(VII) **Elizabeth Danvers** (...)
= ...; **Sir Edward Hoby** (...)
issue ?
(VIII) **Anne Danvers** (...)
(IX) **Mary Danvers** (...)
(X) **Sir John Danvers** (ca.1588 – Apr 1655 London)
=1 1608; **Magdalen Newport** (ca.1568 – Jun 1627) daughter of
Sir Richard Newport& Margaret Bromley; =1st Richard Herbert
=2 10 Jul 1628; **Elizabeth Dauntsey** (1604 – 9 Jul 1636)
daughter of Ambrose Dauntsey & Gertrude Sadler
=3 6 Jan 1648/9; **Grace Hewett** (...)
issue of 2nd (none by 1st):
(A) **Elizabeth Danvers** (1 May 1629 – 1709)
= ...; **Robert Danvers** (ca.1621 – ca.1674) illegitimate son[135] of
Sir Robert Howard & Frances Coke; surnamed Villiers, before
taking wife's family name.
(1) **Robert Villers** (ca.1656 – ca.1684)
= 1676; **Lady Margaret Bourke** (... – Aug 1698 Tonbridge,
Kent) daughter of Ulrick Bourke, 1st Marquess of Clanricarde &
Lady Anne Compton; =1st Charles, Vicount Muskerry; =3rd
Robert Feidling
(a) **John Villers** (1677 – 10 Aug 1723 London)
= 23 Nov 1699; **Frances Moyses** (...) =1st George Heneage
Has further generations of issue
(2) **Edward Villers** (ca.1661 – ca.1691)
= 10 Jul 1685 Worcester; **Joan Heming** (ca.1663 – ...)
daughter of William Heming
(a) **Rev. George Villiers** (11 Apr 1690 Worcester – ca.Apr
1748)
= bef.1724; **Katherine Stephens** (... – ca.1759) daughter of
Thomas Stephens
Has further generations of issue
(3) **Ann Danvers** (...)
= 1655; ♦**Sir Henry Lee, 3rd Baronet** (1633–1959)
Children are listed with other parent
(4) **Frances Danvers** (...)
= ...; **Sir Richard Dereham, 3rd Baronet** (1644 – ca.1710)

---

[135] He was born during the marriage of his mother to Viscount Purbeck. In 1678, the House of
Lords ruled he was the son of Sir Robert instead and therefore not enttitled to inherit the
viscountcy, which he disclaimed in 1658

son of Sir Thomas Dereham, 1st Baronet; suc. brother 1682

(a) **Elizabeth Dereham** (...)

= ...; **Sir Simeon Stuart, 2nd Baronet** (... – 11 Aug 1761) son of Charles Stuart & Clemence Hovell; suc. grandfather 15 Feb 1709/10

Has further generations of issue

(b) **Sir Thomas Dereham, 4th Baronet** (ca.1678 – 16 Jan 1739 Rome) unm. suc. father 1710

(B) **Henry Danvers** (5 Dec 1633 – Nov 1654) unm.

issue of 3rd:

(C) **John Danvers** (10 Aug 1650 – ...)

= ...; **Elizabeth Morewood** (...) =2nd Samuel Danvers

no issue

2) **Margaret Neville** (1525 – 1546) unm.

B) **Margaret Neville** (9 Mar 1494/5 – ...)

= ...; **Edward Willoughby** (ca.1485 – Nov 1517) son of Robert Willoughby, 2nd Baron Willoughby & Elizabeth Beauchamp

1) **Elizabeth Willoughby, 3rd Baroness Willoughby** (... – Nov 1560) suc. grandfather 10 Nov 1521

= bef.11 Apr 1526; **Sir Fulke Greville** (... – 10 Nov 1559) son of Sir Edward Greville & Anne Denton; Kt. bef.1544

a) **Fulke Greville, 4th Baron Willoughby** (ca.1536 – 15 Nov 1606) suc. mother 1560

= ca.1553; **Lady Anne Neville** (...) daughter of Ralph Neville, 4th Earl of Westmorland & Lady Catherine Stafford

(I) **Fulke Greville, 5th Baron Willoughby, Baron Brooke** (1554 – 30 Sep 1628 London) murdered by a servant; unm. suc. father 1606; cr. Baron Brook with special remainder to his Greville uncles 29 Jan 1620/1

(II) **Margaret Greville, 6th Baroness Willoughby** (ca.1561 – 26 Mar 1631) suc. brother 1628

= 29 Oct 1582 Alcester, Warks.; **Sir Richard Verney** (... – 7 Aug 1630) son of George Verney

(A) **Greville Vervey, 7th Baron Willoughby** (ca.1586 – 12 May 1642) suc. mother 1631

= 13 May 1618; **Catherine Southwell** (...) daughter of Sir Richard Southwell

(1) **Greville Verney, 8th Baron Willoughby** (1619 – 9 Dec 1648) suc. father 1642

= ...; **Hon. Elizabeth Wenman** (...) daughter of Richard Wenman, 1st Viscount Wenman & Agnes Fermor

(a) **Greville Verney, 9th Baron Willoughby** (ph.26 Jan 1648/9 – 23 Jul 1668) suc. father at brth

= 29 Aug 1667; ◆**Lady Diana Russell** (... – 13 Dec 1701) daughter of William Russell, 1st Duke of Bedford & Lady Anne Carr; =2nd William Alington, 3rd Baron Alington

Issue extinct 1683
(2) **Richard Verney, 11th Baron Willoughby** (28 Jan
1621/2 – 18 Jul 1711) suc. grand-nephew 11 Aug 1683
=1 Nov 1651; **Mary Pretyman** (...) daughter of Sir John
Pretyman, 1st Baronet
=2 ...; **Frances Dove** (1643 – 17 Sep 1730) daughter of
Thomas Dove
issue of 1st:
  (a) **Hon. John Verney** (ca.1652 – 31 Oct 1707)
    = 13 Jul 1683; **Christian Breton** (...) daughter of John
    Breton
    no surviving issue
  (b) **Hon. Mary Verney** (...)
  (c) **Hon. Sarah Verney** (1660 – 1724)
    = ...; **Sir Edward English** (... – 1697)
    Has further generations of issue
  (d) **George Verney, 12th Baron Willoughby** (10 Mar
    1660/1 – 26 Dec 1728) suc. father 1711
    = 2 Dec 1688; **Margaret Heath** (...) daughter of Sir John
    Heath & Margaret Mennes
    Has further generations of issue
  (e) **Hon. Thomas Verney** (ca.1663 – ... Lisbon, Portugal)
issue of 2nd:
  (f) **Hon. Richard Verney** (ca.1677 – 23 Jun 1698) unm.
  (g) **Hon. Diana Verney** (... – 28 Sep 1725)
    = aft.26 Oct 1684; **Sir Charles Shuckburgh, 2nd Baronet**
    (1659 – 2 Sep 1705) son of Sir John Shuckburgh, 1st Baronet
    & Catharina Fermor; suc. father 1661
    Has further generations of issue
  (3) **Hon. Elizabeth Verney** (...)
  = ...; **William Peyto** (...)
  issue ?
  (B) **Hon. John Verney** (...)
b) **Hon. Robert Greville** (...)
= ...; **Blanche Whitney** (...)
(I) **Fulke Greville** (... – 1632)
= 15 May 1602; **Mary Copley** (...) daughter of Christopher
Copley; =1st Ralph Bosville
  (A) **Dorothy Greville** (... – 28 Jan 1650)
  = ...; **Sir Arthur Hesilrige, 2nd Baronet** (... – 7 Jan 1660/1)
  son of Sir Thomas Hesilrige, 1st Baronet & Frances Gorges; =1st
  Frances Elmes
    (1) **Sir Robert Hesilrige, 5th Baronet** (1640 – 22 May 1713)
    suc. nephew 11 Jul 1700
    = 3 May 1664; **Bridget Rolle** (... – 26 Jul 1697) daughter of
    Samuel Rolle

(a) **Sir Robert Hesilridge, 6ᵗʰ Baronet** (1668 – 19 May 1721) suc. father 1713
= 29 Jul 1696; ◆**Hon. Dorothy Maynard** (... – 11 sep 1748) daughter of Banastre Maynard, 3ʳᵈ Baron Maynard
Has further generations of issue

(B) **Robert Greville, 2ⁿᵈ Baron Brooke** (1607 – 2 Mar 1642/3 Farndon, Ches.) killed in action
= ca.1630; ◆**Lady Catherine Russell** (1618 – 1 Dec 1676) daughter of Francis Russell, 4ᵗʰ Earl of Bedford & Hon. Catherine Brydges

(1) **Francis Greville, 3ʳᵈ Baron Brooke** (bef.1637 – 19 Nov 1658 London) unm. suc. father 1643

(2) **Robert Greville, 4ᵗʰ Baron Brooke** (4 Jan 1638/9 – 17 Feb 1676/7 Bath) suc. brother 1658
= ...; **Ann Dodington** (... – 3 Feb 1690/1) daughter of John Dodington; =2ⁿᵈ Thomas Hoby

  (a) **Hon. Doddington Greville** (... – 16 Feb 1720)
  = 1691; ◆**Charles Montagu, 1ˢᵗ Duke of Manchester** (1662–1722)
  Children are listed with other parent

(3) **Fulke Greville, 5ᵗʰ Baron Brooke** (ph.aft.2 Mar 1642/3 – 22 Oct 1710 London) suc. brother 1677
= 12 Jan 1664/5 London; ◆**Sarah Dashwood** (ca.1646 – 20 Sep 1705) daughter of Francis Dashwood & Alice Sleigh

  (a) **Hon. Catherine Greville** (... – 7 Feb 1703/4)
  =1 1687; ◆**Wriothelsey Baptist Noel, 2ⁿᵈ Earl of Gainsborough** (bef.1665 – 1690)
  =2 12 Mar 1698/9 London; ◆**John Sheffield, 1ˢᵗ Duke of Buckingham**, etc. (85 Sep 1647 – 24 Feb 1721 London) son of Edmund Sheffield, 2ⁿᵈ Earl of Mulgrave & Lady Elizabeth Cranfield; =1ˢᵗ Ursula Stawel; =3ʳᵈ ◆Lady Catherine Darnley; suc. father 24 Aug 1658; cr. Duke 23 Mar 1702/3
  issue of 1ˢᵗ (none by 2ⁿᵈ):
  Children are listed with other parent

  (b) **Hon. Elizabeth Greville** (... – 4 Nov 1699)
  = 25 Feb 1694/5; **Francis North, 2ⁿᵈ Baron of Guilford** (14 Dec 1673 – 17 Oct 1729) son of Francis North, 1ˢᵗ Baron of Guilford & Lady Frances Pope; =2ⁿᵈ Alicia Brownlow; suc. father 5 Sep 1685
  no issue

  (c) **Hon. Francis Greville** (... – 11 Oct 1710)
  = ...; **Lady Anne Wilmot** (1672 – 8 Aug 1703) daughter of John Wilmot, 2ⁿᵈ Earl of Rochester; =1ˢᵗ Henry Bayntun
  Has further generations of issue

  (d) **Hon. Algernon Greville** (ca.1677 – 28 Apr 1720)
  = 24 Dec 1711; ◆**Mary Somerset** (...) daughter of Lord

Arthur Somerset & Mary Russell
Has further generations of issue
 (e) **Hon. Henrietta Greville** (26 Aug 1683 – 18 May 1765 Bath)
 = 9 Jun 1702 London; **Sir James Long, 5ᵗʰ Baronet** (ca.1682 – 16 Mar 1728/9) son of James Long & Susan Strangways; suc. brother 1697
 Has further generations of issue
 (C) **William Greville** (...)
 c) **Hon. Sir Edward Greville** (...)
2) **Anne Willoughby** (... – bef.12 Nov 1528) unm.
3) **Blanche Willoughby** (... – bef.1545)
 = bef. 25 Jan 1535; **Sir Francis Dawtrey** (...)
 no issue
C) **William Neville** (14 Jul 1497 – bef.1545)
= bef.1 Apr 1529; **Elizabeth Greville** (...) daughter of Sir Giles Greville; =1ˢᵗ Richard Wye
1) **Richard Neville** (... – 27 May 1590) erroneously claimed to have succeeded as 5ᵗʰ Baron Latymer
 = ...; **Barbara Arden** (...) daughter of William Arden & Elizabeth Conway
 a) **Edmund Neville** (bef.1555 – ca.1633) erroneously claimed to have succeeded as 6ᵗʰ Baron Latymer
 = 5 Jan 1587/8 London; **Jane Smyth** (... – ca.1646) daughter of Richard Smyth
 no known issue
2) **Mary Neville** (...)
3) **Susan Neville** (...)
D) **Dorothy Neville** (29 Mar 1496 – ...)
= ...; **Sir John Daunay** (... – 2 Mar 1553) son of Sir Guy Daunay & Joan Darrell
1) **Sir Thomas Daunay** (... – 3 Sep 1566)
 = ...; **Edith D'Arcy** (...) daughter of George D'Arcy, 1ˢᵗ Baron D'Arcy
 a) **Sir John Daunay** (ca.1530 – ...)
 = ...; **Elizabeth Tunstall** (...) daughter of Sir Marmaduke Tunstall
 (I) **Sir Thomas Dawnay** (... – May 1642)
 = ...; **Faith Legard** (...) daughter of Sir Richard Legard
 (A) **John Dawnay** (... – 16 Mar 1629)
 = ...; **Elizabeth Hutton** (...) daughter of Sir Richard Hutton
 (1) **George Dawnay** (... – Apr 1639) unm.
 (2) **Sir Christopher Dawnay, 1ˢᵗ Baronet** (... – 13 Jul 1644) cr. Baronet 19 May 1642
 = ...; **Jane Moseley** (...) daughter of Thomas Moseley

(a) **Sir Thomas Dawnay, 2nd Baronet** (... – aft.1644) unm. suc. father 13 Jul 1644. title became extinct upon his death

   (3) **Sir John Dawnay, 1st Viscount Downe** (25 Jan 1624/5 – 1 Oct 1695) Ky. 1660; cr. Viscount 19 Feb 1680/1
=1 4 Aug 1645; **Elizabeth Melton** (... – 21 Feb 1661/2) daughter of Sir John Melton
=2 14 May 1663; **Dorothy Johnson** (...) daughter of William Johnson
issue of 2nd (none by 1st):

     (a) **Henry Dawnay, 2nd Viscount Downe** (bap.7 Jun 1664 – May 1741) suc. father 1 Oct 1695
= 29 Sep 1685; **Mildred Godfrey** (... – Aug 1725) daughter of William Godfrey
Has further generations of issue

(II) **Mary Dawnay** (...)
= ...; **John Legard** (...) son of John Legard & Elizabeth Mallory

  (A) **Sir John Legard, 1st Baronet** (1631 – 1678) cr. Baronet 29 Dec 1660
=1 18 Oct 1655; **Lady Grace Darcy** (... – 1658) daughter of Conyers Darcy, 1st Earl of Holderness & Grace Rokeby
=2 12 Aug 1658; **Frances Widdrington** (...) daughter of Sir Thomas Widdrington
issue of 1st:

   (1) a daughter (...)
issue of 2nd:

   (2) **Dorothy Legard** (...)
= 29 May 1690; **Thomas Grimston** (...)

     (a) **Thomas Grimston** (26 Sep 1702 – 22 Oct 1751)
= 16 Oct 1722; **Jane Close** (...) daughter of John Close
Has further generations of issue

   (3) **Sir John Legard, 2nd Baronet** (bap.16 Jun 1659 – 5 May 1715) suc. father 1678
=1 1682; **Elizabeth Wastell** (... – 1695) daughter of Leonard Wastell
=2 1695; **Dorothy Cayley** (... – 11 Jul 1739) daughter of Sir William Cayley, 2nd Baronet & May Holbech
issue of 2nd (none by 1st):

     (a) **Sir John Legard, 3rd Baronet** (ca.1696 – 14 Apr 1719) unm. suc father 5 May 1715

     (b) **Sir Thomas Legard, 4th Baronet** (ca.1698 – May 1735) suc. brother 14 Apr 1719
= 1726; **Frances Digby** (... – 1 May 1736)
Has further generations of issue

E) **Elizabeth Neville** (28 Apr 1500 – ...)

= bef.1531; ♦**Sir Christopher Danby** (1503 – 1571)
Children are listed with other parent
F) **Susan Neville** (28 Apr 1501 – ca.1560)
= ...; **Richard Norton** (... – 9 Apr 1585) =2nd Philippa Trapps
1) **Edmund Norton** (... – ca.1610)
= ...; **Cecilia Boynton** (...) daughter of Matthew Boynton
a) **William Norton** (...)
= ...; **Margaret Welbury** (...)
(I) **... Norton** (a son) (...)
= ...
(A) **Welbury Norton** (...)
= ...; **Catherine Norton** (...) daughter of Thomas Norton
(1) **William Norton** (...)
= ...
(a) **Margaret Norton** (...)
=1 ...; **Thomas Liddell** (...) son of John Bright & Cordelia
Clutterbuck; changed name
=2 1748; **Sir John Ramsden, 3rd Baronet** (... – 10 Apr
1769) son of Sir William Ramsden, 2nd Baronet & Hon.
Elizabeth Lowther; suc. father 27 Jun 1736
Has further generations of issue by both
(b) has additional unknown issue
(2) **Thomas Norton** (...)
= ...; **Mary Fletcher** (...) daughter of Thomas Fletcher
(a) **Thomas Norton** (ca.1684 – 22 Feb 1719)
= 3 May 1712; **Elizabeth Serjeantson** (ca.1692 – 10 Sep
1774) daughter of William Serjeantson & Jane Walker
Has further generations of issue
(3) **John Norton** (...)
b) **Robert Norton** (
2) **Francis Norton** (...)
= ...; **Albreda Wimbish** (...)
issue ?
G) **Sir Thomas Neville** (24 Dec 1502 – 28 Oct 1544)
= ...; **Mary Teye** (...) daughter of Sir Thomas Teye
1) **Thomas Neville** (...)
H) **Katherine Neville** (...) probably +young
I) **Joan Neville** (...) probably +young
J) **Marmaduke Neville** (1506 – 28 May 1545)
= ...; **Elizabeth Teye** (...) daughter of Sir Thomas Teye
1) **Christopher Neville** (+young)
2) **Alianore Neville** (...)
= ...; **Thomas Teye** (...)
issue ?
K) **George Neville, Archdeacon of Carlisle** (29 Jul 1509 – 6
Sep 1567)

L) **Christopher Neville** (...) probably +young

III) **Thomas Neville** (1468 – 1546)

= ...; **Laetitia Harcourt** (1494 – 1520) daughter of Sir Robert Harcourt & Agnes Lymbrake

has unknown issue

c. **Thomas Neville** (...)

d. **Jane Neville** (...)

12. **Lady Joan Neville** (...) a nun

CHAPTER 14

GASCOIGNE

This chapter is called Gascoigne because that is the family it starts with. However, that name will disappear within two generations. We start with Joan Neville, a great-granddaughter of Lady Joan Beaufort, Countess of Westmorland from the last chapter. The younger Joan married into the Gascoigne family, but the three daughters of her only son will be the end of this line.

The Gascoigne family goes back to the Norman Conquest and is believed to be so named as they came from Gascony in France. The family split into two major branches, the elder settling in Gawthorpe, the younger in Barnow, both in Yorkshire. The younger branch would go on to become Baronets, and both often find themselves somewhere in the ancestral line between Americans and their royal ancestors.

Joan Neville's husband, Sir William, was the head of Gawthorpe line. A man whose only distinction in history was the ownership of Gawthorpe Hall, he only serves our purposes as the father of another lackluster fellow named Sir William. What the two Williams lacked in contributions to history, they made up for in grandeur of their marriages. As we have already seen, William Sr. married a Neville, while his son married Lady Margaret Percy, daughter of the 2nd Earl of Northumberland. The Percy family were at this time at the peak of their prominence. William and Margaret had three daughters, Elizabeth, Margaret, and Anne. This chapter is divided among them.

Elizabeth Gascoigne married a man named George Tailboys. The Tailboys family would have been relegated to the dustbin of history had it not been for their son, Gilbert, going off and doing something extremely foolish. He fell in love with the king's mistress. While serving in a very minor capacity in Henry VIII's court during a period when the king had tired of Katharine of Aragon but not yet taken up with the Boleyn sisters, Gilbert spied His Majesty's current playmate, Bessie Blount. The poor boy was smitten at once.

He contrived reasons to introduce himself to Bessie, but that was the farthest he dared at first. After all, Henry already had a reputation for explosive anger over the most minor perceived slights. Gilbert was petrified at the thought of what Henry would do to a man caught with one of his women. So he waited. And then luck, or more likely Henry's fickleness, turned in his favor.

Bessie Blount gave the King the son he always wanted, although illegitimately. Once Henry proved to himself he was not the problem and that he could indeed father sons, he went looking for more fertile ground to sew his wild oats. Enter Mary Boleyn, soon to be eclipsed by her younger sister, Anne. Bessie and her little bastard, now Duke of Richmond, were on the outside looking in.

Henry Tudor was many things, but oblivious was never one of them. He had a knack—and plenty of gossipy servants—of knowing everything that was going on in his court. He was quite aware of Gilbert Tailboy's unrequited love for Bessie. So when Henry was completely finished with her, he arranged not only for Gilbert to be called to Parliament as a Baron, but also for his marriage to Bessie in order to provide a stable home for his own son, Richmond.

Gilbert and Bessie had three children of their own, all of whom succeeded to the barony in their turn, but none having children of their own. The barony died out with their daughter Elizabeth, Countess of Warwick in 1563.

Gilbert also had four sisters, all who married untitled landowners. One sister, Elizabeth did see her son become Baron Willoughby. His descendants would start marrying into the minor noble families. Other surnames descended from the Tailboys sisters are Lambert, Vernon, Dymoke, Reade and especially noteworthy to Americans, Warner. In 1670 Mildred Reade married Augustine Warner. They would become the great-grandparents of President George Washington.

Margaret Gascoigne married the 3rd Baron Ogle. The Ogle title would pass through marriage to the Cavendish family and end up one of the many titles of the Dukes of Newcastle-upon-Tyme, whose story is outside the scope of this work. Margaret's daughter married a Forester and some of their descendants ended up in Virginia in early 1700s.

Anne Gascoigne married a man named Fairfax. Their descendants would be well-known colonial settlers in Virginia and Fairfax County would be named for them. A very large family, they end up connected to almost all colonial families originating in northeast Virginia. Furthermore, a very large percentage of Americans with colonial roots will find one line or another of their ancestry going through this same region. So, for Americans seeking the royal connection, this is a place to focus their attention.

Edward III
|
John of Gaunt, Duke of Lancaster
|
Joan, Countess of Westmorland
|
Mary, Lady Neville
|
John Neville
|

Joan Neville (ca.1443 Oversley – ...)
= ca.1460 Oversley; **Sir William Gascoigne** (ca.1439 Gawthorpe, Yorks. –
ca.1464) son of William Gascoigne & Margaret Clarell
A) **Sir William Gascoigne** (... – 1486)
= ...; ♦**Lady Margaret Percy** (...) daughter of Henry Percy, 2nd Earl of
Northumberland & Eleanor Poynings, Baroness de Poynings
  1) **Elizabeth Gascoigne** (...)
    = bef.Apr 1493; **Sir George Tailboys** (ca.1467 – 21 Sep 1538) son of Sir
    Robert Tailboys & Elizabeth Heron; =1st Margaret Burgh
    a) **Gilbert Tailboys, 1st Baron Tailboys** (ca.1497 – 30 Apr 1530) cr.
      Baron Nov 1529
      = 18 Jun 1520; **Elizabeth Blount**[136] (ca.1499 Kinlet, Salop. – Jan
      1539/40) daughter of Jir John Blount & Catherine Pershall
      (I) **Elizabeth Tailboys, 4th Baroness Tailboys** (ca.1520 – 1563) suc.
        brother 1542; upon her death the barony became extinct
        =1 ...; **Thomas Wimbish** (... – 1553)
        =2 bef.13 Nov 1553; **Ambrose Dudley, 1st Earl of Warwick KG**
        (ca.1528 – 21 Feb 1489/90) son of John Dudley, 1st Duke of
        Northumberland & Jane Guilford; =1st Anne Whorwood; cr. Earl 26
        Dec 1561; KG 1563
        no issue
      (II) **George Tailboys, 2nd Baron Tailboys** (ca.1523 – 6 Sep 1539)
        suc. father 1530
        = 1539; **Margaret Skipwith** (... – 6 May 1583) daughter of Sir
        William Skipwith & Alice Dymoke; =2nd Sir Peter Carew
        no issue
      (III) **Robert Tailboys, 3rd Baron Tailboys** (ca.1528 – Jun 1542)
        suc. brother 1539; unm.
    b) **Anne Tailboys** (...)
      = ...; **Sir Edward Dymoke** (1508 – 16 Sep 1566) son of Sir Robert

---

[136] Prior to her marriage, Bessie Blount had been mistress to tKing Edward VIII and bore him
his only acknledged bastaard, Henry, Duke of Ricmond.

Tailboys & Jane Sparrow

(I) Margaret Dymoke (...)

= ...; **William Eure, 2ⁿᵈ Baron Eure** (10 May 1529 – 12 Sep 1594) son of Sir Ralph Eure & Margery Bowes; suc. grandfather aft.1544

  (A) Ralph Eure, 3ʳᵈ Baron Eure (24 Sep 1558 – 1 Apr 1617) suc. father 1594

  =1 1578; **Mary Dawnay** (... – Mar 1612) daughter of Sir John Dawnay

  =2 Mar 1612; **Elizabeth Spencer** (29 Jun 1552 Althorp, Northants.– 25 Feb 1618) daughter of Sir John Spencer & Katherine Kitson; =1ˢᵗ George Carey, 2ⁿᵈ Baron Hunsdon

  issue of 1ˢᵗ (none by 2ⁿᵈ):

    (1) William Eure, 4ᵗʰ Baron Eure (ca.1579 – Jun 1646) suc. father 1617

    = 15 Sep 1601 Ingleby Greenhow, Yorks.; **Lucy Noel** (... – 17 Jan 1615) daughter of Sir Andrew Noel & Mabel Harington

      (a) Sir William Eure (ca.1602 – 2 Jul 1644 Marston Moor, Yorks.) killed in battle

      = ...

      Has further generations of issue

      (b) Elizabeth Eure (...)

      = ...; **Sir Francis Ireland** (...)

      Has further generations of issue

      (c) Ralph Eure (ca.1606 – ca.1640)

      = 1 Nov 1627; **Hon. Catherine Arundell** (ca.1612 – 1657) daughter of Thomas Arundell, 1ˢᵗ Baron Arrundell & Anne Philipson

      issue extinct 1652

      (d) Mary Eure (...)

      = ...; ♦**Sir William Howard** (...)

      Children are listed with other parent

  (B) Martha Eure (...)

  = ...; **William Armyne** (ca.1563 – 22 Jan 1621/2)

    (1) Sir William Armyne, 1ˢᵗ Baronet (11 Dec 1593 – 10 Apr 1651) cr. Baronet 28 Nov 1619

    =1 14 Dec 1619; **Elizabeth Hicks** (...) daughter of Sir Michael Hicks & Elizabeth Coulson

    =2 28 Aug 1628; **Mary Talbot** (bef.1595 – 6 Mar 1674/5) daughter of Hon. Henry Talbot & Elizabeth Reyner; =1ˢᵗ Thomas Holcroft

    issue of 1ˢᵗ (none by 2ⁿᵈ):

      (a) Elizabeth Armyne (... – 10 Dec 1679)

      = ...; **Sir Thomas Style, 2ⁿᵈ Baronet** (1624 – 19 Nov 1702) son of Sir Thomas Style, 1ˢᵗ Baronet & Elizabeth Foulkes; =2ⁿᵈ Margaret Twisden; suc. father 18 Oct 1637

      Has further generations of issue

584

    (b) **Sir William Armyne, 2ⁿᵈ Baronet** (14 Jul 1622 Ruckholte, Essex – 2 Jan 1657/8 Londoon) suc. father 1651 = 26 Aug 1649 Clinton, Suffolk; **Anne Crane** (... – 11 Aug 1662) daughter of Sir Robert Crane, Baronet & Susan Alington; =2ⁿᵈ John Belasyse, 1ˢᵗ Baron Belayasyse
Has further generations of issue

    (c) **Anne Armyne** (6 Aug 1624 Osgodby, Lincs. – Aug 1671) = bef.1643; **Sir Thomas Barnardiston, 1ˢᵗ Baronet** (ca.1618 – 4 Oct 1669 Ketton, Suffolk) son of Sir Nathaniel Barnardiston & Jane Soame; cr. Baronet 7 Apr 1663
Has further generations of issue

    (d) **Sir Michael Armyne, 3ʳᵈ Baronet** (21 Sep 1625 Osgodby – 1668) suc. brother 1658; upon his death baronetcy became extinct
= ...; **Hon. Mary Chaworth** (... – 1667) daughter of John Chaworth, 2ⁿᵈ Viscount Chaworth & Hon. Elizabeth Noel
no issue

(C) **Sir Francis Eure** (... – 1 May 1621)
=1 ...; **Elin Morris** (... – 11 Sep 1626) daughter of William Morris; =1ˢᵗ John Owen
=2 ...; **Elizabeth Lennard** (...) daughter of John Lennard
issue of 1ˢᵗ (none by 2ⁿᵈ):

    (1) **Horatio Eure** (ca.1591 – 6 Jan 1636/7)
= ...; **Deborah Brett** (...) daughter of John Brett
    (a) **George Eure, 6ᵗʰ Baron Eure** (... – 21 Oct 1672) unm.; suc. cousin 22 Jun 1652
    (b) **Ralph Eure, 7ᵗʰ Baron Eure** (... – 27 Apr 1707 London) unm.; suc brother 1672; title became extinct upon his death

(D) **Meriol Eure** (...)
= ...; **... Goodricke** (...)
    (1) **Sir Henry Goodricke** (...)
= ...; **Jane Savile** (...) daughter of Sir John Savile & Jane Garth
    (a) **Sir John Goodricke, 1ˢᵗ Baronet** (20 Apr 1617 – Nov 1670) cr. Baronet 14 Aug 1641
=1 7 Oct 1641; **Catherine Norcliffe** (bef.31 Aug 1620 – ...) daughter of Stephen Norcliffe & Elizabeth Udall
=2 ...; **Elizabeth Smith** (...) daughter of Alexander Smith; =1ˢᵗ William Fairfax, 3ʳᵈ Viscount Fairfax
Has further generations of issue by 2ⁿᵈ

(II) **Frances Dymoke** (... – aft.3 Mar 1611)
= 20 Aug 1566; **Sir Thomas Windebank** (... – 24 Oct 1607 Scrivelsby, Lincs.) son of Richard Windebank & Margaret verch Griffith
(A) **Sir Francis Windebank** (1852 – 1646)
= ...
    (1) **Frances Windebank** (...)

= ...; ♦**Sir Edward Hales, 3rd Baronet** (... – 1695)
Children are listed with other parent
(B) **Mildred Windebank** (1584 – aft.15 Aug 1630)
= 31 Jul 1600; **Robert Reade** (ca.1551 – ca.1627) son of
Andrew Reade & Alice Cooke
  (1) **Thomas Reade** (1606 Linkenholt, Hants. – Mar 1669
  London) unm.
  (2) **George Reade** (25 Oct 1608 Linkenholt – aft.1674
  Gloucester Co, VA)
  = 1641 York Co, VA; **Elizabeth Martiau** (... York Co – 1686
  Gloucester Co) daughter of Nichoolas Martinau & Jane ...
    (a) **Mildred Reade** (10 Feb 1642 York Co – 6 Jan 1693
    Warner Hall, Gloucester Co)
      = 1670; **Augustine Warner** (3 Jun 1642 York Co – 19 Jun
      1681 Warner Hall) son of Augustine Warner & Mary Towneley
      Has further generations of issue[137]
    (b) **George Reade** (... – bef.1685)
    (c) **Robert Reade** (...)
    (d) **Thomas Reade** (...)
    (e) **Francis Reade** (... – ca.1694)
    (f) **Benjamin Reade** (...)
    (g) **Elizabeth Reade** (...)
(C) **Edith Windebank** (...)
= 1 Dec 1638 London; **Sir Toby Tyrrell, 2nd Baronet** (9 Oct
1617 Thornton, Bucks. – ...) son of Sir Edward Tyrrell, 1st
Baronet & Elizabeth Kingsmill; =2nd Lucy Barrington; suc.
father 2 Jul 1656
  (1) **Frances Tyrrell** (...)
    =1 ...; **Sir John Hewett, Baronet** (...)
    =2 ...; **Philip Cotton** (ca.1647 – ...) son of Sir Thomas Cotton,
    2nd Baronet & Alice Constable
    issue ?
(D) **Helen Windebank** (1 Feb 1596 Berks. – 1656 Yorks.)
= 16 Nov 1623 Southwark, Surrey; **Richard Denton** (1603 – 1662)
  (1) **Nathaniel Denton** (1629 – 1960)
(III) **Susan Dymoke** (ca.1546 – 5 Jul 1620)
= ...; **Sir Thomas Lambert** (ca.1550 Skipton-in-Craven,
Yorks. – ca.23 Jul 1613)
(A) **Charles Lambert** (ca.1588 Lincs. – ...)
(B) **Tailboys Lambert** (bef.22 Mar 1589 Pinchbeck, Lincs. – ...)
(C) **William Lambert** (bef.28 Nov 1591 Pinchbeck – ...)

---

[137] Augustine & Mildred were great-grandparents to Pres. George Washington.

(D) **John Lambert** (bef.31 Mar 1593 Pinchbeck – ...)

(E) **Samuel Lambert** (bef. 13 Jul 1595 Pinchbeck – ...)

e) **Elizabeth Tailboys** (...)

= ca.May 1512; **Sir Christopher Willoughby** (... – ca.1539) son of Sir Christopher Willoughby & Margaret Jenney

(I) **William Willoughby, 1st Baron Willoughby** (ca.1515 – 30 Jul 1570) cr. Baron 20 Feb 1546/7

=1 ca.1535; **Catherine Heneage** (...) daughter of Sir Thomas Heneage & Catherine Skipwith

=2 aft.1558; **Margaret Garneys** (... – 1599) daughter of John Garneys; =1st Walter Devereux, 1st Viscount Hereford

issue of 1st (none by 2nd):

(A) **Charles Willoughby, 2nd Baron Willoughby** (ca.1537 – 26 Oct 1612) suc. father 1570

= ...; ♦**Lady Margaret Clinton** (...) daughter of Edward Clinton, 1st Earl of Lincoln & Elizabeth Blount

(1) **Hon. William Willoughby** (... – 1 Jun 1601)

= bef.1582; **Elizabeth Hildyard** (...) daughter of Sir Christopher Hildyard

(a) **Catherine Willoughby** (ca.1583 – 15 Aug 1658)

= 15 Jun 1603; **Joseph Godfrey** (... – 30 Jun 1631)

Has further generations of issue

(b) **William Willoughby, 3rd Baron Willoughby** (1584 – 28 Aug 1617 Knaith, Lincs.) suc. grandfather 1612

= aft.4 Feb 1602/3; ♦**Lady Frances Manners** (22 Oct 1588 Winkbourne, Notts. – ca.1643) daughter of John Manners, 4th Earl of Rutland & Elizabeth Charlton

Has further generations of issue

(2) **Hon. Sir Ambrose Willoughby** (... – bef.24 Nov 1608)

= ...; **Susanna Brooke** (...) daughter of Richard Brooke

(a) **Edward Willoughby** (... – bef.30 Sep 1650)

= 5 May 1625; **Rebecca Draper** (...) daughter of Henry Draper

Has further generations of issue

(3) **Hon. Katherine Willoughby** (...)

= ...; **John Savile, 1st Baron Savile** (1556 – 31 Aug 1630) son of Sir Robert Savile & Anne Hussey; =2nd ♦Elizabeth Cary

(a) **Hon. Katherine Savile** (...)

= ...; **Sir Thomas Bland** (...)

Has further generations of issue

(b) **Hon. Edward Savile** (...)

= ...; **Anne Tolson** (...) daughter of Richard Tolson

no issue

(c) **Hon. Elizabeth Savile** (...)

=1 ...; **Alveray Cooper** (...)

=2 ... **Richard Banks** (...)

issue ?

(d) **Hon. Frances Savile** (...)
= ...; **Rev. Thomas Bradley** (...)
issue ?
(4) **Hon. Edward Willoughby** (...)
(5) **Hon. Margaret Willoughby** (...)
(6) **Hon. Sir Thomas Willoughby** (...)
= ...; **Mary Thornhagh** (...) daughter of John Thornhagh
(a) **Thomas Willoughby, 1st Baron Willoughby** (ca. 1602 – 29 Feb 1691/2) cr. Baron 21 Oct 1680[138]
= 22 Feb 1639/40; **Eleanor Whittle** (...) daughter of Hugh Whittle
Has further generations of issue
(7) **Hon. Anne Willoughby** (...)
= ...; ♦**Sir William Pelham** (...)
Children are listed with other parent
d) **Margaret Tailboys** (...)
= ...; **Sir George Vernon** (... – 1565) son of Sir Richard Vernon & Margaret Dymoke; =2nd Maud Longford
(I) **Margaret Vernon** (...)
=1 ...; ♦**Sir Thomas Stanley** (... – 1576)
=2 ...; **William Mather** (...)
issue of 1st (none by 2nd):
Children are listed with other parent
(II) **Dorothy Vernon** (1531 – 24 Jun 1584)
= ...; ♦**Sir John Manners** (1527 – 1611)
Children are listed with other parent
e) **Cecilia Tailboys** (...)
= ...; **William Ingleby** (1494 – 1528) son of John Ingleby & Eleanore Constable
(I) **Sir William Ingleby** (1518 – 1578)
= ...; **Ann Mallory** (... – 1588)
(A) **Samson Ingleby** (... – 1604)
= ...; **Jane Lambert** (... – 1628)
(1) **Sir William Ingleby, 1st Baronet** (ca.1603 – 1653)
= ...; **Anne Agnes Bellingham** (ca.1598 – 1640) daughter of Sir James Bellingham & Agnes Curwen
(a) **Sir William Ingleby, 2nd Baronet** (1621 – 1682) suc. father 1653
= ...; **Margaret Savile** (... – 9 Nov 1697) daughter of John Savile & Margaret Garraway

---

[138] He was created Baron after being called to Parliament erroneously as the heir to the 10th Baron when a senior line existed.

Has further generations of issue

2) **Margaret Gascoigne** (...)
= ...; **Ralph Ogle, 3ʳᵈ Baron Ogle** (1468 – 1513) son of Owen Ogle,
2ⁿᵈ Baron Ogle; suc. father 1486
a) **Dorothy Ogle** (...)
=1 ...; **Sir Thomas Forster** (... – 1526) son of Thomas Firster & ...
Hilton
=2 ...; **Sir Thomas Grey** (...)
issue of 1ˢᵗ (none by 2ⁿᵈ):
(I) **Thomas Forster** (...)
= ...; **Hon. Florence Wharton** (...) daughter of Thomas Wharton, 1ˢᵗ
Baron Wharton & Eleanor Stapleton
(A) **Ralph Forster** (1552 – 1616)
= ...
(1) **William Forster** (...)
= 1 Jan 1626; **Prudence Clark** (...)
(a) **Rev. William Forster** (Dec 1630 – 8 Dec 1679)
= ...; **Alice Coveney** (... – 8 Jan 1694) daughter of William
Coveney; =1ˢᵗ Samuel Forster
Has further generations of issue
(II) **Sir John Forster** (ca.1520 Etherstone Castle, Durham – 13
Jan 1602 Spindlestone Manor, Northumb.)
=1 ...
=2 ...; **Isabel Sheppard** (...)
issue of 1ˢᵗ:
(A) **Sir Nicholas Forster** (...)
= ...; **Jane Radclyffe** (...)
(1) **John Forster** (... – 1625 Bambaugh Castle, Northumb.)
= ...
(a) **Nicholas Forster** (... – 1612 Bambaugh Castle)
= ca.1632 Northumb.; **Agnes Chaytor** (27 Apr 1615 Croft,
Yorks. – Jan 1669) daughter of Sir William Chaytor &
Frances Bellingham
issue ?
issue of 2ⁿᵈ:
(B) **Mary Forster** (...)
= ...; **Henry Stapleton** (...)
(1) **Robert Stapleton** (...)
= ...; **Hon. Katherine Fairfax** (... – 23 Feb 1666) daughter
of Thomas Fairfax, 1ˢᵗ Viscount Fairfax & Catharine Constable; =2ⁿᵈ
Sir Matthew Boynton, 1ˢᵗ Baronet; =3ʳᵈ Sir Arthur Ingram; =4ᵗʰ
Willilam Wickham
(a) **Catherine Stapleton** (1635 – 1694)
= ...; **William Fairfax** (1626 – 1674) son of Sir William
Fairfax & Frances Chaloner
issue ?

b) **Robert Ogle, 4ᵗʰ Baron Ogle** (ca.1491 – 1530) suc. father 1513
= bef.28 Dec 1515; ♦**Anne Lumley** (... – 1487) daughter of
Thomas Lumley & Elizabeth Plantagenet
(I) **... Ogle, 5ᵗʰ Baron Ogle** (ca.1513 – 6 Mar 1544/5) suc. father 1530
(II) **Robert Ogle, 6ᵗʰ Baron Ogle** (... – 1562) suc. brother 1545
= aft.8 Jul 1537; ♦**Jane Radcliffe** (...) daughter of Sir Cuthbert
Radcliffe & Margaret Clifford
(A) **Cuthbert Ogle, 7ᵗʰ Baron Ogle** (ca.1540 – 1597) suc. father
1562

= ca.1565; **Catherine Carnaby** (...) daugh of Sir Reynold
Carnaby & Dorothy Forster
(1) **Catherine Ogle, 8ᵗʰ Baroness Ogle** (... – 18 Apr 1629)
suc. father 1597
= ...; **Sir Charles Cavendish** (ca.1553 – 4 Apr 1617) son of
Rt.Hon. Sir William Cavendish & Elizabeth Hardwicke; =1ˢᵗ
Margaret Kitson
(a) **William Cavendish, 1ˢᵗ Duke of Newcastle-upon-Tyme**
Marquess of Newcastle-upon-Tyme, Earl of Ogle, Earl of
Newcastle-upon-Tyme, Viscount Mansfield, Baron Cavendish, 9ᵗʰ
Baron Ogle **KG** (bef.16 Dec 1593 – 25 Dec 1676) suc. mother
1629;

cr. Viscount 29 Oct 1620, Earl of Newcastle and Baron Cavendish
7 Mar 1627/8, Marquess 27 Oct 1643, Duke etc. 16 Mar 1664/5;

KB

1610, KG 1650
=1 ca.1618; **Elizabeth Basset** (... – 17 Apr 1643) daughter of
William Basset & Judith Austin; =1ˢᵗ ♦Hon. Henry Howard
=2 Dec 1645; **Margaret Lucas** (1617 – 15 Dec 1673)
daughter of Sir Thomas Lucas & Elizabeth Leighton
Has further generations of issue by 1ˢᵗ
3) **Anne Gascoigne** (ca.1474 Gawthorpe, Yorks. – 1504 Walton, Yorks.)
= ca.1495; **Sir Thomas Fairfax** (ca.1575 Walton – 1520 Walton)
son of Sir Thomas Fairfax & Elizabeth Sherburne
a) **Sir Nicholas Fairfax** (1496 Walton – 30 Mar 1571 Walton)
=1 ...; **Alice Harrington** (...) daughter of Sir John Harrington
=2 ...; **Jane Palmes** (...) daughter of Guy Palmes
issue of 2ⁿᵈ (none by 1ˢᵗ):
(I) **Mary Fairfax** (ca.1529 Walton – ... Workington Hall, Cumb.)
= ca.1549 Workington; **Sir Henry Curwen** (May 1528 – 1592)
son of Sir Thomas Curwen & Agnes Strickland; =2ⁿᵈ Catherine
Lambton; =3ʳᵈ Jane Crosby
(A) **Sir Nicholas Curwen** (1550 Gilling, Yorks. – 1605 Workington
Hall)
=1 ...; **Anne Musgrave** (...) daughter of Sir Simon Musgrave
=2 ...; **Elizabeth Carus** (...) daughter of Thomas Carus
issue of 1ˢᵗ:

(1) **Marie Curwen** (...)
= ...; **Sir Henry Widdrington** (... – 4 Sep 1623) daughter of
Edward Widdrington
(a) **William Widdrington, 1ˢᵗ Baron Widdrington** (11 Jul
1610 – 25 Aug 1651) killed in battle; cr. Baron 1643
= 10 Jan 1629; **Mary Thorold** (1610 – aft.1676) daughter of
Sir Anthony Thorold & Elizabeth Molyneux
Has further generations of issue
(2) **Jane Curwen** (...)
= ...; **Sir William Lambton** (... – 2 Jul 1644 Marston Moor)
killed in battle; son of Ralph Lambton & Eleanor Tempest; =2ⁿᵈ
Catherine Widdrington
(a) **Henry Lambton** (... – 1693)
= ...; **Mary Davison** (...) daughter of Sir Alexander Davison
Has further generations of issue
issue of 2ⁿᵈ:
(3) **Sir Henry Curwen** (ca.1581 Workington Hall – 23 Oct
1623 Workington Hall)
=1 1 Jan 1601; **Catherine Dalston** (... – 1 Jul 1605) daughter
of Sir John Dalston & ... Tyrrell
=2 ...; **Margaret Bouskell** (... – 1656) daughter of Thomas
Bouskell; =1ˢᵗ Christopher Wright
issue of 1ˢᵗ:
(a) **Sir Patricius Curwen, 1ˢᵗ Baronet** (23 Apr 1602
Workington
Hall – 1664 Workington Hall) cr. 12 Mar 1627
= 28 Feb 1620; **Isabella Selby** (... – Jan 1667) daughter of
Sir George Selby & Margaret Selby
no surviving issue
(b) **Thomas Curwen** (... – aft.1664) unm.
issue of 2ⁿᵈ:
(c) **Eldred Curwen** (... – aft. 1664)
= ...
Issue extinct in the next generation
(B) **Jane Curwen** (ca.1552 Workington Hall – ...)
= ...; **Christopher Musgrave** (...) son of Sir Simon Musgrave
& Juliana Ellerker
(1) **Sir Richard Musgrave, 1ˢᵗ Baronet KB** (... – 1615) cr.
Baronet 29 Jun 1611; KB 1603
= ...; ♦**Hon. Frances Wharton** (...) daughter of Philip
Wharton, 3ʳᵈ Baron Wharton & Lady Frances Clifford
(a) **Sir Philip Musgrave, 2ⁿᵈ Baronet** (21 May 1607 – 7
Feb 1677/8) suc. father 1615
= ...; **Juliana Hutton** (...) daughter of Sir Richard Hutton
Has further generations of issue
(C) **Agnes Curwen** (ca.1554 Workington Hall – aft.1598)

= ...; **Sir James Bellingham** (... – 1641)

(1) **Sir Henry Bellingham, 1st Baronet** (... – Oct 1650) cr.
Baronet 30 May 1620
= ...; **Dorothy Boynton** (bef.1607 – ...) daughter of Sir
Francis Boynton
  (a) **Elizabeth Bellingham** (...)
  = 1665; **John Lowther** (1628 – bef. Mar 1667/8) son of Sir
  John Lowther, 1st Baronet & Mary Fletcher; =2nd Mary Withins
  Has further generations of issue
  (b) **Sir James Bellingham, 2nd Baronet** (8 Sep 1623 – Oct
  1650 Heversham, Cumb.) suc. father 1650, but baronetcy
  became extinct upon his death
  = ...; ♦**Catherine Willoughby** (...) daughter of Sir Henry
  Willoughby, 1st Baronet & Lettice Darby; =2nd George Purfoy
  no issue

(2) **Frances Bellingham** (... – Nov 1669)
= 9 Jun 1614; **Sir William Chaytor** (2 Aug 1592 Croft, Yorks. –

30

Mar 1640) son of Anthony Chaytor & Margery Thornton
  (a) **Agnes Chaytor** (27 Apr 1615 – Jan 1669)
  = 1632; ♦**Nicholas Forster** (...)
  Children are listed with other parent
  (b) **Thomas Chaytor** (8 Feb 1616 – 25 Mar 1641 Croft)
  = 5 Mar 1635; **Mary Lewis** (... – Jul 1638) daughter of
  Thomas Lewis
  Has further generations of issue
  (c) **Henry Chaytor** (ca.1617 Croft – Oct 1664 Croft)
  = ...; **Margaret Hebburne** (... – 1704) daughter of Arthur
  Hebburne; =1st Robert Dodsworth
  no issue

(3) **Dorothy Bellingham** (ca.1580 – ...)
= 19 Aug 1604; **Sir Ralph Assheton, 1st Baronet** (ca.1581 – Oct
1644 Whalley Abbey, Lancs.) son of Ralph Assheton & Johanna
Radclyffe; =2nd Eleanor Shuttleworth; cr. Baronet 28 Jun 1620
  (a) **Sir Ralph Assheton, 2nd Baronet** (ca.1605 – 30 Jan
  1679/80 London) suc. father 1644
  =1 aft.17 Apr 1630; ♦**Lady Dorothy Tufton** (ca.1606 – 25
  Jan 1635) daughter of Nicholas Tufton, 1st Earl of Thanet &
  Lady Frances Cecil
  =2 3 Feb 1643/4 London; **Elizabeth Harington** (... – 8
  Jun 1686 London) daughter of Sir Sapcote Harington
  no issue

(4) **Ann Agnes Bellingham** (ca.1598 – 1640)
= ...; ♦**Sir William Ingleby, 1st Baronet** (1603 – 1653)
Children are listed with other parent
(D) **Mabel Curwen** (ca.1556 Workington Hall – 29 Nov 1624

Malew, Isle of Man)
=1 ca.1576 Lezayre, Isle of Man; **William Christian** (bef.1561
Milntown, Isle of Man – 1593 Milntown) son of William
McCeystyn & ... Samsbury
=2 1581; **Sir William Fairfax** (...)
issue of 1st:
(1) **Jane Christian** (... – 1629 Malew)
  = ...; **Thomas Samsbury** (...)
  issue ?
(2) **Mary Christian** (...)
  = ...; **John Quayle** (...) son of Nicholas Quayle
  (a) **Robert Quayle** (...)
(3) **Ewan Christian** (1579 Milntown – Sep 1655 Malew)
  = ca.1599 Isle of Man; **Katherine Harrison** (ca.1586 Estholme-
in-
  the-Fylde, Lancs. – bef.1617 Malew)
  (a) **Mabel Christian** (ca.1599 Milntown – ...)
  = 17 Jul 1615 Isle of Man; **John Curghey** (ca.1590
Ballakillinghan,
  Isle of Man – 1952Ballakillinghan) son of John Curghey
  no issue
  (b) **John Christian** (1 Aug 1602 Milntown – 1673 Kirk Lonan)
  = 31 Aug 1622; **Margaret Parker** (1605 Kirkham, Lancs. – 10
Feb
  1661/2 Preston, Lancs.) daughter of John Parker & Alice Mason
  Has further generations of issue
  (c) **Edward Christian** (1603 Milntown – ca.1654)
  = ca.1631; **Dorothy Salkeld** (...)
  no issue
  (d) **Margery Christian** (6 Jun 1604 Milntown – ...)
  = ...; **Syvester Radcliffe** (... – Dec 1631 Patrick, Isle of
  Man) son of Sylvester Radcliffe
  Has further generations of issue
  (e) **William Christian** (14 Apr 1608 Milntown – 2 Jan
  1662/3 Hango Hill, Isle of Man)
  = ca.1632; **Elizabeth Cockshutt** (1606 Great Harwood,
  Lancs. – Nov 1665 Malew) daughter of George Cockshutt
  Has further generations of issue
  (f) **Margaret Christian** (1617 Milntown – 1652 Ballakillinhan)
  = ... **Ewan Curghey** (ca.1613 Ballakillanhan – 1695
  Ballakillinhan) son of John Curghey
  Has further generations of issue
  issue by **Jane Woods** (ca.1600 Maughold, Isle of Man – 4 Sep
1644
  Milntown):
  (g) **William Christian** (ca.1618 Milntown – ca.1706

Whitehaven, Cumb.)
= ca.1643 Whitehaven; **Anne Holshurst** (ca.1622
Whitehaven – ca.1709)
issue ?

(h) **John Christian** (ca.1620 Milntown – ca.1689 Ballaquinnea)
=1 13 Jul 1660 Kirk Marown; **Kathren Clague** (ca.1650 Isle
of Man – ca.1671 Ballaquinnea)
=2 aft.1671 Kirk Marown; **Margaret Kelly** (ca.1650 Isle of
Man – ...)
issue ?

(i) **Jane Christian** (ca.1621 Milntown – May 1694 Ballakilley)
= ca.1647 Maughold; **William Christian** (1612 Maughold –
12 Jun 1668 Ballakilley) son of Rev. John Christian
Has further generations of issue

issue of 2nd:
(4) **Philip Fairfax** (ca.1582 – ...)
= ...; **Frances Sheffield** (1568 –1645)

(a) **Sir William Fairfax** (1609 – 1644)
= ca.1630; **Frances Chaloner** (Feb 1612– 1692) daughter
of Sir Thomas Chaloner & Judith Blount
Has further generations of issue

(II) **Sir William Fairfax** (ca.1531 – 1 Nov 1597)
=1 ...; **Agnes Darcy** (...) daughter of George Darcy, 2nd Baron
=2 ...; **Jane Stapleton** (...) daughter of Bryan Stapleton
issue of 2nd (none by 1st):

(A) **Thomas Fairfax, 1st Viscount Fairfax** (ca.1574 – 23 Dec
1636 Howsham, Yorks.) cr. Viscount 10 Feb 1628/9; Kt.1603
=1 ca.1594; **Catherine Constable** (...) daughter of Sir Henry
Constable & Margaret Dormer
=2 1 Jan 1626/7; **Mary Ford** (... – Mar 1638/9) daughter of
Robert Ford & Frances Glemham
issue of 1st:

(1) **Hon. Katherine Fairfax** (... – 23 Feb 1666)
=1 ...; ♦**Robert Stapleton** (...)
=2 ...; **Sir Matthew Boynton, 1st Baronet** (26 Jann 1591
Barmston, Yorks. – Mar 1646/7 London) son of Sir Francis
Boynton & Dorothy Place; cr. Baronet 15 May 1618; =1st
Frances Griffith
=3 aft.1646/7; **Sir Arthur Ingram** (... – 4 Jul 1655) son of
Sir Arthur Ingram & Susan Brown; =1st Eleonor Slingsby
=4 aft.1665; **William Wickham** (...)
issue of 1st (none by the others):

(a) **Catherine Stapleton** (1635 – 1694)
= ...; ♦**William Fairfax** (1626 – 1674) son of Sir William
Fairfax & Frances Chaloner
no issue

(2) **Thomas Fairfax, 2ⁿᵈ Viscount Fairfax** (ca.1599 – 24 Sep 1641) suc. father 1636
= ...; **Alathea Howard** (...) daughter of Sir Philip Howard
 (a) **William Fairfax, 3ʳᵈ Viscount Fairfax** (6 Jun 1620 – 1648) suc. father 1641
  = ...; **Elizabeth Smith** (...) daughter of Alexander Smith; =2ⁿᵈ Sir John Goodricke, 1ˢᵗ Baronet
  Has further generations of issue¹³⁹
 (b) **Charles Fairfax, 5ᵗʰ Viscount Fairfax** (ca.1621 – 6 Jul 1671) suc. nephew 1651
  = bef.18 Mar 1664; **Abigail Yate** (...) daughter of Sir John Yate, 2ⁿᵈ Baronet
  Has further generations of issue
 (c) **Hon. Nicholas Fairfax** (aft.1622 – ...)
  = ...; **Elizabeth Davison** (...) daughter of Sir Thomas Davison; =1ˢᵗ ♦John Chaytor
  Has further generations of issue
 (d) **Hon. John Fairfax** (...)
  = ...; **Mary Hungate** (...) daughter of Francis Hungate
  issue ?
(3) **Hon. Willliam Fairfax** (...)
= ...; **Mary Cholmeley** (...) daughter of Marmaduke Cholmeley
 (a) **William Fairfax, 8ᵗʰ Viscount Fairfax** (... – Nov 1738) suc. cousin 1719
  = ...; **Elizabeth Gerard** (...)
  Has further generations of issue
(4) **Hon. Henry Fairfax** (...)
= ...; **Frances Baker** (...) daughter of Henry Baker
 (a) **Henry Fairfax** (...) an author with the pen name **Thomas Browne**
  = ...; **Anne Browne** (...) daughter of Sir Thomas Browne
  Has further generations of issue
(5) **Hon. Margaret Fairfax** (...)
=1 ...; **Watkinson Payler** (...)
=2 ...; **John Hotham** (... – 1 Jan 1644/5) executed; son of Sir John Hotham, 1ˢᵗ Baronet & Katherine Rodes
issue ?
issue of 2ⁿᵈ:
(6) **Hon. Dorothy Fairfax** (...)
= 28 Mar 1639 Goodramgate, Yorks.; **Sir Thomas Norcliffe** (1618 – 5 Jan 1679/80 Langton, Yorks.) son of Sir Thomas

---

¹³⁹ Including the 4ᵗʰ Viscount (+25 Feb 1650/1)

Norcliffe & Catherine Bamburgh

(a) **Catherine Norcliffe** (... – 1678)

=1 ...; **Christopher Lister** (...)

=2 ...; **Sir John Wentworth** (...)

=3 10 Apr 1673; ♦**Heneage Finch, 3rd Earl of Winchilsea**, etc. (ca.1627 – 28 Aug 1689) son of Thomas Finch, 2nd Earl of Winchilsea & Cecille Wentworth; =1st ♦Diana Willoughby; =2nd ♦Lady Mary Seymour; =4th Elizabeth Ayres

issue ?

(b) **Elizabeth Nordliffe** (... – 26 Jun 1674)

= ca.1665; **Sir John Bright, Baronet** (14 Oct 1619 Sheffield, Yorks. – 13 Oct 1688 Badsworth, Yorks.) son of Stephen Bright & Jane Westbye; =1st Catherine Hawksworth; =3rd Frances Liddell; and =4th Susanna Wharton; cr. Baronet 16 Jul 1660, but it became extinct upon his death

no issue

(7) **Hon. ...** (a daughter) **Fairfax** (...)

had issue by ...:

(a) **Frances Fairfax** (....)

= ...; **... Herne** (...)

Has further generations of issue

(III) **Margaret Fairfax** (...)

= ...; **Sir William Belasyse** (ca.1523 – 13 Apr 1604) son of Richard Belasyse & Margery Errington

(A) **Sir Henry Belasyse, 1st Baronet** (14 Jun 1555 Coxwold, Yorks. – 16 Aug 1624) cr. Baronet 29 Jun 1611

= ...; **Ursula Fairfax** (... – 25 Aug 1633) daughter of Sir Thomas Fairfax & Dorothy Gale

(1) **Thomas Belasyse, 1st Viscount Fauconberg** Baron Fauconberg, 2nd Baronet (1577 – 1652) suc. father 1624; c r. Baron 25 May 1627 and Viscount 31 Jan 1642/3

= ca.1600; ♦**Barbara Cholmley** (...) daughter of Sir Henry Cholmley & Margaret Babthorpe

(a) **Hon. Mary Belasyse** (... – 14 Sep 1625)

= 7 Nov 1624; **John Darcy, 4th Baron Darcy** (ca.1579 – 5 Jul 1635) son of Hon. Michael Darcy & Margaret Wentworth; =1st Rosamund Frescheville; =2nd Isabel Wray; suc. grandfather 18 Oct 1602

no issue

(b) **Hon. Henry Belasyse** (1604 – 1647)

= ...; **Grace Barton** (...) daughter of Sir Thomas Barton

Has further generations of issue

(c) **Hon. Margaret Belasyse** (... – 7 Nov 1624)

= 1618; **Sir Edward Osborne, 1st Baronet** (bef.12 Dec 1596 London – 9 Sep 1647) son of Sir Hewett Osborne & Joyce

Fleetwood; =2nd Anne Walmesley; cr. Baronet 13 Jul 1620
Issue extinct 1638

(d) **Hon. Barbara Belasyse** (...)
= 7 Jul 1631 London; **Sir Henry Slingsby, 1st Baronet** (14 Jan 1601/2 – 8 Jun 1658 London) executed; son of Sir Henry Slingsby & Frances Vavasour; cr. Baronet 2 Mar 1638 (not forfeited before execution)
Has further generations of issue

(e) **Hon. Frances Belasyse** (...)
= ...; **Thomas Ingram** (...) son of Sir Arthur Ingram & Susan Brown
no issue

(f) **John Belasyse, 1st Baron Belasyse** (24 Jun 1614 Newborough, Yorks. – 10 Sep 1689 London) cr. Baron 27 Jan 1644/5
=1 8 Mar 1636; **Jane Boteler** (20 Jan 1620/1 Aston, Herts. – bef.12 Dec 1657) daughter of Sir Robert Boteler & Frances Drury
=2 11 Jul 1659 London; **Anne Crane** (... – 11 Aug 1662 London) daughter of Sir Robert Crane, Baronet & Susan Alington; =1st ♦Sir William Armyne, 2nd Baronet
=3 aft. 1662; ♦**Lady Anne Paulet** (... – Sep 1694) daughter of John Paulet, 5th Marquess of Winchester & Honora de Burgh
Has further generations of issue by 1st and 3rd

(g) **Hon. Ursula Belasyse** (ca.1617 – ...)
= 1636; ♦**Sir Walter Vavasour, 2nd Baronet** (1612 – 1666)
Children are listed with other parent

(2) **Dorothy Belasyse** (... – 8 May 1653)
= 1594; **Conyers Darcy, 7th Baron Darcy**, 4th Baron Conyers (bef.27 Aug 1570 – 3 Mar 1653/4) son of Thomas Darcy & Elizabeth Conyers; suc. as Baron Darcy 10 Aug 1641 and Baron Conyers 12 Aug 1641 upon the termination of those abeyances

(a) **Hon. Margaret Darcy** (... – 1668)
= ...; **Sir Thomas Harrison** (... – 1664)
Has further generations of issue

(b) **Conyers Darcy, 1st Earl of Holderness** 8th Baron Darcy, etc. (24 Jun 1599 – 14 Jun 1689) suc. father 1654; cr. Earl 5 Dec 1682
= 14 Oct 1616; **Grace Rokeby** (... – 1 Jan 1658) daughter of Thomas Rokeby & Mary Cartwright
Has further generations of issue

(c) **Hon. Dorothy Darcy** (3 May 1600 Hornby Castle, Yorks. – 31 May 1666 West Hauxwell, Yorks.)
= 22 Apr 1627 Hornby; **John Dalton** (Sep 1603 West Hauxwell – 20 Jul 1644 Burton on Trent, Staffs.) died wounds from protecting the Queen
Has further generations of issue

(d) **Hon. Barbara Darcy** (3 May 1600 – 1696)
= 22 Apr 1617; **Matthew Hutton** (20 Oct 1597 – Feb 1666)
son of Sir Timothy Hutton & Elizabeth Bowes
Has further generations of issue

(e) **Hon. Ursula Darcy** (7 Jul 1601 – ...)
= 21 Sep 1620 **John Stillington** (... – bef.1669)
issue ?

(f) **Hon. Sir William Darcy** (bef.15 May 1608 – ...)
= ...; **Dorothy Selby** (...) daughter of Sir George Selby &
Margaret ...
Has further generations of issue

(g) **Hon. Henry Darcy** (ca.1610 – 28 Apr 1662)
= 1628; **Mary Scrope** (... – 1667) daughter of William Scrope
issue ?

(h) **Hon. Anne Darcy** (15 Mar 1611 – ...)
= 4 Aug 1633; **Thomas Metcalfe** (... – 1652)
issue ?

(i) **Hon. Thomas Darcy** (bef.19 Dec 1613 – ...)

(j) **Hon. Marmaduke Darcy** (4 Jun 1615 – 3 Jul 1687) unm.

(k) **Hon. Grace Darcy** (25 Aug 1616 – 1656)
=1 5 Aug 1633; **George Best** (3 Oct 1613 – ca.1638)
=2 ...; **Francis Molyneux** (...) son of Sir Francis Molyneux,
1st Baronet & Theodosia Heron
Has further generations of issue by 1st

(l) **Hon. James Darcy** (30 Nov 1617 – aft.13 Oct 1673)
= bef.1650; **Isabel Wyvill** (...) daughter of Sir Marmaduke
Wyvill, 2nd Baronet & Isabell Gascoigne
Has further generations of issue

(m) **Hon. Mary Darcy** (5 Sep 1624 – 1661)
= 30 Oct 1655 Hornby; **Acton Burnell** (... – 1687)
Has further generations of issue

(3) **Mary Belasyse** (2 Feb 1591/2 – ...)
= 17 Jun 1610 Coxwold; **Sir William Lister** (...)

(a) **William Lister** (ca.1613 – 7 Dec 1642 Tadcaster, Yorks.) killed
= bef.1642; **Catherine Hawksworth** (... – bef.1665) daughter of
Sir Richard Hawksworth & Anne Wentworth; =2nd Sir John
Bright,
Baronet
Has further generations of issue

(b) **Frances Lister** (ca.1622 – 20 Dec 1676 Plymouth, Devon)
= 10 Sep 1639 Thornton in Craven, Yorks.; **John Lambert**
(7 Sep 1619 Kirkby in Malhamdale, Yorks. – 25 Mar 1684 St.
Nicholas Isle, Devon) son of Josias Lambert & Ann Pigott
Has further generations of issue

(B) **Catherine Belasyse** (...)
= ...; **Thomas Metham** (...)

(1) **Frances Metham** (...)
   = 1593; ♦**Sir Marmaduke Constable** (1574–1632)
   Children are listed with other parent
(C) **James Belasyse** (...)
   = ...; **Isabel Chaytor** (ca.1612 Butterby, Durham – ...) daughter
   of Thomas Chaytor & Jame Tempest
   issue ?
(IV) **Edward Fairfax** (...)
   = ...; **Hon. Ursula Mordaunt** (...) daughter of John Mordaunt,
   2nd Baron Mordaunt & Ela FitzLewis
   issue ?
(V) **Rev. Thomas Fairfax** (ca.1537 – 1595)
   = ...; **... Vaux** (...)
   (A) **Rev. Thomas Fairfax** (ca.1570 – 1640)
     = ...; **Grace Hutton** (...) daughter of William Hutton
     (1) **Rev. William Fairfax** (ca.1600 – 1636)
       = ...; **Jane Tolson** (...) daughter of Richard Tolson
       issue ?
     (2) **Katherine Fairfax** (...)
       = ca.1620; **Richard Tickell** (ca.1598 – 1666)
       issue ?
     (3) **Anthony Fairfax** (1608 Caldbeck, Cumb. – ...)
     (4) **Thomas Fairfax** (...)
     (5) **Henry Fairfax** (...)
     (6) **Richard Fairfax** (...)
     (7) **Edward Fairfax** (...)
     (8) **Lancelot Fairfax** (...)
     (9) **Christian Fairfax** (...)
     (10) **Nicholas Fairfax** (...)
     (11) **Robert Fairfax** (...)
   (B) **George Fairfax** (...)
   (C) **Nicholas Fairfax** (...)
(VI) **Nicholas Fairfax** (...)
(VII) **George Fairfax** (...)
(VIII) **Robert Fairfax** (...)
(IX) **Cuthbert Fairfax** (...)
(X) **Henry Fairfax** (...)
(XI) **Anne Fairfax** (...)
(XII) **Eleanor Fairfax** (...)
(XIII) **Elizabeth Fairfax** (...)
b) **William Fairfax** (... – 1588)
= 1542; **Anne Baker** (...)
(I) **John Fairfax** (... – 1614)
   = ...; **Mary Birch** (...) daughter of John Birch
   (A) **Benjamin Fairfax** (1592 – 1675)
     = ...; **Sarah Galliard** (...) daughter of Roger Galliard

(1) **Sarah Fairfax** (...)
= ....; **Bartolomew Allerton**[140] (...) son of Isaac Allerton &
Mary Norris
issue ?
(2) **John Fairfax** (1623 – 1700)
= ...; **Elizabeth Cowper** (...) daughter of William Cowper
(a) **Nathaniel Fairfax** (1661 – 1722)
= ...; **Frances ...** (...)
Has further generations of issue
(3) **Benjamin Fairfax** (1625 – ca.1708)
= ...; **Bridget Stringer** (...)
(a) **Sarah Fairfax** (1654 – 1688)
= ca.1675; **Rev. John Meadows** (7 Apr 1622 Ipswich,
Suffolk – 1697 Bury St. Edmunds, Suffolk) son of Daniel
Meadows & Elizabeth Smith
Has further generations of issue[141]
c) **Margaret Fairfax** (...)
=1 ...; **William Sayre** (
=2 5 Aug 1535; **Richard Maunsell** (... – 6 Nov 1559 Chichley,
Bucks.) son of Richard Maunsell & Elizabeth Wingfield
(I) **Thomas Maunsell** (1536 – Apr 1582)
= 11 Sep 1567; **Agnes Morton** (... – 1603) daughter of John
Morton; =1st William Everett
(A) **Richard Maunsell** (... – 1631)
= 1623; **Dorothy Mordaunt** (...) daughter of Henry
Mordaunt; =1st Humphrey Phipps; =3rd Thomas Halewood
no issue
(B) **Maria Maunsell** (...)
= ...; **Daniel Comry** (...)
issue ?
(C) **Martha Maunsell** (...)
= ...; **Henry Edwards** (...)
issue ?
(D) **Elizabeth Maunsell** (...)
= ...; **... Petit** (...)
issue ?
(E) **John Maunsell** (1575 – 19 Oct 1625)
= 1601; **Katherine Ward** (...) daughter of Sir Richard Ward
(1) **John Maunsell** (12 Mar 1604/5 – 2 May 1677)
= 1626; **Susanna Phipps**[142] (...) daughter of Humphrey Phipps

---

[140] Sailed to America on the *Mayflower* as a boy, but later returned to England.
[141] Including HRH The Duchess of Cambridge (née Kate Middleton).
[142] She was the step-daughter of his uncle, Richard Maunsell.

& Dorothy Mordaunt
(a) **Robert Maunsell** (1629 – 27 May 1705)
= 1656; **Judith Brooke** (1627 – 27 Apr 1709) daughter of
Thomas Brooke & Margaret Walter
no surviving issue
(b) **John Maunsell** (... – 1670 London)
= ca.1664; **Martha ...** (...)
Has further generations of issue
(c) **Humphrey Maunsell** (... – 1676 Montpellier, France) unm.
(d) **Henry Maunsell** (... – 1699 London) unm.
(e) **Dorothy Maunsell** (...)
= ca.1659; **William Wheelowes** (...)
issue ?
(f) **Catherine Maunsell** (... – 27 Jan 1704)
= 1658; **Rev. John Courtman** (... – 9 Apr 1719) son of
John Courtman
Has further generations of issue
(g) **Susan Maunsell** (...)
= 1665; **Edward Hill** (...)
Has further generations of issue[143]
(h) **Elizabeth Maunsell** (...)
= ...; **... Leigh** (...)
issue ?
(i) **Mary Maunsell** (...)
= 1669; **Daniel Blundell** (...)
issue ?
(j) **Thomas Maunsell** (1640 – 1721) unm.
(2) **Thomas Maunsell** (1607 – 25 Feb 1643 Thorpe Malsor,
Northants.) unm.
(F) **Thomas Maunsell** (6 Apr 1577 – ca.1646)
= ...; **Aphra Crayford** (... – 1662) daughter of Sir William
Crayford
(1) **Thomas Maunsell** (... – 13 Mar 1686/7)
= 1641; **Margaret Knoyle** (... – 2 Feb 1679) daughter of
Leonard Knoyle & Francisca Jerard; =1st Thomas Hutchins
(a) **Thomas Maunsell** (... – aft.Jul 1692)
= ...; **Anne Eaton** (...) daughter of Sir Theophilius Eaton; =2nd
Joseph Ormsby; =3rd John Ryves
Has further generations of issue
(b) **John Maunsell** (... – bef.1687)
(c) **Sarah Maunsell** (...)

---

[143] 19 children!!

= ...; **Thomas Seward** (...)
issue ?
 (d) **...** (a daughter) **Maunsell** (...)
 = ...; **Henry Carter** (...)
 issue ?
 (e) **Aphra Maunsell** (...)
 = ...; **John Downing** (...)
 Has further generations of issue
(2) **Walter Maunsell** (... – aft.1672)
(3) **Boyle Maunsell** (... – bef.1705)
 = ...
 (a) **Thomas Maunsell** (...)
 = ...; **Jane Cosby** (...)
 Has further generations of issue
 (b) **...** (a daughter) **Maunsell** (...)
 = ...; **Thomas Bowers** (...)
 issue ?
 (c) **Sarah Maunsell** (...)
 = ...; **John Drew** (...)
 issue ?
(4) **Richard Maunsell** (... – bef.1651) unm.
(5) **Aphra Maunsell** (... – 1678)
 = ...; **George Peacocke** (... – bef.17 Feb 1687)
 no surviving issue
(6) **Anne Maunsell** (...)
 = May 1630; **Very Rev. Robert Naylor** (...) son of Robert
 Naylor; Dean of Lismore
 (a) a daughter
 (b) a daughter
(7) **Sarah Maunsell** (...)
 = ...; **... Ridgate** (...)
 issue ?
(8) **Catherine Maunsell** (...)
 = ...; **Theophilius Eaton** (...)
 issue ?
(9) **Alice Maunsell** (...)
 = ...; **... Andrews** (...)
 issue ?
(10) **Mary Maunsell** (...)
 = ...; **Richard Bettesworth** (...)
 issuse ?
(11) **John Maunsell** (ca.1622 – 14 Nov 1695)
 =1 1656; **Mary Booth** (...) daughter of George Booth
 =2 ...; **Jane Campbell** (...) daughter of John Campbell
 issue of 1st:
 (a) **George Maunsell** (... – 1711)

(b) **John Maunsell** (... – bef.1739)
= 1683; **Anne Foulkes** (...) daughter of Robert Foulkes
Has further generations of issue
issue of 2nd:
(c) **Thomas Maunsell** (... – 27 Sep 1739)
= 1699; **Thomasine Stephens** (... – 3 Apr 1747) daughter of
Richard Stephens
Has further generations of issue
(d) **Jane Maunsell** (...)
= ...; **Joseph Osborn** (...)
issue ?
(e) **Mary Maunsell** (...)
= ...; **Samuel Edmondson** (...)
issue ?
(II) **John Maunsell** (22 Sep 1539 – 25 Jan 1605)
= ...; **Dorothy Smyth** (...) daughter of Samuel Smyth
  (A) **Samuel Maunsell** (13 Sep 1581 – ca.1633)
  = 1621; **Nightingale Furtho** (... – ca.1682) daughter of
  Edward Furtho & Elizabeth Gascoigne; =2nd Francis Longueville
  (1) **Thomas Maunsell** (...)
    = ...
    (a) **Thomas Maunsell** (...)
    (b) **Rev. John Maunsell** (1644 – 1730)
  (2) **Christopher Maunsell** (...)
    = ...
    (a) **Elizabeth Maunsell** (... – 1710)
    = ... **Charles West** (...)
    issue ?
  (3) **Edward Maunsell/Mansel** (1627 – 6 Nov 1696)
  = 1660; **Millicent Draper** (... – Apr 1711) daughter of
  Edward Draper
    (a) **Rev. Edward Mansel** (1661 – ...) unm.
    (b) **John Mansel** (...)
    = ...; **Anne Rawlins** (...)
    issue ?
    (c) **Charles Mansel** (...) unm.
    (d) **Rev. Christopher Mansel** (1686 – 23 Oct 1741)
    = 1717; **Sarah Hoare** (... – 19 Sep 1769) daughter of Edward
    Hoare
    Has further generations of issue
(III) **Olivia Maunsell** (1542 – ...)
(IV) **Elizabeth Maunsell** (1546 – ...)
d) **Thomas Fairfax** (...) unm.

SELECTED SOURCES

Ancestry. numerous pages. *Ancestry.com*. Accessed 2016–2021.

Burke, John. *A Genealogical and Heraldic History of the Commoners of Great Britain and Ireland, Volumes I-III*. London, 1834-1838.

Burke, John and Burke, John Bernard. *A Genealogical and Heraldic History of the Extinct and Dormant Baronetcies of England, Ireland, and Scotland*. London, 1841.

Find-a-grave.com. Accessed 2016–2021.

Freer, Alan. *william1.co.uk*. Accessed 2016–2021.

Geneanet.com Accessed 2021.

Geni. numerous pages. *Geni.com*. Accessed 2016–2021.

Gibbs. Hon. Vicary and Doubleday, H.A, editors. *The Complete Peerage of England, Scotland, Ireland, Great Britain, and the United Kingdom. Volumes I-XIII*. St. Catherine Press, London, 1926.

Hylbom, Tor. "Miles #2606". *hylbom.com*. Revised 7 Sep 2015. Accessed 30 Apr 2016.

Lundy, Darryl. *thepeerage.com*. Accessed 2016–2021.

Mosley, Charles, editor. *Burke's Peerage and Baronetage, 10th Edition*. Burke's Peerage Ltd. 1999.

Ruvigny and Raineval, Marquis of. *The Plantagenet Roll of the Blood Royal*. TC & EC Jack, 1905.

Theroff, Paul. *http://www.angelfire.com/realm/gotha/gotha.htm*. Accessed 2016-2021.

Townsend, Peter, editor. *Burke's Genealogical and Heraldic History of the Landed Gentry, Volumes 1-3*. Burke's Peerage Ltd, 1965, 1969, 1973.

Wikipedia. numerous pages. *wikipedia.com*. Accessed 2016–2021.

INDEX
VOLUME 1

x

CPSIA information can be obtained
at www.ICGtesting.com
Printed in the USA
BVHW081007130921
616662BV00001B/4

9 781955 065085